ROUTLEDGE HANDBOOK OF THE SOUTH ASIAN DIASPORA

South Asia's diaspora is among the world's largest and most widespread, and it is growing exponentially. It is estimated that over 25 million persons of Indian descent live abroad; and many more millions have roots in other countries of the subcontinent, in Pakistan, Bangladesh and Sri Lanka. There are 3 million South Asians in the UK and approximately the same number resides in North America. South Asians are an extremely significant presence in Southeast Asia and Africa, and increasingly visible in the Middle East.

Now available in paperback, this inter-disciplinary handbook on the South Asian diaspora brings together contributions by leading scholars and rising stars on different aspects of its history, anthropology and geography, as well as its contemporary political and socio-cultural implications. The Handbook is split into five main sections, with chapters looking at mobile South Asians in the early modern world before moving on to discuss diaspora in relation to empire, nation, nation state and the neighbourhood, and globalisation and culture.

Contributors highlight how South Asian diaspora has influenced politics, business, labour, marriage, family and culture. This much needed and pioneering venture provides an invaluable reference work for students, scholars and policy makers interested in South Asian Studies.

Joya Chatterji is Reader in Modern South Asian History at the University of Cambridge, UK, and a Fellow of Trinity College. Her publications include *Bengal Divided: Hindu Communalism and Partition 1932–1947* (1995), *The Spoils of Partition: Bengal and India, 1947–67* (2007) and co-author of *The Bengal Diaspora* (forthcoming 2013, Routledge). She is also the editor of the journal *Modern Asian Studies*.

David Washbrook is Senior Research Fellow at Trinity College, University of Cambridge, UK, and he has previously taught at Warwick, Harvard and Oxford Universities and the University of Pennsylvania. His major interests lie in the societies and cultures of southern India on which he has published extensively

ROUTLEDGE HANDBOOK OF THE SOUTH ASIAN DIASPORA

Edited by Joya Chatterji and David Washbrook

Routledge
Taylor & Francis Group

LONDON AND NEW YORK

First published in paperback 2018

First published 2013
by Routledge
2 Park Square, Milton Park, Abingdon, Oxon OX14 4RN

and by Routledge
711 Third Avenue, New York, NY 10017

Routledge is an imprint of the Taylor & Francis Group, an informa business

British Library Cataloguing-in-Publication Data
A catalogue record for this book is available from the British Library

Library of Congress Cataloging-in-Publication Data
Routledge handbook of the South Asian diaspora / edited by Joya Chatterji and David Washbrook. pages cm
Includes bibliographical references and index.
ISBN 978-0-415-48010-9 (hardback) -- ISBN 978-0-203-79652-8 (ebook) 1. South Asian diaspora. 2. South Asians--Foreign countries. 3. South Asia--Emigration and immigration. 4. South Asians--Migrations. I. Chatterji, Joya. II. Washbrook, D. A.
DS339.4.R68 2013
909'.04914--dc23
2013005958

ISBN: 978-0-415-48010-9 (hbk)
ISBN: 978-1-138-31125-1 (pbk)
ISBN: 978-0-203-79652-8 (ebk)

Typeset in Bembo
by Taylor & Francis Books

CONTENTS

Contents

ILLUSTRATIONS

Figures

Tables

CONTRIBUTORS

Ravi Ahuja, having taught at the University of Heidelberg, Germany and the School of Oriental and African Studies in London, is presently Professor of Modern Indian History at the Centre for Modern Indian Studies in Göttingen, Germany. His research interests include the history of work and labour since the eighteenth century and the social histories of 'public works' and warfare.

Claire Alexander is Professor of Sociology at the University of Manchester, UK. Her research interests are in the area of race, ethnicity, masculinity and youth identities. Her main publications include *The Art of Being Black* (1996) and *The Asian Gang* (2000). Claire is also a Trustee of the Runnymede Trust, Britain's foremost race equality thinktank.

Roger Ballard is Director of the Centre for Applied South Asian Studies, UK. His specialist interest is emigration from the Punjab, and hence in Sikh and Hindu settlers from the Jullundur Doab in India, and in Mirpuri Muslims from the Potohar/Azad Kashmir region of northern Pakistan. He has published widely on these subjects.

Joya Chatterji is Reader in Modern South Asian History at the University of Cambridge, UK and a Fellow of Trinity College. Her publications include *Bengal Divided: Hindu Communalism and Partition 1932–1947* (1995); *The Spoils of Partition: Bengal and India, 1947–67* (2007) and (with Claire Alexander and Annu Jalais) *The Bengal Diaspora* (forthcoming 2013, Routledge). She is the editor of the journal *Modern Asian Studies*.

Faisal Devji is Reader in Indian History at the University of Oxford, UK. He is the author of *Landscapes of the Jihad* (2005), and *The Terrorist in Search of Humanity* (2008). His current research is on Gandhi as a thinker of violence and on Jinnah and the making of Pakistan.

Rachel Dwyer is Professor of Indian Cinema and Cultures at SOAS, University of London, UK. Her research publications are mostly on Hindi cinema and she is currently completing her book *Bollywood's India: The Dreams of Hindi Cinema's Imaginary World*. Her next project is the cultural history of the Indian elephant.

John Eade is Professor of Sociology and Anthropology at the University of Roehampton, UK and Visiting Professor at University College London, UK. He works in the areas of urban ethnicity, global migration and pilgrimage. His publications include single-authored *Placing London* (2000) and *The Politics of Community* (1989), single-edited *Living the Global City* (1997) and co-edited *Accession and Migration: Changing Policy, Society, and Culture in an Enlarged Europe* (2009) and *Transnational Ties* (2008).

Michael H. Fisher is Danforth Professor of History at Oberlin College, USA. He has published widely about interactions between Asians and Britons in Asia and Britain, including *The Inordinately Strange Life of Dyce Sombre: Victorian Anglo Indian M.P. and Chancery 'Lunatic'* (2010) and *Counterflows to Colonialism: Indian Travellers and Settlers in Britain, 1600–1857* (2004).

Katy Gardner is Professor of Anthropology at the University of Sussex, UK. Her publications include *Global Migrants, Local Lives: Travel and Transformation in Rural Bangladesh* (1995); *Anthropology, Development and the Post-Modern Challenge* (1996, with David Lewis); *Age, Narrative and Migration: Life Stories and the Life Cycle among Bengali Settlers in London* (2002); and *Discordant Development: Global Capitalism and the Struggle for Survival in Bangladesh* (2012).

David N. Gellner is Professor of Social Anthropology at the University of Oxford, UK. He has worked on Nepal for over 30 years. His publications include *Rebuilding Buddhism: The Theravada Movement in Twentieth-Century Nepal* (2005), *Nationalism and Ethnicity in Nepal* (2008 [1997]) and *Borderlands of Northern South Asia: Non-State Perspectives* (2013).

William Gould is Senior Lecturer in Indian History at the University of Leeds, UK. His research interests include South Asian diasporas, religious and sectarian conflict in India, administrative corruption and Denotified/Nomadic tribal politics. He has published three books, including *Hindu Nationalism and the Language of Politics* (2004) and *Bureaucracy, Community and Influence* (Routledge, 2011).

Douglas Haynes is Professor of History at Dartmouth College, USA. He is the author of *Small Town Capitalism in Western India: Artisans, Merchants and the Making of the Informal Economy, 1870–1960* (2011) and *Rhetoric and Ritual in Colonial India: The Shaping of a Public Culture in Surat City, 1852–1928* (1991).

Isabel Hofmeyr is Professor of African Literature and Acting Director of the Centre for Indian Studies in Africa at the University of the Witwatersrand, South Africa. Her publication *The Portable Bunyan: A Transnational History of The Pilgrim's Progress* won the 2007 Richard L. Greaves Award. She is currently working on a book on textual circulation in the Indian Ocean region.

Ananya Jahanara Kabir is Professor of English Literature at King's College, London, UK. Her publications include *Partition's Post-Amnesias: 1947, 1971 and Modern South Asia* (2013) and (as co-editor) *Writing the British Asian City* (2013). She was co-investigator in the AHRC-funded research network's *Writing the British Asian City* (2006–8), and in the Economic and Social Research Council-funded research network's *Performance, Politics, Piety: Music and Debate in Muslim Societies of North Africa, West Asia, South Asia and their Diasporas* (2008–9).

Helen Kim is currently an Associate Lecturer at the University of Arts, London, UK. She obtained her PhD in the Department of Sociology at the London School of Economics and

Political Science, UK, in 2011. Her research interests are 'race', ethnicity, diaspora and cultural production.

Dirk H.A. Kolff is Emeritus Professor of South Asian History at Leiden University, the Netherlands. His publications include *Naukar, Rajput and Sepoy: The Ethnohistory of the Military Labour Market in Hindustan, 1450–1850* (1990) and *Warfare and Weaponry in South Asia 1000–1800* (co-edited, 2001). His current research is on the peasant history of northern India.

Brij V. Lal is Professor of Pacific and Asian History and Acting Director of the School of Culture, History and Language in the College of Asia and the Pacific at The Australian National University. He has published widely on Indian indenture history and historiography and is the General Editor of the *Encyclopedia of the Indian Diaspora* (2006). His book, *Girmitiyas: The Origins of the Fiji Indians*, is widely regarded as a foundational text in Indian indenture historiography.

Karen Leonard currently chairs the Anthropology department at the University of California, USA. Her publications include *Locating Home: India's Hyderabadis Abroad* (2007) and *Muslims in the United States: The State of Research* (2003).

Claude Markovits is Senior Research Fellow Emeritus at the Centre of Indian and South Asian Studies in France. His publications include *The Global World of Indian Merchants* (2000), *The Un-Gandhian Gandhi: The Life and Afterlife of the Mahatma* (2004) and *Merchants, Traders, Entrepreneurs* (2008).

Magnus Marsden is Senior Lecturer in Social Anthropology with reference to South and Central Asia at SOAS, the University of London, UK. His publications include *Living Islam: Muslim Religious Experience in Pakistan's North-West Frontier* (2005) and, with Benjamin D. Hopkins, *Fragments of the Afghan Frontier* (2012).

Fiona McConnell is Lecturer in Human Geography at Newcastle University, UK. Her research interests lie in the everyday construction of statehood and sovereignty in cases of tenuous territoriality, with a particular focus on the exiled Tibetan community in India. She has published in Geography and South Asia journals and has a forthcoming co-edited book on 'Geographies of Peace', and a monograph on 'Rehearsing the State'.

Perveez Mody is Lecturer at the Division of Social Anthropology, Cambridge University, UK and a Fellow of King's College. She is interested in changes in South Asian kinship, marriage, gender and sexuality, and intimacy more broadly. Her publications include *The Intimate State: Love–Marriage and the Law in Delhi* (Routledge, 2008).

Ali Nobil Ahmad teaches World History at Lahore University of Management Studies, Pakistan. His current research interests include cinema, journalism and the media in Pakistan, and his publications include *Masculinity, Sexuality and Illegal Migration* (2011).

Rosalind (Polly) O'Hanlon is Professor of Indian History and Culture in the Faculty of Oriental Studies, University of Oxford, UK. Her publications include *A Comparison Between Women and Men: Tarabai Shinde and the Critique of Gender Relations in Colonial India* (1994) and numerous articles on the social history of colonial and early modern India.

Tirthankar Roy is Professor of Economic History, London School of Economics and Political Science, UK and the author of *India in the World Economy from Antiquity to the Present* (2012) and *Traditional Industry in the Economy of Colonial India* (1999).

Yunas Samad is Professor of South Asian Studies at the University of Bradford, UK. He is a leading expert on the study of South Asia and its diaspora, and his recent publications include *Pakistan–US Conundrum: Jihadis, Military and the People – The Struggle for Control* (2011) and *Muslim Community Cohesion* (2010).

Samita Sen is Vice Chancellor, Diamond Harbour University, and Professor of History, Jadavpur University, India. Her publications include *Women and Labour in Late Colonial India* (1999) and three jointly edited volumes: *Intimate Others* (2010) and *Mapping the Field* (Vols 1 and 2; 2011 and 2012).

Jayanta Sengupta is Assistant Professor of History at the University of Notre Dame, USA. His primary research interests are the social and cultural history of modern South Asia and intellectual interaction between India and the United States. His latest publication is an article on the culture of the politics of food in colonial Bengal, published in *Modern Asian Studies* in January 2010.

Sandhya Shukla is Associate Professor of American Studies and English at the University of Virginia, USA. Her areas of specialization include diaspora, migration and urban space. She is the author of *India Abroad: Diasporic Cultures of Postwar America and England* (2003) and the co-editor of *Imagining Our Americas: Nation, Empire, and Region* (2007).

Emma Tarlo is a Professor of Anthropology at Goldsmiths, University of London, UK. Her research interests include the anthropology of dress, material culture and the body. She is author of *Clothing Matters: Dress and Identity in India* (1996) and *Visibly Muslim: Fashion, Politics, Faith* (2010). Her new research focuses on the global trade in human hair.

Nicholas Van Hear is Deputy Director at the Centre on Migration, Policy and Society (COMPAS) at the University of Oxford, UK. He works on forced migration, conflict, development, diaspora and transnationalism and has field experience in Africa, the Middle East, South Asia and Europe. His books include *New Diasporas* (Routledge, 1998), *The Migration–Development Nexus* (2003) and *Catching Fire: Containing Forced Migration in a Volatile World* (2006).

David Washbrook is Senior Research Fellow at Trinity College, University of Cambridge, UK. Previously, he has taught at Warwick, Harvard and Oxford Universities and the University of Pennsylvania. His major interests lie in the societies and cultures of southern India on which he has published extensively.

Pnina Werbner is Professor Emerita of Social Anthropology, Keele University, UK and author of *The Manchester Migration Trilogy*, including *The Migration Process: Capital, Gifts and Offerings among British Pakistanis* (1990/2002), *Imagined Diasporas among Manchester Muslims* (2002) and *Pilgrims of Love: The Anthropology of a Global Sufi Cult* (2003).

John Zavos is Senior Lecturer in South Asian Studies at the University of Manchester, UK. His recent publications include *Religious Traditions in Modern South Asia* (Routledge, 2011), co-authored with Jacqueline Suthren Hirst, *Public Hinduisms* (2012), co-edited with several colleagues, and articles on Hinduism and Hindu organisations in the UK and Europe.

ACKNOWLEDGEMENTS

The idea of producing this *Handbook* was first mooted, appropriately enough, over a meal in a Chinese restaurant in Cambridge. That was, we are ashamed to say, in 2008. It goes to press in 2013, and its editors have incurred debts along the way that it is a pleasure finally to acknowledge.

Our first and largest debt is to our contributors, whose patience has been sorely tried; and to our Editorial Committee, whose members have commented wisely on many of these essays. We hope the final product is worth the wait. Both of us owe much to Trinity College, Cambridge, whose Master and Fellows sustained us with food, conversation and coffee (and sometimes with stronger beverages) as we worked together to bring this project to fruition. Dorothea Schaeffer and Jillian Morrison at Taylor and Francis were as supportive and as tolerant as commissioning editors could be.

The students who have attended our graduate seminar on 'mobility, migration and diaspora' stimulated many of the ideas that have found their way into this *Handbook*, and we hope some of them will look at it when it is published. Rosalind O'Hanlon has our gratitude for reading and commenting on it extremely closely at later stages, as does Anil Seal. Kartik Upadhyaya helped type up editorial changes while his mother was too unwell to do so herself and was very relieved (for more than one reason) when she recovered. Roy Sinai kindly gave us permission to use, and to crop, his photograph for the cover. Finally, we must acknowledge the millions of South Asians whose comings and goings, trials and tribulations, successes and sufferings have provided the stuff of this volume, and who have contributed so significantly to the world in which we live.

DAW and JC
Cambridge, 31 January 2013

INTRODUCTION

Concepts and questions

Joya Chatterji and David Washbrook

The South Asian diaspora is the subject of a rich and lively scholarship, reflected in three excellent recent works of synthesis (Brown, 2006; Metcalf, 2008; Amrith, 2011) and a comprehensive *Encyclopaedia of the Indian Diaspora*, (Lal *et al.* ed., 2006). The need today for a *Handbook* on the South Asian diaspora, with contributions from over 30 leading scholars in this field, thus calls for a word or two of explanation.

The *Handbook*'s contents will immediately reveal how this collection differs from other recent works. Its aim is not to provide an encyclopaedic coverage of communities of South Asian origin the world over. Its approach, in contrast, is thematic and deliberately historical, and it draws attention to the long and complex history of human movement *not only from outside but also within* the subcontinent. In so doing, it questions the assumption that internal (or intra-regional) migrations and global diaspora are unrelated and have wholly distinct histories. Instead it suggests that the size and spread of present-day South Asian diaspora around the world – at a conservative estimate, totalling about 40 million people[1] – cannot properly be understood without an appreciation of the longevity, scale and diversity of mobility within the subcontinent since early modern times.

In this respect, this work is rather more than a *Handbook*. Instead of being a compendium that surveys different aspects of the field, this collection of articles is built around key ideas and seeks, in its own way, to redefine that field. Its editors believe that the whole is more than a sum of its parts: while each individual article can be read on its own, taken together these essays draw a powerful and compelling picture which, we hope, will encourage the reader to question conventional assumptions about contemporary diasporas and see them in a new light.

What are these assumptions? The first, and perhaps most ubiquitous, is that migration is something new, an activity that characterises the late-modern, or indeed the postmodern, predicament. Another is that migration is an unusual activity, requiring special explanation: the common perception being that most people stay 'at home' and that migrants break that mould. On the contrary, as the articles in this volume will attest, since early modern times South Asia has possessed an extraordinarily mobile society. Before 1800, perhaps half the total population of the subcontinent was *habitually* itinerant for a substantial part of their adult lives (Ludden, 2003). The mobile lives of the peasant-soldiery, described here by Dirk Kolff, reveal just how common it was for early modern agrarian societies to export young males for months and years at a time, supplying a vibrant subcontinental demand for military labour. We are used to thinking of

1

agrarian societies as being inherently settled, indeed as the least mobile of all communities, their peoples tied eternally to the land. Kolff's essay, among others, encourages us to question this perception. It also draws attention to the complex role of brokers, and their deployment of caste, clan and *biradari* ties both to recruit men and to control the market in soldiering men.

Another group, different in some respects from the armed peasants, were itinerant merchants who travelled far and wide, both within the South Asian region and beyond, in search of markets. With their highly sophisticated skills in accountancy, and tied into complex (and usually closed) networks of trust, the operations of South Asia's merchants criss-crossed the subcontinent as well as the Indian ocean region. Their activities were underpinned by intricate mechanisms of value transfer — *hawala* and *hundi*, described here in all their rich detail by Roger Ballard. David Washbrook looks at the merchant communities resident in the consumption centres of the 'Indian Ocean world' from Cairo to the Malay archipelago, around which all manner of traders, pilgrims and adventurers circulated with considerable ease and in remarkable numbers. The ocean, as Washbrook shows, far from being a barrier to mobility and migration, was a great enabler.

Unlike these migrants, who in the main circulated as single men — albeit within networks afforced by ties of caste and kinship — other groups moved to new places as whole communities, taking their families with them. They deployed specialised skills — often handed down through generations and closely dependent on caste status — to facilitate their movement, particularly during times of political and economic turbulence. Prominent among such were the weaving (and other artisan) communities described by Roy and Haynes, and also the scribal groups whom O'Hanlon discusses. In both cases, the emergence of early modern states and the growth of increasingly sophisticated civil and revenue administrations, as well as the rise of complex courtly and religious cultures, created the context in which men — along with small branches of the extended households from which they acquired their skills and status — moved readily in search of new patrons and employers. These instances, by no means constituting an exhaustive account of all the South Asians who were on the move in early modern times, are likely to be something of an eye-opener for many readers, challenging assumptions about the supposedly static nature of 'traditional' societies.

One important question raised by this series of essays has to do with the role of the state in early modern mobility. South Asian states — their rise and fall, their demands for military labour, administrators, credit, fine commodities and religious legitimation — all helped to provide the context within which many South Asians (and indeed many other migrants from further afield) travelled. But from the essays in this volume and the wider scholarship from which they are derived, we get a clear sense that these migrants (or the agents who recruited them) enjoyed considerable bargaining power vis-à-vis the rulers into whose territories they moved. Rajas and nawabs actively competed to attract talented people born beyond their realms, and the evidence suggests that South Asia in the early modern period was an attractive destination for migrants from far and wide, whether inner, central or west Asia, who had the skills these polities needed. Little is known about the mechanisms — if indeed any existed — used by states to count outsiders (although see Peabody, 2001), or to prevent their entry or exit.

Few of these migrants, however, appeared to regard the kingdoms from which they were drawn as 'home'. While they maintained connections and made remittances, as Markovits, O'Hanlon, Ballard and Washbrook show, these were driven by links to family and household, to eminent towns and to temples. We get little sense of an allegiance to a 'homeland' which Safran (1991) and others have held is a defining feature of diaspora.

The rise of British power in the subcontinent transformed many of these earlier patterns. British rule created a novel kind of state in India, which tried to curtail certain forms of mobility while enabling others. In the nineteenth century in particular, one thrust of British policy was to settle (or 'sedentarise') people on the land (Washbrook, 1993; Bayly, 1988) and to disarm the roving bands who challenged their attempts to impose their rule on the ground. As Kolff's essay shows, after the Rebellion of 1857, the thriving market for mobile mercenaries all but completely collapsed, as the Raj sought to achieve a monopoly over military force. But there remain fascinating hints of continuity with older times. As new demands for labour emerged from plantations, factories and mines across the empire, India included, the recruitment zones tended to replicate the old hinterlands from which the peasant soldiery had been drawn – the very same unwatered tracts of present-day Uttar Pradesh, Bihar, Orissa and Andhra Pradesh that had produced thousands of willing warriors for the armies of the past. The scribal and service groups whom O'Hanlon describes seem to have adapted themselves swiftly to work for the Raj and to migrate far and wide in search of official and professional employment (Chattopadhyaya, 1987; Zachariah, 1964). Young men joined the British Indian Army, a fighting force that not only defended India itself but also projected British power east of Suez. The merchants who are the subjects of Markovits's essay continued to ply their trade, although now increasingly they operated within the British empire, taking advantage of such limited protections afforded by imperial subjecthood and opportunities to trade in markets opened up by European expansion.

Of course, there were significant new developments, and it would be unwise to underestimate their impact. Transport was revolutionised by the railways and steamships. The ships (and trains) themselves became vital vectors of mobility, as Ravi Ahuja shows in his discussion of 'the age of the lascar' (see also Ahuja, 2006). Sprawling new metropolises grew up in Calcutta, Madras and Bombay, and later New Delhi: offices, mills and factories became new magnets drawing migrant labour from their agrarian hinterlands (Chandvarkar, 1994; Sen, 1999; Basu, 2004; Joshi, 2003). These centres also became hubs for recruiting lascars, generating fresh streams of emigration from the Konkan coast and from the Pashtun- and Punjabi-speaking tracts in northern India; while the interior district of Sylhet, bordering on Assam, emerged as the most important source of recruitment by far for Britain's worldwide merchant marine. Pilgrimage, already popular in the early modern era, albeit limited by the huge costs and rigours of travel, now exploded. South Asian Muslims in their thousands flocked to the Hijaz for the Hajj; while, within the subcontinent, religious fairs (such as the Kumbh Mela, see Maclean, 2008), temples and sufi shrines drew ever larger numbers of the devout. New destinations emerged as well: a few lascars jumped ship in British ports, joining the small but significant 'counterflow' of Indians to Europe who, as Michael Fisher shows in his essay, had begun since the early modern era to travel to Europe.

But perhaps the most pronounced change during the imperial period was in the role of the state in migration. As Chatterji points out, the late-colonial government of British India watched over and, where it deemed it to be important for reasons of state, prevented the ingress and egress of persons. But it also actively organised emigration on a huge scale deploying the indenture system, discussed in this volume by Brij Lal and Samita Sen. Famously described by High Tinker as 'a new form of slavery', indenture has traditionally been viewed as a form of forced migration that exploited the poverty of the most disadvantaged Indians and subjected them to harsh and unremitting regimes that they were powerless to resist (Tinker, 1974; Breman, 1990). New scholarship, represented in this volume by Lal and Sen, has begun to refine that picture. As Sen's essay suggests, the Raj's regime of indenture was indeed violent and racist, but it was also incoherent and incompetent. Unquestionably, indentured migrants were subject to brutal exploitation. But they were far more informed about pay and working conditions at different destinations, and more capable of negotiating them, than previous scholarship has assumed.

Sen's women migrants evaded or ignored the blandishments of jobbers and government to travel to destinations that they knew were better avoided. The world of the indentured labourers overseas proves to have been one in which migrants moved more readily to some destinations rather than others, and shared more information about conditions there than was previously recognised. A different, and far more complex, picture of the Indian Ocean world of the late nineteenth and early twentieth centuries is thus emerging from these accounts, with significant questions about the survival of older networks and the agency of 'victims' of the indenture system. But, in its assumption of the role of 'Protectors of Emigrants' (Warhurst, 1984), and 'Protector of Pilgrims' (Singha, 2008), the will of the imperial state to manage migration is apparent.

A fundamental question that these essays raise is whether the mobile South Asian communities of the early modern and imperial periods should be seen as a diaspora at all. Scholarly debates about the definition of diaspora continue to rage (Safran, 1991; Tololyan, 1991; Gilroy, 1997; Clifford, 1997; Cohen, 1999; Sheffer, 2003; Brubaker, 2005). Safran (1991) influentially defined diasporas as 'expatriate minority communities' which share six key features: 1) they are dispersed from an originary centre of origin to at least two 'peripheral places'; 2) they maintain a 'memory, vision or myth about their original homeland'; 3) they 'believe that they are not – and perhaps cannot – be fully accepted by their host country'; 4) the ancestral home is seen as a place to which to return; 5) they are committed to the maintenance or restoration of this homeland; and 6) they share a consciousness and solidarity as a group through a continuing relationship with the homeland. Other scholars have taken issue with this definition but, as Brubaker has noted, most common working definitions of diaspora underline three characteristics – dispersion across space, homeland orientation and boundary maintenance. He stresses how important it is not to regard diaspora as bounded groups of members, 'an ethnodemographic or ethnocultural fact', but has instead urged scholars to think in terms of diasporic 'stances, projects, claims, idioms, practices' (Brubaker, 2005: 13).

How far did mobile South Asians dispersed across space in the early modern and imperial periods develop such stances, projects or claims? It is of course difficult to generalise. For some, such as the Brahmin scribes whom O'Hanlon describes, 'boundary maintenance' across generations, as well as a degree of 'homeland orientation', was a vital part of their migration strategy. Similarly, for the merchant communities discussed by Markovits, Ballard and Washbrook, tightly controlling group boundaries was crucial to their success in regulating complex commercial transactions with minimal state interference. Roy and Haynes's weavers, just as O'Hanlon's scribes, invested much effort in producing migration myths, genealogies and histories that emphasised their distinctiveness from their host society, and their distant origins in glorious places (Roy and Haynes, 1999). 'Boundaries' of caste, clan and *biradari* were critical tools in the recruitment methods of the jobbers who cajoled men and women to travel to work in armies, mills, plantations and ships. But for many others – such as the working women Sen describes, or Kolff's soldiers, or O'Hanlon's Kayasthas, or indeed Leonard's 'Punjabi Mexicans' – migration offered opportunities for reinvention, or even for breaking free from the bonds of home, caste and family. How far the peculiarly South Asian social institutions of caste and *biradari* enabled mobility on this vast scale, and how far these institutions were in turn affected by it, is an important question that remains to be answered. But whatever consensus scholars arrive at, it is difficult to discern instances of diasporic 'claims making' by early modern South Asians in their new settings.

The essays in Part III lend strong support to the idea that forms of diasporic consciousness only began to emerge in the late nineteenth and early twentieth centuries, side by side with the rise of nationalist modes of thinking. Stories of the sexual exploitation of indentured women were drawn in 'a discursive sweep', as Sen shows, into nationalist projects. Opposition to indentured emigration from India culminated in a movement between 1910 and 1920, led by prominent members of the Indian National Congress and notably including Gandhi, which contributed to its abolition. Gandhi's views about the problems of Natal's Indians, while a migrant himself in South Africa, were crucial to his emergence as an Indian nationalist. As Isabel Hofmeyr shows here, where the Mahatma had once couched his arguments for the welfare of Indians in South Africa in terms of a shared imperial subjecthood (i.e. that as subjects of the empire, Indians had a right to be treated as full subjects), increasingly he came to speak in nationalist terms, about 'national' belonging and 'national' boundaries. Sandhya Shukla's essay also reveals how J. J. Singh and Dilip Singh Saund in America proselytised for the cause of India's independence even as they fought for their rights – in a classic act of 'diasporic claims making' – in America. Read together, these essays suggest that nationalism – far from being the 'other' of a hybrid, diasporic consciousness – ought perhaps to be seen instead as a precursor, or even a partner, in the production of diasporic stances. Nationalism at home and diasporic claims making abroad were often interlinked projects, developing side by side, at the same time.

Decolonisation, and the proliferation of nation states after World War II, profoundly affected patterns of South Asian migration and settlement, both within the region and world-wide. The essays in this volume reflect upon these shifts, but also highlight important continuities with the past that have been largely overlooked. In her essay, Chatterji describes how the partition of the British Indian empire into the new nation states of India and Pakistan produced new diaspora on a vast, and hitherto unprecedented, scale, but hints that the sheer magnitude of refugee movements in South Asia after 1947 must be understood in the context of pre-existing migratory flows within the partitioned regions (see also Chatterji 2013). She also demonstrates that the new national states of India and Pakistan were quickly drawn into trying to stem this migration. As they put into place laws designed to restrict the return of partition emigrants, this produced new dilemmas for both new nations in their treatment of 'overseas Indians'; and many of them lost their right to return to their places of origin in the subcontinent, and also their claims to full citizenship in host countries. The central role of post-colonial conflict in generating streams of emigration, and new predicaments of exile, is also discussed in the Sri Lankan context in Nicholas Van Hear's essay. Since 1947, mobility within the subcontinent has been restricted in unprecedented ways by national borders and majoritarian nationalisms. At the same time other parts of the world, whether in the Indian Ocean region or beyond, restricted the entry of South Asians with ever growing zeal, sometimes expelling long-time residents. As Ali Nobil Ahmad shows, migrants have sought and found ways of evading these restrictions. But, together with an unprecedented rise in population and widespread agrarian poverty, these findings help us understand why the migration from countryside to towns and cities inside the countries of South Asia is now the dominant type of movement of peoples in the region.

The essays in this volume also draw attention to another fact that is all too often ignored in the study of South Asian diaspora. After independence, the states of South Asia remained powerful magnets, attracting migrants in vast numbers from across their borders. Sri Lanka's Tamils, Pakistan's Hindus and Sikhs, and India's Muslims moved in their millions not to the wealthier industrialised countries of the West, but to the 'right' country right across the new borders. The Deobandi Muslims, whom Magnus Marsden describes, reestablished their religious school in this period in the Chitral region of Pakistan, with consequences that remain palpable today. Nepalese Gurkhas, as David Gellner shows, continued in large numbers to migrate to, and to settle in, India. A decade later, as Fiona McConnell describes, Tibetans accompanying the Dalai Lama crossed the Himalayas into India, where they have remained ever since as a self-conscious 'nation-in-exile'. Ali Nobil Ahmad highlights the importance of Afghan migrant communities in Pakistan, and it is worth noting that Pakistan is the second most popular destination for Bangladeshi migrants. The states of South Asia, their poverty and under-development notwithstanding, have shown a remarkable capacity to absorb migrants; and even in an age of increasingly unporous borders, South Asians continue to deploy migration as a strategy of coping with poverty, insecurity and political exclusion. These continuities are largely overlooked in our understanding of post-colonial migration. The essays in the *Handbook* suggest that they call urgently to be explored if our understanding of contemporary globalisation is to be based on more secure foundations.

It remains true that restrictionist immigration policies have wrought significant changes upon post-war patterns of migration, and the *Handbook* suggests that it would be unwise to ignore them. Of course, restrictions are not as new as is sometimes thought (see the essays by Fisher, Ahuja and Eade), but there is no doubt that they have grown ever more stringent. South Asians keen to move abroad resort more and more to 'facilitators' who specialise in organising illicit migration to key destinations and who perhaps are replacing (or a least supplementing) the informal migration networks of old. This lucrative business of 'facilitation', as Ahmad shows, has raised the premium on legal migration, whether to the countries of the Persian Gulf or to the countries of the West, the latter now permitting the entry only of 'bona fide' students and the highly skilled. But, even in these new trends, we see legacies of older histories. Washbrook suggests that the flow of highly qualified Indians to the USA draws upon older habits and histories of high-caste, scribal migration. Eade's essay on Bengali migrants in Britain, likewise, is suggestive of how an older stream of Sylheti seafarers has changed and diversified strategies of migration and work in response to changing labour markets and immigration restrictions in the UK, and Yunus Samad considers similar processes among Pakistanis. In a fascinating essay, Gardner throws light on how, in their turn, these changes have transformed the regions which send out migrants of the subcontinent such as 'Londoni' Sylhet, setting up, in their turn, new local streams of immigration from poorer neighbourhoods into the area. It suggests that much more research needs to be done on the transformative effects of large-scale emigration on the 'sending' areas of the subcontinent.

The final group of essays in this collection explore the deeply interesting cultural effects and expressions of the self-consciously diasporic South Asians abroad in the late twentieth and early twenty-first century. They challenge any simplistic notion of the 'creolisation' of religion and culture, or the one-way 'assimilation' of migrants into supposedly homogenous host societies. The variety and complexity of texts produced by South Asian 'diasporic' authors, as Kabir shows, belies common assumptions about 'elitist' 'Indian' writing in English. Introducing readers to literatures in languages other than English, produced by authors writing from a variety of class and subject positions, and indeed from different types of diaspora – whether indentured labour, partition refugees or skilled post-colonial migrants to the West – she shows us how these works reflect, in very different ways, on 'the tension between roots and routes'. Other essays encourage readers to consider 'cultures' abroad as 'fields of power' (Webner); to see them not only as modes of expression but as sites of debate and contestation, whether about dress (Tarlo), music (Kim and Alexander), food (Sengupta), cinema (Dwyer), religion (Werbner and Zavos) or marriage (Mody). They highlight the multifaceted ways in which South Asians self-consciously use markers of identity (dress, food, music and literature) to challenge popular stereotypes about cultures and also structures of power – both within the community and beyond – that sustain and reinforce them.

In our view, many of these articles draw attention to how deeply political even the most everyday cultural practices inevitably become in the context of diaspora. Given strident forms of patriotism prevalent in many host societies, and given the racism and increasingly hysterical attitudes of Western 'receiving' states towards migrants of South Asian, and particularly Muslim, origin (on which the essays of Eade, Devji and Gould throw light), can 'diaspora consciousness' ever be apolitical? It is hard to see how migrants can lead lives that are not affected by the discourses that surround them, even if they wish to do so. Every time a South Asian woman, say, in Britain, wakes up and decides what to wear, as Mody and Tarlo have shown, she has perforce to make a choice about where to position herself in relation to a host of cross-cutting, often shrill, debates about 'right' dress, 'right' conduct, the rights of individuals, families and communities, and the 'duty' of migrants to assimilate. Whatever she does, then, involves adopting a diasporic 'stance', of one sort or another.

This raises questions about Brubaker's influential proposition that 'not all those who are claimed as members of putative diasporas themselves adopt a diasporic stance' (2005: 12). These essays suggest that a putative diaspora is never singular, even if some of its self-proclaimed spokesmen insist that it is. Diasporic stances can be (and perhaps more often are) everyday, and very local, acts of positioning, redefinition and negotiation, as much as they are about declaring an affiliation to a distant 'homeland' or the global '*ummah*'. The political attitudes of receiving societies, then, both at local and national levels, need to be brought back to the centre ground in refining our understanding of how, when and why diasporic cultures and stances come to be fashioned.

Finally, this collection suggests something important about women and diaspora. It has so often been claimed that women migrants abroad reproduce the culture of 'home' that the proposition is now taken for granted. The narrative would have us believe that single male migrants move easily within receiving societies, producing cosmopolitan or convivial cultures. They mix with local people and take on local mistresses and wives; they create none of the problems of self-segregation that characterise diasporic cultures. It is only when 'their' women arrive, importing their inconvenient 'culture' in their tattered suitcases, that ethnicity and culture also problematically begin to be recreated abroad. Women do all the work of boundary maintenance, so it is assumed, through food, dress, religious observance and marriage alliances for their children, thus producing, maintaining and policing the ethnic boundaries of closed and inward-looking diasporic communities.

The essays in this collection suggest that this assumption, as so many others, calls to be re-examined. Sen's essay shows that it was indentured men, not women, who demanded the imposition of religious laws governing marriage in distant lands; and Mody shows how many queer women negotiate and subvert expectations of filial and wifely obedience. Leonard tells us that Mexican American men took great offence at the marriage of 'their' women to Punjabi men, even causing a 'race riot' in 1918. Other essays demonstrate that, since the early modern period, men have been actively involved in the recreation of community in their places of settlement, whether by producing caste histories (Roy and Haynes) and genealogies (O'Hanlon) or by building temples (Washbrook). We need to learn a great deal more about the movement of women, both within and outside the context of marriage, since early modern times.

There are other comparative questions that remain unanswered. How do we account for the sheer scale of South Asia's diaspora, compared with that of other parts of the world? It would seem that South Asians have travelled more readily and in greater numbers than people from many other parts of the world – other than perhaps China (Kuhn, 2008). Why has this been so? Did (and does) South Asia have social institutions – whether caste, *biradari* or exceptionally robust kinship structures – that are particularly enabling to movement? How far have these institutions been shaped by mobility, rather than (as is often assumed) by stasis? And if South Asian society has strong dispositions and institutions favouring mobility, how then do we account for the very large numbers who do not move, even in times of great hardship and danger? (Alexander, Chatterji and Jalais, forthcoming). Does South Asia share features with other societies – such as China – that have produced diaspora on a comparable scale? Has migration from these two great regions indeed been qualitatively different from the 'Atlantic' migrations of the West, as scholars have long believed? All these raise exciting questions for further research and comparative thinking. If this *Handbook* stimulates new investigation into these problems, it will have served a useful purpose.

Note

1   *Report of the High Level Committee on Indian Diaspora*, www.indiandiaspora.nic.in (last accessed on 30 January 2013); *World Bank Migration and Remittances Factbook* 2011, http://siteresources.worldbnk. org/INTLAK/Factbook (last accessed on 30 January 2013).

References

Ahuja, Ravi (2006) 'Mobility and Containment: The Voyages of South Asian Seamen, c. 1900–1960', *International Review of Social History*, 51.

Alexander, Claire, Chatterji, Joya and Jalais, Annu (forthcoming) *The Bengal Diaspora*.

Amrith, Sunil S. (2011) *Migration and Diaspora in Modern Asia*, Cambridge: Cambridge University Press.

Basu, Subho (2004) *Does Class Matter? Colonial Capital and Workers' Resistance in Bengal, 1890–1937*, Delhi: Oxford University Press.

Bayly, C. A. (1988) *Indian Society and the Making of the British Empire*, Cambridge: Cambridge University Press.

Breman, Jan (1990) *Footloose Labour: Working in India's Informal Economy*, Cambridge: Cambridge University Press.

Brown, Judith (2006) *Global South Asians: Introducing the Modern Diaspora*, Cambridge: Cambridge University Press.

Brubaker, R. (2005) 'The "Diaspora" Diaspora', *Ethnic and Racial Studies*, Vol. 28, No. 1, pp. 1–19.

Chandavarkar, Rajnarayan (1994) *The Origins of Industrial Capitalism in India: Business Strategies and the Working Classes in Bombay, 1900–1940*, Cambridge: Cambridge University Press.

Chatterji, Joya (2013) 'Dispositions and Destinations: Refugee Agency and "Mobility Capital" in the Bengal Diaspora, 1947–2007', Vol. 55, No. 2, pp. 273–304.

Chattopadhyaya, Haraprasad (1987) *Internal Migration in India. A Case Study of Bengal*, Calcutta: K.P. Bagchi and Co.

Clifford, J. (1997) *Routes: Travel and Translation in the Late Twentieth Century*, Cambridge, MA: Harvard University Press.

Cohen, P. (1999) 'Rethinking the Diasporama', *Patterns of Prejudice*, Vol. 33, No. 1, pp. 3–22.

Gilroy, P. (1997) 'Diaspora and the Detours of Identity', in K. Woodward (ed.) *Identity and Difference*, London: Sage.

Joshi, Chitra (2003) *Lost Worlds: Indian Labour and its Forgotten Histories*, Rnikhet: Permanent Black Press.

Kuhn, Philip A. (2008) *Chinese Among Others. Emigration in Modern Times*, Maryland: Rowman and Littlefield.

Lal, Brij V., Reeves, Peter and Rai, Rajesh (2006) *The Encyclopedia of the Indian Diaspora*, Singapore: Editions Didier Millet in association with the National University of Singapore.

Ludden, David (2003) 'Presidential Address: Maps in the Mind and Mobility in Asia', *Journal of Asian Studies*, Vol. 62, No. 4.

Maclean, Kama (2008) *Pilgrimage and Power: The Kumbh Mela in Allahabad, 1765–1954*, Oxford: Oxford University Press.

Metcalf, Thomas R. (2008) *Imperial Connections; India in the Indian Ocean Arena, 1860–1920*, Berkeley and Los Angeles: University of California Press.

Peabody, Norbert (2001) 'Cents, Sense, Census: Human Inventories in Late Precolonial and Early Colonial India', *Comparative Studies in Society and History*, Vol. 43, No. 4 (October).

Roy, Tirthankar and Haynes, Douglas (1999) 'Conceiving Mobility: Migration of Handloom Weavers in Precolonial and Colonial India', *Indian Economic and Social History Review*, Vol. 36, No. 1, pp. 35–67.

Safran, W. (1991) 'Diasporas in Modern Societies: Myths of Homeland and Return', *Diaspora*, Vol. 1, No. 1, pp. 83–99.

Sen, Samita (1999) *Women and Labour in Late Colonial India: The Bengal Jute Industry*, Cambridge: Cambridge University Press.

Sheffer, Gabriel (2003) *Diaspora and Diasporism*, Cambridge: Cambridge University Press.

Singha, Radhika (2008) 'Passport, Ticket, and India-rubber Stamp: "The Problem of the Pauper Pilgrim" in Colonial India ca. 1882–1925', in Fischer-Tine, Harald and Tambe, Ashwini (eds) *The Limits of British Colonial Control in South Asia, Spaces of Disorder in the Indian Ocean Region*, New Delhi: Cambridge University Press.

Tinker, Hugh (1974) *A New System of Slavery: The Export of Indian Labour Overseas 1830–1920*, Oxford: Oxford University Press.

Tololyan, K. (1991) 'The Nation State and its Others: In Lieu of a Preface', *Diaspora*, Vol. 1, No. 1, pp. 3–7.

Warhurst, P. R. (1984) 'Obstructing the Protector', *Journal of Natal and Zulu History*, VII.

Washbrook, D. (1993) 'Economic Depression and the Making of Traditional Society in Colonial India', *Transactions of the Royal Historical Society*, Vol. 6, No. 3, pp. 237–63.

Zachariah, K. C. (1964) *A Historical Study of Internal Migration in the Indian Subcontinent, 1901–1931*, New York: Asia Publishing House.

PART I

Mobile South Asians in the early modern world

1

THE WORLD OF THE INDIAN OCEAN

David Washbrook

In the days when the sea was regarded less as a barrier to communication than the easiest means of it, the ocean surrounding the Indian peninsula guaranteed it a significant place in the histories of its adjacent continents. In the ancient world, contacts were especially strong towards the east, where peoples native to India carried their trade, their technologies and, perhaps most of all, their ideas into new lands. Physical evidence of colonization and settlement is, admittedly, scarce: confined, for the most part, to northern Sri Lanka and to relics of the sea-borne empire of the South Indian Chola dynasty (tenth–twelfth centuries CE), found as far away as Java and Sumatra (Hall: 1985). However, 'softer' evidence of cultural influence is much stronger and unmistakable. Two of the great religious traditions of east and south-east Asia had their origins in the Indian subcontinent: Sanskritic Hinduism, whose mark stretched from Angkor Wat in Cambodia to Candi Perumban in Java; and Buddhism, whose reach and remit proved to be greater still.

Recognition of this cultural influence in the nineteenth and early twentieth centuries led many theorists to suppose the sometime existence of a 'Greater India', even a world-empire once centred on the subcontinent, which time and history had come to erode. Yet, as Sheldon Pollock has warned, while flattering contemporary sentiments of nationalism, such theories need to recognize that, if this were an 'empire', it was one like none in the modern world. There is little – beyond the Chola naval expeditions – to suggest an expansionary political drive or even political means to sustain an apparatus of hegemony. Also, there is little to suggest the large-scale physical movement of people. Rather, India's influence was conveyed via the activities of individuals or small groups of merchants, priests, intellectuals and service personnel and it achieved its strength from the willingness with which recipients embraced what they brought with them: sophisticated theories of society and law; a language of unparalleled precision and elegance; in Buddhism, a religion offering a universalistic moral schema. Sanskritic (and related Pali) cultures were rapidly imbibed, 'indigenized' and made independent of the need for continuing institutional links with the subcontinent. 'Greater India' represented a cosmopolis of ideas whose impact vastly outreached the small number of 'Indian-natives' ever physically present at its frontiers (Pollock: 2006).

Moreover, included in this universe of ideas were technologies which forged connections no less deep. The superior quality of Indian cotton textiles was recognized throughout the ancient and medieval worlds, and the technologies producing it also were eventually exported worldwide.

However, it took far longer to replicate these technologies than it did Sanskrit, 'the language of the gods' – in the case of south-east Asia, not until the seventeenth century CE and, in that of Western Europe, not until the eighteenth. In the interim, the subcontinent enjoyed the reputation of 'the workshop of the world' whose goods were conveyed to markets from the Levant (and eventually Western Europe) to Africa, south-east Asia and China – and, very often, conveyed by merchants who were native to India itself. Almost from the time that we first have records, there appear to have been Indian merchant-communities resident in the consumption centres of the Indian Ocean world: Cairo and Baghdad; Zanzibar and East Africa; Sri Lanka; Java, Sumatra and the Malaysian archipelago (Pearson: 2003). The staple of their trade was cotton textiles. However, this put them in a position to profit from other goods which consumers sought from India – especially spices and gem-stones – and also those which were wanted by Indian consumers themselves – coffee, silk, specie and base metals. For more than a millennium, thousands of small ships criss-crossed the Arabian Sea and the Bay of Bengal, articulating a lively commerce in which Indian merchants and ship-owners played a leading role. Indeed, Indian mercantile activities were by no means confined to the sea. Utilizing the 'gateways' into central Asia represented by the 'silk road' east and the 'horse road' north and west, they penetrated deep into the interiors of the Russian and Chinese empires (Dale: 1994). Reflective of the sophisticated commercial knowledges built up in India's then highly developed economy, the equivalent term to 'Indian' was virtually synonymous with 'merchant' in half a dozen languages of the region, much as 'Jew' was with 'banker' in medieval Europe.

Yet the subcontinent's relative economic development did not only give rise to merchant communities. It also drew 'foreign' merchant communities towards India, along with hosts of other groups – soldiers and slaves, priests and literati, artists and artisans. Recent archaeological investigations in both the south-east and south-west have revealed a much more expansive trade with ancient Rome than once was supposed, to match what has long been known about these regions' direct connections with imperial China (Whittaker: 2009). Connections, too, with Jewish merchant communities centred on Cairo and Armenian communities from the Caucuses also can be traced to the first millennium of the Christian era, as can the beginnings of the influx from the Levant represented by the Syrian Christian community of Kerala (Goitein and Friedman: 2007).

The rise of Islam, however, may have marked a new watershed. Arabian-based merchants – who, no doubt, had long conducted trade with Indian ports – became much more visible as a religious mission was added to their pursuit of wealth. From the eighth century CE, the southern peninsula saw a build-up of Muslim merchant communities whose activities moved progressively eastwards – penetrating south-east Asia, too, behind the green flag of Islam. Ports on the south-east and south-west coasts now became staging posts in an elongated set of linkages connecting Arabia to Aceh (Wink: 1991).

In the north, other forces were also at work. The road from central Asia to Punjab became the pathway for successive waves of conquest by armies of Muslim warriors, culminating with the Mughals at the beginning of the sixteenth century. However, it opened the way not only for soldiers but for the full panoply of Islamic civilization, especially in its Persian adumbration. Poets and theologians, sufi pirs and bureaucrats, musicians and artists poured in to service the courts of Muslim rulers and the growing congregation of 'indigenous' converts to Islam. North India, in particular, but also many urban centres dispersed through the subcontinent, became drawn into extended networks of patronage and ideas, making them part of a much wider Islamic ecumene and giving elite levels of several local societies a distinctly Islamicate appearance (Wink: 1991). And, from the turn of the sixteenth century, Western Europeans began to add their own presence to this extraordinary mix – initially from the Catholic Mediterranean but, during the seventeenth century, from the Protestant north as well. While never large in number, their impact immediately added to the forces of commerce driving India into the world – and much of the world into India. They linked the subcontinent to the new flows of specie metal coming out of the Americas (and Japan) and contributed disproportionately to the progressive monetization of the economy in the Mughal Empire under Akbar, which further developed it as a world-significant centre of trade and commerce (Richards: 1987).

In the millennium prior to the onset of colonial rule, Indian society – especially, but by no means exclusively, around its port cities – presented a picture of remarkable cultural plurality. Large parts of it consisted of communities of immigrants from many different quarters of the subcontinent and the Indian Ocean world: each preserving aspects of their language and culture but living side by side in some species of harmony informed, it can be surmised, by social paradigms derived from the Hindu caste system. The nature of this cultural plurality has been brilliantly evoked in Amitav Ghosh's imaginative portrait of medieval Mangalore in his *In An Antique Land* (Ghosh: 1993). However, and importantly, each of these groups was not only part of a single local community, but also linked to wider communities yet which inhabited other locales in other societies and might be influenced by pressures arising there. Social harmony was by no means guaranteed and, in a context of weak state authority, conflict and violence were ever-present dangers: as K.N. Chaudhuri has put it, the strongest guarantor of security was always coercive force (Chaudhuri: 1985). It would be problematic to allow a post-modern angst against the homogenization of national identity to lead to a romanticization of conditions of life in pre-modern cultural pluralities.

It would also be problematic to subject description of the relations of the pre-modern Indian Ocean World to categories derived from latter-day modern nationalism. In many ways, 'India' as a meaningful socio-geographic space, did not exist in this era. Rather, as K. N. Chaudhuri has also argued, the territory represented by India might better be seen as divided between three concentric 'circuits of trade and civilization' connecting parts of its society to parts elsewhere across the Indian Ocean. One circuit linked north India to central Asia and Iran; a second linked western India to Arabia and the Gulf; a third linked south India to south-east Asia (Chaudhuri: 1985). People, goods and ideas moved around these circuits: it being neither meaningful, nor often possible, to specify where any especially originated. The circuits also converged and overlapped at certain points, and they overlay other, more spatially restricted circuits. Although, by the tenth century CE, it had become almost entirely confined to the subcontinent, there was also the circuit represented by 'Bharat' – sacred to Sanskritic Hinduism, centred on the Ganges and stretching out to dispersed temple and pilgrimage centres across India. And, by the twelfth and thirteenth centuries CE, with the rise of vernacular literatures, there were the circuits describing the parameters of discrete regional cultures as well.

Identity was gained by reference to points on these circuits and could be both multiple and contextual: an individual could be a Gujarati, a Hindu, a Vaishya, an Arabic speaker and the agent of a Muslim court all at the same time. The context was one in which, in some senses, every-body was an 'immigrant', referring themselves to locations and sources of authority and value elsewhere: as noted in this volume, virtually all Indian origin myths specify arrival from another place. But, by the same token, being an 'immigrant' was wholly unexceptional where there were no self-evaluating 'indigenes'.

Into this highly mobile, pulsating and variable Indian Ocean world, the Western Europeans 'inrupted' from the sixteenth century CE. Much controversy surrounds how far, in what ways and when they disrupted it and what they built in its place. From the beginning, it can be said that they struggled to understand it and to abide by its norms. With their recent Iberian experience, the Portuguese targeted Islam as 'enemy' at the start and added an edge to religious conflict – even if they were less clear about how to relate to Hindus. Also, their subsequent adoption of counter-reformation theology and nascent ideas of proto-national identity caused migratory ripples down the west coast, as considerable numbers of their would-be subjects in Goa moved away. However, the weakness of the Portuguese on land limited their ability to recast Indian society, at least until they became part of a much stronger European presence in the eighteenth and nineteenth centuries (Subrahmanyam: 1993).

But they were by no means so powerless at sea. From the first, they introduced ideas derived from their European experience, which had radical implications for Indian overseas trade. They sought to 'arm the sea' and to bring profit and power together in the way that they managed their commerce: establishing fortified ports, imposing cartaz (licences) on independent local shipping and treating rivals as 'pirates'. This fundamentally broke with an Indian Ocean tradition which had facilitated freedom of movement and trade. In any event, few of the small states and sultanates bordering the Ocean had possessed the naval power to seek to enforce monopolies. Moreover, the larger states (such as the Mughal Empire), which might have done, had other pre-occupations and regarded the encouragement of trade from multiple sources as a positive good. However, with the costs of running their far-flung empire high and returns from trade at risk from forces of competition, the Portuguese thought otherwise: bringing aggressive principles of mercantilism, forged out of the trade wars of Europe itself, into the Indian Ocean (Subrahmanyam: 1993).

Admittedly, and as Sanjay Subrahmanyam has argued, it would be easy to exaggerate the immediate impact of the Portuguese, whose resources and fleets were limited in scale and often diverted to alternative priorities. Nonetheless, the precedent was set and followed by other European powers as they rounded the Cape later on: the Dutch, the Danish, the French and the English. Over the course of the seventeenth and eighteenth centuries CE, they forced an increasing amount of India-centred trade into the bottoms of their ships, and reduced the scope of Indian-owned shipping, especially in the longer-distance trades. This did not necessarily mean a decline in the total volume of India's commerce – indeed, at times it would seem the reverse. The Europeans often found new markets for Indian goods and expanded India's trade to Africa, China and the New World. However, it did mean the progressive subordination of India-based, foreign-trade agencies to European control, and a dimunition in the scale and energies of Indian-based overseas mercantile organizations. If, in the early seventeenth century, the European companies themselves had rested on, and allied with, the vast commercial empires of the likes of Virji Vora, in Gujarat, and Kasi Viranna, on the Coromandel coast, by the mid-eighteenth century there were no comparable Indian mercantile magnates working the seas – their fall anticipating by half-a-century what was to happen to the land-based commercial empires of the likes of Jagath Seth in Bengal, on which the English Company rested. India-centred trading initiatives were further curtailed by the way in which rising European global power either undermined or destabilized the position of several of the consumer markets which Indian merchants had long served, especially in the Middle East and Iran, or closed them off to Indian-derived goods, as in 'Dutch' Java. If Indian-produced goods still continued to be sold in the eighteenth-century world, it was rather less by people from India itself and rather less around the Indian Ocean (Prakash: 1998).

Moreover, from the turn of the nineteenth century, it was rather less anywhere – at least for a time. While debates continue to rage about the extent to which British rule came to 'deindustrialize' India and destroy its domestic manufacturing, there can be no doubt that the effects of the British industrial revolution were to undermine its overseas textile trade for several generations – thereby suppressing the principal motor-force which had carried its people into the wider world. Indian cloth lost its global premium, and large numbers of the people who had transported and sold it found the demand for their skills and services in sharp decline (Chaudhuri: 1971).

In other ways, too, colonial rule seriously disrupted long-standing patterns of mobility and circulation. Most strikingly, India ceased to attract migrants from overseas on anything like the previous scale. As its economy suffered relative decline, and conversion into an agricultural colony, few people – beyond a handful of British imperial rent-seekers – found much profit in moving to it. While global economic migration may have grown exponentially in the nineteenth century, India was not a large recipient of it.

Also, connections to the Islamic world became attenuated, at least in an India-wards direction. In part, this followed from the extent to which parts of the subcontinent now became Dar-ul-Harb, a 'realm of war' – not just subject to the rule of non-Muslims, but a realm in which it was a Muslim obligation to wage war on their infidel rulers. But, in greater part, this attenuation may have resulted from the decline in the power of Muslim states and the potential patronage of Muslim elites.

If India's new rulers looked for 'service' personnel, it was to Europe, not to the wider Islamic ecumene. Also, British revenue demands progressively reduced the resources available to Muslim 'grandees' to invite poets, artists and musicians from abroad to entertain their courts or Muslim holymen to show them the way to salvation. Of course, this did not entirely break cultural connections with the wider Islamic world: in some ways, it encouraged Indian-based Muslims to emphasize those contacts even more as a means of recovering declining prestige and distinguishing themselves from the non-Muslim communities surrounding them. However, the wider Islamic world may have responded less enthusiastically than in previous eras, and sometimes attempted dialogues became painfully one-sided. When vast numbers of Indian Muslims were mobilized, after the First World War, to protect and save the Ottoman Khalifa, few of their co-religionists located elsewhere – even his notional countrymen – bothered to join them. Indian Islam now circulated in its own local eddies, away from the religion's mainstream, pursuing a more distinctive, but also more separate, existence for itself (Hardy: 1972).

Equally, the British Empire's ideologies of citizenship and nation- and subject-hood functioned towards similar ends. They made an absolute distinction between those – regardless of colour or creed – who had been born within the territories of the British Empire and those – even of the same colour or creed – who had not and who were 'aliens', at risk of deportation or worse. Indeed, the British Empire even extended this distinction inside the subcontinent to those who, whether fortunately or unfortunately, were born within the Princely states. Natality and residence now circumscribed identity and freedom of movement, permitting unwanted 'aliens' to be sent back whence they came without right of redress.

Yet colonial rule did not only block or break linkages around the Indian Ocean world. It also restructured them and created new ones. If, now, fewer 'foreigners' came to India's shores, or at least to settle long term, far more people born in India travelled abroad than ever before – and many still around that Ocean's rim. Indeed, emigration from India was to become one of the major forces of nineteenth- and twentieth-century global history. In part, this followed from the relative decline of the economy: where, for example, many of the first wave of labour migrants from south India to Burma and Malaya in the 1840s were disemployed weavers; and from north India to the Caribbean in the 1850s impoverished agriculturalists. However, in part, emigration was also pulled by new opportunities opened up by the expansion of Pax Britannica across and around the Indian Ocean.

Wherever Europeans conquered or established new port-cities, and set up new colonial states, they created a major need for infrastructure and skilled personnel. Yet Europeans were rarely able to supply this themselves: where the costs of keeping them in the tropics were astronomical and, before the age of modern medicines, they tended to die like flies. India, with its long traditions of a 'paper-state' and commercial economy, met this need on a grand scale. Clerks and accountants, soldiers and policemen, teachers and doctors moved out in large numbers to work in Singapore, Burma and Malaya; Sri Lanka; east and south Africa; Aden and the Persian Gulf – and, sometimes, even farther afield, to Hong Kong and Shanghai (Metcalf: 2008).

They followed, and sometimes led, larger contingents of humbler workers and labourers. Wherever the leading projects of colonial capitalism – in mines, plantations and construction – ran into problems of labour-shortage, whether from under-population or resistance, recourse was quickly had to the supposedly inexhaustible supply of 'coolies' available in India. Recruited mainly through systems of indenture, vast numbers of 'coolies' were exported over the course of the nineteenth century to open the plantations of Natal, Mauritius, Sri Lanka, Burma and Malaya – as well as those of Fiji, Trinidad and Guyana. By some estimates, as many as 5 million 'natives' of India left the subcontinent under British rule, most for other economies around the Indian Ocean. The imperial indentured labour system has been likened to a 'new system of slavery' and so, in distant parts of the world, it may have been (Tinker: 1974). However, in the Indian Ocean, proximity to 'home' eased some of its tensions, making it more a system of circulation – where many labourers took recurrent contracts, moving back and forth across the seas, and others found means to establish permanent communities abroad and, eventually, acquire land and living standards denied to them in British India itself (Amrith: 2009).

Also, if slowly, new economic opportunities emerged. Before the second half of the nineteenth century, these were few and far between – drawn mainly from attendance in a secondary capacity on the institutions of imperial commerce. Nonetheless, they were not entirely negligible. Several of India's currently leading business families – the Tata, the Goenka, the Birla – gained major boosts to their fortunes, and starting points for capital accumulation, in the opium trade to China and south-east Asia, which they served by sending out their own agents to key marketplaces. Also, some older trades survived and even prospered: niche markets for Indian textiles in the Gulf and Middle East were preserved, and Gujarati capital remained heavily involved in the Zanzibar slave trade (Machado: 2003).

However, it was the transport revolution – in steam-shipping and -railways – in the second half of the century that really pushed the Indian economy strongly back into the world. India became a large-scale exporter of wheat, cotton, jute, tea and oil-seeds in global markets. Much of this trade was handled overseas by European merchants and shippers, confining Indian capital to a domestic role. However, some Indian merchant houses carried it into markets where European rivals were fewer or had less interest. In particular, Indian commodities – which were often of low quality – found substantial markets outside the British Empire and in areas on the periphery of global commerce: in Eastern Europe, north-east Asia and around the Indian Ocean littoral. Established Indian merchant communities revived their activities and carried their commerce far and wide, their networks spanning large parts of the world once again (Markovits: 2008).

Also, new opportunities beckoned for new groups. Until the mid-nineteenth century, South India's Nattukottai Chettiars were principally known as 'uppu Chetties' (salt traders) who peddled their basic commodity through interior markets. However, the opening up of the Irrawady delta in Burma created the potential for a huge new 'rice bowl', which colonial capital found difficulty in servicing directly. The Nattukottai Chettiars stepped in as frontline creditors and intermediaries for European banks to take on the role of financiers and to spin out new 'indigenous' banking networks which reached Sri Lanka and Indonesia too. These networks were articulated through family connections which, of necessity, took increasing numbers of

Chettiars to settle (albeit temporarily) across south-east Asia. Natives of South India, especially, not only laboured around the eastern Indian Ocean littoral: some of them came to build significant capital accumulations, and to own large chunks of land as well (Rudner: 1994).

The transport revolution also had an effect in transforming older established relationships, for example with regard to the Hajj. In the past, while it may have been the desire of every Muslim to see 'the Holy Places' of Mecca and Medina at least once in a lifetime, very few had actually been able to accomplish it. In Mughal India, the Hajj had very much been an aristocratic pursuit, undertaken with due ceremony and splendour by royal courts and great nobles. Successive Mughal Emperors, in particular, had made a habit of sending their (several) mothers-in-law on Hajj to escape the stresses and strains of the seraglio. However, the increased availability and cheapness of transit via steam-ship now began to open up the opportunity of the Hajj to much wider Muslim constituencies. By the late nineteenth century CE, the numbers of pilgrims undertaking the Hajj had reached the thousands and, by the 1920s and 1930s, the tens of thousands. Many of those who went never came back: either disappearing into the desert or becoming part of local Indian communities whose size swelled accordingly. Others tried to get home but failed: creating problems of indigence in the port-cities of the Gulf and necessitating the establishment of Indian infrastructures to rescue and protect them. The popularization of the Hajj strengthened yet another tie between the subcontinent and the lands surrounding it (Singha: 2009).

Indeed, by the turn of the twentieth century, it may be no surprise that intellectuals were pondering the long-term historical existence of a 'Greater India' since one such had just come into existence around them. Far from merely rupturing the ties of an older Indian Ocean world, European colonialism had facilitated the development of new ones which were, if anything, even more intense. While its traffic was now more unidirectional – from India to other regions – it brought a strong and distinctively Indian cultural presence to adjacent lands. India's manufacturing economy partly revived on the demand for 'niche' goods coming from Burma, Malaya and Sri Lanka from the later nineteenth century. Commodities such as rice, rubber and tin flowed into the Indian economy from these sources in return. Indian capital supported British capital in the promotion of economic development. And, behind the money and the goods, tens of thousands of Indian-born people sojourned and/or settled every year, carrying their cultures and their life-styles with them. The Indian Ocean lived up to its name, with the subcontinent at the centre of multi-dimensional systems of trade and movement, tying the region together.

Yet if, ultimately, European colonial rule did not undermine the integrity of the Indian Ocean world, there was a threat for a time that its own nemesis might. From the turn of the twentieth century, the rise of nationalist ideologies began to question not just the right of 'foreign' Europeans to rule over other societies, but that of members of 'alien' cultures to be present in them at all. For Indian groups, the problem perhaps began in South Africa where an increasingly aggressive 'white' settler community sought to curb, and then expropriate, the rights of those who had initially been recruited to set up the Natal sugar industry (Bhana: 1998). But it then spread much more widely, targeting Indian groups who had come to provide support for imperial infrastructures or even, as with the Chettiars in Burma, who had played leading roles in the development of colonial capitalism itself (Charney: 2009). The strains were made much worse by the economic consequences of the First World War and of the Great Depression, which disarticulated the colonial economy and created more intense rivalries for work and subsistence in material circumstances marked by serious decline.

For a time, the Government of India attempted the role of imperial hegemon, trying to protect its subjects from threats to their rights and from 'riotous assemblies' wherever they might arise. However, it was compromised by its metropolitan connections and, even before the Second

World War, had ceded best to the new political forces: acknowledging deepening racial segregation (and Indian inferiorization) in Natal and Kenya; separating the government of Burma from that of India; denying 'hill Tamils' full constitutional rights in Sri Lanka. By the 1930s, the 'repatriation' of Indian capital and labour from Burma and Malaya was already under-way – before the Japanese invasion turned it into a tide, severely damaging the remaining links and breaking up what had been left of an eastern Indian Ocean economy.

From the late 1940s, the many new nation states lining up around the Ocean's littoral were by no means friendly to the idea of 'transnational' space either, and did their best to complete the work of the Depression and the War. Most new governments turned inwards, emphasizing their 'autonomy' and 'sovereignty' and reducing erstwhile interdependencies. Burma's rice and rubber no longer found markets in India, as the latter tried to create its own replacements at very considerable cost. Conversely, Indian commodities and labour no longer flowed so freely to south-east Asia and Sri Lanka, creating recurrent shortages there too. How much the disappoint-ing economic performances of most of these countries in the immediate post-colonial decades can be attributed to their respective searches for an illusory economic autarchy can now only be guessed. But, in the case of India, it may even have lain behind the heightened famine risks realized in the early 1960s.

Exacerbating these tensions were disputes over the citizenship and nationality of the residuum of erstwhile Indian Ocean integration, especially those millions with natal ties to India. Faced already with the daunting problems of Partition, India was hardly in a position to take a generous view of the award of its citizenship. It posed Indians overseas with a key dilemma: to abandon their lives abroad and return home or lose their nationality. The dilemma was made worse by the reluctance of many of their host nations to grant them 'full' citizenship or even any citizenship at all. The region became rife with rancorous disputes over nationality and responsibility: in Sri Lanka, 650,000 'hill Tamils' were left stateless for more than 30 years; in Malaysia, long-resident Indians were eventually offered a form of citizenship with restricted rights in relation to 'indigenous' Bhumipatra; in East Africa, especially Uganda, no less long-resident Indians were summarily expelled (Chatterji: 2012).

Nationalism, far more than colonialism, threatened the integrity of the Indian Ocean world. Indeed, and ironically, it started to accomplish a goal which European imperialism undoubtedly possessed but failed effectively to achieve. As their relations with each other deteriorated and became more overtly competitive, most of the new nations of the region turned increasingly towards the developed economies of the West: to strengthen their trade patterns; to encourage inflows of capital; and, in the case of India (which admittedly, did these first two rather less) to find homes and opportunities for their emigrants. For the first post-Independence generation, Bradford became much nearer to Amritsar than Dubai; London to Hyderabad and Madras than Kuala Lumpur.

Yet, even then, by no means all connections were lost and the groundwork was already being laid for another revival. The new state of Pakistan, which looked to the wider Muslim world for support and security, was much less restrictive in its terms of citizenship than was India, at least for Muslims (Talbot: 1999). Also, it benefited from one nexus which had not been broken by the rise of the nation state but which had continued to strengthen. The Hajj provided a direct conduit into the heart of the Islamic world, which the Pakistan government assiduously cultivated – not least, by issuing its own special Hajj banknotes, for use on the journey, between the 1950s and 1970s. Moreover, from 1973, the western Indian Ocean was convulsed by a seismic wave which impacted on the entire global political economy.

Following the 1973 Arab–Israeli war and the use of OPEC to cartelize the global market in oil, the wealth of the oil-producing nations of Arabia and the Persian Gulf increased exponentially, making them the new core centres of regional integration (Crystal: 1990). On the one hand, their development made huge demands for labour and skill, which, as in the colonial era, the Indian subcontinent was best-placed to supply. How many citizens of India, Pakistan, Bangladesh and Sri Lanka now live and work in the oil economies is hard to estimate, but it may be above 2 million. They can be found at virtually all levels of activity from engineers, doctors and businessmen to oil-field workers, cleaners and taxi-drivers. The remittances that they send back play a vital role in the economies of their own countries, especially in certain regions. Even recorded remittances (overlooking *hawala*) have regularly exceeded the annual value of foreign investments from all other sources, and sometimes equated to a third of total export earnings (World Bank: 2009). In places like Kerala, along the south-west Indian coast, remittance earnings during the 1980s equalled a third of per capita income. The oil economies have also become significant sources of regional investment: for example, in property development and urban renewal in Pakistan and India. Equally, they are major partners in trade: providing India and Pakistan with most of their energy imports and taking a wide range of manufactures and goods, including food produce and even flowers, in return. Many of the coastal districts in India and Pakistan are almost as much parts of an Indian Ocean regional economy as of their own national economies.

Moreover, the oil economies have not only drawn people and resources towards themselves. No less, they have exuded forces with equally important consequences. Rising wealth has promoted their cultural and political assertion: often associated with an Islam 'purer' and less constrained by other influences than in the rest of the region; and sometimes involving the export of long-standing, violent conflicts. Lavish patronage from Saudi Arabia and the Gulf has lain behind the prodigious growth of *madrasas* and religious institutions in Pakistan, Bangladesh and south-east Asia since the 1980s and contributed to the radicalization of an Islam which had lost much of its status in earlier colonial times (Noor: 1999). It has also pushed peoples from other parts of the Islamic world into South Asia – often as warriors to fight proxy wars, as in days of yore.

Towards the east, if from a somewhat later date, reconnections, albeit of a very different kind, have also been reforged. Abandoning policies of autarchy much earlier than in India, many of the economies of south-east Asia began to enjoy prodigious economic growth from the 1980s, based especially on industrial manufacture. However, and yet again, they soon ran into constraints on manpower and skills: leading, yet again, to the societies of the subcontinent having to come to their rescue and supply their needs. From the 1980s, demands for highly-educated labour started to draw Indian professionals and business personnel back towards Singapore and Malaysia and, not far behind them, Indian merchants and commodity brokers.

And, finally, the Indian giant itself stirred from its torpor – or overcame its paranoia – and, from 1991, began to reopen its borders to trade, investment and (official) in-migration from the surrounding region. Admittedly, economic integration between the countries comprising South Asia itself remains very tenuous: with the South Asian Association for Regional Co-operation proving itself something of an oxymoron (Batra: 2012). National suspicions, most obviously but not exclusively between India and Pakistan, remain high. Nonetheless, the pressures of globalization have taken down many barriers raised in previous decades and promise to do so increasingly in the future. Moreover, national suspicions apply much less to the countries which were never part of the same imperial state – to east and west – with whom all South Asian countries now appear eager to develop closer contacts.

If the Indian Ocean world today is constituted very differently from its ancient, medieval and colonial predecessors, it nevertheless remains vital and continues to condition each of its constituent parts. Goods, ideas and peoples still circulate around it: finding ways over – and often underneath – barriers of national exclusion wherever those are posted. Tamil may still be heard in the streets of Singapore, Chennai and Natal; just as Gujarati in those of Dubai, Mumbai and Hong Kong. Sacred Arabic texts are read in Oman, Deoband and Aceh; just as sacred Pali texts are read in Ladakh, Kandy and Bangkok. Kerala prawns can still be eaten in Kuala Lumpur and Malaysian palm-oil consumed in Kolkata. The Indian Ocean world is part of the twenty-first century just as it was of the eleventh, and even the first.

References

Amrith, Sunil: 'Tamil Diasporas across the Bay of Bengal', *American Historical Review*, 114:3 (2009), pp. 547–72.

Batra, Amita: *Regional Economic Integration in South Asia*. (London: Routledge, 2012.)

Bhana, Surendra: *Gandhi's Legacy*. (Durban: University of Kwa-Zulu Natal Press, 1998.)

Charney, Michael W: *A History of Modern Burma*. (Cambridge: Cambridge University press, 2009.)

Chatterji, Joya: 'South Asian Histories of Citizenship, 1946–1970', *Historical Journal*, 55:4 (2012), pp. 1–23.

Chaudhuri, K.N: *The Economic Development of India under The East India Company 1814–1858*. (Cambridge: Cambridge University Press, 1971.)

— *Asia Before Europe*. (Cambridge: Cambridge University Press, 1985.)

Crystal, Jill: *Oil and Politics in the Gulf*. (Cambridge: Cambridge University Press, 1990.)

Dale, Stephen F: *South Asian Merchants and Eurasian Trade 1600–1750*. (Cambridge: Cambridge University Press, 1994.)

Ghosh, Amitav: *In An Antique Land*. (New York: Arthur Knopf, 1993.)

Goitein, Shelomo Dov and Friedman, Mordecai: *India Traders of the Early Middle Ages*. (Leiden: E.J. Brill, 2007.)

Hall, Kenneth R: *Maritime Trade and State Development in Early South-East Asia*. (Honolulu: University of Hawaii Press, 1985.)

Hardy, Peter: *The Muslims of British India*. (Cambridge: Cambridge University Press, 1972.)

Machado, Pedro: 'Forgotten Corner of the Indian Ocean', *Slavery & Abolition*, 24:2 (2003), pp. 17–32.

Markovits, Claude: *The Global World of Indian Merchants 1750–1947*. (Cambridge: Cambridge University Press, 2008.)

Metcalf, Thomas R: *Imperial Connections: India in the Indian Ocean Arena 1860–1920*. (Berkeley: University of California Press, 2008.)

Noor, Farish A. (ed.): *The Madrasa in Asia*. (Amsterdam: Amsterdam University Press, 1999.)

Pearson, Michael: *The Indian Ocean*. (London: Routledge, 2003.)

Pollock, Sheldon: *The Language of the Gods in the World of Men*. (Berkeley: University of California Press, 2006.)

Prakash, Om: *European Commercial Enterprise in Pre-Colonial India*. (Cambridge: Cambridge University Press, 1998.)

Richards, John F: *The Imperial Monetary System of the Mughal Empire*. (Oxford: Oxford University Press, 1987.)

Rudner, David West: *Caste and Colonial Capitalism in India*. (Berkeley: University of California Press, 1994.)

Subrahmanyam, Sanjay: *The Portuguese Empire in Asia*. (London: Longmann, 1993.)

Singha, Radhika: 'Passport, Ticket and India Rubber-Stamp' in A. Tambe and H. Fischer-Tine (eds), *The Limits of British Colonial Control in South Asia*. (London: Routledge, 2009.)

Talbot, Ian: *Pakistan: A Modern History*. (London: Hurst and Company, 1999.)

Tinker, Hugh: *A New System of Slavery*. (Oxford: Oxford University Press, 1974.)

Whittaker, Dick: 'Conjunctures and Conjectures: Kerala and Roman Trade', *South Asian Studies*, 25:1, 2009, pp. 1–9.

Wink, Andre: *Al-Hind: The Making of the Indo-Islamic World*. (Leiden: E.J. Brill, 1991.)

World Bank: *Migration and Remittances Fact Book 2008*. (Washington: World Bank, 2009.)

2

THE MARKET FOR MOBILE LABOUR IN EARLY MODERN NORTH INDIA

Dirk H.A. Kolff

It is a long time since historians projected the idea of India as a huge collection of economically self-sufficient and politically autonomous village units. Another image, that of two worlds, one of settled agriculture and another of mobile, often pastoral, labour, and of the dynamic frontiers that held them together, has taken its place. In accepting this model, it should be noted, on the one hand, that the pastoral world never existed independently from town and village markets, while, on the other hand, the management of settled agriculture could rarely do without either an annual exodus of seasonal labour during the post-harvest season or the engagement of manpower from outside during the busiest months of the year (Gommans 2002: ch. 1). Long-term labour mobility, more often than not, was circulatory in character and did not lack an agrarian base in the region of origin; neither were sedentary villagers always unacquainted with far-away service, whether as weavers, soldiers or agricultural labourers. On the other hand, a region's circulatory tradition could, if it appeared attractive to do so, produce little diasporas. Sometimes, a man or a family who had left home with the intention to return would settle down somewhere along the road and it was not unusual for landed communities to invite in their midst stranger families with their ploughs and to integrate them in their systems of exchange of produce and division of labour, though such people might, even after years, be more prone to move on than the rest of the villagers.

It makes sense, therefore, to talk about a market for circulatory-cum-diasporic mobile labour in India as a phenomenon in its own right. It was fed by the interaction of different ecosystems, more especially by the dynamics of the frontiers that linked the worlds of agriculture and pastoralism, of settlement and mobility. That market played a crucial role both in the formation of Indian states at the regional and local levels and, through the distribution of earnings and the sharing of loot, in the survival strategies of peasants and cattle keepers. The mobility and the diasporas of India's villages and regions constituted the great machine of the subcontinent's social history. People never stopped looking for new niches in the labour markets within their migratory reach. The cog wheels of the machine, therefore, changed function over the seasons and the years. Their sizes waxed and waned. Its professional segments – agricultural, industrial, commercial or military – were not closed compartments. Both weavers and peasants, if mobile, were generally skilled in the use of arms and would change occupation or return home whenever it appeared advantageous to do so. To keep such options open was an essential part of their culture of survival and of their contribution to the economies of their communities and home villages.

Not all mobile labour could fall back on agrarian, village-based activity. More often than not such groups of men had their origin in pastoral India. We give only one, extended, example. Seventeenth-century Baluchi cameleers found employment as armed guards with caravan leaders on the main Gujarat to Hindustan routes. Many of them were archers, though some had firearms and swords. One European observer found them an unruly lot and warned against engaging both Baluchis and Jats as one's protectors, as they would likely attack each other instead of co-operating. Another, though convinced that in Baluchistan these people were bloody-minded villains, found that, in Gujarat, and even more towards Agra, there were many honest men among them. In long-distance commercial transport, they were indispensable. They cost 3.5 rupees a month. Their leaders, styled *muqaddam* (a term also used for village leaders) or *mirdahā,* received 4 rupees and travelled with their men.

They did not conduct caravans only. Any journey was inconceivable without them. They were easily hired in towns or *qasbas* along the road. There they had headmen – maybe called *chaudhri*s – who answered for their honesty and received a rupee for each contracted man. With other men of a pastoralist origin, many of them entered the regional military labour market of Gujarat under the denomination of *qasbātis*, townsmen, and, it appears, acquired some land. The *Mirāt-i Ahmadi* says about their activities in eighteenth-century Gujarat:

> They attacked villages, drove away cattle, escorted Mughal officials, took responsibility of collecting tribute from landholders on a small salary, they got enlisted as recruits in the army for a few days, served the chiefs and inspectors of the district police.

Generally reluctant to serve outside Gujarat, some of them nevertheless tried their luck in other provinces and 'made bravery their profession' (Ali Muhammad Khan 1965: 580). Direct employment by the empire could lead to the grant of land, even of entire villages. Aurangzeb, for instance, gave nine villages near Shamli in the Upper Doab to a number of Baluchis on the condition that they exterminate the numerous highway robbers in that part of the country. This made sense. Safety on the roads had all along been their specialty. In the Shamli area, they remained powerful throughout the eighteenth century and, when the East India Company took over the Upper Doab from the Marathas, the land revenue was settled with their chiefs (Kolff 2010: 297). Other Baluchis, however, did not settle down. In 1876, a group of Baluchi peddlers 'tramped through the villages' of the Panjab and the Central Provinces and spent the summer in Banda, Bundelkhand. As with so many travelling people there were rumours about them concerning extortion and thefts (Bhattacharya 2006: 199).

The above case may serve as an example of the social and spatial mobility that was typical of North India in the early modern period. The military labour market was only one aspect, though an important one, of this world pulsating with movement. The flexible entrepreneurship of the pastoralist Baluchis who turned travel guards, then *qasbātis*, regional and imperial soldiers, landholders-cum-policemen and finally village managers in colonial India, is just an illustration of the kind of occupational genealogies one meets along the roads of early modern India. To give one more example, weavers from small Kerala towns

> abandoned weaving and sought employment as day labourers, palanquin carriers and baggage bearers, messengers and peons, until they found a niche in the export economy of the [fifteenth-century] Kotte kingdom by specialising in the peeling of wild cinnamon, which they did in groups under the protection of armed guards because the villagers were not willing to let them enter their lands.
>
> *(Meyer 2006: 61)*

The multiplicity of vocational roles at the disposal of such people often baffled outsiders: only one occupation could be 'real', they thought; the others must be, perhaps criminal, 'disguises'. As late as 1895, the Harnis of the Panjab, 'well-known to be thieving by profession', were typically seen as peddlers who 'go disguised as fakirs, hakims and travelling merchants . . . or cattle merchants' (Bhattacharya 2006: 195). The survival culture of these groups of men always was one of negotiations in more than one direction, of risk-spreading management, of keeping open several occupational options and identities, and of a never fully successful search for wealth and secure patronage.

Especially in the world of settled agriculture, there must have been many cases in which peasants, though able artisans, as skilled in the use of arms as most life-long soldiers and, therefore, fit to set out as journeymen or enter the all-India labour market, never were under the necessity to leave home for long periods or fight over other than local issues. There were always many local issues. It was impossible to retain the respect of and to keep going to negotiations with armed travellers, hostile neighbours or the government itself, without a readiness to risk armed conflict. But even without the threatening presence of hostile outsiders, carefully measured dosages of violence were a necessary part of agrarian management. Armed gangs in the service of rural stakeholders were a phenomenon inseparable from the country scene.

The martial skills of men, however, became essential survival tools in other than strictly local circumstances. In combination with forms of small-scale migration, the use of force was often an integral part of the annual agrarian cycle. Seasonal soldiering or looting enabled quite a number of people in town and countryside to survive the slack agricultural season. In August 1636, soon after the onset of the monsoon, plundering ceased on the roads of Gujarat, partly because the rains made the peasants return to their fields. Similarly, the weavers of the town of Baroda in the 1620s, usually at home during the rainy season, went to serve in the provincial army in the dry months of the year. In times of dearth or famine, this occupational and spatial mobility of labour was the rule rather than the exception and must have saved many lives. No doubt, most of these men were fit to enter the regional or all-India labour markets, military or otherwise. Yet, their services were not in demand there as a matter of course (Kolff 1990: 4ff., 16).

When the rains and harvests failed, in cases of flood or unbearable devastations of war, many would leave their homes and look for work, weaving, ploughing or military, wherever there was food and quiet. In more or less normal years, however, the range of mobility of most settled people remained limited, even though they might hear of great prizes being won by others in far-away lands and felt a push to leave and try their luck. Artisans or armed peasants, in other words, could not always automatically accede to the itineraries of circulatory labour. This is especially true of the all-India level of the military profession that was organised around the elite of the empire. Why was this so?

One reason is that the survival strategy of the state – whether that of the Mughals or their predecessors – and those of the peasantries generally did not meet and suit each other. They had little ground in common. Confrontation was the rule. Strikingly, that confrontation produced a kind of migration, even a diaspora, of its own. Hindustan, the great fertile regions between the Panjab and Bengal, dominated by the rivers Ganga and Yamuna, saw relations between state and peasantry deteriorate. During the 1620s and 1630s, forms of enslavement, deportation and extermination came to mark these relations. It is reported that Abdullah Khan Firuz Jang, then in charge of the Kalpi-Kanauj region, defeated all the hitherto unsubdued Chauhan rajas and rebels there, had the leaders beheaded and the peasant wives, daughters and children, to the number of 200,000, transported to Iran and sold there. Abdullah Khan himself boasted that he had sold half a million women and men. Large numbers of them, also from other areas, were deported across the Indus, while Afghans were forced, though not as slaves, to move east.

Certainly, Abdullah Khan was more given to tyrannical methods of pacification than most of his contemporaries. But many peasant communities left their rulers with no choice but to take stern measures against them. Another aspect of this is the demand for labour in Iran and Central Asia, where many of these deported Indians must have been employed as peasants and artisans, as were the 120 slaves – tillers of grain, diggers of canals for irrigation, bronze and metal workers, a potter, a cook, a tinker, and a bowl maker, 'fathers, sons and grandsons … all Hindustanis', who were employed on an estate near Bukhara towards the end of the fifteenth century (Chekhovich 1974: 172, 233–4; Kolff 1990: 12ff.). Though its remnants may be difficult to trace today, this was a true medieval Indian diaspora involving hundreds of thousands.

Clearly, however, no state could be formed on the basis of the systematic deportation of potential taxpayers, certainly not an 'early modern', military-fiscalist state. Any policy aiming at the actual disarming of the countryside would have been even more impractical. Only the English East India Company would, in the 1798 to 1818 period, achieve something approaching the demilitarisation, though not the disarmament, of India. The Mughal empire, in other words, never overcame the problem of its being faced, not just with recalcitrant individual landholders, but with armed peasantries that represented the backbone of society and could not be destroyed without dire consequences to the agrarian productivity on which the regime depended for its survival. Let us, therefore, examine another course open to the empire, that of engaging as infantry a significant and well-selected number of those it could not otherwise control. This also leads us to a second reason for the difficult access to the all-India level of the military labour market: the fact that employment there was a semi-monopoly of those already active within it.

The question is whether the Mughal government was in a position to make its own choice of recruits from amongst the enormous human resource potential seemingly at its disposal. To an extent it was. A provincial Mughal force, sent against unco-operative subjects in Gujarat in 1684, included

> a numberless multitude of men of the country, consisting of Grasiyas and Kolis, who are tillers of the soil but follow the army by command in exchange for freedom of tribute; as they receive nothing for food, they keep themselves going mostly by theft.
>
> *(Kolff 1990: 17, 18)*

The local knowledge of such men was valuable and they were cheap. But their looting for a living would obviously do more harm than good and they could not easily be turned into units sufficiently dependable for use on a major battlefield.

A more important role was played in Mughal armies by highly mobile professional peasant soldiers. It is clear their services were in demand with the Mughal and the provincial armies of the empire. At the same time, the imperial officers were not entirely free to recruit whomever they wished, any more than the East India Company was when it drafted its sepoy army in the eighteenth century. It was only after 1857, when the modern British colonial state made the radical decision to shift its recruitment away from Hindustan, that such top-down authority was exercised in India. Before that time, the negotiating position of some of the village-based military service traditions was far stronger than, as far as I am aware, that of their contemporaries in Europe. Let me elaborate this theme with respect to the most striking example that can be found, the recruitment history of Avadhi and Bhojpuri Hindi-speaking Hindustan, exactly the part of North India where Abdullah Khan performed his atrocities.

The soldiering tradition of this region deserves to be treated as a whole. For almost four centuries, it tenaciously retained its position as a recruitment area for units of infantry that occupied a crucial role in imperial and regional state formation. As a tradition of peasant soldiering, it is traceable at least to the fifteenth-century Jaunpur sultanate of the Sharqis. Rajput agency made sure the sultans were served by war-bands of peasant soldiers. Evidence of the intimate nature of the alliances between the sultans and their Rajput warlords is that in the latters' households the presence of Muslim women was considered regular. After the last Sharqi sultan lost control of Jaunpur in the 1480s, a clan of local Rajputs spearheaded an insurrection in support of him in which 200,000 or even 300,000 footsoldiers were said to have participated. These were inflated figures no doubt, but, put against the 15,000 horsemen the source mentions, they clearly convey an idea of the enormous manpower called up from the regional peasantries. Subsequently, the conquest of Hindustan by the Lodi Afghans from the west reduced the chances of military employment in their own region for these levies. Many moved west and south in search of *naukari*, the term then and later used for the honourable service of roaming warriors. Thus these professionals made possible the renewed growth and splendour of the royal Tomar Rajput court at Gwaliyar, as well as of courts in Malwa and elsewhere. The term used for these soldiers, Purbiya, not only indicates their origin from the east, but also an identity of their own, an identity that was, however, due to their negotiated settlement with the Tomars who employed them.

After the collapse of Tomar hegemony in Central India, the Purbiya tradition of *naukari* launched its next soldiering incarnation. It now introduced in the north Indian military labour market a more distinct identity and a new brand name, that of 'Ujjainiya'. During the first decades of the sixteenth century, the members of the 'spurious' Rajput clan of the Ujjainiyas of Bhojpur in the south-west of Bihar indeed made themselves indispensable as specialised recruiting agents and jobber-commanders (*jamadārs*) of the peasant soldiers of the area, the Purbiyas. Their mediating role in selling the services of Bhojpuri men, in negotiating for them their conditions of employment and in leading them in the field was a cardinal one and explains how the name 'Ujjainiya' became the trademark and identity of the men they led. The great reputation these units acquired with the pretenders, warlords and rulers of North India was enhanced by the close association that developed between Ujjainiya brokerage and, first, the pilgrimage centre of Baksar near Bhojpur and, second, the Sur Afghans, then at the start of their comet-like emergence as a north Indian dynasty. According to a myth that enshrined the circulatory nature of this North India military service tradition, a bath in a holy tank of Baksar – that is a Tiger Tank – ensured a young peasant *jawān* not only consecration as a Saivite tiger-like warrior, but, importantly, also the promise of a painless deincarnation. The myth's message was that the memory of God's promise at Baksar that, however distant and long a man's service, however abject his duties or miserable his life, the road back home would always be open, was a component part of the Baksariya identity. After perhaps many (traditionally 12) years of service, one would again shed one's tiger nature and be a family man in one's own village. Farid Sur, the future Delhi sultan Sher Shah, depended a great deal on the Ujjainiya Rajputs' ability to muster men by the thousands – by no means all from their own clan, but from the inexhaustible manpower of Hindustan – and on his personal relationship with them. At the battle of Surajgarh, in which Sher defeated the Bengal army, he put 3,000 picked Afghans and 2,000 Ujjainiyas under their leader Gajpat in his first line. After the battle was won,

> all the spoils of war, comprising elephants, horses, and other equipments, which had fallen into the hands of [Gajpat] were allowed to be retained by him. At the time of departure of [Gajpat] he [Sher] tied with his own hand the bejewelled sword to hang round [Gajpat's] waist, bound his arm with a jewelled armlet, gave a string of

pearls round his neck, fixed a bejewelled ornament in his headdress, gave a horse, head-to-foot dress and a sword for prince Bairishal [Gajpat's brother] and gave Baksar as a fief to him.

(Ambashthya 1961: 438)

I have given this long quote, because of what it implies. It articulates and advertises the fame of the Ujjainiya leadership as an agency of much distributive intensity: *naukari* under a man like Gajpat meant a share in spoils that might be huge. In the chronicles telling the story of the great early sixteenth-century Purbiya *jamadār* Silhadi in Malwa, the emphasis on their wealth and largesse is even more explicit. The organised loot of large-scale war could be more profitable than the haphazard local plundering of straggling travellers and small groups of soldiers. Such promise of fortunes to be made far from home was later transferred to the rhetoric of Hindustani circulatory indentured labour, the latter-day successor of the Bhojpuri tradition of *naukari*. *Kantrākis*, contract labourers, engaged to go to Surinam in the nineteenth century were told the name of their destination contained the root *sonā*: gold.

The passage about the Gajpat–Sher relationship suggests that the degree to which one's dream as a *naukar* would come true was dependent on the diplomatic and entrepreneurial talent of the dealer in manpower or the recruiting warlord one joined and entrusted one's fate to. Agency, however, was as fluid as the circulatory labour market it served. In the case of Sher Shah, his bitter struggle with Humayun not only involved North India in civil war, but also split the Ujjainiya agency into rival factions. Both Sher and Humayun needed Ujjainiya subcontractors, in order to reach the best niches of the military labour market, as much as the local Rajput lineages needed the treasure and loot of major campaigns in order to maintain their pivotal position as brokers. Positions easily shifted; for groups of peasant soldiers, there was a constant need to reconsider one's alliance, one's temporary identity as the *naukar* of an Ujjainiya Rajput, and to re-evaluate the status of the lord or ruler whose salt (*namak*) one ate. On the other hand, and perhaps confusingly, the decision to serve an Ujjainiya lord could be a first step to assuming the Ujjainiya Rajput identity for good and be adopted as a member of the clan. In the military labour market, all identities were multiple, flexible, and possibly temporary, which meant that, instead of going home, one just might end one's life at a place that was not one's village of origin and that one might pass on to one's children an identity different from the one received from one's parents.

During the early modern period, neither the Ujjainiyas nor any other group of men could maintain themselves in a dominant position as brokers for very long. Though they hung on as managers of extensive agricultural tracts in western Bihar and as pugnacious leaders of undoubted regional notoriety, by the time of Shahjahan's reign they had been compelled to give up their role as the principal recruiters and middlemen of the military labour of central Hindustan. At least partly, their place was taken by the clan of the Bundela Rajputs of the region east of Gwaliyar and west of the home of the Ujjainiyas. No Bundela leader was ever as spectacularly successful in linking Hindustani peasant soldiering to imperial fiscal resources as Bir Singh Deo. It was his talent to put numerous units, mainly infantry, at the disposal of Jahangir, the emperor, without ever having to relinquish personal command over them. In 1615, his imperial rank was increased to 4,700, at that time a very high figure. Jahangir gave Bir Singh Deo, 'than whom in the rajput caste there is no greater nobleman', as he wrote of him, the title of maharaja. Like his Tomar and Ujjainiya predecessors, the financial means that Bir Singh Deo was able to invest in and extract from the Mughal state were impressive. In 1624, he first contributed a sum of between 200 and 300,000 rupees to the cost of the imperial campaign in eastern Hindustan against the rebellious prince Khurram, the future emperor Shahjahan, and in the end plundered the prince's camp seizing many gold coins, jewels, 3,000 horses and 40 elephants, as booty. Or perhaps it is better to say that he prevented Khurram's enemies from getting hold of these valuables, because, as a Dutch chronicler remarked, Bir Singh Deo was a great friend of the prince. As a manpower agent he had to have friends in both camps.

In Agra he had a palace on the river, next to the famous Man Singh Kachhwaha's mansion. A greater achievement of his was the Keshav Dev temple, devoted to Krishna, at Mathura, which, according to Tavernier, the French traveller, was one of the most sumptuous buildings in all India and was visited by large numbers of pilgrims. Bir Singh Deo himself went to Mathura as a pilgrim to weigh himself against an amount of gold which, together with an additional 81 *man* of gold, probably representing the 81 districts, or *parganas*, that constituted his realm, was then distributed in charity (Kolff and van Santen 1979: 187, 191/2, 225, 249; Kolff 1990: 128–30).

The religious side of the story of Bundela recruitment is further illustrated by the phenomenon of the veneration in which the peasant-soldiers who followed Bir Singh Deo and his successors came to hold Hardaul, one of the sons of the great Bundela. Hardaul was murdered by a brother of his and became the centre of a soldiers' cult that struck root in the core region of Purbiya recruitment, i.e. in all the districts that supplied young men (*jawāāns*) to Bundela middlemen or *jamadārs*. The story is too long to tell it here. The cult was yet another means through which peasant boys came to partake of the Bundela Rajput, or soldiers', identity (Kolff 1990: 145ff.). To some extent, it can be compared to the experience of some of the indentured labourers: that, during the sea voyage that brought them so far from their Indian homes, a kind of solidarity grew amongst them that made them into each others' *jahāzi bhāi*, ship brothers, an awareness that began fading old ritual distinctions and marked the emergence of a new group identity. In this case also, the adoption, in common with his fellow soldiers, of a religious identity provided him with the confidence he needed during his *naukari* years. In addition, however, the Hardaul myth was constructed so as to convey a message of soothing trust. It reassured the long-distance soldier that, whatever the machinations or rivalries in his home village, the women of his family would be cared for and saved from disgrace. It has, in other words, a clear circulatory quality.

After the death of Bir Singh Deo in 1627, Bundela agency would slowly lose its grip on the procurement of military labour for Mughal India. The market for infantry as a *longue durée* phenomenon once more entered a new phase, this time emancipated from clan brokerage. The emphasis shifted to the jobbing and ritual practices at the brahmanical pilgrimage town of Baksar, in a sense the ritual centre, as we saw, of the old Purbiya and Ujjainiya recruiting grounds. As early as 1580 we hear of a Brahman Mughal officer who attempted to draft soldiers at that place or, rather, at the holy tank of that name, and was killed on the bank of the Ganga by the Ujjainiya interest. As the empire consolidated its grip on the profession, however, such intrusions became the rule rather than the exception. Soon, large numbers of soldiers derived their identity from a real or supposed connection with Baksar. Significantly, they became known as Baksariyas, a name that, until the end of the eighteenth century, would almost be synonymous with Hindustani matchlock men. A Mughal source of 1690 still mentions Baksariyas and Bundelas as the categories that summed up the presence of regular matchlock men in the imperial army. But soon one finds only the first identity. The quintessential sepoy was a Baksariya.

Far-reaching as the revolutions in the brokering profession must have been for the clan elites of Hindustan, in the common peasants' experience much remained the same. The Baksariyas, just as the Ujjainiya and Bundela soldiers had done and as their successor incarnations, that of the Company's sepoys and of the indentured labourers of the Bojpuri region, would do, always looked forward to a return to the family farms they had left as boys of perhaps only seventeen years of age. What did not change either, at least for a while, was that, as much as feasible, they kept their options open and were capable of renegotiating their contracts, especially with respect to their pay. In the absence of the old clan brokers, another kind of middleman became prominent: Baksariya *jamadāārs* who had risen from the ranks and performed the task – well-known in the labour history of India – of jobbers, in this case jobber-commanders. These men now became the figures on whose loyalty the political fortunes of the Mughal's successor states often depended. Already in the second decade of the eighteenth century, the British East India Company had some of them in its pay. Inevitably, Baksariya sepoys served under Clive in 1757. Similarly, his adversary at the battle of Plassey, Sirajud-Daula, the ruler of Bengal, depended crucially on his principal sepoy *jamadārs* (Yang 1989: 191–4; Kolff 1990: 170–1, 174, 177, 179).

Then the break came. It is true that the Company's sepoy army was a straight descendant and a new incarnation of the Purbiya–Tomar–Ujjainiya–Bundela–Baksariya tradition of Hindustani peasant soldiering. But the fact that, under the British near-monopoly of military recruitment, independent brokerage by *jamadārs* was no longer possible or tolerated, meant a revolution in the labour market. For centuries, circulatory military labour had contributed to a circulation of states, none of which, except that of the Sharqis and of Sher Shah, had the Bhojpuri recruit-ment region as its centre. With no spokesmen or negotiators to take up their cause and no alternative employer around, every soldier of some experience now acted as a broker in his own right and presented his younger brothers, nephews or fellow villagers to his command-ing officers as recruits, thus rendering the Company's regiments into self-perpetuating and inward-looking institutions. The sepoys of the Bengal army compensated their loss of negotiating power by inventing a cult of themselves as 'high-caste' Brahmans and respectable Rajputs. Sepoys with lesser ritual pretentions, such as the Pasis and Dusadhs, who had contributed much to the centuries-old Purbiya tradition of mobile labour and had helped fight Clive's battles, were soon squeezed out of the labour supply by their 'high-caste' colleagues (Chattopadhyaya 1957: 72; Singh 1976: 157; Kolff 1990: 28, 117ff.). Even then, the Bhumihar Brahman and Rajput sepoys would never reconcile themselves to a condition that deprived them of all alternative options of service other than those one-sidedly imposed upon them by the British. Their last bid to renegotiate their terms of service and regain their old freedom according to the ancient code of honourable *naukari* would come to nought in 1857. After that, as the British shifted recruitment to the Panjab, options on the market for mobile labour would be much more meagre than before; the top-ranking opportunities had gone. For many, there was no alternative but to return to their villages and fields and there push out of the agrarian labour market the lower-status men they had earlier deprived of profitable army service. For the latter, to be sure, and also for a fair number of those who in the recent past would have joined the Company's regiments, other, less rewarding, Bhojpuri traditions of circulatory labour were still available (Servan-Schreiber 2006: 302). A relatively new one among them was that of indentured labour overseas, which, though it assumed (in common with all circulatory labour) a partly, often even a predominantly, diasporic character, must be seen as a new form of the *naukari* tradition that we have traced back to pre-modern times.

The world we have looked at in this chapter was characterised, above all, by its many fluidities: occupational or vocational fluidities, fluidities of negotiated and renegotiated employment rela-tionships, fluid multiple identities and disguises, fluidities of state formation and of the agencies of brokers on the (military) labour markets. To what extent these fluidities were preserved and perhaps transformed when modernity and globalisation, both colonial and post-colonial, turned India's circulatory energies into external diasporas, is an intriguing question.

References

Ambashthya, Brahmadeva Prasad (1961). 'The Accounts of the Ujjainiyas in Bihar', *Journal of the Bihar Research Society* 47, 420–40.

Bhattacharya, Neeladri (2006). 'Predicaments of Mobility: Peddlers and Itinerants in Nineteenth-century Northwestern India', in Claude Markovits, Jaques Pouchepadass and Sanjay Subrahmanyam (eds), *Society and Circulation: Mobile People and Itinerant Cultures in South Asia, 1750–1950*, London: Anthem Press, 163–214.

Chattopadhyaya, Haraprasad (1957). *The Sepoy Mutiny, 1857: A Social Study and Analysis*, Calcutta: Bookland.

Chekhovich, O.D. (1974). *Samarkandskie Dokumenti*, XV–XVI vv, Moscow: Akademija Nauk SSSR.

Gommans, Jos (2002). *Mughal Warfare: Indian Frontiers and High Roads to Empire, 1500–1700*, London and New York: Routledge.

Khan, Ali Muhammad (1965). *Mirāt-i-Ahmadī: A Persian History of Gujarat*, transl. by M.F. Lokhandwala, Baroda: Gaekwad's Oriental Series 146.

Kolff, Dirk H.A. (1990). *Naukar, Rajput and Sepoy: The Ethnohistory of the Military Labour Market in Hindustan, 1450–1850*, Cambridge: Cambridge University Press.

— (2010). *Grass in their Mouths: The Upper Doab of India under the Company's Magna Charta, 1793–1830*, Brill: Leiden.

Kolff, D.H.A. and H.W. van Santen (eds) (1979). *De Geschriften van Francisco Pelsaert over Mughal Indië, 1627: Kroniek en Remonstrantie*, The Hague: Martinus Nijhoff.

Meyer, Eric (2006). 'Labour Circulation between Sri Lanka and South India in Historical Perspective', in Claude Markovits, Jaques Pouchepadass and Sanjay Subrahmanyam (eds) *Society and Circulation: Mobile People and Itinerant Cultures in South Asia, 1750–1950*, London: Anthem Press, 55–88.

Servan-Schreiber, Cathérine (2006). 'Tellers of Tales, Sellers of Tales: Bhojpuri Peddlers in Northern India', in Claude Markovits, Jaques Pouchepadass and Sanjay Subrahmanyam (eds) *Society and Circulation: Mobile People and Itinerant Cultures in South Asia, 1750–1950*, London: Anthem Press, 275–305.

Singh, Madan Paul (1976). *Indian Army under the East India Company*, New Delhi: Sterling Publications.

Yang, Anand A. (1989). *The Limited Raj: Agrarian Relations in Colonial India, Saran District, 1793–1920*, Berkely/Los Angeles/London: University of California Press.

3

SCRIBAL MIGRATIONS IN EARLY MODERN INDIA

Rosalind O'Hanlon

Introduction

One of the most striking aspects of India's recent history, and certainly a vital contributor to India's post-liberalisation economic growth, lies in the mobility of its skilled service communities, above all those in the new communications technologies. Within India, students and young professionals have gravitated to Bangalore, Hyderabad, Pune and other expanding cities where universities and IT companies now collaborate in productive alliance. Even more spectacularly, this mobility takes the form of a diaspora in Europe and above all in the United States, where skilled Indian professionals are in high demand in the IT and technology service industries of the west coast, and in the IT and science departments of American universities. This modern diaspora looks very different from many of the migrations that took place within and from India within the British empire – those that drew from the humbler social strata of small business people and traders, artisans, military men and indentured labourers. India's modern diaspora of highly qualified professional elites might be thought to bear little connection to India's earlier history.

In fact, these modern professional migrations have an important historical precedent within an earlier period of India's history. India's early modern centuries, when regional states and courts flourished within the framework of the Mughal empire, saw the growth of exceptional opportunities for skilled service people willing to travel in search of employment and patronage. India itself was a magnet for such people, drawn from the states of central and west Asia (Subrahmanyam 1992; Alam and Subrahmanyam 2007). Within India, communities of service people – such as Brahmans, kayasthas, khatris, Muslim scribal specialists – developed very effective strategies for such migrations in search of opportunity, patronage and employment (S. Bayly 1999: 64–96; Guha 2004; Alam and Subrahmanyam 2004; O'Hanlon and Washbrook 2011). Key to these strategies was a seemingly contradictory logic, but one which made their migration particularly successful as a means of enhancing family security and opportunity. Scribal families were able simultaneously to indigenise themselves successfully in new settings, while at the same time preserving their own community identities and their links with their past histories.

Scribal specialists and 'early modernity'

Economic, political, religious and intellectual developments intensified the demand for the skills of scribal people of many different kinds in Mughal India. Mughal administration incorporated military as well as economic and revenue dimensions. The shift to a money economy was already under way during the years of the Delhi Sultanate. However, it quickened as the emperor Akbar's government began to collect the imperial state's revenue demand in cash, opening up new opportunities at every level of society and state for men adept in the movement of money and credit. The 'mansabdars' or elite administrative cadres of the Mughal empire, supported by military estates, had military obligations indicated by their rank, but also held a wide range of posts in military, civil, judicial and revenue administration. Biographies of Mughal elites often reveal their postings to different regions in the ever-expanding Mughal empire (Athar Ali 1997: 144–9). Mansabdars themselves also required and supported considerable administrative establishments, to oversee their households and collect revenues from their military estates. Beneath the Mughal imperial umbrella, the consolidation of regional states led to the further growth of state bureaucracies, as well as of ranks of skilled accountants and administrators employed to manage the affairs of substantial gentry and petty lords.

Other kinds of scribal expertise were in demand too. Most royal courts and great households supported men of letters in both of early modern India's cosmopolitan literary traditions, Sanskrit and Persian: intellectuals, translators, poets, chroniclers, newswriters, skilled writers of royal eulogies, astrologers, experts in religious law and ritual specialists able to meet the growing demand of regional courts for more elaborate forms of royal ritual. These specialists were valued not only for their practical skills, but also for the prestige that their presence could confer. Great scholars guaranteed the judicial authority of royal courts, while the the patronage of public disputations between leading intellectuals boosted the reputations of rulers for learning and culture (Deshpande 2011). Powerful merchant patrons, anxious to display their wealth and express their piety, found means to do this through the support of scholars and holy men.

Very many different communities were drawn into providing this wide range of specialist scribal skills. Many Mughal scholar bureaucrats were drawn from migrant communities with homes in various parts of central Asia: Iranians, Turanis, Tajiks, Uzbegs, Afghans and Kashmiris. Others came from *ashraf* Muslim gentry families based in north India's expanding urban centres, who worked also at lower levels of the system as judicial and revenue officers (Richards 1993: 58–78; Subrahmanyam 1992: 340–62; Athar Ali 1997: 136–53; Hasan 2004, Barnett 1987, Alam 1986). Brahman communities of many different kinds also participated. In the south, the worldly *karanam* classes of clerkly niyogi Brahmans predominated (Narayana Rao *et al.* 2001: 92–139). In the Marathi-speaking regions of western India, more conservative Brahman communities rooted in a longstanding Sanskrit culture had long provided the scribal expertise for the region's states (Fukazawa 1991: 1–48; Wink 1986: 67–84). In Bengal, similar functions were discharged by more cosmopolitan and often Persianised Brahmans and Vaidyas (Chatterjee 2009: 445–72). In northern India and the Rajput states, Persian-assimilated kayasthas and khatris were the leading scribal people. These communities were not Brahmans, but had early in the second millennium developed as specialised scribes and clerks. Popular literatures reviled them for the influence they were able to command as royal scribes, but they also appear in inscriptional literature represented as pious donors and great men in their own right. Originally serving medieval 'Hindu' kings, the coming of the Muslim empires opened up new opportunities for them. In these new courtly contexts, their willingness to assimilate themselves to the Persianate language and culture of Muslim courts gave them enormous advantages – although often, in the process, attracting sharp hostility from Brahman scribal rivals (O'Hanlon 2010b: 563–95).

Early modern India's scribal communities therefore comprised many different groups with different ethnic identities, religious cultures and service ethics. At the extremes, the imperial service ethic of Mughal scholar bureaucrats (Richards 1984: 255–89) contrasted sharply with that of the south Indian karanams with whom they might serve on the Deccan fringes of the empire; and both contrasted again with that of the Maratha Brahman intellectuals who migrated to Banaras and different Indian courts. Many scribes exercised their skills only within their own local communities, finding new challenges as local accounting and revenue needs grew in complexity and local power-holders sought them out to help manage their household affairs in the face of growing pressures from the state. However, some were very willing to move, following opportunities for advancement through promotion via Mughal state administration, in the expansion of new regional courts and from the growth of urban and mercantile fortunes seeking outlets for artistic creation and piety. At the same time, movement was often followed by new settlement and local entrenchment. Very often office holders were given lands to support themselves, so offices became hereditary and families built new positions for themselves in new places. But the political fluidity of the epoch guaranteed that no locality would be permanently secure and that the need for movement would be constant. Many families developed long-term practices of sending out new branches to found new households in new places, even while their patriarchs remained firmly located over several generations in one.

Yet the pressures of mobility did not only affect scribal communities locally. In many ways, they reshaped society more broadly, especially favouring the development of forms of identity which could become 'portable' and recognisable across the sub-continent. Some groups, such as Brahmins, already possessed the lineaments from which to make such pan-Indian identities, which strengthened across the period. However, others – most notably kayasthas – had constantly to reinvent themselves to meet the task.

Logics of migration

Where skills were in demand, but the locus of demand fluctuated with the rise and fall of patrons and employers, it was important for service people to be mobile. Transfers were central to Mughal imperial administration, very often with families operating as units and sons inheriting some of the responsibilities of their fathers. The kayastha Bhimsen Saksena grew up in the central Indian town of Burhanpur in the 1650s. His father had been posted there from north India as an accounts officer attached to the artillery of the Mughal army. Bhimsen and his family then moved to the city of Aurangabad in 1658, where he took up work as his father's deputy. He then went on to serve the Mughal officer Daud Khan and then Rao Dalpat, the Raja of Datia (Khobrekar 1972: 1–4).

Ritual and religious specialists also looked to migration for expanded opportunities. Some did so within the framework of religious sects and orders, such as those Muslim sufi orders who had developed a close relation to the Mughal court (Alam 2009: 135–74), or the Hindu monastic organisations who received substantial support from rulers in this period (Minkowski 2011: 127–31). Others could be individual scholars who combined expertise in law with ritual skills. For pandit households in particular, migration for education was built into their traditions of learning. The fame of any pandit household depended not just on sons, but on the numbers of students it was known to have trained, and who went on themselves not only to perpetuate the traditions of learning imbibed in the households of their teachers, but to spread the reputations of those teachers to new centres of learning and patronage (Kelkar 1915: 29–34). When the famous Banaras scholar Kamalakara Bhatta described the achievements of his father Narayana Bhatta, he listed all of those students from different parts of India 'from Dravida, Gurjara, Kanyakubja, Malwa, Braja, Mithila, the Himalayan regions, Karnata, Utkala, the Konkan, Gauda, Andhra, Mathura, Kamarupa and other parts of India' (Shastri 1912: 12). This gives us some idea of the journeys that these scholar families undertook and the intellectual networks they established.

Particularly remarkable was the scholarly diaspora of Maratha Brahmans from western India, which reached up to Banaras and Rajasthan in the north and to Thanjavur, deep in southern India. The old religious centres of western India's Konkan littoral, and the shrine towns that clustered along the Godavari, Bhima and Krishna rivers as they flowed eastward across the plains of central and southern India, clearly offered an environment in which the learned and the pious could flourish. Outside these centres, the relatively poor and famine-prone agrarian economy of the Deccan plateau meant that it was imperative for Brahman families to diversify, to spread their risks beyond the precarious livelihoods to be earned as petty teachers, village priests, astrologers or small farmers. With their skills of literacy and numeracy, it was a natural strategy for Brahman families to send some of their sons to pursue the worldly opportunities in state service and revenue administration as these expanded under the Bahmani kings and their successors in the states of the Deccan Sultanate. The aim was to disperse the family and spread risk. Thus families would often combine continued landholding at their point of origin, but send family members off to different places where they could find employment and patronage. Indeed, these skills applied in the service of states carried them far into central and southern India too, and it became almost a cliché for seventeenth-century observers that what Maratha Brahmans prized above all was secure positions in state service (Sastri 1963: 111–17).

These pressures were intensified by particular events, which precipitated specific waves of migration. It is likely that the fall to Muslim incomers of the central India Yadava court of Devagiri in 1294, and consequent decline of nearby Paithan as an old centre of Brahman piety and learning, was one such stimulus. The fourteenth century saw two catastrophic famines in the Deccan region, in 1346 and again in 1390–1410, which resulted in the very widespread depopulation of Deccan villages. Episodes of temple destruction and forced proselytisation that accompanied the expansion of Portuguese power in the Konkan littoral also resulted in the migration of many Brahman families outside the Portuguese regions, although many also stayed on and prospered (Axelrod and Fuerch 2008).

But scribal families did not only migrate because they were 'pushed'. The emergence of Banaras as a great centre of learning and piety in the sixteenth and seventeenth centuries functioned as a special 'pull' factor, too. Very many pandit families migrated there (O'Hanlon 2011) to meet wealthy patrons who would support their lives as pious scholars. Some had close connections with Mughal courtiers; others with the wealthy monastic institution in the city; others served in judicial assemblies acting as courts of last appeal in religious disputes originating in many other parts of India, dispensing justice to Brahman communities out in the localities. Banares also became a base from which scholars could go to regional courts and display their learning. It is likely that some at least also became involved in Banaras's burgeoning banking and money-lending activities, which expanded with the population of the city and particularly with the growth of the pilgrim trade. When the great Maratha warrior king Sivaji sought refuge in the city in 1666 having escaped from captivity at the Mughal court, he was able to raise an enormous loan from the city's bankers (Sen 1920: 71–2).

Other 'pull' factors included the recruitment needs of states for secular administrators and accountants. Kayasthas provide a prime example here, frequently migrating from northern India to central and western regions, most notably Hyderabad (Leonard 1971). They were encouraged by the preference of many rulers for appointing some outsiders deliberately to provide balance against locals, who otherwise might gain too much control. In Sivaji's Maratha state, contemporaries reported a deliberate policy of appointing a kayastha and a Brahman jointly to head up particular departments, thus limiting the power and influence enjoyed by each (Sen 1920: 29–30).

From the later seventeenth century, several factors promoted even larger flows of scribal specialists with religious expertise. Under the Mughal emperor Aurangzeb, the older flow of Mughal patronage to Brahman scholars in Banaras dried up, as Aurangzeb suspected the city's Brahmans of having aided Sivaji in his escape and developed his own more assertive Islamic religiosity. In this changing climate, ritual specialists and experts in religious law sought alternative patronage in the courts of the southern Maratha country and in the courts of Rajasthan (Horstmann 2009). From the early eighteenth century, the establishment of a Brahman court at Pune in western India further accentuated this regionalisation of migration patterns for ambitious and skilled Brahman scribal specialists.

Paths and patterns of mobility

In the case of Banares, while we know that different families arrived at different times from the early sixteenth century (and even earlier), we have rather less appreciation of the mechanics of their migration. Migration to Banaras was often undertaken through a series of smaller and more local moves. Once a family was established in Banaras, there was commonly a series of comings and goings over several generations, in which family ties and ties of property rights were maintained with natal locations for many decades or longer, before a distinctive 'Banaras' branch of the family emerged as a settled part of the city's population. In addition, Banaras was commonly only one destination for such migrant families, who might despatch further members to establish themselves at other promising courtly or religious centres.

The eminent Sesa family, who emerged in the late sixteenth century as leading grammarians in the city, provides a good example. The family traced their origins back to a thirteenth-century ancestor, Ramakrsna, who held lands in Nanded, an important centre of learning and pilgrimage within the Marathi-speaking regions of the Godaveri river in central India. He had three sons, Ganesapant, Vitthalpant and Bopajipant. Ganesapant and his descendants remained in Nanded, but some at least of Vitthalpant's family left the town for other destinations (Kanole 1950: 58). One Visnu Sesa had moved to Banaras for his education in the later fifteenth century, where he excelled as a grammarian, winning the title of *sabhāpati*, 'lord of the assembly', for his outstanding performances in debate (Kanole 1950: 60–1). Other descendants of Vitthalpant left Nanded for the court of Bijapur, where the family clearly flourished in a range of different avocations. In 1567, one Vaman, the son of Anant Sesa, was appointed royal librarian to Ali Adil Shah I (1558–80) of Bijapur, with the substantial salary of 1,000 gold *hon* per annum. Vaman clearly impressed his royal patron, for his appointment was renewed in 1575 (Joshi 1956–7: 10). Vaman's contemporary Narasimha Sesa also received patronage at the court, not for his library skills, but for his expertise in the family tradition of learning in Sanskrit grammar, for which his Brahman scholar peers at Bijapur rewarded him with the title of *bhaṭṭa-bhaṭṭārakar*, 'revered among scholars' (Aryavaraguru 1912: 248).

Not long afterwards, however, the attractions of Mughal Banaras began to eclipse those of the provincial court of Bijapur. Narasimha's son Krsna Sesa inherited both his father's skills as a grammarian and the family's talent for mobilising social networks in the quest for opportunity and reputation. By the 1580s, Krsna Sesa had moved to Banaras and established himself not only as a formidable grammarian, but as the leader of the growing community of Maharashtrian Brahmans in the city (O'Hanlon 2009: 221). His success may have been attributable, in part at least, to the fact that he had ready-made family contacts in the city, in the descendants of the grammarian Visnu Sesa. Other Sesas from Bijapur followed, although their talents took different forms. The royal librarian Vaman's grandson, also Vaman pandit (1608–95), spent his youth in Bijapur, but then left to pursue his Sanskrit education in Banaras, where he emerged as an outstandingly successful poet (Kanhere 1926: 305–14).

Dispersed as the family became, however, the links with Sesas back in Nanded remained active. When Krsna moved to Banaras, his father Narasimha had clearly gone back to Nanded, for Krsna recorded that he wrote his play *Murārīvijaya* when he himself was in Banaras and his father living on the Godavari. Sesas, who had left Nanded, clearly continued to share in the extended family's rights in land. In a family deed confirming the division of a plot of land in Nanded, dated to 1629, one Vasudeva Pant Sesa, 'resident of Kasi' is mentioned as a party to the document (Kanole 1950: 62). In addition, there was clearly some family tradition whereby important family documents were returned for safekeeping to Nanded. When Kanole, the historian of the Sesa family, was exploring the family's archives in the 1940s, it was here that he found copies of the royal librarian's documents of appointment, dating back to the 1560s and 1570s (Kanole 1950: 64).

The Mahasabde family of scholars and priests offer another example of early modern scribal mobility. They were a Maratha Brahman family who had by the middle of the seventeenth century established themselves sufficiently successfully in Banaras for Devabhatta and Jotirvid Mahasabde to appear in the city's important judicial assembly in 1657. Devabhatta had three sons, Dinkara, Prabhakar and Ratnakar, who grew very close to the royal family of the Rajput court of Amer and came to serve the family as gurus and spiritual guides. Dinkara stayed in Banaras, where his son Vidyadhar grew so wealthy that he was called 'Kuber' after the treasurer to the gods in the Hindu pantheon. The second son, Prabhakar, migrated to the holy city of Mathura, where he was a teacher in the city's great Vaishnava temple. The names he gave his sons – Vrajnatha and Gokulnatha – reflect this influence and the family's adaptation to the local religious culture. These sons became very influential at the Jaipur court of Jaisingh (1688–1743), who was himself a major Vaishavite patron (Gode 1943: 292–306). Adapting themselves to their new religious setting, these Brahman scholars and ritualists became central to what Monika Horstmann has described as the reinvention and revival of Hindu kingship during the course of the eighteenth century (Horstmann 2009).

Migration and the household

The principal institution through which the skills of scribal migrants were transmitted, and their migration translated into active strategy, was the household. Here, skills were learned and transmitted and human capital preserved and concentrated. Young scholars often lived as part of their teacher's household, receiving education alongside his sons, and often for periods of many years, and the relationship between teacher or guru and student seems often to have assumed a quasi-filial form (O'Hanlon 2011: 181–9). This strategy made excellent sense from the point of view of an expanding scholar household, developing its range of potentially valuable social and intellectual connections far beyond the sons of the family.

It was often this extended household that undertook journeys of migration. For example, Ramesvara Bhatta, of the eminent Banaras Bhatta family of scholars, left Paithan in the first decade of the sixteenth century. The family moved some 80 miles west to Sangamner, where Ramesvara set up his own successful establishment as a teacher. His students travelled with Ramesvara and his wife in their subsequent journeys: to Kolhapur to worship the family deity, in the hope of getting a son for the family, and to the Vijayanagar court of Krsnadevaraya, to see its wealth of learning and, perhaps, to explore the opportunities there for suitable patronage. For reasons that are obscure, Ramesvara did not find Vijayanagar congenial. The family left, now with a different purpose – to go to the sacred city of Dwarka in the hope of curing his baby son Narayana, born in 1513, of consumption. Here, to alleviate his worries about his son, Ramesvara spent some time training a local student, and set him up there to carry on his intellectual traditions in that city. From there he returned to Paithan, but not to stay: he left shortly afterwards for Banaras, where he settled, and where his wife bore him the further sons that went on to establish the intellectual pre-eminence of the family in that city (Benson 2001: 105–17). But the Bhatta family continued to maintain its links with the Deccan: by writing works on Hindu law as it applied to the Deccan, by serving in the pandit assemblies to which cases from the Maratha regions were brought, by coming down to advise pandit assemblies within the Maratha country (O'Hanlon 2009: 59) and by visiting the Deccan court itself, most notably when the great ritual specialist Gagabhatta came down to consecrate the Maratha ruler Sivaji at his Raigad court in 1674 (Bendrey 1960).

An even more peripatetic dramatic history lay behind the eventual appointment of the kayastha Balaji Avaji as the principal scribe at Sivaji's court. Balaji Avaji came from a family of writers, the Gholkar family of Gholavadi village in the Konkan. Originally part of the kayastha migration from northern India, they had come down to the Konkan to serve the Siddhis of Janjira as scribes. They then became ministers to a local great household in the Konkan, where Balaji Avaji's father was executed because of suspicions that he had helped cause the death of his patron. He, his mother and his brothers were then sent to the nearby town of Rajapur to be sold as slaves. However, his mother's brother at that time was employed as a writer in the coastal town Rajapur. He rescued the family, putting the boys to work as writers, just at the time that Sivaji's power began to spread into the region. Balaji Avaji's talents were recognised at the rising court and he was offered a post in Sivaji's revenue administration (O'Hanlon 2010b: 578).

Culture and identity

Culture and identity also represented key aspects of the strategy of migrant scribal communities, although their logic could seem at first paradoxical. On the one hand, it was important that identities should be recognisable across different locations and thus 'portable'. But, on the other, it was also important for 'prestige' that identities should remain connected to particular households and places of origin associated with eminence. This twin logic affected the way that, especially, Brahmans and kayasthas came to conceive themselves during the early modern period and actually worked in tandem to enable these communities to maximise their positions.

As Susan Bayly especially has noted, Brahmans in early modern India drew particular advantage from the fact that they were able to tap into subcontinent-wide networks and that, as 'Brahmans', they had a status and employability which was meaningful everywhere (Bayly 1999: 70). To enhance this advantage, Brahman intellectuals further developed at this time a comprehensive 'grid' through which to convey and classify Brahman identities across the subcontinent. This grid divided all Brahmans into 'gauda', or northern Brahmans and 'dravida', or southern Brahmans, and laid out five further subdivisions within each. These subdivisions were derived in part from the lines of regional vernacular language communities then also consolidating themselves during this period (O'Hanlon 2011: 191–4). This grid allowed all Brahmans in theory at least to map themselves and their histories within an all-India frame, which would be comprehensible wherever families moved and needed to establish themselves as skilled and reputable members of the Brahman caste category at large.

Kayasthas also tried to develop this kind of portable identity but, lacking the Brahman religious inheritance, it required a greater modification of history. In the early part of the second millennium, and as they moved from being an occupational to a caste-like grouping, kayastha communities in northern India had strong affiliations to tantric forms of Hindu religious culture. However, their migration south and westwards as servants of expanding Muslim states from the fourteenth century onwards brought them into conflict with long-settled Brahman communities in these regions, who had hitherto enjoyed very much a monopoly of scribal occupations and expertise. These Brahmans sought to portray kayasthas not as accomplished men of culture and close confidants of kings, but rather as low-born servants affiliated with disreputable forms of worship. Under these pressures, kayasthas distanced themselves from tantric ritual. Instead, they 'indigenised' themselves by describing their origins in relation to the god Parashuram, sixth incarnation of Vishnu and everywhere in western India understood to be the creator of its lands and the patron of its indigenous communities. These new identities travelled back to Banaras, where local Brahmans accepted them even while their sometime brothers in western India disputed them and continued to sustain anti-kayastha feuds (O'Hanlon 2010b). Mobility both stretched the need for identity and the means by which it could be constantly reinvented.

Yet reinvention was not without boundaries. While migrating families or communities might 'imagine' themselves in ways which flattered their status and raised their prospects, their respectability continued partly to depend on their places of origin – and these were not necessarily easy to invent. A delicate balance between truth and fiction often needed to be maintained. We can see how delicate, for example, in the case of the Devarukhe community of Maratha Brahmans. They were a rather marginal community back in the Maratha country, with some association with labour on the land and with whom other local Brahman communities often refused to dine. However, Devarukhe families that had moved to Banaras were able to establish impressive reputations for themselves as respectable scholars and ritualists. They also changed their community name slightly, taking advantage of the soft pronunciation of the 'kh' in the local Hindvi dialect, calling themselves 'Devarshi' Brahmans, a much more dignified title implying that they were godly seers. On this basis, other Brahman communities in Banaras accepted them as Brahmans of repute and worthy marriage partners. However, when hints at their true origins belatedly came to light, these produced a major crisis in local relations, with the respectable Banaras families into which they had married facing acute embarrassment. To overcome the problem, large numbers of Banaras's more eminent pandit families found themselves obliged to gather publicly and specifically to declare the 'Devarshis' to be respectable Brahmans – the protests and complaints of critics notwithstanding – and thus to be fit marriage partners for themselves (O'Hanlon 2010a: 220–34).

Whether or not migration was used to improve status and construct new identities, it was often very important for a migratory community also to be able to demonstrate its origins. This could take a variety of forms. Sometimes, it might take the form of family memory relayed via a combination of oral tradition and documents of property right. For example, and remarkably, the kayastha brothers Govind Ramji and Rango Atmaji were living near the western Indian town of Pune during the 1720s. When asked for details of their lineage by a visiting kayastha dignitary, they were able to reconstruct their family history from the first migration of their ancestor, Konda Prabhu, who had come from the north Indian province of Awadh southwards to the Deccan with Muhammad bin Tughlaq in the middle of the fourteenth century, right down to the 1720s. This, they said, was on the basis of a history 'taken from original papers, and heard from the mouths of our fathers and forefathers' (Bendrey 1966, vol. 2: 400). Memory of a community's origins might also take the form of distinctive practices maintained in a new place. As evidence of their family origins in Awadh, the two kayastha brothers pointed to the continued tradition of worship in their family of the goddess Vinzai, whose temple stood on the hill of Vindhyachal near Mirzapur (Bendrey 1966, vol. 2: 401; Enthoven 1922, vol. 3: 238).

Scribal migrations: legacies

How far this culture of scribal mobility continued after the onset of colonial rule remains debatable. By no means all the old sources of patronage and employment were lost: the princely states maintained old features of their royal gloss (especially in the Indian arts) until late into the nineteenth century, and temples and mosques continued to dispense significant endowments. Also, in its early days, the East India Company state drew heavily on inherited practices and spread pockets of Bengali scribes across much of northern India.

Nonetheless, change became progressively radical. Even the Company state was thin on largesse and its patronage activities were heavily constrained. Also, the watchwords of its governance were 'sedentarisation' and 'peasantisation' as it treated mobility within the Indian population with suspicion, fearful that its processes lay beyond state control. Further, as the culture of power became increasingly Anglicised, references to the Indian past and to the etiquettes of Indian religion lost much of their force – at least in creating criteria of respectability and employability. Moreover, in the twentieth century, the vernacularisation of both society and state undermined the practical utility of all-India networks of community and family. Much of the world constituted around the mobility of early modern scribal groups faded away.

But perhaps not all of it. The revival of scribal (or, more properly these days, 'professional') migration in the 'global' twentieth and twenty-first centuries poses many of the individuals and families involved with many of the same dilemmas. How to make host societies aware of one's 'special' abilities and qualities? How both to fit into the society of new locales and to maintain links with one's own distinctive past and identity? The family strategies adopted, and the strains on values and aspirations which they cause, can look very much the same, albeit at a level that is global and now conducted with the aid of air travel and internet connections. It is arguable as to how far these earlier histories of migration may actively have shaped South Asia's global diasporas in the twentieth and twenty-first centuries (Fuller and Narasimhan 2010). Nonetheless, these communities do at least have a very long history of migration and mobility on which they can call.

References

Alam, Muzaffar. (1986) *The Crisis of Empire in Mughal North India. Awadh and the Punjab 1707–1748*. Delhi: Oxford University Press.
— (2009) 'The Mughals, the Sufi Shaikhs and the Formation of the Akbari Dispensation', *Modern Asian Studies* 43 (1): 135–74.
Alam, M. and Sanjay Subrahmanyam. (2004) 'The Making of a Munshi', *Comparative Studies of South Asia, Africa and the Middle East* 24 (2): 61–72.
— (2007) *Indo-Persian Travels in the Age of Discoveries, 1400–1800*. Cambridge: Cambridge University Press.
Aryavaraguru, R. (1912) 'On the Sheshas of Benaras', *Indian Antiquary* 51: 245–53.
Athar Ali, M. (1997) *The Mughal Nobility Under Aurangzeb*. Delhi: Oxford University Press.
Axelrod, Paul and Michelle Fuerch. (2008) 'Flight of the Deities: Hindu Resistance in Portuguese Goa', *The Indian Economic and Social History Review* 45 (3): 439–76.
Barnett, Richard B. (1987) *North India Between Empires: Awadh, the Mughals and the British 1720–1801*. Delhi: Manohar.
Bayly, S. (1999) *Caste, Society and Politics in India from the Eighteenth Century to the Modern Age*. Cambridge: Cambridge University Press.
Bendrey, V.S. (1960) *The Coronation of Shivaji the Great*. Bombay: PPH Bookstall.

— (1966) *Mahārāṣṭretihāsaci Sādhane*, 2 vols. Bombay: Mumbai Marathi Granthasangrahalaya.

Benson, J. (2001) 'Saṃkārabhaṭṭa's Family Chronicle'. In Axel Michaels (ed.), *The Pandit: Traditional Scholarship in India*. Delhi: Manohar.

Chatterjee, Kumkum. (2009) *The Cultures of History in Early Modern India. Persianisation and Mughal Culture in Bengal*. New Delhi: Oxford University Press.

Deshpande, M. (2011) 'Will the Real Winner Stand Up? Conflicting Narratives of a Seventeenth Century Philosophical Debate from Karnataka'. In Cynthia Talbot (ed.), *Knowing India: Colonial and Modern Constructions of the Past. Essays in Honour of Thomas R. Trautman*. New Delhi: Yoda Press.

Enthoven, R.E. (1922) *Tribes and Castes of Bombay*. Bombay: Government Central Press.

Fukazawa, F. (1991) *The Medieval Deccan: Peasants, Social Systems and States, Seventeenth to Eighteenth Centuries*. Delhi: Oxford University Press.

Fuller, C.J. and Haripriya Narasimhan. (2010) 'Traditional Vocations and Modern Professions among Tamil Brahmans in Colonial and Post-colonial South India', *The Indian Economic and Social History Review* 47 (4): 473–96.

Gode, P.K. (1943) 'Some New Evidence Regarding Devabhatta Mahasabde, the Father of Ratnakarabhatta, the Guru of Sevai Jaising of Amber (AD 1699–1743)', *The Poona Orientalist* 8 (3–4) (October 1943–January 1944): 1–10.

Guha, S. (2004) 'Speaking Historically: The Changing Voices of Historical Narration in Western India, 1400–1900', *American Historical Review* 109 (4): 1084–113.

Hasan, Farhat. (2004) *State and Locality in Mughal India. Power Relations in Western India, c. 1572–1730*. Cambridge: Cambridge University Press.

Horstmann, V. (2009) *Der Zusammenhalt des Welts: Religiose Herrschaftslegitimation und Religionspolitik Maharaja Savai Jaisinghs (1700–1743)*. Wiesbaden: Harrassowitz.

Joshi, P.M. (1956–7) ''Ālī 'Ādil Shāh I of Bījāpūr (1558–1580) and His Royal Librarian: Two Ruq'as', *Journal of the Bombay Branch of the Royal Asiatic Society* 31–2: 97–107.

Kanhere, S.G. (1926) 'Waman Pandit: Scholar and Marathi Poet', *Bulletin of the School of Oriental and African Studies* 4 (2), 305–14.

Kanole, V.A. (1950) 'Nāṇḍeḍace śeṣa gharāṇe'. In Surendranath Sen (ed.), *Mahamahopadhyaya Prof. D. V. Potdar Sixty First Birthday Commemoration Volume*. Poona: Samartha Press.

Kelkar, N.C. (1915) 'Mahārāṣṭrātīl kāhī paṇḍit gharāṇī'. In *Kelkarakrt lekh sangraha*, vol. 4: 29–34. Pune: Chitrashala Press.

Khobrekar, V.G. (ed.) (1972) *Tarikh-i Dilkasha of Bhimsen. Sir Jadunath Sarkar Birth Centenary Volume*. Bombay: Department of Archives.

Leonard, Karen. (1971) 'The Hyderabad Political System and Its Participants', *Journal of Asian Studies* 30 (3): 569–82.

Minkowski, Christopher. (2011) 'Advaita Vedanta in Early Modern History'. In Rosalind O'Hanlon and David Washbrook (eds), *Religious Cultures in Early Modern India: New Perspectives*. London: Routledge: 104–142.

Narayana Rao, V., David Shulman and Sanjay Subrahmanyam. (2001) *Textures of Time: Writing History in South India 1600–1800*. Delhi: Permanent Black.

O'Hanlon, Rosalind. (2009) 'Narratives of Penance and Purification in Western India, c. 1650–1850', *The Journal of Hindu Studies* 2: 48–75.

— (2010a) 'Letters Home: Banaras Pandits and the Maratha Regions in Early Modern India', *Modern Asian Studies* 44 (2): 201–40.

— (2010b) 'The Social Worth of Scribes: Brahmins, Kayasthas and the Social Order in Early Modern India', *The Indian Economic and Social History Review* 47 (4): 563–95.

— (2011) 'Speaking from Siva's Temple: Banaras Scholar Households and the Brahman "Ecumene" of Mughal India'. In Rosalind O'Hanlon and David Washbrook (eds), *Religious Cultures in Early Modern India: New Perspectives*. London: Routledge.

O'Hanlon, Rosalind and David Washbrook. (2011) 'Munshis, Pandits and Record Keepers: Scribal Communities and Historical Change in India'. Special Issue of *The Indian Economic and Social History Review* XLVII (4) October–December 2012.

Richards, John F. (1984) 'Norms of Comportment among Imperial Mughal Officials'. In Barbara Daly Metcalf (ed.), *Moral Conduct and Authority: The Place of Adab in South Asian Islam*. Berkeley: University of California Press, 255–89.

— (1993) *The Mughal Empire*. Cambridge: Cambridge University Press.

Sastri, S.N. (ed.) (1963) *Visvagunadarsacampu of Venkatadhvari*. Varanasi, India.

Sen, Surendranath. (1920) *Extracts and Documents Relating to Maratha History, Vol. 1, Siva Chhatrapati.* Calcutta: University of Calcutta.

Shastri, M.H. (1912) 'Dakshini Pandits at Banaras', *Indian Antiquary* 41 (January 1912): 7–13.

Subrahmanyam, S. (1992) 'Iranians Abroad: Intra-Asian Elite Migration and Early Modern State Formation', *Journal of Asian Studies*, 51 (2): 340–62.

Wink, Andre. (1986) *Land and Sovereignty in India. Agrarian Society and Politics under the Eighteenth Century Maratha Svarajya.* Cambridge: Cambridge University Press.

4

MOBILE ARTISANS

Tirthankar Roy and Douglas Haynes

Throughout recorded history, skilled artisans in South Asia have exhibited a high degree of geographic mobility. Craft activity on the subcontinent has generally been characterized by low capital intensity, and workshops have often been highly portable as a result. Handloom weavers, for instance, could usually make, assemble and repair looms almost anywhere, with only minimal support from tool-making artisans, namely, carpenters and blacksmiths. Political and economic developments could thus easily induce small producers to move from one place to another within the subcontinent. The formation of strong empires, the discovery of new trading routes and commercial expansion, and the development of new urban centres strongly attracted skilled artisans, whereas famines, warfare, state failure and political oppression could drive them to seek work in distant locations.

Historians have recognized the mobility of the South Asian artisan during the last two to three decades. Before this, pre-colonial artisans were often thought to be members of self-sufficient, self-contained and highly stable village communities unencumbered by market relations. Artisans in the colonial period, on the other hand, were viewed mainly as victims of industrializing processes, driven back onto the land in their local regions by foreign competition, in contrast to the factory workers who had adapted to the changing economic climate by moving to large cities in search of jobs. As recent scholarship has challenged the traditional view of South Asian society before the imposition of British rule – giving rise to a picture of constant fluidity, social circulation and change – a more differentiated picture of the South Asian artisan has emerged. On the one hand, the advantages of knowledge commanded by those who dealt most directly with raw materials, such as iron-smelters and cotton spinners, remained tied to local natural resource endowments, like iron ore or cotton. On the other, artisans oriented towards the final market for their products were often mobile. Handloom weavers could potentially employ their skills in making designed textiles to create markets for their products, and this prospect sometimes drove them towards points of consumption rather than of material supplies. The record is replete with evidence of movements of such artisans (for sources, see Haynes and Roy 1999).

Nor did artisan mobility cease with the advent of colonialism or the industrial revolution. There may have been a period during the first half of the nineteenth century when dislocations in the economy were so severe that large numbers of artisans were faced with the necessity of giving up their occupations for unskilled labor in the cities or countryside, with little hope of remunerative employment elsewhere. But by the late nineteenth century, the uneven character of commercialization in the subcontinent induced new movements of significant numbers of craftspeople from stagnant regions to more dynamic areas where new demand for artisanal goods had emerged. The history of artisan mobility is thus neither one of sharp disruption nor one of smooth continuity, but instead one of shifting forms of adjustment, some more successful than others, to changes in the South Asian economy that could vary from region to region.

Pre-colonial South Asia

Artisans who catered purely to a peasant clientele are mentioned rarely in the sources that attest to pre-colonial migration. By contrast, those who were involved in urban or export markets, or produced goods for kings and nobilities, seem to have relocated themselves often. Thus iron-smelters, who by and large sold their wares to the peasantry, were usually far less mobile than blacksmiths engaged in making swords and cannons, who circulated over larger territories as demand for their services shifted (Roy 2009). These two kinds of actor remained distinct in their respective levels of technological capability and maintained separate institutional identities. Urban artisans tended to form powerful guilds that carefully nurtured collective memories of their past involvement with their profession. Frequently, a core ingredient in such memories was a migration undertaken when an external threat materialized or when a new state offered security and respect in exchange for their presence in its new capital city.

Most well-recorded instances of the migration of textile artisans before the eighteenth century represent movements away from decaying or unstable polities towards the territory of stable and powerful regimes. One of the earliest pieces of evidence, the inscriptions from Mandasor (located in western India), which were recorded in the fifth century, testify to the movement of a set of silk-weavers, along with their kin and children, from the area of Lata (located in present-day Khandesh) to Dasapura (in present-day Malwa) in the Gupta Empire (Basham 1983: 95). In Dasapura, they were 'honoured by the kings like their own sons' and formed a craft guild, which used its 'hoarded wealth' to build an 'incomparably noble' sun temple in 437–8 CE. The evidence says very little about the weavers' reasons for leaving, but A.L. Basham speculates that declining demand for exports to the Roman empire accounts for the demise of the industry in Lata, which had manufactured considerable cloth for foreign trade (Basham 1983: 93–106).

During the medieval period, the evidence on artisan migration suggests that it largely followed the dynamics of the two great empires of the subcontinent, the Mughal in the north and the Vijayanagara in the south. It is perhaps possible to detect two general forms of migration, the first towards the imperial capitals and the second towards emerging provinces in the empires.

Oral histories recorded around the turn of the twentieth century refer to a large number of weavers' movements in western and northern India, which are vaguely attributed to the late medieval period. They suggest a tendency to leave thinly populated, arid regions of Sind, Rajasthan and perhaps tribal Gujarat, areas where South Asian crafts once seem to have flourished, for the agrarian heartland of the Delhi sultanate and Mughal empire in northern India. Families of printers from Gujarat, for instance, were provided with land grants in Agra around 1530 (Haynes and Roy 1999). Later, many of these families migrated to Jaipur, Kanauj and Benares. Within Gujarat and Bengal, the coastal areas attracted mobile artisans from the interior. Both regions emerged in the sixteenth century as wealthy, if sometimes semi-autonomous, imperial provinces, and as nodal points in the external trade of the subcontinent. Settlements of immigrant artisans emerged in cities founded and developed by the Gujarat sultanate. Khatri weavers living in Gujarat largely trace their ancestry to Champaner in the current Panch Mahals district or Hinglaj in Sind. Community genealogists today preserve the memory of how Khatri families fanned out through much of central and southern Gujarat in the late sixteenth century. Bengal was annexed to the Mughal empire by the general Mansingh during the late sixteenth century. Subsequently, Mughal governors tried, with partial success, to unify what once had been a deeply fragmented and unstable political-economic world. The heavily forested regions of eastern Bengal were transformed into a thickly-settled agrarian landscape characterized by villages extensively involved in production for markets. The urbanization that inevitably followed – Dhaka became an important manufacturing city under Mughal provincial rulers and flourished as a result – drew artisan groups from a wide expanse of the eastern Gangetic plains towards deltaic Bengal. These people formed the axis of an artisan tradition that was to play a pivotal role in eighteenth-century European trade in Bengal.

The collapse of the Mughal empire during the early eighteenth century is no longer seen by historians as an era of decline. While the importance of the imperial centre in north India undoubtedly diminished, a number of regional kingdoms, both large and small, show clear signs of political dynamism and economic growth. Indeed, some scholars have argued that these 'successor' states represented a new form of polity more closely linked than the Mughal state itself to the interests of commercial and financial capital, and more directly involved in the promotion of productive and market activity (Bayly 1983). These states played a special role in encouraging the movements of skilled artisans. According to Bayly (1983: 145–6), the rulers of eighteenth-century Farrukhabad 'made a policy of attracting weavers from disturbed regions of the east Punjab and Delhi territories', while the Rajas of Benares brought in weavers from Gujarat and other distant territories in order to promote the manufacture of high-quality silk cloth and brocades. Weavers of the small town of Shahzadpur 'moved across the Ganges to seek patronage and protection among the taluqdars of south Awadh' (Bayly 1983: 292). There is evidence to suggest that similar developments took place in the regions of Bihar and Orissa that had been part of the Mughal domains.

Much of the evidence on mobility in southern India is connected, in a similar fashion, to the Vijayanagara empire. European travellers commented on the wide range of textiles available in the Vijayanagara capital, especially silks. The dependence of the empire upon maritime trade strengthened its commercial and industrial potential and made it more attractive to skilled artisan communities. Movements of artisans were triggered by the rise and fall of Vijayanagara. Vijaya Ramaswamy attributes the migration of Devanga weavers from Andhra or Karnataka further south into Tamil country to the outward expansion of imperial hegemony (Ramaswamy 1985b). Perhaps the most dramatic example of pre-colonial migration, the entry of the Sourashtra silk-weavers from regions north and west of the empire into southern India, can also be attributed to the pull exerted by the urban consumers of Vijayanagara.

Not all groups, however, experienced imperial expansion in the same way. Branches of the Salis, another major south Indian weaving community found today in different parts of the Andhra–Karnataka regions, were prominent under Chola patronage before the fourteenth century, but appear to have suffered a partial eclipse during the Vijayanagara empire. Imperial consolidation stimulated this effect by intensifying competition among communities for royal patronage. There is considerable evidence of weavers and blacksmiths approaching the Vijayanagara court for the licence to protect their monopoly from encroachment (Ramaswamy 1985a, 1985b; Sinopoli 2003). A somewhat similar instance occurred later in the Nayaka-ruled Madurai, which saw, according to community myths, a deliberate displacement of the Kaikkolar weavers and resettlement of Sourashtras (Roy 1998).

The Kaikkolar or Sengunthar weavers represent a well-known, but somewhat unique, example of mobility. Straddling the Chola and Vijayanagara periods, their prominence in the economic and political life of these two empires owed itself to their role as warriors, merchants and weavers. In one view, they needed to maintain armies in order to guard their itinerant and regional trading enterprise (Mines 1984: 12). The switch from soldiery to weaving cannot be dated precisely, but can be attributed to the group's prior engagement with commercial and urban livelihoods. The Kaikkolars settled within an ever widening territory, almost always as prominent actors in the urban economy, and organized under an elaborate and regionally configured structure of authority.

The settlement of some skilled weaver groups in Tamil Nadu and southern Andhra Pradesh reflects patterns of temple patronage. Temple towns were concentrated points of consumption and purchase. In some cases, the temples themselves could sponsor such moves. Aside from the well-known examples of weavers in Tamil Nadu, varied groups of artisans settling in the temple complexes of Orissa from the twelfth century can be cited in this context (Behura 1965).

The disintegration of the Vijayanagara empire in the mid-sixteenth century, and the subsequent rise of smaller regional polities, such as the Nayaka kingdom of Madura, again connects with stories of dispersal. It is suggested that Tirumala (1623–59), the greatest of the Nayaka kings, invited the Vijayanagara Sourashtras to migrate to Madurai (Rangachari 1914). The Devangas who settled in western India trace their origin to towns formerly under Vijayanagara rule, which they had apparently left due to the decline of the empire. The Devangas of Salem migrated from Hampi, where the head of the community continued to reside for a long time afterwards. Their southern movement, it would seem from fragmentary evidence, was not a single flow, which we can surmise from the fact that there later occurred a segmentation of the Devangas into linguistic subcastes. The expansion of Maratha power southwards after the middle of the seventeenth century encouraged the textile trade of Pune with Burhanpur on the one hand and with Mysore on the other. Under Mysore rule, weavers were exempted from the payment of taxes, and their activity flourished until the fall of Seringapatnam in 1799.

Many of those groups involved in migration organized themselves in guilds or cohesive communities and devised elaborate cultural strategies to preserve their identity. By 1900, Kaikkolar organization had evolved into a guild-like network formed of provinces (nadus), regions and localities, and a hierarchical order of authority structured by region. It is not clear from available descriptions whether or not the organization intervened at all in business disputes. It maintained a powerful presence in Kanchipuram, however, where the most prosperous weaving–trading groups resided. And it did have a visible role in keeping a regionally segmented, yet professionally integrated, community in one fold. The Sourashtras too had a strong sense of collectivity, which spawned a formal association, the Sourashtra Sabha, in the late nineteenth century. Once again, business seems to have strengthened the association, but whether the association also formally contributed to the business is not altogether clear (Roy 1998).

Collective myths played a critical role in defining a sense of community. Typically, such myths attributed origin to a specific locale and suggested that migration was precipitated by some catastrophic socio-political event, such as famine, conquest by outside rulers or the threat of conversion to Islam. Such claims may have provided a kind of 'cover memory' that disguised more diverse places of origins and more gradual processes of movement. An important part of the ritual life of the Sourashtras is a migration fable known as Bhoguluvas (or Baulas in corrupted form), ritually recited as part of the bethrothal proceedings at marriages. This fable suggests 'Sorath', Devagiri, and Vijayanagara as three group settlements prior to the Sourashtras' arrival in

Tamil country. Based upon linguistic and ritual evidence, colonial ethnographic research traces the origin of this group to Gujarat (even present-day Saurashtra) and Maharashtra, but these claims are controversial (Roy 1998). Such highly skilled groups in new locations usually claimed social and ritual privileges and established temples.

Like the pre-colonial rulers before them, the European purchasers of Indian cloth who became involved in the trade of South Asia from the seventeenth century onwards relied upon the encouragement of artisan settlement in territories within easy access. The English East India Company depended on these centres for its own development as a commercial power, and later as a state. Unlike Indian rulers, the Company sought to stimulate weaver migration less to clothe a local nobility and more to gain profits from the sale of textiles in Southeast Asia, the western Indian Ocean and Europe itself. But while the leaders of skilled artisan groups in domestic polities often doubled as their own merchants and strengthened their control on the market, a cleavage between production and trade was present in the case of textile artisans serving Indo–European trade. Insofar as some of the major new markets were controlled by European capitalists, weavers dealing with them retreated into a role of specialist producers, with fewer chances of becoming capitalist actors themselves. The master artisan in such situations was usually at best a headman–contractor, working under a European factor, and at worst a 'henchman' used to enforce contracts by coercion (the term is used by Ramaswamy 1985a). The relationship between artisan communities and their principal client no longer had an association with honour and status, and became purely contractual and pecuniary instead. The enforcement of sale contracts was a serious concern for the Europeans, especially when several companies competed for a limited group of suppliers. The Company, therefore, was keen to invite weavers to live near or within reach of the fortified settlements that they had built in order to gain more control of the suppliers and secure frictionless and timely deliveries.

These settlements became a refuge for weavers escaping stateless, even predatory, conditions on the fringes of the major successor states. Hossain (1989) records that weavers in one town after another in Bengal left areas experiencing Maratha invasions during the 1740s, often to seek refuge in the protected factories of the English. Large numbers of weavers, 'entering the Hon'ble Company's employ', settled in Gorakhpur town in 1803, soon after its absorption into the emerging empire (Pandey 1983). In western India during the 1780s, thousands of weavers appear to have left centres under Maratha influence like Ahmedabad, for Surat, where the British factors enjoyed authority as governors of the castle (*Gazetteer of the Bombay Presidency* 1884). Bombay, too, gradually became populated by weavers producing cloth for export. In southern India, the Company offered inducements to settle in areas surrounding Madras as early as the seventeenth century. Weavers were provided rice at cheap prices and lower taxes. There may even have been a net migration out of temple towns to European settlements by the end of the eighteenth century (Ramaswamy 1985a).

By the late eighteenth century, however, many weavers in southern, eastern and western India were beginning to employ migration as a way to escape or to reduce the Company's demands. As the English consolidated their hold on many coastal regions during the late eighteenth century, they often attempted to bypass existing merchant intermediaries and reduce the prices that weavers received for their cloth. Coercion became a feasible method of contract enforcement when the Company commanded state power. From the perspective of the cloth producers, the Company was itself engaged in 'predatory' behaviour that called for resistance. Parthasarathi (2001) has shown how migration to places outside the territory controlled by the Company, sometimes on quite a large scale, was an important mechanism by which artisans tried to compel the English to accept weavers' concerns (although not always successfully). This also seems to have been the pattern in Bengal during the 1790s.

Colonial migration

Nineteenth-century globalization and industrialization, it is often believed, led to a net decline in artisanal enterprise and to the expansion of peasant production in India. The twin effect is variously designated 'deindustrialization' (the contraction of indigenous industries in the face of competition from imports) and 'peasantization' (the absorption of those once employed in diverse occupational categories into the agricultural sector). Some scholars have further argued that these developments were accompanied by 'sedentarization', that is, the reduction of previously mobile population-segments into settled actors fixed in particular places where they cultivated land and performed agricultural labour (for instance, Washbrook 2010). As a master narrative of the effects of economic change on artisan communities, the deindustrialization thesis has been seriously qualified. While certainly many craftspeople had to give up their occupations in order to subsist, others showed considerable resilience in withstanding the new pressures and in adapting to the changing economic context. Migration was a critical adaptive mechanism, along with shifting techniques, products and markets, which small producers deployed to cope with the dislocations of the global economy. While records of artisan movement no doubt decline in the early nineteenth century, they then pick up again after 1860.

Rather than exhibit a uniform tendency towards sedentary work, artisan accommodations to change diversified along at least five principal tracks. There was, first of all, a significant departure from the ranks of artisans, associated with a spatial movement that one might call artisan-to-labour movement. Much of this probably involved the entry of craftspeople into the rural economy, especially as unskilled workers; in such cases, artisans could become indistinguishable from those with origins in the more purely agricultural occupations (although see Kolff, this volume). In a plausible view of the impact of foreign trade that has taken shape in recent decades, artisans who manufactured inputs, such as cotton yarn, and who served mainly rural and local demand, were more likely to shift towards agricultural pursuits. Still other unemployed artisans probably joined the stream of people migrating overseas as indentured labour.

A second tendency was represented by a few thousand European craftsmen, carpenters and blacksmiths predominant amongst them, who migrated to India to seek their fortunes. A number of artisans travelled from Britain to India after the end of the East India Company's trade charter in 1813. Already, by this date, 'a great number of European artisans [had] established themselves in Calcutta, in Patna, at all our cantonments at Lucknow' (Malcolm 1814: 3). They produced goods to meet the demand from the European settlers and richer members of the Indian residents for goods such as 'carriages, furniture of all kinds, palankeens of a peculiar construction, invented by the Europeans, plate, sadlery, boots and shoes, salting meats, in making guns and pistols, and a variety of other articles', which included watch-making, silverware, and glassware (ibid.: 4). Between 1800 and 1850, tanneries, glass-works, casting and forging shops, and carpentry workshops were being established in significant numbers. In Calcutta, Madras and Bombay could be found 'British artisans and manufacturers of almost every description of trade that is exercised in [Britain]: such as coachmakers, carpenters, cabinetmakers, upholsterers, workers in the different metals, workers in all kinds of tanned leather, tailors, and shoemakers' (ibid.: 10). Unfortunately, the precise scale and composition of European artisan migration to India cannot be measured with certainty. About 1860, the resident Europeans in the three largest port towns numbered about 15,000, but few of them were artisans. The major component of the artisans of foreign extraction had by then been absorbed in the several hundred thousand strong Indo–European population.

After 1860, there was also significant mobility among Indian craftspeople, who maintained their participation in their professions by moving to other parts of the subcontinent. Those involved in the more skill-intensive and urban crafts making finished goods were often able to hold on to their traditional markets or even to explore alternative markets consistent with their productive capacities as artisans. For these kinds of actors, the consolidation of commercial agriculture frequently meant the creation of new markets for manufactures among more prosperous peasants who preferred to buy artisan-produced goods, particularly women's saris and bodice pieces, rather than imported products. Some artisans moved to new locations in order to develop access to consumers or to manufactured raw materials such as mill-made yarn, thus reducing their costs. The migration of gold-thread workers from Benares to Surat, both thread manufacturing towns, probably follows this pattern. According to the collective memory of some communities, such artisan-to-artisan migration was initially induced by famine (see Haynes and Roy 1999 for more discussion).

In some cases, mobile artisans shifted mainly to new places within their local regions. But several artisan-to-artisan movements involved long-distance migration, resettlement and, in a broad sense, urbanization of the artisan communities.

Most cases of long-distance migration can be found among the ranks of highly skilled handloom weavers. By the late nineteenth century, many thousands resisted the prospect of unemployment by moving from stagnant manufacturing regions to areas where their skills were in demand. In interviews conducted by one of the authors in the 1990s, some elderly weavers in western, northern and southern India insisted that few or none of the members of their community had ever taken part in agriculture. The same individuals gave extensive testimony on their past movements, and those of family members, to other textile centres. While such oral accounts are undoubtedly imperfect, they do point to a powerful norm in many weavers' communities that sanctioned migration as a preferable alternative to absorption into the agricultural sector.

Perhaps the best documented cases of large-scale movements of artisan groups concern the migration of weavers out of the impoverished areas of the eastern United Provinces and Hyderabad State. The former consisted mainly of Muslims, often referred to as Julahas in British records, but who increasingly took on the identity of 'Momin' (the faithful). They frequently moved to more dynamic sari-producing weaving towns in western India close to Bombay, such as Dhulia, Malegaon and Bhiwandi. The second involved Hindu Padmashali weavers from Telugu country who migrated to big handloom centres further to the south in the Bombay Presidency, including Sholapur and Ahmednagar. In most cases, particularly when they lacked funds of their own, they sought employment in their new locales on a wage basis in handloom workshops, which could contain from 4 to 150 looms. The more successful among these employees could later deploy personal savings or even loans from their former bosses to set up small enterprises based upon family labour or small numbers of wage workers. Still others moved into the jute mills of Calcutta or the textile mills of Bombay and Sholapur, where their skills sometimes allowed them to become part of the upper rungs of the working class. There is some evidence of Padmasalis and Momins circulating between artisan households, larger handloom workshops and modern factories as they grew older or as conditions changed, in these different types of manufacturing units. Artisans could also move back and forth between their home districts and new centres of employment with the season or with shifts in the employment climate. Ultimately, substantial diaspora of Momins and Padmasalis, stretching from northern or southeastern India into the Bombay Presidency, were forged.

The discussion of the Padmasalis and Momins draws attention to a fourth kind of mobility, which might be called artisan-to-factory movement, and which established the migrant artisan as a wage-earner in the new setting. These movements again involved shifts not only between geographic sites but from one form of organization to another, often located in towns or in major urban centres, with little job loss or expertise. This would include, for instance, weavers who entered the large handloom workshops of western and southern India, but also those who found employment in the factories of Calcutta and Bombay. In Bombay, for instance, there were four dominant social groupings in the cotton mills, the Marathas of peasant background mainly from Konkan, the 'Untouchables', North Indian Muslims and the Pardeshis or North Indian Hindus. Of these groups, those from north India included many ex-handloom weavers.

Artisan-to-factory relocation is also represented by the people from the leather tanning communities of northern India. They came from villages with large livestock supplies, where they had performed their craft as individual or groups of cooperative families, to settle as factory workers in Calcutta, Madras and Bombay, the port towns which, from the end of the nineteenth century, exported large quantities of semi-finished leather. In the case of tanning, the artisan household and the factory both used very similar tools and processes. Another nineteenth-century instance of adaptive migration occurred in northern India, when famine-hit Kashmiri artisans from the hills went to Punjab to start weaving carpets in Amritsar. At first they made shawls for export to Europe, but then shifted to carpet manufacture, which had a steadier and growing export potential.

For those who participated in geographic circulation in search of more secure livelihoods, the advent of employment in modern factories and other new industries added possible options in their constant search for work outside agriculture. Handloom weavers, as persons who already possessed great experience in the production of cloth, often found that their skills were demanded in the mills. Entry into the mills was commonplace during times of recession in weaving, such as the crisis that affected handloom producers in western India during the First World War, when the price of dyes and spun cotton yarn increased dramatically. While historians have tended to view migration to the centres of modern mills as a radical departure from 'pre-industrial' practices, the artisans in declining regions may have seen their movement to these new kinds of venture as an extension of pre-existing forms of migration to hand-loom towns, which they had undertaken whenever new opportunities arose (see Haynes and Roy 1999).

A fifth and final form of mobility was localized peasant-to-artisan movements after the 1920s, especially in the thriving cotton textile towns located in Tamil Nadu. Historically, the phenomenon that some scholars have called 'proto-industrialization', that is, production by peasant households of manufactures for the long-distance market, and which has been illustrated with some eighteenth-century European case studies and that of the peasant silk-makers of late-nineteenth-century Japan, was rather weak in India (see DeVries 1994; Saito 2005). But, in some cases at least, peasants did move into artisan professions once new market opportunities appeared. One of the more famous cases is that of the richer Gounder farmers of Tamil Nadu who converted a part of their farmhouses into textile-making units in the mid-twentieth century, a form of investment that eventually gave rise to very large and dense clusters of the textile industry in the same regions.

Artisans and community

While in pre-colonial India whole communities had seemingly travelled together, the nineteenth-century migrant artisan at first typically moved as a young single male. The railways had vastly increased the scope for a kind of migration that brought an individual job-seeker in contact with an individual employer, and the effect of such hiring possibilities was felt in the artisan job market as well as in the more well-known contexts of tea plantations or mill work. The indenture contract, which enabled such circulation in the plantations especially, was conspicuously rare in industry, including artisanal production; there are occasional reports of a contractual element in the new employment relations that emerged in the mid-twentieth century. But, while artisans moved on their own or in small groups, community did figure in other ways. Larger workshops in the thriving handloom centres were often owned by persons belonging to artisan communities themselves, and these small capitalists tended to hire those from their own community background. Between the capitalist and the wage-earner, the bond of a community at times had a reinforcing effect on the contractual relationship and provided employers with social mechanisms to deepen their hold over workforces.

Not surprisingly, as artisans moved, they often strengthened community solidarities in their new locales with those who shared origins in the same homelands. The role of community was critical in providing the individual migrant with essential resources, for example, a place to stay, a job and the reassuring company of kin in an alien environment. Often artisan-migrants lived together in neighbourhoods populated largely by their caste fellows or co-religionists. They established community-bound charitable deeds and religious institutions, such as mosques or temples, which created sentiments of solidarity and sometimes linked migrants back to their places of origin. They also established community organizations and associations, variously named *panches*, *fands* and *jamaats*, to enforce group codes of conduct, such as those surrounding marriage and employer–employee conduct, and to promote educational upliftment and social reform. After 1900, communities like the Padmasalis and Momins in different towns created inter-regional public associations that connected them with each other and with caste fellows in their homelands. In many of the sources on mass migration of handloom weavers in the nineteenth and twentieth century, the role of the community as a mutual support system appears paramount. Deliberate attempts to revive collective memory and solidarity, in the case of groups that considered themselves alien in their new locales, showed how community could be harnessed to serve the modern need to share risks and to create new forms of social connection in an urban environment.

Conclusion

The world of the South Asian artisan thus has often been a mobile one. Through much of South Asian history, skilled artisans have chosen to adapt to periods of stress on their livelihoods or to changing opportunities by moving to new territories, rather than allowing themselves to be absorbed into the general labour market in their places of origin. As the factors promoting regional decline or dynamism have changed over time, the immediate causes of their movements have altered, as has their mode of travel, but the role of mobility as an adaptive mechanism has remained. In some cases, of course, those who moved gave up their professions and merged with other mobile categories of people, for instance in communities of South Asians living in Africa, Southeast Asia and the Caribbean. But what is striking about so much artisanal mobility within South Asia is the ways that migrants have perpetuated or reinvented an identification with a 'traditional' occupation and a pride in specific manufacturing skills and have so often fashioned strong bonds of community that continue to demarcate them from non-artisanal groups in their new settings, decades or even centuries after their initial migrations. This makes it possible for historians to consider their movements *as artisans* (or at least as persons who maintain artisanal identities) in a way that is often not feasible with many other occupational groups on the move. Modernity, in the form of new kinds of technology, communication and travel, and associational activity, has often only enhanced the capacity of artisans to reproduce community solidarities in novel environments and to strengthen their ability to sustain social connections with their places of origin.

References

Basham, A.L. 1983. 'The Mandasor Inscription of the Silk Weavers', in Bardwell Smith, ed., *Essays on Gupta Culture*, New York: Columbia University Press.

Bayly, C.A. 1983. *Rulers, Townsmen and Bazaars: North Indian Society in the Age of British Expansion*, Cambridge: Cambridge University Press.

Behura, N.K. 1965. 'The Potter Servants of Jagannath at Puri', *Man in India*, 45, pp. 127–133.

De Vries, J. 1994. 'The Industrial Revolution and the Industrious Revolution', *Journal of Economic History*, 54(2), pp. 249–70.

Gazetteer of the Bombay Presidency. 1884. *Surat District*, vol. II, Bombay: Government Press.

Haynes, D. and T. Roy. 1999. 'Conceiving Mobility: Weavers' Migrations in Precolonial and Colonial India', *Indian Economic and Social History Review*, 36(1), pp. 35–67.

Hossain, H. 1989. *The Company Weavers of Bengal: The East India Company and the Organisation of Textile Production in Bengal 1750–1813*, Delhi: Oxford University Press.

Malcolm, J. 1814. *Affairs of the East India Company in the Sessions 1813; Illustrative of the Improvements in the Manufacture of Iron, Steel, Brass, Tin, Copper, Hemp, Cordage, &c. by the Natives of India*, London: J.M. Richardson.

Mines, M. 1984. *The Warrior Merchants: Textiles, Trade, and Territory in South India*, Cambridge: Cambridge University Press.

Pandey, G. 1983. 'Economic Dislocation in Nineteenth Century Eastern Uttar Pradesh: Some Implications of the Decline of Artisanal Industry in Colonial India', in Peter Robb, ed., *Rural South Asia: Linkages, Change and Development*, London: Curzon Press.

Parthasarathi, P. 2001. *The Transition to a Colonial Economy, Weavers, Merchants and Kings in South India, 1720–1800*, Cambridge: Cambridge University Press.

Ramaswamy, V. 1985a. 'The Genesis and Historical Role of the Master Weavers in South Indian Textile Production', *Journal of the Economic and Social History of the Orient*, 28(4), pp. 294–325.

Ramaswamy, V. 1985b. 'Artisans in Vijayanagar Society', *Indian Economic and Social History Review*, 22(4), pp. 417–44.

Rangachari, V. 1914. 'History of the Naick Kingdom of Madura', *Indian Antiquary*, 43.

Roy, T. 1998. 'Capitalism and Community: A Case-study of the Maduari Sourashtras', *Indian Economic and Social History Review*, 34(4), pp. 437–63.

Roy, T. 2009. 'Did Globalization Aid Industrial Development in Colonial India? A Study of Knowledge Transfer in the Iron Industry', *Indian Economic and Social History Review*, 46(4), pp. 579–613.

Saito, O. 2005. 'Pre-Modern Economic Growth Revisited: Japan and the West', Working Paper, Economic History, London School of Economics and Political Science.

Sinopoli, C.M. 2003. *The Political Economy of Craft Production: Crafting Empire in South India, c. 1350–1650*, Cambridge: Cambridge University Press.

Washbrook, David. 2010. 'Merchants, Markets, and Commerce in Early Modern South India', *Journal of the Economic and Social History of the Orient*, 53(3), pp. 266–89.

5

HAWALA AND *HUNDI*

Vehicles for the long-distance transmission of value

Roger Ballard

Hawala and *hundi*: their historical origins

Long-distance trade is in no way a modern phenomenon nor a product of European colonial expansion. Overland trade across the Asiatic landmass has existed for millennia. Given its strategic location midway between Europe and east Asia, the Indian subcontinent has long been a significant player in long-distance oceanic trade. To facilitate this, India developed sophisticated methods for the transfer of value across the many jurisdictions that have come and gone in this vast arena.

Despite intense efforts by Western-style banking systems and related regulatory authorities to suppress them, these methods continue to thrive in the institutions of *hawala* and *hundi*. In recent times, these institutions have attracted much critical attention for their potential as a means of criminal 'money-laundering'. This essay explores how far that is really the case.

Hawala and *hundi* operations arose to serve the same purpose, namely the transfer of value over long distances. Yet there are also differences. The concept of *hawala* is of Arabic and hence Islamic origin, whilst the term *hundi* is firmly rooted in Indic and Hindu tradition. Each therefore reflects the priorities of its own religious and cultural tradition. In the case of *hawala*, the demands of Islamic Law are twofold: first an insistence that unearned profits obtained without shouldering risk are intrinsically exploitative, and hence unlawful, and second the view that, whilst debts are 'real', in that they are grounded in interpersonal obligation, credit is essentially a fiction and as such potentially exploitative.

Hence, as Schacht describes, *hawala* – a term drawn from the Arabic root h-w-l, whose basic meanings include 'change' and 'transform' – is understood in Islamic Law as a means whereby one can extinguish an existing obligation to person A by arranging to transfer it to person B. It

> is in the first place, a mandate to pay, i.e. I owe something to *A* but charge *B* to pay my debt. It can also be an assumption of my debt by *B*. The practical prerequisite in both cases is that I have a claim against *B* which is equal to or higher than the claim of *A* against me. This is not necessarily a debt. It can also be for the return of an object, e.g. a deposit or something taken by usurpation. Normally, therefore, the *hawala* amounts to an assignment: I assign to *A* a claim of mine against *B*, in order to satisfy a claim of *A* against me.

But the existence of a claim by *A* against me is not a necessary prerequisite, and the *hawala* then amounts to a mandate to collect, i.e. I charge *A* to collect my claim against *B*. The element common to all cases is merely that an obligation of *B* towards *A* is created. The acceptance of the *hawala* by *A* extinguishes my obligation; it revives only if *B* dies bankrupt or denies the existence of the *hawala*. Performance of *B* towards *A* extinguishes my claim against him only if the *hawala* was conducted with specific reference to this obligation, not if it was unconditional.

(Schacht 1964: 147)

Thus far *hawala* simply amounts to a straightforward way in which merchants involved in a complex series of transactions in any given (local) marketplace can make a comprehensive settlement of the debts they owe to each other, and those owed by their customers to them, within a given period. Provided that the participating *hawaladars* continue to trust each other even when they are out of touch, *hawala* is also an ideal means by which to implement long-distance value transfers. As Schacht goes on to explain:

One of the practical advantages of this institution is that it enables me to make payments in another place through *B*. Its effect is the same as that of the *suftaja* or bill of exchange. This defined as 'a loan of money in order to avoid the risk of transport'; I lend an amount to *B*, in order that he may pay it to *A* in another place.

The difference between *hawala* and *suftaja* is that the obligation of *B* towards me, which in the case of the *hawala* is normally supposed to be already existing, is, in the case of the *suftaja*, created on purpose by a payment which I make to *B*, which can only be construed as a loan of money; the transaction is reprehensible, because it is a loan of money from which I derive, without giving a counter-value, the advantage avoiding the risk of transport. But it is not invalid. In practice I buy a draft from *B* on the place in question. Historically, the origin of the bill of exchange can be traced to the *suftaja* and the *hawala*.

(Schacht 1964:148–9)

Such bills of exchange have been a commonplace feature of European banking systems since medieval times. Known as *avallo* in Italian and *aval* in French, there is every reason to believe that Islamic practice inspired the use of such instruments. The *hundi* evolved rather differently. The word is etymologically rooted in the Sanskrit term for a bond, *hundika*. Its usage has never been affected by qualms about the payment of interest. Hence, whilst most *hundis* have always been issued interest-free, those who utilised the system to generate liquidity secured against fixed assets (as did rulers and landowners when they found themselves in financial difficulty) frequently found themselves required to pay interest on what amounted to a loan.

Financial instruments, such as promissory notes and bills of exchange, are essential lubricants in the operation of every market economy of any complexity. But *hawala* focuses our attention on the transactional processes to which the rearrangement of obligations gives rise, and in consequence the ways in which such agreements can be utilised to implement financial *settlements*, regardless of the scale of spatial separation between those involved. This represents a vital service for those engaged in activities implying the need for long-distance value transfers.

Trust and the containment of risk

The recent credit crunch has provided a graphic reminder of the importance of trust in all financial systems. How did *hawaladars* manage to maintain trust when those with whom they did business were routinely located in far-distant market places? To understand this, we need to look beyond individual transactions to the systematic way in which they are used to transfer – or better still to *exchange* – value. The essence of all *hawala*-style settlement systems is to obviate the need to transfer money physically from one location to another.

In the long run, long-distance value transfers have a zero-sum outcome. If a financial crisis is to be avoided, the value of goods and services flowing in any given location must ultimately match that of those flowing out in the reverse direction. *Hawala*-style settlement networks build on precisely this insight.

A (highly simplified) model of how such an exchange works is set out below.

i. Customer c^1 indebts *hawaladar* A by handing over v^1 in local currency for onward transfer;
ii. A transfers the debt v^1 to his distant *hawala* partner B;
iii. B discharges the debt either to c^1's agent, or to c^1 himself on his arrival; the debt is discharged in an appropriate local currency;
iv. However, every *hawaladar* has a multiplicity of customers; before long A will have transferred debts to the tune of Σv on behalf of Σp customers to B, who will in due course have discharged the debts he had assumed to the assigned recipients;
v. A is now indebted to B to the tune of Σv;
vi. But B is in the *hawala* business as well, and has simultaneously transmitted debts to the tune of Σw on behalf of Σq customers to A, who will in turn have discharged those debts to the assigned recipients;
vii. And if $\Sigma v = \Sigma w$, the two *hawaladars* can readily extinguish their mutual debts.

Nevertheless, the whole operation is in principle risky. How can customers be sure that either A or B will not abscond with their hard earned assets? As I have argued elsewhere (Ballard 2005a), Greif's analysis of the means by which tenth-century Jewish traders in the southern Mediterranean contained risks of this kind applies equally well to *hawala* networks of Muslim traders which were emerging during the same period down the Red Sea and across the ocean to India. Taking his cue from games theory, Greif concludes that:

> The Maghribi traders overcame the contractual problems associated with agency relationships ... through a non-anonymous organizational framework, the coalition. Within the coalition an internal information-transmission system served to balance asymmetric information, and a reputation mechanism was used to ensure proper conduct. This reputation mechanism explains the observed 'trust' relations among the traders.
>
> The 'trust' did not reflect a social control system or the internalization of norms of behaviour (although these factors play a role in any economic system). Rather, the Maghribi traders established a relationship between past conduct and future economic reward. As a result, agents resisted the short-term gains attainable though deception, since the reduction in future utility resulting from dishonest behaviour outweighed the associated increase in present utility. Since this fact was known beforehand to all traders, agents could acquire a reputation as honest agents.
>
> *(Greif 1989: 880)*

It is quite clear that the preconditions for the emergence of the coalitions of reciprocity that Greif identifies – namely strongly endogamous kinship networks – were already available within the Indian Ocean's many caste, sect and *biraderi*-based networks. A further strength of this system is that such coalitions were intrinsically self-regulating. They had therefore little need to look to outside agencies (of the state, for example) to guarantee system security, even as the transactions they processed reached across a multitude of financial and legal jurisdictions.

Hundi/hawala networks and imperial hegemony

During the first three centuries of their presence in the Indian Ocean region, European Companies and traders relied almost exclusively on indigenous moneylenders or *shroffs*. Shroffs used access to *hundi* networks to facilitate value transfers across the length and breadth of the subcontinent, as well as into neighbouring territories (Bayly 1983). During the course of the nineteenth century, however, the Company and its civilian and military agents made strenuous efforts to free themselves from such indigenous services. In the financial sphere as in all others, the scale and the impact of British hegemony expanded rapidly in the aftermath of the uprising of 1857. Thereafter all government business, as well as the bulk of that implemented by European-controlled business houses, began to be directed through 'formal channels': European-owned and -run banks. But even if this may have pushed indigenous service-providers out of this sector of the market place, there was still plenty left to play for, especially since they enjoyed a significant competitive advantage over their new-found rivals. Besides being able to implement value transfers much more speedily than European-style banks, they did so in ways that were not immediately accessible to the imperial authorities.

This opened up a further contradiction. Hitherto *hundi* and *hawala* networks had operated as autonomous, self-regulating coalitions, governed by their own internal customary conventions. But within the context of the British Raj they found themselves subject to an unprecedentedly intrusive jurisdiction. Pax Britannica sought to regulate virtually all aspects of its newfound subjects' behaviour according to its own preferred norms, to tax them heavily to defray its consequent costs of administration and to prosecute them criminally for failing to adhere to its regulatory prescriptions. Whilst *hundi* and *hawala* networks were by no means the only indigenous institutions to suffer such harassment, the fact that the most affluent subjects of the Raj regularly transferred huge sums of now taxable wealth rendered them an immediate focus of attention.

Hence the objective of the 1879 Indian Stamp Act, which required details of all such transactions to be recorded in writing on expensively stamped officially printed paper, was not just to raise revenue; rather it also served to undermine the position of competitive advantage which highly efficient indigenous modes of value transfer enjoyed in comparison with those provided by formally constituted banks. Although banks did indeed begin to occupy an ever greater proportion of the financial marketplace, the use of *hundis* did not fall into abeyance. Indian agents often simply avoided using stamped paper to record their agreements: insofar as coalitions of reciprocity were self-regulating, conflicts could be resolved through networks of kinship and community, without reference to the courts. Nor did matters change much when India gained its independence. Although no longer subject to an alien Raj, its 'steel frame' was by no means abandoned by the indigenous administrators who took it over. On the contrary, the 'permit Raj' which they eventually created further reinforced state power and sought systematically to drive economic activities of any significance into state-run institutions.

Hundi/hawala networks in post-imperial and contemporary contexts

Despite initial hopes that a planned economy operating within a socialistic pattern of society would generate rapid progress towards prosperity, the Indian economy remained disappointingly stagnant in the immediate post-imperial period. State-run initiatives grew increasingly sclerotic, taxation regimes increasingly punitive and access to foreign exchange ever more tightly rationed. In consequence, India's so-called 'black economy' burgeoned – and so did *hawala/hundi* networks as means of servicing value transfer in the 'invisible' dimensions of India's economy. To be sure, the 'economic liberalisation' of the past two decades has swept away the worst of these regulatory excesses, such that much that was formally 'invisible' has now been rendered 'visible'. Yet *hawala/hundi* networks have survived. Insofar as overenthusiastic efforts to regulate and tax financial activities of all kinds has had – and in many instances still has – a strangulating impact on the prospects for economic growth, many economic agents still rely, of necessity, on informal means of value transfer in order to get their business done. However, in the contemporary world the provision of financial services to strangulated local markets has proved to be only a small part of the game. Where *hawala/hundi* networks have really come into their own in recent years is in the provision of highly efficient international (and hence cross-jurisdictional) value-transfer services. As a result it is the *hawala* as opposed to the *hundi* dimension of the business that has become critical in the contemporary world order.

Four major and interconnected factors have facilitated the resurgence of *hawala*-style value systems in contemporary times:

- the failure of the formal banking system to develop cheap, efficient and accessible global cross-jurisdictional payments systems;
- the explosive growth in the volume of international travel and trade;
- the emergence of the internet as a vehicle for instant (and secure) global communication;
- the huge outflow of migrant workers from South and East Asia to Arabia and Northern America, who have in turn generated a reverse flow of remittances currently running in excess of $US 300 billion per annum (Roth *et al.* 2004).

Moreover, since these inward flows of value are of necessity matched by similarly sized outflows in the reverse direction, these transactions have in turn launched a flood of hard-currency liquidity into precisely the arena in which *hawala* has its longest history. Given the prominence of South Asian diasporic networks in these processes, it is hardly surprising that *hawala* methodologies have enjoyed a huge resurgence. At the same time, these very developments have themselves transformed the way in which the system operates.

Hawala swaps rest on *hawaladars'* capacity to negotiate deals in which the ingoing and outgoing flows of value to and from any given jurisdiction are exactly matched. However, in the contemporary world, few of the inflows of value to the subcontinent are derived from commercial activity. Rather, they take the form of relatively small tranches of value, which migrant workers send to support their families and kinsfolk back home, most of whom are based in remote rural locations. By contrast, the foreign exchange released as a result of the purchase of the rupees due to be delivered to migrants' kinsfolk is a good which is eagerly sought after by all manner of customers. Many are local traders who have imported manufactured goods from elsewhere, and who are in urgent need of foreign exchange to settle dollar-denominated invoices. Others may be well-off families who have similar needs in order to meet the costs of educating their offspring in overseas universities, or the hospital bills of those elders whose illnesses require sophisticated medical treatment abroad. Others still may be high-net-wealth individuals seeking to squirrel away assets in overseas tax havens, well clear of the prying eyes of tax authorities.

Meeting the discrepant needs of these widely varying clients is a challenge. *Hawaladars* meet it, on the one hand, by building globally extended self-regulating transjurisdictionally extended coalitions based on precisely the same principles as those outlined by Greif; and, on the other, by making the most of current electronic technologies to acquire and distribute the information needed to negotiate and execute trust-based transactions on an almost instantaneous basis, all within the context of acephalous but globally distributed networks of reciprocal trust.

A series of linked examples will serve to illustrate how such complex outcomes are achieved. Since migrant remittances are the driving force behind contemporary manifestations of *hawala*, let us begin in Bradford, where there is a large concentration of migrants stemming from Pakistani-controlled Azad Kashmir. As a result, there is a substantial demand for a swift, reliable and low-cost value-transfer system capable of making cash deliveries (in rupees) to recipients based in locations scattered widely across a mountainous and overwhelming rural terrain. The way in which the first arm of what has become a complex system was pioneered was relatively straightforward. A respected – and hence trusted – member of the settlement in Bradford began to take orders for the delivery of cash deposits made with him as rupees to recipients in Azad Kashmir, delivery of which would be organised by his brother back in Mirpur. Since everyone trusted each other, little paperwork was entailed, other than the fax (and subsequently the e-mail) which the Bradford *hawaladar* regularly sent to his overseas partner setting out just how much should be paid to whom in what village. But, although the resultant rupee deliveries, normally implemented within a day or two, led to almost immediate transfers of value as far as their customers were concerned, the two *hawaladars'* position was unsustainable unless some means could be found of reimbursing the disbursing *hawaladar*.

This is where the second arm of the transaction came in. What the two parties also needed to do was to make contact with affluent local Pakistanis who were in urgent need of foreign exchange. It was in this context that a *hawala* deal proper could be implemented: when an affluent businessman in Pakistan agreed to deliver a large tranche of rupees to the *hawaladar* in Mirpur and his Bradford-based partner could transfer an equivalent amount in sterling into an account nominated by the Pakistani businessman. A matched pair of back-to-back transfers were then implemented in a manner which was convenient for all concerned and which gave rise to far lower overhead costs than would have been incurred had the transfer been made though the formally constituted banking system – always providing that it had been capable of making deliveries to such remote locations.

However, these developments were by no means unique to Bradford, to Pakistanis or even to emigrants from elsewhere in South Asia. Similar developments – now routinely identified as Informal Value Transfer Systems (IVTS) – emerged wherever chain migration led to the construction of ethnic colonies. Yet, if the capacity to generate effective transnational coalitions of reciprocity is the principal determinant of the success of such initiatives, the character of the cultural resources on which those involved rely also has a far-reaching impact on the eventual outcomes. Hence the IVTS networks to which all the diasporic outflows from South Asia have given rise are profoundly conditioned, first, by the way in which solidarities of caste, sect and *biraderi* (descent) provide them with ready foundations and, second, by their capacity to connect up with long-standing commercially driven *hawala* networks.

One of the most salient features of contemporary *hawala* networks is the facility with which they have been able to implement the classic financial exercises of consolidation, wholesale settlement and deconsolidation. The costs of making a transaction bear little or no relationship to the size of the sum transferred: hence the bigger the sum transferred, the smaller the proportion of its value will be eaten up in transfer costs. With this in mind, it is worth observing that the secret of the *hawala* system lies in the fact that, even though the remittances which local *hawaladars* transmit on behalf of their migrant worker customers are rarely greater than a few hundred pounds, the back-to-back settlements on which the whole operation ultimately relies are conducted on a hugely greater scale – in multiples of US$100,000.

In the simplistic example given so far, brokering the *hawala* swap was very much a hit and miss activity, since it was far from easy to set up equally sized tranches of value to exchange between the two complementary arms of the transaction. Likewise, the service on offer was inherently inflexible, since by no means all South Asian settlers looking for remittance services are of Mirpuri – or even of Pakistani – origin. It was in response to these challenges that strategies of consolidation and deconsolidation became ever more salient instruments in the *hawala* toolbox, and once again coalitions of reciprocity played a major role in the implementation of these initiatives, at the core of which lay the development of networks of agencies and sub-agencies.

As the operations of pioneer local *hawaladars* grew steadily in scale, leading figures occupying similar positions of trust in Mirpuri communities located elsewhere in the UK began to tap into established initiatives by acting as agents of the initial pioneers, such that transactions emanating from elsewhere were consolidated into the most successful pioneers' steadily expanding operations. Moreover, as this occurred, the bigger operators' activities in Pakistan became steadily less *ad hoc* in character, since they were now in a position to deal with well-entrenched Exchange Houses in Karachi, Pakistan's major financial, commercial and manufacturing centre – in other words the location in which there was by far the strongest demand for foreign exchange. Once relationships of this kind were in place, emergent UK-based *hawaladars* no longer had to look for Pakistani counterparts to implement *hawala*-style swaps on an *ad hoc* basis. They could now begin to broker *hawala* swaps on a global basis and in doing so tap into the financial potential of the equally complex counter-flows of value being generated by the agents of consolidating *hawaladars* located overseas. By now the implementation of a straightforward *hawala* swap (in this case for £100,000) as between the UK and Pakistan had become a complex and increasingly professional business, as the much simplified model set out in Figure 5.1 serves to demonstrate.

Having negotiated an exchange rate (e.g. £1 = 100 rupees), the UK-based consolidating *hawaladar* agrees to swap his obligation to fulfil £100,000 worth of delivery orders in rupees which he has accepted on behalf of his UK-based clients, in return for agreeing to implement £100,000 worth of payments (often to settle his partners' clients' invoices) into a series of nominated bank accounts in the UK. Meanwhile the Pakistani-based consolidator settles his debt to his UK-based partner by arranging to deliver 10 million rupees (often in cash) to his nominated agents in northern Pakistan, ready for further disaggregation and distribution to its ultimate recipients.

As Figure 5.1 serves to illustrate, a large number of actors in at least four separate networks are involved in the process, whose product is the outcome of myriads of independently brokered deals negotiated within and between networks of agents and sub-agents. The system effectively 'pulses' on a daily basis and every such pulse is the result of a series of transjurisdictional flows of *information* passed back and forth along the horizontal axis between UK and Pakistan, which in turn gives rise to two matched and simultaneous local flows of hard cash.

By now it should be clear that the conditions which have rendered this contemporary version of the *hawala* system are not just the capacity of those involved to construct coalitions of reciprocity, nor just the huge volume of liquidity generated by migrant remittances, but also the emergence of a readily accessible vehicle for instantaneous information transfer on a global scale. As internet services have become steadily more ubiquitous, so *hawala* networks have ceased to be restricted to simple bi-directional swaps. The great majority of swaps are now brokered through major Exchange Houses in Dubai, most of which are owned and run by Indian and Pakistani entrepreneurs, and which initially emerged during the 1970s and 1980s to service the financial needs of millions of South Asian migrant workers recruited to build infrastructural developments.

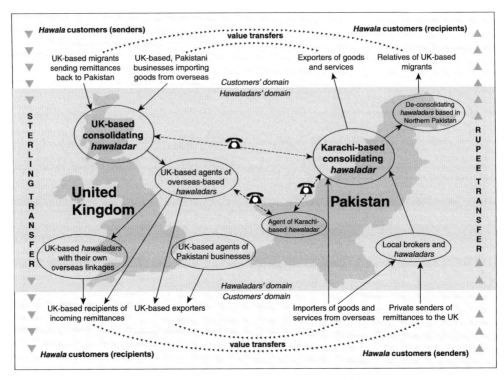

Figure 5.1 Transactions precipitated by a Britain/Pakistan exchange of debt between two consolidating hawaladars

However, with the turn of the millennium, Dubai's most successful Exchange Houses began to act as what can best be described as super-consolidators, providing further a level of brokerage services to the nationally grounded consolidators identified in Figure 5.1. By this stage a huge number of nationally grounded networks of *hawaladars* had emerged in virtually every region supplying labour migrants to the Gulf. By then, this included jurisdictions from Somalia in the west through the Middle East and South Asia to East Asia and the Philippines, further supplemented by settlers from all these regions who had also begun to establish successful footholds in Western Europe and North America. By adding what can be usefully envisaged as yet another layer to the model that I have set out in Figure 5.1, the Exchange Houses of Dubai effectively become a clearing hub standing at the core of a highly efficient global payments system. Its principal source of liquidity arose from its capacity to provide transjurisdictional value-transfer services to members of the regions' many diasporic communities, and most especially – although by no means exclusively – to those of Muslim origin. Moreover, the sums transferred through the system were far from trivial: daily settlements in Dubai reached multi-millions of dollars.

9/11 and after

Whilst these developments attracted little attention in Euro–American contexts prior to the events of 9/11, the wholly unexpected attacks on the Pentagon and the Twin Towers precipitated an immediate search for scapegoats. Everything remotely Islamic in character immediately found itself surrounded by a halo of suspicion. *Hawala* networks – presented in the press as 'a shady underground banking system' – rapidly became the focus of excited attention. One such network, al-Barakat, serving the global Somali diaspora, was promptly closed down by the US authorities on the grounds that its services had been utilised to fund the 9/11 attack. Subsequent investigations revealed that, while originating in Dubai, the bulk of these funds had been processed by the Florida-based Sun Trust Bank (Roth *et al.* 2004: 131–8). Nor was that the end of the matter. Within six weeks of 9/11, the US Congress passed the massive Patriot Act, which sought to render all IVTS networks illegitimate and their perpetrators liable to prosecution not just in the USA, but globally.

The introduction of Anti-Money Laundering (AML) measures (which amongst other things reverse the burden of proof) led to a significant number of successful prosecutions against *hawaladars* operating in both the UK and the USA. However, little or no evidence ever emerged to suggest that these initiatives had enabled the authorities to track down terrorists or drugs smugglers, the nominal objective of the whole exercise (Passas 2007). Despite these setbacks, IVTS networks of all kinds have continued to thrive, not least because the demand for cheap, swift and reliable transjurisdictional value transfers has steadily increased, given the ever rising scale of long-distance migration and trading networks. However, that does not mean that the operation of such networks has remained wholly unchanged.

In the first place, *hawala* networks have comprehensively relabelled themselves. No-one now acknowledges that the services they provide are driven by or articulated through *hawala*. They simply identify themselves as Money Transfer Agents, or some other similarly innocuous term. Second, virtually all the major operators, such as the Exchange Houses in Dubai, have yet further developed their *modus operandi*, not least in an effort to render themselves compliant with AML regulations. One of the principal means by which they have done so is to give their operations a more formal appearance.

The steady erosion of the distinction between 'formal' and 'informal' value transfers

Although *hawala* transfers are routinely described as 'informal', the term is in many respects a misnomer: as we have seen, a fully fledged transjurisdictional *hawala* swap is anything but a simple financial operation. Nor is it an operation of an intrinsically unusual kind. In *structural* terms, formally incorporated banks, as well as major multinational corporations, implement transjurisdictional value transfers on exactly the same basis. *Hawala* networks differ from these Western-style institutions in several interconnected respects – all of which are grounded in their distinctive historical and cultural origins.

In the first place, *hawala* networks have no legal personality in the Euro–American sense: they are not formally incorporated, and instead root their operations in trust-based coalitions of reciprocity. Second, and consequently, they are *distributed systems*: just like the internet, *hawala* networks can operate reliably on a global scale in the absence of a central registry. Third, and most significantly, this facilitates their capacity to implement value transfers on a 'lean and mean' basis, not least because they can eliminate the huge volume of redundant information transfer and storage facilities characteristic of Western-style contract-based banking systems. In other words it is their *technical* capabilities (of a kind that are so often erroneously identified as 'informal') that provide *hawaladars* with their competitive advantage.

But this is not all. Given that information transfer between trusted partners is the key to their whole operation, *hawaladars* have taken to the radical improvements in communication technology that we have witnessed in recent years like ducks to water. The availability of the internet and of mobile phones means that e-mails and spreadsheets can now readily and instantly be distributed to the remotest corners of the world. Nor have *hawaladars* necessarily eschewed opportunities to implement wholesale value transfers through the formal banking system as and when that suits their purposes. The very scale of their resultant operations has in one sense rendered the system steadily more centralised, with the result that Dubai has now emerged as a major global hub. Moreover, the major Exchange Houses have become steadily more 'formal' in character. Most have by now incorporated themselves as limited liability companies (LLCs); many have established formal links with major Euro–American banks; and, to bring their operations into compliance with AML regulations, many have set up LLCs in London and recruited large networks of local agents. But, having formalised themselves in this way, the settlement swaps which they facilitate continue to be ordered within distributed systems underpinned by coalitions of reciprocity – and with an ever greater component of 'back–office' activity being concentrated in Dubai, the subcontinent's *de facto* offshore banking sector.

A vehicle for money-laundering?

Money-laundering is a term which is as vague as it is elastic, given that it is applied to transactions ranging all the way from financial manoeuvres deployed to evade the payment of tax to those which enable criminals to finance their activities and conceal their ill–gotten gains. It is an open question as to whether outright crime takes place on any greater scale in the present than it did in the past. Yet there can be no doubt that, in the face of the ever-growing financial needs of contemporary states (and hence their ever more far-reaching efforts to raise tax) in an increasingly globalised world in which transjurisdictional value transfers have grown exponentially, those wishing to evade taxation by moving their wealth into some distant sovereign jurisdiction can do so with much greater ease than ever before. As a result money-laundering (sometimes euphemistically described as 'wealth management') has become a major activity, to which the best minds in the formal banking sector have paid a great deal of attention. Virtually all major multinational corporations, together with the majority of the world's high-net-wealth individuals, have organised their affairs in such a way as ensure that the largest possible proportion of their profits and financial assets are formally located in 'no-questions-asked', low-tax offshore financial jurisdictions well clear of that within which they are actually domiciled. The scale of the value transfers associated with money-laundering in the most general sense is immense: on the basis of a careful and cautious analysis, Baker (2005) estimated that the annual flow of 'dirty money' through the formal banking sector was as shown in Table 5.1.

Several points are worth noting about these figures. First, Baker concluded that the scale of the 'dirty' transfers made by corporate and commercial bodies was at least three times greater than those which were the outcome of more directly criminal activities. Second, he produced these figures prior to the credit crunch of 2008/9, in which a huge amount of dirty linen previously concealed was brought into public view, so much so that the 'formal' banking system's former reputation for trustworthiness, integrity and probity was comprehensively shredded.

In the aftermath of all these developments, it is now quite clear that 'money-laundering' in all its various formats has become an endemic feature of the contemporary global economic order. Even the most august financial institutions have been heavily implicated in it. To the extent that *hawala* networks also facilitate just the same kind of transjurisdictional value transfers, it would be idle to suggest that they have not been similarly infiltrated by what Baker describes as 'dirty money'. In these circumstances two key questions emerge. Are *hawala* networks intrinsically more vulnerable to penetration by those transferring funds of such origin than their more

Table 5.1 Estimates of cross-border flows of global dirty money in US$ billion

Dirty money	Global transfers		Developing/traditional economies	
	High	Low	High	Low
Criminal				
Drugs	200	120	90	60
Counterfeit goods	120	80	60	45
Counterfeit currency	4	3	2	1
Human trafficking	15	12	12	10
Illegal arms trade	10	6	4	3
Smuggling	100	60	40	30
Racketeering	100	50	30	20
Subtotal	549	331	238	169
Commercial corruption	50	30	40	20
Mispricing	250	200	150	100
Abusive transfer pricing	500	300	150	100
Fake transactions	250	200	200	150
Subtotal	1,000	700	500	350
Total	1,599	1,061	778	539

Source: Baker 2005: 172, Table 4.4

formally constituted counterparts? Given that it is to everyone's collective benefit that 'dirty' transfers of this kind are curtailed, how is this best achieved?

Conclusion

The resurgence of the significance of *hawala-/hundi*-style value transfers in the contemporary world is manifestly an outcome not just of globalisation, but above all of 'globalisation from below', and of the concomitant emergence of webs of ever expanding transjurisdictional diasporic networks from all quarters of the Indian Ocean region (Ballard 2009). These networks have provided the foundations of the coalitions of reciprocity on which *hawala* networks were initially constructed, as well as precipitating a huge flow of liquidity in the form of migrant remittances. As a result, they have made a major impact on economic and commercial development throughout the entire region. Moreover, the 'informal' trust-based networks, which have provided the financial services underpinning these developments, owe their competitive advantage over their more formally constituted competitors to their capacity to implement transjurisdictional value transfers more cheaply, more swiftly, more accessibly and just as reliably as their more formally constituted Western-style counterparts.

It is also worth noting that, although 'formal' banking institutions routinely issue public proclamations to the effect that they would not touch dirty money, and point to their strenuous efforts to comply with AML regulations, their practices reveal otherwise. For them, compliance is not an obligation that they owe to other players in the market place. Compliance is rather obedience to state-imposed regulations specifying the limits within which they must operate. In these circumstances they have hired armies of expensive bankers and lawyers to devise strategies of 'wealth management', 'transfer pricing' and so forth to produce precisely the outcomes which

Baker has highlighted. *Hawala* networks may actually be rather less prone to these excesses. This is partly because they restrict themselves to value transfer rather than to value storage (if even some of those transfers may well still end up in off-shore tax havens). It is also because *hawaladars* are well aware that, if they engage in business which their partners regard as excessively risky, they could find themselves exposed to far reaching sanctions from the entire coalition.

Nevertheless, what is plain is that even if the vast majority of the transfers passing through such trust-based 'Asiatic' networks are wholly legitimate in character, at least some of those transactions will involve funds of a kind which Baker identifies as 'dirty'. However, to identify such networks as criminal conspiracies – as has become increasingly commonplace in the aftermath of 9/11 – appears to be entirely inappropriate, especially since there is clear evidence that their Euro–American counterparts are equally heavily, if not more, involved in facilitating transfers of this kind. In these circumstances, a much more appropriate response would be the initiation of careful policing initiatives which seek to work in close collaboration with those operating all forms of transjurisdictional value transfer in an effort to detect, and in due course to prosecute, those actually seeking to engage in malfeasance. However there is little sign of any such developments taking place. Given that the New York money markets play such a central role in the global economy, and that the Federal Reserve requires all overseas banks maintaining corresponding accounts with Wall Street Banks to strictly apply its AML regulations (which also incorporate the provisions of the Patriot Act) in all aspects of their global operations it follows that the ultimate object of the exercise was to reinforce the global hegemony of the US dollar, whilst simultaneously promulgating what it deemed to be a universally applicable means of distinguishing between 'good' money and 'bad'. This exercise in financial hegemony, which has een designed to distinguish 'good' money from 'bad', has far reaching consequences, not least for *hawaladars* and their migrant worker clients. For money to be deemed to be 'clean', financial institutions must keep records which will enable them to track the course of every financial transaction from end to end: and it goes without saying that the cost of such record-keeping is inversely proportional to the sum being transferred. As a result the rules of AML bear down disproportionately heavily on customers seeking to send small sums of money to distant destinations through the formal sector.

But given that Hawala networks are distributed systems, they do not maintain expensive central registries. As a result their overhead costs for forex transfers remain much lower than those of formally constituted banks, much to the advantage of many millions of small fry. But does this mean that their activities are inherently criminal? Contrary to popular assumptions, *hawala* is in no sense a 'system without records'; on the contrary plentiful records are routinely kept by *hawaladars* at each node in the network. But rather than seeking to devise strategies to monitor these highly efficient global value transfer systems, the preferred strategy emanating from Washington and New York is to enforce the premises of AML on a global scale, and to extract large fines from all financial institutions that in their view have failed to enforce them. Since caution is the greater part of valour, formal financial operators around the globe have meekly complied, not least because they can pass on the extra overheads (and some) directly to their customers.

But whether or not this provides an effective means of keeping terrorists and drugs smugglers at bay is a much more open question. What it does do, however, is escalate the cost of long distance value-transfers made by millions of little fish, whilst enabling the authorities to confiscate large tranches of value being swapped between *hawaladars* on the grounds that 'sensibly' there can be no explanation of the existence of these funds other than cleansing the product of drug smuggling, or failing that, the delivery of funds to finance terrorist activity. Whilst raids of this sort provide the basis for dramatic exercises in public relations, they much more rarely lead to the identification of terrorists – or indeed of drugs smugglers.

Bibliography

Baker, Raymond (2005) *Capitalism's Achilles Heel: Dirty Money and How to Renew the Free-Market System*, New York: Wiley.

Ballard, Roger (2009) 'The Dynamics of Translocal and Transjurisdictional Networks: A Diasporic Perspective' in *South Asian Diaspora*, Vol. 1 (2): 141–66.

— (2006) 'Hawala: Criminal Haven or Vital Financial Network?' in *Newsletter of the International Institute for Asian Studies* (September), University of Leiden, Netherlands: 8–9.

— (2005a) 'Coalitions of Reciprocity and the Maintenance of Financial Integrity within Informal Value Transmission Systems: The Operational Dynamics of Contemporary Hawala Networks' in *Journal of Banking Regulation*, Vol. 6 (4): 319–52.

— (2005b) 'Remittances and Economic Development in India and Pakistan' in Maimbo, S. and Ratha, D. (eds) *Remittances: Development Impact and Future Prospects*, Washington, DC: World Bank, pp. 103–18.

— (2003) 'The South Asian Presence in Britain and its Transnational Connections' in Singh, H. and Vertovec, S. (eds) *Culture and Economy in the Indian Diaspora*, London: Routledge, pp. 197–222.

Bayly, C. A. (1983) *Rulers, Townsmen and Bazaars: North Indian Society in the Age of British Expansion 1770–1870*, New Delhi, India: Oxford University Press.

Greif, Avner (1989) 'Reputation and Coalitions in Medieval Trade: Evidence on the Maghribi Traders' in *The Journal of Economic History*, 49: 857–82.

Passas, Nikos (2007) 'Fighting Terror with Error: The Counter-productive Regulation of Informal Value Transfers' in *Crime, Law and Social Change*, Vol. 45, 315–66.

Roth, John, Greenburg, Douglas and Willie, Serena (2004) *Monograph on Terrorist Financing*, Washington, DC: National Commission on Terrorist Attacks upon the United States.

Schacht, Joseph (1964) *An Introduction to Islamic Law*, Oxford: Clarendon Press.

PART II

Diaspora and empire

6

SOUTH ASIAN BUSINESS IN THE EMPIRE AND BEYOND
c. 1800–1950

Claude Markovits

By 1800, there were colonies of South Asian traders dispersed across the entire Indian Ocean basin, from Mocha in Yemen to Malacca on the Straits. There were also small clusters of money-lenders and merchants in the interior of Asia, in the immense continental space extending from Tibet to the Russian heartland across Central Asia, Afghanistan and Iran. No credible demographic estimate of this population is available, but it was certainly in the several thousands, perhaps even more. Most dispersed South Asian traders originated from Western and Southern India. Prominent amongst those from Western India were various groups of Gujarati traders (including Kutchis), mostly Muslims, both Shi'a (Khojas and Bohras) and Sunni (Memons), but also Hindus (more specifically the Bhatias of Kutch). There were also Hindu traders from Thatta in Sindh and Muslims from the Konkan. South Indian traders came mostly from Kerala on the West Coast, in particular the Muslim Mapillai, as well as Syrian Christians, and from the Coromandel coast of present-day Tamilnadu, mostly the Muslim Marakayyars, often known as Chulias. Along the caravan routes leading to Upper Asia and Central Asia, the dominant element consisted of the Multani–Shikarpuris of the Punjab–Sindh confines (Markovits 2000a; Levi 2002). These various networks did in no way constitute a unified South Asian trading diaspora, and Stephen Dale's view of the existence of an 'Indian world economy' is probably an exaggeration (Dale 1994: 1–7). The reasons why Indian trading networks were, from an early medieval period, able to expand much beyond the subcontinent, remain an under-researched area, but mention must be made, apart from their seafaring abilities (the pilot who guided Vasco de Gama from Malindi to Calicut in 1498 was most probably a Gujarati), of their financial skills. In particular they had developed a credit instrument known as the *hundi*, a kind of bill of exchange and promissory note, which allowed them to maximize their capital assets and to transfer funds in relative safety across long distances. Another advantage they had over their European and Asian competitors was their unrivalled knowledge of the Indian textile industry, which was the main supplier of cotton cloth to the entire Indian Ocean Basin. Indian cloth was such a standard commodity that it was still in use as a kind of currency in the eighteenth century in many areas of the Indian Ocean, and South Asian traders had developed over the centuries an uncanny ability to match supply in India with demand in faraway markets. The question before us therefore is how this dispersed but efficient mercantile universe managed to survive the colonial transition of the first half of the nineteenth century and even to thrive in the period starting around 1860, when British and European capital extended its sway over most of Asia and Africa.

Surviving the colonial transition (*c.* 1800 to *c.* 1860)

By the early 1800s, the East India Company had established its domination, either direct or indirect, over the whole of India's coastal areas, from where most of the expatriate traders originated. Prior to 1858, these traders, although not Crown subjects, were considered British-protected persons and therefore felt the impact of the growing power of the British in the Indian Ocean area, manifested in the increasing presence of the Royal Navy and the establishment of British consulates in various localities. There was a positive aspect to it: when extra-territorial privileges were granted to British subjects, as was the case in China in the wake of the First Opium War (1842), Indians *de facto* enjoyed them; they also enjoyed trading facilities in two major Indian Ocean ports, Singapore and Aden, which were annexed by the British in 1819 and 1839 and were administered as part of the Bengal and Bombay Presidencies. Although there is no instance of a British intervention specifically aimed at protecting Indian traders, their British connection ensured Indian traders a certain degree of protection against local hazards, in particular piracy which was widespread in many parts of the Indian Ocean. But there was also a more negative aspect, from the traders' point of view, to the spread of British influence. In Zanzibar, which became after 1840 the main hub of trade for the entire East African region, following the relocation there of the reigning family of the Oman sultanate, British consuls were bent on suppressing the slave trade, in which local Indian merchants were heavily involved as financiers. Even after the Queen's Proclamation of 1st November 1858 had made residents of British India subjects of the Crown, Indian merchants in Zanzibar, most of whom originated from the tiny Indian State of Kutch, took shelter behind the fact that they were not *stricto sensu* British subjects to continue their activities as financiers of the slave trade. The British had to obtain, in 1869, a *firman* from the ruler of Kutch officially advising his subjects in Africa that they had to conform to British regulations, before they abandoned that activity (some of them shifted to financing the still prosperous slave trade carried out from neighbouring Portuguese-ruled Mozambique). This story tends to epitomize the attitude of most Indian traders towards British imperialism, which was basically instrumentalist. They tried to derive maximum benefits from it, but also to limit the hindrances arising from certain British policies. During the 1840–60 period, a certain correlation can be observed between the expansion of some Indian trading networks and the growth of the 'informal' British Empire characteristic of the 'imperialism of free trade'. Some Indian traders were important actors in the process of gradual integration of areas of Africa and Asia with the then British-dominated world economy. Two cases in point are Zanzibar and China. The role of various South Asian trading networks in the emergence of a Zanzibar-centred commercial economy on the East African coast is well documented (Shariff 1987). Indian financiers, mostly Bhatias from Kutch, largely managed the finances of the Zanzibar sultanate, in particular the customs department, and they played an important role in the development of clove cultivation in the islands of Zanzibar and Pemba, both through the advances they made to the Arab landholders who owned the plantations and through their financing of the slave trade which provided the planters with their manpower. From Zanzibar, they were able to expand their operations across the entire East African littoral, making use of the opportunities offered by the expansion of the Zanzibar state itself. In China, the role of the Indians was mostly commercial, through their participation in the cotton and the opium trades. Bombay Parsis developed a particularly close connection to the China trade. From the 1740s onwards, they started travelling regularly to China, renewing an old trading link between India and China, which had remained dormant during three centuries (following the end, around 1430, of the Ming trading expeditions to Calicut of the early fifteenth century). Their role in the opium trade increased considerably after 1800, and it was of a dual nature. On the one hand, the ships which carried the 'Bengal' or 'Patna' opium, grown in Company territory under Company supervision, to Canton, were often built in the Parsi-owned Wadia Bombay shipyard and were also partly financed by Parsi merchants in association with British private merchants (as the trade was illegal for the Chinese authorities, the East India Company remained in the background). Some of these Parsi merchants started residing in Canton, where they formed a small colony, entirely dedicated to the opium trade. On the other hand, the same Bombay Parsi merchants were as heavily involved (sometimes also in association with British capitalists) in the financing of the contraband trade in 'Malwa' opium, grown in the native states of Central India and exported to China through the Portuguese port of Damao, in violation of East India Company regulations (Markovits 2009). After 1842, when, following the 'opening' of China, the opium trade became 'legal', Parsis continued to play an active role in it, in close association with big British firms. The best-known case is that of Sir Jamsetji Jejeebhoy, the 'First Baronet', a legendary Parsi opium trader, who is said to have supplied the great British trading firm of Jardine Mathesons with a third of the opium lying in their Canton warehouses by the 1830s (Siddiqi 1982). Some Parsis earned considerable fortunes in the opium trade and, after 1860, when they started withdrawing from it, they invested on a big scale in Bombay real estate and in cotton mills. They did not however send all their profits to India, and cities like Hong Kong (where many Parsis moved from Canton after 1842) and Shanghai benefited by their munificence (Markovits 2000b). While the British Empire entered a new phase of unprecedented expansion from the 1870s onwards, British Indian merchants were faced with new challenges, but also new opportunities.

Challenges and opportunities in the high imperial era (1870–1914)

In spite of being subjects of the Crown, theoretically free to move anywhere in the British Empire, and entitled to the protection of HM's consuls in foreign countries, British Indian traders faced increasing obstacles to their movements from the 1880s onwards, as in particular white settlers' colonies, influenced by the example of the United States, passed anti-Asiatic bills. Southern Africa was the place where the hostility of the settlers was the most palpable, particularly in the colony of Natal. Durban, where there was a significant influx of 'passenger' Indians, i.e. traders, in the 1880s, became a flashpoint in the confrontation between those traders, claiming their rights as subjects of the Crown, and local colonial authorities and white settlers. The launching of Gandhi's political career in South Africa in 1894 was closely linked to his taking up the cause of the local Gujarati, mostly Muslim, merchants, in their fight against the settlers' attempts to reduce them to the status of 'coolies' deprived of any rights. In spite of Gandhi's heroic efforts and of the struggles he led from 1906 onwards, by the time the future Mahatma left the Union of South Africa in 1914, new emigration of traders from India had been effectively interdicted and those who had managed to stay were subjected to discriminatory policies, confined in Indian 'locations'. Similar trends were visible in neighbouring Rhodesia (where there had been anti-Indian riots by whites in the town of Umtali in 1898) and in more faraway Kenya, where, however, white settlers were too dependent on the Indian traders to push too far their hostility, at least before 1920. Hostility to Indian traders even spread from British territory into neighbouring Portuguese territory, as Indian merchants in Mozambique faced increasing discrimination on the part of the colonial authorities there. Even before the First World War generalized the use of the passport, it had become difficult for Indian traders to travel abroad without documents, as they had done prior to the 1880s and, since the granting of a passport in India was not a citizen's right but was left to the discretion of the authorities, it enhanced the possibilities of government control over the movement of traders. Authorities could also use international sanitary regulations (there was often a cholera epidemic somewhere in India) to deny landing rights to Indian passengers in British colonial ports, as they often did in South Africa. In spite of these growing obstacles, Indian traders extended the range of their travels in an unprecedented manner in the pre-First World War period. Sindhi traders from Hyderabad, known as Sindworkies, ranged as far as Panama in Central America, Punta Arenas in South America and Honolulu in Hawaï, setting up shops in most ports of call along the steamer routes and selling silk and curios to travellers and tourists (Markovits 2000a). Apart from the hostility of colonial officials and white settlers, Indian traders had also to contend with the growing strength of British and other European banks and commercial firms in their traditional area of operations, the Indian Ocean basin. To cope with it, they tended to seek accommodation, rather than confrontation, and they were not totally devoid of bargaining power. Over the centuries, they had developed an unparalleled knowledge of the societies and markets of that entire area, and British and European bankers and merchants were generally interested in tapping this source of knowledge, especially when entering new, unfamiliar territory. Indians could therefore 'trade' this knowledge to form partnerships with Europeans in which they were not necessarily confined to the role of junior partners. Besides, their financial skills were at a premium in regions where few were familiar with sophisticated techniques, such as double-entry bookkeeping, which Indians mastered as well as Europeans. Hence the position of privileged intermediaries between British capital and local economic agents that Indian traders acquired in different regions of the British Empire. Two stand out particularly: East Africa and Southeast Asia.

Indian traders and their role in East Africa and Southeast Asia

In East Africa, Indians were already well entrenched in trade when the British established their protectorate over the area in 1890, while in Southeast Asia the presence of Indian traders was more directly linked to the expansion of British colonial domination, starting with the foundation of Georgetown on Penang island in 1786. The two regions therefore offer a study in contrasts, and the outcomes in both were largely dissimilar. British East Africa became the region of the Empire where the Indian commercial presence was the most visible. The Indian commercial community in East Africa was the result of two distinct streams of migration. On the one hand, there were those Indian traders, originally hailing from Kutch and Kathiawar (Saurashtra) in Gujarat, who, from their base in Zanzibar, had expanded all over the littoral and started also trading in the interior, where they played an important role in the ivory trade, in close conjunction with African and Arab traders and chiefs. By 1890, they occupied a dominant position in the trade in many commodities and they were the main credit agency. They belonged to various communities, both Muslim, like the Khojas, themselves divided into the Ismaili and Itna'asheri segments (the latter a product of a schism within the Ismaili community, the dissidents having adhered to Twelver Shi'ism), the Shi'a Bohras and the Sunni Memons, and Hindu, like the Kutchi Bhatias who had followed the Omani rulers in their move from Mascat to Zanzibar. The ranks of all these groups were constantly replenished with new arrivals from India, often adolescents who took employment with a relative before setting up their own business. The second stream consisted of those indentured workers, recruited in the 1890s in the Punjab and in Gujarat, to build the Uganda railway, who stayed behind after the expiration of their contracts, a total of 7,000 out of the 38,000 recruited (many of whom died during the construction of the railway). These men, mostly Gujarati Patidars (Patels), belonging to a relatively affluent peasant caste of Central Gujarat, formed the backbone of the class of *dukawallas* who tended general purpose shops in the interior, mostly along the railway line, catering to the needs of both

Africans and white settlers. They sold mostly goods imported from India (some of which had come from Britain and were re-exported to East Africa), which they procured from the Indian traders in the ports. Increasingly they also bought the produce of African and even of some European farms which they sent to the ports from where the wholesalers, often also Indian, exported them abroad. Mention should be made also of a group of poor Jain agriculturists from the Jamnagar area in Kathiawar, often known as Shahs, who migrated to Kenya and became very successful traders there. All in all, by 1914, Indians had established a stranglehold over most retail and some of the wholesale trade in British East Africa, offering a strong challenge to British and other European traders, who could not compete with them because of the very low margins with which they were ready to work, but also tending to block the emergence of a class of African traders. The role of the Indians has been diversely appreciated in the literature on East Africa: some Marxist authors as well as African nationalists have viewed them as typical 'compradores' serving British imperialism in its enterprise of colonial domination and devoid of any significant agency. They emphasize in particular the fact that most Indians, especially those in the main cities, who lived in Indian 'locations' which were like ghettoes, did not plant deep roots in East Africa, retained a mentality of 'sojourners' and exported most of their profits back to India to support their families, and buy land and real estate, thus hindering the process of capital accumulation in the host countries. Others have stressed on the contrary their capacity for autonomous action and feel that their role has been partly misunderstood. They point to the importance of their local investments, the fact that most East African cities were built by a combination of Indian labour and Indian capital, and to the munificence of their charities which endowed many hospitals and schools, benefiting Africans as well as Indians and Europeans (Gregory 1993). The same strictures are often directed at the impact the Indians had in Southeast Asia, particularly in Burma. That colony, which remained administratively part of British India till 1937 (like the colony of Aden), saw a particularly large influx of Indian traders and moneylenders in the wake of its gradual conquest by armies from British India between 1826 and 1885. One group amongst them, the Nattukottai Nagarathars, generally known as Nattukottai Chettiars, or simply Chettiars, hailing from the Pudukottai area of Tamilnadu, have acquired a particular reputation as greedy moneylenders. They first arrived in Moulmein in the late 1820s, but the influx swelled in the 1850s, following the British occupation of Lower Burma in 1852. At first they lent money to local Burmese moneylenders but, as rice cultivation expanded rapidly in the fertile Irrawaddy delta from the 1870s, they took to lending directly to the Burmese peasantry monies that they largely borrowed from British banks. They spared the banks the trouble of collecting information about a myriad of small borrowers generally devoid of collateral, except a small plot of land and family labour. They took risks because, in case of default, their only recourse was to foreclose and seize land, which was useless to them as they did not have direct control over labour. However they covered each other for that risk through a mechanism of caste solidarity which proved very solid (Rudner 1994). They used their Saivaite temples as clearing houses in which compensation took place every year on *hundis* worth millions of rupees, which they also discounted with the banks. While they made large profits, their advances played a major role in the spectacular growth of rice cultivation in Burma, which made that colony the rice bowl of Asia. Other groups of Indians were active in trade in Burma: they included the Marakayyars (Chulias), different communities of Gujarati Muslims (mostly Memons) as well as Hindu Marwaris from Calcutta. Indians clearly dominated commercial life in Rangoon and were also well entrenched in other commercial centres, such as Moulmein or Mandalay. Some of them set up rice mills, but most of the latter were controlled by European firms, as were teak and oil, the other major commodities exported from Burma. The extent of Indian economic domination in Burma was probably exaggerated in many accounts and served partly to direct Burmese resentment towards Indians rather than towards Europeans, but such misperception is understandable in terms of the greater visibility of Indians 'on the ground' in comparison with Europeans. In the other British territories of Southeast Asia, Malaya and the Straits Settlements, the Indian commercial presence, although far from negligible, was less visible than in Burma, partly because the Chinese were present there in greater numbers than the Indians. It is, however, worth noting that Indian traders preceded Chinese traders in Singapore: Narayan Pillai, who accompanied Raffles in 1819, became Singapore's first building contractor and a major textile merchant (Kudaisya 2006). Chettiars entered the area from the 1830s onwards and, in the 1870s, they played a big role in the expansion of tin mining, supplying Chinese miners with advances that the European banks denied them. The pioneer in rubber planting in Malaya, a Chinese, also got started in 1895 thanks to a Chettiar loan. Gujarati Muslims, in particular Kutchi Khojas, were also actively involved in commodity trade, and the Sindworkies started trading in silks in Singapore from the 1870s. In Southeast Asia, the Indian commercial presence spilled into non-British territory: from Penang into Siam as early as the 1850s and from Singapore into Sumatra and Java in the Dutch East Indies from the 1880s. The Chettiars extended their moneylending operations to French Indochina from 1885 onwards, and the Sindworkies established silk shops in Saigon. Sindhi and Punjabi Sikh traders also entered the then Spanish colony of the Philippines in the 1890s and increased their activities after the American annexation in 1899. In the whole of Southeast Asia however, with the exception of Burma, the activities of Indian traders tended to be dwarfed by those of Chinese traders and, in that way, the situation was not comparable to that in East Africa.

Indian traders in the era of imperial decline (1914–47)

In the 1920s, the expansion of Indian trading networks, which had been but slightly slowed down by the First World War, continued along the same lines as in the pre-War era. Burma and East Africa were the two areas of greatest advance. In East Africa, the incorporation of German East Africa (Tanganyika) into the British domain benefited the Indians, who had been kept in check in the pre-War period by the German authorities, which suspected them of being a British fifth column. Indians were thus amongst the main beneficiaries of the sale of confiscated German properties, in particular sisal estates, and they established a dominant position in several branches of trade. Ismaili Khojas were particularly active in that territory. In Uganda, the Asians, especially Hindu Lohanas and Patidars, made significant inroads into the cotton trade at the expense of British firms and they tended to supply increasing volumes of Ugandan long-fibre cotton to the Indian mills. They also pioneered the trucking trade, competing with the railways for the transport of produce. In Kenya, the Indians faced more problems, as white settlers, supported by the colonial authorities, turned increasingly hostile to them and tried, with some measure of success, to diminish their role in the commercialization of agricultural produce. African hostility also became more palpable and some *dukawallas* started moving from the rural areas, where they lived isolated amongst the African masses, toward the safer environment of the partly Indian towns and cities. In spite of these difficulties, Indian traders managed to increase their profits and the level of their activities and started entering industry, mostly at first processing industries, like sisal factories or coconut oil and soap mills. Turning to Burma, it can be shown that, as Indian emigration reached unprecedented numbers in the 1920s, Indian dominance in trading activities became also more marked, especially in Rangoon, and started provoking hostile reactions on the part of the Burmese population, a hostility which was particularly directed at Muslim traders. Indian entry into industrial activities was also noticeable: the number of

Indian-owned rice mills and sawmills increased, and one Indian firm (Adamji Haji Dawood) created in Rangoon one of Asia's largest match factories.

Around 1930, one estimate is that there were some 250,000 Indians engaged in trade and finance outside India (Markovits 1999). Of these, more than 200,000 were in the British Empire, including 96,000 in Burma, 30,000 in Malaya and the Straits Settlements, 25,000 in Ceylon, some 20,000 in East Africa and 12,000 in South Africa. The vast majority were India-born immigrants, but there was a growing category of locally-born Indians, particularly in Burma and Ceylon. They were overwhelmingly male (less than 10,000 were female) and the majority of them were either salaried employees or small shopkeepers. There were few 'capitalists' amongst them, although many worked for firms which were owned by proprietors residing in India. Thus the principals of the Chettiar firms resided in the Pudukottai area, and those in charge of the branches in Burma or Malaya were their agents, remunerated by a complex system which included commissions on profits. Amongst Sindworkies also, the vast majority of those residing abroad were salaried personnel, either managers, or shop assistants or even a category of servants, the principals residing in Hyderabad (Sindh) and making periodic tours of their branches abroad. The proprietors of Marwari firms in Burma were similarly based in Calcutta or in Assam and had agents on the spot. It is only in East Africa and South Africa that one found a significant number of resident Indian capitalists, generally small-scale, but with a few big names; the reason was mostly that the distance from India and restrictive immigration policies by colonial authorities made it difficult to maintain a pattern of regular circulation between India and Africa. But, more generally, the pattern was one of circulation rather than of migration. That is why it is better to talk in terms of a plurality of South Asian trading networks rather than of one Indian trading diaspora.

Two trading networks from South Asia

Ismaili Khojas were a group which developed particularly extended transnational connections in the nineteenth and twentieth centuries. That community, the product of conversions amongst Vaisnava Hindu Lohana traders effected between 1200 and 1400 by Ismaili missionaries, remained located in the small coastal state of Kutch, till the early nineteenth century. In the first decades of that century, there was a fairly massive migration to Bombay, and by 1840 there were some 2,000 Khojas there, mostly small traders in grain, with a few big merchants. In the following decades, Khojas started moving to Zanzibar (a few had gone there from Muscat) and engaging in the China opium trade. Following the relocation of their imam, the Aga Khan, to Bombay from Persia in 1845, and the split which gave birth to the Itna'asheri branch, Khojas were encouraged to move to Zanzibar in greater numbers and, from there, they spread over the whole of East Africa, engaging mostly in the ivory trade and also in finance. By the 1870s, there were some 2,500 Ismaili Khojas in East Africa, and their ranks swelled even further after the establishment of the British Protectorate in 1890. In the 1860s the Khojas also entered the China opium trade in a big way and, by 1890, they had overtaken the Parsis as the most significant Indian operators in this most lucrative of trades. When the opium trade fell drastically after 1910, they shifted to the piece-goods trade, but their numbers in China fell precipitously in the 1920s and 1930s, while they continued to grow at a regular pace in East Africa. Khoja traders were also active in Southeast Asia, particularly in Singapore, and in Japan. Although they moved mostly to territories within the British Empire, they operated also in non-British colonial territories, like in French Madagascar, where their presence had preceded French colonization, and Portuguese Mozambique. A brief life-sketch of a prominent Khoja Ismaili merchant, Taria Topan, will illustrate the range of their activities. He came to Zanzibar in the 1840s, at the age of 12, to serve in the commercial firm of his father, who had close links to American merchants supplying coarse cloth (known as *merkani*) to the local market. He was so successful that in 1876 he was granted the farm of the Sultan of Zanzibar's custom revenues, a highly prestigious if not necessarily very profitable position which he relinquished in 1880. In his position as customs master, he rendered the British services which gained him an OBE, a rare distinction for an Indian trader at the time. Having kept close links with Bombay, he moved there in 1885 and embarked upon a second career as a tea and (probably) opium trader with China, a venture which proved highly profitable. In the case of the Ismaili Khojas, the fact that they were also a closely-knit religious community, ruled by its imam, the Aga Khan, certainly contributed to its cohesion in spite of the enormous distances across which its members–followers ranged. Other groups, with no comparable religious base, nevertheless maintained close links in spite of dispersion.

The Sindworkies of Hyderabad (Sindh) were the South Asian network with the most extended spatial range, as already alluded to. They were mostly a cluster of firms, not more than 100 at their peak, with principals in Hyderabad and branches in many locations between Panama in Central America and Kobe in Japan. Principals, agents and employees were all Sindhi Hindus from Hyderabad and its immediate environs, belonging to the so-called Bhaiband segment of the Lohana caste, the major Hindu caste of Sindh. They started their operations abroad around 1860, selling at first mostly craft productions from small workshops in Sindh which were known in Bombay as 'Sindwork', hence the name of 'Sindworkers' or 'Sindworkies' under which they became known. At first they were peddlers, but, from the 1880s, they started establishing permanent shops in the main ports of call along the steamer routes west and east of India. They showed no particular preference for territories within the British Empire, their movements being mostly dictated by the lure of commercial opportunities. By 1907, according to the *Gazetteer of Sind*, there were some 5,000 of them dispersed across the world, with the largest colonies being in Egypt and the Dutch East Indies. They specialized in the sale of silks and curios, which they increasingly sourced from China and Japan. After the First World War, which barely slowed down their activities, they expanded into new regions, such as the West Indies and British West Africa, and they tended to specialize in the sale of Japanese goods, in particular textiles, a trend which was only strengthened in the 1930s when the devaluation of the yen made purchasing goods in Japan to sell them in sterling and dollar areas a particularly profitable business. This brought them sometimes in direct conflict with British interests, wary of Japanese competition, but, when faced with restrictions on their movements, they did not hesitate to seek the help of British authorities, sometimes with a measure of success. By the late 1930s, there were more than 10,000 of them located outside India at any given time, but only a few had settled abroad for good; the majority circulated, alternating periods in Hyderabad with stints abroad. It is only after the Partition of India led to their leaving their home town for good that they started relocating abroad permanently on a big scale, laying the ground for the emergence of a worldwide Sindhi diaspora.

On the political economy of South Asian traders' circulation

Such significant circulation of traders from the Indian subcontinent has attracted less attention from economic historians than similar movements by Chinese, Lebanese, Armenian or Jewish traders. No coherent analytical framework has emerged which could help give meaning to that phenomenon. Circulation of South Asian traders could be seen as part of what economists call 'international factor mobility', but the problem is that the two factors, capital and labour, are so closely intertwined in this case as to preclude the kind of neat classifications favoured by economists. The circulation of traders from South Asia was not related to significant capital movements: most traders left India with very little capital or no capital at all, and their accumulation occurred generally 'on the spot', thanks to an exceptionally high rate of savings permitted by an abstemious lifestyle. As to profits, when they became significant, which was generally only after a considerable time-lag, their transfer to India, when it occurred, was largely invisible and not easily distinguishable from remittances sent by workers to their families. The overall contributions of such movements of traders to India's balance of payments cannot be measured, even approximately. Given the lack of measurable data, interpretations of these movements have varied according to scholars' ideological preferences. As already mentioned about East Africa, some Marxist authors have tended to analyze the role of Indian traders as that of 'compradores', and to view them as instrumentalized by British imperialism and basically devoid of agency. Indian historian Rajat Ray has proposed to differentiate between auxiliaries of the British, of which he views the Chettiars as the most significant example, and traders less dependent on a British connection, mostly Gujaratis in East Africa (Ray 1995). But the distinction is not very convincing. Chettiars, in spite of their close links to British banks, were not without agency: in the 1930s, in the wake of the Great Depression, which, in Burma, had burdened them with large landholdings for which they had no profitable use, following massive defaults by their peasant debtors, they transferred to India most of their accumulated profits and invested them, not only, as previously, in building elaborate mansions in their home region of Chettinad, but in setting up factories, largely laying out the base for industrial development in Tamilnadu. Such a trajectory is certainly not typical of 'compradores'. An alternative view would be then to see the role of Indian traders as 'sub-imperial': under the umbrella of British imperialism, there would have developed a specific Indian sub-imperialism, siphoning off resources from some colonies to feed the growth of India. This model is not totally devoid of pertinence, but it exaggerates the coherence of the operations of South Asian traders. As argued here, there was a diversity of trading networks with regional or local bases in the subcontinent and they did not as a rule coordinate their activities to achieve a 'domination effect', even in places like Burma or Uganda, where Indian traders occupied a particularly strong position in different sectors of the economy. In spite of the fact that 'Indian economic domination' was more of a rhetorical device used by local nationalists, often cynically abetted by colonial authorities and British businessmen, than an empirical truth, it raised a profound echo amongst local elites and local populations, and in the post-1947 period it would result in a powerful anti-Indian backlash, culminating with Idi Amin Dada's expulsion of Asians from Uganda in 1971.

Glossary

Bhaiband	literally group of brothers, in Sindh, segment of the Lohana caste
Bhatia	Hindu caste of Kutch
Bohras	community of Gujarati Muslims, mostly Shi'a
Chettiars	Nattukottai Chettiars, group of Hindu bankers from Pudukottai area in Tamilnadu
dukawalla	holder of general purpose shop (*duka*) in the interior of East Africa
firman	edict in Persian
hundi	native bill of exchange or promissory note
Ismailis	followers of a branch of Shi'a Islam, disciples of the Aga Khan
Itna'asheri	adherent of Twelver Shi'ism
Jains	adherents of an ancient Indian religion founded by Mahavir
Khojas	Gujarati Shi'a Muslim community, divided between Ismailis and Itna'asheris
Lohana	Hindu caste of Gujarat and Sindh

Mapillai (Moplahs)	community of Kerala Muslims, descendants of unions between Arab seafarers and Malayali women
Marakayyars	Tamilian Muslims, also known as Chulias
Marwaris	traders and moneylenders hailing from an area of Rajasthan, both Hindu and Jain
Memons	Sunni Muslim Gujarati traders from Kutch and Kathiawar
Multanis or Shikarpuris	Indian traders–moneylenders in Central Asia, hailing from the Punjab-Sindh confines
Parsis	Zoroastrians in India
Patidars, Patels	a caste of Gujarati Hindus, originally agriculturists, who became traders in East Africa.

References

Dale, S.F., 1994, *Indian Merchants and Eurasian Trade, 1600–1750*, Cambridge: Cambridge University Press.

Gregory, R.G., 1993, *South Asians in East Africa: An Economic and Social History, 1890–1980*, Boulder, CO, San Francisco, CA, Oxford: Westview Press.

Kudaisya, M., 2006, 'Trading Networks in Southeast Asia', in Lal, B.V. (ed.), *The Encyclopedia of the Indian Diaspora*, Singapore: Didier Millet, pp. 59–65.

Levi, S.C., 2002, *The Indian Diaspora in Central Asia and its Trade 1550–1900*, Leiden, Boston, Cologne: E.J. Brill.

Markovits, C., 1999, 'Indian Merchant Networks Outside India in the Nineteenth and Twentieth Centuries: A Preliminary Survey', *Modern Asian Studies*, 33, 4, pp. 883–911.

—, 2000a, *The Global World of Indian Merchants 1750–1947: Traders of Sind from Bukhara to Panama*, Cambridge: Cambridge University Press.

—, 2000b, 'Indian Communities in China, *c.* 1842–1949', in Bickers, R. and Henriot, C., *New Frontiers: Imperialism's New Communities in East Asia, 1842–1953*, Manchester: Manchester University Press, pp. 55–74.

—, 2009, 'The Political Economy of Opium Smuggling in Early Nineteenth Century India: Leakage or Resistance?', *Modern Asian Studies*, 43, 1, pp. 89–111.

Ray, R.K., 1995, 'Asian Capital in the Age of European Domination: The Rise of the Bazaar, 1800–1914', *Modern Asian Studies*, 49, 3, pp. 449–554.

Rudner, D.W., 1994, *Caste and Capitalism in Colonial India: the Nattukottai Chettiars*, Berkeley, Los Angeles: University of California Press.

Shariff, A., 1987, *Slaves, Spices and Ivory in Zanzibar: Integration of an East African Commercial Empire into the World Economy, 1770–1873*, London: James Currey.

Siddiqi, A., 1982, 'The Business World of Jamsetji Jejeebhoy', *The Indian Economic and Social History Review*, XIX, 3–4, pp. 301–24.

7

INDIAN INDENTURE

Experiment and experience

Brij V. Lal

But the past must live on,
For it is the soul of today
And the strength of the morn;
A break to silent tears
That mourn the dream of stillborn ...
Churamanie Bissundyal, Guyana.[1]

On 9 September 1834, 36 lost-looking Dhangars (tribal people from the Chota Nagpur region) met some recruiters in Calcutta and were asked if they would be willing to go to Mauritius as indentured labourers. The absence would be of short duration and remuneration attractive. *Mirich Dwip* was said to be just off the coast of Bengal, and they would be back home before their absence was noticed in the village. The Dhangars agreed, for they had come to Calcutta looking for employment in the first place. Thereupon, they were taken to the Chief Magistrate at the Calcutta Police Court, who read out and 'explained' the terms and conditions of the contract to be signed. The men affixed their thumb imprints on the document affirming their understanding of what was on offer and that they were emigrating voluntarily. The Vice-President-in-Council of the Government of Bengal approved the transaction and authorised the departure of the indentured labourers. The tentative venture proved successful after the initial teething problems. Between 1 August 1834 and the end of 1835, 14 ships were engaged to transport emigrants from Calcutta to Mauritius. By the end of 1839, over 25,000 Indians had been introduced into the colony. Other colonies elsewhere soon followed suit. Thus began a massive and unprecedented experiment in unskilled labour recruitment and migration. By 1870, Mauritius had 352,401 Indians, British Guiana 79,691, Trinidad 42,519 and Jamaica 15,169. In 1907, Guiana's total population of Indians had swelled to 127,000; that of Trinidad to 103,000; and of Natal to 115,000. By the time indentured emigration ceased in 1917, over 1 million indentured Indian immigrants had been transported across the dark, dreaded seas, the *Kala Pani*, to the 'King Sugar' colonies in the West Indies, Fiji, Mauritius and South Africa. Their descendants now constitute an important segment of the larger mosaic of the Indian diaspora.

Origins

Indian indentured emigration was started in direct response to the shortage of labour in the tropical colonies caused by the abolition of slavery in the British Empire in 1833 and by the termination of the system of apprenticeship (for six years) under which, until 1838, the planters had been able to obtain slave labour. Once freed, the former slaves understandably refused to return to their old jobs. As one official wrote:

> for the greater part of the Negroes abandoned not only field labour, but service of every kind, almost as soon as they were at a liberty to do so. No present kindness, or memory of past benefits, no persuasion or pecuniary inducements could prevail upon them to remain; and it is to be feared that the time is yet distant when motives of interest, or the press of necessity, will bring them back to serve as agricultural labourers.[2]

The apprenticeship system failed because it was riddled with contradictions and paradoxes, the most important of all being the inherent ambivalence in relations between the labourers and the planters. Once freed, the labourers refused to succumb to the regime imposed on the slaves. The pattern of resistance was the same in the West Indies as it was in Mauritius.

The failure of the apprentice experiment forced the planters to look elsewhere, to Africa and Europe. Between 1834 and 1837, some 3,000 English, 1,000 Scots and the same number of Germans and a sprinkling of Irish were introduced into Jamaica and a smaller number into St Lucia. The emigrants were brought privately on contract for three to five years, although Jamaica also offered a bounty from public funds. But this experiment, too, failed because of the high mortality rate caused by insufficient sanitary precautions, 'the unsuitability of raw, unacclimatised Europeans for field work in the tropical sun, with the added temptation of unlimited drink'.[3]

Trinidad attempted to procure labour from neighbouring Grenada, St Christopher and Nevis, engaging captains of small trading vessels with a bounty, with the promise of returning them to their homes after the completion of their contracts. But the bounty system, with no legal provisions specifying the terms and conditions of service, or making the contract enforceable, 'being ill-contrived and injudiciously managed', also succumbed to failure. The planters then turned to Africa but, given its former history of slavery, this was never a realistic prospect.[4]

China proved a better prospect. One official described the Chinese labourers in 1844 as:

> well made, robust, and active, inured to field labour, and able to work during the heat of the day, in fact, they are equal to our best Creole field labourers; they are eager for gain, and will do anything for money; they are quiet and very intelligent for their class, and not lazy. They value money, and are shrewd; and I do think no class of men can be better adapted to our wants than they are.[5]

But the very qualities for which the Chinese were praised made them unsuitable as long-term plantation workers. Being 'further developed in civilisation', as one official put it, the Chinese tended to move out of the plantations at the earliest possible opportunity to set themselves up as market gardeners and small shopkeepers, becoming in time rivals to the very planters whom they were supposed to serve.

These failures focused attention on India as a reliable and enduring source of labour. In the nineteenth century, India remained the principal source of labour supply to the sugar colonies of the British Empire. An important attribute of the Indian indenture was that it was state regulated, not privately contracted. It was conducted on the basis of a written and supposedly voluntarily accepted contract or 'Agreement' (dubbed *Girmit* in Fiji), which the emigrants signed (or, more commonly, affixed their thumb prints to) before leaving India. In the early years of indentured emigration, the terms and conditions were not uniform; indeed they varied widely in content and application. But, by the 1870s, a more or less uniform document was in place for all the indentured labour-recruiting colonies. The contract stipulated, among other things, the nature and conditions of employment (principally dealing with work related to the manufacture of sugar cane), remuneration for labour on the plantations, entitlement to medical and housing facilities and, above all, the availability of a return passage back to India after a period of 'industrial residence' in the colonies, usually ten years after the date of arrival. There can be little doubt that the majority of the emigrants intended their excursion out of India as a brief sojourn, a temporary expedient to cope with their fluctuating economic fortune at home. Many did return: up to 1870, 21 per cent of the emigrants had returned and, in the decade after 1910, one emigrant returned for every two who had embarked for the colonies. But, for the overwhelming majority, an intended sojourn was transformed into permanent displacement in the course of time and in response to prevailing circumstances.

The early shipments of labourers to Mauritius drew attention to reports of neglect and ill-treatment, which led the Government of India, responding to pressure from anti-slavery quarters, to instruct the Indian Law Commissioners to provide a firmer legislative cover to the operation. These were incorporated in Act V of 1837. Among other things, the Act provided that the emigration of contract labourers was to be subject to orders from authorities from India; that the emigrants should be required to appear before an official appointed by the provincial government; that the contract, in English and the mother tongue of the emigrant, must specify wages and the nature of employment in the colonies; that contracts for a period of over five years, which did not include the provision for a return passage, were not to be approved; and that recruiters who obtained labourers through fraudulent means were to be fined or imprisoned.

The imperial dimension

Over the next several years, critics and opponents of Indian indentured emigration pointed to the disparity between the rhetoric on paper and the realities on the ground. Reports continued to reach the public of fraudulence and violence in the recruitment and shipping of labourers and of the terrible conditions of employment on the plantations. For a while, emigration was halted, but it soon became clear that the prohibition of emigration could not be maintained for too long. Reports from the colonies acknowledged hardship and problems but claimed that these were exaggerated by the critics. Indeed, they claimed that emigrants in the colonies were better off than their counterparts in India.

The result of the voluminous correspondence between the colonies, the Imperial Government and the Government of India was the passage of the Government of India's Act XV of 1842, the first comprehensive legislation of its kind to provide control and supervision of the trade. The Act provided for the appointment, on fixed salary, of an Emigration Agent at the ports of embarkation in India. The Agent, who might act for several colonies because the recruitment seasons for different places varied, was required personally to examine each emigrant and to ascertain that he or she fully understood the contract they were signing. All the emigrant ships were to be fully licensed by the government and required to conform to certain prescribed standards; dietary and medical supplies for the emigrants were prescribed, as were the accommodation facilities and indeed the length of the voyage itself. The Act was a good start, but it had no provision for the enforcement of the regulations. Nonetheless, this piece of legislation formed the basis for further reforms and amendments in the latter half of the nineteenth century.

Was there room for further government involvement? In 1875, Lord Salisbury, the Secretary of State for the Colonies, wrote to the Government of India enquiring whether, under proper regulation, and with due regard to the interest of the labourers, the Government of India 'might not more directly encourage emigration and superintend the system under which it was conducted'. In Lord Salisbury's view, indentured emigration, properly regulated, would benefit everyone: India, the United Kingdom and the emigrants themselves:

> While, then, from an Indian point of view, emigration, properly regulated, and accompanied by sufficient assurance of profitable employment and fair treatment, seems a thing to be encouraged on grounds of humanity, with a view to promote the well-being of the poorer classes; we may also consider, from an imperial point of view, the great advantage which must result from peopling the warmer British possessions which are rich in ntural resources and only want population, by an intelligent and industrious race to whom the climate of these countries is well suited, and to whom the culture of the staples suited to the soil, and the modes of labour and settlement, are adapted. In this view also it seems proper to encourage emigration from India to the colonies well fitted for an Indian population.[6]

Salisbury went on to suggest a number of ways in which the Government of India might intervene directly to encourage and facilitate indentured recruitment and emigration and to reduce its various deficiencies. He urged it to exercise direct control over the type of emigrants recruited by allowing the authorities in India to 'help and counsel' the colonial agents and, in times of difficulty, to even directly recruit labourers themselves. It might also directly involve itself in ensuring that the terms and conditions of the contract the emigrants had signed in India were observed in the colonies by appointing its own agents there. In the last paragraph of his Despatch, Salisbury added:

> Above all things we must confidently expect, as an indispensable condition of the proposed arrangements [that] the Colonial laws and their administration will be such that Indian settlers who have completed their terms of service to which they are agreed as return for the expense of bringing them to the Colonies, will be in all respects free men, with privileges no whit inferior to those of any other class of Her Majesty's subjects residents in the colonies.

Salisbury's Despatch was sent to all the Indian provincial governments for their comment and consideration.[7] With the exception of Bengal, all the other provinces were against the proposals. Bombay feared the loss of labour and therefore loss of revenue. Madras thought that greater involvement on its part could be misconstrued as its support for the colonial planters at the expense of the interests of India. The Uttar Pradesh (UP) government doubted if greater encouragement would necessarily give the colonies the kind of emigrants they wanted. And so the Government of India told the Secretary of State for India that greater involvement was not feasible. 'Our policy may be described as one of seeing fair play between the parties to a commercial transaction, while the Government altogether abstains from mixing itself in the bargain.' Emigration would have an 'infinitesimal effect' on the population of the districts where recruitment was most popular. Moreover, direct involvement might put India in the invidious position of having to reconcile the interests of the colonies with those of the emigrants. Perhaps most important, the Government of India feared being held accountable for abuses and irregularities in the recruitment process. It was this reason, more than any other, the fear of being tainted by the evils of the indenture system, that led the Government of India to abolish the indenture system in 1916, despite protest from the colonies.

Origins of indentured labourers

Indian indentured labourers to various parts of the world came from different parts of India. Predominantly, they came from the north and embarked for the colonies from the port of Calcutta. In 1856–61, 66 per cent embarked at Calcutta and 30 per cent from Madras. In 1907–08 and 1916–17, 62 per cent embarked at Calcutta and 30 per cent from Madras.

South India

South India has probably always been the most migration-prone region of India. Even in pre-historic times, its inhabitants were known to have established contact with other countries. Systematic, large-scale labour migration from this region, however, began in the nineteenth century. The largest importers of South Indian labour were the 'Colonies of India System' – Burma, Ceylon and Malaya. The exact volume of numbers emigrating is difficult to ascertain but, according to one source, between 1852 and 1937, 2,595,000 Indian emigrants settled in Burma, 1,529,000 in Ceylon and 1,189,000 in Malaya.[8]

Much of this migration took place under the supervision of the middlemen called *Kanganis* in the case of Ceylon and Malaya and *Maistries* in the case of Burma.[9] In Ceylon, this system was prominent from the outset, while in Malaya it operated alongside indentured emigration. These middlemen, trusted and experienced employees of the plantation or the estate, were sent to their villages to recruit their fellow village and kinsmen. They were usually given an advance to cover the costs of recruitment and transportation, but the labourers were expected to refund the amount spent on them after a period of employment. The middlemen were not mere recruiters, however; at work they were often the sole intermediaries between the workers and their employers, a position which lent itself to the possibility of corruption and extortion. The absence of comprehensive protective legislation which governed indenture, and the absence of written and legally enforceable contracts, served to enhance their grip on the labourers.

Malaya was the largest single importer of South Indian indentured labour: some 250,000 between 1844 and 1910. The predominance of the South Indians was due partly to the reluctance of Government of India in sanctioning recruitment in other parts of the country and the perception that North Indians were 'troublesome elements'. Geography, too, played its part. Indentured immigration to Malaya was different in form, if not in spirit, to that for the sugar colonies. In the case of Malaya, recruitment was carried out by speculators and private agents of the employers, while for the sugar colonies it was carried out by licensed recruiters appointed by the Emigrant Agents and under the supervision, however minimal, of the local authorities in the districts. The contract for Malaya was for one to three years; and it was not always a written document. Further, the Emigration Agents for the colonies assumed responsibility for the cost of recruitment and transportation, while for Malaya, the indentured labourers, like their kangani counterparts, had to repay a certain amount from their wages. Finally, because the indentured emigration to Malaya was not strictly state regulated, the Government of India was unable in many cases to demand the fulfilment of certain conditions stipulated in the Emigration Act. In the case of the sugar colonies, for instance, it was able successfully to insist that 40 women accompany 100 men on each shipment, but was unable to do much in this regard for Malaya.

To the sugar colonies, South India contributed upwards of 290,000 migrants: Mauritius 144,342 (32 per cent of the total going to that country), Natal 103,261 (68 per cent), Guiana 15,065 (6 per cent), Fiji 14,536 (24 per cent), West Indies 12,975 (7 per cent), Reunion 2,131 (8 per cent) and French West Indies 330 (2 per cent). In the case of Mauritius, about 77 per cent had migrated before 1870. It was a similar story for Guiana and the West Indian islands. Emigration to Natal began in 1860 but increased after the 1880s. The first South Indians went to Fiji in 1903.

In South India, the labourers came from certain regions. Malaya and Ceylon drew their recruits mainly from the Tamil-speaking areas, with a sprinkling of Telugus from Andhra Pradesh and Malayalis from the Malabar coast. Migrants to Burma came largely from Vizagapatnam and Godavari in Andhra Pradesh and, to a lesser extent, from Tanjore and Ramnad. The sugar colonies drew their emigrants from these areas as well. For Fiji, for instance, most of the South emigrants were recruited in North Arcot, Madras, Kistna, Godavari, Vizagapatnam, Tanjore, Malabar and Coimbatore.[10]

Bombay

This was not a major port of embarkation. The indentured labourers who left Bombay for the colonies, especially before the 1870s, came mostly from Poona, Satora, Ratnagiri, Nagpur and Sawantwadi.[11] After 1870, Bombay and Karachi (mostly Karachi) accounted for 43,221 embarkations. Of these, 36,902 were bound for Mombasa, 538 for Seychelles and 5,781 for other places. The emigrants for Mombasa came mostly from the Punjab region; they were recruited to work on the railways there, and most returned at the expiry of their contracts. In the wake of indentured emigration, small groups of free migrants (traders, artisans) mostly from Gujarat left from Bombay for other colonies, but theirs is a different history.

French ports

These accounted for the smallest number of indentured embarkations. Altogether, between 1842 and 1916, 49,890 emigrants boarded the ships there for the colonies.[12] Of these, 20,770 (42 per cent) had left before 1870, of whom 16,000 went to the French West Indies and 4,700 to Reunion. After 1870, 29,000 left for the French West Indies, Reunion and French Guiana. Embarkation from French ports was prohibited after the promulgation of the Indian Emigration Act of 1883, which restricted departures to the ports of Calcutta, Madras and Bombay.

Calcutta and North India

Calcutta was, of course, the most important port of embarkation for the indentured emigrants destined for the sugar colonies. Interestingly, there were few Bengalis among the emigrants; indeed, they were conspicuous by their absence.[13] The overwhelming majority of the Calcutta departees were 'upcountry men'. Before the 1870s, many came from the tribal and plains areas of Bihar. The ship lists for the *Hespres* and the *Whitby* which left for British Guiana in 1838 show that of the 405 emigrants abroad those two vessels, 72 came from Hazaribagh, 49 from Bankura, 36 from Ramgarh, 27 from Midnapur and 20 from Nagpur. Dhangars furnished

34 per cent of the emigrants, Muslims 8 per cent, Rajputs and Kurmis 5 per cent each, Bauris and Bhuiyas 4 per cent each and Kshattriyas, Gowalas and Bagdis the rest.

The tribal emigrants proved popular with the colonial planters for their supposed 'docile disposition', for their willingness 'to turn their hands to any labour whatever, as far as they are capable', for their simple way of life and their adaptability to the hard conditions on the plantations. Further, they were in ample supply in the crowded quarters of Calcutta where they had drifted in search of employment as their former homeland came under settled occupation from Hindu and Muslim traders, speculators, moneylenders and others in the early decades of the nineteenth century who began 'to exploit simple and unsophisticated aboriginals, who were dispossessed of their holdings sometimes by legal process and sometimes by illegal means'. But the high mortality rate of the tribals on crowded and unsanitary voyages and the availability of appropriate employment opportunities closer to home, such as in the Assam Tea Gardens and the Bihar indigo plantations and coal mines, reduced the attractiveness of employment on the colonial plantations.

The decline in the volume of tribal emigration shifted colonial recruitment northwards into the settled areas of Bihar. Among the largest recruitment districts in Bihar in the 1850s and 1860s were Arrah (Shahabad), Sahebganj (Gaya), Hazaribagh, Patna, Purulia, Ranchi and Chapra (Saran). But these areas also proved a disappointing hunting ground for colonial recruiters in the long run. Like the tribals, these people too were attracted by employment opportunities nearer home. At the same time, encouraged perhaps by the advent of railways, large numbers of Biharis were turning towards Bengal, especially Calcutta, where they were in great demand as palki-bearers, pankah-pullers, peons, *lathials* (guards) and general labourers. The advantage of internal over colonial migration was that it enabled the immigrants to return to their villages in the planting and harvesting seasons.

From the 1870s onwards, the focus of indentured recruitment shifted to the United Provinces of Agra and Oudh, as they were called, and they remained the principal suppliers of labour for the remaining period of indentured emigration.[14] Within the UP, it was the eastern (*poorbea*) districts which furnished the bulk of the emigrants, districts such as Basti, Gonda, Faizabad, Sultanpur, Azamgarh, Gorakhpur, Allahabad and Ghazipur. Many factors explain their popularity: a depressed economy, dwindling property rights, fragmentation of landholdings, subdivision of property, heavy population density, the effects of periodic droughts, floods and famine and, finally, an established pattern of migration. The number of *poorbeas* enumerated in Bengal increased significantly over the last quarter of the nineteenth century: 351,933 in 1880, 365,248 in 1891 and 496,940 in 1901.[15]

Indeed, according to one informed observer, there was hardly a single family in the entire Benares region which did not have at least one member in employment in other places. It was from this uprooted mass of humanity that the indentured emigrants came. In an important sense, colonial emigration was an extension of the process of emigration. Contrary to popular perception, migration was an established fact of life in the eastern districts of UP. In Azamgarh, it was 'known to be considerable', and in Allahabad, 'at all times an appreciable proportion of the population is absent in search of employment far afield'. In Gonda, migration 'in such [adverse] circumstances was a natural way out of the difficulties with which the population did not know how to cope.'[16]

Migration meant remittance. In Sultanpur, the migrants remitted Rs 1,627,700 between October 1894 and September 1897. In Azamgarh, the Settlement Officer noted that, in the 1890s, yearly remittances amounted to Rs 13 lakh, rising to Rs 22 lakh in years of scarcity. In Ghazipur, an important migration district, emigration since 1901 had assumed 'extraordinary proportions', the proof of which was 'to be found in the immensely increased passenger traffic of the railways, and also in the remarkable amounts remitted to the district through the agency of the post-office'. A result of migration in the district was that labour was becoming dearer each year. Even the cultivating classes 'no longer rely solely on the produce of their fields, for savings of the emigrants are almost equal to the entire rental demands, the same thing occurring in Ballia and Jaunpur'.

It was often asserted by the opponents of the indenture system at the time and by popular writers even today that the recruits were either kidnapped or otherwise fraudulently enticed by unscrupulous recruiters into emigrating.[17] This accords with the conventional view that Indians by nature are not migrants but a sedentary people confined to their familiar surroundings by strictures and protocols of caste and religion. But, by the nineteenth century, migration was not a strange phenomenon in rural India. There can be little doubt that a degree of fraudulence and violence was ever present in the recruitment process, as it is even today. Tall tales of easy opportunity awaiting them in the colonies trapped the greedy and the gullible. But deception should be placed in its proper context. The rural population was already uprooted and in search of employment; the recruiters' soothing words made the decision to migrate easier.

Social background

'I have been assured by every native from whom I have enquired, and by most Europeans, that only the lowest castes emigrate, and that nothing will ever induce men of higher class to leave.' Thus wrote G.A. Grierson in 1882.[18] This view has persisted over time and periodically invoked by the planters and colonial governments to sanction discrimination against their Indian settlers, deny them equal political rights and remind them of their proper place in society – at the bottom. The most comprehensive and exact data on the social background of the indentured migrants is from Fiji, and it can safely be assumed that the pattern for Fiji prevailed in other sugar colonies as well.[19] Of Fiji's 45,000 North Indian migrants, Brahman and allied castes numbered 1,686, Kshattriya and allied castes 4,565, Bania 1,592, middling agricultural and artisan castes (Kurmi, Ahir, Jat, Lodha) 15,800, menial and low castes (Chamar, Pasi, Dusadh) 11,907 and Muslims 6,787.[20] In other words, the emigrating indentured population represented a fair cross-section of rural Indian society. And this is not surprising for it was the cultivating castes, without social or institutional protection, who bore the brunt of the deteriorating economic situation in the country in the late nineteenth century: increase in land rent, often demanded in cash rather than kind, increasing fragmentation of ownership rights and subdivision of property which particularly affected the lower-order cultivators, while the widespread decline in the handicraft industry in UP was ruinous to the artisan class. To many in distress and despair, migration offered a way out. Prolonged absence was not contemplated, but in time an intended sojourn was transformed into permanent separation.

Women migrated as well as men. Migration of men is understandable, but that by rural, illiterate Indian women is less easy to explain. Consequently, stereotype and (male) prejudice become substitute for explanation. It is the common view that the indentured women were people of low moral character, the refuse of society, who fell easy prey to the wily recruiters. C.F. Andrews wrote about Indian indentured women in Fiji:

> The Hindu woman in this country is like a rudderless vessel with its mast broken being whirled down the rapids of a great river without any controlling hand. She passes from one man to another, and has lost even the sense of shame in doing so.[21]

Australian overseer Walter Gill who saw the last days of indenture in Fiji, wrote that the Hindu woman in Fiji was 'as joyously amoral as a doe rabbit. She took her lovers as a ship takes to rough seas, surging up to one who would smother her, then tossing him aside, thirsting for the next'. Indeed, so pervasive was the negative stereotype of Indian women in Fiji that they were held primarily responsible for a high male suicide rate, allegedly because they sold themselves to the highest bidder and then moved to the next, leaving the man to take his own life in despair and shame. The records, when read against the grain, tell a different story: a story of courage, fortitude and defiance against the odds and in the most difficult of circumstances.

Why women emigrated is lost to us, but scattered data provide some clues. We have already mentioned the pervasiveness of migration in the Indo–Gangetic plains. Most of the internal migration within India was male-dominated and, if the amount remitted to the village was not enough or if the man did not return, the life of the wife could become very difficult. Tolerated for a while, she could be tossed out of the household and forced to fend for herself in times of hardship and difficulty. The following folksong captures some of the anguish of the wife:

> The sun is cruel and bright
> A lot of work is still to be done.
> People have returned to their homes
> Yet no call for meals has come for me.
> Here, in these lonely fields
> I, the unfortunate, work alone.
> My lord being in a distant land
> Who will tell me thy lord has come
> The day of their happiness has dawned.[22]

Constant domestic disputes could be another reason to contemplate escape:

> Alas, I will have to run away with another man
> For my beloved has turned his mind away from me
> How eagerly as I cook rice and dal do I pour the ghee
> But as soon as we sit for dinner, you start quarrelling
> My heart is weary of you
> I put hot fire in the basket
> Carefully I make the bed
> But as soon as we lie down to rest, you start quarrelling
> My heart is weary of you.

To women in desperate, distraught circumstances, the recruiters' soothing words must have been a godsend. They left.

Indentured emigration was, by necessity as well as choice, an individualised phenomenon. Nonetheless, there were families migrating on virtually every shipment to the various colonies. In the case of Fiji, 70 per cent of women migrated as individuals, but the remaining 30 per cent migrated as members of families. The majority, 70 per cent of the women, were accompanied by their husbands only, 15 per cent by their husbands and children and 12 per cent by their children only. Some families were formed in the depots at the ports of embarkation and others on the long voyage out and still more on the plantations. The fact that women were prepared to leave a life of drudgery lived on the sufferance of others for distant unknown places across the ocean would suggest that these were women of pride and determination, and enterprise and self respect. These were certainly the values they inculcated in the children and grandchildren.

Once recruited, the potential emigrants would be taken to the District Depot where they would be examined by the District Magistrate or his deputy. Around 18 to 19 per cent would be rejected for various reasons, mostly because they were found to be unfit. At the port of embarkation, a similar percentage would fall off the list because they were found unfit or because they deserted or simply refused to embark. All told, more than a third of those recruited had been dropped, or dropped out, before the ship left.

The journey from districts of recruitment to the ports of embarkation involved more than just physical relocation. For men and women from the land-locked villages, a journey of several hundred miles was a novel, traumatic experience. Many were seeing the sea for the first time. In the crowded country depots and in the living quarters in Madras and Calcutta, people rubbed shoulders with those of unknown castes, something that would have never happened in the villages regulated by age-old norms and protocols of social intercourse that respected hierarchy and separation. Old adhesives of society were slowly loosening, such as the caste system. Occasionally men and women were finding partners from different social backgrounds. A sense of togetherness, of being passengers in the same boat, was slowly taking shape. As K.L. Gillion has written, 'Most of their caste scruples gone, without their traditional leaders and elders and generally without kin, they were resigned to the future and very vulnerable.'[23] New bonds of friendships formed on the long voyages, which could take up to three months on sailing ships. None was more important than the relationship of *Jahajibhai*, brotherhood of the crossing, which provided a degree of much-needed emotional attachment and security in an alien and alienating environment against the alienations and asperities of the outside world, and which persisted long after indenture itself was over. The process of fragmentation and reconstitution would continue apace on the voyage out and on the plantations in the colonies.

Life and work on colonial plantations

Just as recruitment and shipment of labourers was regulated by legislation, so too were the conditions of employment on the plantations. By the late nineteenth century, a uniform set of rules and procedures had been finalised. The provisions of the Guyana Ordinance of 1891 were closely followed in most other colonies, including the Dutch colony of Surinam.[24] It amplified the precise terms and condition of employment, the provision of accommodation and medical facilities, sanctions for breaches of the labour laws, the administration of justice, the terms and conditions of reindenture, and so on. On paper, the Ordinance was as comprehensive a piece of legislation as it was possible to imagine, but it was the glaring disparity between the words on paper and the reality on the ground that became the main source of the problem. It was stated, for instance, that indentured men would get 1 shilling per day's work and women 9 pennies, but it took a long time for the workers to achieve this sum. The days absent at hospital were added to the indenture contract. Once contracted to a particular estate or plantation, the labourer could not change his or her employer no matter how genuine the demand for the change. The penal sanctions for breaches of the labour ordinances were more effectively invoked by the planters than by the workers. Indenture was a system of structured inequality between the workers and their employers.

Upon arrival in the colonies, the indentured labourers would be allocated to the various plantations on the basis of orders placed before the colonial government by the planters the year before. Care was taken not to separate families, although on the same plantation, husband and wife could, and often did, work in different sections. But an effort was made to break up groups of people (who might come from the same district in India, for instance), to prevent strikes. The working day began early. The workers were mustered between 5am and 6am, had a hurried breakfast (or this was had at around 10.30am in Trinidad) and worked late till 4pm.[25] During harvesting time, the hours could be longer. Most of the work related to the cultivation and manufacture of sugar cane: ploughing, hoeing, weeding, harvesting and planting cane.

The labourers were promised that they would do either 'time work' or 'task work'. The new arrivals were usually allotted time work but, as they became accustomed to the working condition on the plantations, they were assigned task work, a task being defined as six hours of continuous work that an able-bodied man could be expected to accomplish. In Trinidad, by 1913, almost 90 per cent of the work was by task.[26] In most cases, it was the overseer who decided what task was appropriate. Sometimes, tasks were defined on the basis of what a few chosen men could accomplish. And tasks could be varied. If a worker accomplished his work in good time, he could return the next day to find his task extended. Sometimes, the standard from one plantation could be applied to another without taking into account the topography of the field. And, sometimes, the workers would be paid nothing at all for a partially completed task.

The Labour Ordinance provided a very large number of offences for which the employers could prosecute their labourers. In Trinidad in 1910–12, the most important prosecutions included desertion (1,668), absence from work without lawful excuse (1,466), refusing to begin or finish work (1,125) and vagrancy (983).[27] Other breaches included malingering, using threatening words and breach of hospital regulations. In Fiji, the employers were able to obtain 82 per cent of all the cases that they brought before the courts. Indentured labourers were punished for not registering their marriages, when the idea of registration probably did not occur to them if their marriages were carried out according to Hindu and Muslim rites. How was desertion defined? And did the labourers know that they could have a week's pay docked or face a month in prison if they 'committed nuisance' within 60 yards of a stream running through a plantation? Indentured labourers convicted of breaching the Labour Ordinance could either be fined or imprisoned. Neither, however, was the end of punishment for indentured labourers, for the planters were legally entitled to recover lost work by extending the contract by the number of days they were absent from the plantation.

Labourers were entitled under the Labour Ordinance to lay charges against their employers for assault and battery, non-payment of wages, not supplying tools or proper rations, using 'insulting language', requiring illegal work, over-tasking, falsifying pay lists and so on. But laying charges involved considerable risk. The labourers had difficulty getting permission to leave their plantations. Those who risked the odds became marked men. And there was no guarantee, after all the risks had been taken, that the courts would give them a sympathetic hearing. In Surinam between 1873 and 1916, only 10 per cent of employers were charged under the labour laws, while the employers were able to secure 75 per cent of the charges they brought against their labourers. After provocation beyond the limits of endurance, the workers either retaliated violently against those in authority, such as by murdering overseers, or striking. But striking was a risky proposition at all times and not easy to organise. The planters had all the power in their hands. The colonial government had a prudent appreciation of the economic contribution of the big companies. The labourers themselves were often disorganised and diffident. When strikes did occur, as Maureen Swann has written of Natal, they were 'short-lived, rarely transcended the accommodation units or work gangs into which plantation work gangs were divided, and were generally concerned with specific abuses of contract'.[28] The strikers were quickly apprehended and dispersed to different locations with the result that, as S.J. Reddy has written of Mauritius, 'experience acquired by one group in wresting some concessions was lost as they dispersed to take employment elsewhere'.[29] The indentured workers had a prudent appreciation of the reality that confronted them. They often engaged in quiet everyday acts of resistance or adopted strategic accommodation with authority as a way out of their difficulties.

Indenture, clearly, was a grim experience for those who experienced it: the relentless pace of work on the plantations, the violence, the disease, the frequent indifference of those in authority, the denial of the humanity of the workers. Many were broken by it, but many also survived. In some places, such as the Caribbean, indenture lasted for generations, with attendant consequences for social and cultural identity. Links with India were broken for long periods of time. People lived in isolation from their ancestral culture for long periods of time, losing their mother tongue in the process. Indenture, in short, was a life sentence. But elsewhere, such as in Fiji, it was a limited detention for five or at most ten years, after which the migrants were free to settle on their own or return to India. And contact with India was never really lost.

It was simultaneously an enslaving as well as a liberating experience for many. There were many in the indentured population whom birth had confined to the lower stratum of Indian society, a fate ordained by divine injunction, it was said, from which there was no escape in this life or the next. To them, migration and indenture offered the possibility to realise their individual humanity. Everywhere they grabbed the opportunity with relish. Indenture was a crucible in which was forged a new society. Old notions of purity and impurity, taboos regarding food, diet, social space, the rituals of prayer and worship collapsed over time to be replaced by new norms and conventions. Caste as a social institution became anachronistic, its protocols of approved behaviour unenforceable.[30] Remuneration during indenture was based on the amount of work accomplished, not on social status. Paucity of women necessitated marriages across caste and sometimes religious lines. Everywhere, people continued to 'play' at caste long after indenture had ceased, but its relevance and legitimacy were gone.

Fragmentation was accompanied by the process of reconstitution. Women everywhere played an important part in that process. Women emerged from indenture as productive workers in their own right, enjoying or negotiating a measure of independence that would have been unimaginable in India. They survived the burdens of racism as well as sexism. They raised families in often inhospitable circumstances and played a critical role in facilitating 'the transmission and practice of folk religion and of tradition-based sanctions'.[31] In Guyana, writes Jeremy Poynting, women 'were the main preservers of Indian domestic culture', which he argues was 'initially the principal means whereby Indians maintained their identity'.[32] The presence of Indian women in the colonies was important in another way: it discouraged relationships between Indian men and non-Indian women to varying degrees in the sugar colonies.

Religion played an equally important role in the protection of Indian culture and identity in the different colonies. It is commonly assumed that religious practices and protocols of Hinduism and Islam collapsed suddenly on the colonial plantations. This is not true. The various groups of people who went to the colonies brought with them their own family (*kul*) or village (*gram*) deities with their own rituals and ceremonies associated with them. Some involved animal sacrifice, while others invoked the dark forces of the underworld. Over time, everywhere, these were replaced by a more universal form of Brahminised Hinduism.[33] And the colonial planters were not always opposed to the perpetuation of the migrants' religious practices. 'As the planters became increasingly dependent on Indian labour', writes Basdeo Mangru about Guiana:

> they correspondingly endeavoured to make estate life as attractive as possible so as to induce the indentured workforce to prolong their residence through re-indenture. One certain way of substituting a temporary sojourn for permanent residence was to permit the Indian labourer to practise his religion, which was an inseparable part of his life.

Further, to 'create a sense of belonging and facilitate reindenture for another five years, some prudent estate managers not only attended the festivals, but generously granted holidays and made regular and substantial contribution towards the festivals'.[34] One festival which was celebrated across all the colonial plantations across the world was Tazia (Fiji), and known as Tadjah (Guiana) or Hosein/Hose/Hosay (Trinidad and Jamaica), commemorating the martyrdom of Hassan and Hussein, grandsons of Prophet Mohammed. Holi, or Phagua, was also regularly celebrated.

In some places, such as the Caribbean, Christianity was able to make significant inroads into the Indian community, promising liberation and the prospect of upward mobility in an environment characterised by closed and low glass ceilings but, in other places, such as Fiji, it was insignificant. In an important sense, religion became a tool of resistance. As Roy Glasgow writes of Guiana, 'The Indians' emphasis upon the value and worthwhileness of his culture was really a mode of expression of his desire to be treated on terms of equality within the Guyanese universe'.[35] This was successful to varying degrees in different places. In Fiji, within a decade of the beginning of indentured migration, the basic texts of popular Hinduism were circulating among the indentured Indians.[36] These included *Satyanarayan ki katha* (a collection of five stories from the Reva chapter of the *Skanda Purana*), *Sukh Sagar* (a discourse on the different incarnations of Lord Vishnu), popular versions of the *Bhagvada Gita*, *Danlila* (a devotional verse in praise of Lord Krishna) and, above all, the *Ramayana*, the story of Lord Rama in some 10,000 lines of verse in the Avadhi dialect of Hindi familiar to most of the North Indian migrants. Rama's story, enacted in *Ramlilas* and sung communally to the accompaniment of rudimentary music, struck a particular chord with the indentured labourers. Rama was exiled for 14 years for no fault of his own, but he did return; good ultimately triumphed over evil. His story gave them hope and consolation: one day, their ordeal, too, would come to an end.

And it did. All indentured emigration ceased in 1916 and the system was abolished soon afterwards although in some places, by the beginning of the twentieth century, the peak of emigration was long over. Reports by C.F. Andrews, among others, drew the attention of the Indian public, slowly awakening to nationalist sentiments, to the social problems of indenture, especially the abuse of women on the plantations, which outraged Indian public opinion and finally forced the Government of India to end indenture despite protests and pleas from the colonies. As Lord Hardinge said:

> No matter how great might be the economic advantages, the political aspect of the question is such that no one who has at heart the interests of British rule in India can afford to neglect it. It is one of the most important subjects in Indian political life today, and its discussion arouses more bitterness, perhaps, than that of any other outstanding question. Few Indian politicians, moderate and extremist alike, do not consider that the existence of this system which they do not hesitate to call by the name of slavery, brands their whole race in the eyes of the British Empire with the stigma of helotry.[37]

Upon the expiry of their indenture, the Indian settlers had no alternative but to be independent. Some experimented with other occupations, but limited opportunities, family obligations, kinship ties and lack of education and marketable skills forced most to depend on agriculture, cultivating rice and sugar principally but also such crops as maize, tobacco, sweet potato and yam, in time monopolising market gardening.[38] Expediency, contingency and tolerance born of need or circumstance, rather than social status and prestige, determined relations among the settlers. They built temples and roads and schools, and tried to create a semblance of life on bits and pieces of a remembered past. The old pattern of village India could not be reproduced in the new environment. The emergence of new settlements of freed Indians, with their temples and mosques, rudimentary schools and established homesteads, was also symbolically important for those still under indenture. They served as beacons of inspiration for them, nurturing the hope that they too would be free one day. It lightened the burden of the relentless plantation routine.

Wherever the Indian indentured labourers went, they encountered people who were either indigenous to those places (such as Fiji) or imported earlier as labourers themselves (as in the West Indies). Relations between the two groups were characterised by prejudice and the suspicion that one was the nemesis of the other. In Trinidad, the blacks could not but notice the degrading conditions in which the Indian indentured labourers lived and worked, their low occupational and social status. The Indians' culture and religion appeared strange and incomprehensible. The Creole and the 'Coolie' found little to admire in each other's way of life. 'The Coolie despises the negro, because he considers him a being not so highly civilized as himself', wrote an observer of Trinidad:

> while the negro, in turn, despises the Coolie, because he is so immensely inferior to him in physical strength. There never will be much danger of seditious disturbances among East Indian immigrants on estates as long as large numbers of negroes continue to be employed with them.[39]

In other places, the perception of Indians working for lower wages than the blacks poisoned relations. In Fiji, the colonial state prohibited social intercourse between Fijians and Indians, and transgressions were punished at law. Everywhere, the seeds of prejudice, suspicion and hostility planted during the early years of indenture continued to bear fruit long after the system itself was abolished. Colonial policies exacerbated the gulf between the communities created by culture and history and circumstances beyond their control. The descendants of the Indian indentured immigrants found themselves living in suffering and on the sufferance of others, excluded from the corridors of power, disempowered. It was a difficult journey; there was a lot of despair and disappointments along the way. But there was also defiance. In the words of Guyanese poet Rooplall Monar:

> Generations nurtured from my seed
> Will clasp their hands and say
> Our ancestors carved those fields
> Which have given us meanings
> meanings to stand tall
> This land is ours too.[40]

Notes

1 In Lloyd Searwar *et al.* (eds), *They Came in Ships: An Anthology of Indo-Guyanese Prose and Poetry* (Leeds: Peepal Tress Press, 1998), 215.
2 Home Legislative Department (Emigration), A. Pros. 14, 8 May 1847, National Archives of India; also D.W.D. Comins, *Note on Emigration from the East Indies to British Guyana* (Calcutta, 1893).
3 Comins, *Note on Emigration from East Indies to St Lucia* (Calcutta, 1893), 3; House of Commons, *Parliamentary Paper*, vol. xxxv (1844), 316.
4 See, generally, David Dabydeen and Brinsley Samaroo (eds), *Across the Dark Waters: Ethnicity and Indian Identity in the Caribbean* (London: MacMallian, 1996), 2–3; Bridget Brereton, *A History of Modern Trinidad, 1783–1962* (Portsmouth, Heinemann, 1989), 96–100.
5 House of Commons, *Parliamentary Paper*, xxxv (1844), 551.

6   K.L. Gillion, *Fiji's Indian Migrants: A History to the End of Indenture in 1920* (Melbourne: Oxford University Press, 1962), 22.

7   For detailed discussion, see Basdeo Mangru, 'Indian Government policy towards indentured labour migration to the sugar colonies', in Dabydeen and Samaroo (eds), *Across the Dark Waters*, op. cit., 162–74.

8   Kingsley Davis, *The Population of India and Pakistan* (Princeton, NJ: Princeton University Press, 1951), 99.

9   See, among others, K.S. Sandhu, *Indians in Malaya: Some Aspects of their Immigration and Settlement, 1786–1957* (Cambridge: Cambridge University Press, 1969); N.R. Chakravarti, *The Indian Minority in Burma: The Rise and Decline of an Immigrant Community* (London: Oxford University Press, 1971); and R. Jayaraman, 'Indian Emigration to Ceylon: Some Aspects of the Historical and Social Background of the Emigrants', *Indian Economic and Social History Review*, vol. IV (1967), 319–59.

10 See, among others, Surendra Bhana, *Indentured Indian Emigrants to Natal, 1860–1902* (New Delhi: Promilla and Co. Publishers, 1991), 41–9; C.G. Hennings, *The Indentured Indian in Natal, 1860–1917* (New Delhi: Promilla and Co. Publishers, 1993), 21.

11 See G. Geoghegan, *Coolie Emigration from India* (Calcutta: Government Printer, 1874); Panchanan Saha, *Emigration of Indian Labour, 1834–1900* (Delhi: Popular Prakashan, 1970); and J.S. Mangat, *A History of Asians in East Africa, c. 1886–1945* (Oxford: Oxford University Press, 1969).

12 Geoghegan, ibid.; House of Commons, *Parliamentary Papers* for various years; and C.L. Tupper, *Note on Colonial Emigration During the Year 1878–1879* (Calcutta, 1879).

13 For discussion of North India, see Lal, *Girmitiyas: The Origins of the Fiji Indians* (Canberra: Journal of Pacific History Monograph, 1983).

14 See also 'Official and Popular Hinduism in the Caribbean: Historical and Contemporary Trends in Surinam, Trinidad and Guyana', in Dabydeen and Samaroo, *Across the Dark Waters*, op. cit., 112–13 for figures for Surinam and Trinidad.

15 Figures derived from the *Census of India* (1921). For a contextualised study of internal migration, see Ranajit Das Gupta, 'Factory Labour in Eastern India: Sources of Supply, 1855–1946. Some Preliminary Findings', *Indian Economic and Social History Review*, vol. XIII, no. 3 (1973), 277–329.

16 Figures and assessment are derived from *Settlement Reports* which are, by far, the most comprehensive sources for the study of rural Indian society.

17 This theme is emphasised in Tinker (1974), *A New System of Slavery* and echoed in the published literature on the subject about a generation ago. More recent studies allow for greater agency for the recruits.

18 In Emigration Proceedings, A. Pros. 12 August 1882, National Archives of India. This view is widely reflected in most official and popular accounts.

19 See, for example, Verene Shepherd, *Transients to Settlers: The Experience of Indians in Jamaica, 1845–1950* (Leeds: Peepal Tree Press, 1993), 47, where she says the Fiji data 'would be replicated in Trinidad, Guyana and Jamaica. What evidence is available supports that assumption.'

20 See my *Girmitiyas*, op. cit., 68–90.

21 This and the Gill quotes are from Lal's *Chalo Jahaji: On a Journey of Indenture through Fiji* (Canberra: Australian National University, 2000), 54.

22 These two folksongs I collected in UP are in my *Girmitiyas*, op. cit., 113–14.

23 Gillion, *Fiji's Indian Migrants*, op. cit., 67.

24 A copy of the Ordinance is reproduced in Lal's *Crossing the Kala Pani: A Documentary History of Indian Indenture in Fiji* (Suva: Fiji Museum, 1998), 49–94.

25 See, generally, Gillion, *Fiji's Indian Migrants*, op. cit.; Marianne Soares Ramesar, *Survivors of Another Crossing: A History of East Indians in Trinidad, 1880–1946* (St Augustine: University of the West Indies, 1994); Verene Shepherd, *Transients to Settlers*, op. cit.; Clem Seecharan, *Tiger in the Stars: The Anatomy of Indian Achievement in British Guyana, 1919–1929* (London: Macmillan, 1997); Ashwin Desai and Goolam Vahed, *Inside Indenture: A South African Story, 1860–1914* (Durban: Madiba Publishers, 2007); and Marina Carter's many works on Mauritius, including *Voices from Indenture: Experiences of Indian Migrants in the British Empire* (London: Leicester University Press, 1996).

26 Shepherd, *Transients to Settlers*, op. cit., 59 has claimed that '[t]asks were generally preferred in all colonies.'

27 See Ramesar, *Survivors of Another Crossing*, op. cit., 44–5; K.O. Laurence, *A Question of Labour: Indentured Immigration into Trinidad and British Guiana, 1875–1916* (Kingston: Ian Randle Publishers, 1994), 131–66; and studies in Kay Saunders (ed.), *Indentured Labour in the British Empire, 1834–1920* (London: Croom Helm, 1984).

28 Maureen Swann, 'Resistance and Accommodation, 1890–1913', in Surendra Bhana (ed.), *Essays on Indentured Indians in Natal* (Leeds: Peepal Tree Press, 1988), 128. See also Lal's 'Non-resistance on Fiji Plantations: The Fiji Indian Experience, 1879–1920', in Brijj V. Lal, Doug Munro and Ed Beechert (eds), *Plantation Workers: Resistance and Accommodation* (Honolulu: University of Hawaii Press, 1993), 187–217.

29 S.J. Reddi, 'Labour Protest Among Indian Immigrants', in U. Bissoondoyal and S.B.C. Servansing (eds), *Indian Labour Immigration* (Moka: Mahatma Gandhi Institute, 1986), 132.

30 See Chandra Jayawardena, 'The Disintegration of Caste in Fiji Indian Rural Society', in Jayawardena and L.R. Hiatt (eds), *Anthropology in Oceania* (Sydney: Angus & Robertson, 1971), 89–119.

31 Marina Carter, *Lakshmi's Legacy: The Testimonies of Indian Women in 19th Century Mauritius* (Stanley-Rose Hill: Editions de L'Océan Indien, 1994), 142.

32 Jeremy Poynting, 'East Indian Women in the Caribbean: Experience and Voice', in David Dabydeen and Brinsley Samaroo (eds), *India in the Caribbean* (London: Hansib, 1987), 234.

33 See Steven Vertovec, 'Official and Popular Hinduism in the Caribbean: Historical and Contemporary Trends in Surinam, Trinidad and Guyana', in Dabydeen and Samaroo (eds), *Across the Dark Waters*, op. cit., 114.

34 Basdeo Mangru, 'Tadjah in British Guiana', in Frank Birbalsingh (ed.), *Indo–Caribbean Resistance* (Toronto: Tsar, 1993), 18.

35 Roy Arthur Glasgow, *Guyana. Race and Politics among Africans and East Indians* (The Hague: Mouton, 1970), 79.

36 See my *Chalo Jahaji*, 'Hinduism Under Indenture', op. cit.

37 Gillion, *Fiji's Indian Migrants*, op. cit., 180. See also Basdeo Mangru, 'Indian Government Policy towards Indentured Labour Migration to the Sugar Colonies', in Dabydeen and Samaroo (eds), *Across the Dark Waters*, op. cit., 171–172. Andrews's role is considered in K.L. Gillion, 'C.F. Andrews and Indians Overseas', in *Visva–Bharti News* (Feb–March, 1971), 206–17.

38 See, for example, Surendra Bhana and Joy Brain, *Setting Down Roots: Indian Immigrants in South Africa* (Hohannesburg: Witwatersrand University Press, 1990), 43–52; Gillion, *Fiji's Indian Migrants*, op. cit., 136–63; Shepherd, *Transients to Settlers*, op. cit., 118–49; Seecharan, *Tiger in the Stars*, op. cit., 147–215; Marian Ramessar, *Survivors of Another Crossing*, op. cit., 77–118.

39 Malcolm Ross, 'East Indian–Creole relations in Trinidad and Guyana in the late 19th Century', in Dabydeen and Samaroo (eds), *Across the Black Water*, op. cit., 28–9; also Brereton, *A History of Modern Trinidad*, op. cit., 110.

40 Lloyd Searwar *et al.* (eds), *They Came in Ships*, op. cit., 205.

References

Bhana, Surendra, *Indentured Indian Emigrants to Natal, 1860–1917* (New Delhi: Promillaand Co. Publishers, 1991).

Bhana, Surendra and Brain, Joy, *Setting Down Roots: Indian Immigrants in South Africa* (Hohannesburg: Witwatersrand University Press, 1990), 43–52.

Brereton, Bridget, *A History of Modern Trinidad, 1783–1962* (Portsmouth: Heinemann, 1989).

Carter, Marina, *Lakshmi's Legacy: The Testimonies of Indian Women in 19th Century Mauritius* (Stanley-Rose Hill: Editions de L'Océan Indien, 1994), 142.

— *Voices from Indenture: Experiences of Indian Migrants in the British Empire* (London: Leicester University Press, 1996).

Chakravarti, N.R., *The Indian Minority in Burma: The Rise and Decline of an Immigrant Community* (London: Oxford University Press, 1971).

Comins, D.W.D., *Note on Emigration from the East Indies to British Guyana* (Calcutta: 1893).

— *Note on Emigration from East Indies to St Lucia* (Calcutta: 1893).

Dabydeen, David and Brinsley Samaroo (eds), *Across the Dark Waters: Ethnicity and Indian Identity in the Caribbean* (London: Macmillan, 1996).

Davis, Kingsley, *The Population of India and Pakistan* (Princeton, NJ: Princeton University Press, 1951).

Desai, Ashwin and Vahed, Goolam, *Inside Indenture: A South African Story, 1860–1914* (Durban: Madiba Publishers, 2007).

Geoghegan, G., *Coolie Emigration from India* (Calcutta: Government Printer, 1874).

Gillion, K.L., *Fiji's Indian Migrants: A History to the End of Indenture in 1920* (Melbourne: Oxford University Press, 1962).

— 'C.F. Andrews and Indians Overseas', in *Visva–Bharti News* (Feb–March, 1971), 206–17.

Glasgow, Roy Arthur, *Guyana. Race and Politics among Africans and East Indians* (The Hague: Mouton, 1970), 79.

Gupta, Ranajit Das, 'Factory Labour in Eastern India: Sources of Supply, 1855–1946: Some Preliminary Findings', *Indian Economic and Social History Review*, vol. XIII, no. 3 (1973), 277–329.

Hennings, C.G., *The Indentured Indian in Natal, 1860–1917* (New Delhi: Promilla and Co. Publishers, 1993).

Jayaraman, R., 'Indian Emigration to Ceylon: Some Aspects of the Historical and Social Background of the Emigrants', *Indian Economic and Social History Review*, vol. IV (1967), 319–59.

Jayawardena, Chandra, 'The Disintegration of Caste in Fiji Indian Rural Society', in Chandra Jayawardena and L.R. Hiatt (eds), *Anthropology in Oceania* (Sydney: Angus & Robertson, 1971), 89–119.

Lal, Brij V., *Girmitiyas: The Origins of the Fiji Indians* (Canberra: Journal of Pacific History Monograph, 1983).

— 'Non-resistance on Fiji Plantations: The Fiji Indian Experience, 1879–1920', in Brijj V. Lal, Doug Munro and Ed Beechert (eds), *Plantation Workers: Resistance and Accommodation* (Honolulu: University of Hawaii Press, 1993), 187–217.

— *Crossing the Kala Pani: A Documentary History of Indian Indenture in Fiji* (Suva: Fiji Museum, 1998), 49–94.

— *Chalo Jahaji: On a Journey of Indenture through Fiji* (Canberra: Australian National University, 2000).

Laurence, K.O., *A Question of Labour: Indentured Immigration into Trinidad and British Guiana, 1875–1916* (Kingston: Ian Randle Publishers, 1994), 131–66.

Mangat, J.S., *A History of Asians in East Africa, c. 1886–1945* (Oxford: Oxford University Press, 1969).

Mangru, Basdeo, 'Tadjah in British Guiana', in Frank Birbalsingh (ed.), *Indo–Caribbean Resistance* (Toronto: Tsar, 1993).

Mangru, Basdeo, 'Indian Government Policy towards Indentured Labour Migration to the Sugar Colonies', in David Dabydeen and Brinsley Samaroo (eds), *Across The Dark Waters: Ethnicity and Indian Identity in the Caribbean* (London: Macmillan, 1996).

Poynting, Jeremy, 'East Indian Women in the Caribbean: Experience and Voice', in David Dabydeen and Brinsley Samaroo (eds), *India in the Caribbean* (London: Hansib, 1987).

Ramesar, Marianne Soares, *Survivors of Another Crossing: A History of East Indians in Trinidad, 1880–1946* (St Augustine: University of the West Indies, 1994).

Reddi, S.J., 'Labour Protest Among Indian Immigrants', in U. Bissoondoyal and S.B.C. Servansing (eds), *Indian Labour Immigration* (Moka: Mahatma Gandhi Institute, 1986).

Ross, Malcolm, 'East Indian–Creole relations in Trinidad and Guyana in the late 19th century', in David Dabydeen and Brinsley Samaroo (eds), *Across the Dark Waters: Ethnicity and Indian Identity in the Caribbean* (London: Macmillan, 1996).

Saha, Panchanan, *Emigration of Indian Labour, 1834–1900* (Delhi: Popular Prakashan, 1970).

Sandhu, K.S., *Indians in Malaya: Some Aspects of the Immigration and Settlement* (Cambridge: Cambridge University Press, 1969).

Saunders, Kay (ed.), *Indentured Labour in the British Empire, 1834–1920* (London: Croom Helm, 1984).

Searwar, Lloyd, Ian McDonald, Laxhmie Kallicharan and Joel Benjamin (eds), *They Came in Ships: An Anthology of Indo-Guyanese Prose and Poetry* (Leeds: Peepal Tree Press, 1998).

Seecharan, Clem, *Tiger in the Stars: The Anatomy of Indian Achievement in British Guiana, 1919–1929* (London: Macmillan, 1997).

Shepherd, Verene, *Transients to Settlers: The Experience of Indians in Jamaica, 1845–1950* (Leeds: Peepal Tree Press, 1993).

Swann, Maureen, 'Resistance and Accommodation, 1890–1913', in Surendra Bhana (ed.), *Essays on Indentured Indians in Natal* (Leeds: Peepal Tree Press, 1988).

Tinker, Hugh, *A New System of Slavery: The Export of Indian Labour Abroad, 1830–1920* (London: Oxford University Press, 1974).

Tupper, C.L., *Note on Colonial Emigration During the Year 1878–1879* (Calcutta: Bengal Secretariat Press, 1879).

Vertovec, S., 'Official and Popular Hinduism in the Caribbean: Historical and Contemporary Trends in Surinam, Trinidad and Guyana', in David Dabydeen and Brinsley Samaroo (eds), *Across the Dark Waters: Ethnicity and Indian Identity in the Caribbean* (London: Macmillan, 1996).

8

WRECKING HOMES, MAKING FAMILIES

Women's recruitment and indentured labour migration from India

Samita Sen

In the nineteenth century, more than a million workers left India to labour under indenture in sugar estates in various parts of the colonial world. Meant to replace the newly freed African slaves, they were tied to the estates by draconian contracts and subjected to harsh labour regimes. Planters preferred to import Indians rather than draw from the locally settled populations in order to be able to command direct labour and avoid the costs of reproduction. These calculations also influenced their import strategy; there was no demand for Indian women. Following in the habits of the slavery regime, planters regarded imported Indians as units of labour and it mattered little to them that their strategy resulted in communities of predominantly male workers. The circulation of persistently unsettled male indentured workers promised, they believed, a better guarantee of docile servitude.

The initial unconcern with settling Indian workers and, therefore, the import of Indian women changed as soon as the basic premise of the early indenture system – the uninterrupted supply of male migrants from India – became open to question. In the 1840s, labour export from India came under a barrage of criticism from various quarters and faltered for a few years. From the 1850s, there was a gradual policy shift towards settling Indian labour. Settlement, however, could not take the route of integrating Indians within existing society in the colonies; to protect the indenture system, separate communities of Indian workers was preferred. The Indian family was imagined as the building block of this diasporic labour sprawl – and the import of Indian women was crucial to the project. The gender strategy of the indenture system, though not wholly reversed, was altered drastically. From the 1860s, policy in London, Calcutta and other colonial capitals focused on the recruitment of Indian women. Their strategies changed over time, but at each stage encountered rough weather; women's migration became grist to the mill of a patriarchal contest – between the productive and reproductive exigencies of the family–household in the Indian countryside and sugar capital's imperative to script family into the indentured labour system.

The significant hyphen between the two successive labour regimes in the sugar estates – slavery and indenture – was gender. Sugar plantations in the Australian colonies had begun to buy Indian workers from the second half of the eighteenth century before the abolition of slavery. It was after the emancipation of the slaves in 1834, however, that a more steady flow of emigration from India began. To offset the cost of recruiting and transporting, and to establish greater control over workers, a system of long-term contracts or indentures (ranging between one and five years) was introduced in 1837.[1] Soon after this, a batch of workers landed in the Caribbean. The freeing of the slaves, planters argued, left them with inadequate labour to sustain cheap production of sugar, not only because the men could opt out of plantation work but even more because the women were expected to withdraw from field labour. Such arguments did not convince some abolitionists, who bitterly opposed the 'new system of slavery', one ground being that it replaced the freedwomen's labour with that of Indian men. In the abolitionist rhetoric, disruption of family, domesticity and gender roles had provided a powerful argument against slavery. In the immediate aftermath of slavery, one measure of the success of emancipation was the formation of family units with established gender and generational roles. In this discourse, the instruments of morality – of social order and control – lay in the domestication of former slave populations through family and, therefore, by marriage. In the Caribbean context, for instance, emancipation was 'celebrated' with 'nearly six thousand marriages' (Kale 1998: 114–15). The absence of women among Indian labourers began to resonate more powerfully as their numbers swelled.

The characterization of women migrants – whether they were victims of force or fraud, or whether they were actively seeking to escape familial discipline to assert sexual and marital agency – spoke to a tension at the very heart of the indenture project. Having initiated this global flow of labour, the British Imperium found it increasingly difficult to reconcile its imperatives with two other major nineteenth-century preoccupations, free labour, on the one hand, and disciplining family and marriage, on the other. It was difficult enough to sustain the argument that labour was free to submit by contract to servitude, i.e. indenture, but, in the case of women, even the principle of freedom of contract had not really been established. Were the debates between competing forms of contract or competing forms of bondage? Were women 'free' as individuals, as units of labour or as agents to sell their labour in the market? Could they, on their own behalf, enter into long-term contracts for migration over long distances, which included the prospect of permanent resettlement? The very process of long-term and long-distance migration unsettled established gender hierarchies. The view of women as free to enter contracts for wage labour disrupted existing modes of control over women's productive and reproductive labour and sexuality. Any large-scale mobilization of individual 'single' women was a challenge to a patriarchal system based on the deployment of women's labour and reproduction exclusively within and through the family–household and the control of their sexuality within marriage. The problem was not only at the recruitment end in India. The notion of women as free agents proved equally inimical for settlement in the colony. The evidence that women could, as indeed some did, use their freedom to become more assertive in choosing and discarding partners raised the spectre of an undesirable 'sexual anarchy', requiring the renewal of the sexual contract and the recreation of the patriarchal family. Herein lay the paradox: to fabricate the Indian family in the colonies, women had to be taken from India; but to encourage women to leave meant wrecking Indian families in India. The collusions and collisions between competing capitalisms and multiple patriarchies – in India and in the colonies – is the subject of this brief essay.

From labour import to colonization: changing gender imperatives of overseas migration

In the 1830s and 1840s planters in Mauritius, the chief receiving colony, focused on recruiting working men, including only about 10 per cent women, ostensibly to be employed in 'cooking and washing up'. Women going to 'Mirich' (Mauritius) were not engaged for field labour.[2] When John Gladstone proposed the import of Indian labour to Demarara, he asked for equal numbers of men and women provided they all agreed to undertake field labour. His labour agents, Gillanders, Arbuthnot & Co., were doubtful of such a prospect, since overseas emigration had become established as a male enterprise (Kale 1998). In both Mauritius and the Caribbean, in the initial years, single male migration rather than family migration became the mainstay of 'coolie export'. The first batch contained some 100 women to 6,000 men (Tinker 1974). Historians have noted that in the Caribbean, as in Mauritius, planters were unwilling to incur the inevitable 'financial disabilities due to the financial risks of child-bearing and rearing' (Reddock 1985; Beall 1990). Gladstone, however, hit a nerve that was to continue to jangle within the indenture system, when he spoke of encouraging marriage, the importation of married couples and families to pre-empt 'improper conduct' and encourage domestic comfort (Kale 1998).

In India, outrage against indentured emigration found expression in a series of petitions and public meetings and raised questions about the fate of the women and children left behind by male migrants. Government produced evidence to 'prove' that families were not left destitute and that single male circular migration was an established practice of long standing. While family contentions were thus summarily settled at the Indian end, it cropped up with greater force in the colonies. The problem of the complete absence of family life in the male world of Indian workers in the receiving colonies raised myriad concerns. Colonial authorities in the receiving countries, concerned with 'social instability', high crime rates and an epidemic of 'wife-murder', gained the ear of the home government in Britain. Not all colonial authorities subscribed to the view that an adverse sex ratio led to more suicides and murders. Sir A. Gordon, Governor of Mauritius, for instance, argued that suicide rates bore no relationship to the sex ratio.[3] Order, however, had to be restored in the plantations; and most colonial governments latched on to the 'family' as a solution.

Between 1858 and 1860, 51,247 workers sailed from Calcutta alone (Tinker 1974: 100, 273). Having failed to increase the proportion of women, varying between 10 and 20 per cent, by incentives and policy directives, the Government of India decided in 1868 to statutorily fix a minimum of 40 women to every 100 men per shipment (Brereton 1974; Moore 1991).[4] Mauritius already had a proportion of 40 and 45 per cent women and was allowed 33 women for every 100 men (Carter 1994).

Caribbean planters first exhibited some interest in women immigrants when it seemed as though labour migration from India might stop altogether. The long-term advantages of a self-reproducing workforce became evident during the sugar crisis of the 1880s, when planters began to encourage cane farming in small family holdings. The women did most of the regular field work, producing cane and undertaking subsistence food production. This allowed a further depression of wages, a ready reserve of labour and an alternative source of cane (Reddock 1985; Tinker 1974).

As the colonies began to demand more women migrants, it became clear that a supply constraint was also at work. The colonies had to pay a premium for women recruits. From 1852 to 1866, the Mauritius Government paid a bonus of a pound for every woman brought into the colony. This bounty encouraged recruiters and returnees to bring multiple wives into

Mauritius. In the case of the Caribbean, recruiters began to charge higher rates for women. By 1910, the disparity was considerable: Rs. 35 for an adult woman (Rs. 25 for an adult man) in some areas; Rs. 40 for adult women (Rs. 30 for adult men) in others; and, in Natal, the Agent paid Rs. 70 for adult women (Rs. 50 for adult men).[5] Neither legislation nor incentives, it appears, brought forth a flow of women migrants (except to some extent in the case of Mauritius). Soon after introducing the statutory gender proportion, the Government of Bengal was forced to open a special file entitled 'Short Shipment of Females' permitting agents to dodge the quota. The shortage in one shipment was supposed to be met in the next, but disparities mounted.[6] Enquiries in the North-Western Provinces and Oudh and in Bihar into the system of emigration from British India to the colonies revealed that, 'admitting that the proportion of 40 women to 100 men was by no means excessive . . . this proportion could not be readily obtained except at the expense of serious abuses'.[7]

Morality, migration and marriage: debates over women's recruitment

The demand for indentured immigration in the 1830s and 1840s had relied not only on representations of 'labour shortage' in the sugar-producing colonies, a claim challenged by abolitionists, but also on the benefits of emigration from India. The latter involved a vision of India as a poor, congested and labour-surplus region, with overseas emigration offering an opportunity to individuals to rise 'from poverty to affluence'.[8] The 'erroneous impression . . . that India is overpopulated' was decried by employers of labour in India,[9] and these arguments gathered momentum with the rapid development of mines and plantations from the late nineteenth century and expansion of industry in the first decades of the twentieth. Within these debates, women's recruitment offered a curious paradox. Colonial and imperial governments wished to recruit more 'honest and decent women' along with their families. In India, however, there appeared to be a shortage of female labour.

By the 1870s, recruiting activities had multiplied, various kinds of commission agents serving the Assam plantations having joined the fray.[10] Both systems of recruitment were characterized by high levels of state regulation, and the gaps between the law and its enforcement remained a matter of bitter contestation. Both sets of employers were keen to mobilize female labour and, in trying to do so, their recruiters became notorious for using fraud and coercion. The recruiters in their turn complained of the scarcity of women willing to migrate under contract and, by their own occasional admission, took recourse to underhand and violent methods, including kidnapping, enticement, deceit and misrepresentation. In the case of colonial Agents, there was the added goad of the statutory requirements, though Assam recruiters also operated under the pressure of an informal gender quota (at least one woman to four men).[11] In the last three decades of the nineteenth century, the 'kidnapping' of women became an officially recognized problem, even though statistical estimates are not available. By the end of the nineteenth century, the issue of women's recruitment, denounced in fiction, by publicists, by the British officials, local employers and the urban Bengali elite, became the stuff of folklore. Doubtless, there were many cases of coercive and fraudulent recruitment but, equally indubitably, many cases of voluntary migration by women became characterized as 'kidnapping' (Sen 2002). Indeed, since women returnees doubled as recruiters and made the journey several times, there must have been some voluntary migration by single women (Carter 1994). Even though evidence spoke of the presence of both, women migrants were characterized either as victims of force and fraud or as immoral women asserting an illegitimate agency.

These stereotypes about women migrants were created in tandem in the colonies and in India. Governments in the colonies attributed social disorder not to the excesses of the indentured labour regime but to the influx of 'prostitutes' and 'lax women', whether in Mauritius (Carter 1994) or the Caribbean (Mohapatra 1995). Imperial government, persuaded by such simple logic, passed on the burden of finding better and more suitable women to the government in India. The project of creating settled communities of Indian workmen had to be through 'family' migration, and single women, if they were to migrate at all, had to meet the primary purpose of colonization. In 1875 Lord Salisbury argued for 'the emigration of a sufficient proportion of women of an honest and decent class' and asked the Government of India to promote such emigration.[12]

The repeated call for 'respectable' women explicitly endorsed the characterization of the female migrant as a disreputable, promiscuous 'prostitute'. Officers in India too were susceptible to these stereotypes since they viewed Indian society through the prism of the closed self-sufficient village economy bound immutably by tradition. Indian peasants, in general, and women, in particular, were perceived as immobile, immune to market incentives (Sen 2010). Administrators imagined all Indian women to be confined within the family and segregated from public spaces, beyond the reach of recruiters. The only women available for recruitment would thus be those already commodified, i.e. bazaar women and prostitutes. By this logic, 'respectable' women would be impossible to recruit outside the family.

Female migration was not, however, atypical. The massive mobilization of labour in the non-agrarian sector in the nineteenth century did not exclude women. They were a numerical minority, but they registered a significant presence in short-term and long-term employment (Anderson 2004), which often involved migration. There were major interactions in the pathways of the different streams of migration, but plantation migration alone involved a determined and directed recruitment of women. Women constituted little less than half of the total 2.5 million (approximately, between 1870 and 1944)[13] in the case of Assam tea plantations and about one-third of the total 1.3 million (1831 to 1920) in the case of overseas migration (Anderson 2004: 424). All of women's migration in this period included a significant pro-portion of family migration, though single women registered the more visible presence. In the case of overseas migration, the proportions varied somewhat. Between 1860 and 1869, the proportion of 'single' women going to Mauritius varied between 35 and 50 per cent, hitting a low of 11 per cent in 1863 (Carter 1994). In the Caribbean, however, in the late nineteenth century, their proportion varied between 75 and 65 per cent (Mohapatra 2004). In 1911, nearly 70 per cent of total female migrants overseas were single;[14] in 1917, the proportion rose to more than 77 per cent.[15]

This preponderance of single women in overseas migration confirmed the colonial stereotypes regarding Indian women, which associated mobility with immorality. At the Indian end, officers as well as emigration Agents also subscribed to these equations.[16] Many emigrating couples were not 'legally' married according to evolving standards of personal law. These partnerships, involving serial and multiple marriages, were often struck at various stages of the long process of migration and settlement.[17]

Who, then, were the 'respectable' women, the desirable but unobtainable subject of migration? Given the ubiquity and early age of marriage, there were no unmarried 'single' women – as Indian publicists and colonial officers repeatedly warned.[18] In a despatch dated 21 September 1917, the Secretary of State admitted that government had not realized how dif-ficult it would be 'under the conditions of early marriage . . . to secure . . . adult single women of respectable antecedents' to take part in overseas migration.[19] If the receiving colonies and the imperial government were concerned over the immoral character of the 'single' women migrants, the British Indian Government had another rather different headache. It was the recruitment of 'respectable' women that was causing all the fuss about 'kidnapping' in India – and their own officers were leading the opposition. Single women migrants were not unmarried; they were either married women or widows, deprived of familial resources due to disinheritance, desertion, neglect, barrenness or the transgression of social norms. These processes were not entirely new, but from the nineteenth century, such women may have been 'pushed' towards migration because they found themselves increasingly marginalized in the village economy. Their traditional occupations were in decline and they were dependent on returns from land, which were controlled by the men in the family. There were also unhappy wives, recalcitrant daughters and adventurous women, who may have been tempted by romance or the prospect of independent wage earning and seized at an opportunity for escape. Proportions are difficult to estimate, but recruiters' complaints seem to indicate that they cannot have been many. It is telling that recruiters found single women more readily in the port towns than in the rural hinterland (Sen 2004; Carter 1994). And yet, the numbers were not negligible. They often accounted for 70 per cent of female migrants. The women going to the cities and to the Assam plantations have to be added to these figures. Such women, even more than the men, were amenable to settlement in the colonies.[20] If we take the figures for Mauritius between 1834 and 1890, about 36 per cent of male migrants returned, but only 28 per cent of the women did so, and Mauritius had the lowest proportion of single women migrants.[21]

The disappearance of wives, daughters and mothers from homes in Indian villages provoked widespread outrage. In India, the migration of 'prostitutes', the flotsam and jetsam of bazaar women, was not a matter of as great concern as was the recruitment of 'respectable' women. Here, the disagreement was between those who upheld a woman's ability to contract and her 'right' to sell her labour and those who emphasized women's 'familial' role, their duties and obligations as wife and mother, and the rights of their husbands or guardians to their person, their labour and sexuality (Sen 1996).

British Indian Government was caught between the demand for, and the resistance to, the recruitment of so-called respectable women. From 1860, government regulation obliged Magistrates to detain possible runaways among the single women. Recruiters complained that Magistrates were too assiduous in this task, wantonly interfering with registration of women. In 1882–3, Major Pitcher and Dr Grierson went against the tenor of official opinion, to argue in favour of single women's migration.[22] Grierson argued that women, married or single, had 'a perfect power to enter a contract binding on herself' and 'at law a right like men to go where they please'.[23] Such a cavalier dismissal of the rights of fathers and husbands, however, placed them in a minority within government. The dismantling of family labour and familial authority was by no means in the interests of the British Indian state. These controversies led finally to the Act of 1901 (applicable to Assam migration), which forbade the recruitment of women without the consent of husband or guardian (Sen 1996).

The justification of such legislation flowed from the British Indian state's other major preoccupation in the nineteenth century, the 'Indian marriage' project. The government was trying to streamline marriage laws, not through homogeneous civil legislation but according to religion-based personal laws, which were grounded in textual scriptural prescriptions. In the case of both Hindus and Muslims, however, there were local caste and class variations in marriage, multiple and informal cohabitation practices and customary variations in systems of divorce and remarriage. The colonial state made a spirited attempt to impose Brahmanical or Sharia prescriptions on these marriage systems, through not only civil but also penal law, criminalizing in the process many of the customary marriage practices common among low-caste, poor and labouring groups. The implementation of marriage laws so much at variance with existing practices did not prove easy, giving rise to a range of contradictions and contestations (Sen 1999b). The gap between the state's agenda and popular usage produced gaps through which emerged the persistent image of the transgressive woman – asserting her rights of mobility – whether in terms of exit and entry into marriage or migration and labour contracts.

In their intentions as well as their effects, the new marriage laws were uneven across the genders and generations. For instance, the definition of monogamy grew more restrictive in relation to women, while men's right to polygamy was extended. Increasingly, women and children were immobilized within the family, their exit options closed by law. The Act of 1901 was a landmark in this process – it sought to prevent women from migrating without or against familial consent. The Act rendered women legal minors in migration decisions, on the grounds that the marriage contract disqualified them from entering a labour contract with an(other) employer. This law, applied primarily to migration under indenture, marked the convergence of legal discourses on labour and marriage, a process not yet addressed adequately in the historiography on South Asia. The Act of 1901 drew on the British notion of coverture, which disqualified married women from entering any contract; but it also cast marriage itself as a contract, thereby placing marriage and labour engagements at par, as contradictory contracts. These processes can be traced to Company regulations in the early nineteenth century, when both marriage and indenture were construed as unequal contracts, in which the subservient party (the woman and the worker) were deemed to have consented to the suspension or curtailment of their rights. Also remarkable is the ease with which this law pertaining to migration affirmed all marriages as contracts, when legal discussions about marriage had hinged so heavily on differentiating between sacramental (Hindu) marriage and contractual (Muslim) marriage.[24] These debates about family and marriage in India fed back into the colonies. Following from policies already set in motion in India, indenture alone was felt to be inadequate for disciplining transgressive women in the colonies; instead, marriage had to be harnessed to the project of disciplining women. The woman in the colony had to be doubly indentured – to their men as well as to their employers.

Disciplining women in the colonies: double indenture

There is now a considerable body of research on the projects to 'restore' or recreate the family among Indian workers in the colonies. Some historians, celebrating the re-establishment of family as a vindication of the rights of indentured Indian workers, have unwittingly affirmed official constructions (Tinker 1974; Cumpston 1969; Mangru 1987). European officials constructed the stereotype of the woman migrant either as the victim of fraud and trickery or as immoral and given to sexual anarchy. At both extremes, the lament was the absence of family to harness women – in monogamous marriage and in domesticity. The restoration of family served the purposes of colonial governments but is believed to have also ameliorated the dehumanizing consequences of indentured emigration. According to other historians, however, migration presented women with an opportunity to escape the 'illiberal, inhibiting and very hierarchical social system in India' (Emmer 1986: 247). Rhoda Reddock (1985) argued that migrant women were able to assert unparalleled social and sexual independence, empowered especially by the adverse sex ratio. They agree, however, that such opportunities coexisted with the exploitation of women's labour and sexuality on the plantations. Yet another group of historians have focused on the abundant evidence of sexually predatory employers, managers, overseers and male workers, dismissing the possibility of women's heightened agency in such circumstances (Beall 1990; Lal 1989). Verene Shepherd (2002) has argued persuasively that accounts of Indian women's sexploitation have to consider the whole experience of migration, including the long voyage on ship. In recent years, the focus has been on the management of gender relations in the plantation colonies: Prabhu Mohapatra (1995) and Madhavi Kale (1998) have argued persuasively, in the context of the Caribbean, for patriarchal reassertion and the domestication of women.

Most colonies, in recreating 'Indian marriage', took a path opposite to the one taken by the British Indian state. While, in India, marriage was being recast through religion-based personal laws, in the colonies, religious authority, destabilized by the conditions of migration, was disregarded altogether and civil marriage regimes with compulsory registration were more common. The state wanted direct mechanisms of control through written records over the Indian working population, who they perceived to be in a dangerous state of marital instability. The instrument they used, however, exacerbated the problem they wished to address. First, it rendered many marriages illegitimate, feeding the frenzy about sexual anarchy. Second, the gaps between law and custom allowed, especially in the initial period, some women easier exit and entry into cohabitation relations, some of which may have been consonant with their customary practices, but were, increasingly, at odds with both British Indian and colonial laws. Third, the dissonances with Indian law and custom regarding marriage became a plank in the movements against indentured migration in India.

The Mauritius government was the first to adopt the colonization project and also was the most successful in creating and maintaining 'Indian families'. Carter shows that women's role in providing wage subsidy was linked to the project of family and its instrument was the Indian Marriage Laws. Government introduced punitive sanctions that husbands could use against transgressive women. In 1853, marriages celebrated according to Indian rites were recognized; and, in 1856, a law was passed to punish those who enticed away wives of migrants. To prevent informal cohabitation practices, all marriages were subjected to civil registration. In the case of women, the marriage certificate and the immigration ticket became instruments of control. These measures did not, as they were supposed to do, reduce violence in marital relationships; rather, they encouraged transactions in women. There was little to distinguish between recruitment commissions and bride-price marriages, though the latter was justified as a cultural continuity. Most crucially, restrictive marriage laws often trapped women into attachments by mis-statement and bureaucratic bungles. On the whole, Carter argues, immobilizing women within conjugal households was given priority over their individual liberty (1994).

On the Caribbean sugar estates, women were engaged for labour, as Gladstone had insisted.[25] Despite the quota of 40 per cent, for most of the period of indentured emigration, women comprised about 25 per cent of indentured labourers. According to Mohapatra, the colonial state became concerned about the skewed sex ratio because of escalating violence against women and an epidemic of wife-murders that came to their notice in the 1870s. At their behest, the Government of India undertook searching enquiries but failed to find a specific Indian custom of 'wife-murder'. Finally convinced that these unhappy incidents were the consequence of colonial indentured migration, they sought a means of providing Indian workers with some social stability. The solution was the same as that prescribed for ex-slaves, the patriarchal family. In the process of creating families, women were transformed from wage workers to unpaid workers in the household. As in Mauritius, the disciplining of women was achieved through a series of Marriage Laws – providing for the formalizing of marriage on the one hand, and setting out penal offences in relation to marriage on the other (Mohapatra 1995: 231). The Indian community did not register marriages before 1887 and intermittently after that. They struggled instead for the recognition of Hindu and Muslim marriage ceremonies, battles that were to be won much later in the 1930s and 40s (Reddock 1985; Mohammed 1995). Through a second set of laws, however, Indian indentured men were able to reclaim some patriarchal authority. Trinidad and British Guiana followed in the footsteps of Mauritius to make it a penal offence to harbour a married woman (Mohapatra 1995). The marriage laws thus sought to empower husbands to control and immobilize women.

The question of women's migration proved an irritant in Natal as well, where women were a little less than one-third for most of the period of indenture.[26] There were, as a result, struggles around the control over women. The option not to work, and a high rate of childbirth, meant that women were economically dependent on men for longer periods. In these circumstances, women sought to negotiate their situation through their relationships with men – by marriage, adultery, desertion and remarriage. In 1872, following the Coolie Commission, the registration of marriages became compulsory. Polygamy became illegal in Natal for Indian men from 1891. These regulations meant that many Indian cohabitation practices remained outside the legal net of the colonial state. Jo Beall shows how the patriarchal collusion between the colonial state, the estate owners and Indian men bore down on women. While this is undoubtedly true, Natal's hesitation to introduce Indian personal laws for the Indian workers, because of their radical divergence from European Christian practices, allowed slippages between Natal law and Indian custom, providing women with some elbow room (Beall 1990).

In the sugar estates, thus, indenture and marriage converged as instruments for the control of women's labour. In 1894, in a report, Surgeon-Major Comins had recommended the reduction of women's indenture from five to two years in the West Indies.[27] In 1897, the recommendation was adopted, but the period was reduced to three years. By 1904, planters began to complain about women seeking release after three years. In their understanding, the indenture – obliging the worker to remain in the estate – ran for the full five years, the three years applied only to labour. The intention behind the change was to encourage women's migration, but its justification was to give women time off for child-bearing. This did not mean that women were eligible for release after three years, planters argued.[28] The British Indian Government upheld this view on moral grounds: married women, if released, would acquire an incentive to desert their husbands.[29]

These tensions meant that there were two options before the colonial government: to abolish indenture for women altogether and depend upon marriage alone to tie the women to the plantation, or to equalize the indenture period again. The Immigration Agent-General of British Guiana opposed the abolition of indenture on the grounds that indenture alone compelled women to learn the work of the sugar estates. If the indenture was retained, however, an early release from labour obligation would be in name only, he believed. Women's desire for release from labour would be countermanded by familial authority:

> having been once initiated into the use of implements, and having become accustomed to regular work, *their husbands may be trusted not to allow them to retain (sic!) idle*, emptiers and not fillers of the family purse. For this purpose a two years' indenture would be sufficient.[30]

But marital authority was still very much in the making in the sugar estates. The Inspector of Immigration had little faith in the power of husbands: 'the idea that husbands can or would venture to put pressure upon their wives is a mistaken one, because owing to the disparity of the sexes, women are too well aware of their value to submit'.[31] In the West Indies, the lines between women's labouring and reproductive functions remained fuzzy. Despite the success of Mauritius in attracting women migrants by exempting them from field labour, the colonies in the West Indies were resistant to the idea of importing women without formal obligation to labour. His solution to the entire issue was gender equalization of labour and bondage; men and women should alike be indentured for five years' labour.[32]

The Indian family abroad: women, honour and the nation

There had been opposition to indentured emigration from India from its very inception. This gathered greater force in the early twentieth century, culminating in a movement led by prominent members of the Congress. Between 1910 and 1920, Indian nationalists seized the political initiative, forcing the British Indian Government into damaging admissions about the conditions of workers in the sugar plantations. Gopal Krishna Gokhale was its first spokesperson; the mantle was later assumed by Mahatma Gandhi. In 1910, after the findings of the Sanderson Committee, indentured emigration to Mauritius and Malaya ceased quietly. In the meanwhile, Gandhi's *satyagraha* had drawn attention to the condition of Indians in South Africa. In 1911, emigration to Natal was stopped. The same year, Gokhale suggested that the penal provisions of the labour contract be explained to intending emigrants to ensure their informed consent. The Government of India had no defence against such a reasonable demand.[33]

The 'slavery' into which Indian labourers emigrated was an emotive plank in anti-indenture rhetoric, and the degradation of women, an imagery already established in the debates over recruitment, provided its most potent symbol. In a discursive sweep, women's recruitment for indentured emigration became connected to nationalism. The voices against the indentured system enunciated a nationalist patriarchy, which spoke of protection of women but also of control and discipline. These linkages had already been made in the heyday of cultural nationalism – with the celebration of women's willed subjection to patriarchal authority, of the unequal and illiberal institution of marriage as the marker of Indian (or Hindu or Muslim) identity, of the hierarchical family as the site of resistance to Westernization and modernization (Sarkar 2000). Thus, existing debates over forms of marriages in the plantation colonies were politicized in new ways. The struggles over the recognition of religion-based marriages in the plantation colonies spoke to nationalist concerns over reconstitution of caste and gender relations in the diasporic 'Indian' communities.

In 1911, Gokhale drew the attention of the government to the disputes over marriage laws in the colonies. In 1897, there had been considerable discussion on marriage between the Governments of India, Britain and Mauritius; and in 1912 the Committee on Emigration from India to the Crown Colonies recommended the recognition of Hindu and Muslim marriages.[34] James McNeil and Chimman Lal's report recommended that marriages prior to 1881 be registered.[35]

In India, the British gave some purchase to localized rights within the larger legal regime, allowing religion-based community law to govern the family, for instance. Even so, the identification of legal authorities within each community involved sweeping homogenization, creating a persistent tension between law and custom in disputes over marriage. Other territories of the Empire, however, which received indentured Indian workers, experienced the imposition of superordinate British imperial law, which privileged civil law based on English ecclesiastical practices.[36] Some of the French colonies had, similarly, been inducted into the metropolitan legal regime. In determining the marital rights of Indian communities in the plantation colonies, these two kinds of imperial policies collided. The Government of Trinidad would not agree to register marriages prior to 1881. In British Guiana, the Registrar-General inverted the logic of this request. His suggestion was that registration be made compulsory and that priests, guardians and the parties be penalized if they neglected to register marriages.[37]

The recalcitrance displayed by the overseas colonial authorities over marriage laws provided the Indian anti-indentured movement with a potent and emotive issue. In elaborating their concerns, they drew on the negative imagery already established in the long and bitter debates around women's recruitment. The indentured woman as a victim of sexual exploitation was the first and perhaps the most evocative symbol in the nationalist battle against the indenture system. If the earlier debates had focused on women as victims of the lust and violence of their own men, now the nationalists shifted the focus to race. White men, plantation bosses and overseers preying on helpless and 'wholly unprotected'[38] women provided a rallying point against emigration. The issue was further sensationalized by the publication of a short account of the travails of Kunti, who jumped into a river to protect herself from the 'beastly assault' of the overseer in a Fiji plantation, entitled 'The Wails of a Woman' in *Bharat Mitra* on 1 August 1913.[39] Around the same time, the Marwari Association (also called the Anti-Indentured Emigration League or the Indentured Cooly Protection Society) published a number of depositions of returning emigrants. The returnees emphasized the way in which Europeans took a fancy to Indian women workers, kept them for some time and then turned them out. According to such testimony, rape and molestation led to frequent suicides by women.[40] Several returnees spoke of a harsh labour regime, underlining that women had to work even in an advanced stage of pregnancy. Totaram Sanadhy swore that he had seen many cases of women being delivered of child while at work.[41] By bringing into play a new dimension of race to the existing gender question, such critics were able to harness to their cause a powerful idiom of national honour (Sen 1994).

The protection of national honour involved disciplining the incipient nation's women. The idea that the women emigrants were 'prostitutes', and were being used as prostitutes in the estates, was an old one repeatedly reaffirmed in the 1910s (Shepherd 2002). Mangal Chand, a Brahmin returning from Trinidad, testified that men and women immigrants lived as husbands and wives 'although they are not married to each other'.[42] Some of the men expressed outrage over widows living in concubinage. Ram Narayan Sharma, a medical doctor, provided a graphic account of such immorality – 'women of loose morals take to many husbands and run away from each after a short period with clothes, cash and jewellery'. Such sexual anarchy led, he argued, much as colonial governments had done some 40 years ago, to suicides and murders. To Sharma, the links were clear: immorality was the inevitable consequence of the derecognition of marriages according to Hindu and Muslim rites and the erosion of social and religious mores.[43] In this upside-down world, gender and caste hierarchy, and the foundation of social order, had been undermined. In its own petition, the Marwari Association dealt with these issues at length. The recruitment of women led to the 'undoing of many a family and the wrecking of many a home in the country' on the one hand; on the other, the exportation of high-caste men and women, who were 'unfit for manual work' meant, under conditions of indenture, intercaste marriages. Not only were the children of such unions unable to return to India, 'a race of Indians of nameless caste' was growing up in the colonies. And, by their 'low standards of social, moral and religious life', they were doing 'incalculable harm to India in many important respects'.[44]

Many of the arguments made in the petitions and publications of anti-indenture lobbyists were premised on the absence of marriage – or, rather, the absence of Hindu and Muslim marriage. And yet, they also supplied the answers themselves. A religion-based marriage system would have played havoc with inter-caste and inter-religious marriages, which had become possible with civil registration. The high rates of inter-caste and inter-religious marriages did not, however, extend to inter-racial marriages (Diptee 2003). By design or default, perhaps a bit of both, the focus on an Indian marriage system did contribute towards the creation of 'Indian' communities in the colonies, albeit with drastically altered caste and gender configurations.

Within a few years of Gokhale's searching questions about consent in contract and the validity of Indian marriages in the colonies, the First World War put a summary stop to shipments of labour. In 1917, government proposed a new scheme to address the most controversial aspects of labour export. In section 8, they proposed to discontinue the women's quota: emigration of 'whole families' was to be encouraged; and women unaccompanied by their families would not be assisted to migrate. Another complementary change was in section 12: marriages celebrated according to 'religion or caste custom of the parties' and 'duly celebrated according to the rites of the particular religion or caste' as long as such was not 'repugnant to the marriage laws of the Colonies' were to be considered valid.[45] The Government of India, in a dispatch to the Secretary of State, admitted, however, that the 'sex question' would not be easily solved.[46] In 1917, indentured emigration ceased, but indentured Indians remained in the many colonies to which they had gone. It took another three years for all the dust to settle. When the system was in its death throes, in 1919, Fiji sent desperate appeals for labour to the Government of India. Unfortunately for them, C. F. Andrews, Gandhi's associate, had done his work too well. In 1918, he had released an admission in a Fiji medical report that Indian women have 'to serve three indentured men, as well as various outsiders' and he continued to bring evidence of 'gross abuse' of Indian women to public notice (Tinker 1974: 359). The resulting furore persuaded the Government of India to request Fiji to cancel outstanding indentures to pave the way for voluntary migration.

The 'sex question' proved to be biggest rock of the many on which indentured emigration foundered after the First World War. If the sugar plantocracy's indifference to women migrants caused the first tensions and anxieties in the early nineteenth century, the change of focus to creating families and the recruiting of respectable women for such purpose turned out to be the bigger challenge. For the entire period of the indenture system, the circumlocutory debates over women's recruitment persisted both in India and the colonies – polarized between control and freedom – and displaced on to 'honour' in the nationalist discourse. The image of the Indian woman migrant as prostitute travelled from India via the ships to the colonial plantations and returned to the country in print, to linger until indenture's very end.

Notes

1 Bihar State Archives, Patna (henceforth, BSA) General Emigration, July 1895, A 1–5, 5-R/13.
2 BSA, Monthly Bundles, February 1874, No. 775.
3 West Bengal State Archives, Calcutta (henceforth, WBSA) General Emigration, April 1872, A 118.
4 These ratios changed over time and for different colonies several times in the nineteenth century.
5 WBSA, General Emigration, December 1912, A 6–19, File 3E/5.
6 Report on the Emigration from the Port of Calcutta to British and Foreign Colonies, 1875–1880.
7 BSA, General Emigration, May 1885, No. 6–8.
8 IOR V/26/820/2, J. P. Grant's *Minute on the Cooly Question*, Vol. 2, 1840.
9 WBSA, General Emigration, January 1862, A6. Letter from W. F. Fergusson, Secretary, Landholders and Commercial Association, to E. H. Lushington, Secretary, Government of Bengal, 30 December 1861.
10 The colonies usually appointed agents in Calcutta, Bombay and Madras, who contracted out recruitment to sub-agents working on commission. The tea planters employed licensed labour contractors and *Garden Sardars*, reliable workers who were paid fees and costs to bring more workers directly to the gardens. The labour contractors employed a labyrinthine network of commissioned agents, sometimes called the *arkathis*.
11 E. Van Cutsem, Emigration Agent for Surinam to the Protector of Emigrants, Calcutta, BSA, General Emigration, May 1885, No. 6–8.
12 Lord Salisbury to the Governor-General of India in Council, 24 March 1875; *Report of the Indian Jute Manufacturers' Association*, Calcutta, 1899.
13 A very rough estimate put together from various sources (Kumar *et al.* 1983 [1989]: 513; Mohapatra 2004; Rao 1946: 445–8).
14 WBSA, General Emigration, July 1912, A 1–6, Report on Emigration from the Port of Calcutta to British and Foreign Colonies for the year 1911.
15 WBSA, Commerce Emigration, July 1918, A 17–18, Report on Emigration from the Port of Calcutta to British and Foreign Colonies for the year 1917.

16 IOR V/26/820/2, J. P. Grant's *Minute on the Cooly Question*, Vol. 2, 1840. Appendix to Minute 2.
17 BSA, General Emigration, March 1885, No. 6–8.
18 WBSA General Emigration, December 1912, A 6–19, 3E/5.
19 WBSA Commerce Emigration, July 1918, A 1–16, File 3E/1–1.
20 The same argument holds for rural–urban migration (Sen 1999a).
21 WBSA General Emigration, July 1895, A 1–5, File 5-R/13.
22 BSA, General Emigration, May 1885, No. 6–8.
23 Quoting Grierson (Kale 1998: 166).
24 The tremendous opposition to the passing of the Act III of 1872 was based largely on the argument that it regarded marriage as a contract (Chakraborty 2009).
25 BSA General Emigration, 1904, A 42–6, File 13C/1/1. Also see Finance Emigration, January 1914 A 30–5, 3E-2.
26 WBSA General Emigration, March 1911, B 13, 3F/2. Government of Bengal contemplated discontinuing emigration to Natal due to the repeated shortfall in the quota of women; Agents raised the commission for women.
27 WBSA General Emigration, January, 1894, A 4–8, File 3E-3.
28 BSA General Emigration, 1904, A 42–6, File 13C/1/1.
29 WBSA Finance Emigration, January 1914, A 30–5, File 3E-2.
30 Note dated 13 June 1910. Ibid. Emphasis in original.
31 F. Gibson, Inspector of Immigrants, Southern Division to the Protector of Immigrants, 1 June 1911. Ibid.
32 Letter from Protector of Emigrants, Calcutta, 5 December 1913. Ibid.
33 WBSA General Emigration, November 1912, A 32–42, 9-R/5.
34 WBSA General Emigration, December 1912, A 6–19, 3E/5, Enclosure 1.
35 WBSA Finance Emigration, January 1914, A 30–5, File 3E-2.
36 Craven and Hay, *Masters, Servants and Magistrates*, Introduction, p. 55.
37 WBSA Finance Emigration, January 1914, A 30–5, File 3E-2.
38 The quote is from the testimony of Buldeo Thakur, a returning migrant from Fiji. Deposition, Calcutta Police Court, 27 July 1914. WBSA Finance Emigration, November 1915, B 5–7, File 3-E/6–6. 'Representation of the Marwari Association, Calcutta, About Recruitment of Indian Labourers for the Colonies' (henceforth, Marwari Association).
39 Reprinted in Marwari Association. The story has been discussed in detail by Brij Lal (1989).
40 Buldeo Thakur, Marwari Association. Also the Ram Narayan Sharma, 'The Law for Coolies in British Guiana', *Bharat Mitra*, 25 March 1914 (included in the same papers).
41 Totaram Sanadhy, deposition in Calcutta Police Court, 13 July 1914. Ibid. Buldeo Thakur, Ibid.
42 Mangal Chand, Calcutta Police Court, 16 July 1914. Marwari Association.
43 Sharma, 'The Law for Coolies in British Guiana'.
44 Ramdeo Chotham, Honorary Secretary, Marwari Association to the Secretary to the Government of Bengal, General Department, 5 August 1915. WBSA Commerce Emigration, July 1918, A1–16. Similar arguments were being made by missionaries. See Richard Piper, 'Indian Indentured Labourers: How they are in Fiji', *The Statesman*, 15 January 1915.
45 WBSA Commerce Emigration, July 1918, A 1–16. Report of the Inter-Departmental Conference on Assisted Emigration from India to British Guiana, Trinidad, Jamaica and Fiji.
46 Despatch No. 5 (Emigration) of 23 March 1917. Ibid.

References

Anderson, M. 2004. 'India, 1858–1930: The Illusion of Free Labour' in Douglas Hay and Paul Craven (eds) *Masters, Servants and Magistrates in Britain and the Empire, 1562–1955*, University of North Carolina Press, Chapel Hill and London.
Beall, J. 1990. 'Women under Indenture in Colonial Natal 1860–1911' in C. Clarke, C. Peach and S. Vertovek (eds) *South Asians Overseas: Migration and Ethnicity*, Cambridge University Press, Cambridge.
Brereton, B. 1974. 'The Experience of Indentureship 1854–1917' in John La Guerre (ed.), *Calcutta to Caroni*, Longmans, Caribbean.
Carter, M. 1994. *Lakshmi's Legacy. The Testimonies of Indian Women in 19th Century Mauritius*, Editions de l'Océan Studies, Stanley, Rose-Hill, Mauritius.

Chakraborty, A. 2009. 'Contract, Consent and Ceremony: The Brahmo Marriage Reform (1868–1920)', *Journal of History*, 26, pp. 64–98.

Cumpston, I. M. 1969. *Indians Overseas in British Territories*, Oxford: Oxford University Press.

Diptee, A. 2003. 'Cultural Transfer and Transformation: Revisiting Indo-African Sexual Relationships in Trinidad and British Guiana in the Late Nineteenth Century' in Sandra Courtman (ed.) The Society for Caribbean Studies Annual Conference Papers, 4, www.scsonline.freeserve.co.uk/olvo14.html (16.8.1010).

Emmer, P. C. 1986. 'The Great Escape: The Migration of Female Indentured Servants from British India to Surinam 1873–1916' in D. Richardson (ed.), *Abolition and Its Aftermath*, London: Frank Cass.

Hay, Douglas and Craven, Paul. 2004. *Masters, Servants and Magistrates in Britain and the Empire, 1562–1955*, University of North Carolina Press, Chapel Hill and London.

Kale, M. 1998. *Fragments of Empire. Capital, Slavery, and Indian Indentured Labor Migration in the British Caribbean*, University of Pennsylvania Press, Philadelphia.

Kumar, D., Tapan Raychaudhuri, Dharma Kumar and Irfan Habib. 1983. *The Cambridge Economic History of India*, 2, Cambridge University Press, Cambridge (reprint 1989).

Lal, B. 1989. 'Kunti's Cry: Indentured Women in Fiji Plantations' in J. Krishnamurty (ed.) *Women in Colonial India: Essays on Survival, Work and the State*, Oxford University Press, Delhi.

Mangru, B. 1987. 'The Sex Ratio Disparity and its Consequences in British Guiana' in D. Dabydeen and B. Samaroo (eds) *India in the Caribbean*, London: Hansib.

Mohammed, P. 1995. 'Writing Gender into History: The Negotiation of Gender Relations Among Indian Men and Women in Post-Indenture Trinidad Society, 1917–1947' in Verene Shepherd, Bridget Brereton and Barbara Bailey (eds) *Engendering History: Caribbean Women in Historical Perspective*, St. Martin's Press, New York, pp. 20–47.

Mohapatra, P. 1995. '"Restoring the Family": Wife Murders and the Making of a Sexual Contract for Indian Immigrant Labour in the British Caribbean Colonies, 1860–1920', *Studies in History*, 11, pp. 227–60.

—— 2004. 'Assam and the West Indies, 1860–1920: Immobilising Plantation Labour' in Douglas Hay and Paul Craven (eds) *Masters, Servants and Magistrates in Britain and the Empire, 1562–1955*, University of North Carolina Press, Chapel Hill and London.

Moore, B. L. 1991. 'Mating Patterns and Gender Relations Among Indians in Nineteenth-Century Guyana', *Guyana Historical Journal*, III, pp. 1–12.

Rao, M. V. S. 1946. 'A Statistical Study of Labour in the Assam Tea Plantation', *Sankhyā: The Indian Journal of Statistics*, 7, 4 (July), pp. 445–8, www.jstor.org/stable/25047893.

Reddock, R. 1985. 'Freedom Denied: Indian Women and Indentureship in Trinidad and Tobago, 1845–1917', *Economic and Political Weekly*, 20, 43.

Sarkar, T. 2000. *Hindu Wife, Hindu Nation. Community, Religion and Cultural Nationalism*, New Delhi: Permanent Black.

Sen, S. 1994. 'Honour and Resistance: Gender, Community and Class in Bengal, 1920–40' in Sekhar Bandopadhyay, Abhijit Dasgupta and Willem van Schendel (eds), *Bengal: Communities, Development and States*, Manohar Publications.

—— 1996. 'Unsettling the Household: Act VI (of 1901) and the Regulation of Women Migrants in Colonial Bengal' in Shahid Amin and Marcel van der Linden (eds) 'Peripheral' Labour? Studies in the History of Partial Proletarianization. *International Review of Social History*, Supplement 4, 41.

—— 1999a. *Women and Labour in Late Colonial India. The Bengal Jute Industry*, Cambridge University Press, Cambridge.

—— 1999b. 'Offences Against Marriage: Negotiating Custom in Colonial Bengal' in Janaki Nair and Mary John (eds), *A Question of Silence? The Sexual Economies of Modern India*, Kali for Women, New Delhi.

—— 2002. 'Questions of Consent: Women's Recruitment for Assam Tea Gardens, 1859–1900', *Studies in History*, 18, 2, pp. 231–60.

—— 2004. '"Without His Consent"? Marriage and Women's Migration in Colonial India' in Rick Halpern *et al.* (ed.) special issue *International Labour and Working Class History*, 65, Spring.

—— 2010. 'Commercial Recruiting and Informal Mediation: Debate over the Sardari System in Assam Tea Plantations, 1860–1900', *Modern Asian Studies*, 44, 1, pp. 3–28.

Shepherd, V. 2002. *Maharani's Misery. Narratives of a Passage from India to the Caribbean*, University of the West Indies Press, Kingston.

Tinker, H. 1974. *A New System of Slavery: The Export of Indian Labour Overseas, 1830–1920*, Oxford University Press, Oxford.

9

THE AGE OF THE 'LASCAR'

South Asian seafarers in the times of imperial steam shipping

Ravi Ahuja

Contexts of shipping and of South Asian seafaring

Oceanic shipping relies on the availability of a spatially mobile maritime workforce to generate conditions for extended circuits and accelerated rhythms of mobility and exchange. This dynamic interdependency has been articulated differentially in changing historical contexts resulting in distinct institutional and socio-spatial arrangements. Steam shipping, in the age of imperialism, thus generated altogether new patterns of circulation, though not from its first appearance and without displacing older patterns altogether.

Famously, the first steamer shipped Asian waters, namely those of the Ganga, as early as in 1821. Yet it took more than half a century to raise the energy-efficiency of the new technology to a level that permitted steamers to compete with wind-driven clippers in intercontinental bulk trade. Sailing vessels were only then gradually relegated to the lower, less profitable, echelons of Indian Ocean maritime traffic. Shipping was turned into a highly capital-intensive industry and contributed to the emergence, in Europe and especially in Britain, of a small number of powerful shipping concerns. Of these, the British India Steam Navigation Company and the Peninsular and Oriental Steam Shipping Company were the most significant in Indian Ocean shipping and reinforced their hold by way of merger in 1914. During the interwar period, this powerful concern alone accounted for up to 30 per cent of the steam shipping in Indian ports. Such trusts were inextricably entangled with their respective imperialist states through means such as mail contracts, troop transports and exchange of management personnel.

Even though the new steamers required heavy initial investment as well as new, expensive and more centralised port facilities, their utilisation permitted a considerable reduction of the costs of maritime transport and facilitated an unprecedented expansion of the carrying capacity of the world merchant fleet (the statistically recognised part of which almost trebled between 1850 and 1910). This accelerated and cheapened not only global commodity trade but also permitted the long- or medium-term supply of labour to areas where capital demanded it on a new scale, including indentured labour for colonial plantation economies. The cheaper, quicker and more regular sea voyages offered by the steamship companies permitted, moreover, the emergence of new forms of transoceanic mobility that involved a wider range of social groups and implied shorter periods of travel and absence from home. Steam shipping also afforded and permitted the utilisation of new infrastructures, namely of the Suez Canal, which reduced the length of the shipping routes between Asia and Europe (between London and Bombay, for instance, by 41 percent), thereby facilitating the integration of their commodity and labour markets. As the tonnage passing the Suez Canal increased tenfold between 1875 and 1914, the maritime circuits of the Indian Ocean and the Atlantic were more directly connected through the Mediterranean and fused to a considerable extent (Ahuja 2004).

Changing patterns of maritime commodity and passenger transport and associated economic and technological transformations of the shipping industry generated equally dynamic work scenarios. Ships are transport facilities as well as work sites, but the work site 'ship' has been transformed almost beyond recognition not once, but twice, over the last two centuries. The sailing vessel is an altogether different work environment from the motorised ship that came to dominate maritime transport in the 1880s and held its own, with substantial technological changes, until the mid-twentieth century. These coal- or oil-fuelled ships have again little in common not only with the aeroplanes that replaced them almost entirely in transcontinental passenger transport in the second half of the twentieth century but also with the container ships that revolutionised freight shipping and ship work around the same time. Numerous South Asians were and are among the crews of all these distinct types of vessels, but their social origins, labour relations, skills, work patterns, rhythms of employment and the modalities of their mobility have varied considerably. This essay mainly explores the forms of South Asian maritime employment and their impact on transoceanic mobility between the 1880s and the 1960s, but begins with a brief account of the preceding scenario and its transformation.

The term 'lascar' is derived from the Persian word 'lashkar' (armed formation) and was used from the sixteenth century to designate both Indian seamen and certain kinds of military labour, mainly camp-followers and inferior artillerymen (Yule and Burnell 1983/1903: 507–9). 'Lascars' were employed on European ships in the Indian Ocean as soon as the Portuguese gained a foothold on the subcontinent. They usually belonged to seafaring and fishing communities inhabiting the coastline where maritime skills were passed down from one generation to the next. Before the latter half of the nineteenth century, the employment of 'lascars' on European sailing vessels remained restricted largely to the so-called 'country trade', i.e. to voyages within the Indian Ocean rim. Even when crews for British men-of-war were in unprecedented demand during the Napoleonic Wars and restrictions on the employment of 'foreign' seafarers were relaxed, the number of 'lascars' reaching Britain increased from a few hundred to about one thousand only. This limited group of 'Asiatics' attracted extraordinary public attention in Britain, especially as naval warfare and the seasonal rhythm of wind-driven shipping caused prolonged and often economically precarious stays of 'lascars' in London and other ports (Fisher 2006; Visram 1986). Moreover, the term 'lascar' was regionally rather unspecific in this period and could refer to seamen not only from the subcontinent but from various regions of the Indian Ocean rim. The proverbial 'motley crew' was fairly common on sailing vessels that recruited labour in the Indian Ocean region: seafarers from Southeast Asia, South Asia, East Africa, the Red Sea and Gulf regions frequently worked together under the supervision of a boatswain or 'sarhang' (Anglicised: 'serang', 'sarong').

This arrangement on board ship was based on equally 'cosmopolitan' maritime labour markets in port cities: large numbers of East African seafarers could be found in Bombay, for instance, well into the latter half of the nineteenth century. There were also no separate labour markets for local and European sailing vessels on the Indian subcontinent: British and other European shipmasters tapped into the existing labour market and had to adjust to local structures of maritime work that included, for instance, the seafarer's customary right to a portion of the freight and to conduct his own petty trade. Finally, there was no clear-cut racial hierarchy with regard to compensation. While the wages of 'lascars' and European seamen could diverge substantially in the eighteenth and early nineteenth centuries to the disadvantage of the former, there is no evidence for a persistent and structured wage discrimination of 'coloured seafarers' of the kind that came to prevail throughout the period of steam shipping and beyond (Dixon 1980; Ewald 2000; Fisher 2006; Ahuja 2008).

The gradual rise to dominance of steam shipping precipitated a fundamental transformation of these patterns of Indian Ocean seafaring. If the opening of the Suez Canal (1869) facilitated an integration of the maritime circuits of the Indian Ocean and the Atlantic, this tendency also encompassed the circuits of maritime employment. 'Lascar' employment ceased to be mainly confined to the Indian Ocean and the numbers of 'Asiatic seafarers' toiling on British merchant ships increased substantially between the 1880s and World War I. While an employment figure of 10,000 to 12,000 'lascars' on British merchant ships (about 60 per cent of them of South Asian origin) has been estimated for 1855, the maritime census data give us 16,673 'lascars' for 1888, 51,616 for 1914 and 50,700 for 1938. The proportional growth is even more pronounced as the British merchant navy's total employment figures expanded from 204,470 men in 1888 to 295,652 in 1914 to decline to 192,375 in the course of the interwar period. Hence 'lascars' represented a proportion among the crews of the British merchant marine of 1 in 12 in 1888, of 1 in 6 in 1914 and of 1 in 4 in both 1938 and 1960. Ten thousands of additional 'lascars' were hired by non-British (and especially German) steamship companies in this period: the 'Hansa Line' of Bremen alone recruited 4,000 'lascars' every year in the early 1900s and the number of Indian seafarers shipped from the ports of Calcutta and Bombay annually in the 1920s ranged between 77,000 and 93,000 (Ahuja 2008). In our own times, the number of Indian seamen has dropped, according to union figures, to about 35,000.[1] Hence the period between 1880 and 1960 may be called, if only for simple quantitative reasons, the 'age of the lascar'.

In this period, the South Asian market for labour on mainly European-owned steamers was separated, to a very considerable extent, from the market for labour on sailing vessels that were mainly owned by Indians and remained sizeable (about 40,000 for Western India alone as late as at the beginning of World War II), though usually below the radar of colonial officialdom. To begin with, steamship workers were recruited almost exclusively in the two main steamer ports Calcutta and Bombay (and, to a minor extent, in Karachi), while sailing vessels continued to operate and draw their crews from small ports, many of them located in princely states of Western India. Moreover, steamship crews were more differentiated in terms of both skill and work organisation than crews of sailing vessels. While most seamen serving on *kotias* and other local sailing craft required specific maritime skills that were the preserve of certain coastal communities, on motorised vessels this was only the case for the deckhands, who accounted for about a third of the steam shipping workforce. As engines had to be kept under steam, and as an increasingly large number of transcontinental passengers wished to be served on board the new and capacious motorised 'liners', two entirely new departments emerged that functioned quite separately from each other and from that of the deck crew. Firemen and stewards required skills other than those passed on by maritime communities. They could be (and were) recruited from regions in the interior of the subcontinent, often hundreds of kilometres away from the recruitment ports – regions without any previous link to seafaring. The majority of the 235,000 men who reportedly looked for employment on steamers in 1930 originated in all likeliness from agricultural, predominantly smallholding, rather than maritime backgrounds (Balachandran 1997; Ahuja 2004, 2008).

Steamship crews were not only divided into these three compartments, under the immediate command of the chief officer, the chief engineer and the purser respectively, there was also a tendency away from the 'motley crew' of the sailing vessel. In Bombay more than in Calcutta, in times of economic crises and maritime labour plenty more than during the World Wars and other periods of maritime labour scarcity, the tendency was instead towards ethnic homogenisation within each department of the steamship. In Bombay, major employers preferred a crew consisting of Gujarati or Konkani deckhands, of Goan catholic stewards and Zanzibari firemen, the latter being systematically replaced by Punjabis and Pashtuns by the end of the nineteenth century. In Calcutta, deckhands were often recruited from Chittagong, Noakhali and other coastal districts of Eastern Bengal but also from the Maldive and Laccadive islands. Stewards frequently originated from urban Northern and Eastern India as well as from Goa. As for firemen, the interior district of Sylhet, bordering on Assam, emerged as the most important recruitment region by far. More detailed investigations show that core regions of recruitment were sometimes highly concentrated – certain village clusters are identifiable both in the case of the uniformly Roman Catholic Goan stewards (who mostly hailed from the *velha conquistas* in the interior) and of Muslim Sylheti firemen (who predominantly lived in what has been called the 'seamen's zone' of the central lowlands of Sylhet). The demise of the 'motley crew' was also reflected in a geographically narrower meaning of the word 'lascar' itself, which was no longer used as a broad designation for all Indian Ocean seafarers by the early twentieth century, but rather as a legal term applicable only to seafarers originating from all territories under the Viceroy of India (including Aden) and other Indian territories such as Goa or the princely states (Adams 1994; Choudhury 1993, 1995; Gardner 2000; Ahuja 2006, 2008).

We have seen that the late nineteenth-century market for South Asian steamship labour was based on the older maritime labour market only to the limited extent that deck crews were still mostly recruited from communities that had been connected to the sailing trade for generations. In the main, this was a *newly generated labour market*, however. It was new, first of all, because about two-thirds of the seafarers originated from social contexts with no previous maritime links. It was new, second, since it was concentrated in the social environment of the recently installed steamer ports of Bombay and Calcutta, where it was interconnected with other sectors of the market for transport labour of these expanding colonial metropolises. It was a new market, third, as its institutional structure was radically different from that of the maritime labour market in the age of sail. The market for South Asian steamship labour was regulated, as we shall see, in novel and particular ways that defined it persistently as a 'sub-market', as the lowest segment in a global labour market that was hierarchically compartmentalised according to criteria of racial difference.

The 'docility' of the 'lascar': structures and contradictions of a segmented labour market

Between 1888 and 1901, the employment of Asian seafarers on British merchant steamers more than doubled, which triggered off a fierce debate among the British public on the desirability of this development. Much of this debate was framed in the language of race by both the proponents and the opponents of 'lascar' employment. Jingoistic critics, including the National Sailor's and Firemen's Union under the leadership of the liberal MP Joseph Havelock Wilson, demanded the exclusion of 'lascars' from employment of British ships as these supposedly weakly, effeminate and rustic Orientals compared unfavourably with the tough, virile and salt-blooded English Jack Tar. The English, they argued, as the most maritime of races, had a birthright to maritime employment and their replacement with 'Asiatics' who could not weather storms, ship accidents or naval battles constituted a grave risk to British lives and property as well as to imperial security. The proponents of 'lascar' employment, among them the directors of leading shipping concerns, readily admitted that 'the Asiatic ocean labourer [was] displacing the European at his own game' (Hood 1903: 12) insisting, however, on the inevitability of this process on equally racial grounds: the British sailor's 'virility' was reinterpreted as a disposition to indiscipline, drunkenness and violence. A contemporary pamphlet condemned the 'blight of insubordination' that the British sailor inflicted on the industry. This, the proponents argued, rendered his employment increasingly untenable in the age of steam, when the profitability of shipping depended on the adherence to temporal schedules, namely on the punctual departure of a ship from a port with a complete crew, to a much higher degree than in the age of sail. As P&O supremo Sir Thomas Sutherland put it before a parliamentary committee: 'a liner, and by that I mean a mail steamer, has to be at each point at a given date, and we found our European crews would not bring us to those given points at those given dates' (Mercantile Marine Committee 1903, vol. 2: 77). The supporters of 'lascar' employment conceded to the critics that unmanly 'docility' was a racial trait of the 'Asiatic', but assigned a different value to it: 'docility', in their view, was not a vice but a virtue that was fully attuned to the need of the new, capital-intensive shipping industry to reduce lay days to an absolute minimum. The following were pointed out as the major advantages: first, the sheer presence of an Asian crew on board ship could be ensured more easily when in port; second, desertion rates were remarkably low; third, the authority of officers was less frequently challenged on board ship.

The superior 'discipline' of the 'lascar' was, however, not construed to imply a greater amenability to industrial time discipline in the labour process itself. Here the argument was fully consonant with the general discourse of colonial industrial employers: 'lascars' worked allegedly less intensively and productively than European seamen, which was adduced as a reason for their consistently lower wages. Further essentialist arguments for the employment of 'lascars' included the assertion that 'native crews' were 'better suited' to work in the 'tropics' than European crews, especially to cope with the excessive heat that developed in the engine room when outside temperatures soared. Even the cost benefits of 'lascar' employment were often justified as mere derivatives of racial difference: 'Asiatics' 'required' smaller and cheaper food rations, 'needed' only half the accommodation space of a European and would actually complain about quarters that were well aired and lit according to European standards. Even more ingeniously, it was also asserted that Indians reached adulthood at an earlier age and could thus be employed young at low pay (Manning Committee 1896; Mercantile Marine Committee 1903; Hood 1903, Ahuja 2005).

The self-interested utility of the assumption of a fundamental racial difference of the 'native' seafarer as a means to naturalise (and hence legitimise) particularly high levels of economic exploitation is clearly evident. Even so, several peculiarities of South Asian maritime employment relations that are ascribed, in this discourse, to an innate 'docility' of the 'lascar', beg explanation. Why is it that South Asian seafarers' wages amounted consistently to between a fifth and a third of a European seaman's pay since the mid-nineteenth century and well into the second half of the twentieth century? Why were desertion rates of 'lascars' reportedly lower than those of European and Chinese seafarers? Why were larger strike movements among Indian seafarers observable only since the late 1930s? These differentials can be explained (to some extent) by reconstructing the internal structure of the South Asian maritime labour market that was constituted by various political and social, legal and extralegal, public and private, articulations of power. States, communities and households were all involved in constituting dynamic *regulatory scenarios* that provided the maritime 'labour market' with concrete historical form and turned it into an operational structure (Ahuja 2005, 2008).

While the attribute 'docility' was predominantly ascribed to the 'oriental' maritime worker, there are interesting instances when it was applied to non-British European sailors, too

(Mercantile Marine Committee 1903, vol. 2: 98). This hints at *political* structures underlying what was perceived and pronounced as 'ethnic' behavioural patterns. Political reforms in Britain had strengthened the citizen rights and bargaining power of the British working classes in the closing decades of the nineteenth century, which expressed itself, in the case of the seamen, in the rise of a new, resolute and vocal trade union (Hyslop 2009). 'Alien' seafarers, whether 'white' or not, were, however, expressly excluded from the political resources newly available to British workers.

Seafarers from India were, moreover, in an even weaker position as colonial subjects whose inferior legal status and rights were specifically and positively defined by an imperialist state that was intimately connected to British employer interests. The racialised hierarchies of the British Empire were clearly reflected in its labour legislation: while the 'master and servant law' was abolished in Britain in 1875, this instrument of establishing unequal labour contracts continued to be the core of 'British Indian' labour law well into the 1920s; while 'new unionism' unfolded in Britain (and especially among maritime workers) from the 1880s, the Indian trade unions were able to gain legal recognition only in 1926; while a National Maritime Board was constituted in Britain in 1917 as a formal platform for negotiations between employers and seamen's unions, a similar institutional arrangement was established in India only 40 years later, or a full decade after the end of the British Raj. More importantly, British maritime law conceived of the Indian seafarer as a distinct and inferior category of labour: he was, for legal purposes, not a 'seaman' but a 'lascar' who was to be employed on the basis of a distinct, standardised and legally sanctioned labour contract, the so-called 'Asiatic Articles', which stipulated rights and conditions consistently inferior to those conceded to 'seamen'. Pay, food rations and accommodation were much less substantial, working hours left legally unregulated, compensation in case of work accidents was lower and more difficult to reclaim, freedom of movement (particularly 'land leave') was more restricted, contract periods longer and any termination of the labour contract outside British India ruled out categorically. The freedom of movement of this potentially highly mobile workforce was further constrained by the immigration legislation of other states, namely the USA and various dominion states of the British Empire, which impinged upon the right to land leave of 'coloured' seafarers. Yet maritime labour law and immigration legislation were not, as we shall see, comprehensively effective in preventing South Asian seafarers from jumping ship and they would have been even less so without the support of 'informal' networks (Mowat 1949; Barnes 1983; Tabili 1994; Aurora 1996; Ahuja 2005, 2006, 2008).

The access to maritime employment and the labour process itself were largely managed through hierarchical recruitment networks based on village neighbourship, religious community, kinship and, crucially, debt. Shipping companies or their agents engaged major recruitment contractors (so-called 'shipping agents' or *ghat serangs*) in the two major recruitment ports, Bombay and Calcutta. These contractors ran their businesses by linking up with jobbers (the so-called *serangs*) and boarding-house keepers *(deravalas or barivalas)* who exerted ground-level control over their respective recruitment network by providing credit to seamen who were, as a rule, also connected to them by bonds of kinship, community or locality. These bonds enabled *serangs* and *barivalas* to recover the unpaid debt of an absconding 'lascar' from his family and thus to further reduce his spatial and occupational mobility. *Serangs* and *barivalas* continued to be the key agents of the recruitment process well into the mid-twentieth century. Various accounts suggest that jobbers, and especially boarding-house keepers, were often regarded by the 'lascars' as prone to abusing their powers for their own benefit and that many of these middlemen succeeded in enhancing both their social and economic position (Kanekar 1928; Desai 1940; Mowat 1949; Balachandran 1996, 1997; Ahuja 2005, 2008).

Yet this mechanism of informal control through intermediaries ran far from smoothly at any time and was severely unsettled in the event of fluctuations in the global demand for maritime labour. Such fluctuations were, moreover, frequent as well as sharp in an industry that was more immediately than most affected by the World Wars and the depressions of international trade. In the recruitment ports of Bombay and Calcutta, about four times as many men were registered as 'lascars' in the early decades of the twentieth century than were annually hired for oceanic steamship work. Even if we take into account that many of these men may not have been looking for maritime employment every year or considered this option only during a certain period of their life cycle, the labour market for 'lascars' appears to have been generally well supplied. During the wars, however, a different scenario emerged: informal networks proved unable to satisfy the Empire's massively increased demand for Indian maritime labour. This implied that crews became more diverse in terms of their origins as jobbers could no longer restrict access to the labour market to members of their own community network. Consequently, *serangs*, who were linked to a declining proportion of their respective labour gangs by informal bonds, found it more difficult to impose control and extract intermediary fees. Conversely, during the post-war crisis and the Great Depression, when demand for maritime labour dropped drastically, *serangs* were seen to fail in providing jobs to their clients, entailing a loss of social standing and power within their respective networks. *Serangs* were accordingly squeezed between the contradictory pressures of the period's frequent and violent labour market fluctuations. The jobber's position was thus beset with risks and more vulnerable than most official accounts allow for, especially since he did not enjoy any formal right to regular employment himself (Balachandran 1996; Ahuja 2005).

Over much of the period, *serangs* responded to the inherent precariousness of maritime employment by spreading risk: they made use of their key position in community-based recruitment networks not exclusively for purposes of seafaring. *Serangs* thus emerged as labour contractors for other maritime as well as non-maritime occupations (including dock, road transport and factory work), as organisers of peddling networks in foreign ports and even as facilitators of illegal immigration into Britain or other countries (Choudhury 1993, 1995; Adams 1994; Ahuja 2006, Balachandran 2007a, 2007b). This diversification of activities allowed for some limited independence from the shipping companies and further emphasised, at the same time, the crucial importance for the *serang* of preserving his reputation as a benevolent, reliable and resourceful leader to the members of his own network. Claims to leadership were sustainable not solely by way of practices of material exchange (namely by providing credit to unemployed 'lascars'). They had to be rendered plausible, too, by a demonstrated ability to resolve conflicts with employers and other authorities. *Serangs* hence played a mediatory role between their labour gangs and the employers. While lasting relationships to a certain shipping company, shipmaster or chief engineer could be upheld only if a *serang* proved his ability to control his men and prevent them from jumping ship, he could (and often did) also function as a spokesman for the crew in negotiations with the ship's officers as well as other employer's agents and port authorities.

Over time, such practices of benefaction and spokesmanship developed their own con-tradictory dynamics. *Serangs* and boarding-house keepers were thus instrumental in creating cooperative societies (the village-based *kurs* or 'seamen's clubs' of Goan Catholics in Bombay and Karachi) as well as trade unions (of which *serangs* and 'butlers' often constituted the crucial middle rung of cadres as well as part of the more visible top-level leadership). After World War I, these trade unions and cooperative societies demanded ever more insistently that informal recruitment through jobbers and brokers be replaced by an institutionalised system based on the formal registration of all employable seamen and on the principles of rotation and union participation. Employers resisted such changes tooth and nail, but the maritime labour shortage during World War II, along with a general political trend towards a new, corporatist labour policy, generated more favourable conditions for a formalisation of the recruitment system. Chances for successful industrial action improved and a series of strikes by Indian seafarers in the early months of World War II turned these chances into pay rises. On an institutional level, Indian seamen's unions consolidated themselves in the course of World War II, achieved recognition by employers and the state, and succeeded in establishing a recruitment system that increasingly bypassed the intermediaries of the informal networks (Mowat 1949; Broeze 1981; Aurora 1996; Balachandran 2002, 2008; Ahuja 2005). That *serangs* were among the chief campaigners against recruitment through middlemen appears contrary to their own and immediate interests at first sight – a paradox that resolves itself if the instable and vulnerable position of the *serang* in the recruitment system is taken into account.

The idea that the 'docility' or total subordination of the 'lascar' was guaranteed by the *serang* whose authority was unassailable, because it was rooted in timeless Indian peasant conceptions of hierarchical order, was regurgitated ceaselessly in employer statements. Yet this notion of the all-powerful 'traditional' middleman was clearly less than compelling by the mid-twentieth century when a more formalised regime of recruitment and labour control could no longer be avoided – a process that has also been observed with regard to factory labour (cf. Chandavarkar 2008). Even so, the combination of maritime labour law, of immigration legislation and of the disciplinarian potential of informal networks created a regulatory scenario that sustained, on the whole effectively and over much of the period under review, the segmentation of the global labour market for maritime labour along the lines of 'race'. The 'lascar' could be perceived and plausibly represented as 'docile' precisely because of this fairly efficient combination of political disenfranchisement, legal discrimination and social control through hierarchical networks. Expressed in the heavily racist social language of contemporary Britain, a historically produced socio-political scenario of labour subordination that sat uncomfortably with the liberal rhetoric of 'free labour' was, however, naturalised as an offshoot of the 'oriental' seafarer's essential ethno-cultural 'identity'. This ideological rendering was politically convenient but failed to grasp the contextual dependency and temporal limitedness of this scenario, as well as the dynamics that set an end to 'docility' by the late 1930s (Ahuja 2005, 2008).

Beyond seafaring: the transformative potential of maritime employment

As shipping interests and the colonial bureaucracy made concerted efforts to keep South Asians within the bounds of the lowest, racially defined segment of the maritime labour market, the limitations of these efforts always remained in sight: segmentation could be aspired to and approximated, but never achieved to the extent of watertight compartmentalisation. Individual 'lascars' did succeed occasionally, and especially in periods of labour scarcity, in being employed on British or other merchant navy ships on the superior standard contracts offered to their 'white' colleagues. Even the most discriminatory immigration regulations of states like the USA, South Africa, Australia or of Britain itself could never fully prevent South Asian seafarers from jumping ship and joining local labour forces (Choudhury 1993, 1995; Adams 1994; Visram 2002; Balachandran 2007a, 2007b; Goodall, Ghosh and Todd 2008; Hyslop 2009). In India, the unpredictable irregularity of steamship work forced many seafarers to maintain non-maritime employment alternatives and enabled them, conversely, to avail themselves of these alternatives even against the wishes of employers and the imperial state, for instance in times of war, when the dangers of seafaring grew exponentially. From the employers' point of view, such perforations of market bounds were not a problem that merited further action if they remained within certain proportions: not every hole in the bucket had to be patched up; labour market segmentation did not have to be 'perfect' to be of practical utility. The imperfect segmentation of the labour market for South Asian maritime labour *did* serve, after all, as a device for imposing very real ceilings on the wages and labour conditions of colonial ship workers over more than one-and-a-half centuries. Even so, the cracks in the regulatory 'bulkheads' dividing the maritime labour market into segments, as well as the porosity of the division between maritime and non-maritime labour markets, bore structural significance, as they conditioned to some extent the potential of maritime employment to serve as an avenue of horizontal and vertical mobility and of social transformation. These levels of porosity varied considerably over the period under review and were contingent on political and economic conjunctures.

The transformative potential of South Asian maritime employment realised itself in two major forms. First, it materialised as *social and spatial mobility of individual members* of South Asian maritime networks, for which cases are observable throughout the period under review. Second, and this type of transformation obtains significance as our period draws to a close, *entire maritime recruitment networks could change their basic functions* and turn into something altogether new. Both forms are interconnected and, as we shall see below: the social ascent of individual seamen generated conditions for larger changes.

The available life accounts of former South Asian seafarers (mostly written by or recorded from men who settled for some time or permanently in Europe or North America) suggest that maritime proletarity was rarely understood, at least in hindsight, as a desirable long-term objective of individual aspiration. Rather, and much more often, it was considered a means of approaching social destinations that lay distinctly outside the world of steamship labour; sometimes it was also recalled as a limited life period of indulgence in a youthful urge to explore the world. Most of these accounts dwell on the circumstances of recruitment, on encounters and exploits in various ports, on instances of ship jumping or the dangers of wartime shipping, but are remarkably silent about the quotidian details of the labour process on board ship (Choudhury 1993, 1995; Adams 1994; Balachandran 2007a, 2007b). Frequent official reports on suicides during voyages of South Asian seafarers, mostly firemen, suggest that the ship (and particularly the blazing hot engine room) was experienced by many as a hostile, oppressive, even satanic, work environment (Ahuja 2012). Moreover, numerous accounts of the violence and racist abuse inflicted by British officers and seafarers on South Asian crews indicate that the ship was more often perceived as a space of humiliation than as a space where a 'black man's' respectability and social standing was likely to grow.

This does not imply that South Asian maritime careers were necessarily brief and transitory or intended to be so. A core of weathered deckhands, firemen and stewards that included highly skilled boatswains (*serangs*), foremen (*tindals*) and helmsmen (*sukhanis*), who knew the nuts and bolts of their vessel, was indispensable for running a steamship economically and safely – a core that was larger or smaller according to the current labour market situation and was rounded out with less experienced and less permanently employed workmen. Shipping companies and agents were acutely aware of this requirement, while shipmasters and chief officers accordingly preferred to work with the same *serangs* and 'core crews' over long periods and tried to cultivate lasting links. A recognisable proportion of South Asian seafarers thus served the same shipping company over a period of decades, slowly rising through the ranks, some to the position of a *serang* (Ahuja 2006). There was thus no doubt the possibility *for some* of an occupational career *within* the global maritime labour market (mostly in its lower segment), which could also be experienced as a basis for respectable masculinity and social standing. This is evident, for instance, in the memoirs of Amir Haider Khan, who joined the engine room crew of a British merchant vessel during World War I as a barely schooled 15-year-old Punjabi peasant boy from the Northwest Frontier.

On jumping ship in New York and enlisting with the US merchant navy, Amir vigorously entered all accessible avenues of technical education and acquired in turn the skills of a ship's engineer, of a car mechanic and of an amateur aircraft pilot. They show that the alienated and super-exploited, but by no means fully deskilled, work of engine-room 'lascars' could be reinterpreted and reappropriated, in this case through the lenses of technophilia and revolutionary socialism, as a source of intense pride, self-assertion and identification – both as a proletarian and, in a wider sense, as a *homo faber* (Khan 2007).

The picture is thus contradictory, but it seems fair to say that maritime work was taken up by many South Asian ship workers (and especially by firemen and stewards) as one of several sources of income that had to be tapped, and as a temporary occupation, rather than a life-long calling. For many of the sons of smallholding peasants, who made up the majority of the maritime workforce, seafaring was a means to make sure that their families could hold on to their property, repay their debts, build a better house and ideally buy more land. Ship work was thus, for many 'lascars', a strategic operation for the defence of their status as petty commodity producers and did not indicate *per se* any inclination to embrace and accept proletarity as a permanent social position. Even those who could not or did not wish to return to the village appear to have looked out for forms of livelihood that permitted them to steer clear of the social relationships constituting 'markets' for waged labour and to rise above the social status attached to these relationships. Doing one's own business appears to have been a major aspiration that could be put into practice in various ways and along a wide spectrum of degrees of economic independence.

At the most basic level, South Asian steamship workers did what Indian Ocean seafarers had done, too, in the early modern period whenever they found sufficient time in a foreign port: they engaged in petty trade and sought to get a good price for textiles, spices or other items they had carried along in their luggage from India. Sideline hawking was, however, not only rendered illegal but even otherwise more difficult in the age of steam, when times in port were considerably reduced. Regardless, this form of supplementing wages (and of partially transcending wage-labour relationships) remained popular, appears to have been considered a customary sailor's right and was resorted to whenever possible.

Such operations were not necessarily conducted on an individual basis: police authorities reported that cheap Indian silk shawls were peddled in an organised manner by Indian seafarers in various British cities in the 1920s and that *serangs* apparently engaged in the coordination of such ventures. The scale of such peddling activities was usually too small to release seafarers from the bonds of 'free labour', though a minority succeeded in opening their own shops, boarding-houses or eateries in recruitment ports in India, in the port areas of cities outside the subcontinent and by the end of the period also in non-maritime industrial towns, for instance in the British Midlands. Many of these aspirants to the urban petty bourgeoisie had been able to accrue the initial capital for their businesses as *serangs*. In Calcutta, a considerable number of former jobbers as well as notables from the main recruitment region for firemen, Sylhet, had emerged as powerful *barivalas* (hostel owners) who controlled much of the maritime recruitment process through moneylending and had a reputation among seafarers for their ruthlessness, while some of them sought to enhance their social status by way of philanthropic activities. In London's East End the first Bangladeshi restaurants were established and run by deserters from British merchant ships (Choudhury 1993, 1995; Adams 1994; Visram 2002; Balachandran 2003; Ahuja 2006).

Establishing one's own business, often outside India, was the most important, but not the only road of individual upward mobility that South Asian seafarers took after World War I. This was also a period when labour emerged as a major issue of public debate in the subcontinent, when new politics of representing labour took shape and when Indian trade unions made political space for themselves in achieving legal recognition from 1926. University educated and high-caste, middle- or even upper-class intellectuals (such as the Servants of India Society's Dinkar Desai) emerged as maritime labour leaders in a pattern familiar from many contemporary trade unions in South Asia. However, Indian seamen's unions were particularly successful during the interwar period in organising a substantial section of the workforce and, crucially, in generating influential rank-and-file leaders in both the major recruitment ports (Broeze 1981). These labour spokesmen were often *serangs*, while managers of cooperative societies (the Goan *kurs* in particular) were also prominent in Bombay; some had the advantage of having attended school or partaken in traditional forms of education; several emerged as leaders from among a crew in the course of ship-level conflicts or industrial action – the type of activist dubbed disparagingly and warily as 'sea lawyers' by British ship's officers.

From among this fairly large category of activists emerged a smaller but recognisable number of 'organic intellectuals' who achieved a considerable degree of public visibility as representatives of their occupational group. Their appearance had far-reaching significance in at least two ways. First, it implied that the labour movement could be appropriated successfully by seafarers as an avenue of *individual* upward mobility in some cases at least. Second, while some of these rank-and-file leaders rose to public prominence only for a fleeting moment to fall (or be cast) into oblivion soon after (Goodall 2008), both major Indian recruitment ports gave rise to seafaring 'organic intellectuals' with more lasting impact. Mohammed Ebrahim Serang was a Muslim seaman originating from Calicut (Kozhikode) whose honorary name 'Khan Saheb' signified his claim to leadership, while his surname 'Serang' suggested that he or a paternal forebear had been a boatswain. In the Bombay of the 1930s, he was merely one of several leading figures of the National Union of Seafarers of India (NUSI) with a seafaring background. His case is unusual only because his family remained involved with the trade union's leadership over several generations: 'Bachhu' Abdul K. Serang inherited his father's role in the 1940s (Aurora 1996), while the present General Secretary, Abdulgani Y. Serang, is his great-grandson.

However, the politically most effective seamen's representative of his generation was surely Aftab Ali. Son of a prosperous if barely educated landowner and boat merchant in the so-called 'seamen's zone' of Sylhet and younger brother of a powerful and unpopular *barivala* in Calcutta, Ali dropped out of school and signed on against his family's wishes as a 'saloon boy', clearly not for reasons of economic constraint. Jumping ship in the USA, he involved himself in trade union politics to re-emerge in Calcutta in the late 1920s as a spokesman of seafarers and particularly of the firemen from his Sylheti home region. By the 1930s, he had established himself as a powerful union leader by effecting the merger of the Bombay and Calcutta seamen's unions, by severally representing Indian labour at International Labour Organization (ILO) conferences and by serving successively as the Vice-President of the All India Trade Union Congress (AITUC), of M. N. Roy's Indian Federation of Labour and, after the partition of India, of the All-Pakistan Confederation of Labour. After 1947, he continued to promote the interests of his Sylheti supporters who now had to cross an international border and submit to increasingly adverse passport regulations to reach the recruitment offices of Calcutta. Exploring alternative employment opportunities, Aftab Ali opened Seamen's Welfare Offices in Sylhet in the 1950s and succeeded from 1956 in negotiating a privileged access of distressed seamen to the British labour market, thus facilitating the emergence of a sizeable Sylheti community in the UK. The organisation of collective migration went hand in hand with the individual upward mobility of the organisers: Abul Lays Chaudhuri is reported to have opened Sylhet's first travel agency, Crescent Travels, right next to the Seamen's Welfare Office he was in charge of on behalf of his maternal uncle Aftab Ali (Broeze 1981; Choudhury 1993, 1995; Adams 1994).

Aftab Ali's story points to a crucial link between the spatial as well as social mobility of individuals and the striking metamorphosis of a network of maritime labour (that had mainly facilitated short-term circulation) into a network of international medium- and long-term resettlement. Throughout the period of imperial steam shipping, staying on in Britain was a less feasible or attractive option for Indian ship jumpers than for other non-European seafarers: no more than 8,000 Indians, it has been estimated, lived in that country before the 1950s (Visram 2002). However, the comparatively small number of 'lascars' that found industrial employment, opened shops, restaurants or boarding-houses and initiated various political, social or religious community associations thereby created crucial anchor points that allowed the relocation and functional transformation of South Asian maritime labour networks as the 'age of the lascar' drew to a close.

Note

1   www.nusi.org.in/aboutnusi.htm (*About NUSI*, accessed 7 September 2010).

References

Adams, C. (ed.) 1994, *Across Seven Seas and Thirteen Rivers. Life Stories of Pioneer Sylhetti Settlers in Britain*, London, Eastside.

Ahuja, R. 2004, 'Lateinsegel und Dampfturbinen. Der Schiffsverkehr des Indischen Ozeans im Zeitalter des Imperialismus', Rothermund, D. and Weigelin-Schwiedrzik, S. (eds), *Der Indische Ozean. Das afro-asiatische Mittelmeer als Kultur- und Wirtschaftsraum*, Wien, Promedia, pp. 207–25.

— 2005, 'Die "Lenksamkeit" des "Lascars". Regulierungsszenarien eines transterritorialen Arbeitsmarktes in der ersten Hälfte des 20. Jahrhunderts', *Geschichte und Gesellschaft*, vol. 31, no. 3, pp. 323–53.

— 2006, 'Mobility and Containment. The Voyages of Indian Seamen, c. 1900–1960', *International Review of Social History*, vol. 51, supplement, pp. 111–41.

— 2008, 'Networks of Subordination – Networks of the Subordinated. The Case of South Asian Maritime Labour under British Imperialism (c. 1890–1947)', Fischer-Tiné, H. and Tambe, A. (eds), *Spaces of Disorder. The Limits of British Colonial Control in South Asia and the Indian Ocean*, London, Routledge, pp. 13–48.

— 2012, 'Capital at Sea, Shaitan Below Decks? A Note on Global Narratives, Narrow Spaces, and the Limits of Experience', *History of the Present*, vol. 2, no. 1, pp. 78–85.

Aurora, A. K. 1996, *Voyage. Chronicle of Seafarers' Movement in India*, Bombay, National Union of Seafarers.

Balachandran, G. 1996, 'Searching for the Sardar: The State, Pre-capitalist Institutions and Human Agency in the Maritime Labour Market, Calcutta, 1880–1935', in Stein, B. and Subrahmanyam, S. (eds), *Institutions and Economic Change in South Asia*, Delhi, OUP.

— 1997, 'Recruitment and Control of Indian Seamen: Calcutta, 1880–1935', *International Journal of Maritime History*, vol. 9, no. 1, pp. 1–18.

— 2002, 'Conflicts in the International Maritime Labour Market: British and Indian Seamen, Employers, and the State, 1890–1939', *Indian Economic and Social History Review*, vol. 39, no. 1, pp. 71–101.

— 2003, 'Circulation through Seafaring: Indian Seamen, 1890–1945', in Markovits, C., Pouchepadass, J. and Subrahmanyam, S. (eds), *Society and Circulation: Mobile People and Itinerant Cultures in South Asia 1750–1950*, Delhi, Permanent Black, pp. 89–130.

— 2007a, 'Crossing the Last Frontier: Transatlantic Movements of Asian Maritime Workers, c. 1900–1945', in Feys, T., Fischer, L. R., Hoste, S. and Vanfraechem, S. (eds), *Maritime Transport and Migration: The Connection between Maritime and Migration Networks* (Research in Maritime History 33), St. John's, Newfoundland, International Maritime Economic History Association, pp. 97–111.

— 2007b, 'South Asian Seafarers and their Worlds, c. 1870–1930s', in Bentley, J. H. et al. (eds), *Seascapes. Maritime Histories, Littoral Cultures and Transoceanic Exchanges*, Honolulu, University of Hawai'i Press, pp. 186–202.

— 2008, 'Cultures of Conflict in Transnational Context, 1886–1945', *Transforming Cultures eJournal*, vol. 3, no. 2, pp. 45–75.

Barnes, L. 1983, *Evolution and Scope of Mercantile Marine Laws Relating to Seamen in India*, New Delhi, Maritime Law Association of India.

Broeze, F. 1981, 'The Muscles of Empire – Indian Seamen and the Raj, 1919–1939', *Indian Economic and Social History Review*, vol. 18, no. 1, pp. 43–67.

Chandavarkar, R. 2008, 'The Decline and Fall of the Jobber System in the Bombay Cotton Textile Industry, 1870–1955', *Modern Asian Studies*, vol. 42, no. 1, pp. 117–210.

Choudhury, Y. 1993, *The Roots and Tales of the Bangladeshi Settlers*, Birmingham, Sylheti Social History Group.

— 1995, *Sons of the Empire. Oral History from the Bangladeshi Seamen who Served on British Ships during the 1939–45 War*, Birmingham, Sylheti Social History Group.

Desai, D. D. 1940, *Maritime Labour in India*, Bombay, Servants of India Society.

Dixon, C. 1980, 'Lascars: The Forgotten Seamen', Ommer, R. and Panting, G. (eds), *Working Men who Got Wet*, Newfoundland, Memorial University of Newfoundland.

Ewald, J. J. 2000, 'Crossers of the Sea: Slaves, Freedmen, and Other Migrants in the Northwestern Indian Ocean, *c.* 1750–1914', *American Historical Review*, vol. 105, no. 1, pp. 69–92.

Fisher, M. H. 2006, 'Working Across the Seas: Indian Maritime Labourers in India, Britain, and in Between, 1600–1857', *International Review of Social History*, vol. 51, supplement, pp. 21–45.

Gardner, K. 2000, *Global Migrants, Local Lives: Travel and Transformation in Rural Bangladesh*, 2nd edn, Oxford: Clarendon Press.

Goodall, H. 2008, 'Port Politics: Indian Seamen, Australian Unions and Indonesian Independence, 1945–47', *Labour History*, no. 94, pp. 43–68.

Goodall, H., Ghosh, D. and Todd, L.R. 2008, 'Jumping Ship – Skirting Empire: Indians, Aborigines and Australians across the Indian Ocean', *Transforming Cultures eJournal*, vol. 3, no. 1, pp. 44–74.

Hood, W. H. 1903, *The Blight of Insubordination. The Lascar Question and Rights and Wrongs of the British Shipmaster*, London, Spottiswoode & Co.

Hyslop, J. 2009, 'Steamship Empire: Asian, African and British Sailors in the Merchant Marine *c.* 1880–1945', *Journal of Asian and African Studies*, vol. 44, no. 1, pp. 49–67.

Kanekar, P. G. 1928, *Seamen in Bombay. Report of an Enquiry into the Conditions of their Life and Work*, Bombay, Servants of India Society.

Khan, A. H. 2007, *Chains to Lose. Life and Struggles of a Revolutionary*, Gardezi, H. N. (ed.), vol. 1, Karachi, Pakistan Study Centre.

Manning Committee 1896, *Reports from the Departmental Committee on Manning of Merchant Ships with Addenda and Statistical Tables*, London, Spottiswoode & Co.

Mercantile Marine Committee 1903, *Report of the Committee Appointed by the Board of Trade to Inquire into Certain Questions Affecting the Mercantile Marine*, 3 vols, London, HM Stationery Office.

Mowat, J. L. 1949, *Seafarers' Conditions in India and Pakistan*, Geneva, ILO.

Tabili, L. 1994, *'We Ask for British Justice'. Workers and Racial Difference in Late Imperial Britain*, Ithaca/London, Cornell University Press.

Visram, Rozina 1986, *Ayahs, Lascars and Princes. The Story of Indians in Britain, 1700–1947*, London, Pluto.

— 2002, *Asians in Britain: The Story of Indians in Britain 1700–1947*, London, Pluto.

Yule, H. and Burnell, A. C. 1983/1903, *Hobson-Jobson. A Glossary of Colloquial Anglo-Indian Words and Phrases* . . . (new 4th edn), New Delhi, Munshiram Manoharlal.

10

SOUTH ASIANS IN BRITAIN UP TO THE MID-NINETEENTH CENTURY

Michael H. Fisher

Overview

The movement of South Asians to Britain dates back to at least the early seventeenth century and changed in character and increased in volume over the subsequent 250 years (Brown 2006; Das 1924; Fisher 2004; Fisher, Lahiri and Thandi 2007; Fryer 1984; Gerzina 1995; Gundara and Duffield 1992; Innes 2002; Ramdin 1999; Visram 1984, 2002). By the mid-nineteenth century, tens of thousands of Indian men and women of all social and economic classes had made the passage to Britain. A substantial number of them remained in Britain for years or for the rest of their lives as settlers. As they married (usually to Britons rather than to other Indians) and had children, the Indian identities of their descendants customarily became more diffuse and they entered British society. Especially from the early nineteenth century, growing numbers joined burgeoning Asian communities in London's docklands and, to a lesser extent, the other major ports of Britain. British class, race and gender dynamics shifted with British social and cultural change, and especially with the expansion of British colonialism over South Asia. Using broader patterns and telling individual examples, we can come to understand the diverse and shifting reception and roles of these South Asians in Britain.

Rich source material of various types reveals aspects of the lives of many of these Asian men and women. The capacious archive of the English East India Company (1600–1858) documents many thousands of lives. Those who became members of Anglican or other Christian congregations appear in lists of marriages, deaths, and baptisms. As the British state moved toward modernity, it attempted to identify and classify all the people within its borders, Indians amongst them. Thus, the comprehensive decennial British censuses (which began in 1841) included Indians and their descendants among other inhabitants of Britain wherever they were living on census day (although inconsistently identified by birthplace). As Indians moved from being colonial subjects to British citizens, they began to appear indiscriminately in official records of law courts and on tax rolls and voter lists. Some British painters portrayed Indians, depending on their class, either as the main subject or as supporting figures to a foregrounded British patron (Tobin 1999). Hundreds more Indians submitted autobiographical letters or petitions to British authorities. By 1857, there were 21 books and pamphlets written by Indians about their experiences in Britain, including fourteen in English, four in Persian (or Arabic), two in Urdu, and one in Nepali, the author's choice of language reflecting his intended readership. Drawing upon all these sources, we can recover some of these Asian lives in Britain, which changed over time in character and possibilities, reflecting and partially shaping popular and official British attitudes toward the Asians in their midst.

As Indians settled in Britain, they negotiated various types of relationships with their host culture. Until the late eighteenth century, British ideas about identity were largely based on religion, class, and other forms of deportment rather than on biological ancestry (Harrison 1999; Ballantyne 2002). This meant that an Indian who converted to Christianity, especially to Anglican Christianity, and joined a parish, who spoke English, and who dressed in British garb appropriate to his or her class, could be accepted. In particular, given British gender constructs, Indian women who married European men, either before coming to Britain or afterward, tended to merge relatively quickly into British society.

The earliest English controls on migration tended to constrain Indians from leaving Britain, not entering it. Starting in 1657, the East India Company tried to exclude unwanted European rivals by ordering that everyone going to India had to purchase a 'Permission' for £12 (whose value in today's currency would be over £1,500, using the retail price index) (Court Minutes, 1657–1813). Inadvertently, this included all Indians travelling from England back to India. Until this requirement ended in 1813, thousands of Indians of all classes – including seamen, servants, slaves, wives, merchants, officers, ambassadors, students, teachers, and others – purchased this 'Permission', had one purchased for them, or else obtained a special exemption from the East India Company's Directors. This expensive requirement apparently proved, for at least some Indians, an incentive to remain as settlers in England rather than return to India.

Working-class seamen, servants, and slaves

South Asians lived in England prior to the first voyages of English ships to India. In an early example, in 1607, five working-class 'Indians' living in London petitioned the recently incorporated East India Company for employment and redress of grievances (Great Britain, Public Record Office 1862, 2: 146–49, 154). At the time, English knowledge of the geography of 'the East' remained sketchy. Further, the English Crown had given the East India Company both a monopoly over trade from southern Africa eastward across South and Southeast Asia all the way to the Philippines, and also responsibility for the management and protection in England of all people (except those of European ancestry) from all those lands, people sometimes collectively designated 'Indians'. Hence, we can never know the actual origins of these five 'Indians'. However, one of them, 'Marcus the Indian', received seaman's clothing and employment for the first voyage to India by English ships. In 1614, for instance, three other Indian seamen working on East India Company ships to India requested permission to bring their English wives with them. However, the Company's authorities deemed it inappropriate to have women living 'among so many unruly sailors', instead arranging for part of these seamen's wages to be paid to their wives until the husbands returned (Court Minutes, 1614 in Great Britain, Public Record Office, 2: 275).

Over the subsequent 250 years, tens of thousands of Indian seamen or *lascars*, would make the voyage to Britain, some settling and marrying, others only as sojourners. When hired in India as part of a maritime labour gang, they received an advance on their pay which thereafter bound them by contract to continue to work throughout the voyage to Britain. Until the mid-seventeenth century, *lascar* wages were markedly larger than those of European seamen sailing to Britain, since ships vitally needed *lascars* to replace European sailors who had deserted, been impressed by the royal navy, or died in Asia. Subsequently, however, Parliament's Navigation Acts (especially those dating from the 1660s and lasting until the 1840s) distorted Britain's maritime labour market, by strongly favouring the employment of British sailors (defined as including African and Afro-Caribbean sailors but not Indians or other Asians). British ships in Asia were still permitted to hire *lascars* for the return voyage to Britain. But on the voyage outward from Britain, ship owners avoided employing *lascars* rather than suffer the official British financial penalties of doing so. This created a pool of unemployable Indian seamen in Britain, whom, if they chose to return, ship owners or the East India Company had reluctantly to send home as unpaid passengers.

For many Britons, especially before colonialism expanded in the late eighteenth century, India represented a rich and prestigious land. Wealthy Britons, despite the considerable expense, began to import Indian servants and slaves. To display their acquisitions, some masters included Indians in portraits by prominent European artists, while others dressed them in oriental or other fanciful garb during soirees or other social occasions. For instance, in 1630, William Feilding, Earl of Denbigh (1582–1643), went to India representing King Charles I. On Denbigh's return in 1633, he brought with him at least one Indian servant or ward. He then commissioned Anthony Van Dyck to paint a joint portrait of him and his finely dressed Indian (National Gallery 1633, NG5633). Subsequently, other Indians, usually servants, appeared in joint portraits with British elites.

In India, domestic slavery remained customary until the mid-nineteenth century (Chatterjee 1999). When British or Indian masters brought slaves to Britain, however, different criteria applied. Some European masters attempted to sell their Indian slaves into the more abusive system of chattel slavery practiced in North and South America. In 1737, for example, a letter to the East India Company's Directors 'from a Black Fellow born in Bengal called Pompey, and brought to Britain by Captain Benfield, and since a servant to Major Woodford at Virginia who now detains him as a Slave' led to an investigation and intervention by the Company to return him to India (Court Minutes, 31/8/1737). Other masters found that their ownership of their Indian slaves ended with arrival in England or conversion to Christianity. Since many Britons believed (especially from the late eighteenth century onward) that slavery should not persist in Britain, particularly for Christians, Indian slaves who converted thereby customarily emancipated themselves, by convention but not necessarily by law. Around 1741, for example, Mr Suthern Davies brought his 10-year-old Indian slave to London from Bengal. After about five years in London, she converted to the Church of England, with the baptismal name Catherine Bengall. Emancipated, she left her master, but became pregnant out of wedlock by a local British man, William Lloyd. She gave birth to her son in her parish workhouse (Barber 2000: 25–34). Thereafter, she either died or disappeared into the undocumented poor of London. But only a relatively small number of Asians came to Britain against their will as slaves. Although the vast majority may have been compelled by economic circumstance in India to have left for Britain, they did so at least nominally as free labour.

Some Indians had special expertise that distinguished them. Rare and delicate Indian animals, like cheetahs, required the attendance of highly trained keepers to escort them to Britain and settle them there. One such expert, Abdullah (who also used the name John Morgan during his life in England), made at least three trips to London in the early 1760s accompanying such valuable felines. Painted vividly by George Stubbs, he also successfully prosecuted his British landlord for theft in Old Bailey court (Court Minutes, 12/3/1760; Manchester City Galleries; Old Bailey 27/2/1765, 1970. 34). His oriental expertise garnered him the solicitous attention of British patrons.

Many Indian working-class women and men, however, learned new trades in Britain. Thus, James 'the Indian' worked as a beer brewer – an English rather than Indian trade. When James died in September 1618, he was respectfully buried in his parish church of St. Botolph without Aldgate, London (Forbes 1971: 3–4).

Over time, working-class Indians became more common in Britain. Many left their masters, willingly or perforce, either finding employment in Britain or eventually becoming destitute. Parliament and the British public blamed the East India Company's Directors for indigent Indians in the streets of London and other British cities and villages. Consequently, from the eighteenth century onward, the Directors paid to house, clothe, and feed growing numbers of indigent Indians in Britain and/or paid their passage home.

In 1769, in order to try to constrain the arrival of Indians who might become a financial burden on the East India Company, the Directors instituted a new requirement: any employer bringing an Indian servant to Britain had to post a bond of £50 which would not be redeemed until the servant either returned to India or died (Court Minutes, 1769–1858). This stricture did not stem the growing number of such servants. In 1807, the Directors doubled it to £100. Company bond records identify many thousands of Indian servants coming to Britain, and this requirement ended only with the dissolution of the East India Company itself in 1858. Hence, unlike the South Asian indentured workers who provided 'cheap labour' in other parts of the Empire, or Indian manual labourers in India itself, those Indian working-class people who came or were brought to Britain in most cases cost their employers more than European ones.

Indian wives and children of Europeans

Indian women ventured to England from at least the early seventeenth century, usually as the wives or servants of Europeans. The first English ship to return from India in 1612 carried Mariam, wife of William Hawkins (1585?–1613), first English ambassador to the Mughal court. She had been a ward of the Mughal Emperor Jahangir and was of Armenian ancestry. She married Hawkins in Agra after he insisted on a Christian bride (Hawkins 1970; Birdwood and Foster 1893). Although Hawkins died during the voyage, Mariam continued to London. There, she negotiated as a respected noblewoman with the East India Company and married another Englishman, Gabriel Towerson (d. 1623). When Towerson was posted to India in 1617, she returned with him but he abandoned her in Agra.

Over time, many other Indians settled in Britain with European husbands and, often, their children. For example, the wife of Gerard Gustavus Ducarel (1745–?) was reportedly a daughter of the Maharaja of Purnea in Bengal and a Hindu widow rescued from concremation as a 'sati' on her first husband's funeral pyre. She had converted to Protestant Christianity, married Ducarel in India around 1780, and then settled with him in Britain. Her contemporary in London was Nur Begam (or Halime Begum, 1770–1853). From a prominent Muslim family of Lucknow, Nur Begum married French mercenary General Benoit de Boigne (1751–1830) with Islamic rites. Her sister had already married William Palmer, an affluent banker of mixed British–Indian ancestry. De Boigne had other Indian wives and mistresses. However, when he retired as a wealthy man to London in 1797, he brought with him Nur Begum and their two children, Banu (c. 1789–1804) and Ali Bakhsh (c. 1790–1853). De Boigne renamed her Hélène Bennett and himself received British denization (partial naturalization) (de Boigne 1956; Compton 1893). They socialized with distinguished members of British society, including Edmund Burke (1729–97). De Boigne's ambitions, however, drove him to seek higher social status. In 1798, he contracted a Catholic marriage with Charlotte d'Osmonde (1781–1866), daughter of exiled and impoverished French nobility. They baptized Nur Begum's children as Catholic, christening them Anna and Charles Alexander. De Boigne then moved Nur Begum out of London, first to Enfield and later to Lower Beeding, Sussex, giving her a modest £300 annual allowance. Many prominent members of British society supported Nur Begum, offering to use British law to enforce her rights to de Boigne's vast wealth. She, however, humbly refused their offers and accepted a quiet retirement. The local villagers and her English maidservant showed her respect, although they thought her exotic, as a mysterious 'dark' lady (Baldwin 1985; Cotton 1933). De Boigne and his new wife eventually established themselves in France. While de Boigne's and Nur Begum's daughter, Anna, died tragically young, their son, Charles, succeeded his father as Count de Boigne in 1830.

Not only did Britons seem to accept Anglicization by Indian wives of Europeans, visiting Indians did so as well. For example, traveller, author, and Persian teacher, Mirza Abu Talib Khan Isfahani (1752–1806) met both Mrs Ducarel and Nur Begum/Hélène Bennett around 1800. He explained patriotically to his Persophone Indian readers that these women had settled in Britain out of devotion to their children, rather than out of love for their European husbands (Abu Talib Khan 1983: 173). But, they appeared to him as virtually English: very fair in complexion, fully Anglophone, and displaying British-style dress and deportment. In particular, the children of Nur Begum/Hélène Bennett impressed Abu Talib as fully English.

Other children of Indian women and European men also made places for themselves in Britain. Lieutenant Colonel James Achilles Kirkpatrick (1764–1805) of the Madras Army sent to England at least three of the children he had with Indian women, leaving their protesting mothers behind in India (Kirkpatrick 1802; Dalrymple 2002). The two younger children, Mir Ghulam Ali, Sahib Allum (1801–28) and Nur un-Nissa, Sahiba Begum (1802–89), attended by an Indian manservant, settled in England in 1805 with Kirkpatrick's relatives. In Kirkpatrick's will, he left them £10,000 each. According to his posthumous directions, they were converted and baptized in 1806, becoming William George and Catherine Aurora Kirkpatrick. Their wealth and connections enabled them to assimilate into British society. Yet, their Indian origins also added to their appeal. Catherine, known as Kitty, was widely known as the 'Hindoo Princess' (illustrating the vague concepts held even in educated British society about Indian culture, since she was neither Hindu nor a princess). She was courted by Thomas Carlyle (1795–1881), who described her as possessing £50,000, 'a strangely-complexioned young lady, with soft brown eyes and floods of bronze-red hair, really a pretty-looking, smiling, and amiable, though most foreign bit of magnificence ... a half-*Begum*; in short, an interesting specimen of the semi-oriental Englishwoman' (Carlyle 1881; Carlyle and Welsh Carlyle 1970–93, 3: 166–7). According to family tradition, the future author Carlyle was dismissed as her suitor since he appeared (wrongly) to have few prospects in life. Portraits of her in Britain reveal nothing about her Indian background, but rather suggest how Anglicized she had become. Indeed, both she and her brother married Britons and died there, leaving children as members of British society. Thus, they, like many other women and men of Indian or part-Indian ancestry, negotiated with the Britons around them, their Indian origins being only one of the many factors comprising their identities.

Indian settlers entering the British middle classes

Some entrepreneurial Indian settlers proved able to Anglicize themselves and enter the middle classes in Britain, often using their Indian origins to distinguish themselves. The settler who wrote most extensively about his diverse careers in Ireland and England was Sake Dean Mahomet (1759–1851). His two-volume autobiographical epistolary travel narrative, *Travels of Dean*

Mahomet, A Native of Patna in Bengal, Through Several Parts of India, While in the Service of The Honorable The East India Company Written by Himself, In a Series of Letters to a Friend (Mahomet 1794), recounts his birth and childhood in a Shi'ite family of Patna, Bihar (Fisher 1996). After Anglo-Irish officer Godfrey Evan Baker (*c.* 1750–86) gave his widowed mother 400 rupees for him, he became Baker's camp follower. Eventually, he rose to be market master then *subedar* (lieutenant) in the 30th Native Infantry Regiment of the Company's Bengal Army. He ends his first autobiographical account with his arrival in Britain in 1784. After settling in Cork, Ireland, he married in 1786 an Anglican gentry-woman, Jane Daly (*c.* 1761–1844), with whom he had several children. While visiting Cork in 1799, Mirza Abu Talib Khan met and described Dean Mahomet and his growing family. Soon after, Dean Mahomet emigrated with his family to London where he worked as a 'shampooer' (doing full body massage therapy). In 1806, he evidently bigamously married another Anglican women, Jane Jeffreys (1780–1850) and had at least seven more children. In 1810, he started London's first Indian restaurant run by an Indian, The Hindostanee Coffee House, also known popularly as 'The Hooka Club', famous for its oriental cuisine and ambiance. After having to declare bankruptcy, Dean Mahomet advertised himself as a butler before moving to the burgeoning seaside resort of Brighton and making himself famous as the 'shampooing surgeon' by appointment to the Crown. He established a fashionable bathhouse on the shorefront and, as part of his self-promotion, he wrote and published two other books *Cases Cured by Sake Deen Mahomed, Shampooing Surgeon, and Inventor of the Indian Medicated Vapour and Sea-Water Bath* (Mahomet 1820) and, in three editions, *Shampooing, or, Benefits Resulting from the Use of the Indian Medicated Vapour Bath* (Mahomet 1822, 1826, 1838). He made a place for himself in Brighton society, qualified to vote for the British Parliament and in local elections, and was buried as a parishioner in an Anglican churchyard. His sons tried to sustain his 'Oriental' medical practice but, having been born in Britain, lacked his image of authenticity. His descendants, however, did succeed in the Western medical profession and clergy. Hence, over his nearly seven decades in Britain, his diverse life, with its movement between social and economic classes, marriage with Britons, and efforts to use his Asian origins to distinguish himself from his European competitors, and his British citizenship all reflected the less well documented experiences of a range of other Asian immigrants.

Similar in origins, Munnoo (1795–183?) had worked in Calcutta since the age of nine as a domestic servant, along with his mother, for lawyer and diarist William Hickey (Hickey 1919–25, 4: 376–473). As Hickey was retiring to England in 1808, he gave 500 rupees to young Munnoo's mother in order to bring him to England. Munnoo settled with Hickey in Beaconsfield, Buckinghamshire, studied in a local school, and eventually converted to Anglican Christianity with the baptismal name William Munnew. He married an Englishwoman, Anne, rose to be a 'licensed victualler' (restaurateur or tavern-keeper), and had at least two children (his son becoming a skilled piano-tuner). Currently, Munnew's portrait (with that of Hickey) hangs in the halls of the British Parliament (National Portrait Gallery 1819, NPG 3249). His descendants displayed little overt connection to Munnoo's origin as an Indian domestic slave. Thus, some Indian men proved able to created new lives for themselves in Britain, with their origins making them distinctively oriental, but their families less so.

Indians seeking justice in Britain

The East India Company's spreading economic and political power in India meant increasingly that people there were aggrieved by colonial authorities. Indian merchants, landholders, and employees of the Company, including soldiers, clerks, and officials, finding no redress in India, travelled to Britain. The dominant British ideology that just authorities in London would overrule any legal or moral injustice committed by British officials in the colonies drew Indians to travel to the metropole and appeal there. Some Indians obtained substantial success but most made a frustratingly futile journey. Of those who came, some stayed on as settlers in Britain.

Among the earliest and most successful of these Indian plaintiffs was Parsi merchant and broker Nowroji Rustamji. In 1721, he sailed to London, accompanied by his wife, children and a dozen Parsi servants. His aim was to protest directly to the Company's Directors against the Bombay Government's refusal to pay a legal debt and imprisonment of his brothers (Court Minutes, 13/5/1724 to 14/10/1724). After years of negotiation, in 1725, the Directors conceded the errors of the Bombay Government and paid the £63,853 debt due to his family, plus in restitution awarded robes of honour, a horse, and tax exemption for Nowroji's houses in Bombay. Relatively few other Indian plaintiffs who followed Nowroji's example proved as successful. Some, however, gained a measure of support in London against East India Company officials and officers in India.

In a later example, Mohammed Ibrahim Palowkar (1811–55) came with his father and servants from Bombay to London in 1833 to make a legal appeal for restoration of land-holdings at Dabhol (from which they had been dispossessed a century earlier by the Marathas) (Board Collections F/4/1371). For 16 years, his family had been vainly protesting to the Bombay Government. While their petition in London had no realistic chance of success, it reflected their desperate faith in British justice if only they could reach London. The Directors quickly repulsed this appeal as they did most by Indian plaintiffs. However, having learned in London about the East India Company's subordinate relationship to Parliament, the family then initiated a new campaign to the Parliamentary Board of Control which oversaw the Directors in political matters. Over time, the family's financial situation deteriorated until they finally accepted £300 from the Directors to pay their debts and passage home. Rather than return to Bombay, however, Mohammed Ibrahim Palowkar, established himself in Britain. Months earlier, he had secretly married a Protestant Irishwoman, Eleanor Deegan, at St. Leonard's Church, Shoreditch. Until his death in 1855, he ran a tobacconist shop in London. His three sons respectively became a merchant's clerk, a gas-fitter then electrician, and a hatter. This family continues in Britain, with some branches taking the surname Wilson, others keeping Palowkar, but with few family traditions about their Indian origins.

From the mid-eighteenth century, increasing numbers of rulers in India came to experience the political power exerted by the East India Company. Consequently, they began to delegate Indian ambassadors and other envoys to London in order to bypass the Company's administration in India and directly influence the British crown and Parliament, as well as influential British public opinion. As early as 1766, Emperor Shah Alam II sent as his political representative Mirza Shaikh I'tisam al-Din (1730–1800) to London. Although diplomatically unsuccessful, he later wrote *Shigrif-namah-i Wilayat* ['Wonder-book of Europe'] describing his time in Britain for Persophone readers. Subsequently, other Indian rulers dispatched their own Indian embassies. Among them, Mughal Emperor Muhammad Akbar II (r. 1806–37) sent the most famous of such ambassadors, Raja Rammohun Roy (1772–1833), already well known in Bengal and Britain as a social and religious reformer. He arrived in 1831, negotiated shrewdly, and never left Britain, dying in Bristol in 1833 (Carpenter 1866). The longest of these Indian diplomatic missions, representing Maratha Maharaja Pratap Singh (r. 1818–39, d. 1847) of Satara, lasted from 1838 to 1851. At its peak, this delegation consisted of four ambassadors, supported by six secretaries and ten servants; Rungoo Bapojee (1804–57/8) was the most effective of these ambassadors, lobbying Parliament and publishing and giving speeches to the British public (Court Minutes, 1838–1851).

Some Indian royalty obtained far better terms by maneuvering in person in London than they could either in India or via representatives. Two of Tipu Sultan's imprisoned sons, Mahomed Jamh ood-Deen (*c.* 1792–1842) and Gholam Mahomed (1795–1872), moved to London in 1835 and 1854 respectively. There, they both negotiated successfully with sympathetic British authorities, including Queen Victoria, for higher pensions and also entered high society, the former permanently. Similarly, deposed Punjabi Maharaja Duleep Singh (1838–93) spent from 1854 until his death mostly based in Britain, although his relations with the British royal family and government varied from cordial to hostile. By the mid-nineteenth century, a total of at least 30 diplomatic or royal missions from Indian rulers (or would-be rulers) had arrived to lobby the British government and savour British pleasures. Thus, a range of Indians ventured to London in order to improve their situations or themselves.

Indian students and teachers

Cultural interactions between Europe and India attracted to Britain Indian students of medicine, engineering, Christianity, and culture generally. In 1614, a young Indian from Surat came to study English and Latin, proving particularly noteworthy to English authorities for his desire for conversion to Christianity. The East India Company allowed him £13 annually for expenses and expected him to return to India as 'an instrument in converting some of his nation' (Court Minutes, 19/8/1614, 18/7/1615). After consultation with the Archbishop of Canterbury, the Lord Mayor, and King James I, this boy was baptized 'Peter Pope' in St. Dionis Backchurch on Fenchurch Street (near the Company's headquarters) on 22 December 1616 (Das 1924: 84–85). This man later returned to India to evangelize, reporting in Latin to his spiritual mentors. Thereafter, many Indian converts to Christianity would likewise travel to Britain for their further education, some returning, others staying on as settlers.

Especially from the early nineteenth century, European technical and scientific developments appeared to some Indians as worthy of study. In the 1830s–40s, British advances in marine steam-engine technology attracted three Parsi naval engineers from Bombay – Jehangeer Nowrojee (1821–66), Hirjeebhoy Merwanjee (1817–83), and Ardaseer Cursetjee (1808–77) (Hinnells 1996). Each authored books about their lives in Britain (Nowrojee and Merwanjee 1841; Cursetjee 1840). Cursetjee would eventually make four trips to Britain, dying there in 1877. From the 1840s, Indian medical students began coming to Britain to qualify as doctors. Some of the first were four graduates of Calcutta Medical College who arrived to study at University College, London in 1845 – Dwarkanath Bose, Bholanath Das Bose, Gopal Chandra Seal, and Soojee Comar Chuckerbutty (later Goodeve). Many other young Indian men, and later women, would go to London for their education thereafter (Brown 1913; Llewellyn-Jones 1990).

British diplomacy and administration in India required mastery over the Persian language and administrative, court, and diplomatic protocols long established by the Mughal Empire over most of India. Hence, from the mid-eighteenth century, Indian teachers of these bodies of knowledge went or were brought to Britain to teach them there to potential British colonial officials and officers. Among the earliest language teachers were Munshi Isma'il in 1772, Mir Muhammad Husain ibn Abdul 'Azim Isfahani in 1775–76, Monshee Mahomet Saeed in 1777, Munshi Muhammad Sami around 1785, and Mirza Mohammed Fitrut of Lucknow in 1797–1801 (Khan 1998). Most famously, Mirza Abu Talib Khan Isfahani (1752–1806) toured Britain in 1799–1802 (Abu Talib Khan 1983). Four of these Indian scholars wrote books (in Persian or Arabic) about their experiences of – and moral judgments about – British faults, as well as accomplishments, for the edification of Indian and British readers. Abu Talib's published articles and books had especially wide audiences in India and Europe. However, he described his years in Britain somewhat differently to two separate audiences. His essay 'Vindication of the Liberties of Asiatic Women' (Abu Talib Khan 1800) attempted to prove to European readers that Asian women had more rights than European ones, hence that Asian culture was superior. This essay was translated into Dutch, German, and French and republished at least ten times in European journals by 1819. In Abu Talib's Persian book *Masir Talibi fi Bilad Afranji*, in contrast, he attempts to show his Persophone readers how they should improve themselves, in at least some measure, by emulating British society.

Most but not all of the scholar-administrators going to Britain were Muslim. A Bengali Hindu by birth but Persian translator by profession, Goneshamdass travelled to England and testified in English before Parliament in 1773 as an expert on Islamic and Hindu legal practices as they related to British colonial courts. A man who moved among cultures, back in Bengal he converted to Christianity as Robert.

Some of these men taught privately, finding students among the many British men who wished to trade or rule in India. Among other Indian teachers in Britain, Mirza Abu Talib Khan came primarily to establish himself as the director of a Persian language academy in Oxford or London. While he awaited government support for his proposal, he took fee-paying private students. He only returned to India when he felt his proposal had permanently stalled (although British authorities belatedly sanctioned his plan, the letter of appointment arriving after Abu Talib's death). More formally, for three decades from 1806, a series of Asian professors held appointments at the East Indian Company's colleges at Haileybury and Addiscombe, teaching Persian and Urdu to its newly appointed civil servants and cadet officers respectively. Three of the Indian immigrant teachers, Sheth Ghoolam Hyder (1776–1823, of Darbhanga, Bihar) Moolvey Meer Abdool Alee (?–1811, of Benaras), and Meer Hassan Ali (of Lucknow) married Englishwomen (in addition to their wives and children back in India). The first two of these men remained in Britain for the rest of their lives. Later, University College, London, appointed a number of Indian language teachers; one of the first was Dadabhai Naoroji (1825–1917), who was Professor of Gujarati (1856–66) there.

Colonial subjects to British citizens and members of civil society

One of the key transitions for Indian settlers in Britain was from being colonial subjects of the British crown to being citizens of the United Kingdom. One measure of citizenship was the right to vote in Britain. Naturalization, while possible by act of Parliament, was expensive and rare, although some Asians succeeded in accomplishing this. Nonetheless, at least from the early nineteenth century onward, Indian-born men and their British-born sons who had sufficient property, were domiciled in a British constituency, and met the religious requirements of the day could vote for local officials and members of the House of Commons like other British citizens. Their wives and other women (whether Indians or British) could not yet vote, however.

Whether India-born men of sufficient property qualified to enter the British Parliament, however, remained moot until 1841. Around 1831, Raja Rammohun Roy was reportedly proposed as a candidate for Parliament by Jeremy Bentham (1748–1832) (Zastoupil 2002). Roy's untimely death, however, precluded his election and thus the test whether, as a Hindu, he could swear the Christian-centered oath necessary for admission to Parliament, should he win. A decade later, however, a Catholic man of mixed ancestry who had been born in the small Indian princely state of Sardhana (outside of British sovereignty), named David Ochterlony Dyce Sombre (1808–51), was elected to Parliament from the English constituency of Sudbury (Fisher 2010). Although Dyce Sombre was extremely wealthy, he owned no landed property in

Britain and could vote neither in India (where no one could vote) or Britain. Nevertheless, he entered Parliament (Catholic men having been permitted to do so since 1829, although Jewish men would not be able to do so until 1858), voted there for nine months, but then was expelled in 1842 due to the excessive electoral corruption of Sudbury. The next Indian elected would be Dadabhai Naoroji half a century later in 1892, from Central Finsbury on the Liberal ticket, after having run and lost in 1886 (Burton 2000). Hence, once in Britain, Asian men acquired the rights of political participation in voting and standing for Parliament based on the laws currently in place about qualifications that applied to all Britons.

Other institutions that Asian men could sometimes join included British societies, including the Freemasons and various British gentlemen's clubs. While in India, some lodges of Freemasons excluded non-whites, others accepted Muslims and Parsis but excluded Hindus (since the oath of admission required acknowledgment of a single divinity, most lodges felt Hindus could not conform). Once an Asian was admitted, the strict hierarchy of Masonic degrees meant that he outranked white Britons of degrees lower than his own. In Britain, however, all branches of Freemasonry seem to have accepted those non-white men whom they deemed socially acceptable. Similarly, some of the gentlemen's clubs of London and other British cities excluded Asians, while others accepted some of them. London's Oriental Club, for example, had been established in 1824, mainly by East India Company officials and officers, for 'gentlemen' who had lived in 'the Orient' (Oriental Club Candidate Books 1824–58). In 1831, the Club had expanded its definition of 'gentlemen' to include selected Asians, but only as 'Honourary Members'. Then, in 1834, it elected as a 'Full Member' a wealthy Parsi merchant of Calcutta, Sirkis Juhannas Sirkis, and four years later, Mahomed Jamh ood-Deen. Further, select Indian elites visiting London were admitted as Honourary Members. These included pretender to the Awadh throne Nawab Iqbal al-Daula Bahadur (1808–88); businessman, banker, social reformer Dwarkanath Tagore (1794–1846) who came twice to Britain and died there; diplomat and author Mohun Lal (1812–77); and deposed Punjabi Maharaja Duleep Singh. The more liberal Reform Club, from early after its founding in 1836 in Pall Mall, London, had elected 'Foreigners of distinction' including Asians and Africans into its membership, although often only on a temporary basis. Thus, class and gender criteria applied to Indians as well as to Britons. However, British concepts of biological race became increasingly determinative from the mid-nineteenth century onward, as growing numbers of Britons brought back colonial concepts and as pseudo-scientific ideas of human and social evolution developed.

Indian communities in Britain

By the late eighteenth century, the number of Asians in Britain, particularly working-class Asians, had grown to the extent that transient communities began to form, especially in the docklands of London. Most of the Asians who travelled to Britain landed in this metropolis. However, paintings, newspaper reports, letters, and books of fiction and non-fiction by Britons depict Asians living across Britain. Many lived in smaller cities, towns, or villages with British families as individual or small groups of servants or slaves, others as a husband or wife to a Briton, with their children moving toward assimilation. Only in London and a few of the other larger port cities, especially from the late eighteenth century onward, were there sufficient numbers of Asians to form communities, even transient ones. Hardening British ideas about class and race also tended to foster such communities of Asians collectively.

From the late eighteenth century, the East India Company contracted with lodging-house keepers to provide for the Indian *lascars* and also those who had become impoverished in

Britain and therefore the responsibility of the Company. From 1799 to 1834, the Company undertook a series of contracts with a Chinese immigrant (who had been naturalized by an act of Parliament, 45 Geo 3 c.4), John Anthony, and his British father-in-law and brother-in-law – Abraham Gole Sr and Jr – to provide and manage a large depot in Shadwell (off the Ratcliffe Highway in east London) for these Indians and other Asians. Over the 1803–13 period alone, the Company paid this family and other contractors a total of £169,795 for food, maintenance, medicine, and clothing for these Indians (plus £200,692 for passage money to Asia) (Marine Department 1793–1818). In 1834, Parliament unintentionally but profoundly transformed the experiences of Indians in Britain when it suspended the East India Company's Charter to trade in Asia for 20 years. This ended the Company's legal responsibility to support indigent Indians and so it terminated its contracts with the Shadwell depot and other suppliers of services to these Indians.

To replace the Shadwell depot, entrepreneurs, including some Indian men and their female British partners, opened and ran lodging houses in Poplar and Limehouse (near London's East India Docks) to accommodate these Asian sailors and other working-class men. This area became known as east London's Oriental Quarter. There, Indians were able to develop their sense of being a part of a diasporic community. In 1856, The Strangers' Home for Asiatics, Africans, and South Sea Islanders opened in Commercial Road, Limehouse, funded by donations from Indians and Britons. This institution then took over many of the functions of lodging and managing Indian *lascars* in London.

By the mid-nineteenth century, expanding British colonial power over non-white peoples in Asia and Africa and the concomitant development of British concepts of biological race as inherited and determinative of moral and civilizational standing of distinct peoples combined to make Indians stand out as separate and appear to many British authorities to be less able to be assimilated in Britain (Mayhew 1861–2; Peggs 1844; Salter 1873). The bloody events of 1857 in India, along with other race-based conflicts elsewhere in the Empire, reinforced these British concepts of non-Britons as essentially 'other'. Further, these same developments simultaneously tended to make Britons assume a solidarity that began to see non-white men as threats to white British womanhood. Also, by this time, the expansion of steam-powered transcontinental ships transformed Indian seamen from skilled workers of wind-powered vessels to become unskilled labour – especially shovellers of coal into boilers or attendants on passengers and crew as servants. Overall, Britain, as the center of an expanding empire, comprised a distinctive host for these Asian settlers and visitors, but one which changed over the centuries.

Bibliography

Abu Talib Khan, Mirza (1800) 'Vindication of the Liberties of Asiatic Women' reprinted in (trans) Charles Stewart (1814) *Travels of Mirza Abu Taleb Khan*, London: Longman *et al.*

— (1983) *Masir Talibi fi Bilad Afranji*, (ed.) Hosein Khadive-Jam, Tehran (Persian reprint).

Baldwin, Marjorie (1985) *Story of the Forest*, Colgate: St Savior's Church.

Ballantyne, Tony (2002) *Orientalism and Race: Aryanism in the British Empire*, Houndmills: Palgrave.

Barber, Jill (2000) *Celebrating the Black Presence*, vol. 2, *Hidden Lives*, Westminster: City of Westminster Archives Centre.

Birdwood, George and Foster, William (1893) *Register of Letters &c. of the Governour and Company of Merchants of London Trading into the East Indies, 1600–16*, London: Bernard Quaritch.

Board Collections F/4/1371 no. 54513, British Library.

de Boigne, Charlotte (1956) *Memoirs*, (ed.) Sylvia de Morsier-Kotthaus, London: Museum Press.

Brown, F. H. (1913) 'Indian Students in Britain', *Edinburgh Review*, 217, 443: 138–56.

Brown, Judith M. (2006) *Global South Asians: Introducing the Modern Diaspora*, Cambridge: Cambridge University Press.

Burton, Antoinette (2000) 'Tongues Untied: Lord Salisbury's "Black Man" and the Boundaries of Imperial Democracy', *Comparative Studies in Society and History*, 42, 3: 632–61.

Carlyle, Thomas (1881) *Reminiscences*, (ed.) James Anthony Froude, New York: Harper and Brothers.

Carlyle, Thomas and Welsh Carlyle, Jane (1970–93), *Collected Letters of Thomas and Jane Welsh Carlyle*, 26 vols, (eds) Charles Richard Sanders *et al.*, Durham: Duke University Press.

Carpenter, Mary (1866) *Last Days in England of the Rajah Rammohun Roy*, London: Trubner.

Chatterjee, Indrani (1999) *Gender, Slavery, and Law in Colonial India*, New Delhi: Oxford University Press.

Compton, Herbert (1893) *Particular Account of the European Military Adventurers in India, from 1784 to 1803*, London: T. Fisher Unwin.

Cotton, Sir Evan (1933) 'Begum in Sussex', *Bengal Past and Present*, 46: 91–4.

Court Minutes, India Office Records, British Library.

Cursetjee, Ardeseer (1840) *Diary of an Overland Journey from Bombay to England and of a Year's Residence in Great Britain*, London: Henington and Galabin.

Dalrymple, William (2002) *White Mughals: Love and Betrayal in Eighteenth-century India*, London: Harper Collins.

Das, Harihar (1924) 'Early Indian Visitors to England', *Calcutta Review*, 3rd series, 13: 83–114.

Fisher, Michael H. (1996) *First Indian Author in English: Dean Mahomed (1759–1851) in India, Ireland, and England*, Delhi: Oxford University Press.

—— (2004) *Counterflows to Colonialism: Indian Travellers and Settlers in Britain, 1600–1857*, Delhi: Permanent Black.

—— (2010) *The Inordinately Strange Life of Dyce Sombre: Victorian Anglo Indian MP and Chancery 'Lunatic'*, London: Hurst.

Fisher, Michael H., Lahiri, Shompa and Thandi, Shinder (2007) *A South Asian History of Britain: Four Centuries of Peoples from the Indian Subcontinent*, London: Greenwood Press.

Forbes, Thomas Roger (1971) *Chronicle from Aldgate: Life and Death in Shakespeare's London*, New Haven, CT: Yale University Press.

Fryer, Peter (1984) *Staying Power: The History of Black People in Britain*, London: Pluto.

Gerzina, Gretchen (1995) *Black London: Life Before Emancipation*, New Brunswick, NJ: Rutgers University Press.

Great Britain, Public Record Office (1862) *Calendar of State Papers, Colonial Series*, vol. 2, *East Indies and Japan, 1513–1616*, ed. W. Noel Sainsbury, London: PRO.

Gundara, Jagdish S. and Duffield, Ian (eds) (1992) *Essays on the History of Blacks in Britain: From Roman Times to the Mid-Twentieth Century*, Aldershot: Avebury.

Harrison, Mark (1999) *Climates and Constitutions: Health, Race, Environment and British Imperialism in India, 1600–1850*, Delhi: Oxford University Press.

Hawkins, William (1970) *Hawkins' Voyages during the Reigns of Henry VIII, Queen Elizabeth, and James I*, (ed.) Clements R. Markham, New York: B. Franklin.

Hickey, William (1919–25) *Memoirs of William Hickey*, 4 vols, (ed.) Alfred Spencer, London: Hurst and Blackett.

Hinnells, John R. (1996) *Zoroastrians in Britain: the Ratanbai Katrak Lectures, University of Oxford 1985*, Oxford: Clarendon Press.

Innes, C. L. (2002) *A History of Black and Asian Writing in Britain, 1700–2000*, Cambridge: Cambridge University Press.

I'tisam al-Din, Mirza Shaikh, *Shigrif-namah-i Wilayat* [Wonder-book of Europe] OR 200, British Library.

Khan, Gulfishan (1998) *Indian Muslim Perceptions of the West during the Eighteenth Century*, Karachi: Oxford University Press.

Kirkpatrick, James Achilles (1802) Letters, MSS EUR F.228/57, British Library.

Llewellyn-Jones, Rosie (1990) 'Indian Travellers in Nineteenth Century England', *Indo-British Review*, 18, 1: 137–41.

Mahomet, Sake Dean (1794) *Travels of Dean Mahomet, A Native of Patna in Bengal, Through Several Parts of India, While in the Service of The Honorable The East India Company Written by Himself, In a Series of Letters to a Friend*, Cork: The Author.

—— (1820) *Cases Cured by Sake Deen Mahomed, Shampooing Surgeon, and Inventor of the Indian Medicated Vapour and Sea-Water Bath*, Brighton: The Author.

—— (1822, 1826, 1838) *Shampooing, or, Benefits Resulting from the Use of the Indian Medicated Vapour Bath*, Brighton: The Author.

Manchester City Galleries, Manchester, 'Cheeta and Stag with Two Indians' by George Stubbs, 1765, 1970.34.

Marine Department, Papers Relating to the Care of Lascars, 1793–1818, L/MAR/C/902, vols. 1–2, British Library.

Mayhew, Henry (1861–2) *London Labour and the London Poor*, 4 vols, London: Griffin, Bohn, and Company.

National Gallery, London (*c.*1633) 'William Feilding, 1st Earl of Denbigh' by Anthony van Dyck, NG5633.

National Portrait Gallery, London (1819) 'William Hickey, His Favourite Black Servant, and Dog', NPG 3249.

Nowrojee, Jehangeer and Merwanjee, Hirjeebhoy (1841) *Journal of a Residence of Two Years and a Half in Great Britain*, London: William H. Allen.

Old Bailey, Proceedings.

Oriental Club Candidate Books (1824–58) LMA/4452/04/01/001–2, London Metropolitan Archives, London.

Peggs, Reverend James (1844) *Lascars' Cry to Britain*, London: The Author.

Ramdin, Ron (1999) *Reimagining Britain: 500 Years of Black and Asian History*, London: Pluto.

Salter, Joseph (1873) *Asiatic in England: Sketches of Sixteen Years' Work among Orientals*, London: Seely, Jackson, and Halliday.

Tobin, Beth Fowkes (1999) *Picturing Imperial Power: Colonial Subjects in Eighteenth-century British Painting*, Durham: Duke University Press.

Visram, Rozina (1984) *Ayahs, Lascars and Princes: Indians in Britain, 1700–1947*, London: Pluto.

— (2002) *Asians in Britain: 400 Years of History*, London: Pluto.

Young, Desmond (1959) *Fountain of the Elephants*, New York: Harper and Brothers.

Zastoupil, Lynn (2002) 'Defining Christians, Making Britons', *Victorian Studies*, 44, 2: 215–43.

11

WARRIORS, WORKERS, TRADERS AND PEASANTS

The Nepali/Gorkhali diaspora since the nineteenth century

David N. Gellner

Defining diaspora

To speak of diaspora implies a scattering of people from a homeland.[1] In the case of the Jews, and other similar cases, this followed a tragic event and expulsion and/or flight. The key event, and the desire for return, were memorialized through rituals. Those rituals become the foundation of collective memory and group identity. In recent decades the term 'diaspora' has been stretched and expanded to refer to any migrant group retaining some memory and some link to their homeland, so that it is no longer possible to insist that diasporas must be born out of suffering and tragedy (Cohen 2008). In this new extended sense, one can even speak of a British diaspora, since there are still people (in New Zealand, for instance) who idealize the home country and whose identity is grounded in maintaining links to it (ibid: 69f). There is certainly a Scottish diaspora, encouraged and courted by the devolved Scottish government in Edinburgh. However, it would be an elementary error to assume that everyone with a Scottish surname shares Sean Connery's level of 'diasporic consciousness'.

In the Nepali case, as with the Tibetans – and unlike the paradigmatic Jews, Greeks, or Armenians (all defined by adherence to a distinctive religious tradition) – it would be anachronistic to speak of a diaspora before the modern period and the age of nationalism. Diaspora is not the same as migration *tout court*. There have been continual waves of migration into and along the Himalayas, and this is likely to have been so even in prehistoric times. Within historic times the dominant trend has been for migration to be in a north-west to south-east direction along the Himalayan foothills, so that the Khas people, who are mentioned in textual sources (the Mahabharata among others) as inhabiting Kashmir, are to be found as the 'indigenous' and majority group in western Nepal today. The predominant eastwards direction can be explained by the greater rainfall and greater fertility of the land, the further east one goes (Whelpton 2005: 13). As the Khas moved east they encountered peoples speaking Tibeto–Burman languages who had settled in Nepal (arriving either from the north or the east) much earlier. There have also been plenty of local eddies and counter-currents in population movements alongside the overall macro west–east trend (Dolfuss *et al.* 2001), with the result that the pattern of ethnic settlement that we have today is thoroughly mixed, not to say Balkanized (Sharma 2008).

For a diaspora to exist there has to be a sense of national or quasi-national (religion-based) identity and the people so concerned must be settled outside the territory with which their identity is bound up. Cultural memories of links to a specific place have to last over the generations (a process much helped if there is continual movement back to that place). Furthermore, there has to be a *boundary*, however conceived. Unless the people are outside that boundary, they can hardly be said to be in diaspora. Where there are no national boundaries – or where the people themselves do not recognize them – they can hardly have a sense of loss at crossing them. The creation of national boundaries in South Asia is still very much a work in progress, a battle that states are waging against ordinary people who are either unaware of them or, if aware, do not much care (van Schendel 2005). It may well be, then, that a 'diasporic consciousness' is more conspicuous or more consistently present in the literary productions of nationalist intellectuals (Hutt 1998) than it is in minds, hearts and actions of the 'working-class cosmopolitans' who actually move and live abroad. It may also be, as we shall see in the Bhutanese, Darjeeling and Sikkimese cases, that, in order to try and establish themselves in their new host societies, people of Nepali cultural background sometimes are obliged to *deny* that they have any diasporic leanings.

Creating Nepal

The modern state of Nepal (though not yet called that) was created in the eighteenth century, largely through the tenacity and strategic vision of one man, Prithvi Narayan Shah (Whelpton 2005). Born in the small hill town of Gorkha in 1722, he became its king in 1743 and immediately travelled to Banaras to buy muskets. Whether or not he anticipated the rise of British power in the subcontinent (as some Nepali historians claim), he was able to create a political unit that dwarfed the tiny kingdom he inherited. At its largest extent, following the conquests of his successors and before the Treaty of Sagauli with the East India Company in 1815, it stretched from the Tista river in the east (now running through Sikkim) to the Satlej river in the west. Thus the Indian divisions of Kumaon and Garhwal (now in Uttarakhand) were under the Gorkhalis for 25 years, a period still remembered for its oppressive rule (Regmi 1999).

The turning point in Prithvi Narayan's career came in 1768–69 with his conquest of the Kathmandu Valley (Stiller 1973; Pradhan 1991; Regmi 1999), which, despite his suspicions of its virility-sapping luxury, he made his capital. It was a wide fertile bowl capable of supporting a higher and denser population than anywhere else in the Himalayas. It was thus an outpost of Indian civilization and a self-constituted sacred centre from at least the third century CE. Its inhabitants were the Newars, an amalgam of local and in-migrating groups ranked in more than 20 castes, with their own language (Newari/Nepal Bhasa) and culture. The new state that Prithvi Narayan created was still quite heavily forested and, by today's standards, thinly populated, but, with peace and unification, the population began to grow rapidly. Economically the state was based on extraction of peasant surplus and on taxing trade (Regmi 1984). The main trade routes from India to Tibet ran through the Kathmandu Valley. Some Newar artisans had been invited to move to Gorkha already in the seventeenth century. Others had long travelled to Tibet and were settled, as artisans and traders, in the cities of Shigatse, Gyantse and Lhasa (some had one wife in Nepal and another in Tibet). The Malla kings of the Kathmandu Valley had provided silver coinage for the Tibetans and gaining control of this contract was one of Prithvi Narayan's motivations for conquest.

No Himalayan migrant peoples thought of themselves as Nepalis before the twentieth century, and for most of the nineteenth century it would have been much more natural to call oneself 'Gorkhali', that is to say, a subject of the Shah dynasty, the 'House of Gorkha' (Whelpton 2008). Their language was also called Gorkhali (an older term was 'Khas Kura' or 'the speech of the Khas'). This was corrupted as 'Gurkha' in British military parlance; often understood as an ethnic term, it is so only in a very weak and extended sense. There is no tribe or caste of 'Gurkhas' in Nepal. In the nineteenth century the name 'Nepal' referred only to the Kathmandu Valley, a usage still current even today in colloquial speech (*(ma) Nepal jāne* is the pithiest and simplest way of saying 'I'm off to Kathmandu'). It was not till the 1920s that Prithvi Narayan's descendants followed much earlier British colonial labelling practice and officially extended the term 'Nepal' to all their possessions. This formed part of the first, hesitant steps towards a new nationalist imagining of the Shah dynasty's subjects as 'Nepalis' (Burghart 1984; Whelpton 2005).

Thus, if one were to speak of a Nepali diaspora before 1850, it could only have referred to the Newars, the inhabitants of the Nepal or Kathmandu Valley. In the course of the nineteenth century many Newars became the traders and shopkeepers of the new Gorkhali kingdom and settled outside the Kathmandu Valley in small bazaars and district capitals throughout the middle hills. The Newars are seen by other Nepalis as a trading diaspora, though many are in fact artisans, peasants and labourers, rather than shopkeepers and merchants.

As far as the modern Nepali diaspora is concerned, three distinct waves and types of migration can be distinguished: first, overland, mainly seeking work and land, and mainly towards the east; second, again overland, but more focused on seeking work in Indian cities; and finally, third, travelling by plane to work in the Persian Gulf (or 'arab' as Nepalis refer to it), in Southeast Asia, and beyond, or for education and work in the developed world.

Creating Nepaliness *(nepālipan)* in diaspora

An assertive sense of Nepali national identity first emerged – as has often been the case (the first Greek uprising against the Ottomans took place in what is now Romania) – in the diaspora. Subsequently, in the twentieth century, the ideas and themes of Nepali nationalism – worked out in Banaras and Darjeeling – were taken up by the Nepali state (Onta 1996; Chalmers 2003). The first writers to think of themselves as Nepalis were scholarly Brahmans in Banaras. There seems to have been a small Nepali quarter in Banaras since at least the eighteenth century, and elite Nepalis came on pilgrimage, or stayed in exile there, even before that (Gaenszle 2002). It was in the 1880s that the movement for Hindi, led by Harishchandra Bharatendu (Orsini 2002), was getting underway in Banaras, and this clearly stimulated some Banaras-based Nepalis to start producing literature in their own vernacular in order to 'uplift' the language, and to establish it as a worthy vehicle for literature.[2] However, 'there remained one overriding limitation of the Nepali literary scene in Banaras: caste and class domination by educated Brahmans who were not reflective of their changing audience' (Chalmers 2002: 90).

In this respect, Darjeeling represented a stark contrast: Bahuns, the priestly and therefore literate caste, were present in much smaller numbers than in Nepal itself (see Table 11.1) but their language became the lingua franca, owned and passionately fought for by Darjeeling Nepalis. One of the key figures was Parasmani Pradhan (1898–1986). His father was a Newar Buddhist (a Shakya) who left home for Banaras and was then sent to sell books in Darjeeling. He adopted the prestigious Hindu surname Pradhan, like most Darjeeling-based Newars. Parasmani was educated in Kalimpong and Darjeeling and became a teacher, schools inspector, writer, publisher and activist. He wrote quantities of Nepali textbooks, dictionaries, grammars, collections of essays, biographies, translations and plays. He helped to bring about the standardization of the

Table 11.1 Ethnic/caste breakdown of Nepali populations in different contexts

Group	Nepal, pop'n census 2001	Proportion of establishment jobs in Nepal	Proportion in Gurkha regiments 1894–1913	Darjeeling 1941	Sikkim 2005–6	UK 2009	Delhi 2000
N =	23.15m	1,526	35,443	236,434*	432,198	18,801+	402#
Bahun	12.7%	} 66.3%		3.5%	9.4%	} 19.3%	} 38.3%
Chhetri (incl. Thakuri)	17.3%			11%	16.45%		
Newar	5.5%	15.2%		5.2%	5%	6.9%	1.2%
Tamang	5.6%			18.3%	9.1%	1.4%	
Magar	7.1%		36.1%	7.3%	3.6%	13.9%	} 34.3%
Gurung	2.4%	} 7.1%¬	23.8%	6.5%	7.9%	22.2%	
Rai	2.8%		14.1%	24%	18%	8.3%	
Limbu	1.6%		13.4%	7.5%	13.2%	9.6%	
Tharu	6.7%						
Yadav	3.9%	} 11.1%				} 0.3%^	} 11.9%^
Muslim	4.3%					0.01%	
Dalit	12.8%	0.3%~		11.5%	8.6%	1.3%	14.1%
Other	17.3%		12.6%	5.2%	8.7%	16.79%	
Proportion of overall pop'n	100%			63%	74.3%	c. 0.01%	c. 0.01%

Sources: Nepal census; Neupane (2000) as adapted in Onta (2006); Ragsdale (1990); Pradhan (1982); Tanka Subba (personal communication, based on Govt of Sikkim socio-economic survey, 2005–6); CNS–UK survey (Nepali Sandesh 8/9/09, pp. 1, 3); Neupane (2005)

* this was 63% of the total Darjeeling population of 376,369.
¬ refers to all Janajatis.
~ refers to hill Dalits only.
^ refers to all Madhesis.
+ number surveyed; total estimated population of Nepalis in the UK in December 2008: 72,173.
# number surveyed, out of a total estimated population of 136,000.

Notes:

Categories are not always exactly equivalent. In column one the Dalit figure is controversial; Dalit organizations claim percentages as high as 20% on the grounds that many Dalits are entered as high castes. In column two Bahuns and Chhetris are not distinguished and hill Janajatis are amalgamated, including some 'other' groups. Separate figures for Yadavs and Muslims are not given, but Madhesis as a whole have 11.1% of the top jobs.

language and he led the campaign to have Nepali recognized by the Indian state (it was accepted as the teaching language for all primary schools with a Nepali majority in Darjeeling district in 1935, as a national literary language in 1973 and as a national language of India by inclusion in Schedule Eight of the Constitution in 1992).

In Darjeeling migration led to a genuine melting pot – at least when viewed from the perspective of Nepal, where caste and ethnic differences were backed by state law until the 1950s. Among those who settled in Darjeeling, tribal languages were lost, many converted to Christianity, and intercaste marriages were commonplace. Other Nepalis practised circular migration, reinvesting what they had earned in Darjeeling back home in Nepal (Ortner 1990). A strong Nepali consciousness based on the language emerged in Darjeeling (Pradhan 1982; Hutt 2008), although ethnic organizations also existed from the 1920s (Shneiderman 2009: 118, 126–27) and began to assume more importance in the 1990s, as the race to achieve state recognition as an ST (Scheduled Tribe) got under way (Shneiderman and Turin 2006). Thanks to the efforts of Parasmani Pradhan and others like him,

> [b]y the late 1930s most of the fundamental questions about Nepaliness had been answered. The Nepali language had adopted a central position in the shared cultural life of Nepalis from different ethnic and linguistic backgrounds. The sense that people from this range of backgrounds could all lay claim to a common identity as 'we Nepalis' had been established and propagated.
>
> *(Chalmers 2003: 24)*

Many Nepalis kept moving, going on to Assam (Russell 2007). As Sinha notes (2009: 15),

> [a] considerable number of high caste Nepalese had moved as herdsmen to the marginal forestlands in Northeast India as graziers. In course of time, they turned out to be the industrious peasant cultivators and pioneering dairymen of the region.

The British made use of the Eighth Gurkha Rifles to put down numerous tribal revolts in north-east India during the course of the nineteenth century (Samaddar 2010: 61), a fact that was not forgotten. With the rise of nativist movements in Assam and the whole of north-east India, Nepalis were

> branded as 'foreigners' and 'migrants' ... [and] nicknamed *Daju*s (coolies or porters), *Bahadur*s (chowkidars) and *Kancha*s (household servants). If they raise any demands – literary, political or economic – they are often told to go to Nepal, as the Governor of Assam did recently.
>
> *(Sinha 2009: 19)*

Some Nepalis moved further on to Burma where an estimated 200,000 still live in their own ethnic enclaves as hill farmers among the Kachin and elsewhere, a largely forgotten diaspora (Haaland and Gurung 2007). They are famous as milk-sellers and cowherds in urban areas. When the Japanese invaded in 1942 many fled back to India and Nepal and some even ended up in Kunming in China (Sadan 2007: 237, 239). Some Nepalis migrated even further, whether before the war or because of it, to Thailand, which is said to have up to 100,000 ethnic Nepalis. Today Thai-born Nepalis are increasingly joined by economic and (occasionally) religious migrants coming directly from Nepal, attracted by Bangkok's high level of development (Haaland 2008) and Theravada Buddhist education (LeVine and Gellner 2005).

Throughout this period the movement of Nepalis into India, and of Indians into Nepal, was free and unhindered – as it remains to this day, guaranteed in the India–Nepal Friendship Treaty of 1950. (Goods, on the other hand, were and are subject both to state control and systematic smuggling.) Indeed, in the nineteenth century the rulers of Nepal were keen to attract peasants from British India into Nepal in order to open up the Tarai region, just as Bhutan welcomed Nepalis into its southern region. In relation to these southern frontier territories, considerations of lingual or religious nationalism were conspicuous by their absence and were to emerge only in the 1950s in Nepal (Gaige 2009) and in the 1980s in Bhutan (Hutt 2003).

This free movement of people meant that by 1871 Nepalis constituted about a third of the 94,712 population of Darjeeling district. Nepali labour from the adjoining districts had started to be attracted to Darjeeling in the 1850s with the establishment of the tea gardens. By 1941 the population of Darjeeling had grown to 376,369 of whom two-thirds were Nepali-speakers. As indicated above and shown in Table 11.1, the ethnic composition of Darjeeling was very different from the Bahun domination of Banaras and was also significantly different from Nepal as a whole. Whereas in Nepal Bahuns are 13 per cent of the population, in Darjeeling, according to the 1951 census, they were only 5 per cent (Hutt 2008: 114) and according to the 1941 census only 3.5 per cent. By contrast, those now called Janajatis and then known as 'hill tribes' – the Magars, Gurungs, Tamangs, Rais and Limbus, along with other smaller groups such as the Sunuwar and Thami (Thangmi) – were in the majority (69 per cent or more compared to 40 per cent or less in Nepal). Not surprisingly, given the proximity of east Nepal, Rais and Limbus were present in large numbers. The figures for Sikkim are similar to those for Darjeeling, though Bahuns and Chhetris are more numerous (but still less than their proportion in Nepal). Accurate figures for the ethnic Nepali population of Bhutan are hard to obtain, but it seems that Bahuns and Chhetris were present in considerable numbers, though whether more or less than their proportion in Nepal is impossible to say (Hutt 2003: 94f).

The overwhelming numbers of Nepalis in Sikkim constitute the brute demographic fact lying behind the absorption of Sikkim as the twenty-second state of India in 1975 (the combination of democracy and absorption into republican India enabled the majority Nepalis to come to power and sideline the indigenous Bhutiyas and Lepchas). Fear that the same might happen in Bhutan was the key driver leading to increasing ethnic tensions and the expulsion of more than 100,000 ethnic Nepalis after 1990 (Hutt 2003). In this context the Sikkimese and Darjeeling Nepalis have wanted to demonstrate their allegiance to India, and to deflect the charge that they were a fifth column for 'Greater Nepal', so they have wished to downplay their links to Nepal. Some have insisted that they be called Gorkhas, not Nepalis, while others have tried to popularize the label 'Nepamul' ('of Nepali origin').[3]

Demands for a separate administrative unit for Lepchas, Bhutias and Nepalis within India go back as far as 1907, but the movement for a separate Gorkhaland state (separate from Bengali domination as part of West Bengal) began in earnest in the 1980s, led by Subhas Ghising and his Gorkha National Liberation Front (GNLF) (Subba 1992). The height of the violence occurred between May 1986 and July 1988 in which over 1,000 people are supposed to have died. The bulk of the violence occurred between the GNLF and local cadres of the CPI(M) (Communist Party of India (Marxist)), which opposed the movement, and between the police and the GNLF, but there were also internal clashes within the GNLF (ibid: ch. 6). In 1988 a Darjeeling Gorkha Hill Council (DGHC) was conceded with powers over primary education, roads, graveyards, irrigation, tourism, and so on; it covered the three hill subdivisions and those parts of Siliguri where Nepalis are in the majority. Subhas Ghising and his GNLF went on to dominate the DGHC until 2008, when Bimal Gurung and his Gorkha Janamukti Morcha (GJM) replaced

Ghising. The GJM again raised the demand for a separate state, encouraged by moves elsewhere in India to allow smaller states to be carved out of larger ones.

In 1991 Gorkhaland campaigners destroyed the bust of Bhanubhakta Acharya, the 'adikavi' (founding poet) of the Nepali language, in Darjeeling's Chowrasta, on the grounds that he was a 'foreign poet'. This was a particularly shocking act since it was the Darjeeling Nepalis who had made a hero out of Bhanubhakta in the first place (Hutt 2008: 110; Onta 1996). Bhanubhakta had been made a Darjeeling hero, Subba writes (2008: 222), because 'for every Nepali family in Darjeeling, the Bengalis were a reference group' and the Bengalis had their own national poet in Rabindranath Tagore. In Bhutan the same nationalist and anti-diasporic logic led to Nepali-speakers accepting, to some extent and in certain contexts, the official epithet 'Lhotshampa' ('southerner' in Bhutanese) and wearing the Bhutanese national dress while living in refugee camps in south-east Nepal.

The 'brave' and 'suffering' Gurkhas

One of main ways in which Nepalis moved abroad, often deciding to stay there, was through service as Gurkha soldiers. The 1815 Treaty of Sagauli (or Segowli, as the British rendered it) between the British East India Company and Nepal made no explicit mention of the recruitment of Gurkhas, but it was during the war that preceded it that 'the British "discovered" the Gurkhas' (Caplan 1995: 15). The Nepalese regime (for fear of losing its own fighting men) initially discouraged recruitment and would not allow them to be recruited inside Nepal. As they came to trust the British more, and the diplomatic relationship grew closer, the number of Gurkhas expanded.

The British generally recruited from those they (and the Nepalis) considered 'martial races' (Caplan 1995; Streets 2004). In the early years, British and indigenous ideas more or less coincided, so that Kshatriya groups and those allied to them were the main recruits. In the Nepal context, this meant largely Thakuris and Chhetris (as Kshatriyas are called in Nepal) and the associated western tribes, the Magars and Gurungs, who had provided the soldiers of Prithvi Narayan's armies. After 1857 British policy shifted markedly away from north Indian plainsmen and towards peripheral populations like the Sikhs and the Gurkhas. Within the Gurkhas, this was expressed as a definite preference for Magars and Gurungs. Nepali hill groups began to be seen as 'warrior gentlemen', similar to the British in their hardiness, sense of humour and not taking religion too seriously – in other words, they were not fanatical like Muslims nor were they ritualistic (and supposedly effeminate) like Hindus. The eastern tribes, Rai and Limbu, were finally accepted as martial towards the end of the nineteenth century. The Tamangs, however, resident principally in the hills around Kathmandu, were not recruited, because the Nepalese elite wished to keep them as their reserve army of labour. Some managed to sneak in by passing as Gurungs (a strategy adopted also by some other ethnic groups not favoured by the recruiters).

From 1908 there were ten Gurkha regiments: the first regiment was based in Dharamsala, the second and ninth in Dehra Doon, the third at Almora, the fourth at Bakloh, the fifth and sixth in Abbotabad, the seventh and tenth at Quetta, and the eighth in Shillong. In all these places Nepali settlements grew up as retired soldiers acquired land or businesses in the areas they knew, preferring to stay on there rather than return to Nepal. More than 200,000 Gurkhas participated in World War 1 (WW1) and over 20,000 died. Of the 11,000 Gurkhas discharged after WW1, only a third chose to return to Nepal, the rest remaining in India (Hutt 2008: 113). It is important to note that, in the early and middle years of the twentieth century, service in the Gurkhas was not always perceived as the greatly sought-after career that it later became – the pursuit of fame, glory, glamour and wealth in foreign parts as celebrated in Nepali folk songs.

Rather, having one's son sent away by the state was something to be avoided and many sought to hide their extra sons by sending them to the mountains as shepherds or to childless aunts and uncles to pretend to be their only son (Des Chene 1991: 276).

After Indian and Pakistani independence the Gurkhas were split between India and the UK, with the second, sixth, seventh, and tenth regiments going to the UK and being transferred to Singapore and Malaya. It was a shock to Gurkha officers when large numbers of the soldiers in these regiments voted to join the Indian Army rather than continue to be officered by the British (Gurkha histories written by the British tend to explain this by claiming that the men had been 'got at' by agitators, but the real motivation may have been greater opportunity to settle in India at retirement). Des Chene (1991: 207) comments that the British Gurkha regiments had to be reconstructed from scratch in Malaya. A Tripartite Agreement was signed between India, the UK and Nepal to allow recruitment from Nepal to continue. As the conditions of British Gurkhas gradually improved, and the numbers recruited decreased, it came to be seen as the most attractive option, with intense competition for places. At the same time, there were considerable misgivings from leftist activists, on combined nationalist and socialist internationalist grounds: it was and is felt that Nepali nationals should not be serving in imperialist armies abroad (Hutt 1989). For those, increasingly numerous, who served in the Indian army, there was also the objection that they were serving the regional hegemon, which – to put it at its mildest – could not be trusted to act in Nepal's best interests.

Labour migration to India

Thus far, I have distinguished two waves of Nepali emigration. A first wave occurred, in increasing numbers, throughout the nineteenth and early twentieth centuries. It consisted of Nepalis seeking land and fleeing oppressive tax and labour demands (Pradhan 1991 stresses the latter; cf. Shrestha 1990). They went to Darjeeling, Bhutan, Assam, Arunachal Pradesh, and on to Burma. Mixed in with this diaspora were retired Gurkha soldiers who preferred to stay where they had served rather than return where they would have to face traditional hierarchies of kinship, caste and clan. Hutt notes that, 'in this diaspora, as in many others, much of the "common culture" was constructed after the migrations, not prior to them' (Hutt 2008: 103).

A second wave of migration overlapped with these earlier movements, starting from the 1950s or perhaps even earlier. The distinctive characteristic of this migration was that it was for work in cities rather than in search of land and other agricultural opportunities (work in tea gardens or herding cattle). It started with Nepalis from the far west of Nepal migrating, in a circular fashion, to Indian cities or to nearby Indian districts to work as labourers on roads and building projects. The far west is the poorest and least fertile part of Nepal, where seasonal migration for work has long been part of household survival strategies, with those capable of 'eating outside' absenting themselves for six to eight months of the year. They are famous as doormen (*chowkidars*) throughout India (they also work as porters, waiters and other unskilled labour). Chain migration has meant that specific districts specialize in particular Indian cities: Bajhangis go to Bangalore, for example (Pfaff-Czarnecka 1995). High-altitude populations of Tibetan ethnicity for whom trade between Tibet and the lowlands had been part of their livelihood were also obliged, when the Nepal–Tibet border was closed in 1959, to adapt by spending longer in India, often working as urban peddlers and street traders. Manangis (Nyishangbas), from north-central Nepal, were given special permission in the 1960s by King Mahendra to trade in Southeast Asia, though in fact this was a recognition of trading links that were much older (van Spengen 2000; Ratanapruck 2007). Many Nepalis from all over western Nepal have gone to Delhi, Mumbai and other Indian cities in recent decades (Sharma 2007;

Thieme 2006; Thieme and Müller-Böker 2004). Officially, both India and Nepal insist that one can have only one nationality. Many of their citizens are ahead of them in this, happily holding ration cards and voting in Delhi, while also returning to Nepal to vote in general elections there.[4]

The total number of people of Nepali origin in India has often been wildly exaggerated, either by the literary activists seeking official recognition of Nepalis under Schedule Eight of the Indian Constitution or by those wishing to legitimate the actions of the Bhutanese state in expelling Lhotshampas. One more sober estimate made in the mid-1990s put the figure at between 1.5 and 2 million (Hutt 2008). Today the Non-Resident Nepali (NRN) organization posts a figure of 5 million Nepalis in all the SAARC countries (most would be in India).

Modern labour and education migration

A distinct third wave of labour migration began in the 1980s and gathered strength in the 1990s, with middlemen and manpower offices in Kathmandu and Nepalganj arranging for men (and a few women) to find work in the Gulf countries (Bruslé 2010, 2012a), Thailand, Malaysia, Taiwan and South Korea. Others managed to migrate on to Europe, Japan (Yamanaka 2000), Australia, New Zealand and North America, either going to study, or by joining relatives, or by travelling illegally and then claiming asylum. A dark side to this movement of labour migration has been the trafficking of Nepali women to brothels in India, though the extent and the definition of the phenomenon remain controversial (Hausner 2005).

Nepalis are one of the fastest growing ethnic minorities in the UK (Adhikari 2012). A few arrived already in the 1970s and '80s: among them, there are around 300 Nepali doctors working for the National Health Service. Although the 2001 census recorded only 5,938 people born in Nepal, this was certainly an underestimate. The Centre for Nepal Studies UK carried out a detailed survey of 18,801 Nepalis, and a larger more schematic survey of all larger settlements, during 2008 on the basis of which they estimated the total Nepali population in the UK at 72,173 (the 2011 UK census recorded 60,202 Nepalis in England and Wales). An increasing number of Nepali men serving in the British Army and their families along with a growing number of students, nurses and other professionals are settling in London, Manchester, Reading and towns close to army bases (Ashford and Folkestone in Kent, Farnborough and Aldershot in Hampshire – an echo of settlement patterns in India). The first Nepali local councillor (Dhan Gurung, an ex-Gurkha) was elected (for the Liberal Democrats) in 2007 to Folkestone Council. Campaigns for greater UK residency and pension rights have been going on for many years. From 2008 the campaign for all ex-Gurkhas to have the right to settle in the UK was fronted by the actress Joanna Lumley, whose father had been a major in the 6th Gurkha Rifles. In April 2009 the government was defeated in the House of Commons on the issue. The following month it conceded the right for all ex-Gurkhas with four years' service (not just those retiring post-1997 when the brigade's headquarters were moved from Hong Kong to the UK, and not just those with 'special personal links') to settle in the UK.

Over 400 Nepali organizations have sprung up. A few are overtly religious, but many more define themselves by ethnicity (e.g. Tamu Dhee [Gurung] Association UK, Thakali Samaj UK, Kirat Rai Yayokkha UK, etc.) or (a more recent trend) in terms of a district or smaller region in Nepal (e.g. Gulmi Zilla Samaj UK, bringing together people from Gulmi district, or the Mauja Bijaypur Samaj UK, based on two villages near Pokhara). Other organizations are simply local community organizations for all Nepalis in a given town or borough of the UK (e.g. Burnt Oak Nepali Samaj, London; Sussex Nepalese Society; or Greater Rushmoor Nepalese Community, which brings together Nepalis in the Aldershot and Farnborough area). There are also some professional organizations (e.g. Nepalese Doctors Association, UK and various ex-Gurkha organizations). In addition there are other organizations that aim to speak for or to all Nepalis in the UK, such as Nepali Samaj UK, Yeti Association UK, NRN-UK, and so on.

Table 11.1 shows that the ethnic/caste make-up of the UK population is subtly different from that in the home country. Dalits, Muslims and inhabitants of the Tarai are very under-represented; 'high' castes are somewhat under-represented; Magars, Gurungs, Rais, and Limbus – the groups favoured for recruitment to the British Gurkhas – are all over-represented, with the Gurungs' proportion nine times that of their population of Nepal. Ethnic breakdown figures for the USA are not available, but it is likely that there is not the same degree of bias towards Gurungs and other Gurkha groups. It is also very likely that the average levels of education and income are higher among US Nepalis, given that so many middle-class and elite Nepalis go every year to the USA for college study and then stay on to work (the same may apply to Nepalis in Canada, Australia and New Zealand).

Between them the diaspora in India and the more recent diaspora populations around the world have contributed enormous remittances that have effectively kept Nepal going as an economy through the disastrous lost years of civil war (1996–2006) (Adhikari 2001; Seddon *et al.* 2002; Graner and Gurung 2003; Singh 2006). This was precisely the time at which export-oriented manufactures (garments, carpets) went into decline, tourism stagnated and investment in hydro power (for years lauded as the country's future) stalled.

In the 1990s and 2000s a series of diasporas within the diaspora began to emerge, paralleling, and contributing to, the process of ethnicization within the home country (Gellner *et al.* 2008; Minami 2007). Thus, in countries with substantial Nepali populations there emerged organizations speaking for all the major ethnic groups. Since 1990 these ethnic groups are known as Janajatis (the Hindi term that was created to translate the English 'tribe'; Nepali activists prefer to translate the word back into English as 'nationality' following the Chinese nomenclature for minorities). These diasporic ethnic organizations formed international links and networks among themselves (Gurung, Magar, Tamang, Rai, Limbu, Newar, Thakali; latterly Madhesis and Dalits, who are not normally considered Janajatis, have also organized). Alongside these, organizations in which membership was open to all regardless of ethnicity – regional organizations and local organizations (local to the 'host' country), as well as professional and party political organizations, as noted above in the UK example – were very common as well. In all these new associations, the facilitating role of the internet and other new technologies has often been crucial (Bruslé 2012a, 2012b).

Just as the ethnic make-up of the diaspora population is subtly different from that of the homeland, so also religious affiliation is rather different. Nepal was an officially Hindu kingdom from 1962 to 2006, and for long before 1962 Hinduism had formed a central part of the rulers' and the elite's legitimation, both in their own eyes and in those of the ruled. Since the late 1980s antibrahmanism has formed a part of the Janajati movement, and activists have campaigned for Magars and Tharus (who have no history of Buddhist affiliation) to return themselves as Buddhists in national censuses, rather than as Hindus. Gurungs, who have traditionally had multiple religious affiliations, are now more than ever inclined to return themselves as Buddhists. One consequence of this politicization and ethnicization of religious identity is that, while the proportion of Buddhists has risen from a state-encouraged 5.3 per cent in 1981 to 10.7 per cent in 2001, the proportion within the UK population is more like 29.3 per cent, with a further 9.2 per cent saying they are Hindu–Buddhist and 2.3 per cent saying they are Kirant–Buddhist (Hausner and Gellner 2012; Gellner, Hausner, and Shrestha forthcoming). Hindus are still the largest single group at 41.4 per cent (roughly half their 80.6 per cent total in the 2001 Nepal census) (figures from CNS–UK survey).

145

Figure 11.1 Gurungs resident in Britain wait outside the Baptist Chapel next door to Thrangu House in Magdalen Rd, Oxford, on the occasion of the visit of Thrangu Rinpoche on 26 July 2009

Source: Photo by David N. Gellner

With the blossoming of diverse groups, new coordinating organizations began to appear, both at national and international levels, aiming to bring them all together. A worldwide NRN organization was set up at a meeting in London in August 2003 and it was formally launched in Kathmandu the following October. Initial leadership was provided by Upendra Mahato, who had gone to the USSR as a student in the 1980s and is now one of the leading manufacturers of electronics in Russia and Belarus (one of many successful Nepali entrepreneurs in Russia). Thanks to NRN lobbying, an NRN Bill was passed in Nepal in August 2007: it defined NRNs as any Nepali living in a non-SAARC country for more than two years, whether holding Nepali or foreign citizenship. By 2009 there were affiliated NRN national associations in 55 countries, including such unexpected locations as Lesotho and Libya. At the Fourth NRN Global Conference in Kathmandu in October 2009, Mahato, having served two three-year terms, stood down and was replaced as President of the Association by Dev Man Hirachan from Japan.

The position of Nepali diasporas varies according to country. The assertiveness and degree of organization on the part of diaspora activists is greater where multiculturalism is favoured, at least in practice if not in official discourse (e.g. in the UK or USA), compared to countries where it is more frowned upon (e.g. Japan). The position of Nepalis in India is particularly difficult because, however many generations they have lived there, they are seen as coming from a foreign country and are vulnerable to vicissitudes in Nepal–India relations (Hutt 2008; Subba 2008).

Indra Bahadur Rai, himself an outstanding Nepali Indian poet, writes about another such poet, Agam Singh Giri:

> Giri dealt with the keynote of Nepalese life in India – the search for self-identity. Nepalis are a martial but maligned race; they have all along been fighting other men's battles; it is not at all pleasant to be branded as 'mercenaries of war'.
>
> *(Rai 2009: 179)*

Tanka Subba concludes his autobiographical survey:

> Whether or not to go back to Nepal has never been an issue for consideration of the Indian Nepalis. Most of them are born in India and have no memories – collective or otherwise – of Nepal. They have neither visited Nepal nor do they particularly wish to do so. They may be poor, starving, and living under inhuman conditions in India. They may be harassed and humiliated at immigration check-gates or elsewhere in Northeast India. Some rowdy local boys may empty their milk cans or slap them on the street. Yet they cannot think of going back for they have nowhere to go.
>
> *(Subba 2008: 230–31)*

Brubaker (2005: 7) points out that any diaspora worth its name has to last beyond a generation: if second and subsequent generations are wholly assimilated, then it is not a diaspora. Much of the Nepali diaspora in India passed this test long ago. Only time will tell whether the Nepali diaspora elsewhere persists, but the much older diasporas from other parts of South Asia suggest that it will.

Notes

1   For helpful comments I would like to thank D.P. Martinez, J. Whelpton, S. Subedi, M. Hutt, C. Laksamba, S. Hausner, T. Subba, M. Sadan, K. Leonard, J. Chatterjee and C. Stewart.
2   On the history of Nepali literature (principally poetry and inscriptions) before this period, see Hutt (1988).
3   Prem Poddar (2009: 11) comments, 'I use the term "Gorkha" ... as a self-descriptive term that has gained currency as a marker of difference for Nepalis living in India as opposed to their brethren and sistren in Nepal ... While this counters the irredentism of a Greater Nepal thesis, it cannot completely exorcise the spectres or temptations of an ethnic absolutism for diasporic subjects.'
4   Sijapati (forthcoming) indicates that holding dual nationality in practice without admitting it to the Nepalese state is common among Nepalis in the USA also.

References

Adhikari, J. (2001) 'Mobility and Agrarian Change in Central Nepal', *Contributions to Nepalese Studies*, 28(2): 247–67.
Adhikari, K. (2012) *Nepalis in the United Kingdom: An Overview*, Reading: Centre for Nepal Studies UK.
Brubaker, R. (2005) 'The "Diaspora" Diaspora', *Ethnic and Racial Studies*, 28(1): 1–19.
Bruslé, T. (2010) 'Who's in a Labour Camp? A Socio-economic Analysis of Labour Migrants in Qatar', *European Bulletin of Himalayan Research*, 35–36: 154–70.
— (2012a) 'What's New in the Gulf? New Technologies, Consumption and Display of Modernity among Nepali Workers in Qatar', *e-migrinter*, 8: 59–73.
— (2012b) 'Nepalese Diasporic Websites: Signs and Conditions of a Diaspora in the Making?', *Social Science Information*, 51(4): 593–610.

Burghart, R. (1984) 'The Formation of the Concept of Nation–State in Nepal', *Journal of Asian Studies*, 44: 101–25; reprinted in Fuller, C.J. and Spencer, J. (eds) (1996) *The Conditions of Listening: Essays on Religion, History and Politics in South Asia*, Delhi: Oxford University Press.

Caplan, L. (1995) *Warrior Gentlemen: 'Gurkhas' in the Western Imagination*, Oxford: Berghahn.

Chalmers, R. (2002) 'Pandits and Pulp Fiction: Popular Publishing and the Birth of Nepali Print-Capitalism in Banaras', *Studies in Nepali History and Society*, 7(1): 31–97.

— (2003) '"We Nepalis": Language, Literature and the Formation of a Nepali Public Sphere in India, 1914–40', unpublished thesis, SOAS, University of London.

Cohen, R. (2008) *Global Diasporas: An Introduction*, 2nd edn, Abingdon and New York: Routledge.

Des Chene, M.K. (1991) 'Relics of Empire: A Cultural History of the Gurkhas 1815–1987', unpublished thesis, Stanford University, CA.

Dolfuss, P., Lecomte-Tilouine, M. and Aubriot, O. (2001) 'Un araire dans la tête: Réflexions sur la répartition géographique de l'outil en Himalaya', *Techniques & Cultures*, 37: 3–50.

Gaenszle, M. (2002) 'Nepali Kings and Kasi: On the Changing Significance of a Sacred Centre', *Studies in Nepali History and Society*, 7(1): 1–33.

Gaige, F.H. (2009) [1975] *Regionalism and National Unity in Nepal*. Kathmandu: Himal.

Gellner, D.N., Pfaff-Czarnecka, J. and Whelpton, J. (2008) *Nationalism and Ethnicity in Nepal*, Kathmandu: Vajra Books; previously published as *Nationalism and Ethnicity in a Hindu Kingdom*, 1997, Amsterdam: Harwood.

Gellner, D.N., Hausner, S., and Shrestha, B.G. (forthcoming) 'Buddhist, Hindu, Kirati, or Something Else? Nepali Strategies of Religious Belonging in the UK and Belgium', in E. Gallo (ed.), *Migration and Religion in Europe: Comparative Perspectives on South Asian Experiences*, Aldershot: Ashgate.

Graner, E. and Gurung, G. (2003) 'Arab ko Lahure: Looking at Nepali Labour Migrants to Arabian Countries', *Contributions to Nepalese Studies*, 30(2): 295–325.

Haaland, G. (2008) 'Explaining Causes in Evolving Contexts: From Nepali Hill Farmers to Business Managers in Thailand', in Walters, B.B., McCruy, B.J., West, P. and Lees, S. (eds), *Against the Grain: The Vayda Tradition in Human Ecology and Ecological Anthropology*, Lanham, MD: Altamira, pp. 43–66.

Haaland, G. and Gurung, P. (2007) 'Globalization of Interaction Systems and the Culture in Ethnicity: Popular Songs and the Production of Nepali Ethnoscapes in South-East Asia', *The International Journal of Diversity in Organisations, Communities and Nations*, 7(3): 77–84.

Hausner, S.L. (2005) *The Movement of Women: Migration, Trafficking, and Prostitution in the Context of Nepal's Armed Conflict*, Kathmandu: Save the Children USA.

Hausner, S.L. and Gellner, D.N. (2012) 'Category and Practice as Two Aspects of Religion: The Case of Nepalis in Britain', *Journal of the American Academy of Religion*, 80(4): 971–97.

Hutt, M.J. (1988) *Nepali: A National Language and its Literature*, London/Delhi: SOAS/Sterling.

— (1989) 'A Hero or a Traitor? The Gurkha Soldier in Nepali Literature', *South Asia Research*, 9(1): 21–32.

— (1998) 'Going to Mugalan: Nepali Literary Representations of Migration to India and Bhutan', *South Asia Research*, 18: 195–214.

— (2003) *Unbecoming Citizens: Culture, Nationhood, and the Flight of Refugees from Bhutan*, Delhi: OUP.

— (2008) [1997] 'Being Nepali without Nepal: Reflections on a South Asian Diaspora', in Gellner *et al.* (eds), *Nationalism and Ethnicity in a Hindu Kingdom*, op. cit., pp. 101–44.

LeVine, S. and Gellner, D.N. (2005) *Rebuilding Buddhism: The Theravada Movement in Twentieth-Century Nepal*, Cambridge: Harvard University Press.

Minami, M. (2007) 'From *tika* to *kata*? Ethnic Movements among the Magars in an Age of Globalization', in Ishii, H., Gellner, D.N., and Nawa, K. (eds), *Nepalis Inside and Outside Nepal: Social Dynamics in Northern South Asia, Volume 1*, Delhi: Manohar, pp. 477–502.

Neupane, G. (2000) *Nepālko Jātiya Prasna: Sāmājik Banot ra Sājhedāriko Sambhāvanā* (Nepal's Nationality Question: Social Structure and the Possibilities of Compromise), Kathmandu: Centre for Development Studies.

— (2005) *Nepalese Migrants in Delhi*, Kathmandu: Centre for Nepalese Studies.

Onta, P.R. (1996) 'Creating a Brave Nation in British India: The Rhetoric of Jati Movement, Rediscovery of Bhanubhakta and the Writing of Bir History', *Studies in Nepali History and Society*, 1(1): 37–76.

— (2006) 'The Growth of the *Adivasi Janajati* Movement in Nepal after 1990: The Non-Political Institutional Agents', *Studies in Nepali History and Society*, 11(2): 303–54.

Orsini, F. (2002) *The Hindi Public Sphere 1920–1940: Language and Literature in the Age of Nationalism*, New Delhi: Oxford University Press.

Ortner, S.B. (1990) *High Religion: A Cultural and Political History of Sherpa Buddhism*, Princeton: Princeton University Press.

Pfaff-Czarnecka, J. (1995) 'Migration Under Marginality Conditions: The Case of Bajhang', in Interdisciplinary Consulting Group (eds), *Rural-Urban Interlinkages: A Challenge for Swiss Development Cooperation*, Zurich/Kathmandu, INFRAS, pp. 97–108.

Poddar, P. (2009) 'Afterlife of the Original: Gorkhaness (or Indian Nepaleseness) and I.B. Rai in Translation', in Poddar, P. and Prasad, A. (eds) *Gorkhas Imagined: Indra Bahadur Rai in Translation*, Kalimpong: Mukti Prakashan, pp. 11–37.

Pradhan, K. (1982) *Pahilo Pahar* (First Watch), Darjeeling: Shyam Prakashan.

— (1991) *The Gorkha Conquests: The Process and Consequences of the Unification of Nepal with Particular Reference to Eastern Nepal*, Calcutta: Oxford University Press.

Ragsdale, T. (1990) 'Gurungs, Goorkhalis, Gurkhas: Speculations on a Nepalese Ethno-history', *Contributions to Nepalese Studies*, 17(1): 1–24.

Rai, I.B. (2009 [1994]) 'Indian Nepali Nationalism and Nepali Poetry', in Poddar, P. and Prasad, A. (eds) *Gorkhas Imagined: Indra Bahadur Rai in Translation*, Kalimpong: Mukti Prakashan, pp. 171–80.

Ratanapruck, P. (2007) 'Kinship and Religious Practices as Institutionalization of Trade Networks: Manangi Trade Communities in South and Southeast Asia', *Journal of the Social and Economic History of the Orient*, 50(2–3): 325–46.

Regmi, M.C. (1984) *The State and Economic Surplus: Production, Trade, and Resource-Mobilization in Early 19th Century Nepal*, Varanasi: Nath.

— (1999) *Imperial Gorkha: An Account of Gorkhali Rule in Kumaon (1791–1815)*, Delhi: Adroit.

Russell, R. (2007) 'Writing Traveling Cultures: Travel and Ethnography among the Yakha of East Nepal', *Ethnos*, 72(3): 361–82.

Sadan, M. (2007) *A Guide to Colonial Sources on Burma: Ethnic and Minority Histories of Burma in the India Office Records, British Library*, Bangkok: Orchid.

Samaddar, R. (2010) 'The Insecure World of the Nation' in Samaddar, R. and Banerjee, P., *Migration and Circles of Insecurity*, New Delhi: Rupa & Co, pp. 1–69.

Seddon, D., Adhikari, J. and Gurung, G. (2002) 'Foreign Labour Migration and the Remittance Economy of Nepal', *Critical Asian Studies*, 34(1): 19–40.

Sharma, J. (2007) 'Mobility, Pathology and Livelihoods: An Ethnography of Forms of Mobility in/from Nepal', PhD dissertation, University of Edinburgh.

Sharma, P. (2008) *Unravelling the Mosaic: Spatial Aspects of Ethnicity in Nepal*, Kathmandu: Social Science Baha/Himal Books.

Shneiderman, S. (2009) 'Ethnic (P)reservations: Comparing Thangmi Ethnic Activism in Nepal and India', in D.N. Gellner (ed.), *Ethnic Activism and Civil Society in South Asia*, Delhi: Sage, pp. 115–41.

Shneiderman, S. and Turin, M. (2006) 'Seeking the Tribe: Ethno-Politics in Darjeeling and Sikkim', *Himal Southasian*, 19(2): 54–58, March–April (www.himalmag.com/2006).

Shrestha, N.R. (1990) *Landlessness and Migration in Nepal*, Boulder: Westview.

Sijapati, B. (forthcoming) 'Multiple Locations, Multiple Identities: Nepali Experiences in the USA', in Pfaff-Czarnecka, J. and Toffin, G. (eds), *Facing Globalization: Belonging and the Politics of the Self*, Delhi: Sage.

Singh, P.M. (2006) 'Remittance Economy Nepal's Evolution towards Accepting and Incorporating the Labour of its Overseas Workers', *Himal Southasian*, 18(5): 73–77.

Sinha, A.C. (2009) 'Introduction', in Subba, T.B., Sinha, A.C., Nepal, G.S., and Nepal, D.R. (eds), *Indian Nepalis: Issues and Perspectives*, Delhi: Concept, pp. 2–27.

Stiller, L.F. (1973) *The Rise of the House of Gorkha: A Study in the Unification of Nepal, 1768–1816*, New Delhi: Manjusri.

Streets, H. (2004) *Martial Races: The Military, Race and Masculinity in British Imperial Culture, 1857–1914*, Manchester: Manchester University Press.

Subba, T.B. (1992) *Caste, Ethnicity, State and Development: A Case Study of Gorkhaland Movement*, Delhi: Har-Anand and Vikas.

— (2008) 'Living the Nepali Diaspora in India: An Autobiographical Essay', *Zeitschrift für Ethnologie*, 133(2): 213–32.

Thieme, S. (2006) *Social Networks and Migration: Far West Nepalese Labour Migrants in Delhi*, Münster: LIT Publishing.

Thieme, S. and Müller-Böker, U. (2004) 'Financial Self-help Associations among Far-west Nepalese Labor Migrants in Delhi, India', *Asian and Pacific Migration Journal*, 13(3): 339–61.

van Schendel, W. (2005) *The Bengal Borderland: Beyond State and Nation in South Asia*, London: Anthem.

van Spengen, W. (2000) *Tibetan Border Worlds: A Geohistorical Analysis of Trade and Traders*, London: Kegan Paul.

Whelpton, J. (2005) *A History of Nepal*, Cambridge: Cambridge University Press.

— (2008) [1997] 'Political Identity in Nepal: State, Nation, and Community', in Gellner *et al.* (eds), *Nationalism and Ethnicity in Nepal*, op. cit., pp. 39–78.

Yamanaka, K. (2000) 'Nepalese Labour Migration to Japan: From Global Warriors to Global Workers', *Ethnic and Racial Studies*, 23(1): 62–93.

PART III

Diaspora and nation

12

SEEKING EMPIRE, FINDING NATION

Gandhi and Indianness in South Africa

Isabel Hofmeyr

Reading through the pages of *Indian Opinion*, one is often momentarily disorientated as time and space between 'South Africa' and 'India' combine in unexpected ways. A headline, 'Loyalty of Native Chiefs', refers not to local African rulers as I first assumed but to the princely states (*Indian Opinion* July 30 1903). Under the headline, 'The National Congress and Indians in South Africa', a report of Dec. 13 1903 indicated that a meeting was to be held at 'Tata Mansions, Waudby Road'. Are we in Durban or Bombay? An article in the edition of Sept. 26 1910 reads:

> Mr GA Natesan writes in the *Indian Review* [a Madras publication]:- A cable from South Africa brings the news that the British Indians in the Transvaal are taking a vow of passive resistance as a protest against the recent Asiatic Amendment Bill.

While the cutting validates local struggles by demonstrating international interest in the event, it also makes it seem as if the event were happening in 'India' and 'South Africa' at the same time.

One could adduce other examples. Caste oppression in 'India' becomes intermeshed with racial oppression in 'South Africa' creating a continuum along which the two can slide. At times, the 'Transvaal question outside India, [had become] a Transvaal within India itself' (*Indian Opinion* April 23 1910). The cry of oppressed Indians in the Transvaal resonates so acutely in the ears of Indian sympathizers on the mainland, one might think that they occupied the same house (*Modern Review* Aug. 6 1910).

In some senses, this time–space configuration may appear unremarkable, the stuff of diasporic communities or long-distance nationalisms all over the world. Yet, these articles all appear before nations had emerged from colonies and modern diasporas (a post-1960s term) had taken precise shape. The articles cited above speak to an era in which ideas of political community have to shape themselves in a world of empires, princely states, colonies, republics, chiefdoms and kingdoms (McKeown 2008). Most of these political units were hostile or reluctant to accept migrants (including British India itself, which was chary about taking back deported and repatriated lower-caste migrants). Migrants had to manoeuvre between these political systems as best they could, an experience that produced a range of experimental modes of belonging, many of which disappear from view as the nation state takes hold and produces its own hindsight.

Gandhi's years in what subsequently became South Africa were characterized by this mosaic-like complexity. Coming from a princely state in Gujarat, Gandhi looked to Durban, a destination that made more sense in the regional circuits of the world from which he came than Delhi or Calcutta. Gandhi initially operated between the self-governing colony of Natal and the independent Boer Republic of the Transvaal (Zuid Afrikaanse Republiek, ZAR) within which the mining metropolis of Johannesburg formed a kind of city state. The other major units in what was to become South Africa comprised the Orange Free State (a second independent Boer republic) and, south of that, the Cape Colony, self-governing since 1872. To the north of Natal was the Zulu kingdom, annexed as a crown colony in 1887 and then incorporated into Natal in 1897.

With the exception of the princely states and the Boer Republics (until their defeat in the Anglo–Boer war of 1899–1902), these units were in the British Empire. However, any ideals of imperial rights and citizenship had steadily been eroded by the racism of white settler self-ruled colonies which had come to define their sovereignty by the right to exclude or control Asian mobility (McKeown 2008). Indeed much of Gandhi's first years in southern Africa involved a desperate search for any toehold in which imperial rights might be claimed. However, in the wake of the Anglo–Boer War as British rule proved as harsh, if not harsher than that of the Boers, Gandhi had to make recourse to different forms of political imagining. His satyagraha campaigns and related activities in South Africa constitute a series of experiments in what kinds of political communities and ideas of 'India' could be constructed in the interstices of empire, colony, erstwhile Boer republic, African chiefdom.

Engaging with Gandhi's South African sojourn presents an opportunity to investigate these experimental forms more fully. Hitherto political and academic alignments have militated against a detailed investigation of these modes of political imagination. The most prominent obstacle has been apartheid itself which prevented scholars from outside using archival sources in South Africa. On the academic front, national and area studies historiographies tended to misalign the story of Gandhi in South Africa and India in teleological and/or nationalist ways. On the one hand, Gandhi's South African experience becomes a simple prelude to a longer epic of Indian nationalism. On the other, accounts of Gandhi in southern Africa tend to downplay India in an attempt to claim Gandhi for South Africa (Swan 1985; Meer 1996).

Another fallout of such nationalist approaches has been the tendency to read Gandhi's ideas on Indianness as necessarily and self-evidently national and to subsume any support for his vision into the same framework. As many have pointed out, such assumptions obscure the populist and millenarian inspiration of the indentured workers strike of 1913 (Mongia 2006; Bhana and Vahed 2005; Desai and Vahed 2007).

With the transnational turn in the academy and the demise of the apartheid state, the possibilities for a more nuanced view of Gandhi's South African context have started to emerge. Within this body of transnational work, two recent streams are especially pertinent. The first pertains to work on Asian mobility and its interaction with colonial white settler self-rule, an encounter which produces modern ideas of border control and identity documentation. As Adam McKeown (2008) and Jonathan Klaaren (2004) have demonstrated, these ideas of border policing become seen as the defining feature of modern national sovereignty.

A second strand of work pertains to what one might call 'Bandung revisionism'. On one level, this work seeks to revisit Bandung and non-alignment and produce new histories of these moments (Abraham 2008; Burton *et al.* 2006; Lee 2010; Tan and Acharya 2008). On a second and for us, more pertinent level, this work re-engages with older ideas of non-alignment and

Afro-Asian solidarity, not to reintroduce them as working political concepts, but as a way of posing revisionist questions to the present day realities of the 'global south'. While these terms are certainly superannuated, they do still point to persistent and important areas of transnational interactions, namely between Africa and India and within the global south more generally. The older non-aligned way of dealing with these interactions was largely through ideas of anti-colonial, and then south–south solidarity. However, as divisions within the south become ever greater, such shoulder-to-shoulder narratives lose their analytical purchase. Yet, at the same time, understanding such lateral linkages becomes ever more important as we enter a post-American world (Zakaria 2008) in which parts of the south and especially China and India become pivotal in the new emerging world order. How then do we think simultaneously about the growing relations of inequality alongside forms of interaction and exchange within the global south?

In his analysis of the Bandung moment, Christopher Lee has suggested some answers to this dilemma. He directs our attention to the hitherto unrecognized diversity of forms of trans-national political community that emerge within the purview of the Bandung nations (largely the Indian Ocean arena). These involve the constellations of political community that have 'cut across the Asian-African divide for the twentieth and early twenty-first century' (Lee 2010: 27) and that transcend the political geographies and the imagination of the nation state. While Lee's focus is on the latter half of the twentieth century, these ideas can be pushed backward with a view to examining the 'variety, complexity and wide ranging geographies of Afro-Asian relations during the last century' and their 'multiple histories of connection' (2010: 27).

Important in this regard is the idea of examining flows between Africa and India that go in both directions. As Uma Dhupelia-Mesthrie points out (2007), most studies of diasporic com-munities track developments from India outwards without asking what the reverse flow might mean or what the political meanings of the diaspora means back on the mainland. This trend is starting to shift as scholars like John Kelly (1991) and Tejaswini Niranjana (1999) demonstrate the centrality of debates about indenture, and the position of Hindu women within it, to the growth of Indian nationalism. These works extend revisionist post-colonial debates on empire, which argued for an integration of 'centre' and 'periphery' into one integrated space, to India itself as a sub-imperial power enabling us to better integrate the Indian 'metropolis' and its indentured peripheries (see also Metcalf 2007). Also important is recent work on cross-cutting diasporas (Amrith 2009; Harper 2002) which demonstrate the limitations of looking at one diaspora in isolation from other diasporas or surrounding groups. Jon Soske's pathbreaking work on Natal demonstrates the need to consider the Indian diaspora in relation to African communities, or what he terms the 'also-colonized other' (2009).

This paper takes forward this configuration with a view to understanding Gandhi's southern African years as a period of intense transnational experiment that took shape between a variety of forms of sovereignty that persisted within empire and on its fringes. These experiments pro-duced different forms of 'Indianness' many of which have subsequently fallen from view as the nation state and nationalist historiographies became universalized. The horizon against which these experiments took place was that of empire within which Gandhi experimented with ideas of deterritorialized self-rule that was both anti-colonial and imperial at the same time.

There is now a growing body of work which suggests that Gandhi's ideas of India need to be understood less as an automatic expression of some prior Indianness and more as the product of his South African experience (Parel 1996; Itzkin 2008; Markovits 2003; Bhana and Vahed 2005; Mongia 2006; Breckenridge 2011; Hyslop 2008; Natarajan 2009).

In brief, this work argues that Gandhi arrived in South Africa without a well-developed idea of 'India' as a political unit. Encountering a small South Asian minority whose broad outline comprised Gujarati Muslim merchants, Tamil Hindu hawkers and petty traders, an underclass of indentured labourers and a tiny group of ex-indentured white-collar workers, Gandhi experimented with different forms of political community. Initially captive to the interests of the Natal and Transvaal merchant class, Gandhi's political imaginings expanded (or had expansion forced upon them), incorporating first the petty traders and ex-indentured petty bourgeoisie and, in 1913, the indentured labourers. The cosmopolitan world of Johannesburg, a gold-mining centre brought into being by migration is identified as an important influence in broadening Gandhi's thinking. Through these political apprenticeships that crossed boundaries of religion, language, caste and status (even if only tenuously), Gandhi was able to grasp an idea of 'India' in a way that was not possible on the vast sub-continent itself. On the basis of this experience, Gandhi positioned himself as a transnational political figure and gained access to the upper reaches of the nationalist movement back in India. In Claude Markovits's words, 'Gandhi's construction of his Indianness was an outcome of his South African stay' (2003: 81). Surendra Bhana and Goolam Vahed comment: 'The ethnic, caste, religious, and cultural make-up of the Indian communities in South Africa afforded Gandhi a laboratory in which to experiment and to develop his ideas' (2005: 149).

What forms of political community did these experiments produce? One route into this question is to start with Gandhi's two major bases, the Transvaal and Natal. In both these locales, Gandhi initially represented an interlinked network of merchants who sought to defend their rights as desirable citizens and British subjects. Yet, as Maureen Swan's study notes, the legal definitions of different categories of 'Asians' in both places created different possibilities for manouevre. In Natal, where legislation differentiated between merchants and indentured labourers ('passengers' and 'immigrants'), this involved creating distinctions between these two groups as well as distance from 'natives'. In the Transvaal, which made no legal distinctions between 'passenger' and 'immigrant', the major boundary became that between 'Indians' and 'natives'. These boundaries had to be defended and dramatized lest all people of colour be lumped together and disenfranchized to the level of 'natives'. The division in Natal between the merchant class and labourers mitigated against mass-based politics and the adoption of Indian nationalist ideas, while these constraints were not as strong in the Transvaal, which was not a destination for Indian indentured labourers (Swan 1985: 50, 83).

This cross-cutting mesh of 'merchant', 'immigrant', 'white' and 'non-white', 'civilized' and 'uncivilized' created a set of shifting frontiers in which different ideas of belonging could be tried out. Added to this complex mix were boundaries of caste, religion, gender and class. These frontiers became the place where Gandhi had to invent his politics. Indeed one might argue that they made him the thinker that he became: an activist roving between categories, recasting them in relation to each other as a way of creating strategic openings. The political horizons against which these intersections took shape were those of empire, an ideal to which Gandhi remained deeply wedded even as ideals of imperial citizenship evaporated before his eyes. His response to these changing circumstances was less that of anti-colonial nationalism than a set of manoeuvres around the categories of imperial authority, white settlers, 'Africans' and 'Indians' in which versions of a nation emerge as a strategy for trying to salvage ideas of empire.

Scavenging for empire

Gandhi's fervent attachment to ideas of British constitutionalism and imperial citizenship are well known and dominated his South African years (Huttenback 1971). For our purposes it is worth highlighting both the negative and positive definitions of empire that Gandhi forged, i.e. what were the limits of empire and what were the sites and places in which the positive substance of imperial citizenship could be realized.

Starting with the latter point, in Natal and the Transvaal, imperial rights were hard to find. A self-governing colony since 1893, Natal had become a pioneer in sophisticating methods of excluding migrants (McKeown 2008; Klaaren 2004) and eroding the rights of those who did gain entry. While appeals to London could at times deliver evidence that British constitutionalism still prevailed, to claim rights as a British citizen in the Transvaal was 'only to invite ridicule', as Gandhi noted in *Satyagraha in South Africa* (1928: 28).

Despite experiencing the direct violence of these exclusionary measures, most notably in 1896–7 when he returned from Bombay and was held hostage on the *SS Courland* through quarantine measures and then attacked by a white lynch mob, Gandhi interpreted such violence as only 'temporary and local' (Gandhi n.d: 91) rather than systemic. In such circumstances, one challenge was to find ways of actualizing such rights. Indeed much of Gandhi's first years in southern Africa involved a search for any toehold in which imperial rights might be claimed.

In the chapter entitled 'The Boer War' in *Satyagraha in South Africa*, Gandhi remarks: 'It is true that we are helots in the Empire but so far we have tried to better our condition, continuing the while to remain in the Empire' (Gandhi 1928: 51). Empire exists only in tenuous pockets or in a poem sent by an 'Englishman' [in Natal] in response to witnessing the Indian volunteer ambulance contingent set off for the field and quoted by Gandhi in *Satyagraha in South Africa*. The poem's refrain reads 'We are sons of the Empire after all' (Gandhi 1928: 53). These sons of Empire were so keen to prove their loyalty that they 'had expressed [their] willingness even to do sweepers' or scavengers' work in hospitals' (Gandhi 1928: 52). Gandhi had to scavenge for empire in every sense of the word.

Indeed Gandhi's love for nursing might be seen as a thwarted expression of imperial loyalty. The more empire neglected him, the more he cared for others, creating in this therapeutic relationship his idea of what British constitutionalism should be. Not surprisingly, in his autobiography, Gandhi links nursing and the British constitution as his key passions (Gandhi n.d.: 90–92). Interestingly if nursing, a highly polluting activity, can be considered as a displaced model for imperial citizenship, then anti-caste ideologies inform ideas of imperial obligation and vice versa.

If Indians were to be excluded from empire on grounds of race, then one response was to counterclaim membership on grounds of civilization. In such an imagined dispensation, India formed a part of empire and shared a boundary with it. This boundary was marked by the 'native' who stood beyond civilization and empire with its promise of 'equal rights for all civilized men'. Underlining this idea was Gandhi's reliance on ideas of civilizationism which ranked civilizations in a competitive hierarchy: Africans with their 'massacre, assegai and fire' (to use Gandhi's words) inevitably came last (quoted in Bhana and Vahed 2005: 41). Like all Congress moderates, Gandhi hoped that India would realize itself as a dominion within empire. In this scenario, 'Africa'/'the native' marked the limits of empire and hence also of India, becoming one of its boundaries.

Gandhi's writing frequently dramatizes this boundary. His prison writings are especially pertinent and focus on a world made up of Indian political prisoners, Indian criminal prisoners and African criminal prisoners. Gandhi worries about the fraternization between these two latter groups and seeks to draw the Indian criminal prisoners into his ambit. He also dramatizes the social distance of the 'natives', describing them in standard colonial terms: they are savage, dirty, noisy, animal-like (Gandhi 1909: 562).

This frontier created by the 'natives' appears to be the line between the civilized and the savage; between those entitled to imperial citizenship and British subjecthood and those who are not. Indeed the blurring of this line furnishes the basis of Gandhi's activism. He comments: 'I had made up my mind to fight against the rule by which Indians are made to live with Kaffirs and others' (Gandhi 1909: 559).

Within the enclave marked off by the 'native' in prison, a nation-in-miniature can start to take shape. Its criteria for membership are set out and exclude: 'those who are addicted to bad habits (smoking &C.) [this category includes the Indian prisoners who fraternize with Africans], those who stick to false distinctions of caste, who are quarrelsome, those who see difference between a Hindu and a Mohammedan, and those who are ill'. These 'are not proper persons to go to jail, or having gone likely to remain there long. Those who consider it a distinction to go to prison out of patriotism should be sound in body, mind and soul' (Gandhi 1909: 563).

This model of shaping possible nations both against and within the horizon of civilization/empire became the hallmark of Gandhi's South African years. The view of nation that emerged was necessarily deterritorialized and portable and could unfold in 'South Africa', 'Greater India' and, according to *Hind Swaraj*, just about anywhere.

'India' in 'South Africa'

The strategies and tactics that Gandhi used to shape an idea of 'India' in 'South Africa' have been well documented. As much of the South African historiography has stressed, he drew on a network of existing organizations, both elite and popular (Swan 1985; Bhana and Vahed 2005). These included the secular and merchant-dominated British Indian Association and a range of elite religious and cultural organizations like the Hindu Gujarati Society, Sanatan Veda Dharma, the Hamidia Islamic Society and Hamdarde Islamic Society (Swan 1985: 10). Bhana and Vahed enumerate 166 organizations operating with the South African Indian community which include the Aryan Literary Society, Kathiawad Arya Samaj, Dhabel Anjuman Islam and Ladysmith Islam Society (Bhana and Vahed 2005: 157–61). The small class of educated professionals and white-collar workers (the descendants of indentured labourers) sustained a number of organizations like the Hindu Young Mens' Association, Durban Indian Society, Natal Indian Patriotic Union and Colonial Born Indian Association (Swan 1985: 13). While indentured workers had no formal organizations, they congregated in leisure activities of dancing, drinking, gambling, smoking marijuana, music, sport and religiously oriented theatre (Desai and Vahed 2007: 287–306).

By stressing this network, the South African historiography (Meer 1996: 87–102; Swan 1985) underlines that the story of Indians in South Africa is not a one-man affair, in contrast to the patronizing view emerging from more hagiographical Gandhi-centred works (see, for example, Sanghavi 2006). The South African historiography also underlines the contingent nature of the different 'Indian' groups that were thrown together (Itzkin 2008; Hyslop 2008). First, there was nothing automatically 'Indian' or indeed systematically representative about the South Asian groups who congregated in Durban and Johannesburg. Part of Gandhi's genius in both his politics and journalism was to make the whole greater than the sum of its parts by insisting that these groups were representative of 'India'.

> To be invited thus to take part was a new experience for the community, all distinctions such as high and low, small and great, master and servant, Hindus, Musalmans, Parsis, Christians, Gujaratis, Madrasis, Sindhis, etc., were forgotten. All were alike the children and servants of the motherland.
>
> *(Gandhi n.d: 74)*

This insistence required a degree of ventriloquization and *trompe l'oeil* politics. Indentured workers who were dragooned by their employers into Gandhi's Boer War ambulance brigade became portrayed as loyal followers of empire and hence worthy 'Indians' (Desai and Vahed 2007). Indentured strikers espousing millenarian ideas are translated into Indian patriots (Swan 1985: 252). Members of the colonial-born white-collar workers who often spoke no Indian language and had lost caste were terrified of being deported to 'India' in whose name they had apparently joined the satyagraha struggle and gone to gaol (Gandhi 1928: 138).

By showcasing different organizations on the same platform, each person and the organization they represented could become metonymic of a portfolio 'nation' comprising a repertoire of distinct but related categories which could be expanded or contracted as the need arose. These parts are in turn invested with affective sentiment which make the whole much more moving than its pedestrian parts: the alliance is not simply a collection of mere organizations but rather an implied spectacle of large swathes of humanity who then submerge their distinctiveness in an act of becoming 'Indian'. Unsurprisingly, Gandhi often makes recourse to the language of evangelical revival in which groups 'awaken' to a new sense of national belonging.

> The Indian community became better organized. I got into closer touch with the indentured Indians. There came a greater awakening amongst them, and the feeling that Hindus, Musalmans, Christians, Tamilians, Gujaratis and Sindhis were all Indians and children of the same motherland took deep root amongst them.
>
> *(Gandhi 1928: 112)*

Importantly, this idea of 'nation' which was linked to civil rights rather than claims to the franchise could be flexible, floating and deterritorialized.

This ability to mobilize sentiment and affect is especially apparent in the 1913 satyagraha campaign and its use of the ongoing issue of the rights of polygamous families in terms of immigration, as Radika Mongia (2006) has shown. This issue had previously been contested in terms of principles of liberal non-interference in the religious rights of imperial citizens. In 1913 Gandhi translated it into an emotive question of the national honour of Indian women and hence the nation itself, enabling outpourings of devotion to the motherland to reach a crescendo.

Yet, as in the case of Gandhi's idea of empire, this 'nation' also has its limits, in this case marked off by the colonial-born Indians, descendants of the indentured labourers who had stayed on in South Africa. Gandhi subsequently expressed clear views on this class: 'The men are neither Indian nor Colonial. They have no Indian culture in the foreign lands they go to, save what they pick up from their uncultured half-dis-Indianized parents' (*Young India* Sept. 9 1926). His close colleague Henry Polak shared similar sentiments: 'There they were, helpless in the midst of an alien population, whose civilization was incomprehensible to their generally limited intellects, and whose mental attitude was coloured by the long contact with a savage race of aboriginals' (Polak 1910: 422).

Colonial-born Indians constituted a dangerous point at which the nation might be compromised. One response was to educate them via organizations like the Natal Indian Educational Association under the aegis of the Natal Indian Congress which included debates, lectures and newspaper articles on domestic sanitation and personal hygiene, as well as classes on Indian history 'to create a love for the mother country' (Gandhi 1928: 36). These ventures were intended 'to impress upon [colonial-born Indians] that free Indians considered them as their own kith and kind, and to create respect for the latter in the minds of the former' (Gandhi 1928: 36).

Greater India

This portable formulation of empire/nation was important in establishing one of Gandhi's enduring political contributions, namely validating what today we call diaspora as a legitimate domain of nationalist political activity. Today the idea seems self-evident but in the early 1900s, the obstacles to such a notion were not inconsiderable. On his brief return to India in 1901 when Gandhi sought to enter Indian nationalist politics, he had attempted to persuade Pherozeshah Mehta to support a South African campaign. Mehta replied that, while India was not free, South Africa remained a non-issue (Swan 1985: 91). In 1906 Dadabhai Naoroji was still maintaining that the question of South Africa was 'a small one' and that 'the real issue for Indians was India' (Swan 1985: 102). This position attracted critical comment from different quarters in the Indian diaspora – Taraknath Das in the USA criticized the 'Isolationists' with their 'frog in the well' position and urged politicians to take an interest in the 'overseas Indians' (*Hindi* 16 Jan. 1925). Gandhi had to work hard to overcome such isolationist prejudices which were in part tied up with social disdain for indentured workers. For some sections of the Indian elite, indenture had been a social good, helping to rid the subcontinent of the 'sweepings of the bazaar' (Niranjana 1999).

By the 1920s, terms like Greater India, overseas Indians, colonial-born Indians, emigrant Indians and Indians in the dominion had become recognized coinage (Bayly 2004; Subramanian 2009). Today, these terms have largely been lost, obscured by discussions of diaspora, shaped by post-1960s migration to Europe and the USA which was more middle class than the indentured migrations which fed into the earlier sets of terms.

The idea of Indians overseas as a political category also lost ground as ideas of empire and imperial citizenship waned, driven on the one hand by white settler self-government and growing anti-colonial nationalism on the other. Gandhi's idea of nation-within-empire was being eaten from under his feet and, shortly after his return to India, the catastrophe of Jallianwala Bagh shattered any lingering fidelity to ideas of imperial citizenship.

Or, so at least, run the dominant accounts. Yet, if we consider his ideas on nation/empire as deterritorialized, the picture might look somewhat different, as a look at *Hind Swaraj* reveals.

Hind Swaraj: rethinking self-rule

The centenary of *Hind Swaraj* in 2009 produced a welter of scholarship. One strand within this explores the South African context of the book's production and explores themes of how Gandhi's idea of Western civilization owes as much to Johannesburg as to British India or London. At the time of writing *Hind Swaraj*, Johannesburg with its massive mining complex was the most advanced industrial centre in the world. Its forms of governmental control – fingerprinting being an apt example – were likewise cutting-edge (Breckenridge 2011; Hyslop 2008).

Another 'South African' dimension of *Hind Swaraj* emerges if we consider the text at the intersection of the vectors we have thus far been discussing, namely white settler rule, imperialism, colonial-born Indians and, by default, Africans. The text can be seen as an exercise that defines a radically deterritorialized idea of nation by using these categories for definition whilst announcing its superiority to them.

With regard to white settlers, the book formulates a radical idea of self-rule which is realized in the individual rather than a territory: the locus of the true nation is the satyagrahi. One way to read this idea is as a sideways comment on the abomination of territorialized white settler rule. (Gandhi's comment on white settler rule delivered on the deck of *SS Courland* on Christmas day

1896, while lynch mobs gathered on the foreshore capture this sentiment well: 'I therefore deplored the civilization of which the Natal whites were the fruit, and which they represented and championed' (Gandhi n.d: 99). Central to this white settler culture is its love of hyper-boundary and exclusion. Indeed in the conclusion of *Satyagraha in South Africa*, Gandhi comes to define satyagraha as a kind of anti-boundary:

> the reader of these pages has seen that had it not been for this great struggle and for the untold sufferings which many Indians invited upon their devoted heads, the Indians today would have been hounded out of South Africa. Nay, the victory achieved by Indians in South Africa more or less served as a shield for Indian emigrants in other parts of the British Empire, who, if they are suppressed, will be suppressed thanks to the absence of Satyagraha among themselves.
>
> (Gandhi 1928: 208)

With regard to the industrialized civilization of the imperial metropolis, *Hind Swaraj* posits the superiority of Indian civilization, thereby redefining the civilizational frame of empire and claiming it on behalf of 'India' (Africans by default remain excluded). While this form of civilization takes territorial expression, claiming allegiance to it doesn't necessarily. *Hind Swaraj* itself is extremely diaspora-friendly: according to its dictates, anyone (although probably not Africans) can make themselves Indian by practising self-rule and identifying with Indian civilization. This idea of placeless loyalty (apparent in the form of the text itself which famously unfolds in no unspecified space) seems to owe something to ideas of imperial citizenship whilst seeking to trump it. The version for realizing one's right to self-rule offered in *Hind Swaraj* has more substance and capacity to be put into action than the chimera of imperial rights that Gandhi encountered.

The colonial-born Indian forms an import addressee in the text with early editions identifying the 'Reader' as the subscriber of *Indian Opinion*. These early prefaces have disappeared, as has this definition of the 'Reader', to be supplanted by the interpretation of this figure as one or more of the Indian 'extremists' that Gandhi encountered on his trip to London on the return leg of which he wrote *Hind Swaraj* (Parel 2009: xxiv–xxix).

One can nonetheless usefully consider the 'Reader' as referring to both of these (the colonial-born reader and the extremist) simultaneously since both represent different points at which the nation is made vulnerable and might be breached. The colonial-born reader is ill-infomed and gullible and stands in danger of being taken in by the propaganda of the extremist who is cynical, violent and worldly. These two weak points, on the face of it so different, come to mirror each other. They may represent weakness and strength, naivety and cynicism, submission and rebellion, but they share a trait of being boundary markers and outer limits of the nation. Both kinds of readers need to come under the tutelage of the Editor who can instruct them in how to make themselves self-ruled satyagrahis (Hofmeyr 2011).

While *Hind Swaraj* never mentions Africans, their presence as boundary markers can be felt. They stand outside civilization and the deterritorialized self-rule that *Hind Swaraj* proposes. In *Satyagraha in South Africa*, Gandhi does indeed mention Africans and retrospectively brings them within the ambit of *Hind Swaraj*. In the following passage, he sets out what is in effect a summary of *Hind Swaraj* and indicates how Africans have suffered under the processes he describes:

> Western thinkers claim that the foundation of Western civilization is the pre-dominance of might over right. Therefore it is that protagonists of that civilization devote most of their time to the conservation of brute force. These thinkers … assert

that the nations which do not increase material wants are doomed to destruction. It is in pursuance of these principles that Western nations have settled in South Africa and subdued the numerically overwhelmingly superior races of South Africa.

(Gandhi 1928: 62)

In the Gandhian scheme of things satyagraha is the proper weapon to counter this Western greed and might. Implicitly then, the passage urges satyagraha as a remedy for Africans. However, it is clear that if such a struggle should occur it will not share a coeval time and place with Indian struggles.

In *Hind Swaraj* we can see the traces of Gandhi's South African experiments which come together to assume an anti-colonial imperial character. Claiming a civilizational superiority over both Britons (and Africans), Gandhi would position 'India' as a reconstituted space of 'imperial' noblesse oblige which would care for its diasporic subjects in appropriately paternalistic ways. Within this larger confederacy, humble subjects like the colonial-born Indians could be 'nursed' and educated towards subjecthood, thereby securing the frontiers of this widely dispersed nation. This larger space of 'Greater India' provides an arena in which self-rule could be realized not in a territory but in individuals who would carry out a prescribed set of spiritual and ethical procedures. In this way, Gandhi could trump white settlers and their territorial and narrowly racist ideas of self-rule by positing a more elevated and spiritual terrain of nationhood which could effectively unfold anywhere.

What were some of the consequences of these ideas in South Africa after Gandhi's departure?

Gandhi's afterlives in South Africa

There is a strong strand of historiography in South Africa which seeks to celebrate Gandhi's legacy in sentimental terms. This work paints a heartening narrative of the African National Congress (ANC) taking on Gandhian 'passive resistance' techniques in the Defiance Campaign in the early 1950s, and of growing Indian–African co-operation through the political alliances of the ANC and South African Indian Congress (SAIC). The apogee of this story links Gandhi and Mandela, two monumental world historical figures, through the connected histories of South African and Indian struggles (Gupta 2003).

Part of an anti-apartheid historiography invested in ideals of non-racialism, this narrative certainly has substance and there is no doubt that Gandhi's satyagraha techniques became an enduring and important part of South Africa's political idiom. Yet, this sentimental narrative is somewhat one-sided as more complex and subtle forms of analysis, made possible by the political transition in South Africa, are starting to reveal (Soske 2009). The picture of Gandhi's legacy that emerges is more ambiguous.

The first theme in this new historiography concerns Gandhi's opposition to African–Indian political co-operation, a position he shifted only towards the very end of his life and then only partially. This long-standing opposition, even as Nehru strongly backed co-operation, points to a residue of civilizational/imperial thinking. By insisting on political separateness for Indians in South Africa, it is as if Gandhi continued to understand diasporic Indians as operating in the deterritorialized space of 'Greater India'. The possibility of them deserting this space to join an anti-colonial struggle (of sorts) with Africans would 'demote' them from the realm of civilization and empire. These ideas remained influential in some quarters of Indian society in South Africa and probably meant that some leaders like Manilal Gandhi maintained an arm's-length attitude to African political organizations for longer than he might otherwise have done (Dhupelia–Mesthrie 2004: 350–55).

Nehru of course took a different position, urging African–Indian co-operation. African leaders in both South Africa and beyond paid considerable attention to his writings and the ideas of other Indian anti-colonial thinkers. Within this line up, the precise details of Gandhi's thought on African–Indian co-operation were not well known and Gandhi, despite his avowed opposition to co-operation, assumed a place in this anti-colonial gallery.

Yet, this African use of Indian anti-colonial luminaries as a source of political inspiration was complicated by the everyday realities of African–Indian tensions. Jon Soske's analysis of African nationalism and the Indian diaspora in Natal in the 1940s to 1960s (2009) paints a picture of more intractable divisions. Politically, there were cleavages between the Transvaal ANC, which favoured political alliances with the SAIC, and the Natal ANC, which did not, its members having more critical views on this question. These views were in turn informed by urban slum experiences in which the 'Gujarati and Hindi merchant and landlord class provided the ersatz urban infrastructure utilized by both Tamil-speaking workers and Zulu migrants' (Soske 2009: ii). While there were certainly daily interactions of sociality, friendship and shared public space, 'African migrants experienced urban life in terms of a haphazard and fragile hierarchy of "Indian" over "African"' (Soske 2009: 7).

A second aspect of Gandhian 'fallout' pertains to colonial-born Indians whom Gandhi continued to regard as weak points of the nation. As anti-colonial nationalism gained momentum and started to erase earlier ideas of Greater India, the diaspora began to lose its cachet. This shift was particularly painfully experienced by the descendents of indentured labourers who took up cash-incentivized repatriation schemes from South Africa to India in 1920s and 1930s. Having lost caste and Indian languages, they could find little foothold in Indian society and tended to gather in the slums of Madras and Calcutta appealing for help to whomever they could (Mesthrie 1985). They became something of an embarrassment which most politicians and organizations including Gandhi tried to sidestep. Yet, as John Kelly and Martha Kaplan have recently argued, within these repatriation schemes, there were people who did reintegrate, but there was an investment in exaggerating the extent to which such returnees couldn't fit in (Kelly and Kaplan 2007). The moral was clear: those in the indentured diaspora were better off staying where they were. Indeed Nehru's subsequent insistence that Indians in the diaspora should identify with the independent nations in which they found themselves has a touch of this patrician dislike of the indentured diaspora.

The plight of these marooned repatriates captures well the contradictions of Gandhi's political experiments. Imagined as the outer limit of a nation-in-empire, these descendents of the indentured diaspora had value as remote boundary markers of 'India'. They were never intended to become actual citizens of a real nation state but rather to signify the limits of the placeless nation that Gandhi was forced to find as a substitute for the empire he so fervently desired.

References

Abraham, I. (2008) 'From Bandung to NAM: Non-alignment and Indian Foreign Policy, 1947–65'. *Commonwealth and Comparative Politics* 46 (2): 195–219.

Amrith, S. (2009) 'Tamil Diasporas across the Bay of Bengal'. *American Historical Review* 114 (3): 547–72.

Bayly, S. (2004) 'Imagining "Greater India": French and Indian Visions of Colonialism in the Indic Mode'. *Modern Asian Studies* 38 (3): 703–44.

Bhana, S. and G. Vahed. (2005) *The Making of a Political Reformer: Gandhi in South Africa, 1893–1914*. New Delhi: Manohar.

Breckenridge, K. (2011) 'Gandhi's Progressive Disillusionment: Thumbs, Fingers, and the Rejection of Scientific Modernism in Hind Swaraj'. *Public Culture* 23 (2): 331–48.

Burton, A., A. Espiritu and F. C. Wilkins. (2006) 'Introduction: The Fate of Nationalisms in the Age of Bandung'. *Radical History Review* 95: 145–8.

Desai, A. and G. Vahed. (2007) *Inside Indenture: A South African Story, 1860–1914*. Durban: Madiba Publishers.

Dhupelia-Mesthrie, U. (2007) 'The Place of India in South African History: Academic Scholarship, Past, Present and Future'. *South African Historical Journal* 57: 12–34.

—. (2004) *Gandhi's Prisoner? The Life of Gandhi's Son Manilal*. Cape Town: Kwela.

Gandhi, M. K. (1928) *Satyagraha in South Africa*. Ahmedabad: Navajivan.

—. (1909) 'Mr. Gandhi's Second Jail Experience', *Modern Review* 6 (6) Dec: 553–64.

—. (n.d.) *An Autobiography or A Story of my Experiments with Truth*. Tr. Mahadev Desai. Bombay: Navajivan.

Gupta, Vijay (ed.) (2003) *Dhanyavaad India: A Tribute to the Heroes and Heroines of India who Supported the Liberation Struggle of South Africa*. New Delhi: High Commission of the Republic of South Africa in India.

Harper, T. N. (2002) 'Empire, Diaspora and the Languages of Globalism, 1850–1914'. *Globalization in World History*. Ed. A. G. Hopkins. London: Pimlico: 141–66.

Hofmeyr, I. (2011) 'Violent Texts, Vulnerable Readers: *Hind Swaraj* and its South African Audiences'. *Public Culture*, 23 (2): 285–97.

Huttenback, R. A. (1971) *Gandhi in South Africa: British Imperialism and the Indian Question, 1860–1914*. Ithaca and London: Cornell University Press.

Hyslop, J. (2008) 'Gandhi, Mandela and the African Modern'. *Johannesburg: The Elusive Metropolis*. Eds A. Mbembe and S. Nuttall. Durham: Duke University Press: 119–36.

Itzkin, E. (2008) 'The Transformation of Gandhi Square: The Search for Socially Inclusive Heritage and Public Space in the Johannesburg City Centre'. University of the Witwatersrand: MA Thesis.

Kelly, J. (1991) *A Politics of Virtue: Hinduism, Sexuality and Countercolonial Discourse in Fiji*. Chicago: University of Chicago Press.

Kelly, J. D. and M. Kaplan. (2007) 'Diaspora and Swaraj, Swaraj and Diaspora'. *From the Colonial to the Post-colonial: India and Pakistan in Transition*. Eds D. Chakrabarty and R. Majumdar. New Delhi: Permanent Black: 311–31.

Klaaren, J. (2004) 'Migrating to Citizenship: Mobility, Law, and Nationality in South Africa, 1897–1937'. Yale University: PhD Thesis.

Lee, C. J. (ed.) (2010) *Making a World After Empire: The Bandung Moment and its Political Afterlives*. Athens: Ohio University Press.

Markovits, C. (2003) *The Un-Gandhian Gandhi: The Life and Afterlife of the Mahatma*. New Delhi: Permanent Black.

McKeown, A. (2008) *Melancholy Order: Asian Migration and the Globalization of Borders*. New York: Columbia University Press.

Meer, F. (ed.) (1996) *The South African Gandhi: An Abstract of the Speeches and Writings of M. K. Gandhi 1893–1914*. Durban: Madiba Publishers/Institute for Black Research.

Mesthrie, U. (1985) 'Reducing the Indian Population to a "Manageable Compass": A Study of the South African Assisted Emigration Scheme of 1927'. *Natalia* (15): 36–56.

Metcalf, T. R. (2007) *Imperial Connections: India and the Indian Ocean Arena, 1860–1920*. Berkeley: University of California Press.

Mongia, R. (2006) 'Gender and the Historiography of Satyagraha in South Africa', *Gender and History* 18 (1): 130–49.

Natarajan, N. (2009) 'Atlantic Gandhi, Caribbean Gandhi'. *Economic and Political Weekly* (18): 43–52.

Niranjana, T. (1999) 'Left to the Imagination: Indian Nationalism and Female Sexuality in Trinidad'. *Public Culture* 11 (1): 223–43.

Parel, A. (ed.) (2009) *Hind Swaraj And Other Writings*. Cambridge: Cambridge University Press.

Parel, A. J. (1996) 'The Origins of Hind Swaraj.' *Gandhi and South Africa: Principles and Politics*. Eds J. Brown and M. Prozesky. Pietermaritzburg: University of Natal Press: 35–68.

Polak, H. S. L. (1910) 'The Transvaal Indians'. *Modern Review* 7 (5): 422–6.

Sanghavi, N. (2006) *The Agony of Arrival: Gandhi: The South African Years*. New Delhi: Rupa.

Soske. J. (2009) '"Wash Me Black Again": African Nationalism, the Indian Diaspora, and Kwa-Zulu Natal, 1944–60'. University of Toronto: PhD Dissertation.

Subramanian, L. (2009) 'Reflections on the "Overseas Indian": At Home in the World', paper presented to a conference, 'Print Cultures, Nationalisms and Publics in the Indian Ocean', University of the Witwatersrand, Johannesburg, Jan 15–17.

Swan, M. (1985) *Gandhi: The South African Experience*. Johannesburg: Ravan Press.

Tan, S. S. and A. Acharya. (eds) (2008) *Bandung Revisited: The Legacy of the 1955 Asian African Conference for International Order*. Singapore: National University of Singapore Press.

Zakaria, F. (2008) *The Post-American World*. London: Allen Lane.

13

SOUTH ASIAN MIGRATION TO THE UNITED STATES
Diasporic and national formations

Sandhya Shukla

Migration to the United States from India, Pakistan, Bangladesh, Sri Lanka and other smaller countries in the subcontinent has increased exponentially since the 1965 Immigration and Naturalization Act. Over the last decade especially, South Asians have become more and more visible, in cultural spheres, in political representation, in economic activity and, more generally, too, in broader national debates about race, ethnicity and difference. They have been part of a significant rewriting of America's story about itself as a land of immigrants. Because of the historical conjuncture of the explosion of South Asian populations and the multiple histories embedded in the experience of South Asianness in the world, South Asian migration has also brought issues of globality and diaspora to discussions of America's identity. South Asian diaspora has of course had a similar impact on other countries, whether Britain or Canada or Trinidad. But the absence of a colonial connection between South Asians and the USA, alongside the pervasiveness of the discourse of US multiculturalism, makes this case particularly interesting for reconceptualizing the shape and form of the nation, and for rethinking America more generally.

This essay maps the histories and cultures of diaspora and nation as they have taken shape through South Asian migrant formations in the United States. Despite the directed gaze on the United States, more than one country comes into view as we consider South Asian migration. South Asian countries like India or Pakistan – nations and national fantasies – are part of the everyday lives and imagined worlds of migrants and successive generations of their descendants. Britain must also be considered, both as imperial ruler and former colonial power, since this legacy shapes South Asians in ways that are far removed from any experience of habitation or interaction. Other spaces of settlement, whether in the Indian ocean region, or further afield in parts of Africa, Australia, Canada and the Caribbean, also have generated South Asian diasporic conceptions and vocabularies that have influenced migrants in the United States.

This migration necessitates an understanding of globality, geopolitical relations and international imaginations; and if that reality is not new, it has nonetheless brought to the fore theoretical languages that diverge from nationality. 'Diaspora' is the most prominent term associated with the South Asian migrant cultures that this essay seeks to represent; others include transnationality, cosmopolitanism, third-world ethnicity and race. South Asian migrant formations are seen here as symptoms of globalization, in ways that throw the boundaries of nationality into question. South Asianness, this essay will suggest, has opened up and changed 'America'.

The unbounded nature of South Asian diasporic cultures is seen here in more than merely geographic terms. Inasmuch as diaspora constructs relationships between people, places and ideas far removed from one another, it is to a great extent felt and lived in the realm of the imagination. Fantasy, projection and nostalgia are central modes for diasporic culture and are made vivid through representation – narrative productions which express that which cannot be easily observed. This essay will attend therefore as much to how the *story* of South Asian migration has been told, as it will to the broad details of the migration and settlement of people from South Asia in the United States. What that narrative includes or omits, and why, is every bit as important as the demographic details of the populations. Approaching South Asian migration in this interdisciplinary mode, this essay seeks to interpret the ruptures and continuities in a historical trajectory as well as the narratives about it.

The early years

Most narratives of migration are shaped and fissured by class, and South Asian migration is no exception. While the contemporary evocation of South Asians in the USA conjures forth images of successful Silicon Valley entrepreneurs or Indian American schoolchildren winning spelling bees, the reality, as always, is less simple. Although there have been some attempts to construct a linear trajectory from more working-class origins, beginning with Punjabi rural migrants settling on the west coast of North America in the early 1900s[1] and moving toward the highly skilled and middle-class migrations of the last few decades, many recent works have opened up and complicated both ends of that account.[2]

The early history of South Asian migration to the United States undoubtedly lies in a stream of labour migration. Between 1830 and 1920, the British empire established a system to supply indentured labour from the Indian subcontinent to agricultural enterprises in the colonies, and Indians went to work on sugar and rice plantations in the Caribbean, Southeast Asia and Africa (see Brij Lal, this volume). After the indenture system ended, the free movement of immigrants to North America was associated with the flows and eddies of global capitalism.

As Punjab suffered poor agricultural conditions in the early 1900s, North America's developing fisheries, railroads and agricultural plantations needed labour, and so a number of men left the Doaba and Malwa regions of Punjab for the west coast of the USA and Canada during this period. While the earliest years saw Punjabis being attracted to Canada's lumber industry, by 1909 when Canadian laws became more restrictive, more of them came to the US west, over the border in a second migration, and, as well, directly to Washington and all the way down to California.[3] In many ways this was the classic push–pull dynamic of US immigration. Punjabis came to work on California farms, in mining and canning factories up to Canada, and joined Chinese, Japanese and Filipino workers to constitute a low-wage 'Asian' labour force. Though the majority of the Indians were Punjabi Sikh, they were classified by local white residents as 'Hindoo', which became less a religious or ethnic term than a racial epithet (see Leonard, this volume). These Indians were subjects of the familiar suspicion that immigrants were taking jobs away from white workers, and they often became victims of racial violence. During this period small numbers of Indians came, too, as students and professionals not only to the west coast but also to other urban areas like New York City. And recent scholarship has uncovered a fascinating and heretofore little documented migration of Bengali seamen who escaped from British ships into multiracial urban spaces like Harlem, Detroit and New Orleans; these Bengalis, though, were by and large invisible because of their transient and concealed status.[4]

Early Indian migrants were affected by American laws restricting immigration from Asian countries. While the 1882 Chinese Exclusion Act, as its name implies, specifically concerned itself with the perceived 'invasion' of Chinese labourers, the 1917 Asiatic Barred Zone Act banned immigration from a region that now included Asia, Pacific Islands and also British India. This political–administrative construction of a region of 'Asia' has been one contributing factor in the broad and inclusive identity itself of 'Asian–Americanness', to which South Asian Americans have at times been drawn. The judicial system, meanwhile, was also involved in the sticky business of determining who could belong to the nation and why. In 1923, the United States Supreme Court ruled in the case *US vs. Bhagat Singh Thind* that, while Indians might be 'Aryan' according to the reigning racial science of the day, they were not white in terms of popular perception, and the latter is what formed the basis for citizenship and inclusion. In this way, an early South Asian migrant presence in the United States was rendered visible through its place in a national narrative of immigrant labour, racial minoritization and US legal doctrine.[5]

When the notion of a South Asian diaspora in the United States is more broadly imagined to include not only the movement of peoples, but the traffic in ideas (which John Kuo Tchen has also shown to be true for Chineseness in America),[6] we can see that South Asians arrived in an America that was itself becoming more global in its outlook. Some intellectuals had developed an affinity for what we might call 'Indianness': Ralph Waldo Emerson and Henry David Thoreau were influenced by Hinduism, and the visit of Swami Vivekananda to the 1893 World's Fair generated significant interest in many circles.[7] And testament to the fluidity of intellectual circuitry is the fact that Thoreau influenced Mohandas Gandhi, who in turn inspired Martin Luther King, Jr.[8]

American law continued to exclude women migrants: regulations aimed to prevent the mass settlement of Asians in America gave rise to largely bachelor communities in a variety of immigrant spaces.[9] The gender imbalance made for some interesting alliances. In California, Punjabis worked alongside Mexican migrants, and attachments grew between Mexican women and these Punjabi men. Karen Leonard has studied the formation and consequences of unions between these similarly coloured and racially positioned, but culturally very different, subjects. (Also see her essay in this volume.)[10] What emerged were astonishing examples of the confluence of social and personal interests – in Punjabi men's needs for companionship and belonging in a hostile new world, and Mexican women's desires for a form of financial stability that was more difficult to achieve in their own community – and also an occasion of cross-cultural intimacy. South Asian migrants have been criticized for their culturally protective behaviour in various parts of the diaspora, but they have also been part of broad racial coalitions and diversely ethnic coalitions in many places, particularly in England, Canada and the United States.[11] And inasmuch as the category of South Asian itself is constituted by heterogeneous national, regional, ethnic, and religious groups, the notion of *crossing* through rigid boundaries of identification is central to how this migration experience must be understood and imagined. It is a mistake, therefore, to view South Asian migration through the lens of single-ethnicity formation; we must interpret it as a hybrid, and hybridizing, phenomenon. Identifying cross-cultural inclinations from the 'beginning' of South Asian migration to the USA also challenges the received view that diversity and multiplicity are only achieved in the second and third generations of migrant culture.

Old and new nations

This author has argued elsewhere that South Asian migrant cultures in the USA were profoundly shaped by parallel processes of constructing multiple nations: America, India, and Britain.[12] The period between the early migration to the west coast and the later, and larger, movement of peoples following the 1965 Immigration and Naturalization Act proffers a useful set of coincidences of nation-formation. When Amitav Ghosh writes of an 'epic relationship' between India and her diaspora,[13] he evokes the hold that the imaginary of India has on its peoples everywhere, as well as the importance of the dispersed population to how the nation sees itself. And ironically, as India and Pakistan, and later Bangladesh, became nations, so too did those from South Asia become national citizens of the United States. It was this very coincidence, I would suggest, that was part, though not all, of the absence of a need to 'choose' national affiliation or attachment, that choice so fundamental a part of American national mythology, that immigrants leave the old land behind for their new American-ness.

It is plain that the desire for nationhood animated migrants who were contending with complicated and contentious histories of colonial rule. Students and workers on the west coast of the United States militated early and aggressively for Indian independence from Britain. The Ghadar Party was formed in 1913 and achieved worldwide importance as an ideological and political vehicle for the 'revolt' or 'mutiny' that its title signified. The publication *Ghadar*, that originated from a group house that the organization created in San Francisco, circulated throughout the diaspora, in North America, the Caribbean, East Asia and more. As Hofmeyr suggests in her essay in this volume, Indian nationalist discourse emerged and developed in diasporic formations and settings.

In the early decades of the twentieth century, small populations of Indian migrants, in association with non-migrant Americans, also formed organizations in other parts of the United States to promote Indian independence. Many migrants who played a central role in translating the cause of overthrowing British colonialism to American political officials and the more mainstream media often had first arrived in places like New York as merchants or writers. J.J. Singh, who came to the United States in 1926, built an Indian import business in Manhattan and devoted himself to appealing to media moguls such as Henry Luce and William Hearst for support of the overthrow of British rule in India. A 1951 article in *The New Yorker* magazine described Singh as a 'one-man lobby', invoking US-style interest politics, and also commented on the confluence of 'American' and 'Indian' identities, in the description: 'As a living refutation of Kipling's never-the-twain-shall-meet thesis, he eclectically embraces India and the United States with equal and unflagging devotion.'[14] As a Punjabi who had actively participated in the independence movement before going to Britain, and then the United States, Singh proselytized for his homeland as both incipient and developing nation-state. He corresponded with Mohandas Gandhi well before 1947 and then helped to organize prime minister Jawaharlal Nehru's visit to the United States in 1949.

Notably, Singh's devotion to India complemented rather than contradicted his commitment to America, as the *New Yorker* piece also recognized. As the leader of the India Home Rule League, which had been built around the goal of national independence, Singh deployed his ties to prominent government officials in the 1940s to organize on behalf of Indians' naturalization rights in the United States. While the eventual legal case was decided in domestic terms, Indians' status as colonized subjects was also a backdrop for their sense of who they were in the world. The remarkable coincidence of the Luce-Celler Act in 1946, which established the right for Indians to become naturalized Americans, and Indian national independence in 1947 can be read through the lens of, on the one hand, multiple nationalities and, on the other, an increasingly expansive and encompassing Americanism. As subcontinental freedom from British colonialism loomed large, so too, did efforts toward civil rights closer to home gain momentum among Indian Americans in this period: the fight for the status of being *from* an independent homeland appeared to translate into expectations of rights in the land of settlement. Nationality, even nationalism, was experienced multiply, without the conflict of interest that is often ascribed to 'homeland–new land' attachments among immigrants to the United States. Just as the South Asian diaspora was transformed by nation–making in the subcontinent, so too were the nations where they settled shaped by migrant experiences. In this way, it is important to recognize that the United States was porous and dynamic, and just as much a 'work in progress' as post-colonial nations.

Various elements of the Indian migrant experience and its complex relationship with nation formation in both South Asia and America are reflected in the story of Dalip Singh Saund. The first Indian American elected to the US Congress, Saund held office from 1956 until 1963. Saund, as a Punjabi migrant to the US west, provides a link to the labour migrants of the early years of the century, yet his actual arrival in 1920, his class background and his further education at the University of California at Berkeley allow for comparisons with the highly skilled migrants who came to the USA years later.

With a remarkably prescient sensibility about dual nationality, Saund wrote in his auto-biography: 'My guideposts were two of the most beloved men in history, Abraham Lincoln and Mahatma Gandhi.'[15] Saund chose icons of American and Indian nationality to construct himself as a multiply formed subject. In this rhetorical gesture, Saund presumed the trajectory of an anti-colonial Indian nation to be fully compatible with that of an America that had overcome the legacy of slavery and emerged as multicultural, so much so that he, a Punjabi Indian immigrant, could even aspire to become a congressional representative. Importantly, an affiliation to Indian anti-colonialism for Saund, as well as for a number of Indian migrants of an earlier period, did not preclude an attachment to a Western power that to a large extent had not actively supported their political causes back home. This was a rather different attitude than the one adopted by South Asian migrants towards Britain, the nation that effected their colonial oppression. In the United States, by contrast, the openness of national ideologies that created a broad and inclusive notion of 'America, a land of immigrants', captured the imaginations of South Asians. To be sure, Indian Americans, after a period of formal exclusion, certainly experienced less widespread forms of racism than their counterparts in England. But, beyond this fact, there has also been the allure of America, not only for South Asians, but for many other groups who migrated to the USA. This attachment to national stories, and the US nation's use, even exploitation, of that sentiment, is a central feature of the migrant cultural experience in America.

Dalip Saund took on Americanism as a defining ideology and reshaped it to make a space for Indians in America. He wrote constantly about his admiration for America in his autobiography and cited a developing loyalty as a reason for his decision to permanently settle in the United States after finishing his doctoral degree. Those attachments persisted through his represented life, even despite being denied citizenship in 1924. Benedict Anderson's discussion of the 'love for nation'[16] can be seen in Saund, and in generations of South Asian and other migrants who have come to the United States. But, if Anderson and other theorists of nation have focused on how singular loyalties have inspired participation in wars and other boundary-preserving activities, the multiple attachments of South Asian migrants in the USA provide instances that enable us to rethink the limits and possibilities of the nation. In this particular case, Dalip Saund developed a form of the trans- or multiple nationality long before increased access to communications and transport associated with a longing for nations perceived to be in formation.

Like Saund, many South Asians took with them wherever they went a profound desire for a new independent India (and later, Pakistan, Bangladesh or Sri Lanka). Although the United States was not a new nation, it would, after World War II and through the beginning of the civil rights era, undergo a dramatic transformation in terms of self-conception and also its status in the world. Both post-war USA and anti-colonial and then independent India, incorporated discourses of multiculturalism that diasporic and migrant peoples could utilize to build their own identities. Multiculturalism, while a *national* organizing principle, also employed stories of origin to establish membership in the whole. And so it seemed possible, preferable, and maybe even necessary, for those desirous of belonging in the USA to be able to claim national status *elsewhere*. Saund's much-publicized trip to India while he was a sitting Congressman spectacularized the idea that to be part of another nation you must be from an independent nation and, in this way, his going to India was a way to think about representing America. But Saund was well aware of his own symbolic importance for another part of the world, too, writing: 'The people of India and the Asiatic world knew the story of my election to the United States Congress in 1956 and were proud of the fact that a man born in India had been elected to that high office.'[17] In this we see the beginnings of the politics of visibility that would play an important part in South Asian migrant identity in the following decades.

If Dalip Singh Saund saw himself as anomalous or exceptional, it was because his own entry into the USA was part of a relatively minor migration of students, and the small communities of South Asians in California that were nearby had been formed by different waves of immigration from his own. The shape of South Asian migration to the United States, of course, would change dramatically, beginning in 1965 with the passage of the Immigration and Naturalization Act. Allowing for 170,000 immigrants from the eastern hemisphere, and 20,000 per country annually, the Act of 1965 transformed the character of the United States. South Asians were part of a broader phenomenon of large entering populations of migrants, from Asia, Africa and Latin America and the Caribbean and, in this early stage, mostly skilled and credentialled peoples, settling not just in California, but in urban and suburban areas all over the United States. The year 1965, then, was a flashpoint in the continuous rethinking of race and ethnicity in America. In response to it, middle-class Asian migrants reinterpreted their history using new conceptual frames.

South Asians' place in the US racial palimpsest continued to be unclear. Simultaneously 'Asian', in terms of region of origin, and 'coloured', through the history of British colonialism, and also 'white' (or Aryan), in a discussion of old models of racial science, South Asians self-presented, and were seen, in multiple ways. With a history of *not* being properly seen in the US social landscape, Indian Americans, especially after 1965, strove to develop for themselves a space within a symbolically powerful, but also practically material, institution, of the US census. Achieving the category of Asian Indian by 1980 was seen as a step in the development of a public identity that felt accurate, or true. The question of who and what a citizen was in the United States that had been ignited for South Asian Americans with the Thind case now changed to encompass notions of recognition, first, and then visibility. The struggle for belonging – a key element of cultural citizenship – became progressively less focused on legal rights (that had already been won) and more directed toward developing a group identity within the national ethnic–racial landscape.

Importantly, too, after 1965, those migrating from the Indian subcontinent came from independent and various nations, of India, Pakistan, Sri Lanka, Nepal and, eventually, after 1971, Bangladesh. So it is difficult to interpret the term 'South Asian' without a nod to its constructed nature, and also its deployment as a racial category for those seeking to bridge the colonial and national periods, as well as to propose diasporic solidarities. Indian American, Pakistani American and Bangladeshi American histories proceeded along similar trajectories, but had particularized logics and manifestations.

The nations of South Asia exerted a symbolic and real hold on migrants. The massive migration to the United States after 1965 of skilled and educated Indians, and the changing shape of patterns of migration to Britain beginning in the late 1960s, meant the departure of those peoples from the developing economies of South Asia. This 'brain drain', or human capital flight, was the source of some anxiety for developing nations in terms of perceived effects and also in the way that this confounded post-colonial nationalisms that rested on ideas of autonomy and strength in the face of richer and dominant countries like Britain and the United States. In response to such shifts, the Indian government developed the official category of the non-resident Indian, or NRI. Largely proposed to address a balance of payments issue in the Indian economy, the formalization of the traditional family remittances appealed to both Indians in India and abroad as an acknowledgment of profound connection with diasporic formations. By 1975, an institution called the Indian Investment Center was running meetings for Indian American immigrant groups to solicit funds for Indian industry.[18] What began as a relatively narrow economic programme soon became a more general process of signification – the figure of the NRI conjured complex, and reciprocal, desires of migrant Indians for their homeland, and the homeland nation-state's claim on peoples outside its borders. Of course the middle-class migrants in the first world with which the Indian state was so eager to develop a formalized relationship may have had little in common, indeed, with their working-class counterparts in their own countries of settlement or with those, say, in the Caribbean, or Africa. When Indians in India and elsewhere spoke of 'NRIs', they evinced a mixture of irony, admiration, longing and derision. In this way, the NRI can be seen as not only a kind of short-hand for the complicated relationship of South Asian migrants to South Asian countries, but a key to the divergences of class and racial experience among South Asians in the diaspora.

The class background of the first large wave of migrants to the United States contrasted sharply with South Asian migrants in most other countries. The position of South Asians in the USA after 1965 was often juxtaposed to that of South Asians in Britain beginning in the 1950s. The latter, a more working-class migration, garnered a great deal of attention back home in India because of a number of racist incidents and political tensions in Britain in the 1960s. An article in the April 22, 1973 issue of *Illustrated Weekly of India*, a magazine published in India, makes this point: 'There are 50,000 Indians and Pakistanis in New York. Unlike their compatriots in Europe who do menial jobs and live in congested lodging houses, those in the States are educated, affluent and believe in gracious living.'[19] South Asians in the United States in this period not only were more likely to have more education and better work opportunities, they also went to a country without the weight of a colonial relationship, if not free of the effects of racialization.

It is significant that in 1972, East Indians were expelled from Uganda, just as Indian Americans were beginning to establish their presence as a relatively new, and successful, immigrant group. What calls to be underlined in this fact is that the flow of ideas back and forth between the 'home country', whether of India, or Pakistan, or Bangladesh, and its circulation in other diasporas would now constitute the central theme of the South Asian diasporic experience. Also important here is the way that South Asians in and for the United States were simultaneously racial, ethnic and diasporic subjects and, while this phenomenon was not entirely new – all sorts of Asians and Latin Americans had been in the United States for many years – it was marked as a large-scale experience and became part of how America was reimagining itself as a nation.

As more middle-class South Asians settled in the United States in the late 1960s and early 1970s, they created communities that were rather different from South Asian west coast communities of the early 1900s. Wheareas, previously, immigrant–ethnic residential and com-mercial spaces had often been built inside the core areas of cities (Chinatowns in San Francisco and New York, for example), post-1965 immigrant places were less like enclaves and rather more designated areas that had once been occupied by other ethnic groups. One example of this trend is the 'Little India' in Jackson Heights in Queens, New York. This 'Indian' space sprung up around a consumer entity, the legendary electronics store 'Sam and Raj'. After the store was established in 1973, other stores providing South Asian goods (saris, foods) and services opened up in the area. Much later, some South Asians were drawn to live in the area; but, notably, it was not primarily a place of South Asian residential concentration. Jackson Heights became famous, attracting South Asians not only from Queens and the other boroughs of New York City, but also from New Jersey, Pennsylvania and other places in the region, but as consumers, not residents.

A number of features of this story bear closer analysis. First, it is striking that the anchor of this community was an electronics store, announcing a new generation, a new relationship of communication and exchange, and of migration to the USA from technologically ascendant Asian countries (and the Indian subcontinent). Second, and relatedly, this store could be seen as a point in the physical and symbolic traversal of boundaries by migrants: South Asians stopped over at 'Sam and Raj' to pick up gifts on their way to Kennedy International Airport, as they returned home for a visit; they also bought video and music players from the store to partake in the process of imagining a homeland through forms like the Bollywood film, or the CD of hybrid music (see Alexander, this volume). (Later, of course, the technology would relate more to computers and their networking possibilities.) This kind of South Asian migrant 'community' is a symptom of globalization – consumption-driven and diffusely experienced, with reference points all around the world.

Other 'Little Indias' emerged in the suburban areas where migrants settled. This marks a shift, too, in how post-1965 immigration was seen in general. Since the nineteenth century, immigrants had occupied less desirable regions of US urban centers, the lower east side of New York, the Tenderloin district of San Francisco, Harlem, and the like. Largely working-class, and working in heavy industry and other jobs located in the city, immigrants, like all Americans, lived close to work. But middle-class Asian and other immigrants of this later period worked in a variety of occupations and all over cities and suburbs. They increasingly lived in areas that ringed cities, or suburbs a commute away. Writers like Junot Diaz and Chang-rae Lee have used the imaginary of the suburb to tell new stories of race and ethnicity.[20] Large numbers of South Asian migrants settled in New Jersey and, by the 1990s a business and residential concentration formed in Edison. Edison now conjures up 'Indianness' for South Asians and non-South Asians alike, not as an urban ethnic enclave, but as a suburban ethnic space. And while Artesia, a Los Angeles-area 'Little India', is largely a business rather than residential concentration, it is a symptom of the new spatiality of the migrant-ethnic subject.[21]

Diasporic futures

Though many scholars have been keen to separate South Asian *migrant* formations from interest in *South Asia* (or India, or Pakistan), it seems that, if we take the model of diaspora seriously, we must acknowledge not only the connection between, but the simultaneity of, various forms of rendered South Asianness. In this sense, the interest in things Indian, say, cannot be decoupled from actual Indians. Literary fiction often announces a new generation and, in the case of South Asians, it signalled the 'coming of age' of diasporic subjects, writing and expressing themselves in new and old lands and asking questions about the shape and content of dispersal. In 1997, the magazine *The New Yorker* published a special Indian fiction issue that highlighted the work of Indians writing in English. While there had certainly been American fascination with India, dating back to Henry David Thoreau's interest in the *Bhagavad Gita*,[22] and extending through the influence of Indian musics and philosophies on 1950s and 1960s radicals, the efflorescence of Indian writing in the 1990s was coincident with a growing presence of South Asians in countries like Britain and the United States and, as such, assumed a kind of weight and substance that flashes of attention to the exotic did not carry. Writers like Salman Rushdie, Abraham Verghese and Kiran Desai, who all lived outside India, in the *New Yorker* issue outlined the flow among countries around the world; they created imaginaries that illuminated the affect of diaspora – constituted by loss and freedom.

A new generation of South Asian diaspora could also be seen in the emergence of youth cultures in the 1980s and 1990s. South Asian youth who had either been born in the United States or immigrated with their parents at a very young age by the 1980s were exploring questions of subjectivity in a rapidly changing racial landscape. South Asian youth self-presented as ethnic Americans, on the one hand, but, with the literal legacy of their parents' experiences as post-colonials, they also staked the ground of a racialism that was other to the black–white dynamics of the United States. Like their parents, these youth were developing new vocabularies for identification, but with a significantly expanded repertoire of possibilities in the 1980s. This generation had absorbed and lived diaspora and now utilized a variety of media, new and old, to illuminate that experience. In doing so they overturned the old presumption that the first is the immigrant generation, and the second is the ethnic; diaspora bridged that divide but also spoke to the globality that ethnic Americans and others lived. The homeland is not a stable point of reference, nor is the language of identity (South Asian, Indian, Asian American, something else?) clear-cut. This ambiguity has made for rich scholarly exploration and cultural production.[23]

South Asian youth turned to music and film, as well as fictional writing, to illuminate and instantiate diasporic experience. Music, especially, because of its inherent ability to move and be transported, provided an exemplary form for those second-generation South Asians who felt either out of place or multiply placed. And those in the United States could, with music, be linked up with and learn from, youth who had, perhaps, deeper or wider familiarity with a style of life that many sought to express. The emergence of the musical cultures of *bhangra* has been well documented,[24] and particular attention has been paid to the way that this Punjabi folk music found a home in the multi-generational, but also oppositional, space of South Asian racialized immigrants in England. What is also important is how South Asian *American* youth found a lexicon for articulating their own concerns about race and ethnicity, in British Asian cultural forms (see Alexander, this volume). In the 1980s and 1990s, South Asian deejays, musicians and other artists in the United States connected up with their counterparts in Britain. This traffic gave a real substance to diaspora, one that did not exist in the same way for first-generation migrants.[25] British Asian films, too, like *Bhaji on the Beach,*[26] which explored questions of generation and identity, beginning in the 1990s, crossed over into the South Asian American cultural sphere, and helped to construct new transatlantic dialogues and formations. By the end of the twentieth century, South Asians had been in countries like the United States for more than one generation, and there was an awareness through American culture not only about the fact of South Asians being there, but about what it meant when those whose parents had come over from the subcontinent grew up to inhabit 'Americanness'.

When Jhumpa Lahiri won the 2000 Pulitzer Prize for Literature for her short story collection *Interpreter of Maladies,* which explored questions of loss and nostalgia in migrant lives, it seemed that a new literature of diaspora had arrived. While related, certainly, to the musings of writers like Rushdie who had been shaped by India and other South Asian countries, Lahiri's imaginary was also more solidly located in the United States and as such broke open questions of migrant identity and the dilemmas for a population caught between homeland attachment and Americanization more widely than those who preceded her. In many respects, new South Asian American writing produced a fuller theoretical toolkit for subjectivity including all the concepts of race, ethnicity, post-colonialism and diaspora. The publicity of this rethinking of migrant identity – Lahiri's subsequent novel *The Namesake*, for example, was made into a film with significant circulation in 2006 – signalled changes in US cultural formations more generally.[27]

The broadening expanse for South Asian culture allowed for the discussion of other forms of diversity, of gender and sexuality, and also region, linguistic background and caste.[28] No longer could it be assumed that the representative South Asian was an Indian nationalist man, nor that 'his' only pressing concern was how to retain ties to the homeland. Groups like the South Asian Lesbian and Gay Association (SALGA) in New York and Trikone in San Francisco brought issues of sexuality to the fore and, not surprisingly, elicited discomfort from more traditional South Asians whose stake in a particular form of representation was deep. For ten years, SALGA was prevented from participating in the India Day Parade, an event that celebrates Indian independence and is a major focus for a number of immigrant organizations, but, in 2010, was allowed to join; yet it is still at the time of writing unable to march in the Pakistan Day Parade. This echoes the long-standing controversy around gays and lesbians marching in the St Patrick's Day Parade in Manhattan. What all these conflicts illustrate is the intense struggle over representation and visibility, about who is in charge of determining who and what it is to be a South Asian American.

Since the first wave of migrants after 1965, South Asians have continued to migrate to the United States. The characteristics of the migration have changed dramatically. The earliest group in this period was to a large extent middle class. Given the nature of the US economy at the time, many of these South Asians were high achievers (as were their children). But subsequent waves of migrants have included many more working-class and less skilled people, who also encountered the effects of the recession through the 1970s. These migrants came from countries like Pakistan and Bangladesh that had been less successful at providing educational resources to their citizens (see Washbrook essay, this volume). South Asian migrants were now not only doctors and bankers, but also hotel, restaurant and gas station owners and employees, taxi-drivers, food service employees, domestic workers and factory labourers.

The landscape of immigrant organizations shifted to accommodate these new interests. Early South Asian organizations had included those directed to culture and political and professional representation, like the Association of Indians in America (formed in 1971), the India Cultural Society of New Jersey in 1973, and associations for Indian and Pakistani physicians. But, more recently, a number of groups have addressed working-class and other political interests and have, too, organized a broader range of ethnic and racial groups. The New York Taxi Workers Alliance includes a large number of South Asians, but also other immigrant drivers from Latin America, the Caribbean and Africa. Workers' Awaaaz addresses concerns of largely South Asian domestic workers. The move here is also from organizations that are largely national (Indian, Pakistani) in nature, to those that utilize the rubric of South Asianness, as a regional–racial category, for a more diverse and cross-cultural set of goals.

The recent diversification of the South Asian American population has made it resemble more closely the British Asian population. While, throughout the 1970s, and even through the 1980s, there was a great deal of emphasis on the differences between the two diasporic sites, now that visible South Asian working-class groups have emerged in the USA, the two sites of diaspora seem more alike. The entry of South Asians from Caribbean countries, like Guyana and Trinidad, into the USA, further complicated the discussion about the complex legacies of post-colonialism. This of course proceeded with the increase and unpredictability of all sorts of flows of people and capital; 'twice migrant' became a more common experience, as did continual movements back and forth, between the USA and India, or other places. Who and what a modern diasporic subject was, in this context, was more complex than ever.

Perhaps the greatest challenge to established notions of modernity is religious identity. At once deeply linked to homeland attachments, and operating in a changed world of communication and affect, Hindu, Muslim and Christian peoples from South Asia have lived in truly diasporic formations. Religion itself is an institution that can articulate to both national and international forces, and religious cultures and religious practices actively militate against all kinds of borders.[29] The Hindu or Christian or Muslim spiritual imaginary is often cast as superseding divisions 'on the ground'. But, inasmuch as Hinduism, for example, has been associated with particular forms of Indian nationalism, it has also prescribed forms of exclusivity among migrants, wherein Indian Hindus have seen themselves as more authentic and authoritative in terms of the representation of 'India' abroad. This religious self-presentation has been inflected by national, class and caste prejudices as well, functioning for upper-middle class Indians as a way to distance themselves from working-class South Asian populations.

Certainly in the period after 2011, South Asian migrants were situated in the popular imagination very differently from before, both in the United States and globally. The Islamophobia following the attacks on the Twin Towers in New York, the London metro, trains in Madrid and buildings in Mumbai captured South Asians partly because they *looked* like Middle Eastern people (Sikhs with turbans were vilified, for example), but also because many of them were Muslim. And the South Asian migrants who were poor or working class and undocumented were particularly vulnerable to US governmental sweeps of communities to investigate terrorism. South Asians reported being stopped and searched at US airports and, regardless of national or regional origin, or religious background, being considered Pakistani Muslim. Many reacted by re-iterating their Hindu background, and this articulation accessed reactionary anti-Muslim sentiments and political formations (Vishva Hindu Parishad, among others) that may have originated in the subcontinent but circulated throughout the diaspora.

Around the same time, there was a great deal of attention paid to the rise of Indian billionaires in the Silicon Valley of California.[30] Lodged in the high-technology sector of the economy, many of these Indians had benefitted from the resources of the Indian state, receiving their education at the Indian Institutes of Technology, coming to the United States to work in the computer industry and starting up companies that rose to prominence in the 1990s and 2000s, during a boom period for the US economy. They hailed, moreover, from a rapidly developing India, which was providing labour for overseas companies who were 'outsourcing', as well as building their own successful enterprises. These very wealthy and successful Indians who were *exceptional* – in both senses of that term, for their highest achievement and their peculiarity – became symbols of a reworked 'model minority' myth and US immigrant dream stories at precisely the moment when poorer immigrants were being targeted as unworthy of membership in America because of their suspicious connections to fundamentalist groups back home.

Diaspora has become a complicated, and contradictory, proposition for the United States and for the world more generally. A form of belonging that traverses boundaries of the nation–state illuminates the experiences of many in the world, and so the concept of diaspora has importantly and successfully intervened in discussions of modern nations. The questions of who and what a modern citizen is, where does he or she rest and what cultures does he or she inhabit are all urgent ones as globalization proceeds with speed and intensity. American social, cultural, and political institutions manifest a keen awareness of migrants' connections to places around the world. But actual diasporas also produce anxiety. Who will migrants root for in soccer matches that pit the US team against Mexico or Brazil, in areas like Los Angeles or Newark, where there are large populations of Latin Americans? And which national or religious imaginaries make sense to those racialized peoples who are alienated from US society and economy? If diaspora signals freedom or a way out for those who feel constrained by their new place of residence, it is also, for the state, a peril.[31]

It has become increasingly difficult to make any winning claims about South Asian diaspora in the United States, so varied and multiple are its current formations. The struggles for recognition in the early 1970s can easily be forgotten in the face of the contemporary ubiquity of South Asians in popular culture (television, film, music) and political life (Congressional representatives, governors) and other social and educational institutions. Importantly, however, visibility and the continuing migrant generations have not made for a simplistic form of assimilation, nor for any waning of ties to countries in South Asia. Diasporic attachment and affect continue to define the South Asian in the United States.

Notes

1 Joan Jensen, *Passage from India: Asian Indian Immigrants in North America* (New Haven: Yale University Press, 1988) and Ronald Takaki, *Strangers from a Different Shore: A History of Asian Americans* (New York: Little, Brown and Company, 1989).

2 Maia Ramnath's *Haj to Utopia: How the Ghadar Movement Charted Global Radicalism and Attempted to Overthrow the British Empire* (Berkeley: University of California Press, 2011) is a recent example of globalizing early Indian immigration history; and Shalini Shankar's *Desi Land: Teen Culture, Class and Success in Silicon Valley* (Durham and London: Duke University Press, 2008) undoes a number of popular and academic preconceptions about Indian middle-class youth in the contemporary period.

3 Karen Isaksen Leonard, *Making Ethnic Choices* (Philadelphia: Temple University Press, 1992); Bruce La Brack, *The Sikhs of Northern California, 1904–1975* (New York: AMS Press, 1988).

4 Vivek Bald, *Bengali Harlem and the Lost Histories of South Asian America* (Cambridge and London: Harvard University Press, 2013).

5 Mae Ngai, *Illegal Aliens and the Making of Modern America* (Princeton: Princeton University Press, 2005).

6 John Kuo Tchen, *New York Before Chinatown: Orientalism and the Shaping of American Culture 1776–1882* (Baltimore: Johns Hopkins University Press, 2001).

7 Arthur Versluis, *American Transcendentalism and Asian Religions* (Oxford and London: Oxford University Press, 1993).

8 Roger Daniels, 'History of Indian Immigration to the United States: An Interpretive Essay', a paper presented to the conference, 'India in America: The Immigrant Experience', Asia Society, New York, April 17, 1989, p. 33.

9 See, for example, Erika Lee, *At America's Gates: Chinese Immigration during the Exclusion Era* (Chapel Hill: University of North Carolina Press, 2007).

10 Leonard, *Making Ethnic Choices*, op. cit.

11 Vijay Prashad, *Everybody Was Kung Fu Fighting: Afro-Asian Connections and the Myth of Cultural Purity* (Boston: Beacon Press, 2001).

12 Sandhya Shukla, *India Abroad: Diasporic Cultures of Postwar America and England* (Princeton, NJ: Princeton University Press, 2003).

13 Amitav Ghosh, 'The Diaspora in Indian Culture', in *Public Culture* 2, No. 1 (Fall 1989), pp. 73–8.

14 Robert Shaplen, 'Profiles: One-Man Lobby', in *The New Yorker*, March 24, 1951, pp. 35–55. Quote is on p. 35. See also Robert Shaffer, 'J.J. Singh and the India League of America 1945–1959: Pressing at the Margins of the Cold War Consensus', *Journal of American Ethnic History*, Vol. 31, No. 2 (Winter 2012) pp. 68–103.

15 D.S. Saund, *Congressman from India* (New York: E.P. Dutton, 1960). I have done a more extensive reading of this text in *India Abroad*, op. cit.

16 Benedict Anderson, *Imagined Communities: Reflections on the Origin and Spread of Nationalism* (London and New York: Verso, 1983).

17 Saund, op. cit., p. 183.

18 Sandhya Shukla, 'New Immigrants, New Forms of Transnational Community: Post-1965 Indian Migrations', *Amerasia Journal*, Vol. 25, No. 3 (1999–2000), pp. 19–36; Maxine Fisher, *Indians of New York City* (Columbia, MO: South Asia Books, 1980), p. 68; V. Balusubramanian, *Indians Abroad: The NRI Syndrome* (Bombay: Business Book Publishing House, 1987); Johanna Lessinger, 'Non-resident-Indian

Investment and India's Drive for Industrial Modernization', in *Anthropology and the Global Factory: Studies of the New Industrialization in the Late Twentieth Century*, ed. Frances Abrahamer Rothstein and Michael L. Blim (New York: Bergin and Garvey, 1992), pp. 62–82.

19 Khalid H. Shah and Linda Shah, 'Indians in New York', *Illustrated Weekly of India*, April 22, 1973, pp. 19–22.

20 Junot Diaz, *The Brief Wondrous Life of Oscar Wao* (New York: Riverhead, 2007); Chang-rae Lee, *A Gesture Life: A Novel* (New York: Riverhead, 1999); Ming Wen, Diane S. Lauderdale and Namratha K. Kandula, 'Ethnic Neighborhoods in Multi-Ethnic America, 1990–2000: Resurgent Ethnicity in the Ethnoburbs?' in *Social Forces*, Vol. 88, No. 1 (September 2009): 425–60. Cindy I-Fen Cheng argues in 'Out of Chinatown and into the Suburbs: Chinese Americans and the Politics of Cultural Citizenship in early Cold War America', *American Quarterly*, Vol. 58, No. 4 (2006), 1067–90, that Chinese Americans moved into some suburbs earlier.

21 S. Mitra Kalita, *Suburban Sahibs: Three Immigrant Families and Their Passage from India to America* (New Brunswick: Rutgers University Press, 2005).

22 Carl T. Jackson, *The Oriental Religions and American Thought: Nineteenth-Century Experiences* (Westport, CO: Greenwood Press, 1981).

23 Shilpa Dave, Pavan Dhingra, Sunaina Maira, *et al.*, 'De-privileging Positions: Indian Americans, South Asian Americans and the Politics of Asian American Studies', *Journal of Asian American Studies*, Vol. 3, No. 1 (2000), 67–100.

24 Sanjay Sharma, John Hutnyk and Ashwani Sharma, *Dis-orienting Rhythms: The Politics of the New Asian Dance Music* (London: Zed Books, 1996); Rupa Huq, *Beyond Subculture: Pop, Youth and Identity in a Postcolonial World* (New York: Routledge, 2006).

25 My own fieldwork among first-generation Indian migrants in England and the United States in the 1990s suggested that the connections between these two groups were felt through an imagined Indianness, that, indeed, is one important aspect of diaspora, but not, necessarily, through a more material set of connections.

26 *Bhaji on the Beach*, dir. Gurinder Chadha, 1993.

27 See Sunaina Maira, *Desis in the House: Indian American Youth Culture in New York City* (Philadelphia: Temple University Press, 2002); Bandana Purkayastha, *Negotiating Ethnicity: Second-Generation South Asians Traverse a Transnational World* (New Brunswick: Rutgers University Press, 2005); and others.

28 Monisha Das Gupta, *Unruly Immigrants: Rights, Activism, and Transnational South Asian Politics in the United States* (Durham and London: Duke University Press, 2006).

29 Prema Kurien, *A Place at the Table: Multiculturalism and the Development of an American Hinduism* (New Brunswick: Rutgers University Press, 2007).

30 Though the reality, on the ground, is more complicated, as Shalini Shankar explores in *Desi Land: Teen Culture, Class and Success in Silicon Valley*, op. cit.

31 Brian Keith Axel has written about diaspora as both 'promise' and 'threat,' in *The Nation's Tortured Body: Violence, Representation, and the Formation of a Sikh 'Diaspora'* (Durham and London: Duke University Press, 2000).

References

Anderson, B 1983, *Imagined Communities: Reflections on the Origin and Spread of Nationalism*, Verso, London.

Axel, BA 2000, *The Nation's Tortured Body: Violence, Representation, and the Formation of a Sikh 'Diaspora'*, Duke University Press, Durham.

Bald, V 2013, *Bengali Harlem and the Lost Histories of South Asian America*, Harvard University Press, Cambridge.

Balusubramanian, V 1987, *Indians Abroad: The NRI Syndrome*, Business Book Publishing House, Bombay.

Chadha, G 1993, *Bhaji on the Beach*.

Cheng, CI 2006, 'Out of Chinatown and into the Suburbs: Chinese Americans and the Politics of Cultural Citizenship in Early Cold War America', *American Quarterly* 58:4, pp. 1067–90.

Daniels, R 1989, 'History of Indian Immigration to the United States: An Interpretive Essay', a paper presented to the conference 'India in America: The Immigrant Experience', Asia Society, New York.

Das Gupta, M 2006, *Unruly Immigrants: Rights, Activism, and Transnational South Asian Politics in the United States*, Duke University Press, Durham.

Dave, S, Dhingra, P, Maira, S, Mazumdar, P, Shankar, L, Singh, J and Srikanth, R 2000, 'De-Privileging Positions: Indian Americans, South Asian Americans and the Politics of Asian American Studies', *Journal of Asian American Studies* 3:1, pp. 67–100.

Diaz, J 2007, *The Brief Wondrous Life of Oscar Wao*, Riverhead, New York.

Fisher, M 1980, *Indians of New York City*, South Asia Books, Columbia, MO.

Ghosh, A 1989, 'The Diaspora in Indian Culture', *Public Culture* 2:1, pp. 73–8.

Huq, R 2006, *Beyond Subculture: Pop, Youth and Identity in a Postcolonial World*, Routledge, New York.

Jackson, C 1981, *The Oriental Religions and American Thought: Nineteenth-Century Experiences*, Greenwood Press, Westport, CT.

Jensen, J 1988, *Passage from India: Asian Indian Immigrants in North America*, Yale University Press, New Haven, CT.

Kalita, SM 2005, *Suburban Sahibs: Three Immigrant Families and Their Passage from India to America*, Rutgers University Press, New Brunswick, NJ.

Kurien, P 2007, *A Place at the Table: Multiculturalism and the Development of an American Hinduism*, Rutgers University Press, New Brunswick, NJ.

La Brack, B 1988, *The Sikhs of Northern California, 1904–1975*, AMS Press, New York.

Lee, C 1999, *A Gesture Life: A Novel*, Riverhead, New York.

Lee, E 2007, *At America's Gates: Chinese Immigration during the Exclusion Era*, University of North Carolina Press, Chapel Hill.

Leonard, KI 1992, *Making Ethnic Choices*, Temple University Press, Philadelphia, PA.

Lessinger, J 1992, 'Non-resident-Indian Investment and India's Drive for Industrial Modernization', in Rothstein, F and Blim, M, *Anthropology and the Global Factory: Studies of the New Industrialization in the Late Twentieth Century*, Bergin and Garvey, New York.

Maira, S 2002, *Desis in the House: Indian American Youth Culture in New York City*, Temple University Press, Philadelphia, PA.

Ngai, M 2005, *Illegal Aliens and the Making of Modern America*, Princeton University Press, Princeton, NJ.

Prashad, V 2001, *Everybody Was Kung Fu Fighting: Afro-Asian Connections and the Myth of Cultural Purity*, Beacon Press, Boston, MA.

Purkayastha, B 2005, *Negotiating Ethnicity: Second-Generation South Asians Traverse a Transnational World*, Rutgers University Press, New Brunswick, NJ.

Ramnath, M 2011, *Haj to Utopia: How the Ghadar Movement Charted Global Radicalism and Attempted to Overthrow the British Empire*, University of California Press, Berkeley.

Saund, DS 1960, *Congressman from India*, EP Dutton, New York.

Shaffer, R 2012, 'JJ Singh and the India League of America 1945–1959: Pressing at the Margins of the Cold War Consensus', *Journal of American Ethnic History* 31:2, pp. 68–103.

Shah, KH and Shah, L 1973, 'Indians in New York', *Illustrated Weekly of India* pp. 19–22.

Shankar S 2008, *Desi Land: Teen Culture, Class and Success in Silicon Valley*, Duke University Press, Durham.

Shaplen, R 1951, 'Profiles: One-Man Lobby', *The New Yorker* March 24, pp. 35–55.

Sharma, S, Hutnyk, J, Sharma, A 1996, *Dis-Orienting Rhythms: The Politics of the New Asian Dance Music*, Zed Books, London.

Shukla, S 1999/2000, 'New Immigrants, New Forms of Transnational Community: Post-1965 Indian Migrations', *Amerasia Journal* 25:3, pp. 19–36.

—— 2003, *India Abroad: Diasporic Cultures in Postwar England and America*, Princeton University Press, Princeton, NJ.

Takaki, R 1989, *Strangers from a Different Shore: A History of Asian Americans*, Little, Brown and Company, New York.

Tchen, JK 2001, *New York Before Chinatown: Orientalism and the Shaping of American Culture 1776–1882*, John Hopkins University Press, Baltimore, MD.

Versluis, A 1993, *American Transcendentalism and Asian Religions*, Oxford University Press, Oxford.

Wen, M, Lauderdale, D, Kandula, N 2009, 'Ethnic Neighborhoods in Multi-Ethnic America, 1990–2000: Resurgent Ethnicity in the Ethnoburbs?' *Social Forces* 88:1, pp. 425–60.

PART IV

Diaspora, nation states and the neighbourhood

14

FROM IMPERIAL SUBJECTS TO NATIONAL CITIZENS

South Asians and the international migration regime since 1947[1]

Joya Chatterji

By the end of the Second World War, some 3.5 million Indians were spread unevenly across 58 countries of the world (see Table 14.1). The largest numbers – not surprisingly, given the imperial role in managing Indian migration – had migrated to other colonies within the British Empire.

Two regions accounted for most of these migrants. The first included territories in the close neighbourhood across the Bay of Bengal in South and Southeast Asia and the Malay archipelago: by 1948, there were 2 million 'Overseas Indians' (as they were known) in Ceylon, Burma, Malaya and Singapore. The second included parts of Africa across the Arabian Sea: almost 700,000 Indians were in Mauritius, British East Africa and South Africa. The remaining million were more unevenly distributed: more than 100,000 respectively dwelt in Trinidad and Tobago, British Guyana and Fiji, and there were sizable communities in Jamaica, Indonesia, Siam and Madagascar. Only a few thousand, by contrast, lived in Canada and Australia.

This diaspora was in no sense a homogenous community; nor was it settled or static. 'Overseas Indians' were drawn from different parts of the subcontinent; they spoke different languages; they prayed to different gods. They were divided by class and status – the wealthier, better-educated, fare-paying, 'passenger class' Indians abroad always anxious not to be mistaken for the lowly 'coolies' who far outnumbered them. Almost all had travelled abroad deploying networks of circulation (Markovits *et al.*, 2003) with their own internal mechanisms of regulation and control (Ahuja, 2006). But some enjoyed greater freedom of mobility than others: the 'passenger' classes were, in theory at least, free to travel when they pleased, whereas indentured coolies were legally obliged to serve out their contracts abroad, and 'assisted' migrants recruited by agents known as *kanganis* (Lal, this volume; Tinker, 1974) were shackled even more firmly by the bonds of debt. Differences of legal status, but also of wealth and literacy, meant that some migrants were better able than others to maintain links with the 'homeland' (Lal, this volume; Amrith, 2009). By 1945, political divisions in India, in particular the clash between the Congress and the Muslim League, were mirrored and played out in many distant parts of the world where well-to-do Indians had settled.[2]

Table 14.1 Statement of Indian population in overseas countries

Country	Overseas Indian population	Year of estimate
South Africa	232,407	1946
of which, Natal	228,492	
Transvaal	37,000	
Cape Province	16,901	
Orange Free State	14	
East Africa	184,000	
of which, Kenya	90,295	1946
Uganda	33,820	1948
Zanzibar and Pembo	16,000	1946
Nyasaland	1,851	1946
British Somaliland	520	1946
Italian Somaliland	1,000	1947
Southern Rhodesia	2,547	1947
Northern Rhodesia	1,484	1946
Ethiopia	500	1949
Nigeria	375	1947
Sierra Leone	76	1948
Rwanda Burundi	66	1948
Madagascar	14,945	1950
Ceylon	732,258	1946
Malaya and Singapore	604,508	1947
Burma	700,000	
Indonesia	27,638	1940
Indo–China	1,310	1949
Sarawak	2,300	1949
Brunei	436	1949
British North Borneo	1,298	1947
Siam	20,000	
Philippines	1,258	1948
Hongkong	1,900	1946
Japan	170	1940
Fiji	133,941	
Australia	4544	1933
New Zealand	1,116	1945
Mauritius	285,111	1950
Seychelles	285	1947
Maldives	550	1933
Iran	2,500	1948
Iraq	650	1948
Afghanistan	200	1948
Bahrein	1,138	1948
Muscat	1,145	1948
Kuwait	1,250	1948
Egypt	1,000	1948
Palestine Turkey	} Less than 100 each	

Country	Overseas Indian population	Year of estimate
Syria	} Less than 100 each	
Lebanon		
Transjordan		
Aden	5,594	
Gibraltar	41	1946
United Kingdom	7,128	1932
USA	1,465	1941
Canada	1,465	1941
Trinidad and Tobago	214,177	1949
Jamaica	22,821	1949
British Honduras	1,366	1946
Granada	5,000	1932
St Lucia	2,189	1946
Windward Islands	7,948	1946
Leeward Islands	99	1950
Barbados	100	1950
Panama	450	1948
Brazil	21	1948

Source: Memo by B. F. H. B. Tyabji dated 23 August 1952, Government of India, Ministry of External Affairs, AFR II Branch, AII/53/6491/31/Secret

This essay will consider the impact of decolonisation upon these far-flung and diverse populations. Britain's retreat, in fits and starts, from empire after World War II had large consequences for 'British Indian subjects' scattered throughout her erstwhile possessions. The transfer of power in 1947, India's independence, partition and Pakistan's emergence as a separate nation state, independence for Ceylon and Burma in 1948, the wave of nation-making in Africa in the 1950s and 1960s, and the breakaway of Bangladesh from Pakistan in 1971 all had a profound, albeit complex and uneven, impact on Indians living in these new nations. Each of these developments helped to produce a new world characterised by more formidable, less porous, frontiers. The new nation states of the later twentieth century – *including those of the subcontinent* – had a greater stake than their imperial predecessor in controlling the entry and exit of outsiders and in stopping, or at least regulating, flows across borders. They also had far more pressing reasons than the empire to define who was, and who was not, a citizen. This forced migrants to decide (and publicly declare) where they 'belonged', and generated fresh impetuses for migration. All of these changes added up to what can best be described as a new 'migration regime', whose interlocking and overlapping laws, policies and practices came to be a crucial part of the international context in which South Asians have migrated abroad since 1947. A short essay cannot explore all the complex ramifications of this regime for the South Asian diaspora, but within the constraints of space it will attempt to sketch, with a broad brush, how the world of the migrants was changed by it.

First, however, a few words call to be said about what 'British Indian subjecthood' had come to mean by the mid-twentieth century. Much had changed since 1608 when Sir Edward Coke, in *Calvin's Case*, had insisted that all the King's subjects were equal (Parry, 1951; Kim, 2004). Three centuries later, at the end of the nineteenth century, this equality of status no longer existed: as Caitlin Anderson has shown, some British subjects were more equal than others, and 'natural born' Britons enjoyed greater rights and more consular protection than those born in the empire (2008). Nor did Britain's Indian subjects, as some commentators suggest, have an unfettered right to move wherever they wanted within an empire on which the sun never set (Sherman, 2011). During World War I, Defence of India rules required all travellers leaving India by sea to carry a passport. The Passport Act of 1920 entrenched these rules in the statute book, while deliberately leaving government with the latitude to exempt from its provisions certain classes of Indians (soldiers and sailors, for instance, as Singha (n.d.) has shown), whose skills were needed in the wider empire. In 1922, the Indian Emigration Act at last ended the notorious system of indenture by which unskilled labourers had been sent abroad under what Tinker (1974) described as 'a new system of slavery'. But there were still many ways in which so called 'free', but unwanted, persons from South Asia could be prevented from entering Europe and America. *Lascar* contracts that specifically prohibited Indian seamen from leaving ships (Ahuja, 2006; Balachandran, 1997) and the Continuous Passage Act which prevented the *Komagata Maru* from docking at Vancouver harbour, were only the most notorious among many stratagems deployed (Mongia, 1999) by the 'white dominions' to keep out brown British subjects.[3] After 1916, 'pilgrim passports' for pious Muslims undertaking the Hajj pilgrimage had to be attached to a prepaid return ticket or deposit, an arrangement that was put onto the statute book in 1925 (Singha 2009). By the 1930s, even the territories of the Indian Ocean rim had begun to restrict the immigration of Indians. Malaya and the Straits Settlement now imposed controls. After its separation from British India in 1937 (Amrith, 2010), Burma too began negotiations for a treaty to limit Indian migration; and in 1939 Ceylon banned it altogether.

Nor was entry into India unregulated. Wars in the twentieth century provided justification for a regime of controls designed to keep out of India persons seen as a threat to imperial security. Since the Great War, 'troublemakers' of Indian origin were denied 'ingress into India'; and the Passport Act of 1920 made travel documents compulsory for travel to India (Singha, n.d.). In 1939, 'the needs of the war emergency' led to the enactment of a Foreigners Ordinance and an Enemy Foreigners Order,[4] powers to detain and expel foreigners which India's Interim Government arrogated for independent India in a Foreigners Act in 1946 (Sen, 2010).

So the imperial past was not some halcyon age of unrestricted mobility. Yet there is no doubt that shift from empire to nations brought about far-reaching changes for South Asian migrants the world over.

Independence and partition at 'home'

Paradoxically, it was in the subcontinent itself that the most dramatic changes took place, impinging on the rights of millions of South Asians to travel abroad or to return home. In its transfer of power, Britain was able to persuade India and Pakistan to stay within the Commonwealth. Consequently, the architects of the complex agreements surrounding partition assumed that citizens of the two successor states, India and Pakistan, would remain British subjects and as such continue to have 'free' access to all other parts of the empire. The Partition Council optimistically concluded that 'no immediate change was called for as a result of partition'. India and Pakistan could formulate their respective nationality laws in due course, and in the meantime, passport rules should be so amended to permit free movement of persons from one dominion to the other.[5] Astonishing as it may seem in retrospect, in August 1947 the leaders of India and Pakistan still believed that, partition notwithstanding, the peoples of the subcontinent would stay where they were. The consensus was that open borders between the two states would facilitate the transfer of power to two separate dominions, with little or no social and economic disruption.

Instead, as we now know, massive migrations followed, the largest recorded in history. Often following in the grooves carved by earlier sojourners (Chatterji, 2013), millions began to head to the 'right' nation state. Ministers on both sides of the new borders, bombarded with reports about killings on a genocidal scale and of a huge influx of refugees, began to rethink these assumptions. This was the context in which the Military Evacuation Organisation (MEO) was set up to provide protection and safe passage across the borders to 'stranded refugees'. By the end of 1947, the MEO had evacuated 5 million refugees across the borders between India and Pakistan (Randhawa, 1954) and, by 1951, over 20 million refugees had fled their homes and crossed into the other country.

This was the first move towards a new policy, which was to have significant ramifications. If partition's refugees in their millions were to be allowed to move across borders between India and Pakistan (and indeed to be assisted by government in so doing), this raised the question of what was to happen to the property they left behind. What was its status, who was to protect it and by what means? Again, it seems that both states started out with the firm intention of protecting these vacant properties within their own territories, keeping out looters and squatters. The plan was to 'preserve' the 'property and effects of evacuees', and to guarantee their continued rights of ownership. At the Lahore Conference at the end of August 1947, Nehru and Liaquat Ali Khan, the prime ministers of India and Pakistan respectively, jointly declared that 'illegal seizure of property [would] not be recognized and both Governments [would] take steps to look after the property of refugees and restore it to its rightful owners'. On 9 September 1947, the authorities of West Punjab in Pakistan appointed a Custodian of Evacuee Property 'to take possession of the property and effects of evacuees and to take such measures as he considers necessary or expedient for preserving such property or effects'. Within days, East Punjab in India followed suit.[6]

But problems soon arose about how to deal with incoming refugees who had already occupied property abandoned by people (described as 'evacuees') who had fled from their homes in the opposite direction during the riots. In Delhi, Calcutta and Karachi, incoming refugees had begun to break into and squat in any vacant property they could find, resolutely resisting efforts to oust them. Local authorities proved inclined to protect members of their own communities and reluctant to take action to evict refugees in illegal possession until they had somewhere else to live, citing a wider 'public' perception that they ought to be allowed to remain. Increasingly, government had to draw a distinction between refugees and 'ordinary looters',[7] which acknowledged the special claims of refugees. However, this in its turn raised another conundrum: what would happen if Muslim evacuees came back home to India once order was restored (and many were known to want to return[8])? Where would they go if their houses had been taken over by refugees? And what would happen to Hindu and Sikh refugees who wanted to return to the homes they had abandoned in Pakistan?

Faced with these dilemmas, Nehru's government came to the conclusion that *the only way forward was to prevent evacuees from returning to reclaim their homes*. In the summer of 1948, India promulgated the Influx from Pakistan (Control) Ordinance, which held that 'no person shall enter India from any place in Pakistan, whether directly or indirectly unless . . . he is in possession of a permit'.[9] This had profound implications for millions of Muslims born in India who had fled to Pakistan in order to protect their families from violence, but who hoped to return when peace and order were restored. The 'permit system' (Zamindar, 2007) denied them the right to return to the land of their birth.

By October 1948, however, it was becoming evident that the permit system was impossible to enforce in a society where few people had proper identity documents, or indeed any kind of paper records at all. Intelligence agencies in India charged with policing the system found that many permits were being forged or improperly issued;[10] and the Indian government struggled to send back to Pakistan Muslim 'returnees' who claimed never to have left India in the first place. In December 1948, the Rehabilitation Department in New Delhi ordered all provincial governments to stop issuing permits for permanent resettlement. In April 1949, and again in May 1949,[11] stern reminders were sent, but government still found it almost impossible to enforce the system and to keep out Muslim evacuees who wished to return to India.

This was the context for the promulgation of India's Evacuee Property Ordinance in June 1949. The ordinance empowered provincial governments in *every* part of India (except in the eastern states of West Bengal, Assam and Tripura[12]) to acquire evacuee property 'as it may need for a public purpose which may include the rehabilitation of refugees, or economic rehabilitation of the province, or payment of fair compensation'. At a stroke, the ordinance nationalised all evacuee Muslim property and made it an essential part of the pool of resources out of which India would seek to house and rehabilitate incoming Hindu and Sikh refugees. So, even if Muslim refugees in Pakistan somehow managed to get a permit to return to India, they now were dispossessed and had nowhere to go. Pakistan's officials protested vociferously and with justification that these measures effectively 'disinherited' India's Muslims who had moved from their homes. But very soon Pakistan followed with its own identical legislative and executive measures.[13] Faced with a situation in which India had slammed the door shut on Muslims refugees and made it impossible to recover their properties, Pakistan could see that it had little option but to appropriate all evacuee Hindu and Sikh property in its turn (Chatterji, 2012).

These measures had a profound impact on the millions of South Asians affected by them. They made migration – indeed even 'circular' or temporary movement – an irrevocable step. Once the very act of leaving one's home rendered it liable to seizure, many South Asians were forced to stay where they were. And, for those who had already left, they had no alternative but to remain where they now found themselves, or to seek some new destination outside South Asia where they could settle, since they no longer had homes back in India or Pakistan to which they could return. The action of migration now was endowed with a new finality and with novel political consequences. Muslim migrants to Pakistan were deemed by India to have adopted citizenship of Pakistan *by the very act of* moving there and to have renounced forever their right to Indian citizenship. Hindus and Sikh refugees, likewise, were banned from returning to their homes in Pakistan.

This regulatory regime had the result of sealing the western borders between India and Pakistan, making it one of the least permeable and most violently policed borders in the world (van Schendel, 2007). The eastern borders too, would gradually come to be closed. After 1952, passports and visas were required for travel between India and East Pakistan. The Enemy Property Acts of 1967, promulgated by both countries, applied to *all* their territories, bringing East Pakistan, West Bengal, Assam and Tripura (hitherto excluded from the purview of the evacuee property regime) firmly within its remit. These Acts not only made it more difficult than ever to cross the borders; it also made it hazardous even to maintain contact with relatives on the other side, since fraternising with 'the enemy' across the border rendered property liable to seizure (Chatterji, 2012). In 1972, Bangladesh enacted its own Vested Property Ordinance, which mirrored the provisions of the evacuee property acts of its neighbours, with dire implications for its large Hindu population, and also for its Urdu-speaking minorities (Barkat *et al.*, 1997; Farooqui, 2000, Ghosh, 2007).

By leaving people stranded and homeless on the 'wrong' sides of these borders, and by rupturing the age-old circulatory networks of people whose worlds had previously straddled them, these new citizenship regimes in South Asia built up pressures for fresh diasporas. Take the case of Sylheti migrants, who for generations had travelled in two distinct streams in search of work: westwards to Calcutta, where they found work as boiler-room men on British merchant ships and eastwards to join the labour force in the tea gardens of Assam. In 1947, Sylhet became part of East Pakistan, while Calcutta and Assam went to India. Since Sylhetis were now deemed to be 'Pakistanis', it became much harder than before for them to stay on as lascars on ships sailing out of Calcutta.[14] The climate in Assam – long fraught with tension between migrants from Bengal and the 'sons of the soil' (Baruah, 2005; Weiner, 1978) – after partition turned bitterly hostile to Bengali Muslim 'interlopers', who now began physically to be driven out of the state.[15] Against this backdrop, in the 1950s some Sylhetis sought employment in British mills they had been told about by former 'lascar' comrades. This began one of several new streams of migration from a far-flung part of the British empire to the metropole (Adams, 1987; Choudhury, 1993; Eade, this volume).

Independence, partition and the diaspora

These upheavals back at home also had large implications for migrants of South Asian origin living in other parts of the world. In 1950, the Indian constitution bestowed Indian citizenship on persons already living abroad, if he himself, or either of his parents, or any of his grandparents, had been born on Indian soil (Sinha, 1962, 83). But, as the External Affairs Ministry's figures showed, perhaps one in three of these 'Overseas Indians' were Muslims.[16] Many of them came from parts of the subcontinent that were now in India, not in Pakistan, and they had relatives and properties there. Questions were now raised about their nationality. The External Affairs Ministry was much exercised, for instance, by the case of one Mr Gardee, a Muslim of Indian origin and long-time resident of Johannesburg. Mr Gardee, reputedly one of South Africa's richest men, came from Bombay, where also he had substantial properties. His 'pro-Pak leanings' were apparently 'well established'. Indian officials believed that he had travelled to Pakistan to buy property there. This led to a move to enlarge the scope of the Evacuee Property Act to apply to Indian Muslims overseas of 'doubtful loyalty'.[17] It failed, but Gardee's properties in Bombay were nonetheless seized by the Custodian of Evacuee Property,[18] as were the properties of many other Indian Muslims living abroad.

Not surprisingly, many Overseas Indians, finding themselves in a similar position to Mr Gardee, rushed to register themselves as Indian citizens. But the position of those among them whose homes were in the erstwhile princely states[19] was further complicated by the passage of the British Nationality Act of 1948 (of which more later), which extended British nationality to all former British Indian subjects. Since inhabitants of the princely states had technically never been British Indian subjects – owing allegiance first and foremost to their own rulers rather than the King Emperor – they now found themselves at risk of being rendered stateless by the new legislation.[20] This prompted a flood of applications for Indian citizenship, to which many were technically entitled under the Constitution of 1950, even though mandarins in the External Affairs Ministry now sought ways and means of frustrating them.[21]

Their rush for Indian citizenship did not, however, go unnoticed by nationalists in East and South Africa, who seized on the phenomenon as evidence that Indian migrants had no loyalty to their countries of adoption.[22] In South Africa, where the Afrikaner National Party had long been pressing for the repatriation of 'Asiatics', the question of whether or not they were Indian nationals had other more delicate ramifications. If South Africa's 'Asiatics' *were* Indian nationals, then, the National Party claimed, it was well within South Africa's rights to ask them to leave. If, on the other hand, they were South African citizens by virtue of birth and domicile, then India had no business interfering in South Africa's internal affairs by offering its people an alternative citizenship and focus for them.[23]

For its part, the Indian government also began to see compelling reasons why its diasporic peoples should be encouraged to take on the citizenship of their host country. This would allow India to sidestep the sticky question of who, among these 3 million-odd people abroad, was entitled to Indian citizenship; who among them was a 'closet' Pakistani and whom it was safe to allow back to India. It would – or so the officials in New Delhi's South Block hoped – give these people more secure status and rights, human and political, in their new nations than if they were deemed to be citizens of these new nations. It would also prevent a flood of returning migrants seeking shelter back in India at a time when government was stretched to the limit by the challenge of rehabilitating the partition refugees. But, as the subsequent events would show, this policy was no guarantee that the 'host' countries would accept Indian migrants as their own people.

Nationality in the neighbourhood and wider empire

In 1948, Burma and Ceylon gained independence and stood forward as new nations. Both countries set immediately to drafting new citizenship laws that distinguished between 'ethnic' citizens and immigrants (Kanapathipillai, 2009). In August 1949, Sri Lanka enacted an Indian and Pakistani Residents (Citizenship) Act, which allowed persons of Indian and Pakistani origin to register, within two years of the passage of the Act, for citizenship of Ceylon. But it distinguished between citizens 'by descent' and citizens by registration, who were not entitled – as defined by various new development initiatives – to the 'goods' of development.[24] According to the Indian Mission in Colombo, Sri Lankan officials had no intention of making registration easy for Indian migrants, 'deliberately dragging their feet in registration of Indians as citizens of their voting rights'.[25] Already in 1939, the further migration of Tamil plantation workers to Ceylon had been banned. But among the seven or eight lakh Tamils who had already migrated to Ceylon before this date, many had left their wives and children behind in South India. This population, for the most part unlettered and unorganised (few independent unions were allowed to operate on the plantations[26]), had now to negotiate the complex business of acquiring Sri Lankan citizenship for themselves and their families. As the Indian Mission in Colombo concluded, 'the best thing would be for all Indians who were qualified to be Sri Lankan citizens to apply for citizenship without hesitation',[27] but the mandarins could do little to help them in this process without compromising its own position. Nor, 'in view of the unnecessary lurking and growing suspicion of the Sri Lankan Government authorities, of any aid from [India], official or unofficial', was New Delhi able to support the Ceylon Indian Congress in fighting a test case in the Privy Council to challenge this discriminatory legislation.[28]

For its part, in 1948 Burma defined its own nationality law on frankly ethnic grounds, giving citizenship only to persons deemed to belong to an 'indigenous race' or having one grandparent from an 'indigenous race'. Indians who had lived in British Burma since before 1942 – a category that included a significant community of Natukottai Chettiars (Adas, 1974) – could register as citizens, but were soon to be victims of government drives forcibly to acquire their land without fair compensation.[29] This generated a new wave of migration (or rather repatriation), as Indians from Burma began to trickle back into India as refugees and, in the case of Arakanese Muslims, to East Pakistan. Neither India nor Pakistan – both still struggling to rehabilitate millions of partition refugees – was able to do much to help them, beyond allowing them (with greater or lesser degrees of reluctance) the right to enter and remain in their countries of origin. In the case of 'Anglo-Indian' residents of Burma, even this limited concession was rather more than the Indian government was prepared to make: the Indian Mission in Burma was advised only to issue these hapless relics of the Raj with temporary papers, rather than to register them as full-fledged Indian citizens. Their loyalty to India, too, was suspect, as indeed were their claims to have ethnic Indian antecedents.[30] The rising tides of ethnically-defined nationalisms throughout the Indian Ocean region meant that the Anglo–Indians too would now have to seek new destinations in other parts of the world where their British subjecthood still allowed them entry, in yet another new stream of migration in the South Asian diaspora (Andrews, 2007).

The decline, revival and fall of 'British subjecthood'

By 1948, Canada and Australia too had adopted their own citizenship laws. Even as they paid lip service to the idea of a shared British subjecthood in the empire and Commonwealth, they reaffirmed their commitment to keeping out non-white migrants – whether from the Commonwealth or elsewhere – from their territories. Australia and Canada stuck obstinately to their position, invoking their sovereign right to determine who could, and could not, enter their territories, and they held fast, until the mid-1960s, to an immigration policy in which colour and race were the determinants. 'British imperial subjecthood' was beginning to look like a tattered inheritance, its inherent contradictions exposed to the world.

These were the circumstances under which the metropole brought about its own legislation responding to these changes in its former empire. The British Nationality Act came onto the statute book in 1948. The Act introduced the new legal statuses of 'Citizens of the UK and Commonwealth' (CUKC) and 'Citizens of Independent Commonwealth Countries' (CICC).[31] It allowed both categories (CUKCs and CICCs) free entry into the UK, with the right to take employment, while citizens of the old (white) dominions were given the right to register as British citizens after a year's residence (Hansen, 2000; Karatani, 2003). It therefore extended, on paper at least, free access to the UK to all citizens of both the 'old' and 'new' Commonwealth, and hence to Indians, Pakistanis, Burmese and Sri Lankans.

Enacted at a time of cross-party consensus about the importance of defending the traditional ideal of British subjecthood and on the necessity of maintaining close relations with the Commonwealth, the Act was passed before the possibility of large-scale immigration from the 'new' Commonwealth had become a concern in Britain. But the context changed almost immediately with the arrival on British shores of 492 Jamaicans on board the *Empire Windrush* in June 1948. After this 'incursion', as Attlee famously described it, (Hansen, 2000, 57) every UK government would now face demands that Britain's doors be closed to 'coloured immigrants'.[32]

Between 1948 and 1962, Whitehall admittedly resisted pressures to introduce controls that were openly discriminatory. But it is not the case, as is often claimed, that Britain in this period remained open to all comers. Interestingly, in a throwback to imperial times when the British Indian Government had introduced emigration controls in response to pressures from other British colonies, Britain now used its good offices with governments in the 'source' countries to encourage them to introduce their own controls to prevent unregulated emigration from their shores. In the mid-1950s, when South Asian migrants replaced those from the Caribbean as the prime focus of official concern, the governments of both India and Pakistan were persuaded not freely to issue passports for travel to the UK. They agreed to deny passports to their own citizens if they lacked adequate resources (financial guarantees) and if they did not have proof of literacy and knowledge of English. Both initiated a system by which the police looked into the character and antecedents of would-be migrants. Significantly, India began to vet and weed out applications for passports from 'low class citizens' – by unpublicised arrangements with the UK Home Office – to scrutinise their claims that they had secure work and accommodation in Britain.[33] It was only in 1960, when India's Supreme Court declared it to be discriminatory that this strange practice – of the 'outsourcing' of UK migration controls against Indians to India – came to an end. In 1961, Pakistan, too, lifted restrictions on emigration, instead promoting the migration to Britain of 5,000 people in Mirpur district uprooted by the construction of the Mangla dam (Brown, 2006, 42).

Finally, after a decade of mounting domestic pressure for restrictions (Kershaw and Pearsall, 2004, 14), the Commonwealth Immigrants Act went onto the statute book in 1962. Although it did not openly discriminate on the grounds of race, it was specifically designed to restrict the admission of 'coloured immigrants', and this was the outcome in practice. Prospective migrants from South Asia now had to obtain employment vouchers from the Ministry of Labour before being allowed into Britain. These were given mainly to people who had specific jobs to go to in Britain, or to those who had particular skills and qualifications which Britain wanted. Only the wives and children of migrants already in Britain still had an absolute right to entry into the UK.

This was the first in a series of measures that would change the character of South Asian migration to Britain. Hitherto that flow had been dominated by single, able-bodied but relatively un-skilled working men who were sojourners rather than settlers, circulating fairly regularly between Britain and their homes back in the subcontinent. Forced to choose between bringing their families to Britain or returning once and for all to the subcontinent, many chose to settle permanently in Britain.

In consequence, in the decades after 1962, new migrants from South Asia tended to have rather different profiles from those who came before them. The men among them were highly qualified, with particular skills: many were doctors, dentists, and graduates in science and technology.[34] Increasingly, however, women outnumbered men: brides or young married women, often accompanied by their children. Latterly, as Katy Gardner (2002) has shown, elderly people have started to migrate to Britain as well, to join their emigrant children to pass their twilight years on its grey shores.

Since 1962, the immigration laws of Britain have become ever more complex and restrictionist, even, for a brief and inglorious episode in the 1980s, subjecting migrant brides from South Asia to virginity tests. Space does not permit a detailed discussion of these laws, but two points call to be noted. In 1963, Kenya gained independence and, four years later, in 1967, passed an Immigration Act that obliged all those without Kenyan citizenship to acquire work permits. It also introduced laws that deliberately targeted South Asians in business and trade. This followed a drive to 'Africanise' the newly independent national government and economy of Kenya. Many of the South Asians who left the country at this time were British citizens, having opted to retain their CUKC status in 1963. In 1968, Britain passed a new Commonwealth Immigration Act, which restricted the number of Asian families from East Africa permitted to enter the UK to 1,500. This broke an explicit pledge, given in 1963 to East African Asians who retained their CUKC status, that they would have unrestricted rights of entry into the UK. It also meant that Britain now had denied the right of entry to a specific class of *Britain's own citizens*.

In 1971, a Conservative government passed an Immigration Act which introduced 'patriality' as a condition for the right of abode in the UK. This was a thinly disguised form of ethnic qualification – 'patriality' being 'indigenous' antecedent by another name. Commonwealth citizens were now deemed to have the same status as 'aliens' in Britain. After a quarter of a century of prevarication, with this step Britain finally turned its back on its own historical conception of subjecthood. Faced with the triple challenge of economic and geopolitical decline and potentially huge post-colonial immigration, Britain, as Joppke (1998) has suggested, refashioned itself from a 'civic' to an 'ethnic' nation, in which membership has come to be defined by the tests of birth and ancestry. Finally, it can be argued, Britain joined the new world of ethnic nation-states as a full-fledged member, abandoning the last shreds of her legacy as architect of a liberal and (in this matter) universalist empire and turning upon itself to keep outsiders at bay.

The world of the 'green card' and 'Gulf subordination'

Since the mid-1960s, the international migration regime (as it affects South Asians) has been dominated by two main trends. The first is the move – heralded by the passage of the Hart-Celler Act by the USA in 1965 – explicitly to embrace a hierarchy of preferences for certain *types* of migrants within a system of controls which caps overall numbers. In the US, preference has been given to two groups.[35] The first, based on the notion of 'family reunion', are the children and dependents of migrants who are already legal permanent residents. The second is for highly accomplished migrants whose skills match the needs of the domestic economy. By and large, with local and temporal variations, these preferences have also guided the immigration policies of the developed countries of the English-speaking West. Australia, Canada and Britain have all adopted this model. Although the common perception is that Britain 'closed' her doors to South Asians at the same time that the rest of the world began to welcome them (Shukla, 2003, 49, for instance), this paper suggests that the facts point to a different conclusion: widely different regimes have converged since the 1960s and 1970s upon common ground.

The second trend has been the resurgence of familiar forms of subordination among poor and unskilled migrants from the subcontinent, mainly but by no means solely in the Gulf. These migrants are predominantly young and able-bodied men, although increasingly large numbers of single women have joined the flow as cooks, maids and child-minders or ayahs. The oil-rich emirates have become the hub of a system which is characterised by race and hierarchy (Ballard, 1987), giving skilled jobs and freedoms to small numbers of Europeans (and a few highly skilled South Asian 'expats'), while employing much larger numbers of poor Asian workers on astonishingly illiberal terms. These new helots enjoy few, if any, rights (Nichols, 2008). The noxious practice of employers confiscating the passports of 'labour-class' employees has become commonplace (in the past, indentured migrants were simply denied passports by the British Indian government). 'Assisted' poor migrants travel to destinations in Malaysia or Dubai, or indeed Britain, only to have their papers confiscated on arrival and their pay withheld. Their employers in effect incarcerate them until they have worked enough notionally to pay off the (inflated) costs of their passage. Human trafficking in the twenty-first century recalls many of the features of indenture and *kangani* in the 1900s (Nobil Ahmad, this volume).

On the face of it, then, the migration regimes of the twenty-first century bear an uncanny resemblance to those of the old imperial world. Just as the old order was stratified by class and status, with a clear legal distinction between the self-funded free 'passenger class' and 'assisted', unfree 'coolie class', the new order is characterised by the chasm that separates the legal status of 'green-card holders' (and their ilk) and trafficked or otherwise 'assisted' migrants.

But there are important distinctions, and this essay concludes by pointing to them. In the nineteenth and early twentieth centuries, the migration of unskilled South Asian workers abroad was managed by the imperial state in its capacity as 'Protector of Emigrants', if with limited success. Today's national governments seem less willing and less able to take on that regulatory role. The poor South Asian migrants of today not only face far greater challenges in breaking through the much tougher border controls of contemporary host nations, they also are much more dependent upon the uncertain goodwill of labour contractors and traffickers who 'assist' their passage. This renders them more vulnerable to abuse, or at least to new forms of abuse, by agents and employers.

A second distinction is that, in the nineteenth century, it was well understood that free and 'assisted' migrants alike would usually leave families behind, remitting monies home and returning periodically. Now the tendency (for Western governments) is to promote 'family reunion'. It would be churlish to deny that this bias owes something to genuine humane concerns in receiving states. But it would be naïve to believe that when Western governments endorse 'family reunion', they are not also concerned to ensure that those few migrants whom they have been forced to accept as permanent inhabitants have all their eggs in one basket, and that is the basket which the host nation controls. These states are anxious to ensure that migrants deposit all their emotional ties and loyalties safely within the borders of the nation state in which they now live.

The final distinction between the old and the new is the preference today for 'permanent settlement', by those chosen few deemed eligible for entry and who have 'earned' their right to stay in Western industrialised nation-states. To get a 'green card' in the USA, the applicant has to demonstrate *continuous unbroken residence* and legal employment. In Britain, those with 'leave to remain' have not only to demonstrate an unbroken stretch of domicile before they are granted that leave, but also cannot leave the UK for any length of time *without losing that entitlement*. The paradox for today's skilled migrants is that they can only regain their freedom to come and go by taking the ultimate step, of applying for the citizenship of their host country and renouncing affiliation with their homeland. Only by professing unalloyed loyalty to the adopted nation, through ever more elaborate rituals of citizenship, can today's migrant regain the right freely to leave it. And yet, ironically, the technologies of today also enable him ever more easily to resort to the many forms of subversion that are collectively understood as 'transnationalism'.

Notes

1 Claire Davies carried out primary research on my behalf, supported by a Trinity College Summer Studentship, on the evolution of UK and US immigration and nationality law. Parts of this paper draw on that investigation.

2 Note by B.N. Nanda, Additional Secretary, Government of India Ministry of External Affairs, File No. 17–39/49-AFRI, (hereafter MEAI/17–39/49-AFRI).

3 Australia's Immigration Restriction Act of 1901 used a dictation test to exclude the unwanted; Canada had an exclusionary head tax aimed at non-whites, and the Union of South Africa in 1913 had passed an Immigrants Regulation Act which prohibited from entering persons whose 'standards and habits of life' rendered them 'unsuited to the requirements of the Union'. *Question of Treatment of Indians in the Union of South Africa before the United Nations. Documents and Proceedings*, Government of India Press, Simla, 1947, MEAI/F. 3–1/OSI-1948. Also see Mongia, 1999, for a discussion of the emergence of Canadian regulations excluding Indian migrants.

4 'Statement of Objectives and Reasons', *The Foreigners Act, 1946 (Act No. 31 of 1946). An Act to confer upon the Central Government certain powers in respect of foreigners.*

5 Statement on Partition by the Deputy Prime Minister in the Constituent Assembly, 12 Dec, 1947, in MEAI/F. 9–2/48-Pak I.

6 See the introduction to the *Government of East Punjab Evacuees (Administration of Property) Act, 1947 (Act XIV of 1947).*

7 As Nehru wrote to Patel, 'It is common knowledge that empty houses are being occupied not only by the refugees but by others who do so with the intention of profiteering. Indeed Punjab refugees have come to me to complain that these empty houses have been occupied by others who charge heavy rent for them. . . . This profiteering at the expense both of the original owner of the house and the Punjab

refugee is scandalous and I hope something will be done to put an end to it.' Nehru to Patel, 6 October 1947. Durga Das (ed.), *Sardar Patel's Correspondence (SPC)*, (10 Volumes, Ahmedabad 1971), vol. iv, p. 400.

8 'Another question of policy arises about Muslim refugees in the city. I imagine that of the 120,000 persons in the Purana Qila [Old Fort] and Humayun's Tomb, about half will go away to Pakistan. Where will the other half go? According to our policy they will return to Delhi. To what parts of Delhi? Some [Muslim-dominated] parts of Delhi … are already full. … Where else then are they to go except to certain areas from which they were evacuated? These areas thus cannot be considered as reserved completely for non-Muslims. This matter must be carefully thought out' (Ibid.).

9 Ordinance XXXIV of 1948, NAI/MEACR/F. 26–189/48-Pak I Secret.

10 See, for instance, the secret memo No 1/ Pass/48(6) from Waryam Singh, Deputy Director, Intelligence Branch, Ministry of Home Affairs, to all Central Intelligence Departments, dated 3 August 1948. NAI/ MEA, Pak I Section, File No. F. 26–189/48/Pak I Secret.

11 C. N. Chandra, Secretary, Government of India, Ministry of Rehabilitation to all Chief Secretaries, 9 May 1948, Government of Bengal Intelligence Branch File No. 1210–48 (4).

12 The reasons for the exclusion of West Bengal, Assam and Tripura from the emerging evacuee property regime is a complex subject in itself which cannot, for reasons of space, be discussed here.

13 Pakistan promulgated a central Evacuee Property Ordinance in October 1949. 'The Problem of Evacuee Property and Efforts Made to Solve it', enclosure in Memo from the Indian Ministry of External Affairs to India's Permanent Representative at the UN, 31 December 1949, MEAI/11(21)/49-Pak III (Secret).

14 In May 1952, at a meeting of the Pakistani Seamen's Association in Chittagong, the Chairman 'accused India of following a policy by which Pakistani seamen in search of employment in Indian ports are put to immense hardships caused by filling up new vacancies by unemployed Hindu youths' (Fortnightly Report from the Deputy High Commissioner of India at Dacca for 1–15 May, 1952, MEA/L/52/1321/202).

15 See, for instance, MEAI/F.30(6)-Pak III/49; MEAI/F.12(31)/49-Pak III; and MEAI/F.8–7/48-Pak I.

16 Memo by BFHB Tyabji dated 23 August 1952, MEAI (AFR II Branch)/AII/53/6491,31 (Secret).

17 MEA/AII/52/6423/31 (1952, Secret).

18 File note dated 20 April 1950, MEA/17–39/49-AFRI (Secret).

19 These were small and large states, about 560 in all, that the British governed informally, but had their own rajas and nawabs. See Ian Copland, *The Princes of India in the Endgame of Empire*, (Cambridge: Cambridge University Press), 1997.

20 Technically, they were 'British Protected Persons'. After the Nationality Act of 1948, they could become citizens of the UK and Colonies by naturalisation, but did not get this citizenship automatically as did other British Indian subjects (Parry, *British Nationality*, 1951, p. 95).

21 File note dated 20 April 1950/MEAI/17–39/49-AFRI (Secret).

22 MEA/17–39/49-AFRI (Secret) and MEA/AII/ 52/6423/31 (1952, Secret).

23 India had been campaigning against the Asiatic Land Tenure Act since its promulgation in 1946 and took the matter to the United Nations.

24 No Indian (or Pakistani) registered under the Act would have rights under the Land Development Ordinance, the Fisheries Ordinance and the Omnibus Licensing Ordinances, designed to promote the welfare of Ceylonese citizens. Note by M.L. Mehta dated 5 April 1950, MEAI/7/49/BCI (C) (Secret).

25 Ministry of External Affairs (CAP Branch) 5/1951, MEAI/7/49-BCI (C).

26 Peebles, Patrick, *The Plantation Tamils of Ceylon*, London: Leicester University Press, 2001.

27 Note by M.L. Mehta dated 5 April 1950, ibid.

28 MEAI(CAP Branch)/5/1951, MEA/F.7/49-BCI (C).

29 'Note on Land Nationalisation in Burma'. GOI/MEA/F. 9–8/48–0.s.II/1948.

30 Writing to the Ministry of External Affairs on 5 April 1949, R. Jaipal asked whether Anglo-Indian residents of Burma should be issued Indian passports. '[T]hough of partial Indian stock and origin, [they] have not hitherto evinced any ultimate intention of settling down in India, nor have they expressed any marked desire to be regarded as Indians. We were therefore not inclined to treat them in the same manner as Indian residents of Burma.' The Ministry of Home Affairs ruled that they could be issued only with emergency certificates for India and 'restricted passports' for other countries (Indian Ministry of Home Affairs (MHAI)/33/32/49-FII, 1949).

31 The Act created five different categories of citizens. In addition to CUKC and CICC, these included 'Irish British subjects', 'British subjects without citizenship' and 'British Protected Persons'. The latter category included former subjects of Indian princely states.

32 This is not the place to enter the heated debate about the place, or indeed the source, of racism in the framing of British policy. See Hampshire, 2005 and Hansen, 2000.

33 Pakistan agreed, in addition, to give publicity to the difficulties encountered by Pakistanis in finding work in Britain. Cabinet Memorandum. Commonwealth Immigrants. Memorandum by the Lord President of the Council, 20 June, 1958, UK PRO/CAB/129/93.

34 After 1965, 'Category B' vouchers were issued only to doctors, dentists, trained nurses, suitably qualified teachers, science and technology graduates, as well as skilled, qualified and experienced non-graduates. UK NA/HO 344/196.

35 Refugees and asylum seekers are the third category of migrants who still have access under these systems, but for reasons of space, cannot be discussed here. See, however, Van Hear in this volume.

References

Adams, Caroline, (1987), *Across Seven Seas and Thirteen Rivers. Life Stories of Sylheti Settlers in Britain*, London: Thap Books.

Adas, Michael, (1974), *The Burma Delta: Economic Development and Social Change on an Asian Rice Frontier, 1852–1941*, Madison: University of Wisconsin Press.

Ahuja, Ravi, (2006), 'Mobility and Containment: The Voyages of South Asian Seamen, *c.* 1900–1960', *International Review of Social History*, 51.

Anderson, Caitlin, (2008), 'Aliens at Home, Subjects Abroad: British Nationality Law and Policy, 1815–1870', University of Cambridge PhD thesis.

Andrews, R. A., (2007), 'Quitting India: The Anglo–Indian Culture of Migration', *Sites*, 4: 2.

Amrith, Sunil, (2009), 'Tamil Diasporas across the Bay of Bengal', *American Historical Review*, 114: 3 (June), pp. 547–72.

—, (2010), 'Indians Overseas? Governing Tamil Migration to Malaya, 1870–1941', *Past and Present*, 208, pp. 231–61.

Balachandran, G., (1997), 'Recruitment and Control of Indian Seamen, Calcutta, 1880–1935', *International Journal of Maritime History*, 9.

Ballard, Roger, (1987), 'The Political Economy of Migration: Pakistan, Britain and the Middle East', in J. Eades, *Migrants, Workers and the Social Order*, London: Tavistock.

Barkat, Abul, Zaman, Shafique uz, Rahman, Azizur, Poddar, Avijit, (1997), *Political Economy of the Vested Property Act in Rural Bangladesh*, Dhaka: ALRD.

Baruah, Sanjib, (2005), *Durable Disorder. Understanding the Politics of Northeast India*, New Delhi: Oxford University Press.

Brown, Judith, (2006), *Global South Asians. Introducing the Modern Diaspora*, Cambridge: Cambridge University Press.

Chatterji, Joya, (2012), 'South Asian Histories of Citizenship', *Historical Journal*, 55: 4.

—, (2013), 'Dispositions and Destinations: Refugee Agency and "Mobility capital" in the Bengal Diaspora, 1947–2007', *Comparative Studies in Society and History*, 55: 2.

Choudhury, Yousuf, (1993), *The Roots and Tales of Bangladeshi Settlers*, London: Sylheti Social History Group.

Copland, Ian, (1997) *The Princes of India in the Endgame of Empire, 1917–1947*, Cambridge: Cambridge University Press.

Farooqui, M. I., (2000), *Law of Abandoned Property*, Dhaka: Khaja Art Press.

Gardner, Katy, (2002), *Age, Narrative and Migration: The Life Course and Life Histories amongst Bengali Elders in London*, London: Berg.

Ghosh, P., (2007), *Partition and the South Asian Diaspora. Extending the Subcontinent*, London, New York and Delhi: Routledge.

Hampshire, James, (2005), *Citizenship and Belonging. Immigration and the Politics of Demographic Governance in Postwar Britain*, London: Palgrave Macmillan.

Hansen, Randall, (2000), *Citizenship and Immigration in Post-War Britain. The Institutional Origins of a Multicultural Nation*, Oxford: Oxford University Press.

Joppke, Christian, (1998), 'Multiculturalism and Immigration: A Comparison of the United States, Germany and Great Britain', in David Jacobsen (ed.), *The Immigration Reader: America in Multidiciplinary Perspective*, Oxford: Blackwell.

Kanapathipillai, Valli, (2009), *Citizenship and Statelessness in Sri Lanka. The Case of Tamil Estate Workers*, London: Anthem.

Karatani, Rieko, (2003), *Defining British Citizenship: Empire, Commonwealth and Modern Britain*, London: Frank Cass.

Kershaw, Roger and Pearsall, Mark, (2004), *Immigrants and Aliens. A Guide to Sources on UK Immigration and Citizenship*, Kew: PRO.

Kim, Keechang, (2004), *Aliens in Medieval Law. The Origins of Modern Citizenship*, Cambridge: Cambridge University Press.

Markovits, C., Pouchepadass, J. and Subrahmanyam, S., (2003), *Society and Circulation: Mobile People and Itinerant Cultures in South Asia, 1750–1950*, Delhi: Permanent Black.

Mongia, Radhika, (1999), 'Race, Nationality, Mobility: A History of the Passport', *Public Culture*, 11: 3, Fall.

Nichols, Robert, (2008), *A Study of Pashtun Migration, 1775–2006*, Karachi: Oxford University Press.

Parry, Clive, (1951), *British Nationality Including Citizenship of the United Kingdom and Colonies and the Status of Aliens*, London: Steven and Sons.

Randhawa, M. S., (1954), *Out of the Ashes; An Account of the Rehabilitation of Refugees from West Pakistan in Rural Areas of East Punjab*, Government of India Press.

Sen, U., (2010), 'The Nation and its Exclusions. The Repatriation of European Refugees from Independent India, 1947–48', working paper presented at a conference on 'Society and the Everyday State in India and Pakistan', London, 9 September.

Sherman, Taylor C., (2011), 'Migration, Citizenship and Belonging in Hyderabad (Deccan), 1946–1956', *Modern Asian Studies*, 45: 1.

Shukla, Sandhya, (2003), *India Abroad*, Princeton, NJ: Princeton University Press.

Singha, Radhika, (n.d.), 'A "Proper Passport" for the Colony: Border Crossing in British India, 1882–1920', unpublished paper.

—, (2009), 'Passport, Ticket and India-Rubber Stamp: "The Problem of the Paper Pilgrim" in Colonial India, 1882–1925', in Harald Fischer-Tine and Ashwini Tambe (eds), *British Colonial Control in South Asia: Spaces of Disorder in the Indian Ocean*, London: Taylor & Francis.

Sinha, A. N., (1962), *Law of Citizenship and Aliens in India*, London: Asia Publishing House.

Tinker, Hugh, (1974), *A New System of Slavery. The Export of Indian Labour Overseas 1830–1920*, London: Hansib.

van Schendel, W., (2007), 'The Wagah Syndrome: Territorial Roots of Contemporary Violence in South Asia', in Amrita Basu and Srirupa Roy (eds), *Violence and Democracy in India*, Calcutta: Seagull Press.

Weiner, Myron, (1978), *Sons Of The Soil: Migration And Ethnic Conflict In India*, Princeton, NJ: Princeton University Press.

Zamindar, Vazira F., (2007), *The Long Partition and the Making of Modern South Asia. Refugees, Boundaries, Histories*, New York: Columbia University Press.

15

THE PRODUCTION OF ILLEGALITY IN MIGRATION AND DIASPORA

State policies and human smuggling from Pakistan

Ali Nobil Ahmad

Introduction

Human smuggling and illegal migration are today issues of paramount concern to policymakers and electorates across Western Europe, where the presence of migrants and asylum seekers from South Asia and other parts of the developing world has become a matter of relentless and often vitriolic public debate in countries as diverse in their respective migration histories as Britain, Italy, the Netherlands and Sweden. Dominant academic, technocratic and media discourse in all these contexts tends to construct irregular border-crossing and economic activity as novel forms of criminality produced by 'globalisation' – the unfettered movement of capital, goods and people in an apparently new era of increased human mobility and diminishing state sovereignty. In truth, the political wind as far as migration control has blown exclusively in restrictionist directions since the 1970s; capital might traverse the globe with an ease that compresses time and space in unprecedented ways, but state control over the movement of labour reached its zenith in human history during the first decade of the twenty-first century.

That human smuggling might in some sense be a product of this imbalance is often lost in mainstream debates about illegal migration, frequently and misleadingly conflated with and maligned as illegal work. The finger-pointing focus of right-wing politicians and interior ministries on criminal gangs as the sole beneficiaries of smuggling is hardly coincidental, and reflects the well-established tendency of states to misrepresent the source of immigration 'problems' by locating their origin in parallel political–economic universes. Convenient though it may be to blame something called the Russian mafia for the presence of illegal migrants in Western Europe, the question of how, when and why the contemporary global 'migration business' (Salt and Stein, 1997) has developed – legally and otherwise – makes sense only in relation to the formal economy's historical interface with changing political and institutional contexts.

The particular story about human smuggling that is the subject of this chapter begins, as so often in discussions about modern South Asia, during the colonial period when passports, state control of immigration from the global economic periphery and organised brokerage of international travel were first institutionalised. What follows is an historical account of these formative processes based on secondary sources, commencing with a critical reinterpretation of several of the earliest, seminal accounts of South Asian migration to Britain. These, it will be seen, are surprisingly rich in data on the antecedents of contemporary human smuggling, brokerage and facilitation, none of which are specific to the contemporary, twenty-first century, scenario. The latter is analysed on the basis of investigative news reports and interview data produced in qualitative research conducted in London, Italy and Lahore.[1]

This discussion makes close reference to Pakistan, but the story, as will be made clear in its telling, resonates with other cases and contexts in South Asia and beyond: human smuggling is hardly specific to any country or region. Conversely, the diversity in nationalities, ethnic groups, ages and genders that produce the South Asian diaspora is such that this chapter cannot possibly cover illegal migration in any exhaustive sense. What follows, rather, is a specific case study, in which various groups are underrepresented: women, children, the elderly and poorest members of Pakistani society, for whom independent emigration of any kind is rare.

A word on the terminology: the term irregularity (used synonymously, in this chapter, with illegality) refers to a status into (and out of) which individual migrants can move over time throughout the migration process. It can occur at the sending context if the bureaucratic procedures stipulated as necessary by the sending state in order to emigrate are not respected. More often, it becomes relevant in transit and contexts of reception where irregularity derives from the fact that migrants *either* enter without compliance with the legal procedures required by the receiving country *and/or* do not comply with the legal conditions attached to their residency and/or employment. Not all irregular migrants are smuggled, and as Ghosh points out, migrants may move from regularity to irregularity and *vice versa* over time (1998: 1–4). The relation between different sorts of irregularity, modes of travel and entry is always complex: they are not mutually exclusive, but nor does the existence of one imply that any of the others will necessarily follow. The implications of this complexity for the quantitative study of illegal migratory flows and stocks is to compound an already acute set of problems in measuring phenomena that by definition 'elude registration and statistical coverage' (Tapinos 1999). And given that the very methods used to estimate illegally resident populations are contested (Pinkerton *et al.* 2004), the importance of qualitative research of the sort provided in this chapter is now widely accepted in migration studies, as is the frequent impossibility of providing meaningful numbers.

Brokerage and human smuggling: the colonial period

The facilitation of migration has always been subject to varying degrees of profiteering at both ends of the migratory process and, ever since state restrictions were put in place, it involved breaking the law. The seamen (lascars) who forged the beginnings of Britain's South Asian diaspora in the early decades of the twentieth century migrated in an epoch of relatively little red tape and limited immigration control through a system of indirect recruitment first estab-lished in Calcutta and Bombay. Even so, they did encounter bureaucratic hurdles which they overcame using professional intermediaries – chiefly labour recruiters, moneylenders and lodging-housekeepers rolled into one. These agents extended credit and ran a loosely organised but lucrative migration business that operated, for the most part, within the law (Ansari, 2004: 38; Adams, 1987; Ajuha, this volume).

Restrictionist state policies pursued by Britain in the early decades of the twentieth century, however, triggered the development of profiteering by facilitating both legal and illegal migration. The earliest attempts of the state to impose immigration controls on Indians date back to 1919 when the Home Office passed the 'Coloured Alien Seaman Act' in response to the growing official and public hostility toward the presence of Indians in cities and seaports (Visram, 2002, 199, 213).[2] Commercial trafficking of lascar discharge papers was cited as a reason for refusing to accept them as proof of identity, which suggests profiteering from the provision of documents was already underway before 1919. The passing of the Act, however, increased the scope for facilitation considerably and when, in 1930, steps were taken to restrict the issuing of passports in British India itself, a burgeoning trade in passports developed (Visram, 2002: 205–8, 224).

Brokerage thrived in both sending and receiving contexts: 'coloured seamen' resident in Britain were required to obtain a certificate of identity and nationality and had to appeal to the British India Office to have their nationality verified, a process that took three to four months; to have a passport made required verification of birth and could take eleven months (Visram, 2002: 210–15). The acquisition of these documents was organised with the contacts and expertise of Indian men who ran local boarding-houses near the docks, where seaman could find shelter and share notes with other Indians whilst they found their feet. Police records suggest owners of East London boarding houses helped lascars obtain the requisite documents for them to obtain the legal right to reside and work in Britain in exchange for money. A peddler in Chatham, according to one report cited by Visram, is claimed to have discharged his debt of 400 rupees to a moneylender at 25 per cent interest per annum for his fare from Jullundur to England via Bombay and Marseilles (Visram, 2002: 262–7).

Marseilles itself, incidentally, was by this time already a hub of trans-Mediterranean smuggling: French colonialism had sprouted its own parallel and intertwined migration business. Although Algeria was a *département* (extension of French territory), migrants at the turn of the century needed to procure various official documents such as identity cards, medical certificates and work contracts at the same time as negotiating their way to Algiers and purchasing boat tickets (MacMaster, 1997: 48–9). Inevitably, brokering emerged at sending and receiving ports, and when controls were tightened in 1924, the costs of migration became much higher. Moroccans, who lacked legal channels to migrate, are known to have stowed away or resorted to criminal networks that specialised in the supply of forged documents or arranged for illegal passage through payments of dockers and sailors. The risks were high: fraud proliferated (many hundreds crossed into Algeria on foot, 'only to fall victim to every kind of confidence trick in Oran and other ports'); many died during the passage, including ten who were found asphyxiated in 1926 as they attempted to make the crossing (MacMaster, 1997: 74).

An international migration business of sorts thus arguably already existed in the colonial period (for a detailed discussion see Ajuha, this volume). Its limited nature in Britain (and France) is likely a reflection of the fact that restrictionism remained limited at this time; the policy of the British state, for example, was ambiguous given the constraints placed by employers and other economic interests on the Home Office's determination to curb migratory flows. As is the case today, migration controls did not prevent people from moving; rather, they acted as a kind of filter, segmenting modes of travel by class-background and ensuring that the less educated paid more than the wealthy to travel. Like today's points-based system privileging the highly skilled, the restrictions of 1930 distinguished between those of 'good character and established position' who remained eligible for passports and those 'with a low standard of education' or without a 'definite offer of employment', who were barred. The Hunter Inquiry of 1939 reported the inevitable consequences of this discriminatory logic: significant numbers of 'semi-legal passport traders' offering passports 'at exorbitant charges to the lower classes' and the 'generally illiterate' (Visram, 2002: 205–8, 222–4).

Aurora's (1967: 41–5) little-known out-of-print study of lascar and early post-colonial migration contains important evidence that many other aspects of smuggling, which are usually thought of as recent developments (e.g. the changing of passport photos, the usage of indirect travel and transit routes) were also already extant in the early 1950s. By around 1953–4, he explains, 'certain spurious travel agents' and their sub-agents were stationed in ports of embarkation such as Bombay and Karachi, where they had access to some of the staff in Indian consulates and 'used devious ways to get over the official hurdles':

> First they would get their clients to apply for passports with initial endorsements to Singapore and Mauritius ... then from Singapore they took their clients to Britain without any endorsement .... In this way, an immigrant would have to travel for two months before he could reach Britain. Another simpler and quicker, but more risky way was to smuggle Indian immigrants through Pakistan as Pakistani citizens with forged Pakistani passports. Still another way was to charter planes from Bombay to London, give the immigrants forged passports and get their agents to receive them at London to avoid any 'unpleasant' detection or questioning. To forge a passport, real passports were bought from persons who had already reached England, and new photographs were attached to these. In this way each passport was used to smuggle across many persons.
>
> *(Aurora, 1967: 43)*

All this suggests the religious, ethnic, regional, national and kinship solidarities and networks that feature so prominently in most classical anthropological accounts of the migration process from South Asia since the 1980s were by this time already competing with, and/or mediated by, a general commerciality that extended across the subcontinental migration networks to Britain at this time. Indeed, the fact that Sikhs passing through Pakistan were shaved and their hair cut to avoid the arousal of suspicion (42–4) and that they paid between 3,000 and 5,000 rupees (three to four times the cost of travelling by sea in the tourist class) suggests the late-colonial period and the early post-colonial period until 1962 can be loosely characterised as a single era of 'proto-restrictionism' in which smuggling from South Asia emerged as a response to sporadic immigration controls.[3]

Another important reason for its emergence was the establishment of a new migration regime in South Asia, where a combination of exclusionary restrictionist policies and citizenship arrangements left hundreds of thousands of evacuees and refugees either stranded or socially excluded in India and Pakistan (see Chatterji, this volume). These were newly formed enemy nations in which emigratory pressures were building as a result of red tape, inefficiency and deliberate slow processing of legitimate requests for passports and other travel documents: 'official circles generally do their best to discourage migrants', so a 'forged passport racket' developed, as Aurora explains (1967: 42). He goes on to provide evidence of travellers being forced to pay bribes in order to process legitimate requests for travel documents, underlining the difference in attitude of sending states towards emigration before the 1980s, after which Pakistan took steps to facilitate a remittance-based economy with institutional arrangements for 'Overseas Pakistanis' to travel and remit money with greater ease.

Smuggling networks: an historical sociology

Having turned on the migratory tap to meet the needs of postwar reconstruction in the early post-colonial period with its proto-restrictionist Open Door policy in the early 1950s, the

Commonwealth Immigration Act of 1962 initiated a pattern of criminalisation of international migration from Pakistan and other former colonies to Europe. Thousands rushed to 'beat the ban'. The introduction of a voucher system in which prospective immigrants were effectively required to have a sponsor in Britain to arrange a job for them before they could enter created new opportunities for brokerage among those settled in Britain, who were placed in positions of power and privilege within their communities of origin. Human smuggling now flourished as a direct consequence of restrictive policy. Nadir,[4] a British migrant from the village of Dinga in the Gujrat district of Pakistan, describes how returnees initiated a process of commodification within and parallel to kinship networks:

> They would have a reference [voucher], and would take one or two. Then subsequently, group migration started. People would adopt kids, declare that so and so is their son just to help someone in their village. *It started as help. But then a business developed* [my italics]. Someone clever would take 10–12, and work out a way to get them to the UK. This was the early sixties. Even graduates and educated boys would look for a way to leave. A van which would take five or six to the UK, would go through Turkey.

The very term 'smuggler' as it is understood nowadays in media and policy circles is misleading: as the above passage makes clear; differentiating sharply between migrants and smugglers ignores the fact that many 'smugglers' are in fact migrants who, upon their arrival, facilitate the illegal travel, entry and/or regularisation of family members, friends, acquaintances and fee-paying strangers. Also noteworthy is the fact that this commodification of the migration chain was socially embedded and that its effects were uneven. The extent to which agents would seek to profit depended upon the type and strength of ties between themselves and given individuals. Where the migration of close kin might be facilitated at no cost, or even at a loss (i.e. a cost to the migrant himself), travellers with only weak ties to the smuggling network were expected to pay their way plus a fee. Those without strong kinship connections, it is likely, effectively subsidised the migration of those who did. The importance of kinship and ethnicity as economic resources in human smuggling, in other words, has always been unclear – even more so than in regular migration and immigrant entrepreneurship, which has been the subject of polarised debates between researchers of diverse ideological leanings since the 1980s (Bun and Hui, 1995).

Recent evidence suggests the profits to be had from facilitation grew impressively in the 1960s; the migration business became more professionalised. In their turn, these trends made kinship and ethnicity less relevant in determining migration outcomes (Ahmad 2011). Irregular migration was facilitated in an ever more systematic manner: a growing number of enterprising individuals made facilitation ('*agenti*') a full-time occupation, charging around 10–12,000 rupees in the mid/late 1960s – a price that, Nadir recounts, went up and up with inflation so that by 'the early seventies you could buy a good plot of urban land' with what it cost to reach the UK. Demand was such that agents could insist on being paid up front; after entry point, contact with the smuggler would be terminated. 'Slave-importing' debt bondage of the sort frequently associated with trafficking (Kyle and Dale, 2001) was, and remains, uncommon. In the long-term, the success of agents depended on their reputations, which would be built up over time through word of mouth; to be sustained, agents had to conduct many successful operations; if they failed, they would be less likely to attract custom in the future. This is a general pattern in human smuggling as it operates today in various contexts, as other studies have shown (Bilger *et al.*, 2006: 66–7).

This is not to suggest that the smuggling business ran itself 'efficiently' through the work of innocent market mechanisms and networks, or that its various agents and customers were motivated by rational economic calculations bringing obvious net benefits to all involved. Agents (themselves often returnees) were preaching to an audience that was highly susceptible to mythical accounts of what emigration entailed. They actively spread *rumours* about the benefits of emigration that were to a large extent, misleading (for a discussion, see Ahmad, 2008). The point is that agents were often beneficiaries of the privileged status they had in the migration process and exerted power relations over their customers. If an operation failed, the agent was supposed to refund the payment that had been given in advance but often, as Nadir remembers: 'they would not return the money, especially if you had no influence'. Helweg's study of India (1979: 27–8) relates shocking tales about agents who, in the 1960s, 'gloriously exaggerated stories about England as the land of opportunity' and extended easy credit to clients. Upon the arrival of these hopefuls in England, their representatives would demand every pound they earned until the debt was paid off. Some villagers, he adds, were 'smuggled into England' without realising it. Such migrants were often informed, once they started working in the UK, that they would have to pay much more to keep their 'sponsors' from telling the British authorities about their illegal entry. In addition to blackmail and extortion, Helweg also reports cases of fraud in which bogus 'agents' extracted sums of money as great as £800 without providing the promised services.

Facilitation of illegal migration, in other words, can involve levels of coercion that blur the distinctions between smuggling and trafficking. At one end of the spectrum, smuggling can take place smoothly, often within the ostensible framework of the law, and sometimes without recourse to the services of agents: declaring a family member's child as one's own, travelling on a dead man's passport or even setting off overland to complete at least some part of the journey legally and independently were all strategies adopted in this period. Smuggling took diverse forms along a continuum that blurs into trafficking. To put it somewhat differently, smuggling and trafficking can be visualised as two circles in a Venn diagram between which there exist numerous points of intersection.

Furthermore, Nadir's reference to 'Turkey' in the passage above hints at a dramatic geographical transformation of the Eurasian migration system which was taking place: the revival of pre-modern overland Central Asian travel routes connecting Asia and the West though Afghanistan, Iran, Turkey and Greece. Agents stationed themselves permanently in ancient trade cities like Peshawar, Kabul, Istanbul and a number of sites in Greece, learning local languages and developing relationships with individuals who developed important stakes in the smuggling business: corrupt border guards and immigration officials, but also small hotel owners (B&Bs would come to play an important role in housing migrants during transit migration). The smuggling business thus became increasingly cosmopolitan and organically embedded within a series of nodal transit points connecting the Grand Trunk road to the Silk Route, the Mediterranean and Western Europe. These nodal hubs were feeding labour into north-western Europe long before the current phase of globalisation and its new technologies of time-space compression:

> There was an area where they used to go and wait in France for an opening to the UK.
> Another was go up to Holland and wait for an opportunity to go to the UK. In doing
> so, people started staying in these transitory places. They got dumped there.

As Britain's borders became increasingly difficult to permeate in the late 1970s and early 1980s, growing numbers of men holed up in continental transit nodes accepted the impossibility of reaching their intended destination and opted instead to take advantage of the labour markets, differing legal conditions and state policies in other nearby countries. What began as a patchwork of travel and transit stopovers began, over time, to produce new patterns of settlement. At a 1982 convention held by the UK-based Centre for Pakistan Studies, a report from France refers to the presence of 3,800 Pakistanis officially registered in the country 'and several thousand more whose legal situation is in the process of being regularised' (Rahmatoullah, 1982: 83); 1,500 were reported to have been residing in Belgium, flows having begun in 1973 ('Pakistanis in Belgium', Unattributed, 1982: 86–87). A fairly sizeable community of 10,000 are reported to have been resident in Holland (Shamsi, 1982: 91–93), whilst a paper on Denmark records the number of Pakistani passport holders in the country, most of whom hailed from Thesil Karian, at around 7,000 ('Pakistanis in Denmark', Unattributed, 1982: 84). In Norway too, there were 7,000 Pakistanis, according to a more detailed report which states that 2,000 of them had entered between 1970 and 1973, having 'travelled through so-called agents' (Mujahid Ali, 1982: 88–90).

Human smuggling since the 1960s has thus been central to the breakup of the bi-lateral, colonial migration system connecting Britain to Pakistan and accompanying dispersal of Pakistanis around Europe and the world. Other factors influencing this process include the 1973 Middle-Eastern oil boom, which drew more of Pakistan's labour force than ever before into a rapidly expanding global diaspora (Nichols 2010). The latter's centre of gravity shifted to West Asia and with it the orientation of Pakistan's economy, which has since remained heavily dependent on remittances from Saudi Arabia, Qatar, Oman and other migratory destinations in the Gulf. Increasingly, the Pakistani state began to actively encourage emigration, a fact reflected in the establishment of the Overseas Pakistanis Foundation, established in 1979 under the Emigration Ordinance to support the welfare concerns of Pakistanis working abroad and their families in Pakistan.

The precise extent of human smuggling and trafficking within West Asia is a (vastly under-researched) topic in its own right, beyond the scope of this chapter. Existing research on the Gulf migration system and journalistic reports suggest, however, that the South-West Asian migration system subjects many migrants to appalling labour conditions, often legally. Here the term 'trafficking' has more relevance. The Punjabi film 'Dubai Chulo' (1979),[5] in which cruel and exploitative agents make a notable on-screen appearance, seems to reflect popular perceptions of these changing trends.

At the same time, this new axis has brought new forms of consumerism, wealth and inequality to parts of Pakistan that were previously peripheral to the international migration system, not to mention a social conservatism which has if anything reinforced the male-breadwinner migration model (Ahmad, 2008). These developments, along with geopolitical and economic transformations in Pakistan and neighbouring Afghanistan since the 1990s, have had important implications for contemporary human smuggling to Europe and elsewhere. To these we now turn.

Contemporary human smuggling: a global business

The passage of laws in Britain to curb transnational subcontinental marriages following the Nationality Act of 1981 abruptly curtailed the possibilities of entry by legal means to the UK even further, reinforcing the flows of migratory traffic to continental Europe, the Americas, Australasia and to other destinations that remained relatively open until more recently. The states in these regions too, since the 1990s, have become increasingly prohibitive in their immigration policies. A confluence of increased economic, political and cultural 'push' or supply factors from global economic peripheries like Pakistan and contracting 'pull' or demand for workers in the West has shaped the relationship between rich countries and their immigrants for nearly four decades now; it looks set to continue given the xenophobic tone of public debates surrounding immigration in Europe before, and especially since, the recession of the early twenty-first century.

In truth, immigration – legal and illegal – has in all likelihood been of considerable net economic benefit to the industrially advanced economies during and since the 1970s. The partial failure of restrictionist policies has been an important part of their overall success: control of migration not only filters out the world's poorest (while squeezing those able to travel for ever higher entry visa tariffs); in failing to stop the most determined it funnels a steady trickle of pliant, low-skilled workers who lack citizenship rights and enjoy only limited access to welfare provision into European labour markets, allowing countries like Britain to manage their transition to service-sector economies and the neoliberal reforms of their national labour markets with relative ease.

Meanwhile, the premium on legal routes has created a goldmine for various actors, most obviously Western states, which now charge spiralling fees for processing visa requests. Private institutions and agencies such as universities have also cashed in: by 2004, foreign students were estimated to be worth a staggering £3 billion a year to the UK economy by Home Office Minister Des Browne (Cowan, 2004). That year, overseas students were charged between £8,000 and £20,000 for courses for which British students paid just over £1,000. Some universities have been accused of preferring foreign students to British ones (O'Reilly and Robertson, 2004). The Saudi Arabian embassy actually advised its nationals to boycott British universities in 2004 in protest over exorbitant fees and 'financial irregularities', according to *The Observer*, which reported that 'degrees were being sold to failing foreign students in return for tuition fees' (Hill, 2004).

More generally, the lengthy bureaucratic process by which spouse, student, visitor and business visas are acquired has led to a proliferation of brokers, rendering these legal channels of migration increasingly subject to commercialisation, fraud and increasing levels of legal 'hybridity'. Two months after the Home Office under David Blunkett set up a register to verify the authenticity of 'colleges' that issue places to foreign students in 2004, over one in four of the first 100 were exposed as vehicles for immigration scams (Travis, 2004).

A parallel business has long been known to exist in 'bogus' (inauthentic) marriages. In June 2004, the *Daily Jang*'s English *News International* reported the exposure of a racket worth tens of thousands of pounds following the confession of a Pakistani student that he had procured one such arrangement to remain in the UK when his student visa expired (*The News*, 2004a). The following month, a network that charged £10,000 for flying in women from the Netherlands to marry West African men in order to secure EU citizenship was infiltrated by undercover immigration officers. Mark Rimmer, a director of registrars in Brent, was quoted saying that as many as 10–12,000 bogus marriages are likely to take place for immigration purposes every year. Around 8,000 of these are in London – one in five of all marriages in the capital (*The News*, 2004b). Many are likely to be individual arrangements rather than organised by professional networks, as shown dramatically by the somewhat extreme case of a Glasgow-born Punjabi woman who married up to 23 Indian men for around £8,000 each for a life in the UK and a British passport (Rahman and Gillani, 2004).

In Pakistan, where the state has historically had little interest in reinforcing transparency and regularity, evidence of profiteering from commercialised legal and pseudo-legal channels of migration to Britain and elsewhere is ample. In 2004 an investigation by *The Dawn Review* reported 'immigration consultant centres' with 'sub-offices abroad' had multiplied greatly in recent years. These centres, which often hire foreigners to give lectures on immigration rules, advertise in the print media and specialise in immigration to Canada, the USA, Australia, New Zealand and the UK (Tahir, 2004: 9). The promise, 'UK study visa offer, 100% confirmed for on the spot admission, available today', has a familiar ring to mobile phone owners in cities like Lahore, where receiving text-messages from unknown senders touting unmissable opportunities to make careers in the West has become commonplace. So it will, too, for the thousands of email account-holders targeted by online marketing campaigns from visa vendors, or, for that matter, anyone who reads newspapers, where classified advertisements offering 'consultancy services' relating to international migration have become ubiquitous. If advice on how to circumvent immigration law is not in itself illegal, irregularity and fraud are pervasive in this kind of brokerage.

Indeed, the facilitation of 'legal' migration in sending and receiving contexts is in many ways no less subject to corruption, fraud and profiteering than the illegal overland routes that grab news headlines, problematising the very notion of smuggling as a distinct form of travel. The latter, for their part, have increased considerably in importance during recent years. Tighter measures to curb illegal emigration since the mid 1990s – especially from airports after 9/11 – have ushered in a new era of high-tech surveillance and 'hard restrictionism', reflected most obviously in the life-endangering risks now entailed in illegal border-crossing, along with the growing numbers of migrants detained and deported. There is also the revival in sourcing out migration controls to sending countries, a development which has brought the Pakistani state into the metropolitan restrictive apparatus for the first time since the mid-1950s (see Chatterji, this volume, for a discussion on the outsourcing of migration controls in the colonial period and early postwar decades). In 1996, the role of the Federal Investigation Agency (FIA), set up in 1974 to control the smuggling of drugs and goods as well as people, was officially changed so that it became an organisation devoted exclusively to combating human smuggling, a measure of its growing political importance by the end of the Cold War. In 2004 *The Dawn* reported that the FIA had launched a major operation against 'human trafficking' (as smuggling is often referred to within the media) in Gujrat after 'growing complaints of the European countries' (Raza, 2004). That month it was also announced that Pakistan would take part in a joint naval patrol with a US-led naval fleet of Western ships in the Arabian sea to combat human smuggling and deter the movement of Islamic militants and arms around the world, a development which underlined the growing convergence of anti-'terrorist' operations with the drive against illegal migration (Reuters, 2004). Also in this vein, state-of-the-art finger and face recognition technology to Pakistan's passport and national identity programme, which is now biometric (*The News*, 2004).

None of this has stamped out smuggling entirely, or even significantly reduced it. Hard restrictionism has merely increased the political stakes involved, and with it the possibilities for individuals and groups to profit. As ever, the biggest shareholders work closely with states. 'We do this', a Lahore-based smuggler told me in 2003, 'with the co-operation of the authorities at airports'. 'Big agents' invariably have contacts within officialdom, elements of which, it should come as no surprise, have built up a considerable stake in the success of their activities. The involvement of Pakistani officials and politicians in smuggling has been widely reported within the media. In September 2004, the outgoing Minister of the Interior, Faisal Saleh Hayat, claimed that '90 per cent of human smuggling to the UK and other foreign countries was being done by recruiting agents of a [specific] Punjab district and adjoining areas' with 'powerful backing of local politicians virtually rendering it impossible for him to take any action against them during his 21 months tenure'. These politicians, he explained, prevented the prosecution of FIA officials working with smugglers by ensuring their posting elsewhere within Punjab government when he attempted to expose their crimes (Klasra, 2004). Later that same month, the British High Commissioner to Pakistan announced that he had told Islamabad that senior government officials in Pakistan were involved in the smuggling business (Raza, 2004). In January of the following year, the details of a big-time agent's arrest, reported in *The News*, revealed the extent of the problem: from 1994, Choudhry Hanif ran a business with 15 to 20 sub-agents working for him nation-wide and, having established links with politicians in Punjab, sent thousands of Punjabi migrants abroad with fake documents. His influential friends, it was reported, were already clamouring for his release (Khanzada, 2005).

What then, is the FIA doing when it routinely arrests smugglers and migrants intercepted at airports,[6] and what does this tell us about the changing role of sending states in the global smuggling business? Controlling emigration consists of catching small fish: migrants and agents without the right contacts or sufficient resources to ensure successful emigration. Imprisonment of these marginal freelancers is punishment for challenging the state's monopoly on what might arguably be described, paradoxically, as 'legitimate smuggling'. Not infrequently, they are forced to offer bribes before being tossed back in the pond to continue their operations. The state thus protects 'big agents', who are themselves networked to a Eurasian migration system which, since the end of the Cold War and the incorporation of Eastern Europe into that system, has expanded considerably. It now is extensively intertwined with other continents (most notably, Mediterranean Africa).

The increasing number of refugees from diverse locations across the 'Third World' using channels historically associated with labour migration has further complicated the geographical pattern. Afghanistan, of course, is of particular importance to Pakistani in outflows as well as the Eurasian system as a whole. The upshot is that 'bi-national' and 'bi-continental' smuggling flows (e.g. Pakistan–Britain, South Asia–Europe, respectively) are increasingly often mediated by, funnelled and filtered through global networks that span several continents. Overland journeys and sea routes thus involve collaboration between agents in Pakistan with operators in locations such as North Africa, and final destinations include North Western, Mediterranean and Scandinavian Europe and other parts of the world. Sea and land-border crossings bring Pakistanis into close proximity with travellers and locally situated facilitators based in locations as diverse as Turkey, Morocco and, should they wish to enter Britain, France and Belgium.

How might we charaterise change and continuity in contemporary human smuggling at the world level? Despite the breadth, diversity and complexity in smuggling routes and labour markets which absorb migrants who work illegally, one thing unifies them: the people who travel or die trying are mostly, if not exclusively young, non-white and bent on reaching some wealthier part of the planet from which they are barred.

In this sense, human smuggling today must be seen within the wider context of its place in the edifice and operation of an older world order of capital (see Ballard, this volume). Yet it would be a mistake to rely too heavily upon macro-economic arguments to explain this phenomenon, since many of these travellers are from middle- (or lower-middle-) class backgrounds in their countries of origin.

The consequences of migration's increased commodification for travellers from all of Asia and Africa (not to speak of Latin America) have been mixed: for all the mansions built and cars purchased with remittances in countries of origin, the exponential increase in human smuggling and illegal work has tended to mean increased vulnerability to exploitation, coercion and trafficking within the labour process. Bodily harm and death in illegal overland and maritime travel and transit are widely reported. Detentions and deportations are now integral to migration control, as are raids on small businesses and other places of illegal work within countries such as Britain and the Netherlands. Regularisation of legal status has added considerably to the already spiralling costs of travel, adding further scope for facilitation by lawyers, employers and migrants who recuperate their own costs by 'helping' newcomers find their way through red tape. Legally hybrid arrangements are thriving as never before. In 1967 Aurora (45) calculated on the basis of the five migrants he interviewed that it would take ten months for a typical migrant in the England of the 1960s earning an average factory income to pay off the costs of travel. That was already a considerable price. What might it be today? (See Ahmad, 2007 for a discussion.)

Yet, whatever the losses and costs of illegal migration, the fact is that it fails to deter a seemingly endless pool of enthusiastic travellers, many of whom are young Muslim men (who, particularly since 9/11, tend to be the least enthusiastically received). This should impel us to consider whether the causes and consequences of migration ought to be read in purely rational, economistic, utilitarian terms. New research on smuggling and migration is increasingly considering the subjective, agentive and experiential aspects of travel and work, mediated by gender and sexuality (Mai and King, 2009). Subjectivity is likely to play a more important role than previously thought in driving migration: in Pakistan, for instance, a mythological masculinist ideology has managed to firmly fix associations of upwardly mobile arrival in the West (and successful return to one's community of origin) to a journey which often delivers neither (Ahmad, 2007). The decision to migrate is often contentious within households, and the general lack of any singular cause that can be isolated in migrant testimonies as *the* driving factor underlines the importance of thinking beyond narrow conceptions of the economic (Ahmad, 2008).

Conclusion

Studies of contemporary smuggling report diverse kinds of relations between smugglers and migrants (Liempt and Doomernik, 2006), arguing that smuggling networks are far less organised and centrally co-ordinated then previously thought (Pastore *et al.*, 2006). This chapter goes further, questioning the radical distinction between smugglers and migrants often posited by talk of criminal gangs and agents within the media. The gerund, *smuggling*, is a more useful term altogether than the noun, 'agent', since it refers to a processual activity in a manner more reflective of sociological realities, without fixing responsibility on a single individual. In practice, smuggling seldom involves a single smuggler or 'agent'. Historically, the two have always been mutually permeable and organically linked categories; today they are more blurred than ever through the practice of '*agenti*' (profiteering from facilitation), in which more and more migrants are involved thanks to the expansion of the migration business into one of regularisation in increasingly inhospitable host countries.

Agenti is a product of political and economic contexts in which networks of individuals – migrants, state officials and many others involved in organising accommodation – co-operate to facilitate various forms of legal and/or illegal residency, work and travel throughout the migration process. Its proliferation in times of restrictionism underlines the fact that illegal migration cannot be isolated from the institutional framework of international migration: it is precisely an essential component of the political framework in and through which labour is disciplined, filtered, funnelled westwards and extracted on terms favourable to capital. Human smuggling, then, is a racket with numerous shareholders who profit in different ways. We hear a good deal about Snakeheads, Russian Mafias and Kurdish gangs, unscrupulous recruiters, callous truck drivers and corrupt FIA officials. But we seldom consider the principal institutional and private beneficiaries which have historically produced and driven human smuggling and illegal migration.

Despite smuggling's increasingly complex ethnic, national and spatial geographies, these have remained constant in shaping migration outcomes ever since the colonial period. It was the restrictionism of colonial states that produced smuggling in the early decades of the twentieth century, and the restrictionism of post-colonial advanced and industrialised states that triggered the dispersal of Pakistanis and South Asians across the globe from 1962, as this chapter has sought to demonstrate. This pivotal role of the state is key to understanding the changes and continuities in the experience of human smuggling and illegal migration, not least for many tens of thousands from Pakistan. Since 9/11 in 2001, they have faced a particular set of constraints that make their continued desire and ability to enter, live and work without authorisation in some of the richest and most powerful states one of the most remarkable, untold and still poorly understood stories in the history of postwar globalisation.

Notes

1 The empirical material presented here is based primarily upon doctoral research conducted over a period of three years between 2003 and 2006 in London and Italy under the supervision of Laurence Fontaine and Pnina Werbner at the European University Institute in Florence. Additional research was funded by the Leverhulme Trust as part of the Leverhulme Programme on Migration and Citizenship (UCL and Bristol) during my time with John Salt and Khalid Koser at the Migration Research Unit at UCL in 2003–04. My main source of data consists of 60 life-stories narrated in Urdu by 'old' and 'new' Pakistani migrants from Punjab, North West Frontier Province (NWFP) and Mirpur. This qualitative material can be divided into three data sets, each of which is based on the testimonies of 20 respondents. The first cohort is made up of British citizens, now middle-aged and elderly, who migrated to Britain as young adults between 1960 and 1980, and who were interviewed in their London homes. The second cohort is men currently in their twenties and thirties who migrated to Britain between 1991 and 2004. The final Italian cohort was composed entirely of men between the ages 20 and 54, interviewed in Florence and Prato, who had first left Pakistan in their twenties and thirties.
2 The Act, which required lascars to register with the police and effectively prove that their birth place and residence was within the British Empire, was used as a means of justifying stop and search, and increasing surveillance and control of the small Indian (and wider non-white) migrant worker population. It also served as a device to effectively denationalise lascars, whose discharge papers would no longer be accepted as proof of identity, rendering them stateless; voluntary repatriation schemes were launched at the same time (Visram, 2002: 199, 213).
3 A separate study of Sikh migration across the border in Indian Punjab conducted by Helweg is replete with evidence of profiteering from facilitation (1979: 27–8); so, too, Gardner's sketch of the equivalent process in Sylhet (East Pakistan) in the 1960s (1995: 45–6).
4 All the names of my research informants and participants are pseudonyms.
5 Released in 1979, the film was directed by Haider Chaudhary.
6 In 2004 alone, the Lahore Passport Cell registered 1,451 cases to add to the 1,399 ones pending (Raza, 2004).

References

Adams, C. (1987) *Across seven seas and thirteen rivers: life stories of pioneer Sylhetti settlers in Britain*, London: Thap Books.
Ahmad, A. N. (2007) 'The myth of arrival: Pakistanis in Italy', in Kalra, Virinder S., *Pakistani diasporas: culture, conflict, and change*, Readings in Sociology and Social Anthropology, Pakistan: Oxford.
—— (2008) 'The romantic appeal of illegal migration: gender, masculinity and human smuggling from Pakistan' in Schrover, M., van der Leun, J., Lucassen, L. and Quispel, C. (eds) *Illegal migration and gender in a global and historical perspective*, Amsterdam: Amsterdam University Press, pp. 126–50.
—— (2011) *Masculinity, sexuality and illegal migration*, London: Ashgate.
Ansari, H. (2004) *The infidel within: Muslims in Britain since 1800*, London: Hurst & Company.
Aurora, G. (1967) *The new frontiersmen: a sociological study of Indian immigrants in the United Kingdom*, Bombay: Popular Prakashan.
Bilger, V., Hofmann, M. and Jandl, M. (2006) 'Human smuggling as a transnational service industry', *International Migration*, 44(4): 59–93.
Bun, C. K. and Hui, O. J. (1995) 'The many faces of ethnic entrepreneurship' in Cohen, R. (ed.) *The Cambridge survey of world migration*, Cambridge: CUP, pp. 523–31.

Cowan, R. (2004) 'Police hit South African visa scam: suspected illegal immigration racket targeted as Home Office cracks down on bogus colleges believed to be issuing counterfeit student visas', *The Guardian*, 17 June.

Gardner, K. (1995) *Global migrants, local lives*, Oxford: Clarendon Press.

Ghosh, B. (1998) *Huddled masses and uncertain shores: insights into irregular migration*, The Hague: M. Nijhoff.

Helweg, A. (1979) *Sikhs in England*, Delhi: OUP.

Hill, A. (2004) 'Saudis to boycott British universities', *The Observer*, London: 15 August.

Khanzada, A. (2005) 'Human trafficker handed over to Lahore FIA', *The News (Daily Jang)*, Lahore: 15 January.

Klasra, R. (2004) 'Faisal says he is victim of conspiracy'. *The News (Daily Jang)*, Lahore: 3 September.

Kyle, D. and Dale, J. (2001) 'Smuggling the state back in: agents of human smuggling reconsidered' in Kyle, D. and Koslowski, R. (eds) *Global human smuggling: comparative perspectives*, Baltimore; Johns Hopkins University Press.

Liempt, I. and Doomernik, J. (2006) 'Migrant's agency in the smuggling process: the perspectives of smuggled migrants in the Netherlands', *International Migration*, 44(4): 165–89.

MacMaster, N. (1997) *Colonial migrants and racism: Algerians in France, 1900–62*, London and New York: Macmillan.

Mai, N. and King, R. (2009) 'Love, sexuality and migration' in *Mobilities* Vol. 4, No. 3: 295–307.

Mujahid Ali, S. (1982) 'Pakistanis in Norway' in Centre for Pakistan Studies (eds) (introduced by Muazzam Ali), *Pakistanis in Europe*, Manchester: New Century Publishers, pp. 88–90.

The News (Daily Jang) (2004a) 'Pakistani student blows whistle on bogus marriage racket', London edition: 18 August.

—— (2004b) 'Bogus marriages network smashed', London edition, 24 September.

Nichols, R. (2010) *A history of Pashtun migration 1775–2006*, New York: OUP.

O'Reilly, J. and Robertson, D. (2004) 'Foreign students preferred', *Sunday Times*, London: 30 May.

Pastore, F., Monzini, P., and Sciortino, G. (2006) 'Schengen's soft underbelly? Irregular migration and human smuggling across land and sea borders to Italy', *International Migration*, 44: 95–119.

Pinkerton, C., McCloughlin, G. and Salt, J. (2004) 'Sizing the illegally resident population in the UK', Home Office online report, 58:4.

Rahman, M. and Gillani, A. (2004) 'High-flying bygamist scandalises Indian society', *The Guardian*, 31 January.

Rahmatoullah (1982) 'Pakistanis in France', in Centre for Pakistan Studies (eds) (introduced by Muazzam Ali), *Pakistanis in Europe*, Manchester: New Century Publishers, p. 83.

Raza, S. (2004) 'UK claims top figures involved in human trade', *The Dawn*, Lahore edition: 24 September.

Reuters (2004) 'Pakistan navy to join US-led patrol: Official', *The News (Daily Jang)*, London: 20 April.

Salt, J. and Stein, J. (1997) 'Migration as a business: the case of trafficking', *International migration*, 35(4): 467–94.

Shamsi, Mohammad Fasih (1982), 'Pakistanis in Holland', in Centre for Pakistan Studies (eds) (introduced by Muazzam Ali), *Pakistanis in Europe*, Manchester, New Century Publishers, pp. 91–3.

Tahir, Z. (2004) 'The allure of greener pastures'. *The Dawn Review*, Report on human smuggling, 14–20 October: 4–10.

Tapinos, G. (1999) 'Clandestine immigration: economic and political issues' in OECD (ed.) *Trends in International Migration 1999*, Paris: OECD Publications, pp. 229–51.

Travis, A. (2004) '100 fake colleges in visa scam', *The Guardian*, 22 June.

Unattributed (1982) 'Pakistanis in Belgium', in Centre for Pakistan Studies (eds) (introduced by Muazzam Ali), *Pakistanis in Europe*, Manchester, New Century Publishers, pp. 91–3.

Unattributed (1982) 'Pakistanis in Denmark', in Centre for Pakistan Studies (eds) (introduced by Muazzam Ali), *Pakistanis in Europe*, Manchester, New Century Publishers, pp. 91–3.

Visram, R. (2002) *Asians in Britain: 400 years of history*, London: Pluto.

16

OUT OF INDIA

Deobandi Islam, radicalism and the globalisation of 'South Asian Islam'

Magnus Marsden

Introduction

By the mid-1990s scholars of South Asian Islam had begun to ask what impact its migration to Pakistan had had on the nature of Deobandi Islam. Historical studies of the Deoband *madrassa* (*daru'l-ulum*), established in India in 1856/7, emphasised its status as an intellectual context in which north Indian Muslims responded to the pressures and constraints of colonialism. They also underscored the depth of the connections between its scholars and established Sufi brotherhoods, notably the Chishtis (Metcalf 1982). The Deoband was inspired by British educational models, yet sought to exclude the Western sciences from its curriculum. Its scholars focused their teaching on a revival of the Islamic sciences rooted in a deeper philosophy of reformed Sufism, emphasising teaching through a spiritual master without the emphasis on the cult of the saints. Initially, the Deoband 'school' focused on the need for Muslims to engage in acts of 'reform' (*islah*), which, in the context of colonial India, involved especially the purification of Islamic traditions and practices from what were increasingly interpreted as illegal, Islamic innovations (*bid'a*). Over the course of the twentieth century, however, Deobandi thinking and learning focused its attention more and more on the impermissibility, according to Deobandi scholars' understanding of Islamic teachings, of Sufi-influenced forms of faith and practice; they also highlighted the dangers posed by non-Sunni Muslim communities and practices to the faith, belief and religious conviction of 'properly Muslim societies'. After partition, and the migration of the Deoband's ulema to Pakistan, they targeted Ahmedi Muslims as infidels and denounced their belief as deviant. They also played a major role in the Pakistani government's decision to strip Ahmadis of their civic rights in 1972 and in 1984.

The Deobandi ullama have also been regarded as central to the ideologies, as well as social and religious networks, of Afghanistan's Taliban movement and government, known also for its deeply anti-Shi'a attitudes and policies. Many of the Taliban's senior leadership had studied together in Deobandi *madrassa*s in Pakistan's North-West Frontier, notably the Dar al-Haqqania run by Sami-ul Haq in the town of Akhora Khattack. Key figures of authority within the Taliban, moreover, continued to maintain connections with these nodes in wider religious–political networks of Deobandis during and after the Taliban's regime in Afghanistan. The very term 'Deobandi' became, in short, synonymous for many commentators on Pakistan and Islam in South Asia with the extreme forms of Islam of the Taliban, and their conservative attitudes and policies towards women, urban populations, and non-Sunni Muslims.

Parallel to these developments in 'political Islam', however, the Deobandi style (*maslak*) of thought was also coming to be known to wider Muslim and non-Muslim audiences through the activities of the politically 'quietist' Tablighi Jama'at, a global movement of Islamic reform and purification, launched around 1922 by a Deoband-trained scholar, Muhammad Illyas (1885–1944). The Tablighis, whose religious activities focus on the strengthening of Muslim faith through teaching the importance of the correct practice of Islamic rituals, has been identified by scholars not simply as another form of 'Islamism', but, rather, a dimension of 'neo-fundamentalism' (Roy 1994) and is now described as a 'piety movement' (Mahmood 2004). Movements of piety-minded Muslims, rather than focusing on public politics or state capture, focus their activities more on the Islamisation of 'the self' – calling upon Muslims to perfect their practice of Islam and fashion their selves according to a pure form of Islamic doctrine and practice (Roy 2004). The Deoband 'school', thus, has come to shape the nature of personal and collective self-consciously 'Muslim' forms of identities, politics and publics in such complex and diverse ways that the analytical value of the very category 'Deoband' is questionable. For Barbara Metcalf, what these different expressions of 'Deobandi Islam' all share, however, is an 'overriding emphasis on encouraging a range of ritual and personal behavioural practices linked to worship, dress, and everyday behaviour' (Metcalf 2001: 1).

The goals of this chapter are twofold. First, it seeks to outline the transformations that Deobandi forms of Islam underwent during their passage to Pakistan and beyond. It will focus on the active participation in Pakistan's electoral politics of the Deobandi political party (the Jam'iyyat-e ullama'-e Islam, JUI). It will also describe the complex connections between Deobandi thought styles and sectarian violence in Pakistan, and the emphasis that the Tablighi Jama'at is now having on the emergence of new understandings of personal piety and self-hood within and beyond Pakistan. Second, it seeks to explore the connections between these expressions of Deobandi Islam and migration patterns within and beyond South Asia, as well as forms of mobility that are better characterised as diasporic dispersion. Deobandi activities, practices and organisation-building have been shaped by dispersal of Deobandi activists, sojourners and scholars over the past century. These activities range from the organisation of collective public events celebrating the Deoaband's historical achievements to the school's 'Old Boys' Association'. They can meaningfully be compared with the 'collective work of memory and commemoration, the performance of difference, the cultivation of ideologies of identity' (Tölöyan 2007) that have been seen elsewhere as critical in defining those diasporas that endure both through time and across multilocal and polycentric spaces. They can also form part of the history of the emergence of another type of 'Islamic ecumene'.[1]

Deobandi and militant Islam: the Jam'iyyat-e ullama'-e Islam

The impact of Deobandi thinking on Pakistan's political culture has been perhaps most powerfully felt through the actions and policies of the Jam'iyyat-e ullama'-e Islam (Association of Religious Scholars) founded in 1945. After the creation of Pakistan, however, the JUI initially focused its activities on the social and religious domains, only eventually fully involving itself in electoral politics in the 1970s (Reetz 2007: 145).[2] Importantly, the creation of the JUI in 1945 signalled major political divisions between the Deobandi ullama: the powerful Jam'iyyat-e ullama'-e Hind (Association of Religious Scholars of India, founded in 1919) remained opposed to partition, focusing instead on the religious rights of Muslims rather than territorial claims, although many JUH scholars did move to Pakistan after partition, regardless.

From the 1970s onwards, the JUI focused its attentions on the cultural Islamisation of Pakistan society, although its leaders simultaneously came to be known by both Pakistani voters and scholars of the country for their pragmatism. This often centred on their willingness to enter into political agreements with parties and leaders who held ideas about Islam's role in society that were very different from their own; this is something that Qasim Zaman suggests is an important indication of the party's complex relationship with plural politics (Zaman 2007). Famously, for example, the JUI first held power in a coalition government in the North-West Frontier Province in 1972 together with the secular and Pushtun nationalist National Awami Party. During this period, the JUI leader, Mufi Mahmud, banned alcohol and required government servants to dress according to Islamic standards (White 2008).

The JUI continued to grow in power and importance throughout the 1980s, largely as a result of the central role that Pakistan played in the anti-Soviet 'jihad' in Afghanistan. Deobandi *madrasa*s were connected to the US-funded 'jihad'; they were also swelled with an influx of students both from villages across the Frontier and Afghanistan, as well as the children of the millions of Afghans who became 'religious refugees' in Pakistan (Shahrani 1995): between 1980 and 1986 the number of *madrassa*s in Pakistan increased from approximately 700 to 7,000 (Jalal 2008: 276). During the eighties, however, the JUI continued to show their willingness to engage in 'pragmatic pluralism', entering into alliance with the Benazir Bhutto government during her second tenure as Prime Minster (1993–6), a political decision further illustrating their reputation for having 'seldom allowed their formal discourses to foreclose the range of political options that might be open to them' (Zaman 2005: 70).[3]

A combination of the growing dispersal and political influence of the Deobandi might well have led to the organisation, in April 2001, of a gathering of Deobandi scholars in Taru Jabba near Peshawar. The gathering aimed to mark the school's one hundred and thirty-fifth birthday, celebrating 'the achievements of the Daru'l-'ulum Deoband during the past 150 years'. The gathering saw a crowd of thousands gather to watch Deobandi delegates speak on matters ranging from the need to develop a moderate Deobandi Islam to calls for commitment for the Taliban (Reetz 2007: 145), and was widely covered in Pakistan's print and television media. Delegates attended the conference from India, Iran, Afghanistan, the Gulf, United Kingdom, Libya, Saudi Arabia and Malaysia, reflecting the fact that, by the turn of the century, Deobandi networks of religious learning and transmission, as well as its ullama-centred form of political activism, had become truly global. The event has recently been described in the memoirs of Mullah Zaeef, the Taliban government's ambassador to Pakistan at the time, as the most 'interesting' of all conferences he attended (Zaeef 2010: 118). The Taru Jabba event marked one of the high points of formal Deobandi political influence: in Pakistan's elections of 2002, the JUI, as part of a coalition group (called the Muttahida Majlis-e Amal) that included both other Sunni and Shi'a religious parties, was elected to provincial government in Pakistan's North-West Frontier Province in the wake of the war on terror and the military defeat of Afghanistan's Taliban government.

More interestingly, the celebratory gathering at Taru Jabba also raises important questions concerning how helpful concepts related to the study of diasporas are for understanding the Deoband. The expansion of Deobandi networks across South Asia, into Afghanistan and beyond – often through highly itinerant refugee carriers – seems to have prompted prominent Deoband scholars to recognise the diasporic dispersal of their school, and to have alerted them to the need to organise memorable public events that would enable the production of vivid and shared collective representations of 'the Deoband'. In addition to such events, 'the Deoband' was also active in producing 'mobilizing structures and practices' (Sökefeld 2006: 270) that scholars of diaspora have argued are central to the maintenance of the collective identity of dispersed people. The Deoband established in 1991 its own 'Old Boys' Association' (Tanzim-e Abna'-e Qadim), initially imagined as a 'springboard for the introduction of an Islamic system of governance' and eventually taking the form of a 'modern networking endeavour' that helps to prepare graduates for the 'job market' (Reetz 2007: 147–8).[4]

Understanding the Deoband as an increasingly diasporic form of identity and community requires, however, a parallel recognition of the existence of other processes in the Deoband diaspora. It is crucial to note the importance of more linear forms of migration in shared images of a Deobandi identity. In Chitral, a large administrative district in the North-West Frontier Province where I conducted fieldwork between 1995 and 2007, villagers distinguished between scholars trained in Deoband itself (the last I met having studied there in the 1960s) and those who had attended Deobandi *madrassa*s in Peshawar. 'Original' (*asli*) Deobandis were referred to by local villagers as 'true scholars' (*sahi 'alim*), known and respected for their relatively relaxed *fatwa*s about issues such as the permissibility of music and dance that more recent (Peshawar-trained) Deobandi scholars all saw as being 'against Islam'. The 'sophisticated humanity' (*insaniyat*) of the original scholars was understood by many Chitralis as reflecting the experiences of these men in India, and their descent from 'people of good family' (*khandani roye*). Other, newer, Deobandi religious authorities, by contrast, hailed from families that were once the serfs (*chermuzh*) of gentry-like lords (*lal*), and who had migrated from particular Chitrali valleys to Peshawar's *madrassa*s from the 1950s onwards, staying in the city to work, and were believed to have been shaped by their migratory pathways in much more negative ways. Local theories suggested that the extremism or *imtihai pasandi* of these men, manifested in their anti-music and Ismai'li ideas, was best understood in relation to their migration to the city, rather than to their passive reception of religious ideology. This migration entailed living in close proximity with 'Pakhtuns', eating mixed-up left-over food (*sharal*) from collective tin dishes (*tash*), and becoming shops owners who sold the Chitrali woollen hats (*pakol*) which, by the 1980s, had become the key symbol of Afghanistan's domestic anti-Soviet jihad: this was a way of life that Chitralis regarded nonetheless as low-status, deadening the senses and intellects of the *dukandaran* (shopkeepers).[5]

In the light of this rather pejorative view of them held by those from their 'home' region, it is hardly surprising that these Peshawar-based shopkeeper-Deobandi mullahs increasingly emphasised the primacy of their attachments to the Deoband, and of reformist Islam, over distinctively Chitral cultural practices. Yet, as is the case with other migrant communities that increasingly come to see themselves as different from their 'fellow people' back home, the Peshawar–Chitralis also talked of Chitral as their homeland (*watan*). They have started to play a major role in the JUI mullah-politicians' efforts to bring non-Pushtun Chitral – by frontier standards, a religiously heterogeneous space – more squarely within predominantly Pukhtun forms of Islamism. They helped finance the successful Muttahida Majli-i Amal (MMA – United Action Front) campaign in Chitral in 2002 and travelled to their home region, where they stayed in the mosques they had also often helped to build in their ancestral villages and campaigned for MMA. It was this group of migrant mullahs who, appropriately, carried on their shoulders the victorious MMA mullah from Chitral through Peshawar's old city streets.

Deobandi Islam and Pakistani 'sectarianism'

Sitting with these Deobandi-affiliated bazaar traders in their shops, I first encountered another defining feature of Deobandi thought and identity: its anti-Shi'a (and anti-Ismai'li) sectarianism. These Sunni shopkeepers told me that they had 'found' cassettes in which Ismai'li preachers from Chitral said unthinkable things about Islam. They also said that they intended to play these cassettes to Chitral's Sunnis in order to launch a jihad against the district's Ismai'lis. Between the 1970s and the 1980s, Deobandi forms of Islam came to be closely associated with sectarian conflict in Pakistan. The role of Deobandi Islam in sectarian violence is connected to the Khatm-e Nabuwwat, an international organisation that sought to raise the awareness of Muslims about the religious profanities taught and believed by followers of Ahmadi Muslims. It sought to rally and unite radical ullama and reformist teaching around 'preaching hatred against dissenters of Islam' (Reetz 2007: 146). Originally founded by a Barelwi scholar, Abdul Sattar Niazi, the general secretariat of the Khatm-e Nabuwwat by the 1980s was located in Pakistan and dominated by the Deobandi ullama, although non-Deobandi ullama did also continually seek to retake control of it (Jalal 2008: 282).[6] The relationship between such preaching of hatred by Deobandis and actual incidences of sectarian violence in Pakistan has been the focus of considerable scholarly debate.

Much scholarship focuses on direct organisational links between Deobandi *madrassa*s and movements in Pakistan who played a key role in sectarian violence. These organisations include the Anjuman-e-Sipah-e Sahaba (SSP), founded in 1984 by Maulana Haq Nawaz Jhangvi in Jhang, Punjab, which was involved in countless incidents of violence against Shi'a Muslims during the 1980s and 1990s. The SSP controlled a 'string of *madrassa*s in Punjab'. After the execution of its founder, Jhangvi, its leader Azam Tariq took an oath of allegiance to the Deobandi scholar Maulana Yusuf Ludhiviani. Another movement connected to Deoband thought and also known for its role in sectarian violence is the Harakat-ul-Ansar (renamed Harakartul Mujahideen after it was declared a terrorist organisation by the USA in 1997). This organisation is known to have dispatched 80,000 Taliban students from Deobandi seminaries in Federally Associated Tribal Areas and the North-West Frontier Province to fight against the Northern Alliance and Shi'a militias in Afghanistan. Later, other paramilitary organisations were founded by Shi'as to counter Sunnis, such as the Sipah-i Mohammadi founded in the 1990s, as well as by non-Deobandi Sunnis, notably Barelvi-linked Sunni Tehrik, to counter the spread of Deobandi influence.[7]

Major questions remain, however, about the nature of the link between Deobandi attitudes to internal theological difference within Islam and sectarian violence in Pakistan. This debate turns especially on the degree to which the shift by Deobandi scholars towards vocal sectarianism can be explained in terms of their experience of migrating to Pakistan from India. Nasr (2000), most notably, argues that the JUI's role in the escalation of sectarian conflict between Sunnis, Ahmadis and Shi'as in Pakistan should be analysed in terms of the party's political history, as well as the life trajectories of the Deobandi ullama involved within it. Many of the Deoband's earlier leaders, he argues, were tainted in the eyes of the Pakistani public because of the decision of the JUH to oppose the creation of Pakistan in 1947. Yet, having moved to the country after its creation, JUI scholars, Nasr argues, sought to vilify Shi'a and Ahmadi Muslims in Pakistan, depicting them as a threat to a Sunni-dominated and -inspired Pakistan. Their aim was to create a legitimate space within Pakistani politics for their party, given the suspicion with which they were regarded in Pakistan, and to do so by representing themselves as the ultimate protector of Pakistan and its Sunni Islam.

Zaman, however, suggests that the role of the Deobandi ullama in Pakistan's sectarian conflict cannot be reduced to the JUI's political strategy in the wake of their migration to Pakistan. This approach fails to address the broader aims and goals of the sectarian-oriented and ullama-based parties in Pakistan. Through a consideration of sectarian politics in the Jhang district of Pakistan's Punjab, Zaman argues that the ullama have sought to generate anti-Shi'a sentiment there in order to accomplish two major goals. First, by 'radicalising' Muslim identities through their focus on sectarianism, the Sunni-Deobandi ullama have sought to weaken the political status and fortunes of wealthy Shi'a landlords and create a niche for an expanding Sunni merchant middle class, a significant proportion of whom are also first-generation migrants into towns (see also Abou Zahab 2002).

Yet, as Zaman also shows, such a class analysis can only go so far: if many of Jhang's merchant middle class are Sunnis, there are also considerable numbers of Shi'a amongst them. Second, then, he argues that, by radicalising Sunni identities in this and other regions of Pakistan, anti-Shi'a Sunni ullama have also sought to expand the influence of reform-minded schools of Islamic thought, especially the Deoband, in the country's rural regions and small towns. Far from dominating the religious world views of rural populations in Pakistan, the Deoband ullama have often only managed to cultivate a thin support base in such contexts, where more regional forms of Islam and modes of being Muslim have remained vital and resilient to reform-minded Islamising processes (e.g. Marsden 2005). More than simply being the outcome of the JUI's political instrumentalism, then, Sunni–Shi'a sectarianism in Pakistan has created greater awareness amongst diverse communities about Islamic reformism and played a critical role in the extension of Deobandi Islam into rural Pakistan (Zaman 2002: 135). The direction of the flow of Deobandi influence on society in Pakistan from this reading, then, needs to take into account circular movements of scholars and Deobandi activists to and from towns and villages, rather than focusing solely on the impact of the migration to Pakistan from India of key Deobandi ullama, or seeing the embrace of reform-minded Islam as the one-dimensional product of 'urbanisation' and 'middle-class' identity formation.

There is now also a growing and much needed recognition of the importance to Deobandi self-identities of equally violent tensions between Sunni Muslims. At one level, scholars have sought to show that a relatively diverse range of opinions and perspectives exist within 'Deobandi Islam' itself. Zaman documents significant differences in the thinking of Pakistani Deobandi scholars over the issue of sectarian violence. Some madrasas, like the Jami'at-al 'Ulum-al Islamiyya in Karachi, have played an active role in the 'exclusion of the Shi'a from the community of Muslims' (Zaman 2007: 73); others like the Dar-al 'Ulum (also in Karachi) have a much more 'extensive, continued and varied' intellectual output that cannot be reduced to its participation in the politics of sectarianism alone (Zaman 2007: 75). Increasing attention is also being directed towards conflicts between Deobandi and non-Deobandi Sunni Muslims. Scholars have drawn attention to the role these conflicts are playing in the formation of self and identity in Pakistan and, especially critical for this chapter, to their importance to South Asian diasporic identity formations beyond. Naveeda Khan (2006) has documented the complex ways in which individual Sunni Muslims might shift between different forms of 'Sunni' Islamic teaching and affiliation over the course of their lives in Lahore.[8] They move from devotional Barelwi Islam (Sanyal 1996), for example, to Deobandi or even Ahl-i Hadith reformism: it is a serious oversimplification to depict Deobandi religio-political activists as always invoking their distinctiveness in opposition to Shi'a Muslims. In diasporic communities of Muslims of South Asian descent, religious differences between Deobandis and Barelwis are foregrounded and are often associated with concerns about 'authenticity'. In Mauritius, South Asian diasporic identity formations focus on competing claims to represent the authenticity of Islam and about which so-called 'ancestral languages' should be taught in government schools. Deobandis, who are 'suspicious of the authenticity of South Asian Islamic practice' and see Mauritian Islamic practice as being equally in 'serious need of purification and reform', favour Arabic over Urdu, arguing it to be 'connected to the original sources of Islam' (Eisenlohr 2006: 402). By contrast, Barelwis see South Asia as a pre-eminent space of authentic Indo-Muslim practice and advocate the teaching of Urdu in schools.

Deoband, Pashtun identity politics and the Taliban

One of the trickiest of issues surrounding the Deoband is its relationship to Pushtun identity dynamics and politics. Not only is the Frontier a critically important political space for Deobandi self-identity in Pakistan (I have suggested above that the frontier regions of Pakistan and Afghanistan might indeed have been treated as a type of Deobandi homeland at the turn of the millennium), so too have Pushtun politico-religious activism and Deobandi thought been connected to one another outside the Frontier itself, notably in Karachi.

Many studies have noted the importance of Deobandi religious teachings, institutions and social networks to the Frontier and the Taliban. Yet the precise nature of the relationship between Deobandi Islam and Pushtun identity dynamics remains poorly understood. At one level, 'the Frontier' is not a homogenously Pushtun space: frontier populations might be deeply influenced by Deobandi forms of Islam, without being Pushtun or publicly supporting the Taliban (Marsden 2005; Marsden and Hopkins 2012). The relationship between Pushtun ethnicity and Deobandi religious-political activism, however, is one that has been for several decades openly reflected upon and conceptualised as 'special' by Deobandi scholars themselves. Most recently, a Taliban leader is reported to have said that 'all Afghans are Deobandi' (Metcalf 2001). Over the twentieth century, moreover, complex interactions unfolded between Pushtun self-understandings and images of Pushtuns that were developed and transmitted by Deobandi ullama (Haroon 2007). Sana Haroon emphasises the ways in which Deobandi religious scholars constructed images of Pushtun tribesmen as independent, free-loving men of honour who were automatically predisposed to anti-colonial militancy and jihad (Haroon 2007: 94).

The connections between Deobandi Islam and Pushtun identity politics should not, thus, be treated in a seamless or historically teleological manner and may be as much about representations of 'Pathans' and 'Deobandis' as they are about 'identity politics'. The lived relationship between reformist Islam and Pushtun communities has, after all, been more defined by their tensions than by any simple overlapping of ideological and religious aspirations. The bands of Indian Muslim anti-colonial fighters who sought to ally themselves with, and reform, the Pushtun tribesmen in a *jihad* against the British in the nineteenth century frequently complained of being let down by their erstwhile tribal supporters, prone as they were to inter-tribal conflict, temptation by financial inducements and attachments to their local 'Pushtun' traditions (Jalal 2008: 101–5). Such complex relations, however, tend to be erased in the titles of books about the Frontier today, which define it homogenously in terms of its connections to Islamism and insurgency, the title of White's *Pakistan's Islamist Frontier* (White 2008) embodying this trend especially vividly. After Pakistan's independence, moreover, the Frontier was an important space of leftist worker activism: Swat – at the centre of successive and well documented Islamic uprisings over the past 150 years (most recently in 2008/09) – saw leftist, Maoist informed peasant agitations into the 1970s (Asdar-Ali 2009). The Frontier, thus, has a been a critical backdrop for the emergence of a creative spectrum of political movements, uprisings and attacks by charismatic leaders on 'the state', which surely derive partly from its significance as a connective space between Central and South Asia, and a destination to which diverse peoples have fled to over centuries.

This point is underscored when we consider the degree to which the Deoband is a critical dimension of the religious identities, not only of Pushtun communities along the Frontier, but also to many others who identify with different ethnic identity markers but who also live in the Frontier as migrants, itinerant students, sojourners and exiles. Indeed, these same communities have also been central to anti-Taliban 'resistance' movements. Many of northern Afghanistan's Sunni ullama, for example, are Deobandi: these Dari-speaking Tajiks studied in predominantly Pushtun *madrassa*s when they were exiles in Pakistan.[9] Their relationship to Deobandi networks and associations are fraught and complex, especially in terms of their memories of the experience of being Dari-speaking migrant/refugee *taliban* (students) in these schools. On the one hand, young men whom I have met from Panjshir and Badakshan say that they studied in Deobandi *madrassa*s in the Frontier because it was their religious duty as Muslims to do so. Yet they also remember being fearful of the Pukhtun scholars and teachers in whose midst they lived, especially during the period when the Taliban launched an assault on the northern regions of Afghanistan where their ancestral homes were located. I was even told by one young man how he had pretended to be Chitrali by speaking only in Khowar during his time in a Peshawar *madrassa*, fearing that the Pukhtun-speaking students might be hostile to him if they discovered he were Panjshiri: they accused Panjshiris of being Russian spies opposed to jihad. Today young Panjshiri men living in Kabul continue to travel for study to Peshawar's *madrassa*s and make choices about which *madrassa*s to study in on the basis of which are 'racist' (*nejad-parast*) and which more 'enlightened' (*rowshan-fikr*) towards 'Tajiks'.

The Tablighi Jama'at, and South Asian Islam in South-East Asia, central Asia and beyond

The images I have discussed above of Deobandi political activism and campaigns for the exclusion of Ahmadis and Shi'a from the Muslim community are constantly offset by another set of images of 'Deoband': those of the Tablighi Jama'at. As mentioned above, the Jama'at is a Deobandi organisation that focuses 'on individual character building through acts of piety and spiritual devotion, which would then lead to religious revival' and, more controversially in the light of recent scholarship, the 'establishment of an Islamic state' (Jalal 2008: 267). The movement is especially well represented in Pakistan, where its capacity to transcend boundaries of class, ethnicity, nationality and culture, and to forge different forms of personal and collective affiliation, have made it a focus of much discussion. If, as Ayesha Jalal argues, the ethnic profile of the Tablighi Jama'at in Pakistan is heavily Pushtun (90,000 of 2 million people who converge in annual meeting in Lahore are Pushtuns from North-West Frontier Province and Federally Associated Tribal Areas – FATA), then it is also a movement that 'casts its net widely among all classes of Muslim South Asian society', partly because its assumed political neutrality has helped it recruit among state bureaucrats and army personnel in Pakistan (Jalal 2008: 268–9).

The remarkable range and depth of the Tablighi Jama'at's influence on the Muslim world is now the focus of a body of comparative scholarship focusing on Tablighi identities and practices in different geographical locales. These are all places where 'Deobandi thought and institution building' has received a 'strong boost from the activities of the Tablighi Jama'at' (Reetz 2007: 155). The Tablighi Jama'at's activities have been explored in northern Pakistan (Knudsen 2009), Afghanistan (Marsden 2009), Malaysia (Noor 2007), Thailand (Horstmann 2007), Tajikistan and Iran (Dudoignon 2009), and the Gambia (Janson 2005). The Tablighi Jama'at's is at the centre of a range of different scholarly debates concerning its relationship to the domain of 'the political' broadly and to Pakistan-based jihadi movements in particular (e.g. Jalal 2008: 280). Scholars have also been interested in its missionary-preaching style and the impact of that style on local understandings of Muslims' selfhood (Knudsen 2009), as well as the degree to which it needs to be understood in terms of generational conflicts (Janson 2005: 465).

The Tablighi Jama'at reveals much about new scales of religious thought and their relationship to old and new forms of mobility. The work of the Tablighi Jama'at highlights the complex relationship between religious transformation and changes in concepts of 'the self' in particular Muslim communities. The Tablighi Jama'at emphasises above all the importance of the individual Muslim following Islamic doctrinal practice, so that he/she may experience and properly embody Islamic ethical states in their full power and significance, notably those associated with the pious nexus (*taqwa*) of the fear of, love for and submission to God. But this needs to be considered alongside another dimension of the movement that is critical to the way in which it operates, which is much less theorised and less well understood: the ceaseless mobility of its (especially male) activists. The mobility of Tablighi activists is frequently the focus of moral critique by those opposed to the movement. Family members accuse Tablighi activists of behaving in a manner that wantonly ignores the emphasis that Islam places on a man's responsibility to the family. Tablighi Jama'at manuals, for example, offer guidance to men about the precise ways in which they should persuade their wives to give them permission to travel (Janson 2005: 462). The emphasis is partly a reflection of the movement's youth dimensions: movement is one way in which young men mark themselves out as autonomous individuals in relationship to their parents. Yet besides reducing complex religious motivations for travel to sociological causes, this approach is also less helpful in settings where mobility is a feature of daily life for young and old people alike, such as in northern Afghanistan. In this setting, the mobility of the Tablighi Jama'at is questioned for reasons other than the doubts that it casts on a man's commitment to family: the Tablighi Jama'at is widely associated by Dari-speakers in northern Afghanistan with Pakistan and Pushtuns. Dari-speaking men in the north who frequently embark on preaching tours to predominantly 'Pushtun' regions with their fellow activists (who are also often Pushtun) are considered problematic, not because of their mobility or time away from home, but the specific places to which they travel and the identities of the men with whom they travel. Indeed, given that many people in this region talk about journeys or *safar* as practices to be deployed in order to come to know friends and business partners 'truly', the forms of companionship established during preaching tours are also held to be especially strong and threatening to pre-existing friendships and relations.

A second critical issue concerns the role played by the networks and mobile lives of Tablighi Jama'at activists in connecting places hitherto not thought about as being a part of 'Deobandi' religious space and forming new nodes at the meeting points of such networks. The social and religious networks of Deobandi scholars, *madrassas* linked to Pakistan's Deobandi centres and religious activists from the Tablighi Jama'at are converging at particular nodes in ways that also have complex political effects. Dudoignon has explored the importance of Deobandi teachings and networks to the emergence of forms of Sunni identity in Shi'a-majority Iran that transcend ethnic differences between Kurds, Baluchis and Turkomans (Dudoignon 2009). Whilst the Tablighi Jama'at does not feature by name, ideas of conversion to Islam that are distinctively Tablighi 'can be felt across the whole Iranian Sunni cyberspace' (Dudoignon 2009: 41). Such forms of influence are also evident at particular nodes within networks of Deobandi religious activism, where Muslims converge from very different directions, such as Zahedan in Iran's Baluchistan Province. Zahedan's *madrassas* have been connected to Karachi's Deobandi religious seminaries by flows of Baluchi religious scholars since the 1930s; they are now also becoming critical nodes of religious learning for other Sunni, Persian-speaking people, especially from Tajikistan. After the collapse of the Soviet Union, many Tajiki students travelled to Iran to study Islam in the country's Deobandi *madrassas*, as do wealthy Tajik merchants, who are seeking both to improve their knowledge of Islam and to educate their wives and children in Islamic teaching and doctrine. These forms of mobility coincide with new trading routes, as merchants visiting their children in *madrassas* in Iran also buy Iranian goods to sell in Dushanbe's bazaars. In addition, the people travelling along these routes include new religious specialists in Tajikistan, who live in the houses of wealthy merchants, teaching their children, and sometimes also using them as unofficial centres of religious instruction more generally.

Not only religious ideology or *dawa* flows down the dispersed Deoband and Tablighi Jama'at networks: the cultural forms, practices and values that move along the Tablighi Jama'at's networks are more diverse in composition than those of 'transnational' or 'deterritorialised' Islam alone (Mandaville 2003; Roy 2004). Given Pakistan's status as a political space where tensions between deterritorialised and bounded understandings of Islam have been particularly visibly played out (Jalal 1995), it is not surprising that the Tablighi Jama'at's most important *markaz* (religious centre) is located in the country at Raiwind.

Yet to think of the Tablighi Jama'at only or even primarily as a movement of deterritorialised Islam overlooks its role in the spreading of distinctively South Asian practices and artefacts. Farish Noor has noted how the Tablighi Jama'at has become active in north-east Malaysia through South Asian Muslim families who, indeed, often refer to their ancestry as 'Pathan'. According to Noor, the Tablighi Jama'at is a powerful and active force behind the transmission of particularly South Asian modes of food and clothing and, importantly, bodily comportment, to South-East Asia. The Tablighi Jama'at deploys these to 'maintain a sense of identity and unity of purpose by emphasising the distinctly South Asian character of its outward appearance and identity': Tablighi students and teachers in the religious education centre wear South Asian clothing and turbans, and eat out of communal open food pots during their time in school, so much so that the Tablighi Jama'at 'outward appearance' appears to be a form of 'Indian Islam' (Noor 2007: 25). Yet the maintenance of this distinct identity, reminiscent of what Tölöyan argues are central dimensions of diasporic identity formation (the performance of difference and cultivation of ideologies of identity) (Tölöyan 2007), set it out as 'alien', and lead it to sit 'uncomfortably with local expressions and norms of popular Islam' (Noor 2007: 9). The distinctiveness of the Tablighi Jama'at, then, needs to be understood not only in relationship to the forms of Islamic ethical practice that are embodied by its followers, but also within a framework that pays close attention to the ways in which its activists 'perform difference', using 'Pakistani' clothing such as the *shalwar kamiz*, turbans and rosary beads. The fact that these 'Islamic commodities' are, increasingly, made in China, rather than South Asia, raises further questions about the multiple migrations and diasporic dispersals connected to 'Deobandi Islam'.

Notes

1 On the relationship between diasporic forms of mobility and dispersion and the making of another very different form of Islamic ecumene, see Ho 2006.
2 Later, a breakaway faction led by Samiul Haq of the JUI also became an important part of the Deobandi political scene in Pakistan.
3 Importantly, the JUI's visions of a Pakistan society shaped by Islamic teachings were marked by their differences from the more middle-class and urban 'Islamism' of Mawlana Mawdudi's Jama'at-e Islami party: the JUI was associated with rural areas, whilst the JI's failure to forge a support base amongst the rural poor reflected its untainted hostility as a result of its urban intellectual cadres' dislike of 'popular Islam' (Nasr 2000).
4 On the importance of memory to collective identity, especially of religious cults, see Whitehouse 1996.
5 See Dresch 1998 on the wariness of exchange in Muslim societies of the Middle East and Central Asia.
6 Barelwi refers to a 'school' of Islamic thought important across South Asia that was founded and established in British India during the nineteenth century by Ahmed Riza Khan Barelwi. Barelwi scholars emphasise the centrality to Islam of the teachings and traditions of the Prophet (see Sanyal 1996).
7 Between the 1980s and 1990s an estimated 30,000 Pakistanis were martyred in Afghanistan and Kashmir, more than 2,000 were killed in the country during Sunni-Shi'a conflicts and over 200,000 belonged to militant organisations (Jalal 2008: 278–81).

8 For an excellent critique of the tendency of South Asian Islam specialists to neatly place Muslims as belonging to different categories of believer on the basis of their 'belief' see Simpson 2007.
9 On the historical connections between Deoband and the Afghan ullama, see Olesen 1995: 43–50.

References

Abou Zahab, M. (2002). 'The Sunni-Shia Conflict in Jhang (Pakistan)', in I. Ahmad and Reifeld, H. (eds) *Lived Islam in South Asia*, Delhi: Social Science Press, pp. 135–48.
Asdar-Ali, K. (2009). 'Pakistan's Troubled Paradise on Earth', *Middle East Report*, April 29, www.merip.org/mero/mero042909.html. Accessed 22/2/10.
Dresch, Paul (1998). 'Mutual Deception: Totality, Exchange and Islam in the Middle East', in W. James and N. Allen (eds), *Marcel Mauss: A Centenary Tribute*, New York: Berghahn Books, pp. 111–33 and 126–7.
Dudoignon, S.A. (2009). 'Sunnis on Line: The Sunni Confessional Internet in Iran', *Asiatische Studien*, 63 (1): 29–66.
Eisenlohr, P. (2006). 'The Politics of Diaspora and the Morality of Secularism: Muslim Identities and Islamic Authority in Mauritius', *Journal of the Royal Anthropological Institute*, 12 (2): 395–412.
Haroon, S. (2007). *Frontier of Faith: Islam in the Indo-Afghan Borderland*, London: Hurst and Co.
Ho, E. (2006). *Graves of Tarim: Genealogy and Mobility across the Indian Ocean*, Berkeley: University of California Press.
Horstmann, A. (2007). 'The Tablighi Jama'at, Transnational Islam, and the Transformation of the Self between Southern Thailand and South Asia', *Comparative Studies of South Asia, Africa and the Middle East*, 27 (1): 26–40.
Jalal, A. (2008). *Partisans of Allah: Jihad in South Asia*, Harvard: Harvard University Press.
— (1995). 'Conjuring Pakistan: History as Official Imagining', *International Journal of Middle East Studies*, 27: 73–89.
Janson, M. (2005). 'Roaming about for God's Sake: The Upsurge of the Tabligh Jama'at in The Gambia', *Journal of Religion in Africa*, 35 (4): 450–81.
Khan, N. (2006). 'Of Children and Jinns: An Inquiry into an Unexpected Friendship in Uncertain Times', *Cultural Anthropology*, 21 (2): 234–64.
Knudsen, A. (2009). *Violence and Belonging: Land, Love and Lethal Conflict in the North-West Frontier Province of Pakistan*, Copenhagen: Nordic Institute of Asian Studies Press.
Mahmood, S. (2004). *Politics of Piety: The Islamic Revival and the Feminist Subject*, Princeton, NJ: Princeton University Press.
Mandaville, P.G. (2003). *Transnational Islam: Reimagining the Umma*, London and New York: Routledge.
Marsden, M. (2009). 'Talking the Talk: Debating Debate in Northern Afghanistan', *Anthropology Today*, 25 (2): 20–4.
— (2005). *Living Islam: Muslim Religious Experience in Pakistan's North-West Frontier*, Cambridge: Cambridge University Press.
Marsden, M. and B. Hopkins (2012). *Fragments of the Frontier*, London: Hurst and Co.
Metcalf, B. (2001). 'Traditionalist' Islamic Activism: Deoband, Tablighis and Talibs', Social Science Research Council Publication After September 11th: http://essays.ssrc.org/sept11/essays/metcalf_text_only.html. Accessed 22/2/10.
— (1982). *Islamic Revival in British India: Deoband, 1860–1900*, Oxford: Oxford University Press.
Nasr, S.V.R. (2000). 'The Rise of Sunni Militancy in Pakistan: The Changing Role of Islamism and the Ulama in Society and Politics', *Modern Asian Studies*, 34 (1): 139–80.
Noor, F. (2007). 'Pathans to the East! The Development of the Tablighi Jama'at Movement in Malaysia and Southern Thailand', *Comparative Studies of South Asia, Africa and the Middle East*, 27 (1): 7–24.
Olesen, A. (1995). *Islam and Politics in Afghanistan*, London: Curzon.
Reetz, D. (2007). 'The Deoband Universe: What Makes a Transcultural and Transnational Educational Movement of Islam', *Comparative Studies of South Asia, Africa and the Middle East*, 27 (1): 139–59.
Roy, O. (2004). *Globalised Islam: The Search for a New Umma*, Columbia: Columbia University Press.
— (1994). *The Failure of Political Islam*, London and New York: I.B. Tauris.
Sanyal, U. (1996). *Devotional Islam and Politics in British India: Ahmed Riza Khan Barelwi and His Movement, 1870–1920*, Oxford: Oxford University Press.
Shahrani, M.N. (1995). 'Afghanistan's Muhajirin (Muslim "Refugee-Warriors"): Politics of Mistrust and Distrust of Politics', in E. Valentine Daniel and John Chr. Knudsen (eds) *Mistrusting Refugees*, Berkeley and Los Angeles: University of California Press, pp. 187–206.

Simpson, E. (2007). 'The Changing Perspectives on Three Muslim Men on the Question of Saint Worship over a 10-year Period in Gujarat, Western India', *Modern Asian Studies*, 42 (2 and 3): 377–403.

Sökefeld, M. (2006). 'Mobilizing in Transnational Space: A Social Movement Approach to the Formation of Diaspora', *Global Network*, 6 (3): 265–84.

Tölöyan, K. (2007). 'The Contemporary Discourse of Diaspora Studies', *Comparative Studies of South Asia, Africa and the Middle East*, 27 (3): 647–55.

White, J. (2008). 'Pakistan's Islamist Frontier: Islamic Politics and US Policy in Pakistan's North-West Frontier', in *Religion & Security Monograph Series* (1), Arlington, VA: Center on Faith and International Affairs.

Whitehouse, H. (1996). 'Rites of Terror: Emotion, Metaphor, and Memory in Melanesian Initiation Cults', *Journal of the Royal Anthropological Institute*, 2 (4): 703–15.

Zaeef, A.S. (2010). *My Life with the Taliban*, London: Hurst and Co.

Zaman, M.Q. (2007). 'Tradition and Authority in Deobandi Madrasas of South Asia', in R.W. Hefner and M.Q. Zaman (eds) *Schooling Islam: The Culture and Politics of Modern Muslim Education*, Princeton, NJ: Princeton University Press.

— (2005). 'Pluralism, Democracy and the "Ulama"', in R.W. Hefner (ed.) *Remaking Muslim Politics: Pluralism, Contestation, Democratization*, Princeton, NJ: Princeton University Press.

— (2002). *The Ulama in Contemporary Islam: Custodians of Change*, Princeton, NJ: Princeton University Press.

17

NATIONALISING A DIASPORA

The Tibetan government-in-exile in India

Fiona McConnell

Clinging to the mountainside, mid-way between the bustling Indian town of Dharamsala and the former British hill-station of McLeod Ganj, is the headquarters of the Tibetan Government-in-Exile. The talk in the Department of Home is of infrastructure problems in Arunachal Pradesh, agricultural yields in Orissa and eviction notices in Delhi. At the Department of Education they are rolling out the new 'Tibetan Education Policy' and across the courtyard the Department of Health is concerned with rising tuberculosis cases and the recruitment of Tibetan doctors. Things are more upbeat in the Department of Finance. The government budget is in surplus for the first time, and the voluntary taxation contributions are on the rise. Meanwhile, staff on the ground floor are processing applications for the exile Tibetan 'passport', *the rangzen lagteb*, which every 'bona fide Tibetan' must hold, but which neither permits the holder to travel, nor offers any legal security.[1]

The history of the Tibetan presence in India is a long and complex one, comprised of fluid territorial borders, historic religious exchanges and seasonal trading. However, following China's declaration of the 'peaceful liberation' of Tibet in 1951 and its crushing of the Tibetan national uprising in Lhasa in 1959, the situation changed dramatically. Tibet's spiritual and political leader, the Dalai Lama, sought asylum in India and, today, the Tibetan diaspora numbers approximately 122,000. In 1960, the Dalai Lama re-established the Tibetan Government in the hill-station of Dharamsala, Himachal Pradesh, with the twin tasks of rehabilitating Tibetan refugees and restoring freedom in Tibet. Over the decades, the exile government has been institution-alised according to democratic principles, and the current administration consists of a cabinet, parliament and seven governmental departments.[2] In performing a number of state-like functions, the Tibetan Government-in-Exile (TGiE) runs schools and clinics in its 39 settlements across India, issues identity documents to and collects 'voluntary' taxes from its diaspora and organises democratic parliamentary elections. Such claims to legitimacy as the official representative of the Tibetan population are thus made despite being internationally unrecognised, having limited judicial powers and lacking *de jure* sovereignty over territory in Tibet and in exile.

In general, diasporic communities navigate between nations and across space, cross-cutting the dominant framing of territorial sovereignty and thereby challenging the hegemony of the nation-state (Appadurai 1996). However, whilst acknowledging that transnational flows have disrupted the significance of national boundaries, attention has also focused on the active role of states in defining the terms under which transnational processes are played out (see Smith and Guarnizo 1998; Jackson *et al.* 2004). This includes the expansion of home state links with their expatriate communities (Levitt *et al.* 2003) and the impact of host state political contexts on the transnational practices of migrants and refugees (Ostergaard-Nielsen 2001). The institution of TGiE adds an important angle to this literature. As I have argued elsewhere, this case of an unrecognised government operating within another sovereign state and yet performing a number of state-like functions for its diaspora raises vital questions regarding the nature of sovereign authority and the relationship between sovereignty and territory (McConnell 2009). In addition, alongside supporting calls for a sustained focus on the internal dynamics of immigrant groups (Veronis 2007), the state-like functioning of TGiE turns attention to the important political structures that transnational communities bring with them and (re)establish in exile (see Al-Ali *et al.* 2001). Moreover, with its defined political agenda, established bureaucratic structures, welfare provision and construction of Tibetan citizenship, this case has the potential to offer a more robust and contextualised conceptualisation of diaspora (Anand 2003).

Based on in-depth interviews and focus groups undertaken in 2005–7 in Dharamsala and Tibetan settlements in Ladakh, Uttarakhand, Delhi and Karnataka, this chapter examines the strategies through which the exile Tibetan government fosters relations with its diaspora and how such connections are distinctively state-like. After outlining the context of Tibet in exile, two aspects of TGiE's nation-building will be explored. Attention will first turn to the strategies through which TGiE seeks to preserve Tibetan culture and identity in exile, including the construction of pan-Tibetan nationalism in exile, the institutionalisation of Tibetan citizenship and the role of education in attempting to standardise this 'national' identity. Secondly, attending to the establishment and functioning of Tibetan settlements in India, the role that these spaces play vis-à-vis TGiE's nation-building project in exile will be discussed and the complex relations between the settlements, the temporality of exile and the homeland explored. The chapter concludes by considering the wider implications of this state-like exilic government and community.

Tibet in exile

Controversy surrounds the legal, territorial and political status of Tibet. Chinese authorities maintain that Tibet has been and remains an inalienable part of China's territory (People's Republic of China 1992), whilst Tibetans assert that Tibet existed as an independent sovereign state prior to the Chinese 'occupation' in 1949 (DIIR 1996). In October 1950, 40,000 troops from China's People's Liberation Army (PLA) entered Eastern Tibet and, after 12 days, defeated the 8,000-strong Tibetan army. Six months later the so-called 'Seventeen-Point Agreement for the Peaceful Liberation of Tibet' affirming Chinese sovereignty over Tibet was signed, albeit with Tibetan officials considering it as having been signed under duress and therefore invalid (Powers 2004). By 1959, growing popular resentment to Chinese rule culminated in an open revolt in Lhasa which, in March that year, was crushed by the PLA with over 80,000 Tibetans killed and thousands imprisoned. A week later, the Dalai Lama, most of his senior government officials and over 80,000 Tibetans fled the capital and crossed the Himalayas to seek refuge in India, Nepal and Bhutan.

Upon his arrival in India, the Dalai Lama announced the re-establishment of the Tibetan Government in exile. Whilst, in the first half of the twentieth century, Tibetans were ruled by what has been described as a feudal theocracy with the central government headed by the Dalai Lama and the national assembly consisting of both religious and lay representatives (Kharat 2003), the exile government was based on democratic principles as documented in the 1963 'Constitution of Tibet'. The 1991 'Charter of Tibetans in Exile' further institutionalised the exile government, establishing an executive body (*Kashag*), legislature (Tibetan Parliament-in-Exile) and judiciary. In terms of political leadership, whilst the Dalai Lama continues to be the central unifying element within the diasporic community (Kolås 1996), he has reduced his political role substantially through devolving his authority to the directly elected *Sikyong* (Prime Minister) and exile parliament. Besides the official organs of the state, the Tibetan community in exile has also seen the development of institutions of civil society. Numerous non-governmental organisations have been established across the diaspora alongside exile media including newspapers, magazines, radio services[3] and web-forums which have linked the internationally dispersed diaspora.

Turning to the diaspora itself, after the peak years of exodus from 1959 to 1961, the borders of Tibet were effectively closed and there was 'little contact between Tibetans inside Tibet and the refugee community for more than two decades' (Yeh 2007: 652). The second wave of refugees began in the 1980s, with 25,000 Tibetans arriving in India between 1986 and 1996 as a result of reforms in China and the loosening of travel restrictions. Members of this second exodus – 'newcomers', as they are commonly referred to – left for a variety of reasons including religious persecution, political repression and a lack of educational opportunities (Hess 2006). The principle escape route was, and continues to be, an arduous and dangerous journey across the Himalayas on foot to Nepal and then on to Dharamsala where TGiE arranges an audience with the Dalai Lama, provides short-term accommodation and organises placements in religious and educational institutions. An estimated 2,000–3,000 Tibetans left illegally for India every year from the late 1990s until 2008, with increasing numbers of young people seeking better employment opportunities and individuals visiting family in exile. However, since the protests across the Tibetan plateau in March 2008, the flow of Tibetan refugees from Tibet to India via Nepal has all but stopped due to stringent border controls. The migration of Tibetan refugees from South Asia to the West began in the 1960s with the resettlement of around 1,500 Tibetans in Switzerland. Meanwhile, movement to the USA occurred after the passage of the 1990 US Immigration Act, with the 'Tibetan U.S. Resettlement Program' granting permanent resident status to 1,000 'displaced' Tibetans living in India and Nepal (Hess 2006)[4]. Remittances sent back to India, subsequent family reunification schemes and the lack of employment opportunities for Tibetans in India has encouraged further migration to the West, including to other European countries, Taiwan, Japan and Australia. In these host states most Tibetans are in contact with Tibetan community organisations and Offices of Tibet run by the TGiE.

In terms of the relationship between the exiled Tibetan administration and the Indian Government, whilst largely contingent on ever-changing Indo–Sino relations, the latter has been an extraordinarily generous and tolerant host, and exile Tibetans have been grateful and largely obedient guests (Diehl 2002). Such a relationship is founded on the basis of a long-standing spiritual and cultural connection between Tibet and India, the fact that Tibetans are largely seen as model refugees (Fürer-Haimendorf 1990) and India's use of TGiE as a bargaining chip to regulate its relations with Beijing (Norbu 1996). Such a relationship is also in many ways mutually beneficial. The TGiE has relied on Indian political and bureaucratic expertise for the development of its constitution, election system and training its civil servants, and the presence of the exile Tibetan community and its institutions has, in turn, instigated a cultural and religious revival in India's Buddhist Himalayan regions. However, despite such hospitality, India has never afforded TGiE formal legal or political recognition as a government, nor the Dalai Lama the status of a legitimate political leader. Yet, at the same time, the Indian Government grants TGiE tacit approval to speak for the Tibetan refugees, manage the exile settlements and engage with international donor agencies. In light of such contradictions, both Tibetan and Indian inter-viewees described a relationship in which the boundaries of authority, legitimacy and legality are constantly being negotiated (McConnell 2009).

Whilst other states where Tibetan exiles reside do not host TGiE institutions, or at least not beyond Offices of Tibet, this tacit approval of the exiled government's representation of the Tibetan diaspora can also be traced. For example, in acknowledging the TGiE's role in validating individual Tibetans' identity, the Immigration and Refugee Board of Canada (1998) declared that 'one of the best ways to determine if a person is a bona fide Tibetan in exile is to see if they have a "Green Book" . . . the authenticity [of which] can be verified by the Office of Tibet that issued the document'.

Identity in exile: nationalism, citizenship and education

In light of the threatened 'loss of purpose and Tibetan language and identity' (Tibetan Government-in-Exile 2004) within the homeland, the diaspora is perceived by the exile government as having a series of interlinked and distinct purposes: as a 'resource' which is under threat in Tibet and thus needs to be preserved in exile; as a population in waiting and in training ready to return to govern a future Tibet; and as a cultural repository, preserving a unified and essentialised Tibetan national identity outside the home territory (McConnell 2012). My focus here is on the latter 'purpose' and the strategies through which the exile government strives to foster this idealised Tibetan diaspora.

In order to construct the diasporic population as a cultural repository, TGiE needed to foster a very particular kind of population in exile: a cohesive, united and homogenous community which shares a single *national* identity. Tibetan nationalism is broadly understood as constructed through the process of the Chinese occupation of Tibet and flight into exile (Shakya 1999) and solidified by Tibetans' 'sudden immersion into the midst of a sea of Indians' (Goldstein 1975: 21). A standardised version of Tibetan nationalism has been promoted in exile through a range of 'national' traditions and rituals which construct a powerful imagined sense of solidarity and belonging. These patriotic yet banal acts (Billig 1995) include singing the national anthem, flying the national flag, staging debates on the legitimacy of Tibet's claim to independence and participation in national holidays such as the anniversary of the national uprising on 10th March 1959 and the Dalai Lama's birthday on 6th July. Such performances of Tibetan nationhood therefore perpetuate the myth of national unity across the diaspora, instilling a collective sensibility and a uniform definition of Tibetan identity (Kolås 1996). In doing so, the exile government has sought to subsume fractious regional and sectarian identities which dominated pre-1950s Tibet under a homogenous and pan-Buddhist national Tibetan identity which had previously not existed beyond the Lhasa elite. It is a strategy which has been largely successful for, whilst regional identities and divisions remain in the community, most interviewees spoke of 'Tibetanness' being their most important identity marker, reflecting Yeh's observation that regional identities are 'largely papered over in the transnational nation-building' (2007: 650). However, it is also imperative to remember that this construction of a nationalised population generates a new national body formed primarily in exile. As such, an increasingly significant division arises between the exile population and Tibetans in Tibet. The decades-long project of cultural preservation in exile has produced, confusingly, both a static and conservative version of Tibetan culture, and one increasingly influenced by Indian and Western cultures (Yeh and Lama 2006). Meanwhile, Tibetan culture and identity within the homeland has been suppressed and increasingly sinicised and, where exile and homeland cultures come together, there are often tensions over issues of identity and authenticity (Yeh 2007)[5].

The essentialising of national identity in exile and politicising of Tibetan ethnicity can thus be seen as forming a key part of TGiE's nation-building project and perhaps the most obvious mechanism through which this identity construction is managed is through its establishment of

Tibetan citizenship. Developed in exile and enshrined in the 1991 Charter, Tibetan citizenship is granted to 'any person whose biological mother or biological father is of Tibetan descent' (Article 8).[6] Although this citizenship has no legal standing due to the TGiE's lack of law-making abilities, its practical implications are widely understood and engaged with McConnell 2013. Tibetan citizenship is materialised in the *Rangzen Lagteb* or 'Green Book' which Tibetans refer to as a pseudo passport and the annual payment of *chatrel* or 'voluntary contributions' to TGiE,[7] both of which are essential to functioning in the exiled community. This includes gaining admission to Tibetan schools, accessing TGiE-run welfare services, being eligible for TGiE stipends and jobs and voting in exile Tibetan elections. Crucially, the Green Book and *chatrel* are key signifiers of authenticity and legitimacy through which the TGiE and Tibetans in exile reaffirm each other's status as a 'legitimate government' and 'bona fide Tibetans' respectively (see McConnell 2013). This establishment of a social contract between exile Tibetans and TGiE through the rights and obligations of citizenship in effect creates state-like political subjects and provides a degree of security for the exile community. With the *legal* identity regime of Tibetan citizenship thus synonymous with the *political* identity regime of Tibetan nationality (see Isin and Turner 2007), this creation of 'universal' Tibetan citizenship can thus be read as the statist aspect of a broader project of nation-building in exile.

Another key arena in which Tibetan identity is standardised and regulated is education. It is widely accepted that school curricula construct a citizen's moral order, worldview and sense of national identity (Radcliffe 2001). In the Tibetan case, education has been accorded the highest priority since the early years of exile and the Department of Education administers 73 schools in India, Nepal and Bhutan, serving around 24,000 Tibetan children in exile. In these schools 'Tibetan textbooks and teachers ... transmit a curriculum of Tibetan[n]ess' (Kolås 1996: 57) alongside the Indian Central Board of Secondary Education-approved syllabus. In documenting the role of this exilic education system in promoting an essentialised notion of Tibetan nationalism, Nowak notes that this was a 'systematic attempt to shape a more cohesive group identity in exile' (1978: 71) especially amongst second generation Tibetans in India. Such is the pivotal role of education in the eyes of TGiE that failings in the education system, such as declining standards in written Tibetan, are perceived to jeopardise the broader project of preserving Tibetan culture and identity. In light of such concerns, TGiE launched a 'Basic Education Policy' in 2005 which (re-)emphasises traditional Tibetan education and values taught in Tibetan language (Department of Education 2005). As a result, this policy aims to produce a very specific and idealised 'type' of Tibetan citizen – both traditional and modern, non-violent and truthful – through a series of disciplinary institutions (schools) and technologies (curriculum).

In summary, on the one hand there have been notable limitations and challenges to the construction of Tibetan nationalism in exile. These range from deeply entrenched regional and sectarian divisions within the ethnically Tibetan population, the spatial scattering of the exiled community both within India and internationally, and the relatively limited resources of the TGiE, especially in the early years of exile. Yet, on the other hand and despite these challenges, the TGiE has been broadly successful in constructing a sense of Tibetan nationalism in exile and creating a relatively cohesive diaspora. Crucially, with the exile government as the primary architect of these re-workings and reinventions of Tibetan nationalism, this is a process which both constructs and goes some way to legitimising TGiE as a governing authority. For, without territory to call their own, it is the population which has followed the Dalai Lama into exile over the past 50 years which has validated the exile administration's existence and continued functioning. Moreover, such deliberate construction and fostering of Tibetan nationalism in exile both challenges post-structuralist dismissals of essentialised identities and the resurgence of patriotism (Brah 1996; Clifford 1997) and supports the idea of a 'creative tension' between diaspora and nationalism (Ong 1999: 17).

Settlements in exile: nation, temporality and homeland

Central to this project of nation-building in exile are the 58 official Tibetan settlements in India, Nepal and Bhutan. Established on land granted to TGiE by the Indian Government, these settlements range from large agricultural townships in Karnataka to small handicraft communities in Himachal Pradesh and several city colonies (see Figure 17.1). Within each of these

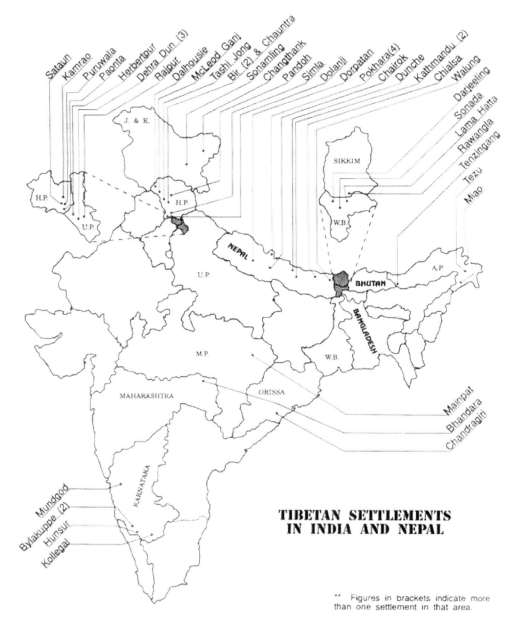

Figure 17.1 Map of the Tibetan settlements

Source: Central Tibetan Administration, Dharamsala, 1995

non-contiguous and highly dispersed settlements, TGiE has autonomy over its own affairs in terms of administering land distribution, agriculture, clinics and schools. This section explores the symbolic importance of the settlements as exilic Tibetan spaces associated in complex ways with nationalism, the temporality of exile and the homeland.

In addition to the pragmatic aim of creating economically self-sufficient Tibetan communities within the host state, the rationale most frequently articulated by TGiE is that of the settlements providing space for protecting and preserving Tibetan culture, identity and way of life in exile (CTRC 2003). 'Deliberately designed in such a way as to recreate Tibetan society with its core values intact' (Norbu 2001: 15), these 'national spaces' are therefore key to the exile government's project of reconstructing 'Tibet' in exile and, as the time in exile extends, they are increasingly seen as places where the community can pass on 'authentic' Tibetan traditions to the next generation. Indeed, a number of interviewees spoke of the 'real Tibetan community' being in the settlements which are in effect spaces where 'Tibetans can be Tibetans' (farmer, Lugsum-Samdupling, Karnataka, 2007). As part of the promotion of a pan-Tibetan identity, TGiE has adopted a policy of locating refugees from different regions in Tibet together in the same settlement (Ström 1995). Such a deliberate nationalising project has obvious connections with the idea of homeland in terms of keeping the collective memory of Tibet alive through sustaining a cohesive national community in exile. In turn, as Gupta and Ferguson argue, place-making is ubiquitous in collective political mobilisation with '"homeland" ... remain[ing] one of the most powerful unifying symbols for mobile and displaced peoples' (1992: 11). Thus, through these discourses TGiE uses the spaces of the settlements to foster essentialised and nationalised Tibetan identities in exile (see Lavie and Swedenburg 1996).

However, the connection between the settlements and the Tibetan nation and homeland is not only imposed upon the diaspora by the TGiE. Reflecting the 'complexity of ... ways in which people construct, remember, and lay claim to particular places as "homelands" or "nations"' (Malkki 1992: 25), settlers themselves have also created the settlements as spaces of nationalism through important material associations with the homeland. Despite the majority of Tibetan settlements in India being located in environments starkly different from those of Tibet, each settlement is 'Tibetanised' through the recurrent use of Buddhist structures and Tibetan architectural styles (see Figures 17.2 and 17.3). In addition to the cluster of Tibetan offices, schools and clinics which form the heart of each settlement, these include the monasteries, small temples for the protector deity of each village, archways decorated with auspicious Tibetan symbols and prayer-flags atop each building. The consistency of these structures across different settlements is strikingly evident as, while the building materials of the houses reflects the climate of their location within India, the unfailing recurrence of these cultural markers means each settlement can be read in a similar way and feels 'familiar' to exiled Tibetans. For example, Majnuka Tilla Tibetan colony is frequently described by newcomer refugees as a reassuring Tibetan 'sanctuary' within the very Indian – and therefore alien – city of Delhi. Thus, in reading the landscape of the settlements as socially constructed cultural texts (Barnes and Duncan 1992), the playing out of these symbolic links to the homeland can be seen as vindicating the TGiE's settlement programme in terms of recreating a 'mini' Tibet in exile.

However, the emotive and material attachments that exile Tibetans have to 'their' settlement also highlights an important and pressing issue within the community. What was intended as a temporary sojourn in exile is becoming increasingly permanent. This uprooted diasporic community is growing roots (see Malkki 1992). As such, this raises the crucial question of how easy and desirable it will be for the exiled community to 'up sticks' and leave India for Tibet

Figure 17.2 Chortens, Lugsum-Samdupling, Karnataka
Source: photo taken by author

should the situation in the homeland be resolved. One view, articulated by a young college graduate in Dharamsala, was that:

> Of course we will leave India if one day we have a free Tibet. . . . As we say, 'if it's written on your forehead then you go' – these are just buildings. People have a stronger attachment to their homeland . . . even those like me who have never seen it. So of course we will leave here and go back.
>
> *(2006)*

However, other interviewees were sceptical that such an upheaval would be easy or even possible, arguing instead that the exiled community and TGiE have become too established and comfortable in exile to the detriment of the greater project of fighting (in whatever way) for the future of the homeland. Indeed, opposition to forming attachments to places in exile has been a recurrent issue within the community, with an older resident in Dekyiling settlement explaining how:

> when land was first given to the Tibetans in South [India] the people they begged our leaders not to give them land. They thought you see . . . having land in India, it would mean they would not return to Tibet, that they would always be in India.
>
> *(2007)*

Figure 17.3 Large prayer-wheel, Dharamsala, Himachal Pradesh
Source: photo taken by author

Such fears of putting down roots in exile continue within the community today, even from those born in India. For example, one politically active interviewee in Dharamsala explained how, though enviously admiring the houses in Kangra Valley below Dharamsala, he refuses to own anything in India with this maintenance of a state of limbo helping inspire his dedication to the freedom struggle. Such decisions – to rent rather than own property, to be mobile rather than settled – which are repeated often within the community, can therefore be seen as deliberate deterritorialising strategies. In directly contradicting current TGiE policies of encouraging young Tibetans to return to the settlements, these beliefs and actions indicate that for some within the exile community the balance has tipped too far in the direction of providing for and settling the exile population, to the detriment of furthering the struggle for the homeland.

At the same time, this relationship between the settlements, nationalism and homeland is further complicated in this case. Not only have the settlements been constructed and performed as a series of temporary homelands in exile, but these Tibetan spaces in India in effect constitute a second or pseudo homeland. This is especially the case for second-generation Tibetans who have moved from India to the West, for whom the network of Tibetan settlements in India, the array of cultural and educational institutions and the seat of the Dalai Lama are in effect a surrogate spatial grounding for these individuals who have never seen the historic homeland.

Such a displacement of ideas of 'homeland' requires a shift in conventional frames of reference. Whilst in essence Tibetans in exile are as a whole a diasporic population, the role of TGiE and its base in India has effectively created a 'domestic' population (those residing in Tibetan spaces in India and Nepal) and a (second) diaspora of Tibetans who have moved from South Asia to the West. As such, TGiE acts as a 'home state', managing the transnational practices of their diaspora in the West: remittances flowing back to India and Nepal; participation in exile parliamentary elections; and the acquiring of 'dual' citizenship. This is therefore a situation which fundamentally dislocates conventional understandings of diaspora and territory, thereby confirming the assertion that exile politics disrupts the division between national and international politics (Mandaville 1999, McConnell 2009).

Such a displacement of ideas of 'homeland' not only requires a shift in conventional frames of reference regarding transnational practices and the concept of diaspora but disrupts the relationship between sovereignty and territory. Following Agnew's observation that 'the negotiation and redefinition of political authority in geographically complex ways suggests the need to change the terms of debate about sovereignty' (2005: 438), these dislocations force us to think beyond binaries of state/non-state, homeland/diaspora, national/transnational and enable us instead to consider the notion of *displaced* sovereignties (McConnell 2009). This is sovereignty which has both been constructed in exile – de facto authority over the 'real' territories of the exile settlements – and which has travelled into exile – TGiE's inherent sovereignty based on its legitimacy as a continuation of the Government of Tibet. This dislocation of the source and enactment of sovereignty therefore breaks down the assumed correlation of sovereignty with a single bounded territory, yet does not eschew the link between sovereignty and territory altogether. Rather, it is reconfigured in complex and contradictory ways. What TGiE lacks in official jurisdiction over territory in exile it compensates for by incorporating a symbolic and imagined territory into its sovereign practices. Indeed, tensions between authority articulated over 'real' territories and legitimacy claims based on symbolic links to a distant homeland get to the heart of TGiE's spatialised authority and the core dilemmas of life in exile: between retaining the desire to return home by maintaining a sense of the temporariness of exile and the community becoming increasingly attached to and rooted in the 'real' spaces of exile as their sojourn there extends (Diehl 2002).

Conclusion

Far from a stateless nation, the Tibetan community in exile has established not only an institutionalised and functioning government-in-exile, but also a state-like polity in exile which strives to nationalise its diaspora. As a polity and diaspora which fundamentally disrupts the fixed binaries of statehood/statelessness, sovereign/non-sovereign, refugee/citizen this case is therefore a useful lens through which these divergent issues can be viewed simultaneously and offers a productive way to rethink issues of authority, legitimacy, governance, identity, territory and statehood. However, it should also be noted that such an achievement says as much about the pluralist nature of the Indian state as that of the exile Tibetan community. For, whilst there are significant uncertainties regarding the future of the Tibetan community and government based in India especially when the current Dalai Lama passes on, TGiE's construction of socio-cultural boundaries between Tibetans and the host society corroborates and enacts India's liberal 'non-assimilative' framework (Goldstein 1975), with Tibetans broadly regarded as a pseudo caste community which can maintain its cultural identity and practices (Norbu 2004).

Finally, I want to posit that TGiE's state-like practices should not be seen simply as an exotic anomaly or theoretical experiment. Rather, this case should be de-exceptionalisd in order to open up the possibility of using it as a framework for an alternative 'durable solution' for refugee groups. Conventionally conceived as distinct stages in a refugee 'cycle', the three primary 'durable solutions' which the UN High Commissioner for Refugees (UNHCR) is charged with pursuing for refugees are: integration in the country of first asylum: resettlement in a third country: or return to the homeland, of which repatriation is the currently prioritised option (Van Hear 2003). However, for the majority of exile Tibetans, a fourth 'solution' has been sought in the form of autonomy within the host state. Distinct from integration or assimilation, TGiE can provide a pragmatic, viable and durable model of self-governance in exile whereby refugees preserve their culture and identity and the burden on the host state is significantly reduced over time. In addition, though distinctly limited in the legal realm, the institution of TGiE also provides a degree of security for this refugee community, both in tangible terms with regards to the provision of welfare and conferment of pseudo-legal status, but also by constituting a focal point for the diaspora to rebuild their lives, sustain traditional cultural practices and provide a sense of belonging. Alongside the territorialising strategies that TGiE has engaged with in India, these practices provide an important empirical grounding for Van Hear's assertion that 'transnationalism may in itself be a "durable solution" for conditions of displacement – or at least an "enduring" solution' (ibid: 14). Considering implications of this case beyond refugee communities, as a lived reality of reconfigured and constantly negotiated sovereignty, the TGiE's structures and ideologies and its operations within the state of India could be instructive for other communities and polities traditionally marginalised from the interstate system. If tolerated by a host state, such de facto autonomy within mutually agreed legal boundaries, organised networks of cultural and educational institutions, state-*ness* without statehood and practicing of democracy could be a valuable template for other diasporas, or even for indigenous populations and national minority groups.

Notes

1   This narrative is based on the author's field diary notes from 2007.
2   These are the Departments of Home; Health; Religion and Culture; Information and International Relations; Security; Education; and Finance.
3   The launch of Tibetan service radio gave exiles the ability to reach out to Tibetans in Tibet, which has proved to be a powerful unifying and nation-building tool (Samphel 2004).
4   The TGiE's estimate of the number of Tibetans in the USA was around 9,000 in 2008 (Macpherson *et al* 2008).
5   It should be noted that there is a trend towards increasing cultural solidarity between Tibetans in Tibet and those in the diaspora, expressed in particular through the emergence of the *Lhakar* movement since 2007–8. See www.lhakar.org
6   Whilst in theory such Tibetan citizenship extends to all Tibetans both in Tibet and in exile, in practice it is only those in exile who are able to enact the obligations and enjoy the rights of this citizenship.
7   The Green Book and *chatrel* system were started by a group of exiles in 1972. Whilst *chatrel* payments are technically voluntary as there is no legal means of enforcing payment, TGiE is careful to stress that this is not a 'donation' as this connotes a different form of relationship, and crucially one not based on obligation and duty (Department of Finance 2005).

References

Agnew, J. (2005). Sovereignty Regimes: Territoriality and State Authority in Contemporary World Politics. *Annals of the Association of American Geographers* 95 (2):437–61.
Al-Ali, N., R. Black and K. Koser (2001). The Limits to 'Transnationalism': Bosnian and Eritrean Refugees in Europe as Emerging Transnational Communities. *Ethnic and Racial Studies* 24 (4): 578–600.
Anand, D. (2003). A Contemporary Story of 'Diaspora': The Tibetan Version. *Diaspora* 12 (2):211–29.

Appadurai, A. (1996). *Modernity at Large: Cultural Dimensions of Globalisation*. Minneapolis: University of Minnesota Press.

Barnes, T. J. and J. S. Duncan (eds) (1992). *Writing Worlds: Discourse, Text and Metaphor in the Representation of Landscape*. Oxford: Routledge.

Billig, M. (1995). *Banal Nationalism*. London: Sage.

Brah, A. (1996). *Cartographies of Diaspora: Contesting Identities*. London: Routledge.

Clifford, J. (1997). *Routes: Travel and Translation in the Late Twentieth Century*. Cambridge, MA: Harvard University Press.

CTRC (2003). *His Holiness the Dalai Lama's Central Tibetan Relief Committee: Building Sustainable Communities in Exile*. Dharamsala: CTRC.

Department of Education (2005). *Basic Education Policy for Tibetans in Exile*. Dharamsala: Department of Education, CTA.

Department of Finance (2005). *The Chatrel System in Exile*. Dharamsala: Department of Finance, CTA.

Diehl, K. (2002). *Echoes from Dharamsala: Music in the Life of a Tibetan Refugee*. Berkeley: University of California Press.

DIIR (1996). *Tibet: Proving Truth from Facts*. Dharamsala: DIIR, CTA.

Fürer-Haimendorf, C. (1990). *The Renaissance of the Tibetan Civilisation*. London: Synergetic Press.

Goldstein, M. C. (1975). Tibetan Refugees in South India: A New Face to the Indo-Tibetan Interface. *The Tibet Society Bulletin* 9:12–29.

Gupta, A. and J. Ferguson (1992). Beyond 'Culture': Space, Identity, and the Politics of Difference. *Cultural Anthropology* 7 (1):6–23.

Hess, J. M. (2006). Statelessness and the State: Tibetans, Citizenship, and Nationalist Activism in a Transnational World. *International Migration* 44 (1):79–101.

Isin, E. F. and B. S. Turner (2007). Investigating Citizenship: An Agenda for Citizenship Studies. *Citizenship Studies* 11 (1):5–17.

Jackson, P., P. Crang and C. Dwyer (eds) (2004). *Transnational Spaces*. London: Routledge.

Kharat, R. (2003). *Tibetan Refugees in India*. New Delhi: Kaveri Books.

Kolås, A. (1996). Tibetan Nationalism: The Politics of Religion. *Journal of Peace Research* 33 (1): 51–66.

Lavie, S. and T. Swedenburg (eds) (1996). *Displacement, Diaspora, and Geographies of Identity*. Durham, NC: Duke University Press.

Levitt, P., J. DeWind and S. Vertovec (2003). International Perspectives on Transnational Migration: An Introduction. *International Migration Review* 37 (3):565–75.

MacPherson, S., A.-S. Bentz and D. B. Ghoso (2008). Global Nomads: The Emergence of the Tibetan Diaspora (Part 1). *Migration Information* www.migrationinformation.org/Feature/display.cfm?id=693 Accessed: 22 September 2010.

Malkki, L. (1992). National Geographic: The Rooting of Peoples and the Territorialisation of National Identity among Scholars and Refugees. *Cultural Anthropology* 7 (1):24–44.

Mandaville, P. G. (1999). Territory and Translocality: Discrepant Idioms of Political Identity. *Millennium: Journal of International Studies* 28 (3):653–73.

McConnell, F. (2009). De Facto, Displaced, Tacit: The Sovereign Articulations of the Tibetan Government-in-Exile. *Political Geography* 28 (6):343–52.

— (2012). Governmentality to practise the state? Constructing a Tibetan population in exile. *Environment and Planning D: Society and Space* 30 (1): 78–95.

— (2013) Citizens and Refugees: Constructing and Negotiating Tibetan Identities in Exile. *Annals of the Association of American Geographers* 103 (4): 967–83.

Norbu, D. (1996). Tibetan Refugees in South Asia: A Case of Peaceful Adjustment. In *Refugees and Regional Security in South Asia*, (eds) S. D. Muni and L. R. Baral. Delhi: Konark Publishers, 78–98.

— (2001). Refugees from Tibet: Structural Causes of Successful Settlements. *The Tibet Journal* 26 (2): 3–25.

— (2004). The Settlements: Participation and Integration. In *Exile as Challenge: The Tibetan Diaspora*, (eds) D. Bernstorff and H. Von Welck. New Delhi: Orient Longman, 186–212.

Nowak, M. (1978). Liminal 'Self', Ambiguous 'Power': The Genesis of the 'Rangzen' Metaphor among Tibetan Youth in India. Unpublished thesis, Department of Anthropology, University of Washington.

Ong, A. (1999). *Flexible Citizenship: The Cultural Logic of Transnationality*. Durham, NC: Duke University Press.

Ostergaard-Nielsen, E. K. (2001). Transnational Political Practices and the Receiving State: Turks and Kurds in Germany and the Netherlands. *Global Networks* 1 (3):261–81.

People's Republic of China (1992) *Tibet – Its Ownership and Human Rights Situation, PRC Government White Paper, September 1992*. Information Office of the State Council of The People's Republic of China.

Powers, J. (2004). *History as Propaganda: Tibetan Exiles versus the People's Republic of China*. Oxford: Oxford University Press.

Radcliffe, S. (2001). Imagining the State as Space: Territoriality and the Formation of the State in Ecuador. In *States of Imagination: Ethnographic Explorations of the Postcolonial State*, (eds) T. B. Hansen and F. Stepputat, 123–48. Durham, NC: Duke University Press.

Samphel, T. (2004). Virtual Tibet: The Media. In *Exile as Challenge: The Tibetan Diaspora*, (eds) D. Bernstorff and H. Von Welck, 167–85. New Delhi: Orient Longman.

Shakya, T. (1999). *The Dragon in the Land of Snows: A History of Modern Tibet Since 1947*. New York: Columbia University Press.

Smith, M. P. and L. E. Guarnizo (eds) (1998). *Transnationalism from Below: Comparative Urban and Community Research*. New Brunswick, NJ: Transaction Publishers.

Ström, A. K. (1995). The Quest for Grace: Identification and Cultural Continuity in the Tibetan Diaspora. *Oslo Occasional Papers in Social Anthropology* 24.

Tibetan Government-in-Exile (2004). *Integrated Development Plan III: 2004–2007*. Dharamsala: Planning Commission.

Van Hear, N. (2003). From Durable Solutions to Transnational Relations: Home and Exile among Refugee Diasporas. New Issues in Refugee Research. Working Paper No. 83, March 2003. Geneva: UNHCR Evaluation and Policy Analysis Unit.

Veronis, L. (2007). Strategic Spatial Essentialism: Latin Americans' Real and Imagined Geographies of Belonging in Toronto. *Social and Cultural Geography* 8 (3):455–73.

Yeh, E. T. (2007). Exile meets Homeland: Politics, Performance and Authenticity in the Tibetan Diaspora. *Environment and Planning D: Society and Space* 25 (4):648–67.

Yeh, E. T. and K. T. Lama (2006). Hip-hop Gangsta or Most Deserving Victims? Transnational Migrant Identities and the Paradox of Tibetan Racialization in the USA. *Environment and Planning A* 38 (5):809–29.

18

SRI LANKA'S DIASPORAS

Nicholas Van Hear

Sri Lanka's diaspora populations have formed as a result of a complex mix of migration since colonial times, gathering momentum after the civil war took off in the 1980s. A number of waves of emigration and dispersal may be identified which have contributed to the emergence of diaspora formations – plural because, as the ethnic divide between majority Sinhalese and minority Tamils has hardened, distinct transnational communities have emerged.

Since the conflict has become cast in terms of ethnicity, Sri Lanka's population figures are controversial. Sinhalese form the majority, at just under three-quarters of the total population. Just under a fifth are Tamils, comprising two groups: about two-thirds are long established and known as 'Sri Lankan Tamils', while those known as 'Indian Tamils' were brought by the British from the nineteenth century to work in plantations. About seven percent of the population are Muslims, many of whom are Tamil speakers and are regarded as an ethnic group in their own right.[1] People from all of these groups, but especially the Tamils, have become mobile internationally and their migration has led to the formation of a number of transnational communities. It is a moot point as to whether these constitute one 'Sri Lankan diaspora' or a number of ethnically based diasporas or transnational communities.[2]

This chapter traces the emergence of the transnational social formations hailing from and remaining connected to the island of Sri Lanka, formerly Ceylon. The first sections sketch the migratory streams that gave rise to the various transnational communities that constitute what may be seen in aggregate and in a loose sense as the 'Sri Lankan diaspora'. Later sections look at the activities and forms of engagement pursued by these different transnational social formations. Brief reflection on the unsettled relationship between the diaspora and the homeland is offered in the conclusion.

The formation of the 'Sri Lankan diaspora'

Early migration

During the colonial period there was some relocation of Tamils from the island then known as Ceylon, particularly to British Malaya, now Malaysia and Singapore (Gunatilleke 1995). Tamils worked as 'colonial auxiliaries' on the railways, in hospitals, in engineering and as clerical staff. Separately, there was migration of educated Sinhalese and Tamils to the colonial metropole,

Britain, to further their studies or pursue their professions, before and after independence in 1948. Migration of students, mainly to the UK, continued in the 1950s, 1960s and 1970s; many of these were Tamils who found their educational pathways increasingly blocked in Ceylon, largely as a result of discriminatory legislation and practices by the majority Sinhalese-dominated, post-independence government (de Silva 1998).

Labour migration

Migration of labour migrants to the oil-rich countries of the Middle East took off from the 1970s. By the later 1990s about 150,000 Sri Lankans went each year to work in the Middle East, as well as in south-east and east Asia; in 2008 more than 250,000 left to work abroad (Van Hear 2002; Department of Census and Statistics 2011). These were mainly Sinhalese from the rural south, although Tamils and Muslims also became labour migrants. Most of these labour migrants were female domestic workers (Gamburd 2000). Usually on contracts of two years, these migrants did not settle; but since many of them had several successive contracts, they formed part of a substantial presence in the Middle East and can arguably be considered as part of the Sri Lankan diaspora, or at least as a transnational community linked to the island. Just as labour migrants became a structural element in the labour markets and demographic make-up of destination countries like Saudi Arabia, Kuwait and the UAE, their absence from their Sri Lankan homes likewise became a structural part of many origin communities, consolidating the formation of transnational households and extended families.

Conflict-related migration

After the civil war between the Sri Lankan armed forces and the separatist Liberation Tigers of Tamil Eelam (LTTE) took off in 1983, a large outflow of refugees, mainly Tamils, took place (McDowell 1996; Fuglerud 1999; Van Hear 2002, 2006). While much of this movement was initially to Tamil Nadu in southern India, many Sri Lankan Tamils sought asylum further afield, adding to the prior dispersal of Sri Lankan migrants who left for the purposes of education or to take up professional positions abroad. Drawn from lower castes and classes of Tamil society than the earlier arrivals, many of these asylum seekers received some help from the established Tamils, initially at least. The UK was the principal destination until it introduced stricter immigration legislation. Thereafter asylum seekers made for more diverse destinations in Europe and particularly Canada. There was a smaller-scale but significant outflow of Sinhalese who fled in the wake of the Janatha Vimukthu Peramuna (JVP) uprisings in the early 1970s and late 1980s. In addition to these migrations motivated directly by conflict, some of the labour migration to the Gulf should be seen in the context of the conflict, since some of the Sinhalese, Muslims and Tamils living near or in the conflict areas were motivated to migrate to the Gulf as much by the search for security as by the need for household income; labour migration can be seen as the less well-off households' 'asylum option' in such settings.

Diaspora formation, migration strategies and the hierarchy of destinations

The outcome of these various forms of migration, and of subsequent 'secondary' migration in the form of family reunion and migration for marriage, was the formation of various transnational groupings. The Tamils were the largest of these formations and can be said to have consolidated into a diaspora. By the 1990s, there were some 110,000 Sri Lankan Tamil refugees in southern India, 200,000 Tamils in Europe, and 250,000 in North America, mainly Canada.

Perhaps a quarter of the Sri Lankan Tamil population of about 2.7 million was outside Sri Lanka (Venugopal 2006): not all of these were refugees, but the war was a significant factor in driving most abroad. The reach of this wider diaspora has become substantial. Statistics are not always consistent, but the most important destinations for Sri Lankan asylum seekers and refugees in Europe and North America appear to be the UK, Canada, Scandinavian countries, France, Germany and Switzerland (McDowell 1996; Van Hear 2006). These countries are therefore significant bases from which Tamil refugees can influence Sri Lanka economically and politically.

Thus a number of migration strategies have been used by Sri Lankans against the background of conflict since the early 1980s (Van Hear 2006): internal migration to safer parts of Sri Lanka, accentuating rural-urban migration; labour migration, mainly to oil-rich countries in the Middle East, but also to southeast Asia; seeking asylum, initially in India and later in Europe, North America and Australia; migration for educational or professional purposes; and marriage to a partner abroad in Europe, North America or Australasia and other forms of family reunion or formation.

Partly because the different migration strategies have required very different levels of outlay or investment, these strategies have divided broadly along class lines, or at least according to the scale of resources that a household could muster. Class was not the only, nor perhaps even the most important, dimension: migration strategies also varied along ethnic, gender, caste and other lines. But wealth and thereby class became an increasingly important factor from the 1990s when the cost of seeking asylum in the West escalated as asylum seekers increasingly had to resort to smugglers or 'agents' to move across international borders and to navigate the immigration system of Western states.

Migration for work in the Middle East and elsewhere required considerable outlays, but was within the reach of farming and labouring households with some resources: it was (and is) pursued by poorer (though not the poorest) rural and urban Sinhalese families and by poorer Muslim and Tamil households who had been displaced. In the 1980s, Tamil households displaced by the conflict were able to find refuge in south India with relatively modest outlays. That option diminished with the assassination of Rajiv Gandhi by the LTTE in 1991, after which India's tolerance of Tamil asylum seekers faded and far fewer were admitted. Meanwhile, asylum migration to other destinations, particularly to Europe, North America or Australia, became increasingly costly: with agents' fees and other costs at US$5,000 or more in the mid- to late 1990s, upwards of US$10,000 by 2000–2, and more than US$15,000 by 2010, this was perhaps 20 times the cost of labour migration and thus out of the reach of poorer households (Van Hear 2002, 2003). Asylum migration therefore became largely (though not exclusively) the preserve of well-to-do Tamils, who had the grounds, resources and networks to pursue it. Migration for marriage also often became costly, for the outlay that had to be found was likely to be high when the spouse-to-be had residence status abroad.[3] Migration for other forms of family reunion also tended to involve substantial costs. Likewise, migration for educational or professional advancement required large outlays and was also pursued by the relatively well-to-do.

International migration then has usually involved substantial household investment. Money needed for migration had to be raised from savings or from relatives. Resources accumulated for dowries might have to be invested in migration, meaning that marriage might have to be delayed well beyond the usual marrying age. Substantial numbers of households, especially those displaced or otherwise war-affected, had to resort to moneylenders, or to sell or pawn assets like land, houses, shops or jewellery. For those who had been displaced or otherwise affected by conflict, raising such resources could be especially difficult. Some Tamils who could ill afford it managed to scrape together enough to send one of their children abroad. Earlier Tamil arrivals sometimes helped some of the less wealthy to seek asylum, but as the 1990s progressed the costs of navigating the migration/asylum regime became prohibitive for the less well-off.

As the cost of migration to the West inflated, largely as a result of increasing restrictions on immigration imposed by Western countries, movement to such destinations since the early 1990s increasingly then became the preserve of those that could mobilise substantial resources: there was a hierarchy of destinations that could be reached according to the resources mobilised (Van Hear 2006). For the less well-off, labour migration might be an option, but even this required large outlays for low income households. In a way, labour migration could thus become poorer households' asylum migration, if the purpose of that migration is thought of as being broadly the security of the whole household, rather than more narrowly as a source of protection for an individual. For the poorest households, migration outside the country was rarely an option, since such households could not afford to send any members abroad.

Sri Lankan Tamils in the UK

Some of these dynamics are illustrated by the formation of the Sri Lankan Tamil community in the UK, reproduced with variations elsewhere in the diaspora. The following account draws on and modifies Valentine Daniel and Thangaraj (1995), who tracked the formation of the Tamil community in the UK up to the early 1990s. Their article forms a baseline from which we can construct a migration history of the Tamils in the UK. Findings from fieldwork by the author are used to bring the story up to date.

Following Valentine Daniel and Thangaraj, we can distinguish the following phases, each of which has helped to shape subsequent periods of migration:

Early phase

The first wave of Sri Lankans arrived around and after independence in 1948, a mix of Sinhalese and Tamils mainly from upper-class and upper-caste backgrounds and educated at elite schools in Ceylon. They came to study for professional degrees in law, medicine or engineering with the idea that they could pursue careers in the universities or civil service at home: most did not intend to stay in Britain, initially at least. But as the Sinhalese-dominated government introduced increasingly discriminatory measures against the Tamil minority, in particular making Sinhalese rather than English the official language and devaluing the Tamil language, many Tamils decided to stay and practise their professions in the UK.

Second phase

As discrimination against Tamils continued in the 1960s and 1970s, seen particularly in difficulties in securing places in universities and employment in the civil service at home, increasing numbers sought to go abroad, particularly to pursue their studies in Britain. The newer arrivals were more mixed in class and caste background than the first wave. Many supported themselves by working as night security guards or in petrol stations. Anticipation of further restrictive immigration legislation also stimulated this second wave of migration to Britain (Pirouet 2001). The exodus accelerated as relations between the two main ethnic groups, the Sinhalese majority and the Tamil minority, degenerated into rival nationalisms.

Third phase

The escalation of communal strife into civil war between government forces and the LTTE in the early 1980s brought a third wave of migration. Anti-terrorist legislation in Sri Lanka heavily affected Tamil youth, and many of these came initially to Britain as students, following the example of the earlier wave. When this channel was stifled they began formally to seek asylum. Many from the second wave of arrivals, who were knowledgeable about how to navigate the immigration system, helped the new arrivals. The earliest wave of elite migrants, now well established in British society, were discomforted by the increasing numbers of new lower-class and lower-caste arrivals with poor English and (to the more well-to-do earlier arrivals) unsophisticated life styles.

According to Valentine Daniel and Thangaraj (1995), the earlier arrivals in the first and second waves adhered to a status-driven vision of Tamil society, based on caste and class. Newcomers were expected to conform to this set-up, to move up the social ladder through education and above all to keep a low social profile so as to avoid tarnishing the image of Tamils in British society. The new arrivals in the third wave did not fit into this mode of getting on. Their education was seriously disrupted by the war and so social mobility through education was not an easy option. Moreover they had heavy financial responsibilities to their families: much of the resources of the household back home had been spent on getting them to the UK, and they had to earn and save to bring their parents, siblings and spouses out of war-torn Sri Lanka. Further they had to finance the dowries of their female kin since those back home in conflict areas had no resources to do so.

Tamils from the second wave of arrivals, who were mainly on student visas, but who worked night shifts in petrol stations and as security guards, introduced the newer arrivals to this kind of employment. The asylum seekers lived frugally in crowded accommodation and were able to save and even get onto the property ladder. Some were able to move up into management of petrol stations and mini markets; at least they learned the elements of retail trade. As time went on tensions between the second and third waves emerged as competition for employment and resentment over the greater prosperity of the new arrivals developed.

As Valentine Daniel and Thangaraj note (1995: 244), the attitude of the established Tamils to the poorer, later arrivals was somewhat ironic, since at home the fighters against the Sri Lankan and later the Indian army were drawn from among their ranks. It was these fighters that the established Tamils were supporting through their substantial financial contributions to the militant groups back home. Some harboured fantasies that they would play a role in the new nation state – Eelam – that they believed would emerge from this struggle. However the elite exiles had failed to realise that power at home had moved away from the old order which they felt part of to a new dispensation in which lower classes held sway. The new arrivals from such social strata, who were highly politicised, for their part saw the 'gerontocracy' as patronising and irrelevant.

Valentine Daniel and Thangaraj suggest that the arrivals who made it through working in petrol stations and retail stores mainly arrived before the mid 1980s. Thereafter things got much tighter as the UK pushed through more restrictive immigration legislation, including the introduction of visa restrictions on Tamils (1985) and the Carriers' Liability Act (1987), introduced largely as a result of increasing flows of Tamil asylum seekers without papers. Partly as a con-sequence, smugglers became increasingly prominent in moving people out of Sri Lanka: the cost of getting to the UK rose tenfold in as many years. For poorer arrivals in the later 1980s, it was a case of getting one member of the family out of Sri Lanka, at the cost of deep debt and/or the sale of property and other assets by the household back home.

Valentine Daniel and Thangaraj note a further change in the composition of asylum seekers in the early 1990s. In addition to those escaping the Sri Lankan army and the war were war-hardened and often disillusioned militants escaping the militant groups they had been part of as these groups engaged in internecine war. The LTTE emerged the winner from this intra-Tamil conflict, largely eliminating its opponents and rivals. Thereafter escape from the clutches of the LTTE – particularly recruitment – became a reason for escape as much as the violence of the war itself.

This is the point in the story which Valentine Daniel and Thangaraj reach. Further phases unfolded in the 1990s and early 2000s.

Fourth phase

The 1990s were marked by an acceleration of asylum migration, as more Tamils fled fighting and intolerable living conditions in northern and eastern Sri Lanka. There were peaks of flight in the early and mid-1990s associated with heavy fighting, reflected in peaks of asylum seeker arrivals in the UK. There was a further peak of asylum seeker arrivals in the UK, much greater than earlier ones, in the late 1990s. Many of those fleeing used the services of smugglers or 'agents'.

The socio-economic backgrounds of migrants in the later periods appear to have been more diverse than is suggested by Valentine Daniel and Thangaraj for earlier phases. Indeed their scheme is arguably too neat: professionals, students and asylum seekers all featured in the later phases. Later arrivals seem to feature a combination of Valentine Daniel and Thangaraj's types. However, as the 1990s wore on and smugglers' charges rose in response to ever greater restrictions on immigration by Western states, only those with substantial funds or connections could afford to undertake the journey. This would often mean that a household could send only one family member abroad to seek asylum. Thus the pattern outlined above – of migration to affluent countries by the relatively well-resourced – took hold.

The period of substantial migration of Tamil asylum seekers to the UK (and other Western states) may then be summarised as follows. In 1985–2003 there were around 50,000 asylum applications made by Sri Lankans to the UK, almost all of whom were Tamils (Home Office Statistical Bulletin, various years). During this period there appear to have been three peaks of asylum migration to the UK, which broadly correspond to upsurges in the fighting. The first was in the mid-1980s, when arrivals were of the order of 2,000 per year: this is the group referred to by Valentine Daniel and Thangaraj as 'phase 3' arrivals. The second peak occurred in the early 1990s when applications were of the order of 3–4,000 a year. A further peak occurred in 1999–2001, with applications at 5–6,000 a year (Home Office Statistical Bulletin various years).

The steep rise in applications from the late 1990s until about 2001 was shaped by a number of factors. First, fighting in Sri Lanka escalated in this period and with it intolerable living conditions and large-scale displacement. Second, the period saw the growth in the popularity of the UK as a destination as others grew less attractive, principally perhaps in terms of access to employment or business opportunities: this appears to have been the case for asylum seekers generally and not just Tamils.

Fifth phase

A ceasefire in late 2001 and early in 2002 between the government and the LTTE, coupled with ever greater restrictions on asylum seekers by the UK government, marked the end of this phase of substantial asylum migration. Though still high relative to earlier periods, the numbers of asylum seekers declined from 2001, a fall which accelerated after the ceasefire of early 2002, after which establishing a case for claiming asylum became increasingly difficult if not impossible. In 2002 applications dropped back to 4,000 and then to less than 1,000 in 2003 (Home Office Statistical Bulletin various years). For the first time in two decades, Tamils were no longer in the top ten of asylum seekers to the UK.

While asylum seeking has become increasingly difficult and expensive, other forms of migration have continued. Notably, family reunion accompanied each of the phases identified above, as spouses, fiancé(e)s and children joined the primary migrants. However this also became increasingly restricted. Migration for study continued to be important and Sri Lankan migration has diversified into other forms, such as those who have entered under the (now restricted) working holiday visa scheme: some of the latter would probably earlier have taken the asylum route.

Recent trends: regrouping and the end of the civil war

In recent years there has been a substantial inflow of Tamils to the UK from other European Union states (Lindley and Van Hear 2007). These are mainly people who have gained EU citizenship and have decided to move, but may also include failed asylum seekers trying their luck again in Britain. The scale of this secondary migration is unclear since new arrivals are recorded as EU nationals rather than as Tamils, but anecdotally it is significant. The aspiration for education in English is given as one reason for this secondary migration. Another is the easier conversion of professional qualifications in the UK than in some other EU states, because initial qualifications gained in the Sri Lankan educational system were based on the British model. Easier access to the labour market and business opportunities is another likely reason. This form of 'regrouping' gathered momentum and became one of the main ways in which the Tamil community was replenished from outside the UK. In the run-up to the defeat of the LTTE in May 2009 there was an increase in asylum applications to more than 1,000 a year, but this was nowhere near the level of the late 1990s and early 2000s. While most people displaced within Sri Lanka during the war have returned to or near their home areas, there has not been a significant return of Tamil refugees since the end of the war; nor at the time of writing does such a return of diasporans seem likely against the background of a triumphant and triumphalist government firmly in control, with the strong support of the majority Sinhalese population.

Transnational communities among the Sinhalese and Sri Lankan Muslims

Census and other population figures commonly do not disaggregate Tamils, Sinhalese and Muslims from the general category of 'Sri Lankan-born'. While there are approximations of the size of the large Tamil diaspora, it is difficult to estimate the size of the Sinhalese and Muslim populations outside Sri Lanka. Looking at UK census data, Siddhisena and White (1999) found that just under 6,500 people recorded in the 1951 census were born in what was then Ceylon. By 1971 the figure was just over 17,000, in 1981 it was 26,000 and in 1991 39,400. In 2001 nearly 50,000 Sri Lankan-born were living in London. We may guess that in the 1950s and 1960s Sinhalese were well represented among the small (relative to other South Asian populations) numbers of Sri Lankan-born living in the UK, while from the 1970s Tamils came to predominate. There are significant Sinhalese populations in Canada (especially Toronto), Australia and continental Europe (especially Italy). Some of these Sinhalese expatriates are active in homeland politics, supporting one or other of the mainstream Sinhalese-dominated political parties. There are small numbers of Sri Lankan Muslims abroad, but there appears to be sufficient critical mass in the UK to support a number of Sri Lankan Muslim organisations. As already mentioned, there are large numbers of Sinhalese and Muslim (as well as some Tamil) migrant workers in the Middle East and Southeast Asia, forming significant transnational communities of these ethnic groups.

Diaspora engagement

Having considered the formation of the 'Sri Lankan diaspora' – or Sri Lankan transnational communities – the chapter now turns to forms of transnational activities undertaken by them. As with other diasporas, activities and engagement by Sri Lankan diaspora groupings can be considered in three spheres:

- the sphere of the individual, the household and the extended family, which is largely private and personal;
- the more public sphere of the 'known community', by which is meant collectivities of people that know each other or know of each other;
- the largely public sphere of the 'imagined community' (Anderson 1983/91), which includes the political field.

The individual/household/extended family sphere

Engagement in the first sphere is likely to be the most sustained of the three. The most common, principal and most tangible form of engagement is sending money – remittances – to assist extended family members to survive and cope in conflict settings. The money sent may be used for everyday needs, housing, schooling, health care and sometimes to help people get out of zones of danger – this can involve paying an agent to organise migration abroad. Besides such transfers in cash and kind, diaspora members participate in life course events such as births, marriages and funerals either 'virtually' or in person. Such engagement may involve visits, such as those by second generation Tamils (as well as the so-called '1.5 generation' of those born in Sri Lanka but brought up abroad) who visited Jaffna for the first time during the 2002–4 ceasefire (Vimalarajah and Cheran 2010: 23; Brun and Van Hear 2012). However, often of necessity in conflict settings, online connections and telephony replace face-to-face physical connection. Circulation of money transnationally has been incorporated into migration in other ways than remittances. For example, to finance a son's migration abroad, which is often expensive if it involves an agent as we have seen, it has sometimes been the practice to use money accumulated for dowries set aside to marry off a household's daughters. Once established and earning abroad, the son's first obligation is to accumulate and pay back the money for those dowries – he has to attend to this before thinking of his own future (Fuglerud 1999).

The 'known community sphere'

Engagement in the '*known community sphere*' takes place in spaces where one lives or has lived (for example, in London or Jaffna or both) and includes involvement in residentially and ethnically based associations and clubs, schools, religious bodies, mutual aid and welfare organisations and community-based and civil society organisations. Home town and home village associations and in particular old school associations – or 'past pupil associations' (PPAs) – have been an important form of organisation and engagement, but their influence is perhaps declining as time passes and connections grow weaker and the cohorts or 'batches' of schoolmates are not reproduced. At the same time, engagement in these and other forms of associational life has expanded with the use of electronic media.

Transfers to wider collectivities than households and extended families can be considered here: examples include donations made in temples, churches or mosques for relief in the home country, for an orphanage or a clinic; the home town association or old school association that collects funds to rebuild a school, equip a hospital, or refurbish a library; collections by welfare organisations to provide relief for the victims of conflict; or, more darkly, the collections by supporters of insurgent groups for funds to buy weapons or otherwise support insurgency. These transfers, for more public or collective purposes, are somewhat different in nature from the more private remittances described above in the first, family sphere. In aggregate they are also probably smaller in scale than such private remittances. In conflict settings, however, the significance of such collective transfers goes beyond their immediate economic and material effects, since they can help repair the social fabric shredded by years of conflict, not least by helping to re-establish social linkages ruptured during war and rebuilding trust and confidence.

The 'imagined community'

In coining the notion 'the imagined community', Anderson referred to the nation to which one has an affinity without necessarily knowing its members personally.[4] The notion can be extended to other collectivities such as classes, co-religionists and co-ethnics, and arguably political movements. Engagement here includes membership of or involvement in political parties and movements, and support for insurgent or oppositional groups, such as the LTTE or JVP. It might involve lobbying politicians or other influential people in the host country and/or at home and engagement in political, social or cultural debate in cyberspace or the blogosphere, media which are highly developed and intensively deployed by Sri Lankan Tamils, Sinhalese and Muslims.

'Big P' politics is located in this sphere, but the political field (Bourdieu 1991) impinges on or encompasses all three spheres. What happens in the imagined community sphere influences what can happen in the 'known community' sphere and in the household – and vice versa. The political field extends over the community and imagined community spheres and at times reaches into the personal, family and household. Moreover, the political field shifts in its centre of gravity over time. The following section considers ways in which the political field has shifted among the Tamil diaspora in recent years.

Transnational Tamil politics since the end of the war

Since the end of the war in May 2009, the Tamil transnational political field has reconfigured, with various different interests emerging (Brun and Van Hear 2012). Following the defeat of the LTTE in Sri Lanka, a number of groupings could be identified in the Tamil diaspora, reflecting different strands of thinking and ideology, and manifested organisationally to different degrees. One such grouping was the LTTE 'old guard', the rump of the LTTE, which included the remnants of the organisation that got out before the end-game in Sri Lanka or who were already outside the country at the end of the war. Related to but distinct from this grouping was what might be called the 'LTTE legacy' or 'LTTE heritage'. Many of these were younger generation activists, who came to the fore during the large-scale mobilisations of 2009 and 2010 in most diaspora locations over the conduct of the final stages of the war and its aftermath. More liberal and democratic than the hard core rump, they promoted a more moderate nationalism: 'swapping bombs for Blackberrys', as a *Financial Times* feature put it, highlighting the newly mobilised 20- and 30-year-olds in the diaspora (Asokan 2009). Meanwhile, there has also been a modest resurgence outside the LTTE of more open discussion of the way forward after the war, with various fora emerging which reached out with varying success to some of the new younger activists and at times to some liberal Sinhalese and Muslims. At the same time, there was a harder opposition to the LTTE, principally the remnants of groups that had rivalled or splintered away from the LTTE in the 1980s and more recently. These were the main activist factions. The Tamil diaspora population at large varied in its orientation, from enthusiastic to passive or grudging support for one or other of these positions – or none of them.

Within this complex milieu, several significant institutional initiatives emerged from mid-2009, mainly from within the 'LTTE legacy' as the defeat of the LTTE sank in among the diaspora. First, the Global Tamil Forum (GTF) was set up as an umbrella grouping for national-level Tamil groupings, including the British Tamil Forum, the Canadian Tamil Congress and similar French, Australian, Norwegian and other national groupings. The GTF held a successful launch in February 2010 in the British parliament, attended by delegates from 15 countries with significant Tamil diaspora populations and addressed by high-profile British politicians. Second, a referendum which reasserted the need for an independent Tamil homeland was held in most major diaspora locations from mid-2009 to early 2010. In a process that monitors attested was well run, most of those who voted appeared to reaffirm the need for a separate state of Tamil Eelam. Third, there were moves towards the formation of a Transnational Government of Tamil Eelam (TGTE). The TGTE's founding documents drew heavily on scholarly discourse on transnationalism and diaspora (Advisory Committee of the TGTE 2010). The initiative was met with scepticism both among hardliners in the LTTE rump and among more liberal elements in the diaspora who saw it as an attempt to revive a defunct LTTE. In the event, a number of the LTTE rump stood and were elected as representatives. Elections were held in early May 2010, and the inaugural meeting of the TGTE constituent assembly was held in transnational session in Philadelphia, London, Geneva and other diaspora constituencies in mid-May 2010 (Office of the Interim Chief Executive of the TGTE 2010).

Conclusion

While these initiatives had varying levels of support among different fractions of the Tamil diaspora, they had very little purchase among the Tamils in Sri Lanka whose cause they claimed to espouse, underlining the apparently large disconnection between the Tamil diaspora and those back home whose main concern after the end of the war was to return to some kind of normal life. This disparity of view – sometimes dubbed as 'long distance nationalism' (Anderson 1998) – is not unusual among diasporas. Like many south Asian and other diasporas, the 'Sri Lankan diaspora' – or rather the various transnational communities which constitute it – has had a chequered relationship with the homeland, Sri Lanka. At times the Tamil diaspora has played a key role in supported insurgents fighting for a homeland – Tamil Eelam – within the island of Sri Lanka. Though less numerous, Sinhalese transnational communities have also had considerable influence abroad, largely in support of the government. Members of both communities have also worked for peace and reconciliation, however.

In the wake of the defeat of the LTTE in May 2009, much of the Tamil diaspora remained committed to the idea of a separate homeland. In holding this position, they were largely out of step with the Tamils in Sri Lanka, who, while wanting rights and justice, no longer appeared to aspire to a separate Tamil Eelam. In contrast, with some notable exceptions, much of the Sinhalese diaspora was in tune with the triumphalism of the current government and the Sinhalese population at large. Divisions at home and abroad thus reflected and reproduced each other, in a cycle that is seemingly very difficult to break.

Notes

1   These proportions are extrapolated from the last complete national census in 1981 and are therefore just approximations: Department of Census and Statistics: www.statistics.gov.lk. A further census is planned which might provide more definitive population figures.
2   See Van Hear (1998: 5–6) for a discussion of the distinction between 'diaspora' and 'transnational communities'; see also Safran (1991) and Cohen (2008) for definition of diaspora, and Brubaker (2005) for a critique of the concept.
3   On migration, transnational marriage and changes to the dowry system, see Fuglerud 1999 and 2002.
4   A nation 'is imagined because the members of even the smallest nation will never know most of their fellow-members, meet them, or even hear of them, yet in the minds of each lives the image of their communion' (Anderson 1983: 15).

References

Advisory Committee of the TGTE (2010). *Formation of a Transnational Government of Tamil Eelam: final report based on the study by the Advisory Committee.*
Anderson, B. (1983/91). *Imagined communities: reflections on the origin and spread of nationalism* (revised and extended edition), London: Verso.
—— (1998). 'Long distance nationalism', in B. Anderson (ed.) *The Spectre of Comparisons: Nationalism, Southeast Asia and the World*, London: Verso, pp. 58–74.
Asokan, S. (2009). 'War by other means'. *Financial Times Weekend Magazine, Financial Times*, October 17/18: 30–5.
Bourdieu, P. (1991). *Language and Symbolic Power*. Edited and introduced by R. Thompson. Cambridge: Polity.
Brubaker, R. (2005). 'The "Diaspora" Diaspora', *Ethnic and Racial Studies*, 28: 1–19.
Brun, C. and N. Van Hear (2012). 'Between the local and the diasporic: the shifting centre of gravity in war-torn Sri Lanka's transnational politics', *Contemporary South Asia*, 20 (1): 65–71.
Cohen, R. (2008, 2nd edn). *Global Diasporas: an introduction*, London: Routledge.
Department of Census and Statistics, National Centre for Migration Statistics (2011). *Departures for Foreign Employment 1986–2008*, Colombo: Department of Census and Statistics, www.statistics.gov.lk/NCMS/RepNTab/Tables/SLBFE/Tab1.pdf (accessed 27 July 2011).
de Silva, K. M. (1998). *Reaping the Whirlwind: ethnic conflict, ethnic politics in Sri Lanka*, New Delhi: Penguin.
Fuglerud, Ø. (1999). *Life on the Outside: the Tamil diaspora and long distance nationalism*, London: Pluto Press.
—— (2002). *Marriage and Migration: making place in the Sri Lankan conflict*, Oslo: Centre for Development and the Environment, University of Oslo.
Gamburd, M. (2000). *The Kitchen Spoon's Handle: transnationalism and Sri Lanka's migrant housemaids*, Ithaca, NY: Cornell University Press.
Gunatilleke, G. (1995). 'The economic, demographic, socio-cultural and political setting for emigration from Sri Lanka', *International Migration*, 33 (3–4): 667–97.
Home Office (various years). *Home Office Statistical Bulletin*, London: Research and Statistics Department, Home Office.
Lindley, A. and N. Van Hear (2007). *New Europeans on the Move: a preliminary review of the onward migration of refugees within the European Union*, COMPAS Working Paper 57, Oxford: COMPAS.
McDowell, C. (1996). *A Tamil Asylum Diaspora: Sri Lankan migration, settlement and politics in Switzerland*, Providence and Oxford: Berghahn.
Office of the Interim Chief Executive of the TGTE (2010). *The Inaugural Sessions of the Transnational Government of Tamil Eelam*. Press release, 20 May, www.tamilnet.com (accessed 20 May 2010).
Pirouet, L. (2001). *Whatever Happened to Asylum in Britain? A tale of two walls*, New York, Oxford: Berghahn.
Safran, W. (1991). 'Diasporas in modern societies: myths of homeland and return', *Diaspora: a journal of transnational studies*, 1 (1): 83–99.
Siddhisena, K. A. P. and P. White (1999). 'The Sri Lankan population of Great Britain: migration and settlement', *Asian and Pacific Migration Journal*, 8 (4): 511–36.
Valentine Daniel, E. and Y. Thangaraj (1995). 'Forms, formations, and transformations of the Tamil refugee', in *Mistrusting Refugees*, eds E. Valentine Daniel and J. C. Knudsen, Berkeley, Los Angeles and London: University of California Press, pp. 225–56.
Van Hear, N. (1998): *New Diasporas*, London: Taylor and Francis.

— (2002). 'Sustaining societies under strain: remittances as a form of transnational exchange in Sri Lanka and Ghana', in *New Approaches to Migration: transnational communities and the transformation of home*, N. Al-Ali and K. Koser, London and New York: Routledge, pp. 202–23.

— (2003). 'From "durable solutions" to "transnational relations": home and exile among refugee diasporas', *UNHCR Evaluation and Policy Analysis Unit, New Issues in Refugee Research, Working Paper 83*, Geneva: UNHCR.

— (2006). '"I went as far as my money would take me": conflict, forced migration and class', in *Forced Migration and Global Processes: a view from forced migration studies*, eds F. Crepeau, D. Nakache and M. Collyer, Lanham, MA: Lexington/Rowman and Littlefield, pp. 125–58.

Venugopal, R. (2006). 'The global dimensions of conflict in Sri Lanka', in *Globalization, Violent Conflict and Self-Determination*, eds V. FitzGerald, F. Stewart and R. Venugopal, Basingstoke: Palgrave.

Vimalarajah, L. and R. Cheran (2010). 'Empowering diasporas: the dynamics of post-war transnational Tamil politics', *Berghof Occasional Paper 31*, Berlin: Berghof Conflict Research, Berghof Peace Support.

PART V

Diaspora, globalisation and culture

19

BRAIN DRAIN, EXCHANGE AND GAIN

'Hi-skill' migrants and the developed economies

David Washbrook

I

A global phenomenon of the second half of the twentieth century has been the flow of highly skilled labour from the developing to the developed economies, especially to the United States (US) and Europe. Within this flow, migrants from South Asia (especially India) have figured particularly large. The case of the US, for which data are better and more refined, makes the point most clearly. The Luce-Celler Act of 1946 first opened the US to significant immigration from India but limited numbers to 2,000 per year. The Immigration and Nationality Act of 1965 widened the quota to 20,000 but set rigorous standards of required education and skill-training. Subsequently, the size of the quota has expanded several times and been supplemented by the H1–B visa, enabling short-term immigration for specific work purposes, but with opportunities to convert to permanent residence (Lowe: 1996). In 2000, the number of H1–B visas available to foreign workers was raised to 195,000, of which Indians took over 60,000. Also, opportunities for higher education (with parallel possibilities of settlement) increased rapidly over the period. In 2006, 76,000 students from India were studying at US universities (US, DHS: 2010).

In response, the number of 'Asian-Indians' settled in the US has grown exponentially over the last four decades. When the category was first introduced to the US Census in 1980, the number recorded was 322,000. By 1990, it had risen to 815,000 and, by 2000, to 1.7 million. In 2010, there were 2.8 million 'Asian-Indians' in the US, representing a decadal increase of nearly 70 per cent. Between 2000 and 2006 alone, 421,000 new immigrants from India were admitted to the country (US, CB: 2010). Moreover, skill-restrictions on entry have meant that the 'community' is marked by extraordinarily positive socio-economic indicators. In 2000, 67 per cent of adult 'Asian-Indians' possessed at least a Bachelor's degree against a US national average of 28 per cent. Some 40 per cent also possessed a Master's or higher degree against a national average of 8 per cent. A total of 57.7 per cent of employed 'Asian-Indians' worked in managerial or professional jobs. Median income for men of US $51,000 and, for women, of $35,000 was the highest for any ethnic group in the US, including 'White-Caucasians' (US, CB: 2009).

The 'Asian-Indian' contribution to the US's recent economic and social development has been very considerable. At least 35,000 medical doctors with Indian primary qualifications now work in US health systems. In 2002, 'Asian-Indians' owned 223,000 registered companies with combined revenues in excess of US $88 billion. At least 200,000 members of the community

251

were millionaires (US, CB: 2009). In many ways, the influx of highly skilled labour from South Asia has brought new talent to, and sharpened scientific and entrepreneurial energies in, the US itself – as well as compensating for the deficiencies of a domestic educational system which has failed to produce sufficient skills to sustain economic growth and public services.

Nor has the US experience been unique, although statistical problems make it harder to quantify in other cases, where distinctions between high- and low-skilled immigrants are less clear. In the UK, for example, large-scale immigration dates back to the 1950s and was initially dominated by unskilled workers, obscuring the specific role played by smaller groups of 'professionals'. The total population of Indian origin in the UK in 2009 was 1.4 million with an additional 990,000 from Pakistan and 384,000 from Bangladesh (UK, ONS: 2009). Nonetheless, with regard to 'hi-skills', in 2010 about 25,000 (or 30 per cent) of the medical doctors working in the UK National Health Service had Indian primary qualifications; in 1999, one-third of the workers in the UK IT industry were of Indian origin; in 2010, there were about 40,000 Indian 'foreign-students' studying at UK universities (GMC: 2010; UKCISA: 2011).

Migration to non-Anglophone Europe has doubtless been much smaller. However, Germany currently possesses a population of Indian origin approaching 45,000, which has doubled in size since 2001 as a result of 20,000 special visas created to support the IT industry (Goel: 2007). Moreover, in recent years, migration to some of the more developed economies around the Indian Ocean has grown prodigiously – or revived again after decades of post-colonial hiatus. An estimated 20,000 medical doctors of Indian origin now practise in the states of the Persian Gulf, along with many thousand engineers, scientists and managerial professionals. South-east Asia has once again become a target area for the export of Indian skills (Khadria: 2006). In Australia in June 2011, 343,000 people present had been born in India, including 51,200 registered at Australian universities (AG, DIC: 2012). Overall, the Indian diaspora around the world is estimated at 20–25 million and, of these, at least 20–25 per cent (or 4–6 million) probably belong in the 'hi-skills' category.

Since the onset of the 2007–9 global financial crisis and economic recession, the issue of 'hi-skill' immigration has become contentious in most of the developed economies, and some countries (most notably, the UK) appear bent on 'capping' it almost regardless of economic and social consequences. Here, race and nationality now threaten to trump class where, at least for the last half-century, exceptions had been made for the educated and 'desirable' to overcome barriers increasingly placed against the ill-educated and 'undesirable'. In many ways, the situation appears to be turning back to an earlier age when, for example, the USA posted blanket bans on immigrants from specific parts of the world, regardless of their skills.

Yet, in the developing economies and, particularly, India, the issues raised by 'hi-skill' *emigration* have always been somewhat different. Here, the questions turn on the profit/loss account of exporting so much high-quality human capital and paying for educational services which support not the advance of a deeply impoverished India, but that of the rich, already-developed world. Also, at least before the epoch of self-avowed 'globalization' beginning in the 1990s, it is not immediately obvious why India should have 'over-developed' its educational system beyond its own needs nor why large numbers of people should have invested their time and capital in acquiring skills which they would then have to wander the world in order to use.

II

To an extent, India's current situation reflects a long-term past spent as a crucial part of Britain's imperial system. Always seen by its colonizers as possessing a more 'civilized' society than other parts of the 'non-white' empire, it was developed from the mid-nineteenth century to supply wider ancillary services not only for its own support but for other parts of the empire as well (Metcalf: 2008). Indian universities were first established in 1857 and, even before, law, medical and engineering schools to whose mysteries Indians were progressively admitted. Their products were encouraged to seek service in government and professional organizations which reached out beyond India's shores. Some came to the UK for higher training, and a few stayed on – or later returned – to practise their skills. Muhammad Ali Jinnah, the founding father of Pakistan, for example, practised law in London in the 1920s and Lord S.P. Sinha even served as a UK government minister in 1919. More broadly, many others followed the flag to parts of the empire where white men were few – either because they were very expensive or because they could not survive in the tropics. In 1931, half of all the registered doctors in Burma had medical degrees from the Indian mainland (Taylor: 1987) and, in 1893, Mohandas Karamchand Gandhi went, via London, to Natal to join many other Indians practising at its bar. Indeed, outside British India – where an embattled colonial government made an increasing fetish of British qualifications for senior positions – the opportunities for Indian-trained doctors, lawyers and engineers were often better than inside.

However, the total resources that British rule was ever prepared to commit to Indian higher education, especially in science and technology, were always very limited and the real explosion in 'modern' learning waited on national independence and the era of Jawaharlal Nehru. India's new 'planned' economy sought a rapid transformation out of poverty and gave pride of place among its weapons to higher education, science and technology, which could support industrialization and mark out the passage to modernization. The number of universities in India grew from 32 in 1950–1 to 56 in 1960–1 and 102 in 1970–1, while that of affiliated colleges grew from 727 to 3,706. Especially significant was the creation of centres of excellence, designed to be of 'first-world' standard and to attract the best and brightest in the land. In particular, the seven Indian Institutes of Technology (IITs) established by 1961 symbolized Nehru's vision of the future. Public spending on higher education grew accordingly, rising from 9.3 per cent of the total education budget in 1951–61 to 11.8 per cent in 1961–71 (Gupta and Gupta: 2012).

Yet, even by the early 1960s, Nehru's vision was starting to be questioned as India faced a recurrence of famine and GDP growth began to slump towards the notorious 'Hindu rate' of 3.5 per cent. Nehruvian planning fell under heavy criticism for its 'top-down' approach to development, which neglected issues such as agriculture and employment and promoted higher education at the expense of primary schooling. As late as 1991, scarcely half of the Indian population could read or write. Moreover, what developmental achievements there were in the period, most notably the Green Revolution, tended to owe more to the importation of 'foreign' than the newly released creativity of 'Indian' science and technology.

Nonetheless, public spending on higher education continued to grow and to absorb ever more of the overall education budget. In 1971–81, it reached 14.0 per cent of the total and, in 1981–91, 14.2 per cent. The number of universities leapt from 102 in 1971 to 190 by 1991, and of affiliated colleges from 3,706 to 7,346. If ever there was testimony that the Nehruvian approach to planning was elitist not only in conception, but also in result, the history of Indian education provides it (Gupta and Gupta: 2012).

However, the palpable 'over-development' of India's higher education sector in these years left an obvious question: What, exactly, was its rapidly proliferating graduate cadre to do in a stagnant economy and a formally 'socialist' state, which deprecated private enterprise and individual achievement? Apart from continuing to train the next generation of graduates in equally inapplicable skills, the prospects were only for employment in India's vast government bureaucracy or heavily protected industries, where Research and Development (R&D) were painfully neglected and scientific and technological expertise sacrificed to pen-pushing and paper management. Moreover, such employment while offering (not-to-be-undervalued) security also brought remuneration far below the entitlement of equivalent skills in most other economies of the non-communist world.

Hardly surprisingly, large numbers of 'Nehru's children' chose to emigrate, especially to the developed economies where the rapid pace of post-war economic growth was creating new demands for 'hi-skills'. Just how many 'hi-skilled' Indians left the country between the 1960s and 1980s, after enjoying publicly funded tertiary education, remains a mystery since no systematic effort was ever made by the Indian state to count them. Indeed, not only did it not count them but successive Indian governments resisted all popular demands either to ban their emigration or to force them to repay the costs of their education. Rather, vehement protests were launched whenever immigration restrictions in the developed economies (such as the UK Immigration Act of 1962), threatened to delay their departure.

Nonetheless, as processes of democratization increasingly overtook the Indian political system after Nehru's death in 1964, voices of concern came to be raised and, in the absence of firm data, to promote conjectures that were seriously alarming. Popular estimates in the 1970s and 1980s put the proportion of the graduates of the prestigious IITs, and other leading scientific and medical establishments, who emigrated shortly after graduation at 65–70 per cent. If the capital costs of their education and lost skills over a career were calculated, the numbers suggested a 'brain drain' scarcely less significant than the infamous 'drain of wealth' by which Britain was held to have profited at India's expense during the colonial era – but, this time, freely given (Oommen: 1989).

Moreover, the arguments put up by defenders of the system at the time appeared very lame. Claims that India would benefit from the more advanced skills of 'returnee' migrants were belied by the very small numbers, in this era, who ever did return. Also, hopes that the remittances and investments of 'Non-Resident Indians' (NRIs) located abroad would revitalize the economy proved much exaggerated. Remittances certainly grew rapidly from the 1970s and came to play an important role in balancing India's often problematic current account. However, the bulk of them came from the Persian Gulf economies where the overwhelming majority of migrants were low-skilled. Equally, special NRI deposit schemes, introduced in 1970, did attract capital inflows from the US and Europe, which were strategically crucial at times of international financial crisis. But, in normal times, they were very expensive and, after 20 years, had still only reached US $12 billion. A popular perception of the times, especially in 'leftist' Indian political circles, was that India's top-heavy public education system, coupled with freedom of emigration, was leading the country to 'underdevelop' itself (Oommen: 1989).

Subsequently, more detailed – although still partial and patchy – research has put the issue into somewhat clearer perspective. For example, one study of the graduates of IIT Bombay between 1973 and 1977 found that, within a decade, 31 per cent of them had migrated abroad – although, for those graduating in the top 25 per cent of their class, the proportion rose to 43 per cent (Sukhatme and Mahadevan: 1988). Another 1989 study of IIT Madras found that 26 per cent of those graduating between 1964 and 1987 had left the country (Ananth: 1989). Another 1976 estimate of the number of medical doctors emigrating between 1971 and 1974 equated to about 30 per cent of those newly graduated in the period (Kalra: 1992).

The proportions are not quite on the scale of popular imaginings, and the total numbers involved in these most elite of elite institutions were very small – where, for example, the combined 1973–7 cohorts at IIT Bombay represented just 1,262 students. Nonetheless, for a country where, at the time, over 35 per cent of the population lived below the official international poverty line, the loss was scarcely insignificant, not least because there was a close positive correlation between the degree of qualification and skill and the propensity to migrate:

the 'best' left first. India's support of economic growth and public services in the already developed economies was by no means without cost to itself.

III

Since the turn of the 1990s, the volume of skilled labour outflow from India has increased rapidly – as witnessed by the phenomenal growth of the 'Asian–Indian' community in the US. However, circumstances have also changed, with the onset of an era of vastly expanded 'globalization', and neither the meaning of the numbers nor their impact on India's own development can be judged entirely the same. In the first place, higher education is much less supported by public expenditure and sustained at the expense of distortions to public investment in the primary and secondary sectors. The proportion of the total education budget devoted to higher education peaked in 1989–90 and has since been falling, reaching just 12.8 per cent in 1991–2001. In real terms, per student expenditure on higher and technical education dropped by 19 per cent between 1993/4 and 1998/9 alone. By contrast, per capita expenditure on primary and secondary education has been rising, including a 35 per cent increase on the primary and 17 per cent on the secondary sectors across the same five-year period (Gupta and Gupta: 2012).

Admittedly, in 2006 under pressure from lower-caste/class aspirants, the Congress Party-led United Progressive Alliance (UPA) government promised an enormous expansion in public sector higher education, including a doubling in the number and tripling in the size of the IITs. However, it is unclear where not merely the funding, but the expert teaching personnel to meet this electoral pledge is going to come from and, thus far, its main achievement may only have been to increase the salaries of existing staff.

Nonetheless, the number of universities and colleges in India, as well as the proportion of the population engaged in higher education, has risen faster than ever before. By 2004–5, there were 343 universities and 17,625 colleges. The scale of enrolments increased during this period from 4.3 to 10.5 million. In effect, the gap between aspiration and reality was covered by the rapid growth of a privately funded tertiary sector, especially in medicine and engineering, where the expansion of opportunities has been stunning. In 2005, India graduated over 200,000 new first-degree engineers and, in 2007, 30,000 new medical doctors (Gupta and Gupta: 2012). Private funding has also driven the expansion of Indians seeking to study abroad, increasingly even for first degrees. As ever, precise numbers are missing. However, by repute, 150,000 new students travel overseas every year and the total population of Indian students abroad is in the region of 450,000. The face of higher education in India has radically changed over the last 20 years.

As, also, has the economic context in which higher educational studies now take place. The era of globalization, inaugurated by the fall of the Soviet Union in 1991 and primed by the revolution in information technology (IT), has given rise also to an era of economic 'liberalization' affecting India itself. Protectionist barriers to transnational trade and capital flows have fallen, and new opportunities have opened out to labour, at least where it possesses 'hi-skills'. India has profited greatly as a result: its GDP growth rates rising to 8–9 per cent and a 'trickle down' of the resulting wealth at least beginning to alleviate its poverty rate, which by some calculations has fallen to 23 per cent. In particular, the pool of 'over-developed' higher educational skills, which once was its curse, has now turned into its virtue. Utilizing this pool, an IT industry of world-significance has been built within India: in 2010, employing upwards of 2.5 million people and earning US $9 billion in export revenues alone (NASSCOM: 2011). Other 'hi-tech' industries, in pharmaceuticals, bio-technology, chemistry, medicine and engineering, have followed suit, attracting both export contracts and inflows of foreign capital. In many ways, the outflow of

Indian 'human capital' now lubricates – or is part of – an economic system which brings tangible rewards of trade and investment to India itself.

And, equally and third, this system is now starting to bring home Indians themselves with new capital and even more refined 'hi-skills'. In the last two decades, the long-extended promise of the 'returnee' has finally begun to be fulfilled. Most famously, perhaps, two of the most successful, multi-billion-dollar companies thrown up by the IT revolution – Infosys and WIPRO – were established by 'returnee' NRIs. Also, the new global medical chains – represented, for example, by Apollo Hospitals – which are creating a large 'medical tourist' industry in India draw heavily on NRI doctors. More broadly, as India's R&D capacities develop (not least, through the transfer of work by foreign companies), increasing numbers of foreign-trained Indians are electing to come back. By recent estimates, 15 per cent of the research-grade hirings by the pharmaceutical giant, Dr Reddy's Laboratories, in the last five years have consisted of sometime NRIs; and, for foreign-owned companies such as GE-Capital, the proportions are even higher, approaching 50 per cent (Venkatraghavan: 2012). A visa to study and/or work abroad no longer represents a one-way ticket.

In effect, India's old problem of 'brain drain' has been submerged beneath processes of 'brain exchange' and even 'brain gain' and is no longer as potentially costly as once it was. Yet, if one set of problems has been resolved, it cannot be said that the shapes either of India's new 'hi-tech' economy nor its expanding tertiary education sector do not give cause for other concerns. The product of globalization, the success of the 'hi-tech' economy now depends on the continuation of that process: especially, on the openness of the markets for 'services' and labour in the developed economies. The effects of a sudden closing down of these markets would be catastrophic. However, since the 2007–9 global financial crisis and economic recession, that is precisely what has started to happen. There are growing signs in the global economy of a return to protectionism and, especially in Europe, of a clampdown on immigration. The rewards of India's increased global integration have also brought risks of increased vulnerability to global 'contagions'.

Also, in India itself, political pressures have emerged at two points. On the one hand, while the profits of the 'hi-skill' economy may be rising, they are necessarily available to only a small section of society. India's urban middle classes may have 'never-had-it-so-good', with salary levels increasing by 15 per cent a year for over a decade, but elsewhere rewards have been much more modest. The rural:urban ratio of value-added to labour, for example, has widened from 1:3.8 to 1:5.3 over the last 20 years, and the proportion of the population qualifying as 'urban' remains below 30 per cent (MOSPI: 2005). In effect, India's pattern of economic growth, led by 'hi-tech' industries, is producing deepening inequalities between town and countryside, as also between 'forward' and 'backward' regions and states. This is starting to fuel heightened political tensions manifested not only in revolutionary 'Maoist' movements, aimed at the violent overthrow of capitalism, but more significantly in increasing democratic protest at the corruptions of wealth and the hidden costs of modern, consumer society. The lop-sided social consequences of India's 'hi-skill' growth trajectory could yet find it out.

And this is especially so if its efforts at improving 'social inclusion' fail, as they very well might. The success of the 'hi-skill' economy has promoted a huge increase in the demand for higher education, especially among lower caste/class sections of the population who were excluded previously. As noted earlier, since 2006, the UPA government has promised to meet this demand by a no less huge increase in the availability of publicly funded higher education. Yet its position rests on a contradiction. While meeting its promise would entail a massive increase in public authority over, and expenditure on, education, the conditions of 'neo-liberalism' promoting economic growth in the first place are based on a reduction, precisely, in the scale of that authority and expenditure. Both higher education and the 'hi-skill' economy have been driven in recent years by 'privatization' – which would be put at risk by a reassertion of the public domain, but which also threatens to continue the exclusion of the lower castes/classes on grounds of cost. The contradiction is very much reflected in other aspects of recent education policy, where the promise to expand publicly funded higher education has its counterpart in an agreement, for the first time, to license foreign universities operating on Indian soil and charging high, private fees to the privileged few who can afford them.

Moreover, there is also the issue of whether, even if the publicly funded tertiary sector can be expanded rapidly, the quality of the resulting education can be maintained – where recent evidence is pessimistic. For example, a Nasscom study has found that two-thirds of those qualifying as graduate engineers in 2005–7 did not have adequate skills even to enter the IT industry (NASSCOM: 2010). Both economic and institutional change over the last 20 years may have solved the conundrum of the 'brain drain'. However, they have done so only at the expense of making higher education an even more complex and controversial social issue, but one on which India's future increasingly depends.

IV

Yet India's history of 'hi-skills' emigration is only very partially understood in terms of economic incentives and rationalities, and may be quite misunderstood if read, teleologically, in terms of the successes – thus far – of the twenty-first century. Ironically, it was a condition for the economic growth of the last 20 years that a pool of under-utilized and cheap 'hi-skill' labour should exist in India, waiting for post-1990s globalization and the IT revolution to draw on its potential. But, if it were under-utilized and cheap prior to the 1990s, why should it have been there in the first place: in particular, why should several million people have devoted long, painful years to studies which promised them very limited economic rewards – except for the few who could 'escape' to foreign countries?

Prior to present times, higher education and wealth never correlated very easily. From the colonial era, and even before, India's wealthiest classes belonged to merchant or banking communities, or else to those of warriors-turned-landlords, who were inclined to shun higher learning whether of the traditional or the neo-Western kind. Conversely, the 'learned' classes no less frequently shunned mercantile pursuits and commerce – a posture brilliantly satirized in Satyajit Ray's 1960s film, 'The Middleman'. This is not to say, of course, that the 'learned' classes were poor: their incomes always tended to distinguish them from the peasant and labouring 'masses'. However, they did not do what they did necessarily to maximize wealth and, for every rich lawyer or doctor, there were thousands of petty clerks or teachers living on the proverbial pittance (Sarkar: 2002).

Rather, the issue turned on questions of status. From pre-colonial times down almost to the present, higher education was dominated by upper caste groups – Brahmins in South India and the Brahmin-Baidya-Kayasth complex in the North – who traditionally lived by the pen and, certainly, distanced themselves from manual labour. Other essays in this volume have explored the worlds of early modern 'scribes', their practices and long established pathways of internal migration. The Western-educated of the colonial epoch, and the 'hi-skilled' workers and migrants of the immediate post-colonial decades, tended to come from much the same caste backgrounds. Indeed, the continuities with the past have led many authors to surmise an especially facile transition between 'tradition' and 'modernity': where, for example, mathematical practices acquired for the purposes of astrology would provide a basis for the mathematics of science or even, as seen by Amartya Sen, the discipline of learning Sanskrit would support the discipline of 'learning' IT (Sen: 2006).

Yet, while the fact of genealogical continuity cannot be disputed, the issue of meaningful 'facilitation' between past and present may be more difficult. Brahmanic traditions of learning were very closely related to religion and, even in pre-colonial times, the shift to scribal roles in 'secular' forms of administration could give rise to tensions. These problems became even worse where 'Yavana' (foreign) forms of learning were involved and, no less, 'polluting' physical contact with Yavanas themselves, be they Muslim rulers or the colonial British. The question of 'pollution' is raised again by the nature of the activities implied by modern forms of science and technology. Max Weber once famously doubted that Brahmins would ever be strongly represented in fields such as medicine or engineering, which deeply violated traditional 'purity' norms (Washbrook: 2010). Also, there were long-standing interdictions against travelling outside Bharat (India) and crossing the 'Kala Pani' (black water), which provoked furious controversies in the mid-nineteenth century – when upper-caste Indians first began to travel to Britain for higher education.

From this vantage point, it might be held that the only upper castes (and Brahmins in particular) capable of acquiring expertise in 'Western' science and technology and freely travelling overseas would be those who also became thoroughly deracinated and were in open revolt against their cultural pasts. However, the paradox then only becomes the greater because, in fact, it has been the most upper-caste, 'hi-skilled' immigrant community of all – that in the US – which has most strongly promoted the veneration of Hindu neo-tradition represented by Hindu nationalism (Prashad: 2001). Indeed, in India too, the last 20 years have been marked by a major revival of Hinduism, precisely among the 'hi-tech' cognoscenti of the urban middle classes.

The way in which these paradoxes unravel is no doubt very different between the many different communities whose histories are represented in India's 'hi-skilled' diaspora. Yet some general insights may be gleaned by looking more closely at one, whose experience particularly exemplifies the issues. As Fuller and Narasimhan have recently argued, Tamil Brahmins today stand out as the vanguard both of 'hi-tech' learning and of transnational migration in India. While representing only 3 per cent of the population of Tamil Nadu state, they are widely taken to have pioneered the IT and other 'science-based' industries, whose centres lie in the South, and to have led the recent exodus to the US. Yet, until the middle of the nineteenth century, they were among the most 'traditional' of all Brahmin communities in India (Fuller and Narasimhan: 2010). Living mainly off their landed endowments in the agriculturally rich Kaveri delta, they had largely eschewed the earlier shift to 'secular' scribal administration – whether for local rulers or the British – and continued to devote themselves principally to religion and the service of the gods. They had also put up fierce resistance to the encroachments of Western learning and culture, leading major public campaigns against missionary Christianity (Pandian: 2007).

However, when, from the later nineteenth century, they began to adopt Western education, the effects were dramatic. Within two generations, their members had come to dominate the local universities, government employment and the professions – where, for example, 80 per cent of the graduates of Madras University in 1920 were Tamil Brahmins. At the same time, they also began to move into the new science-based employments of engineering and medicine – in spite of interdictions against 'pollution' – and, by the 1940s and 1950s, they had gravitated into the first science-based industries – in spite of the status implications of 'commerce'. In terms of migration, their initial move from the Kaveri countryside to the main urban centres of South India was followed by a shift to the national capital of Delhi, after independence, where legendarily they filled a disproportionate share of positions in the new Secretariats and national Institutes – and thence, from the 1960s, towards the US. Fuller and Narasimhan see Tamil Brahmins as a veritable paradigm of the hi-skilled, transnational migrant community (Fuller and Narasimhan: 2010).

Yet their history and trajectory from the Kaveri delta in the mid-nineteenth century was anything but obvious or clearly facilitated by their pasts. Rather, when historically examined, it can be seen to have involved more 'push' than 'pull' factors, and also to have reflected subtle transformations in culture. The initial move out of the delta in the later nineteenth century, for example, was precipitated by agricultural decline which began with the opening out of the Burma 'ricebowl' and culminated in the Great Depression of the 1930s. Kaveri agriculture could no longer support their 'traditional' ways of life. Equally, their later shift towards medicine, engineering and science, and even the beginnings of their exodus, can be related to emerging political pressures. From the turn of the twentieth century, popular 'non-Brahmin' and 'Dravidian' movements developed, highly critical of their elitism and privilege. These led onto the imposition of ever-expanding caste-based quotas in public education and employment, which cut back Tamil Brahmin opportunities. However, initially, the quotas did not apply in areas such as medicine and engineering, where other applicants were scarce, or in private sector industry, then beginning to develop. Local political pressures also did not apply in national-level arenas, such as the institutions of the post-independence state in New Delhi, nor abroad (Washbrook: 2010).

Nonetheless, even if 'pushed', the Tamil Brahmin trajectory required heroic efforts in cultural reconstruction to marry the continuation of Hindu religiosity – crucial to Brahmin identity – to the pursuit of modern scientific knowledge and skill. This can be seen to have taken place through a remarkable adumbration of religion and science, which informed southern intellectual discourse from the later nineteenth century. Missionary Christianity challenged Hinduism, *inter alia*, on the scientific adequacy of its beliefs and Hindu protagonists responded in kind: by counter-challenging Christianity on the same grounds in circumstances where the arguments of the great British atheist, Charles Bradlaugh, became favoured tools of Hindu apologetics. This discourse developed further with the advent of the Theosophical Society, which was hugely influential in the South. Situated as part of the West's own 'flight from reason' and drawing on the authority of the West's own intellectual traditions (embodied in the person of the long-term President, Annie Besant), Theosophy sought to use scientific methods to establish the claims of Hinduism as a world religion, replacing a discredited Christianity. At a stroke, science became the servant – not the enemy – of religion, and Tamil Brahmins might conscientiously preserve their identities while, at the same time, practising its arts (Pandian: 2007). Indeed, where unique knowledge of the language and mysteries of the gods (Sanskrit) once underpinned their claims to privilege and status, now those underpinnings could be rebuilt in terms of the no less arcane language and mysteries of science (Washbrook: 2010).

In effect, and in contrast to recent polemics against 'hi-skilled' immigrants in the developed economies, migration has rarely been the result of 'simple' incentives to gain superior material rewards. Shifting global and cultural location involves hardships and painful dislocations. Those who undertake it usually have complex histories where problems in their old environments play at least as much of a role as attractions in their new. Equally, cultural adjustments can involve subtle and sophisticated reappraisals of self-'traditions'. While such factors have long been seen as relevant to the condition of poorer immigrants and 'refugees', they may be no less true of peoples with the highest levels of education and scientific skills, as well.

References

AG, DIC (2012): *Country Profile: the Republic of India*. (Canberra: Australian Government, Department of Immigration and Citizenship.)

Ananth, M.S. (1989): *Data Base for Brain Drain. Institution-based Study, IIT Madras*. (Madras: Government of India.)

Fuller, Christopher and Narasimhan, Haripriya (2010): 'Traditional Vocations and Modern Professions among Tamil Brahmans in Colonial and Postcolonial South India', *Indian Economic and Social History Review*, 47:3, pp. 473–96

GMC (2010): *The State of Medical Education and Practice*. (London: General Medical Council.)

Goel, Urmila (2007): 'Indians in Germany' in Brij Lal (ed.), *Encylcopedia of the Indian Diaspora*. (Honolulu: University of Hawaii Press.)

Gupta, Dipti and Gupta, Navneet (2012): 'Higher Education in India: Structure, Statistics and Challenges', *Journal of Education and Practice*, 3:2.

Kalra, Veena (1992): *Pilot Study to Evaluate the Phenomenon of Brain Drain among the Graduates of the All India Institute of Medical Sciences*. (New Delhi: Government of India.)

Khadria, Binod (2006): 'Skilled Migration to Developed Countries: Labour Migration to the Gulf', *Migracion y Desarallo*, 7:2.

Lowe, Lisa (1996): *Immigration Acts: On Asian American Cultural Politics*. (Durham: Duke University Press.)

Metcalf, Thomas R. (2008): *Imperial Connections*. (Berkeley: University of California Press.)

MOSPI (2005): *Economic Census 2005*. (New Delhi: Ministry of Statistics and Programme Implementation.)

NASSCOM (2010): *Human Resources Survey*. (Bangalore: National Association of Software and Services Companies.)

— (2011): *Strategic Review 2010*. (Bangalore: National Association of Software and Services Companies.)

Oommen, T.K. (1989): 'India: The Brain Drain or the Migration of Talent?', *International Migration*, 27:3.

Pandian, M.S.S. (2007): *Brahmin and Non-Brahmin: Genealogies of the Tamil Political Present*. (New Delhi: Permanent Black Limited.)

Prashad, Vijay (2001): *The Karma of Brown Folk*. (Minneapolis: University of Minnesota Press.)

Sarkar, Sumit (2002): *Beyond Nationalist Frames*. (New Delhi: Permanent Black Limited.)

Sen, Amartya (2006): *The Argumentative Indian*. (London: Picador Books.)

Sukhatme, S.P. and Mahadevan, I. (1988): 'Brain Drain and IIT Graduates', *Economic and Political Weekly*, 23:24.

Taylor, Robert H. (1987): *The State in Burma*. (London: Hurst and Company.)

UK, ONS (2009): *Resident Population Estimates by Ethnic Group, All Persons*. (London: Office of National Statistics.)

UKCISA (2011): *International Students in UK Higher Education: Statistics*. (London: UK Council for International Student Affairs.)

US, CB (2009): *American Community Survey*. (Washington, DC: US Census Bureau.)

— (2010): *The Asian Population 2010*. (Washington, DC: US Census Bureau.)

US, DHS (2010): *Yearbook of Immigration Statistics, 2009*. (Washington, DC: US Department of Homeland Security.)

Venkatraghavan, Deepa (2012): '5 Sectors in India that are Hiring NRIs and Expats Right Now', *Economic Times*, 2 February.

Washbrook, David (2010): 'The Maratha Brahmin Model in South India', *Indian Economic and Social History Review*, 47:4, pp. 597–615.

20

TRANSNATIONALISM AND THE TRANSFORMATION OF 'HOME' BY 'ABROAD' IN SYLHET, BANGLADESH

Katy Gardner

Transnational transformations: a visit to the desh

Take the N1 Highway out of Dhaka. Drive for an hour or so through the peri-industrial ribbons of garment factories and brick fields until the landscape turns green with padi; cross the vast Meghna and, after another few hours, head through surprising clumps of forest and tea gardens for Sree Mongal, capital of the Bangladeshi tea industry. It's around here, as the highway returns you to the flat green landscape of the lowlands, that you may start to notice something unusual. You will have passed plenty of villages on the way: some of the houses will have tin roofs, but most will be thatch. Yet here, as you grow closer to Sylhet Town, you will start to see huge mansions, set back from the road and surrounded by walls and gates. Turn off the highway, perhaps towards Beani Bazaar, or Biswanath, and, amongst the more humble rural dwellings built with waddle and straw, will be houses like those found in the wealthiest areas of Dhaka: three storeys high, with smoked glass windows, Arabesque pillars and satellite dishes. Stone aeroplanes can sometimes be seen on top of these houses, testimony to their owner's status as a successful migrant. The fields surrounding them are noteworthy too, for unlike the usual Bangladeshi vista of patchwork green and gold, the landscape is cut across by boundary walls. These walls are a sure sign that you have arrived in a *Londoni gao* (village of people who come from London, or the UK), for they have been erected to ensure that no-one encroaches on the land of the non-resident owner. Without exception, the large brick houses, many of them empty, or inhabited by caretakers, are owned by families who have largely settled in the UK. The contrast with other villages, situated outside what we might think of as these clusters of transnationalism[1] in Sylhet and Habiganj districts could not be more striking.

The apparent wealth of the *Londoni gaos*, with their large houses and splendid mosques[2] would seem to be physical evidence of how contact with *bidesh* ('abroad') has led to social and material transformations impossible to attain by staying put at home (the *desh*). In what follows I shall trace the history of Sylheti involvement with '*bidesh*' in general, and *London* (ie the UK) in particular, arguing that what we might think of as a 'transnational habitus' (Vertovec, 2004) has developed since the mid-twentieth century, in which access to *bidesh* is generally thought of as the only way to get on in life: geographical, social and economic mobility intrinsically interwoven. From the perspectives of those who only dream of such movement, the cultural construction of

261

place is central to this process, for imagined futures are inseparable from imagined places: witness the rickshaw paintings of Big Ben or the Tower of London, the restaurants named 'London Fried Chicken' and shopping malls filled with foreign consumer goods with swanky Arab names (the largest shopping mall in Sylhet Town is named Al Hamera).

I shall return to the issue of transnational habitus in a short while. First, however, some background to the special relationship that has developed between Sylhet and the UK.

Bangladeshi movement and migration

In his account of 'the marginal nation', Ranabir Samaddar describes the turmoil and physical upheaval that has characterised the history of Bangladesh. As he argues, it is impossible to study migration in the contemporary period without being dragged back to the horrors of Indian partition, when millions were violently displaced and there was large-scale bloodshed across the border with West Bengal (Samaddar, 1999; Van Schendel, 2005). Since then, the region has suffered a war of independence from Pakistan, a series of coups and political crises over the 1970s, a military dictatorship in the 1980s and, despite the establishment of democracy in the 1990s, ongoing and often violent political tension which led to a caretaker military government from 2006–8.[3] This is manifested not only in constant general strikes in which, in urban areas at least, normal life grinds to a halt and it is unsafe to move around the streets, but also bombings, civil disorder and political violence. The country was rated at the top of Transparency International's Corruption Perception Index in 2005 and has a distinctly unhappy human rights record.[4]

The physical landscape of Bangladesh is equally insecure. The deltaic terrain often floods, and some parts of the country are seasonally inundated. Flooding can mean the loss of crops, livestock and homes, sometimes even lives. Invariably it is the poorest, who can afford neither *pucca* (stone) houses nor higher land, who are the worst affected. Population pressure has meant that the most risky locations are inhabited by those without access to more secure locations. Add to this the potentially catastrophic effects of global warming and deforestation in the Himalayan region and Samaddar's characterisation of the country as 'an insecure environment inhabited by insecure families' reads like an understatement (1999: 87).

It is partly due to this insecurity that the rural population of Bangladesh is so mobile. Migration within rural areas as well as from rural to urban areas has long been a livelihood strategy of many of the country's poorest people (Gardner and Ahmed, 2006; Siddiqui, 2003; Hossain *et al.*, 2005). In contrast, migration overseas is generally the domain of the more prosperous. Air fares, visas and the services of agents all cost money, but once the initial investment has been made men can earn wages in the Middle East or South East Asia that are substantially higher than those in Bangladesh. This type of migration is in itself risky and *can* lead to net losses for the households that send men abroad, but the profits are generally high enough to make temporary labour migration to destinations in the Middle East and South East Asia worthwhile. Indeed, temporary labour migration is one of the few economic opportunities available for rural men, a trend which has spread from particular areas of Bangladesh such as Sylhet, to much of the country. In 1976–2002 more than 3 million Bangladeshis migrated overseas for employment (Siddiqui, 2003). Siddiqui cites figures from 2003 that show that the net export earnings from ready-made garments were between US $2.29 billion and $2.52 billion, whilst net earnings from remittances were $3.063 billion. In 2004, earnings from remittances amounted to twice that of Bangladesh's aid budget (Siddiqui, 2005). In September 2009 BBC News reported that Bangladesh earnt $937 million from migrant workers.

Ships, factories and restaurants: Sylhetis in the UK

Whilst most regions of Bangladesh now send migrants to work as labourers in the Middle East and South East Asia, for many generations Sylhetis have monopolised migration to Britain.[5] Indeed, Sylhet's special relationship with the UK is just one reason why the district is seen by many Bangladeshis as significantly different from the rest of the country.[6] Over the nineteenth and into the twentieth century, many Sylheti *lascars* 'jumped ship' in London, where they stayed, seeking work as peddlers or in London's hotels and restaurants (Choudhury, 1993: 33). Although originally men from districts such as Noakhali and Chittagong were also *lascars*, by the twentieth century Sylhetis dominated (ibid: 33–5).[7] The reasons why are unclear: both geographical conditions (what were to become *Londoni* areas being situated close to rivers, a characteristic common to many places in Bangladesh) and regional cultures (the independence and adventurous nature of Sylhetis; again, similar characteristics could be applied to most of South Asia) have been cited as explanations,[8] but neither seems convincing. More crucially perhaps, particular individuals dominated the recruitment of labour, leading to a 'chain' effect whereby men from particular villages and lineages gained employment through the patronage of their relatives and neighbours. This has led to the 'clustering' of *Londoni* villages in areas such as Beani Bazaar, Biswanath, Mouliv Bazaar and Sylhet Town. Indeed, in the area where I conducted my doctoral fieldwork (Nobiganj), the migratory chain can be traced to one *bari* (collection of related households, usually sharing a common patrlineal ancestor) which in the late 1980s was still known as *'sareng bari'* (ship's foreman, who would have played an important role in recruiting local labour). Most surrounding villages had also sent ship workers by the mid-twentieth century; these men were often, though not always, part of the same lineage as the original *sareng*, but one village never sent anyone. Today, this village is extremely poor and only has one *Londoni* household.[9]

The vast majority of Sylhetis came to Britain in the 1950s and 1960s when the second phase of migration to the UK took place. Prompted by a labour shortage after World War Two the British authorities actively encouraged labour migration from its previous colonies and thousands of migrants embarked for the UK (Adams, 1987; Choudhury, 1993). Again, the chains instituted by the ship workers led to a particular constellation of UK-bound men coming from particular areas of Sylhet. Most of these men initially found employment in factories in cities such as Birmingham, Luton, Manchester and Newcastle. The men were 'transnationals' par excellence: they worked and lived in Britain, but returned home as often as they could, where they were still heavily involved in social networks of kinship and village community. Over the 1970s and into the 1980s conditions started to change. Britain's heavy industry was in decline and many Sylheti men moved to London to seek employment in the garment or restaurant trades. Crucially, a growing number started to bring their wives and children to the UK (Peach, 1996). This shift was partly the result of changing immigration laws, which many rightly feared would soon make primary migration to Britain (without it involving marriage to a British citizen) increasingly difficult. It also reflected wider changes in the areas where many Bengalis were settled, in which mosques, shops selling *halal* meat and other community facilities were becoming established. When I was doing my original fieldwork in Talukpur in the late 1980s, many families were in the process of reunification. Today, these households have completely settled in the UK, children who were toddlers at the time of settlement in the UK having completed school and had their own children in the various cities where they live (most notably, Newcastle, Manchester and London).

In 2009 the Bangladeshi population is one of the youngest and fastest growing in Britain[10] and the process of family reunification is complete. If not classed as a 'family dependant', it is extremely difficult to obtain an entry visa to Britain from Sylhet. Indeed, figures from the British High Commission in Dhaka show that, of the Bangladeshis seeking work permits over 2005–6, 90 per cent were from Sylhet and the vast majority were refused.[11] New links with the *desh* (homeland) are, however, still being made, via transnational marriages.[12] Indeed, marriage to a British-based man or woman is now one of the only ways of gaining entry to the UK.[13] Whilst in the 1970s and 1980s it was mostly wives who travelled to the UK to join their husbands, today almost as many men apply for settlement visas to join their British-based wives. Foreign Office (FO) figures show that, in 2005, 1,530 settlement visas were granted to Bangladeshi grooms (with 330 refused), in contrast to 2,133 issued to brides (with 590 refused). These figures have remained relatively stable since 2001.[14] A 2004 Report from the Home Office[15] cites a rise of 14 per cent of husbands admitted from the Indian subcontinent since 2003, compared to a rise of 12 per cent of wives. Whilst marriage is a way in which trans-national ties are reinvigorated and/or instituted, it is the catering industry that provides economic sustenance to the transnational community. Since the 1980s, many of the UK-based families have been involved in the 'Indian' restaurant business, which is almost wholly dominated by Sylhetis. Indeed, it would be fair to say that, via its restaurants, the British Sylheti population is represented in almost every small town and area of Britain.

In sum, what has developed is therefore less a diaspora (in the sense of a globally dispersed population, though one could certainly talk more generally of a Bengali diaspora) and, more, a transnational relationship that links particular areas of Sylhet with the UK. Whilst this has changed in character over the last 50 years, the links between places remain strong and people, ideas, goods and practices continue to flow between them. In their marriages, journeys between *desh* and *bidesh* (however defined), gifts sent back and forth, phone calls and religious rituals the British Sylheti transnational social field is as vibrant as ever, albeit in an ever changing form. Yet, as we shall see, the different locations within this flow of people and things are far from equal, and, in the case of villages in rural Sylhet, have been transformed in very specific ways.

Transnational transformations: village-based research in Sylhet

The broader history of Sylheti migration is linked to dramatic changes within the villages that originally sent men to Britain. In Talukpur, I found that households that had gained access to Britain in the 1960s had, by the 1980s, accumulated large amounts of land. In contrast, those who had neither the inclination nor the wherewithal to send members abroad had, from the 1960s to the late 1980s, tended to lose it, usually to their *Londoni* neighbours. There was thus a direct correlation between migration to Britain and the accumulation of wealth: the stronger a household's links with Britain, the more land could be acquired, whilst non-migrants were pushed, through processes of land division and rural impoverishment, to sell up. Gains were concentrated in particular villages, which, as noted earlier, were clustered in particular areas of Greater Sylhet. Within *Londoni* villages these gains were further concentrated in the hands of particular families. Significantly, *Londoni* households were involved in intense projects of social transformation: marrying into higher status families, building impressive houses and sometimes changing their family names from the lower status 'Ullah' or 'Ahmed' to 'Saiyed' or 'Sheikh', thereby asserting a blood link to Shah Jalal, the Muslim saint who is said to have originally introduced Islam to the region. A proportion of these upwardly mobile families also claimed to be descendents of local saints (*pir*): claims which were often strenuously contested by their sceptical neighbours (Gardner, 1993, 1995).

In Talukpur, the use of remittances tended to follow a particular pattern. After paying off any debts that the original migration incurred and covering household subsistence needs, foreign earnings tended to be invested in land, the arbiter of wealth, power and security. After this, they were generally used to build new *pucca* (stone) houses, an important asset in an environment liable to cyclonic storms and flooding. Remittances were also invested in further migration, funding the movement of close kin to the Middle East, as well as business enterprises and property in Britain. What was taking place was a process in which successful *Londonis* and their immediate families were making themselves as secure as possible, both by accumulating land in the village and laying down strong connections with Britain and other sources of foreign earnings. Social resources were important too; the processes of 'Ashrafisation'[16] and other signifiers of upward mobility were not empty 'vanity projects', but part of a wider context in which one's status directly affected the claims one could make on others (Gardner, 1995).

A similar story can be told in another village where I have recently been involved in research: Jalalgaon, in Biswanath.[17] Here the outward effects of *Londoni* migration are even more extreme[18] than in Talukpur. Situated only a short bus ride away from Sylhet, Biswanath Town is one of the wealthiest *Londoni* areas in the region, its bustling town filled with smart shopping malls, banks and fast food outlets. Jalalgaon is only a few miles away, its large, ostentatious houses confirming that this is a *Londoni* village par excellence. As in Talukpur, the local economic hierarchy in Jalalgaon is directly correlated with migration to Britain. Those who originally sent members to the UK have, over the last 30 years or so, accumulated large amounts of land, as well as assets such as shops, 'colonies' (*bustee*-style dwellings where poor in-migrant labourers live)[19] and other business interests. Of the 98 households native to the village (i.e. they are not in-migrant labourers who live in 'colonies' on the periphery of the village) 34 are *Londonis* (i.e. they have members in Britain). Another seven households are, using local terminology, classified as 'Dubai', meaning that they have had experience of migration to the Gulf. Of these, three have been moderately successful and own some land. The rest are landless. The remaining 57 households have no members abroad.

When landholding in the village is correlated with these household types, the results speak for themselves. Of the total local agricultural land, 79 per cent is owned by *Londoni* households, 6.9 per cent by 'Dubai' households and 13.9 per cent by non-migrants. Put another way, 100 per cent (34) of *Londoni* households own land, compared to 50 per cent (6) of Dubai households and 10 per cent (6) of non-migrant insider households. Of the non-migrant insiders, one household owns five *kiare* (nearly two acres) and the rest one *kiare* or less (i.e. less than 0.3 acres). Amongst the *Londoni* households, whilst 23.5 per cent own up to one acre and 26.47 per cent own between one and two acres, the rest own over 2 acres, with 23.5 per cent owning over 5 acres. Whilst the Biswanath research did not produce longitudinal data on village landholding, it is likely that, as in Talukpur, those who initially migrated to the UK were originally middle-income farmers who, with their foreign earnings, were able to buy up land over the 1960s–80s, creating a new local hierarchy in which those with access to the UK owned the majority of the local land. In sum, by the 1980s the local economic hierarchy was structured by peoples' access to *place*.

These changes have contributed to local imaginings of different places which, in turn, structure peoples' aspirations and dreams. For non-migrants in Jalalgaon and Talukpur, 'London' is constructed as a place of economic opportunity and security. The highly visible achievements of *Londoni* households are, from the vantage of the village, testimony to the wealth that can be made in the UK. Exchange rates mean that even a modest wage in Britain is a fortune in Bangladesh. For example (in 2009), a labourer's wages averaged 130 taka a day (about £1). Crucially, competition over land and property between *Londoni* families has pushed local prices up so high that one needs a British income to afford them. A third of an acre of land (one *kiare*) near the centre of the village costs up to 1 *crore* (1 million) *taka*: around £8,264. In other areas of Bangladesh, one might pay around £600 to £700 for an acre.[20]

Paradoxically, as the price of land has risen, the intensity with which it is cultivated has decreased. Of the 34 *Londoni* households in Jalalgaon, 26.5 per cent had no involvement in cultivation, either leaving their land fallow (usually because of a planned building project) or using it for 'colony' housing. Of the remaining 73.5 per cent, only 32.4 per cent of households (11, in total) were directly involved. The rest sharecropped their land out, usually to poorer relatives. It should be noted that those who *were* cultivating land were not actually doing this themselves; rather, they were hiring labourers from outside the village. Indeed, during the winter harvesting season the village is completely reliant on wage labourers from outside the village. This shift from direct cultivation into a more mixed 'portfolio' of livelihood strategies, which may include the management of some agricultural activities but is no longer wholly based on farming, is not confined to the wealthier *Londoni* households. Out of 57 non-migrant households, the research team found that 84 per cent were not directly engaged in agriculture, gaining their income from other sources, such as day labouring, small businesses, or driving vehicles.

There is another notable difference between agriculture in Jalalgaon and other regions in Bangladesh. This is that, whilst in most of the country cultivating two crops a year is the norm, in Jalalgaon there is only one. The reason for this, villagers said, is that agriculture is not profitable ('*laab nai*'). Since cultivation is reliant on hired labour, the costs of organising two crops are seen as too high for the amount of produce gained. If one is receiving regular remittances from Britain, or is largely absent in the UK, the hard work and worry involved in organising labour, selling surplus crops in the market, and so on, is generally seen as not worth it.

Changing connections: shifts in the remittance economy

As the above implies, *Londoni* village economies are largely dependent upon migration, both to the UK and involving the movement of labourers *into* the area to cultivate the land. Crucially, however, the nature of transnational connectedness with Britain is changing. Whilst Britain was once the source of regular remittances, processes of family reunification mean that by 2009 those households who have settled in Britain are unlikely to send money back on a regular basis. This has had a major impact on other family members who have become dependent upon British earnings. In Talukpur, for example, a family who have two sons in Britain bemoan the dwindling financial returns. The oldest son, who went to Oldham in the 1970s, has stopped remitting altogether, whilst his younger brother, recently married to his British-based cousin and with a young child, can hardly afford to send anything back. In Jalalgaon, an elderly woman told a similar story: 'We are very poor', she said. 'We took the decision to send my son to London because we needed the money. But that was 20 years ago and he hasn't sent us anything for a long time.'

In Jalalgaon in 2005 the main source of British funds was pensions rather than remittances, paid by the British government through the Sonali Bank to return migrants or their widows. Whilst this means that cash is still flowing from the UK to Bangladesh, it will only last as long as the older generation. Unless they are replaced by more pensioners who have decided to retire in the *desh*,[21] the income source will dry up. Other money that comes from the UK is usually in the form of informal 'help' in times of need rather than as an assured source of income. Many households rely on the patronage of *Londoni* relatives, whether in paying for the weddings of children, in times of crisis, or in allowing them to cultivate their land whilst they are away. Out of 16 men involved in business in the Biswanath area that were interviewed, for example, ten mentioned that they had been assisted in setting up their businesses (usually shops) by close relatives settled in Britain. Of the many young men in Jalalgaon who are hoping to go abroad, all anticipate the assistance of close relatives already in the UK. This support might be financial but also extends to help in finding ways into Britain, largely through helping them apply for the limited work permit schemes that are available for Bangladeshis[22] or organising marriages with British Bangladeshi brides. Such support clearly depends upon the goodwill and financial abilities of British-based relatives.

It is thus hardly surprising that for those who remain in Bangladesh their relationships to *Londonis* are so important for they are tied to long-term livelihood strategies in which access to the earnings of foreign countries is the main determinant of economic security. If, over the time and distance that separates family members, relations turn sour, Bangladesh-based kin may find that support is withdrawn. It is very much in Bangladesh-based kin's interest to make sure that the relationship is kept up. One way of doing this is through the arrangement of marriage between cousins based in Bangladesh and Britain. If this can be satisfactorily carried out, the links between different sections of the family are reinforced and the primary migration of a bride or groom becomes possible. The expectations of family members concerning prospective marriages (and the pressure which Bangladeshi kin sometimes put on their British-based cousins and uncles) can, however, lead to rifts. For example, Mr Ali, a Biswanath businessman, described how his household had fallen out with his British-based uncle and aunt over the arrangement of a marriage between his brother and his British cousin. Whilst he and his brothers were keen for the marriage to take place, both the aunt and her daughter resisted the alliance, arguing that a Sylheti groom would not be suitable for a British-born girl. Allegations of the misappropriation of money quickly followed and today the British-based wing of the family no longer sends any form of support.

Security, place and 'transnational habitus'

In sum, although the majority of villagers in both Talukpur and Jalagoan have never moved beyond Bangladesh's state boundaries, the net effect of 30 or 40 years of connectedness to Britain has created what Steve Vertovec has dubbed a 'transnational habitus', in which geographical movement and economic success are inextricably linked in the minds of migrants and non-migrants alike (Vertovec, 2004: 22–3). As we have seen, this need for connectedness is not simply 'imagined'; the economies of villages such as Jalalgaon and Talukpur have become largely dependent upon remittances from foreign countries.

Yet, whilst overseas migration is associated with upward mobility and success there is also a clear hierarchy of places within local imaginings. Although in the late 1980s in Talukpur many young men were migrating to the Middle East for temporary employment, by 2005 the Middle East was no longer seen as a particularly desirable destination amongst the more prosperous households in either Talukpur or Jalalgaon. This is because, in general, the wages to be earned there are not high enough to enable one to invest in property or businesses at home. In addition, the Middle East is often perceived as a risky destination in which would-be migrants are cheated by agents, or go as insecure 'unlegals'. Migrants to the Middle East are thus the more vulnerable lower-income households who lack the social links to get to the UK yet are prepared to take the gamble of investing savings or credit on temporary labour migration. This is usually organised by an agent, who may or may not be trustworthy. Yet, whilst migration to the Gulf or to South East Asia is a risky enterprise, Britain is seen as a secure and profitable destination. Once in Britain, one's security is far greater than in the Middle East, for there is an existing network of Bangladeshi businesses to work in, often run by people to whom one is related. There is also the social protection provided by the British state: health care, education for one's children, benefits for the unemployed and pensions for the retired. Even if by British standards a household is living below the poverty line,[23] from the perspective of Bangladesh – where extreme insecurity and desperate poverty mean that those without assets may struggle to satisfy their day-to-day calorific needs – it is seen as enjoying plenty.

The destinations of would-be migrants are therefore arranged hierarchically in Sylhet with the UK at the top. Let us not confuse this with a love of things 'English' or 'Westernisation'. The 'London' that people wish to join is the Sylheti community in Britain, not British society per se. Let us also not confuse these perspectives with those of Sylhetis settled in the UK, who may feel neither secure nor wealthy. Despite these caveats, it is generally true to say that the majority of young, unmarried men from middle-income households in *Londoni* villages dream of migrating to Britain, a plan encouraged by their close family, who, facing the insecurity of dwindling remittances from long-departed relatives, are keen to forge new links with the sources of capital. Rather than investing their time in further education or seeking work in Dhaka or Sylhet Town, many of these young men say they are 'waiting' to go to London and regularly visit the British High Commission in Dhaka in an attempt to get a visa, something that will only materialise with either the sponsorship and assistance of a *Londoni* relative, or marriage with a British-based woman. Sadid is a good example of a would-be *Londoni*. Aged 30, he is keen to follow in the footsteps of his oldest brother, who, with the help of their British based sister-in-law, married a *Londoni* bride and now lives in the UK. Whilst the family are pleased to finally have a London connection, Sadid is also pursuing marriage with a *Londoni* woman. As he said:

> If I can get to London my luck will change. I'll be helped by my in-laws who can find me a job. . . . After that my next step will be to arrange a marriage with my younger two brothers as soon as I arrive in London. I really don't think there's any point in them staying here. They have to get to the UK. Here there's nothing: no income, no security, no certainty.

Conclusion: transnational social fields and local realities

In their important discussion of transnational social fields, Levitt and Glick-Schiller rightly point out how power plays a vital role in structuring transnational relationships. This power is held in varying degrees by the states that transnational subjects come into contact with as well as individuals who gain social power through migrating (Levitt and Glick-Schiller, 2004: 1014). What is less central to their analysis is the way that these relationships lead to particular, located, material realities, or indeed the role that *places* – themselves structured by unequal global relationships – play in producing and reproducing hierarchy and inequality between people within the transnational social field. These places do not stay the same, but are continually transformed, both by the transnational movements that take place between them and by wider processes.

Rather than focussing upon flows, networks or relationships between places, what I have attempted to describe in this paper is how these flows, networks and relationships have helped to transform a particular location within the Sylheti transnational field: the rural areas from which *Londonis* originated (the *desh*, according to most *Londonis*, if not their children). Here, we find a situation in which poverty plus economic, political and environmental insecurity in Bangladesh have contributed to a 'transnational habitus' in which connectedness to the global labour market is seen as virtually the only avenue for success. This is closely associated with the economic dependence of the region on remittances. Social capital, in the form of relationships with those who have established links with Britain, is a vital resource for non-migrants, for it is only through *Londonis* that they can gain access to financial 'help' or that their plans of future migration may be realised. These links are, however, increasingly fragile, for, as the children and grandchildren of the original pioneers marry and establish their own families and careers in the UK, their ability, not to say their willingness, to remit regularly or even send money irregularly as 'gifts' is likely to wane significantly, as is their interest in regular visits to the *desh*. What this means is that, whilst we might talk of 'transnational social fields' and, by doing so, recognise the interdependence of places in transnational worlds (thereby avoiding a simplistic dualism in which the 'local' and 'global' are opposed and contrasting categories), different places within the transnational relationships have very different material realities.

Notes

1 These 'Londoni' clusters can largely be found in the communities and neighbourhoods of Maulvi Bazaar, Biswanath, Beani Bazaar, Nobigang and Sylhet Town.

2 Sometimes the houses have their own private mosques.

3 Bangladesh's current government, which is formed by the Awami League, was democratically elected at the end of 2008.

4 For more details, see The Home Office Operational Guidance Note on Bangladesh (www.ind. homeoffice.gov.uk/ind/en/home/laws_policy/country_information/operation_guidance.Main content.0004.file.tmp/Bangladesh%20v3.0%20December%202005.pdf).

5 The House of Commons Report 1986–7 estimates that 95 per cent of Bangladeshis in Britain originate from Sylhet. There have been no major demographic shifts in the last 20 years that would suggest that this figure has changed.

6 Other reasons include the district's distinctive dialect and its historical links to Assam; under British rule, from 1874–1947, it was administered as part of Assam rather than Bengal.

7 The reasons are complex and dealt with in detail elsewhere (Gardner, 1995).

8 See Gardner, 1995; Adams, 1987; Choudhury, 1993.

9 For more details of the relationship between local hierarchies and UK migration, see Gardner, 1995.

10 The 2001 Census enumerated a total population of 283,063, of which 38 per cent were under 16.

11 For detailed information concerning the options for Bangladeshi migrants to the UK see McPhee, 2006.

12 See Shaw and Charsley, 2006.

13 There are other opportunities for highly skilled workers or students in higher education.

14 Unfortunately the FO were not able to provide data for previous years.

15 *Control of Immigration Statistics*.

16 Vreede-de Stuers, 1968; see also Osella and Osella 2000 for discussion of these processes in Kerala.

17 This research was funded by the Department for International Development's (DFID) Development Research Centre on Migration, Poverty and Globalisation, at the University of Sussex. Fieldwork was conducted by a team of researchers from Jahangirnagar University, Dhaka: Zahir Ahmed, Abdul Mannan and Rownek Rasheed.

18 In contrast to Jalalgaon, Talukpur is about two hours away from Sylhet, in a less prosperous area in the interior of Nobiganj. Most British-based villagers live in Oldham.

19 The term 'colony' is used locally and may have spread from India, where low-cost, slum-style 'colonies' were built for scheduled castes after independence (personal communication: F. Osella).

20 These prices are based on data gathered in 2005.

21 Although many older people dream of returning to Bangladesh, the need for good health care, acclimatisation to Britain and the settlement of children in the UK mean that few actually do (Gardner, 2002).

22 For more details, see McPhee, 2006.

23 According to national census data, over 60 per cent of people of Bangladeshi and Pakistani origin were living in low-income households in 2001 (www.statistics.gov.uk/cci/nugget.asp?id=269).

References

Adams, C. (1987) *Across Seven Seas and Thirteen Rivers: Life Stories of Pioneer Sylheti Settlers in Britain*, London: Tower Hamlets Arts Project.

Choudhury, Y. (1993) *The Routes and Tales of the Bangladeshi Settlers*, Birmingham: Sylhet Social History Group.

Gardner, K. (1993) 'Desh–Bidesh: Sylheti images of home and away', *MAN (Journal of Royal Anthropological Institute)* N:S 28, vol. 1, pp. 1–15.

— (1995) *Global Migrants, Local Lives: Travel and Transformation in Rural Bangladesh*, Oxford: Oxford University Press.

— (2002) *Age, Narrative and Migration: The Life Course and Life Histories of Bengali Elders in London*, Oxford: Berg.

Gardner, K. and Ahmed, Z. (2006) 'Place, Social Protection and Migration in Bangladesh: A Londoni village in Biswanath', *DRC in Migration, Poverty and Globalisation*, Working Paper, University of Sussex.

Hossain, M., Khan, I.A., Seeley, J. (2005) 'Migration as a Form of Livelihood for the Poor' in Khan, I.A. and Seeley, J. (eds) *Making a Living: The Livelihoods of the Rural Poor in Bangladesh*, Dhaka: Dhaka University Press, pp. 199–224.

Levitt, P. and Glick-Schiller, N. (2004) 'Conceptualising Simultaneity: A transnational social field perspective on society', *International Migration Review*, vol. 38, no. 3, pp. 1002–39.

McPhee, S. (2006) *Avenues for Legal Migration from Bangladesh to the UK: Labour Migration*, Dhaka: Refugee and Migratory Movement Unit (RMMRU).

Osella, F. and Osella, C. (2000) *Social Mobility in Kerala: Modernity and Identity in Conflict*, London: Pluto Press.

Peach, C. (ed.) (1996) *Ethnicity in the 1991 Census*, The Ethnic Minority Populations of Britain Vol. 2, London: HMSO.

Samaddar, R. (1999) *The Marginal Nation: Transborder Migration from Bangladesh to West Bengal*, Dhaka: Dhaka University Press.

Shaw, A. and Charsley, K. (eds) (2006) Special Issue: South Asian Transnational Marriages, *Global Networks* Vol. 6, No. 4.

Siddiqui, T. (2003) 'Migration as a Livelihood Strategy of the Poor: The Bangladesh case', paper presented to the Regional Conference on Migration, Development and Pro-Poor Policy Choices in Asia, RMMRU, June.

— (2005) *International Labour Migration from Bangladesh: A Decent Work Perspective*, International Labour Office: Working Paper 66.

Van Schendel, W. (2005) *The Bengal Borderland: Beyond State and Nation in South Asia*, London: Anthem Press.

Vertovec, S. (2004) 'Trends and Impacts of Migrant Transnationalism', Centre on Migration, Policy and Society Working Paper no. 3, University of Oxford.

Vreede-de Stuers, C. (1968) *Parda: A Study of Muslim Women's Life in North India*, Assen: Van Gorcum.

21

INDIANS ABROAD

Mixing it up

Karen Leonard

How should one conceptualize Indian-descended collectivities abroad, especially when focusing on those that are hybrid? This collection is entitled South Asian diasporas, and my topic is hybridity. 'South Asian' can include people from India, Pakistan, Bangladesh, Sri Lanka, Nepal, Bhutan, the Maldive Islands, Afghanistan and even those of Indian origin from places like Fiji and the West Indies, but since most of my material concerns those who migrated before 1947, I will usually refer to Indians in what follows. Diaspora has become the term used loosely for sets of immigrants abroad and their descendants, and I too will use it in that way. Yet the original meaning of diaspora, and the meaning still implicit for many scholars, suggests that those abroad retain active connections and an ideological allegiance to the homeland, share a desire to return to it and display strong cultural continuities in belief and behaviour. Scholars typically have 'compared South Asian diasporas with conditions "back home" on the Indian subcontinent and sought to determine processes of cultural retention and attenuation' and, more recently, they have looked at interactions in the new environments, stressing the effects of new political contexts and focusing less on objective documentation of diasporas than on their production through the labour of memory (Eisenlohr 2007: 773–4). This means that diasporas can emerge, be invented if you will, over time, an insight that nicely complements Arjun Appadurai's discussion (1996) of the unstable nature of transnational ethnic identities, of concepts shifting and no longer bound by territory, history, or cultural homogeneity. My point is that definitions and policies concerning 'Indians' are often at the mercy of both old and new states and their changing policies over time, and immigrants can become diasporic if they were not so at first.

Hybridity is another term in need of careful definition and application when discussing Indians abroad. Many scholars of Indian diasporas limit their research and their reviews of secondary work to 'real Indians', those whom they see as remaining more or less true to their traditions and homeland communities. These works celebrate the transmission and maintenance of Indian culture abroad, excluding discussions of men and women who marry outside their religion, caste or community, those who produce hybridity in the primary sense of breeding across races or species. A good example is the essay by Vinay Lal in an *Indian Diaspora* volume, where discussion of the Punjabis who migrated to the US before 1965 is cursory and dismissive. Lal states (2006: 319): 'Indians showed considerable, if not always successful, ability to innovate in their social life. Punjabi men took Mexican women as wives, adapted to differences in language,

271

cuisine, dress and religion, and together they created an unusual biethnic community.' Other authors give more space and respect to that so-called Mexican Hindu or Punjabi Mexican community but just as clearly view this hybrid community as not the 'real subject of research' on Indian immigrants abroad.

Evidence abounds, however, that hybrid or intermarried Indian diasporic families and communities developed in many places.[1] The indentured labourers in the West Indies, the Fiji Islands, South Africa and Australia clearly constituted new families and communities, ones that have been more readily accepted as 'Indian' because the marital boundaries crossed were between Indians rather than between Indians and others. Some authors celebrate hybridity. Karthiyaini Devarajoo, based in Malaysia, mentions a ChinIndian community, a whole group of mixed Chinese and Indian parentage, and she says (2009: 139): 'Hybridity is the catalytic element that supports the transformation of an individual or community from being a diaspora to being the citizen of the host country and to finally being a world citizen.' In some cases, the hybridity is deliberate and intended to deny membership in a diaspora. For example, many of the Indian Muslim *muhajirs* (refugees, exiles) who went to Pakistan 'married out', Hyderabadi Muslims marrying Kashmiris, Punjabis and Sindhis, deliberately becoming hybrid to claim membership in a new nation. In fact, one Hyderabadi Muslim going to Pakistan rejected the term *muhajir*: 'How could we be refugees, coming to our homeland?' (Leonard 2007: 57). India's Jews who migrated to Israel might fit this model as well.

Some diasporic communities are not only racially or ethnically hybrid but hybrid in other ways, because hybridity can mean other sorts of mixed origins, like languages, religions or ancestral homes. The Zoroastrians or Parsis who left India (or Pakistan or East Africa) have become part of new communities in North America as they meet Zoroastrian immigrants from Iran. Indian Parsis and Iranian Zoroastrians are worshipping together and are working to constitute a new 'Zarthusti' community. The Zarthusti community relies upon priests trained in India, and the priests in North America, unlike those in India, are beginning to consecrate mixed marriages and recognize the children of mixed marriages as Parsi, changing the rules in the diaspora governing religious and marital boundaries (Leonard 2006). John Hinnells's work (1994) on Parsi migrants in Australia, Britain and North America shows that diasporic patterns differ by destination, with intermarriage and community membership issues being crucial everywhere. Another example would be South Asian Muslims in the US, working to constitute an American Muslim community and sometimes marrying Arab or African American Muslims. And what about those who cross gender boundaries? Freddy Mercury, born in Zanzibar of Parsi parentage and brought up in India, became the spectacularly successful frontman of the British rock band Queen. Like most South Asian Indian gay men abroad, he formed partnerships beyond the boundaries traditional to his parental community. Gay and lesbian South Asians have become visible in the diaspora but have yet to be studied.

Indian immigrants abroad have also become hybrid by mixing and changing ancestral homelands, languages and religions. Some have written that there is no diasporic second generation, the children always becoming culturally hybrid and no longer 'really Indian' (Bhatia and Ram 2007; Leonard 2009). Leaving aside the argument that the diaspora is always only one generation deep, linguistic and religious hybridity prevails throughout the old and new Indian diasporas. Much depends on the context and the timing of arrival, but everywhere communities with new identities have been formed. Indian and Sri Lankan Christians abroad have mixed their religious beliefs and practices with those in Europe and North America in fascinating ways (Jacobsen and Raj 2008). Those indentured laborers going to the West Indies, to Surinam, Trinidad, Jamaica and Guyana, travelled together on ships and lived on plantations in conditions that erased distinctions of caste, leading to intermarriage and commingling of musical and religious traditions. In Trinidad, where Hindus are second to Roman Catholics in number, Divali is second to Carnival as the largest national festival. Hosay/Muharram (the Shia Muslim commemoration of the death of the Prophet's grandsons) is one of the largest national events in Jamaica, one that involves many Hindus and Africans as well. The smaller Caribbean Islands, St. Vincent, St. Lucia, Belize, Grenada, Guadeloupe and Martinique, display a variety of cultural interactions. Although the Indians tend to form separate and identifiable groups in most of these countries, few vestiges of Indian culture are actually retained. In Cuba, where most of the Indians came from Jamaica rather than India, everyday cultural practices including cuisine reflect widely shared Cuban patterns. Christian traditions, Cuban traditions, black traditions, are said to characterize many of these West Indian groups (Mahabir 2009). In some places, 'revivals' of Indian traditions are underway. When I visited Trinidad for a conference in 2000, I had read up on hybrid musical developments among Trinidadian Indians, noting that an Indian music concert in a village was on the programme. However, when we arrived at a small rural temple, the musicians had performed in North America the previous week and played classical Hindustani music for us.

Mauritius offers a fascinating case of the 'emergence' (Eisenlohr 2007:774) of Indian diasporas, of hybridities transformed (Hookoomsing 2009; Eisenlohr 2007). The indentured Indian laborers of diverse but chiefly North Indian origins ended up speaking Bhojpuri or Creole–Bhojpuri. According to the linguistic anthropologist Patrick Eisenlohr, nearly all Mauritians actually speak French-lexicon Mauritian Creole, with Bhojpuri being the second language of almost a quarter of the population, the language of Hindus and Muslims from both northern and southern India. Yet the Mauritian state has decided to support teaching, propagation and celebration of 'ancestral languages', thus instigating notions of diasporas. The state-designated ancestral languages are not diasporic languages in the sense that they were actually spoken by the indentured laborers, and these 'ancestral languages' cut across intermarriage patterns long-standing among Indo-Mauritians. Eisesnlohr traces the disintegration of the earlier hybrid Creole–Bhojpuri-speaking Indo–Mauritian community: by the 1940s a Hindu–Muslim split had been produced by religious nationalism and missionaries from the subcontinent and by the 1970s the state had subdivided the Hindus into separate Hindi-, Tamil-, Telugu- and Marathi-speaking groups, while Muslims, reaching for languages they had never spoken, reported not only Urdu but Arabic as ancestral languages! Interestingly, 'Indian' in Mauritius now means Hindus and never Muslims. In contrast, 'Hindu' in the US before the 1970s meant all Indians, including Muslims and Sikhs, as discussed below.

Another striking illustration of diasporic identities subject to shifting political contexts comes from Nasreen Ali (2007), who analyzes Kashmiris in Britain. She points to four somewhat overlapping but sometimes competing discourses that identify them differently: as a nation, a people with a right to a state of their own; as an oppressed people, victims undertaking a liberation struggle; as a distinct non-Pakistani ethnicity within the context of Britain; and, as Muslims, part of a global Islamic community. Ali sees the first, the nationalist discourse, as based upon the territorialization of Kashmiriyat, a shared political culture; the second discourse demonizes India; and the third attempts to separate Kashmiris from Pakistanis within Britain. The fourth discourse is most problematic, directly conflicting with the nationalist discourse by excluding non-Muslim Kashmiris. Finally, she notes that the Kashmiri diasporic identity in Britain is distinct from the Kashmiri identity expressed in Kashmir, and one might speculate that it would be different again in the US, given the very different constellation of Muslim and South Asian identities there.

These considerations, of Indians in Mauritius and Kashmiris abroad, point to the role of the state in shaping diasporic discourses of linguistic, cultural and religious hybridities and bring me to the so-called Mexican Hindu or Punjabi Mexican community in early twentieth-century California. Given the discussions above, I submit that this was not a diasporic community, nor has it emerged as one. However, it is a fine example of hybridity, of Indians abroad who constituted a new and thoroughly hybrid community in a new social and political context. The remainder of this essay speaks to the limits of the diaspora concept, a theme also addressed in Oonk (2007: 10); I delineate the ways in which the lives of the earliest Indian immigrants to the US diverged from that concept in interesting ways.

Making Ethnic Choices was the title of my 1992 book about the Punjabi pioneers (Leonard 1992), but it was an ironic title, because the early immigrants from India could not choose freely when it came to many aspects of their lives in early twentieth-century America. Constrained by laws based on national origin and race that prevented them from bringing their wives and families from India and that limited their choice of spouses in the US, the men who wanted a family life married predominantly Spanish-speaking women, producing families known in southern California as 'Mexican Hindus'. The demographic patterns of marriage and childbearing testify to the difficult conditions the men and their families experienced in rural California, and their testimonies of conflict and accommodation speak vividly about the social world in which the Punjabi pioneers lived. Their children, the second generation, grew up valuing their 'Hindu' heritage highly, but they were also proud to be American and, when they met with disbelief and disapproval from the post-1965 immigrants from India and Pakistan, they affirmed the new homeland rather than the old.

The Punjabi Mexican story began in California's Imperial Valley, a desert along the Mexican border east of San Diego that was transformed into a major center of irrigation agriculture in the early twentieth century by diversion of the Colorado River. Native-born whites controlled the developing political economy, but men from many nations came to work in the valley. Cocopah Indians were among the first laborers. With the 1910 Revolution in Mexico, Mexicans began moving across the border, and blacks were recruited from the south to pick cotton. Japanese and Punjabis showed up as farmers and farm labourers in the 1910 Census, where 18 unmistakably Punjabi names appeared (US National Archives 1910). In 1920, Indians were not counted separately in the census, but an educated Indian estimated there were 268 Punjabis in the valley in 1924 (Hoover Institution 1924). In other parts of California, Punjabi men stayed in labour camps or rooming houses, but, in the Imperial Valley, they began to settle down. They sent foreign money orders from the local post offices, were listed as 'ranchers' in local directories and were early telephone subscribers. They lived in wooden shacks on the land they were farming, typically in households of two to four persons. Better housing usually was not available to them or even desired, since many leased different acreage from year to year. Many became successful farmers. Leases recorded in the county courthouse show many Punjabi partnerships; court cases, with Hindoo or Hindu as a category in the records, show disputes over property and finances (Leonard 1992: 48–52). But in 1923 the US Supreme Court's decision that, while persons from India were Caucasian they were not 'white persons', meant that they were subjected to California's Alien Land Laws. Access to American citizenship at the time depended on race – one had to be white or black (this was true until the 1940s when, group by group, access was extended to Asians). The Alien Land Laws, dating from 1910 and aimed at the increasingly successful Japanese immigrant farmers, prevented 'aliens ineligible for citizenship' from leasing or owning agricultural land. After the 1923 decision, these laws were applied to the Punjabi farmers too.

Yet many Punjabis persevered and settled down. People called them 'Hindus', meaning immigrants from Hindustan or India, and the Punjabis (85 percent of them Sikhs by religion) accepted the name and used it for themselves. When post-1965 immigrants from South Asia began arriving much later, people called the Punjabi pioneers the 'old Hindus'. The pioneers worked hard to cultivate local relationships with white farmers, lawyers and judges to gain access to land and resources. They had a very good reputation in the Imperial Valley and elsewhere in the American southwest, noted for their hard work, dependability and honesty.

The Punjabi farmers looked for women to marry. Women were scarce in the Imperial Valley in those early years, with a sex ratio in the 1910 Census of almost 2 to 1 (8,900 males to 4,691 females). By 1920 the population was 40 percent female, but there were greater imbalances among the Asian immigrants and there were no women from India.[2] Men returned to their homelands for brides or sent for them: the Swiss got 'mail-order brides' and the Japanese got 'picture brides'. California's anti-miscegenation laws (repealed only in 1948) prohibited marriages between people of different races, and Punjabis were generally classified as non-white. The first few Punjabi marriages in the valley were front-page news. Sher Singh, a wealthy Holtville cotton farmer, secured a licence for a Mexican bride in March of 1916, and his partner Gopal Singh married the sister of Sher Singh's wife in 1917. These sisters, Antonia and Anna Anita Alvarez, had moved from Mexico with their mother to El Paso and then the Imperial Valley, where they had got jobs picking cotton for Punjabi farmers. (Cotton brought together Punjabis and many of the women they married, and cotton picking was the only outdoor work done by Jat Sikh women in the central Punjab in India.) By 1919, two more Alvarez sisters and a niece of theirs had also married Punjabis. These civil ceremonies and others with Hispanic women were often witnessed by leading Anglo farmers. But when another well-to-do Holtville cotton farmer married the young daughter of one of his white tenants in 1918, he had to go to Arizona because Imperial County would not issue a marriage licence, attracting headlines such as 'Hindu Weds White Girl by Stealing Away to Arizona'. While Punjabis secured marriage licences for Hispanic women without problems, the growing Mexican American community in the valley objected to their women being taken away by Punjabi men, and there were conflicts. A Punjabi's marriage to a Mexican woman caused a 'race riot' in a cotton field near Heber in 1918, and four years later two Mexican men abducted two Mexican sisters who had married Punjabis (Leonard 1992: 62–5).

The Punjabi–Mexican marriage networks extended from El Paso, Texas, to Las Cruces, New Mexico, Phoenix, Arizona and the Imperial Valley. The men not only married across ethnic lines but related to each other across religious lines that were hardening back in India. Sikhs, Muslims and Hindus were partners and brothers-in-law and godparents to each others' children, and their families constituted a new ethnic group called the Mexican Hindus or Mexidus. One marriage led to another as the women arranged matches with relatives and friends, the women usually being much younger than the men. Partners often married sisters, and couples shared households with each other and with bachelors who became 'uncles' to the many children born of the marriages. Based in the Imperial Valley, where 93 percent of the wives were Spanish-speakers, marriages elsewhere reflected the prevailing demographic patterns. Thus in northern California 40 percent of the wives were white and black English-speakers and a very few wives from India had managed to migrate there (see the table in Leonard 1992: 67).

Post-1965 Indian immigrants frequently state that these marriages outside traditional community boundaries took place because they helped the men secure land, either through wives who were American citizens or the children who were citizens by birth. But this is not true, because the men only lost access to land in 1923 when the Supreme Court declared them ineligible to citizenship, and the biethnic marriage pattern was well established before that. Also, the wives acquired the status of their husbands upon marriage, not the reverse (the Cable Act, in effect from 1922 through 1931, provided that female citizens marrying aliens ineligible for citizenship lost their citizenship). The Punjabi fathers did not begin putting land in the names of their children (with themselves as guardians) until 1934, well after many, many children had been born. Before 1934, only three Imperial Valley farmers had registered as guardians, but many more did after the 1933 Imperial County indictment of some Punjabis and Anglos for conspiring to evade the Alien Land Law by forming corporations (Leonard 1992: 7–19).

The biethnic community was a very visible one in many of California's farm towns. Patterns of childbearing, fertility and mortality show large families: 80 percent of the children born to the 69 women for whom I have good information in the Imperial Valley had four or more siblings and 42 percent had eight or more siblings. Infant, child and maternal mortality rates were relatively high, with the county records showing most births occurring in homes with midwives in attendance rather than in hospitals with doctors. Often, the names of children and parents were misspelled and the ages of the parents were inaccurate on the birth certificates (Leonard 1992: 74–8). But the naming pattern was clear: Hispanic first names followed by Sikh, Muslim and Hindu surnames. Thus, children with names like Angelita Singh, Jesusita Mohammed or Fernando Chand, along with stepchildren brought into the marriages by their Hispanic mothers from previous relationships, helped give the growing community the local name 'Mexican Hindu' or 'Mexidu'.

The hybridity of family life was also reflected in food, religion and languages. The men taught the women how to cook Punjabi dishes, like 'chicken *murghi*' (literally chicken chicken) or chicken curry, *roti* or bread, vegetables and pickles. However, they found Mexican food similar to Indian and mixed the cuisines in homes and at public events. Some of the women, cut off from their families, proclaimed themselves 'Hindu', and others called them that too, as they were the wives of the Hindus. The women's kinship networks organized affiliations to the Catholic Church through *compadrazgo* or godparent relationships sanctioned by that church, and almost all the godparents were drawn from within the Punjabi Mexican community. The Sikh, Muslim and Hindu men did not convert to Catholicism, but they were recorded, sometimes with Hispanic first names (Miguel Singh for Maghyar Singh), as godparents to each others' children. The men, themselves often illiterate and without religious texts of their own, entrusted the childrens' religious upbringing to their wives, saying that all religions were to be respected, that all were ways to the one God. A Sikh temple was established in 1912 in northern California in Stockton, and Punjabis of all backgrounds met there with their wives and children for social as well as religious purposes. Languages within the families tended to be Spanish and English. Since the men not only married Hispanic women but worked with or employed Mexicans, they learned Spanish and did not try to teach their wives or children Punjabi. Coming from British India, most of the men spoke some English and many of the wives spoke it as well, and the children were schooled in English.

Did these early Indian migrants constitute a diaspora? Most of the Punjabi pioneers were Sikhs, and Sikh scholars and laymen alike have proudly claimed this early migration of Punjabis as a Sikh diaspora. This is a misnomer, since the men's networks were based on their shared Punjabi language and regional origin: if anything, this was a Punjabi diaspora. Further, I would argue that it was not really a diaspora at all. The Punjabi men did not intend to return to India, although many did send remittances to their families in India and some sent money for schools or other improvements in their home villages. Given the chance to go back after access to citizenship was obtained in 1946, very few did. Relatives in India were far more eager to resume contact with the Punjabis in America than vice versa, on the whole (Leonard 1992: 212). The women, many from Mexico, also had no intentions of returning there, although some retained connections to relatives there and occasionally visited them.

Moreover, the men's political allegiances and efforts shifted over time from India to America. The men were immensely proud of their Indian origin and many retained a keen interest in Indian politics and some degree of connection to relatives in India. Much has been made of the militant anti-British Ghadar party that these Punjabi men formed in California in 1913, but it was very short lived. Internal conflicts based on regional origins in the Punjab and US government persecution led to its decline; in actuality, it contributed little to the nationalist movement in India. Instead, Punjabi farmers focused their strongest and most sustained political efforts on gaining access to American citizenship, working with other Indians across the US in a lobbying campaign that succeeded in 1946 with the passage of the Luce Celler Bill. Many old-timers became citizens then, claiming the new homeland in large numbers and, significantly, claiming farmland for their own since the Alien Land Law no longer applied to them (Leonard 1992: 211, 164). Despite their support of Indian nationalist leaders who visited California to raise money for the Congress party in the 1940s, most Punjabis in California were taken by surprise by the partition of British India in 1947 into India and Pakistan. Networks formed in America were somewhat disrupted after that event, and a new name was invented, Spanish Pakistani, for the families whose Punjabi founders' villages ended up in Pakistan (Leonard 1992: 173).

The men made little effort to transmit Indian cultural traditions to their wives and children, in some cases telling them it would be useless as they were all American now. They did pass on some food preferences and they continued habits of work and play brought from India: a strong work ethic, a propensity to drink and talk together after work and a keen interest in politics. Later, when the children matured and began dating, the fathers attempted to apply regional and religious preferences and avoidances brought from India (saying, for example, that a young man's father was from Malwa not the Doab, a young woman's father was an untouchable Sikh and not a Jat, or a young person's father was Sikh and not Muslim), but both the wives and the children resisted these unfamiliar notions. When members of the second generation began marrying, the biethnic community proved to be transitional, as most Mexican Hindu youth married whites or Hispanics rather than each other. This new pattern of outmarriages was partly a result of fatherly pressure against marriages within the Mexican Hindu community but across Punjabi religious, caste and regional lines (above). Such lines seem to have been resurrected in the minds of the fathers when the Luce Celler Bill of 1946 gave them access to American citizenship and consequently to their relatives in India once again. Whether or not the fathers might be seen as trying at that point to reverse the hybridity they had themselves created, trying to reinvent themselves as diasporic, is a moot point because they did not succeed in arranging marriages for their children with potential immigrants from the homeland.

As the children grew up, the young people took great pride in their 'Hindu' heritage, but they knew virtually nothing of Punjabi or Indian culture. They did represent India (and Pakistan, after 1947) in county fairs, beauty pageants and the like. But the arrival of the post-1965 immigrants from India and Pakistan jolted and challenged them, as the new immigrants from all over India questioned their Indianness. An example is when Joe Mallobox, son of an 'old Hindu' in the Imperial Valley, introduced himself at Disneyland to a family he took to be from India because the woman was wearing a sari. Saying, 'I'm a Hindu too', he offered to show them around, but they clearly failed to acknowledge him as Indian and rebuffed his offer. To some extent this reaction was understandable: 'members of the second generation often could not give a recognizable name for their fathers' villages or sometimes not even for their [own] fathers (Bleth Heather? Ali Singh?). And it is hard to forget the third-generation youngster in the Imperial Valley who had Singh as her last name but asked me, "I know I'm a Hindu and I'm proud of that, but was my grandfather a Muslim, Sikh, or Hindu?"'

The new immigrants were critical of the descendants of the old ones, but those descendants were also critical of the new immigrants. In their view, the newcomers were not becoming American fast enough and were retaining old-fashioned or superstitious practices from India. Even worse, the newcomers failed to recognize the considerable achievements of the Punjabi pioneers despite the legal and social constraints they had faced. As I concluded in my 1992 book, most of the descendants of the 'old Hindus' saw themselves at the end of the twentieth century as part of a larger unhyphenated white or American category (Leonard 1992: 218). The Punjabi pioneers and their descendants seem to exemplify Devaroo's predicted movement to citizenship in the host country, without having been diasporic in the ways commonly accepted by scholarly definitions, but having been hybrid in multiple and compelling ways.

Notes

1   Instances of boundary-crossing appear also in non-academic writings: in Samarasan's compelling novel (2008), the chief male Tamil immigrant in Malaysia has children with a Chinese Malaysian woman; and Hajratwala's fine family history (2009) of diasporic Gujaratis (a notoriously insular group) documents numerous instances of outmarriages among her kin in North America.
2   US Department of Commerce, Bureau of the Census, *Thirteenth Census of the United States taken in the year of 1910; Abstract of the Census with Supplement for California* (Washington, DC: Government Printing Office, 1913), 601 for the 1910 ratio; for 1920, US Department of Commerce, *Fourteenth Census: Population, 1920*, III: 113, 131.

References

Ali, Nasreen (2007). 'Diaspora and Nation: Displacement and the Politics of Kashmiri Identity in Britain', in Ajaya Kumar Sahoo and Brij Maharaj (eds) *Sociology of Diaspora: A Reader*, New Delhi: Rawat Publications, II, 888–901.

Appadurai, Arjun (1996). *Modernity at Large: Cultural Dimensions of Globalisation*, Minneapolis, MN: University of Minnesota Press.

Bhatia, Sunil and Anjali Ram (2007). 'Culture, Hybridity, and the Dialogical Self: Cases from the South Asian Diaspora', in Ajaya Kumar Sahoo and Brij Maharaj (eds) *Sociology of Diaspora: A Reader*, New Delhi: Rawat Publications, II, 618–42.

Devarajoo, Karthiyaini (2009). 'Transforming Diaspora', in Laxmi Narayan Kadekar, Ajaya Kumar Sahoo and Gauri Bhattacharya (eds) *The Indian Diaspora: Historical and Contemporary Context*, New Delhi: Rawat Publications, 135–47.

Eisenlohr, Patrick (2007). 'Language and Identity in an Indian Diaspora: Multiculturalism and Ethno-Linguistic Communities in Mauritius', in Ajaya Kumar Sahoo and Brij Maharaj (eds) *Sociology of Diaspora: A Reader*, New Delhi: Rawat Publications, II, 773–86.

Hajratwala, Minal (2009). *Five Families: My Family's Journey from Five Villages to Five Continents*, New York: Houghton Mifflin Harcourt.

Hinnels, John R. (1994). 'The Modern Zoroastrian Diaspora', in Judith M. Brown and Rosemary Foot (eds) *Migration: The Asian Experience*, Oxford: St. Martin's Press, 56–82.

Hookoomsing, Vinesh (2009). 'Language Loss, Language Maintenance: The Case of Bhojpuri and Hindi in Mauritius', in Laxmi Narayan Kadekar, Ajaya Kumar Sahoo and Gauri Bhattacharya (eds) *The Indian Diaspora: Historical and Contemporary Context*, New Delhi: Rawat Publications, 35–53.

Hoover Institution (1924). *Survey of Race Relations*, Hoover Institution Archives, Stanford, California, no. 232, Ram Chand, p. 4, interviewed by W.C. Smith, June 1, El Centro.

Jacobsen, Knut A. and Selva J. Raj (eds) (2008). *South Asian Christian Diaspora: Invisible Diaspora in Europe and North America*, Surrey: Ashgate.

Lal, Vinay (2006). 'United States of America', in Brij V. Lal (ed.) *The Enycyclopedia of the Indian Diaspora*, Honolulu: University of Hawai'i Press, 314–26.

Leonard, Karen Isaksen (1992). *Making Ethnic Choices: California's Punjabi Mexican Americans*, Philadelphia: Temple University Press.

— (2006). 'South Asian Religions in the US: New Contexts and Configurations', in Gita Rajan and Shailja Sharma (eds) *New Cosmopolitanisms: South Asians in the United States at the Turn of the 21st Century*, Palo Alto: Stanford University Press, 91–114.

— (2007). *Locating Home: India's Hyderabadis Abroad*, Palo Alto: Stanford University Press.

— (2009). 'Is There a Second Diasporic Generation? The Case of India's Hyderabadis', in Laxmi Narayan Kadekar, Ajaya Kumar Sahoo and Gauri Bhattacharya (eds) *The Indian Diaspora: Historical and Contemporary Context*, New Delhi: Rawat Publications, 232–43.

Mahabir, Kumar (2009). 'The Indian Diaspora in the West Indies/Caribbean', in Laxmi Narayan Kadekar, Ajaya Kumar Sahoo and Gauri Bhattacharya (eds) *The Indian Diaspora: Historical and Contemporary Context*, New Delhi: Rawat Publications, 113–34.

Oonk, Gijsbert (2007). 'Global Indian Diasporas: Exploring Trajectories of Migration and Theory' in Gijsbert Oonk (ed.) *Global Indian Diasporas: Exploring Trajectories of Migration and Theory*, Amsterdam: Amsterdam University Press.

Samarasan, Preeta (2008). *Evening is the Whole Day*, Boston: Houghton Mifflin Company.

US Department of Commerce (1913). Bureau of the Census. *Thirteenth Census of the United States Taken in the Year of 1910*; *Abstract of the Census with Supplement for California*, Washington, DC: Government Printing Office.

— (1920). *Fourteenth Census: Population*, III.

US National Archives (1910). [manuscript census] *Record Group 29, Census of US Population*, Imperial County, California.

22

BENGALIS IN BRITAIN

Migration, state controls and settlement

John Eade

Preparing the ground: colonialism and global flows

The Bengali presence in Britain long precedes the end of the British Indian empire. In 1616 the Mayor of London attended the baptism of 'Peter', an East Indian from the Bay of Bengal, who had arrived in 1614 and whose 'Christian' name was chosen by James I. As Rosina Visram reveals in her pioneering book, *Ayahs, Lascars and Princes* (1986), British involvement in the Bengal delta soon led to servants being brought to Britain, to be followed by sailors (*lascars*), aristocrats and university students. Hence, by 'the time the first Indian students came to Britain in the mid-nineteenth century, an itinerant Indian population of ayahs and lascars already existed' (Lahiri 2000: 3). The first record of a specifically Bengali student presence in Britain appears in 1845, when 'four Bengali Hindus accompanied Dr Goodeve, Professor of Anatomy in Calcutta, to University College, London' (Visram 1986). The most renowned Bengali visitor was India's first Nobel Prize winner, the poet Rabindranath Tagore (1861–1941), who attended a public school in Brighton and studied law at University College London before returning to Bengal in 1880. An inveterate traveller, he visited Britain again in 1912 and 1930 during subsequent tours of Europe.

Like Tagore, most Bengalis returned to their homeland. However, a few stayed on and survived as street musicians in London's East End. Some became involved with local women. One of the celebrated offspring from these early mixed relationships was Albert Mahomet:

> Born in 1858 at Sophia Street in Bow, East London, to an English mother and an ex-seaman from Calcutta. Mahomet grew up in a world of crime and poverty that claimed many of his siblings. Eventually, he moved to the city of Wells and became a respected Methodist preacher and photographer.[1]

The *lascars* benefitted from the strengthening ties between Calcutta and the British merchant fleet and contributed to mixed relationships in London's East End:

> In 1856, Calcutta became the headquarters of the British India Steam Navigation Company (BISNC). This greatly increased the employment of Bengali Lascars in the British Merchant Navy. By 1873 there is mention of a lodge run by an Englishwoman

called 'Calcutta' Louisa and another run by 'Lascar' Sally, for Indian Lascars at the riverside of the High Street at Wapping. 'Lascar' Sally's real name was Sarah Graham. These English women lived with their Indian partners and often even spoke Bengali or Hindi.[2]

Since Calcutta was closely connected to the Bengali hinterland through a complex network of rivers and sea connections to other ports along the Bay of Bengal, many of these *lascars* were Muslims recruited from Noakhali in East Bengal, the port of Chittagong and the up-country district of Sylhet, which was then in the province of Assam (see Ahuja, this volume and Visram 1986: 191). Sylhetis were recorded as 'working in London restaurants since at least 1873' and they contributed to the growing numbers of 'Muslim seamen' who 'formed a substantial section of the "visible" migrant population in Britain' (Ansari 2004: 40), especially the ports.[3]

By the end of the 1930s, a more permanent and visible Bengali presence had emerged in London and some of Britain's other cities – a presence which was shaped by class, caste, religion and regional differences. The main emergent groups were not only the Muslim *lascars* but also high-caste Hindus from Calcutta, who entered professional jobs after university in Bengal and/or Britain. Relatively little is known about the latter group of educated Bengali Hindus but it may be assumed that they contributed to the community of Indian doctors, approximately 1,000 strong, who were practising in Britain by 1947, of whom 200 were in London (Visram 1986: 191).

Much more is known about the *lascars'* presence during the first half of the twentieth century. They first appeared in the seaports – not just London but also 'Glasgow, Newcastle, Liverpool, Southampton and London' (Visram 1986: 190). However, some moved away from these ports to find jobs in factories, foundries, hotels and hospitals, for example, across England or sold goods as pedlars (see Adams 1987: 45–46; and Ahuja, this volume). Yousuf Choudhury notes:

> The Bangladeshi job seekers, including the new-comers from ships, were unable to find jobs in London. They began to find their way to the Midlands and also to the further north in the industrial and cotton mills belt. Birmingham the heart-land of industries, already had a few Bangladeshis long before the second world war.
>
> *(1993: 71)*

By the 1930s some had emerged as 'ethnic entrepreneurs':

> At least one Sylheti ex-sailor Ayub Ali, arrived in London and established a restaurant at 76 Commercial Street in Whitechapel. Another Sylheti ex-sailor, Syed Tofussil Ally, opened the British Indian Sailors' Home and seaman's outfitting shop at 32–3 Victoria Dock Road, in Canning Town.[4]

The outbreak of the Second World War and the Bengali famine of 1941 both pulled and pushed young Bengali Muslims into serving on British merchant ships. Their presence in London's docks while they waited for a ship to take them back to Calcutta encouraged Ayub Ali to collaborate with another Bengali Muslim colleague to set up 'the Indian Seaman's Welfare League at 66, Christian Street'.[5] Significantly the membership of this organisation appears to have been predominantly Sylheti.[6]

British attempts to control flows from India to Britain during the colonial period

Although the literature on the colonial period primarily focuses on migrants themselves, attention must also be paid to the political and economic structures within which the migrants moved. Clearly, the links between the Indian subcontinent and Britain were forged by Britain's expanding empire, which involved more than just a one-way flow of capital, goods, ideas and images. The flow of British administrators, military, traders, industrialists, planters and professionals (teachers, lawyers, doctors, engineers), for example, was accompanied by the reverse flow described above (also see Fisher, this volume). The flows were unequal, of course, and the British government sought to control the influx as part of the long debate about 'immigrants'. This debate was arguably not only about foreigners, but also about sections of the indigenous population who were considered a danger to respectable society. Anxieties about immigration were, then as now, closely linked to concerns about poverty, criminality and the rapid growth of cities.

Initially, the East India Company tried to restrict Indian seamen to 'trading from India to Burma, China, the Malay Archipelago and east Africa' (Ahuja, this volume; and Adams 1987: 15). However, as early as the seventeenth century they had also been 'used for the return voyage to Britain for ships whose crews had been decimated by disease and desertion' (Adams 1987: 15). During the nineteenth century, the practice rapidly strengthened; and, after the Company's demise, 'the practice was continued by the shipping lines', so that, as Ahuja (this volume) has shown, 'the heyday of steam shipping, the 1850's to the 1950's, was also the heyday of the lascar seamen' (Adams 1987: 16). The presence of rootless, impoverished and racially different *lascars* was particularly disturbing to British officials, not only in Britain but also back in India. After first ignoring the issue, from 1795 the East India Company began to provide some basic accommodation in the East End and the central government also introduced legislation – the 1832 Lascar Act – to make the Company 'theoretically responsible . . . for the accommodation and repatriation of lascars' (Adams 1987: 18). Although the India Office inherited the Company's responsibilities, it was merchants and Indian princes (Adams 1987: 20), who helped to provide a 200-bed 'Stranger's Home for Asiatics, Africans, South Sea Islanders and other occasionally residing in the Metropolis' (Visram 1986: 49) in the East End.

As Tabili (1994) has pointed out, government legislation played a crucial role in the changing construction of racial difference during the colonial period. Moreover, it has deeply influenced the development of racialised discourses and practices during the unravelling of empire after the Second World War. The presence of Bengali and other seamen from the colonies was the focus of 'the first instance of state-sanctioned race discrimination inside Britain to come to widespread notice' (Tabili 1994: 56) – the Coloured Alien Seamen Order of 1925, which required 'undocumented Black seamen' to 'register as aliens in Britain' (Tabili 1994: 56). The category 'Black' was applied to seamen from a wide range of colonial territories (India, Africa and the Caribbean) in ways which not only excluded them as aliens but also shaped racial hierarchies within Britain. The effect of the order:

> was the codification of a hierarchical definition of British nationality dependent on race, class and occupation, and, implicitly, gender, a definition shaped by the demands of the shipping industry, the vagaries of the interwar economy, local and national politics, and state policy decisions.
>
> *(Tabili 1994: 86)*

At the same time, the seamen challenged and tried to subvert the Order, 'prompting continual reshaping of official definitions of entitlement and of racial difference itself' (Tabili 1994: 87).

The Order was renewed in 1938 and 1942 before being abolished to widen the net of those who could be conscripted to help the war effort. This interweaving of local and global forces ensured that definitions of British subjecthood could expand or contract very quickly. The extension of 'British citizenship ... to all colonial and Commonwealth subjects' in 1948 was restricted by the legislation controlling immigration and citizenship from 1962 (Tabili 1994: 94).

Although the regulation of *lascars* and 'Black' seamen from the colonies was very important, other factors played a part in government attempts to control flows from the empire to Britain. Growing unrest with British control in India led to the introduction of passport stop lists during the 1920s 'to exclude political activists with a history of anti-British activity in India'. These lists were also used to control 'the entry of Indians of "limited means" from the early 1930s' and were directed 'primarily at Indian peddlars from the Punjab who sought to bring family members to Britain to assist them with their businesses, selling goods door-to-door'. [7]

Migration after the Second World War: from sojourners to settlers

While many *lascars* returned to Calcutta at the end of the war, the flow reversed during the 1950s. The British economy began to recover from the effects of the Second World War and the indigenous workforce took advantage of the improved labour demand to move away from low-paid, menial jobs in factories, foundries, hotels, hospitals and transport. Initially, European workers, who had been displaced by the war or faced bleak prospects in their countries of origin, stepped into these jobs, but the demand remained high and so, for a brief period in the mid-1950s, the British government actively encouraged labour migration from the Commonwealth. As Ahuja has shown (this volume), Sylheti former *lascars* were able to garner many of the 'vouchers issued to Commonwealth workers during London's post-war boom'.

Although doctors from West Bengal were also recruited at this time to fill vacancies in the National Health Service (NHS), the majority of Bengalis came from Sylhet, which had become a district in East Pakistan from 1947. The key organisations involved in negotiating Sylheti recruitment were the Overseas Seamen's Welfare Association, led by Aftab Ali, and the Pakistan Welfare Association. Under pressure from the UK government (Chatterji, this volume), Pakistan had restricted access to passports in the early 1950s, but in 1956 it 'agreed to grant one thousand passports to "distressed seamen", their survivors [and] nominated dependents (sic)' (Adams 1987: 62). Travel agencies in both Bangladesh and London eased the process and, after further pressure from Aftab Ali, the Pakistan government allowed Sylhetis other than former seamen to obtain passports. Adams claims that:

> 1956, the year of the passports, brought about a sudden change, as the three hundred or so ex-seamen in East London were joined by two to three thousand more men.... After the first arrivals there was a steady stream of migration until by 1962 the community was perhaps five thousand strong.
>
> *(Adams 1987: 64)*

The Sylhet connection was also strengthened by the long-established ties between Calcutta and the up-country district noted above. After the 1947 partition, ships continued to sail from Calcutta to Sylhet during the rainy season to collect rice and jute. Gardner cites the regular arrival of 'huge cargo ships from Calcutta' up to 1965 at places which became 'key

Londoni areas' (Gardner 1995: 41). Links between Sylhet and Calcutta were reinforced by the Sylheti brokers who had long been established in the metropolis.

Land ownership also appears to have played a role. Unlike other areas of the Bengal delta a 'large proportion of farmers were independent owner–cultivators rather than tenants' (Gardner 1995: 38). Competition over land and related status was a prime feature of this *talukdar* system and Gardner suggests that 'migration may have been a means to compete, enabling families to improve their economic position through earning foreign wages' (Gardner 1995: 40). Migrants were not pushed by poverty, therefore, since they enjoyed the financial means to take the opportunity through their position as rich 'or middle income rural families' (Gardner 1995: 40). Gardner notes that similar socio-economic conditions underpinned Pakistani migration to Britain and Punjabi Hindu migration from India (Gardner 1995: 42).

The 1950s can be characterised as the 'early pioneer period' (see Robinson 1986), where 'a steady stream of single men' arrived in Britain to work 'once they had obtained an identity card' (Gardner 1995: 43). During the early 1960s, this period of sojourning gave way to the process of settling. British state legislation hastened this development since concern about white British hostility towards black migrants encouraged the introduction of the Commonwealth Immigrants Act in 1962, which required migrants from the Commonwealth to acquire employment vouchers (Gardner 1995: 44). Rather than limiting migration as it had hoped to do, it encouraged people to apply for permits before it was too late, using their family networks, and Gardner claims that 'thousands of Sylheti men went to Manchester, Bradford, Newcastle, and countless other towns to work in the factories' (Gardner 1995: 45).

British Bengali involvement in the E. Pakistan crisis of 1971 and the creation of an independent Bangladesh later that year largely engaged this first generation of settlers. They worked with white activists, politicians and journalists to highlight 'the atrocities taking place' there, lobbied the 'British government and international community' and raised 'funds for refugees and Bengali freedom fighters' (Ullah and Eade 2006: 8).[8] However, by the late 1970s, younger Sylhetis from what would prove to be a second generation of settlers, entered the local political and community arena (see Eade 1989; Forman 1989; Ullah and Eade 2006). Significantly, these new community representatives and activists mainly came from London's East End and Tower Hamlets, in particular, indicating the ways in which the metropolis was becoming the main centre of political and cultural life – a process strengthened by industrial decline in the North and Midlands and the better opportunities available in London and the Home Counties.

The first reliable data on the Bangladeshi, as opposed to the Bengali, presence in Britain were provided by the 1991 national census. A question on ethnicity enabled respondents to refer to their country of birth and 162,835 people were recorded as Bangladeshi (see Eade *et al.* 1996, 150). Approximately 40 per cent of this 1991 total had been born in Britain – the beginnings of the third generation (Eade *et al.* 1996). A total of 97 per cent of these Bangladeshis were located within England, and over half were in Greater London. Half of these Londoners were confined to one borough – Tower Hamlets (Eade *et al.* 1996: 157).

The rapid expansion of the Bangladeshi population has continued with the arrival of wives and dependants during the late 1980s and early 1990s, and through the natural growth of a third generation. Between 1991 and 2011 the Bangladeshi population in England and Wales increased from 157,950 to 447,201, i.e. by 183 per cent. London continued to dominate demographically since, by 2011, it contained 221,227 or just under half the total Bangladeshi population in England and Wales. Although Tower Hamlets was still the most important in terms of population and political weight – 81,377 or 18 per cent of the England and Wales Bangladeshi population lived there – Bangladeshis were spreading across the inner and outer boroughs north of the Thames. They also formed substantial concentrations in the metropolitan areas of the Midlands,

North West and Yorkshire. Luton had also attracted substantial numbers, while Cardiff, Newcastle and Portsmouth – with strong histories as ports – were also the home of long established Bangladeshi settlements[9].

Entering the public arena

The movement from temporary to permanent settlement from the 1970s onwards has been reflected in the changing characteristics of British Bangladeshi political engagement. Diasporic ties with Bangladesh have been maintained over generations, so, until today, political developments in the country of origin reverberate in the British diaspora. These continuing links have been sustained by the competition for influence and prestige (*izzat*) between lineages through projects for development (*jonokollan*). Competition between community leaders has overlapped with the divisions in Bangladeshi party politics, since leaders of Bangladeshi parties have played a central role in the *jonokollan* committees (Eade and Garbin 2006). Major parties such as the Awami League and the Bangladesh National Party (BNP) have kept in close touch with their supporters in Britain and other areas of the diaspora, such as the Middle East and North America, through fund-raising campaigns and visits by leaders. President Ershad visited Britain in the 1980s, and Sheikh Hasina, whose sister lives in Britain, has visited on many occasions.

Links between present and past are also sustained by organisations that may be described as diasporic 'heritage' groups such as Swadhinata, the UK Bangabandhu Society (which seeks to keep alive the memory of Sheikh Mujibur Rahman, the country's first Prime Minister), the Bangladesh Mutijoddha Sangshad UK (Bangladesh Freedom Fighter Association, UK) and the Nirmul Committee, which campaigns for the punishment of 'war crimes' committed during the 1971 struggle and is informally connected to Swadhinata.

Diasporic links are also strengthened by the ways in which politics and religion interweave. The issue of Muslim identity has been a central theme of politics both before and after the creation of Bangladesh. Although the break-up of East Pakistan led to the adoption of a constitution modelled on secular nation-state regimes of the West, Sheikh Mujib drew on Muslim identity before his death and, despite the Awami League's self-presentation as a secular party, it has acknowledged the power of Muslim identity politics through pragmatic alliances with Jamaat-i-Islami Bangladesh in order to outflank its main rival, the BNP.

This diasporic relationship between politics and religion is not confined to party institutions and struggles for control of state institutions back in Bangladesh. It is linked to notions of prestige in rural and urban society and to the way people express Muslim identity in everyday life (clothing, education, language and food). Prestige projects such as the building of mosques and *madrassahs* also express a more widespread process of Islamisation, which has influenced developments among British Bangladeshis. Religious leaders inevitably play a part in politics, directly or indirectly, through the example they provide as 'good Muslims'. Their visits to Britain to meet their supporters have had considerable political impact, since they are wooed by political leaders and their teachings encourage their followers to see Muslim identity in distinct ways: so, for instance, Abdul Latif Chowdhury, the Bangladeshi 'Pir of Fultoli', advocates a syncretic approach towards Islam, which differs from the more exclusive or purificatory approach pursued by many Deobandi leaders (see Eade and Garbin 2002, 2006 and Marsden, this volume). Highly visible mosques in areas of Bengali concentration, such as the East London Mosque and Jamme Masjid in Tower Hamlets, the Shah Jalal mosque in Birmingham and the Al Jalaliah *madrassah* in Oldham, have exercised influence on religion and politics at both local and global levels.

British domestic politics have also exerted a considerable influence on the political life of the Bangladeshi diaspora. Government attempts to control Bengali immigration from the 1960s prompted an engagement between British political and administrative structures and Bangladeshi diasporic politics. The 1971 crisis played a key role, since East Bengalis were mobilised across Britain in public demonstrations, lobbying MPs and central government (Ullah and Eade 2006). A range of people came together in a coalition that included women, Hindus from both sides of the border, British politicians, journalists and community leaders; and the Pakistan Welfare Association was taken over and renamed the Bangladesh Welfare Association (BWA).

During the 1970s, British Bangladeshi community leaders continued to be involved in competition for prestige through leadership contests within the BWA. But the local British political arena provided another space where this competition was played out, and where outside funding was being made available. Government funding of inner city redevelopment also played a role here and in turn encouraged the process of permanent settlement. Both Labour and Conservative parties supported a strategy of multiculturalism which promoted the growth of minority ethnic leaders claiming to represent 'their community' at local and central state levels.

One issue that preoccupied them was housing. Bangladeshis had been initially confined to cheap private accommodation in areas where council housing predominated. Unlike the Pakistani migrants, they were concentrated in areas where they did not own their properties. In Tower Hamlets and other inner London boroughs, council housing predominated and had been allocated to local white residents during the large-scale redevelopment programmes of the 1950s and 1960s. Although newcomers could apply for this accommodation after five years' residency, a number of factors conspired against them, such as language problems, correct paperwork and local hostility to newcomers (see Phillips 1986; Eade 1989).

Other economic problems were politically significant. Despite the similarities between inner city London and the Northern and Midlands towns, the reliance on industrial production was less intense. Services, such as shops, restaurants, taxis, hotels, travel agencies and public services (local government, hospitals, schools), tended to offset the decline in the garment industry, which took place during the 1990s in the East End. Oldham relied far more heavily on one industry – cotton manufacturing – which began its inexorable decline during the 1980s. Tower Hamlets attracted massive injections of capital during the 1980s which largely passed Bangladeshis and other 'locals' by. Yet the sale of council housing partly compensated for this during the 1990s, when Bangladeshis had entered the council housing sector, as well as the housing cooperatives, in substantial numbers.

The emergence of Bangladeshi ethnic enclaves in London and other cities promoted a process of political representation, which relied on the organisational efforts of community activists and voluntary organisations supported by local residents, such as the youth groups of the 1970s and 1980s, as well as housing cooperatives (of which the Spitalfields Housing Cooperative was a notable example). Given the local and central government's financing of council housing, the state was a major target of Bangladeshi lobbying. Even though the government withdrew from its involvement during the 1990s through the right-to-buy scheme, the state continued to be a focus of Bengali pressure groups, since some Bangladeshi residents wanted to share in the sale, while others wanted to access the social housing which remained available. Government-funded urban redevelopment projects also strengthened the ties between Bangladeshi representatives and government, such as the massive Olympic Games redevelopment projects in London's East End. Consequently, by 2008 the Bangladesh High Commission estimated that there were 75 councillors across Britain, of which 32 came from Tower Hamlets alone. In 1998 one of Tower Hamlets' prominent community activists, Pola Uddin, became the first Muslim peer.

Controlling immigration

The rapid influx of wives and dependants during the late 1980s and early 1990s was again a response to British government legislation. As Gardner notes, the 1972 Immigration Act and subsequent legislation 'completely halted primary immigration: to get to Britain migrants now had to be the dependants of those already resident' (1995: 47). The Act also broke with previous legislation by ending the distinction between 'aliens' and Commonwealth citizens (Biersteker and Weber 1996) and enabled free entry to those of British descent who were living in the Commonwealth by introducing the category of patrials – a parent or grandparent who was born in Britain. Patrials could also gain access to the European Community and were predominantly white, reflecting the racial thrust of this legislation.

The 1981 British Nationality Act continued the process by making it impossible to gain citizenship by birth (Gardner 1995: 49). Next, attention turned towards preventing marriages of convenience being used to get round stricter visa controls – the 'primary purpose' rule – while the 1988 Immigration Act denied guaranteed entry to dependants. During the 1990s the focus of government controls moved towards asylum seekers and refugees, but pressure was still exercised through visa controls and the issue of 'forced marriage', where British assumptions failed to recognise arranged marriage customs (see Gardner 2002; Mody, this volume). More recently, Bangladeshi activists have focussed on the introduction of an Australian-based points system designed to prevent the influx of low-skilled migrants. The claim was made that this would prevent the customary recruitment of Bangladeshi chefs and, thereby, adversely affect the catering industry. These controls built on a long history of work permits and employment vouchers going back to the Victorian period as we have seen in the case of the *lascars* and the White Paper on Immigration from the Commonwealth of 1965.

Government, Muslim representation and 'social cohesion'

Since the 1990s 'Islamophobia' has largely replaced racism as the main concern for Bangladeshi activists. This has coincided with the growing influence of the East London Mosque (ELM) and also the London Muslim Centre, built on a site next to the mosque. The ELM was used as a base by several Islamist groups, particularly the Islamic Forum Europe (IFE), which also has bases in Birmingham and Oldham (Eade and Garbin 2006: 188). Youth groups with ties to these groups began to rival the secular Bangladeshi organisations from the 1980s: the Young Muslim Organisation (YMO), linked to the ELM and IFE, now has a powerful presence. These links not only radiated across Britain but, not surprisingly, were part of a global network which involved the *Jamaat-i-Islami* and its student wing (*Islami Chatra Shibir* or Muslim Student Camp Organisation) in Bangladesh and Middle Eastern organisations.

Both local and central government have played a part in the growth of these activist groups from the 1990s onwards. At the local level, borough councils supported the outreach work of certain mosques, such as the ELM, on drug addiction. Central government also encouraged the growth of Muslim groups through its ideological commitment to 'faith communities'. The establishment of the Muslim Council of Britain (MCB) in 1997 found favour with the British government, partly because it was seen as more 'moderate' than the Muslim Parliament founded by Dr Siddiqui in 1992.

Another key development has been the growing influence of the ELM and the London Muslim Centre beyond East London. The election of Dr Bari as Secretary-General of the MCB in 2006 has had significant ramifications, as has the establishment of the MCB's offices near the East London Mosque. Although Dr Bari was born in Bangladesh, he is different in a number of respects from many of his compatriots. Not only does he *not* come from Sylhet, he is one of relatively few members of the second generation. He is also highly educated, and mixes easily with non-Bangladeshi Muslim activists across Britain and further afield.

Dr Bari's leadership of the MCB, and the establishment of its offices in Tower Hamlets, strengthened even further the image of the borough as the heartland of the Bangladeshi Muslim community. However, it is important to remember that the ELM and the London Muslim Centre has not been the only focus of Muslim activity. There has been a significant growth of mosques and *madrassahs* beyond the borough. Other religious and community centres were developed, for example, at the Jamme Masjid or London Great Mosque on Brick Lane and the Christian Street mosque in nearby St Katharine's ward, which is used by the Tabligh-i-Jamaat. The establishment and expansion of these religious centres has been a contested process, since mosque leaders have to satisfy objections made by non-Muslim residents as well as the regulations and requirements of local government, especially planning officers (Eade 1997, 2010). When the Tabligh-i-Jamaat moved to the neighbouring borough of Newham and sought to develop a site near the emerging Olympic Village, it encountered objections inspired by environmental and regulatory concerns, as well as by the agendas of other political leaders (Eade 2010; DeHanas and Pieri 2011).

Similar developments were taking place in other cities where Bangladeshis had settled in substantial numbers. Here the influence of the YMO and the IFE was weaker, while the Tabligh-i-Jamaat had a firm base in Birmingham and Oldham, drawing together Muslims from Bangladeshi and other S. Asian countries (see Eade and Garbin 2006: 189). Some mosques in Tower Hamlets, Birmingham and Oldham also provided a welcome to the Sylheti spiritual leader, Pir Abdul Latif Chowdhury, during his regular visits to meet his supporters in Britain (Eade and Garbin 2006:190).

As we have seen, the British government has encouraged the growth of what it saw as a moderate Muslim leadership in order to counter the influence of more radical groups. From the late 1990s onwards, the most prominent radical political groups were Hizb ut-Tahrir and two groups related to Al Muhajiroun – the Saviour Sect and Al-Ghurabaa. These radical organisations had little Bangladeshi local support (see Begum and Eade 2005), although Hizb ut-Tahrir was successful in dominating local student politics, for example, at Tower Hamlets College (Hussain 2007).

Central government has approached Bangladeshis in terms of its general social cohesion policies directed towards 'faith communities'. Its discursive construction of Bangladeshis as members of a particular 'faith community' has stimulated, and in turn been supported by, those claiming to represent that community, especially the Muslim Council of Britain. Since such events as '9/11', '7/7' and civil disturbances in Oldham, Bradford, Leeds and Rochdale in 2006, a key theme in government rhetoric has been the importance of 'social cohesion'. The sharp divide between white residents, on the one hand, and Bangladeshi and Pakistani residents, on the other, in these cities was seen as a prime factor in the the disturbances. Official enquiries into their causes (see, for example, the 2005 Ouseley Report[10] and the 2009 Cantle Report[11]) made recommendations designed to encourage cooperation across ethnic divisions.

The encouragement of social cohesion was also linked to the government's effort to prevent violent extremism (PVE), which in turn was part of its counter-terrorism strategy (CONTEST). It controversially provided extra funds to persons or organisations who could deliver its prime objective of preventing 'people becoming or supporting terrorists or violent extremists'.[12] In 2008 and 2009, local councils funded a variety of schemes, involving many mosques and voluntary groups, across the country, and these inevitably involved Bangladeshis as part of a wider Muslim constituency.

The drive to win the hearts and minds of Bangladeshis and other British Muslims was soon challenged by Muslim organisations, however. The An-Nisa Society, for example, in February 2009 declared that:

> the government's approach to dealing with terrorism by targeting the whole Muslim community as 'potential terrorists' in its **Prevent Strategy** is flawed and fraught with perils. We believe that rather than creating community cohesion and eliminating terrorism it has the potential to create discord and inflame community tensions.
>
> *(Khan 2009: 3, bold text in original)*

The Labour government sought to allay these kinds of fears by broadening Prevent's focus to include all forms of extremism. After its election to power, the coalition government retained the anti-terrorism programme but sought to correct two major flaws – a confusion between government policies concerning integration and the prevention of terrorism and a failure to 'tackle the extremist ideology at the heart of the threat we face'.[13] The new government claimed that 'in trying to reach those at risk of radicalisation, funding sometimes even reached the very extremist organisations that Prevent should have been confronting'.[14]

Keeping below the radar or trying to be heard: Bangladeshi Hindus, the Jumma people and W. Bengali Hindus

By the early twenty-first century Muslims from the Sylhet district of Bangladesh had thus become highly visible in the British public arena through a combination of insider and outsider political representation. They had become the prime focus of various attempts by the British state to regulate their presence not only since the anti-terrorism campaign following '9/11' but also over decades stretching back to their recruitment to work in ships trading between India and Britain. At the same time this population of Sylheti Muslims had generated a wide range of community organisations, especially in London, which have sought to represent the interests of British Bangladeshis to outsiders, and to state officials in particular.

Yet Sylheti Muslims were not the only people from the Bengal delta to settle in Britain. Muslims have migrated from other districts in contemporary Bangladesh, such as Noakhali and Mymensingh, and from the cities of Dhaka and Chittagong. The most celebrated (if controversial) fictional representation of Bangladeshi life in London – *Brick Lane* – was written by Monica Ali, whose father came from Mymensingh but moved to Bolton in N. England with his British wife and his three-year-old daughter in 1970.

Bangladeshi Hindus have also come to this country, in small but significant numbers. Migrants from the 'tribal areas' of the Chittagong Hill Tracts have also arrived in Britain. The presence of Hindus in London from the Bengal delta can be traced back to at least the nineteenth century:

> blue plaques mark the houses of Raja Ram Mohan Roy, and Swami Vivikananda. The tomb of Rabindranath Tagore's grandfather, Prince Dwarkanath Tagore is in Kensal Green Cemetery. This scattering of notables along with many more ordinarily employed Bengalis indicates the range of Bengalis who have been present in this country for a couple of centuries.[15]

During the first half of the twentieth century, university students and political activists enriched Bengali Hindu life in London and other major cities, with a minority settling down to pursue mostly middle-class occupations. As we have already seen, during the 1960s the ranks of the Bengali Hindu middle class were strengthened by the arrival of doctors recruited by the NHS.

In striking contrast to Bangladeshi Muslims, Hindus have largely eschewed identity politics and have little direct contact with the British state. They are relatively prosperous and scattered across suburban areas, so there is little cause to define themselves in terms of deprivation or, relatedly, in need of state support. Their engagement with local government has largely been confined to gaining funding and recognition for community organisations and public events. The Tagore Centre in North London's suburbs, one of the prominent community centres, was founded in 1985 and relied on 'donations, membership fees, ticket sales, funding and publication sales' rather than public funding.[16] It hosted a library, organised cultural events, lectures, seminars and workshops and also supported a branch in Glasgow.

There are exceptions, of course. Bithika Raha, for example, who was born in Assam but came to Britain in 1974 and established a classical dance school currently based in the North London suburb of Totteridge, in 2007 made a successful application to the Heritage Lottery Fund to undertake an oral history of West Bengalis in Britain. The project resulted in a film, shown in Kolkata and London – *Londone Probashi* – on 'first generation Bengalis in Britain'. Its explicit purpose was 'to make other communities more aware of Bengali cultural heritage and history and Bengal's contribution on national and international platforms' and to 'sensitise the present generation of Bengalis who are British citizens [but] unaware of their ethnicity'.[17]

Raha also wanted to challenge widespread ignorance about West Bengalis in Britain. In an interview in Kolkata, she explained the widespread conflation of Bengalis and Bangladeshis, and firmly linked Bengali cultural heritage with Tagore:

> In England the word Bengali spells confusion. They think Bengalis are all people from Bangladesh. Few are even aware of a place called West Bengal. They have stereotyped ideas about us. . . . I am sure the film will generate respect for the Bengali. Britons will understand that Bengal is different from Bangladesh though I do not mean any disrespect to the neighbouring country. . . . What comes out through the film full of dances and Rabindranath Tagore songs is how the Bengalis in London preserved their culture.[18]

The presence of Bangladeshi Hindus has been less publicised than that of West Bengali Hindus. At the time of writing, the only community group using the internet to announce its representation of Bangladeshi Hindus was the Bangladesh Hindu Association which, significantly, was located in Tower Hamlets, the heartland of Britain's Bangladeshi Muslim community. Although the first two of its charitable aims were directed to Bengali Hindus in general, its third goal was directed at Bangladeshi Hindus in both Britain and Bangladesh:

> 1) The advancement of the Hindu religion in the United Kingdom. 2) The advancement of the education of the public, in particular among the Bengali Hindu community in the Hindu culture and religion. 3) The relief of financial need and suffering among victims of natural disaster in the United Kingdom and in Bangladesh.[19]

Bangladeshi Hindus in Tower Hamlets shared the W. Bengali strategy of relying on self-help rather than state support. For example, another voluntary organisation based in London's East End – the Sanaton Association (UK), founded in 1983 – tried to improve the educational standards of young Hindus in Tower Hamlets by running self-funded Saturday and summer schools. When in 2005 it did collaborate with an outside organisation it was with Civitas, 'a free-market think tank', rather than the local state.[20] The extra schooling was necessary according to the association's secretary because local state schools were not insisting on homework:

> Our children aren't given homework in their regular schools because the other kids are Muslims and the schools imagine they have religious study to do in the mosque.... It's a form of political correctness.[21]

Those who had migrated from the Chittagong Hill Tracts were even more scattered than Hindus in Britain. Their relationship to the British state was principally defined through campaigns to raise awareness about 'land grabs' by Muslims from outside the area in Bangladesh, which were reportedly accompanied by violence aided and abetted by the Bangladesh government. These campaigns were directed at the British and Bangladeshi governments as well as through such global organisations as Amnesty International, the Anti-Slavery Society, Survival International, Global Human Rights Defence and the United Nations. Interestingly, in an example of the complex inter-relationships that characterise politics in the diaspora, their grievances have been supported by the secular heritage organisation, Swadhinata, led by a Sylheti Muslim activist of the second generation in Tower Hamlets.

Conclusion

This chapter has explored the ways in which the British state has responded to those migrating from the Bengal delta during the period of British colonial control and since independence. During the nineteenth century and the first half of the twentieth century British officials were preoccupied by the presence of *lascars* in London and other ports and the growing numbers of Bengalis who were staying on rather than returning to Calcutta or their ancestral homes in the Bengal countryside. Bengali settlement became entangled, therefore, in a racialised array of changing state policies and practices concerning immigration, which emerged during the second half of the nineteenth century and became ever more stringent during the twentieth century.

Bengalis were not passive subjects of state control, however. Despite the 1832 Lascar Act and subsequent legislation intended to control the presence of *lascars* and other seamen together in British ports and return them to their countries of origin, by the 1920s and 1930s it was clear that some of these (predominantly) young men had stayed on and were surviving as pedlars, factory workers and owners of small businesses in British urban working-class neighbourhoods. Unlike the Bengali female servants (ayahs) and university students, these men transgressed the boundaries established by the British state. They were neither fully under the supervision of their white employers in Britain, nor did they enjoy the financial means and desire to return to India which characterised the students. Furthermore, they settled in poor urban localities which had become the sites of state surveillance and regulation during the rapid urbanisation and industrialisation of nineteenth-century Britain. They were doubly disturbing, i.e. in terms of both race and class, and in cases where they formed families with local white women they added another unsettling transgression through racial mixture.

During the second half of the twentieth century, Bengali migration was shaped by economic forces encouraged by the state – the demand for cheap labour during the 1950s and early 1960s, which provided opportunities predominantly for the descendants of Sylheti Muslim *lascars*. Likewise, the demand for doctors within the NHS which led to a much smaller influx of West Bengali Hindus. Political tensions around immigration during the 1960s resulted in renewed controls on migration, which encouraged the formation of a dominant Sylheti Muslim group.

From the 1980s this group has engaged with the British state at local and central levels through vigorous political and community activism. This engagement has enabled members of competing Sylheti lineages to dominate access to state-funded resources such as jobs in public services, social housing and amenities in particular urban neighbourhoods. They have also played a major role in representing 'British Muslims' to government after '9/11' as policy focused on anti-terrorism and forging alliances with 'moderate' Muslims in Britain's urban areas.

The migration from the Bengal delta includes other groups besides Sylheti Muslims from what is now called Bangladesh, of course. It is easy to forget their long-established presence in Britain, since many live in middle-class neighbourhoods and have largely been ignored by the state. Muslims from other Bangladeshi districts and Hindus from both Bangladesh and W. Bengal have distanced themselves either through location or, as in the case of Bengali Hindus in Tower Hamlets, by religion and educational aspiration. Those from the 'tribal areas' of the Chittagong Hill Tracts are far more eager to represent their particular needs and grievances to both the British and Bangladeshi state, but here they significantly draw on the expertise of a secular Bangladeshi organisation from Tower Hamlets as well as international agencies. Unlike the other non-Sylheti Muslim groups, they need to call on the state to help them and draw on the support of secular British Bangladeshis in the process.

Notes

1 'Bengali-speaking community in the Port of London', www.portcities.org.uk/london/server/show/ ConNarrative.126/chapterId/2600/Bengalispeaking-community-in-the-Port-of-London.html, accessed September 7, 2012.
2 'History of Bengalis in UK', http://saikatspeak.blogspot.com/2007/12/history-of-bengalis-in-uk. html, accessed December 31, 2007.
3 Exact numbers are impossible to guage, partly because the term *lascar* was used to describe seamen recruited mainly through colonial links and included Arabs, Egyptians, Yemenis, Somalis, Malays and those from across the Indian subcontinent (see Ansari 2004: 35). Furthermore, it is not known how many of these visitors to Britain's ports stayed on. Yousuf Choudhury notes that before the Second World War the 'Bangladeshi population in London numbered only two or three hundred' (1993: 4).
4 'Bengal-speaking community in the Port of London', www.portcities.org.uk/london/server/show/ ConNarrative.126/chapterId/2600/Bengalispeaking-community-in-the-Port-of-London.html, accessed January 22, 2013.
5 Ibid.
6 Ibid.
7 'Moving here migration histories', www.movinghere.org.uk/galleries/histories/asian/settling/settling. htm, accessed September 7, 2012.
8 Ullah and Eade note: 'It is said that some people donated their entire week's salary and at least in one case where a woman donated her entire wedding gift of gold jewellery' (2006).
9 Based on England and Wales 2011 Census, Table KS201EW, www.ons.gov.uk/ons/rel/census/2011-census/, accessed May 3, 2013.
10 'Community pride not prejudice – making diversity work in Bradford, Sir Herman Ouseley – The Ouseley Report', http://resources.cohesioninstitute.org.uk/Publications/Documents/Document/ Default.aspx?recordId=98, accessed January 22, 2013.
11 'The Cantle Report – Community cohesion: a report of the Independent Review Team', http:// resources.cohesioninstitute.org.uk/Publications/Documents/Document/Default.aspx?recordId=96, accessed January 22, 2013.
12 'The Prevent strategy: a guide for local partners in England', www.tedcantle.co.uk/publications/039%20 CLG%20Prevent%20Guide%20guide%20for%20local%20partners%202008.pdf, accessed January 22, 2013.
13 'The Prevent strategy', www.homeoffice.gov.uk/counter-terrorism/review-of-prevent-strategy/, accessed September 8, 2012.
14 Ibid.

15 'Bengali history in London', April 13, 2006, Culture 24, www.culture24.org.uk/sector+info/campaigns/art36298, accessed September 6, 2012.
16 www.tagorecentre.org.uk/about-us.html, accessed September 6, 2012.
17 'Film on London's Bengali diaspora', *Hindustan Times*, March 21, 2006, www.hindustantimes.com/News-Feed/NM8/Film-on-London-s-Bengali-diaspora/Article1-77301.aspx, accessed September 6, 2012.
18 Ibid.
19 See https://www.cafonline.org/system/charity-profile.aspx?friendlyUrl=BANGLADESH-HINDU-ASSOCIATION-UK/CCRegNo1128209, accessed September 11, 2012.
20 Damian Green, 'A summer school that aims to overturn multicultural dogma is a hit with pupils', 27 August, 2005, *The Telegraph*, www.telegraph.co.uk/education/expateducation/4197298/Give-them-the-tools-to-get-on-in-life.html, accessed September 6, 2012. For a discussion of social mobility among Bengali Hindus in Tower Hamlets see a report on an LSE Roundtable, 'The "diversity of diversity": Cohesion, integration, and social mobility amongst British Asians', September 3, 2012, http://blogs.lse.ac.uk/indiaatlse/2012/09/03/cohesion-integration-and-social-mobility-amongst-british-asians/, accessed September 6, 2012.
21 See Damian Green reference above.

References

Adams, Caroline, *Across Seven Seas and Thirteen Rivers. Life Stories of Sylheti Settlers in Britain*, (London: THAP Books), 1987.

Ansari, Humayun, *'The Infidel Within': Muslims in Britain since 1800*, (London: Hurst and Co.), 2004.

Begum, Halima and John Eade, 'All Quiet on the Eastern Front?' Bangladeshi Reactions to September 11 in Tower Hamlets' in T. Abbas (ed.), *British Muslims and September 11*, (London: Zed Press), 2005.

Biersteker, Thomas and Cynthia Weber, *State Sovereignty as Social Construct*, (Cambridge: Cambridge University Press), 1996.

Choudhury, Yousuf, *The Roots and Tales of Bangladeshi Settlers*, (London: Sylheti Social History Group), 1993.

DeHanas, Daniel and Zacharias Pieri, 'Olympic Proportions: The Expanding Scalar Politics of the London "Olympics Mega-Mosque" Controversy', *Sociology*, 45 (5): 798–814, 2011.

Eade, John, 'Debating Fundamentalisms in the Global City: Christian and Muslim Migrants in London' in Nesar AlSayyad and Megaan Massoumi (eds), *The Fundamentalist City: Religiosity and the Remaking of Urban Space*, (New York: Routledge), 2010.

— 'Nationalism, Community and the Islamization of Space in London' in Barbara Metcalf (ed.), *Making Muslim Space in North America and Europe*, (Berkeley and Los Angeles: University of California Press), 1997.

— *The Politics of Community: The Bangladeshi Community in East London*, (Aldershot: Ashgate), 1989.

Eade, John and David Garbin, 'Competing Visions of Identity and Space: Bangladeshi Muslims in Britain', *Contemporary South Asia*, 15 (2): 181–93, 2006.

Eade, John and D. Garbin, 'Changing Narratives of Violence, Struggle and Resistance: Bangladeshis and the Competition for Resources in the Global City', *Oxford Development Studies*, 30 (2): 137–49, 2002.

Eade, John, Tim Vamplew and Ceri Peach, 'The Bangladeshis: The Encapsulated Community' in Ceri Peach (ed.), *Ethnicity in the 1991 Census*, Vol. 3 (London: HMSO), 1996.

Forman, Charlie, *Spitalfields: A Battle for Land*, (London: Hilary Shipman), 1989.

Gardner, Katy, *Age, Narrative and Migration: The Life Course and Life Histories amongst Bengali Elders in London* (London: Berg), 2002.

— *Global Migrants, Local Lives: Travel and Transformation in Rural Bangladesh* (Oxford: Oxford University Press), 1995.

Hussain, Ed, *The Islamist* (London: Penguin), 2007.

Khan, Khalida, 'Preventing Violent Extremism (PVE) and PREVENT. A Response from the Muslim Community', *An-Nisa Society*, February 2009, www.an-nisa.org/downloads/PVE_&_Prevent-A_Muslim_response.pdf, accessed September 7, 2012.

Lahiri, Shompa, *Indians in Britain: Anglo-Indian Encounters, Race and Identity, 1880–1930*, (London and Portland, OR: Frank Cass), 2000.

Phillips, Deborah, *What Price Equality? A Report on the Allocation of GLC Housing in Tower Hamlets*, (London: GLC), 1986.

Robinson, Vaughan, *Transients, Settlers, and Refugees: Asians in Britain*, (Oxford: Oxford University Press), 1986.

Tabili, Laura, 'The Construction of Racial Difference in Twentieth-Century Britain: The Special Restriction (Coloured Alien Seamen) Order, 1925', *Journal of British Studies*, 33, (1): 54–98, 1994.

Ullah, Ansar Ahmed and John Eade, 'Introduction to 1st Strand' in John Eade, Ansar Ahmed Ullah, Jamil Iqbal and Marissa Hey, *Tales of Three Generations of Bengalis in Britain* (London: Nirmal Committee), 2006.

Visram, Rosina, *Ayahs, Lascars and Princes: Indians in Britain 1700–1947*, (London: Pluto Press), 1986.

23

THE PAKISTANI DIASPORA: USA AND UK

Yunas Samad

Introduction

The global Pakistani diaspora contains most of the features elaborated in Cohen's (2008) comprehensive typology of diaspora but primarily consists of labour migrations, high-end workers, trading networks, long-distance nationalists and cultural producers. In spatial terms, the largest concentration of Pakistanis in the diasapora is found in the Middle East, Europe and North America. There are no accurate records of numbers for the Pakistani diaspora, but the Government of Pakistan claims that there are just fewer than 4 million Pakistanis living aboard and under 1.9 million in the Middle East (with the largest contingent found in Saudi Arabia), under 1.7 million in Europe (largest settlement found in Great Britain) and around 0.85 million in North America (with the largest aggregation found in the USA) (Government of Pakistan 2004). The key difference in the populations found in Europe and North America and the Middle East is citizenship. Permanent settlement and citizenship rights give the Pakistani population in the Atlantic economies a different trajectory and characteristics than those found in the Middle East, where the denial of citizenship rights and permanent settlement leads to circular migration, transmigration and guest-worker status. However the US/UK comparison does have a number of difficulties in that the categories recognised and used in the censuses in the two countries are not the same and thus the comparison is only indicative of general trends found in the two countries.

In the UK, identification of the numbers of Pakistanis in the population is now relatively straightforward. Having moved from generic categories such as Asians to ethnic categories in the 1990s, the census makes enumeration straightforward and accurate. The 2001 census estimated that there were almost three-quarters of a million Pakistanis (749,000) out of a total population of visible minorities which was just over 4.6 million (55 per cent of whom where born in Britain), making Pakistanis around 1 per cent of the total population in the country and the second largest minority after the Indians. The overwhelming majority are citizens (Dobbs *et al.* 2006: 30). Controversy in the 1990s over the size of the Muslim population led to a campaign, run successfully by a number of religious organisations, lobbying for a question about religious identity to be included in the most recent census of 2001. It revealed that Muslims were the largest faith community in Britain after Christians (72 per cent), making up nearly 3 per cent of the population, or almost 1.6 million people, of which the Pakistanis are the largest component at 43 per cent. Around 1 per cent of Pakistanis belong to other faiths: primarily Christians, some Hindus, Sikhs, Jews and Buddhists, with 1 per cent having no religion (Dobbs *et al.* 2006: 20–1).

For the USA, estimating the Pakistani population is not that straightforward. The US Census 2000 estimated that 4.21 per cent or 11,859,446 were Asian (alone or in combination with one or more other races) – the largest proportion being Chinese at 1.02 per cent, followed by Filipino at 0.85 per cent and Pakistanis numbering 209,273 or 0.07 per cent of the US population. Of this figure, around 24.5 per cent of Pakistanis were born in the USA and around 44.8 per cent are not citizens (Reeves and Bennett 2004: 1, 9). The figures for Pakistanis are believed seriously to underestimate the population. The US Census 2000 included a question on 'race' which included the option 'Asian Indian' but not 'Pakistani', and allowed respondents to write in their preference, while another question sought information on ancestry. Critics have argued that the census undercounts Pakistanis because the question is open-ended and requires self-identification. Pakistanis can fall into multiple categories including 'Asian Indian', and the large difference between the two questions raises issues of reliability of the data. According to Najam (2006: 56–8) the study conducted by the Pakistan Embassy in Washington probably provides the best estimate of the Pakistani population in the USA. The study based on the Census 2000 and on the Embassy's consular records arrived at a figure of around 500,000 in 2002. These figures were similar to Najam's own estimates, which he considers are conservative given the growth rate of the community. Alternative estimates of the Pakistani population have been based on estimates of the Muslim population. The America Religious Identification Survey (ARIS) survey of 2008 estimated that there were 1,349,000 Muslims representing 0.06 per cent of the total US population (Kosmin and Keysar 2009: 5). Many consider this to be too low an estimation. Nimer's (2002) calculations lead him to estimate that the population in 2002 was between 2.1 and 3.6 million. Najam (2006) takes the higher figure and estimates that 15 per cent of the Muslim population is from Pakistan. This corroborates his estimate of 525,000 Pakistanis. The difficulty is that, unlike the categories used in the UK, neither 'Pakistani' nor 'Muslim' are explicit categories in the census. This has a number of implications, particularly for social policy.

Pakistani (inhabitants from those areas of India which are now in Pakistan) presence in Britain is inextricably associated with imperialism and colonialism. It goes back to the eighteenth century, when sailors, students and professionals had been entering Britain. This trickle became more substantial in post-war Britain, which suffered a major shortage of labour, particularly in mature industries such as textiles where working conditions were poor. In 1951 there were 5,000 Pakistanis (including Bangladeshis). By 1961, this figure had risen to 24,900 and by 1966 it had grown to 119,700. Numbers increased significantly as Pakistanis joined the 'beat-the-ban-rush' to come to Britain before the Immigration Act 1962 closed the door. It also shifted the demographics from a population consisting primarily of male workers who originally came only to work, to a more rounded population as they were joined by their families intent on settling permanently (Anwar 1996). By 1971, primary immigration was almost brought to a halt and only holders of family reunification and special vouchers and asylum seekers and refugees were allowed (Layton-Henry 1992). With primary migratory flow to Britain halted, immigration fluctuated between peaks and troughs. The troughs coincided with administrative measures designed to restrict applications for immigration being processed quickly, followed by peaks as these restrictions were relaxed. The introduction of the 1971 Immigration Act resulted in a significant number of applications being unsuccessful, until challenged in the courts. This forced the new government to change the regulation allowing the backlog to be cleared during the years 1976–8. Similarly, the demand for medical evidence supporting claims of relationships was used as an administrative measure to regulate migratory flows. Introduction of DNA testing at the point of entry to the UK resulted in an increase of immigration in 1989. The overall effect of immigration regulations is that the numbers admitted for settlement has been declining and there is very little primary immigration from Pakistan, which today is mainly restricted to entry of spouses (Anwar 1996: 12).

Large-scale Pakistani migration began in the 1960s and was heavily represented by populations from Azad Kashmir. It is estimated that anywhere between 50 and 75 per cent of the population living in Britain originated from Mirpur (Ballard 1991) with the remainder from the Punjab and a smaller number from Khyber–Pakhtunkhwa Province. Mirpuris were sailors in the merchant navy, often working in the engine rooms, prior to the Second World War. With the outbreak of hostilities, many came to work in munitions factories in South Shields and established a bridgehead, which facilitated the arrivals of fellow countrymen. Two factors played a role in encouraging migration: partition, and the building of the Mangla Dam. The partition of British India into India and Pakistan resulted in forced transfer of populations and in this climate certain groups were drawn into international migration. The other major impetus for migration from Pakistan came with the establishment of the Mangla Dam (1961–7), funded by the World Bank, in which the lake formed by the dam flooded the original town of Mirpur along with 250 villages. The money received in compensation allowed a large number of Kashmiris to migrate and eventually settle in Britain. In the northern mill towns of Yorkshire and Lancashire, there were opportunities in the woollen and cotton mills, and in the West Midlands, particularly Birmingham, this was complemented by factory work. The majority of immigrants from Pakistan had low levels of education and skills and many were unable to speak English on arrival. There was, however, a small group of professionals – in particular, physicians – who joined the National Health Service. Large Pakistani communities, mainly Kashmiri, can be found in Birmingham, Bradford, Oldham and the surrounding northern towns, while Manchester's population hails mainly from the Punjab. Luton and Slough, in the south of England, have the largest Kashmiri communities. London has a more diverse cohort than found elsewhere, consisting of Punjabis, Kashmiris, Pukhtuns, Sindhis and Urdu speakers. The largest concentrations, mainly working class, are found in East London. London also has the largest middle-class professional conglomeration of Pakistanis in the country, composed of health professionals, scientists, IT and financial sector workers and business professionals. The British Pakistani population is diverse and differs from region to region. It is also affected by Britain's 'North–South divide', which reinforces class characteristics. This means that, in London and the South East, the community is socially mobile and educational achievement is at or above the national average. On the other hand, in the West Midlands and the north of England, the community has generally suffered from the decline in the manufacturing industry and the change to a service economy.

South Asian presence in the USA dates back to the mid-nineteenth century, when mainly Punjabi men (85 per cent Sikh and 10–12 per cent Muslim) settled primarily in California. By the early twentieth century, discrimination against South Asians was formalised in the Immigration Act of 1917 with its 'barred Asiatic zone' and in 1923 a US Supreme Court ruling defined them as aliens ineligible for citizenship as they were not White. As a result many Punjabis married Mexican women and settled around El Centro in California's Imperial Valley. This began to change only with the signing of the Luce-Celler Bill by President Truman in 1946, which allowed South Asians the right to become citizens, own property and bring in relatives under national quotas. A slow trickle entered the USA from 1948 onwards, mainly following Pakistanis already settled there and accompanied by a trickle of students and professionals. By the 1960s, a clearly definable Pakistani community distinct from 'East Indians' was discernible.

It was, however, only with the passage of the 1965 Immigration and Naturalization Act that there was a significant increase in the number of arrivals. The Act increased the number of immigrant visas from Pakistan to 20,000 per year under a number of categories, including preferred occupational skills, family reunification and victims of political and religious persecution. The numbers of arrivals from Pakistan were in the 1950s around 100 a year; this rose to just under 200 in the early 1960s and to under 700 in the late 1960s when the Act came into force. By the 1970s the figure had risen to 1,528 and by the 1980s was averaging around 5,000 a year. By the 1990s, there were just under 10,000 arrivals a year. The introduction of the Visa Lottery in 1990 (it had low educational and work experience thresholds that attracted a diverse range of participants) and the Special Agricultural Worker clause (phased out in 1994) in the 1986 Immigration Reform and Control Act (IRCA) increased the rate of immigration from Pakistan. By 2001, the immigration rates were around 16,500 per annum. After 9/11, however, there was a squeeze on entry from Pakistan and numbers by 2003 were just below the 10,000 mark. There was a similar squeeze on visitor visas and student visas during this period, but it is not clear whether this will be a permanent trend or just a short-term blip (Helweg and Helweg 1990; Najam 2006).

Most Pakistanis arriving in the USA from the late 1980s onward were from Lahore, Karachi, Rawalpindi, Faisalabad, Hyderabad and Peshawar. Around 50 per cent were from the Punjab. Of these, 30 per cent are Urdu speakers and there are some small numbers of Sindhis and Pukhtuns (Mohammad-Arif 2000: 35). Those arriving were high-end professionals, physicians, engineers, IT workers, scientists, who either came directly because of demand in their profession or as students who stayed after qualifying. Along with these professionals came less-educated relatives who were eligible under immigration visa preference for relatives or via the Visa Lottery. As immigration rules changed, less-qualified and less-skilled workers migrated, and they chose the self-employment routes and started up small businesses, retail stores, petrol pumps and taxis. Furthermore, a sizable minority of Pakistani Christians and Zoroastrians established themselves in the USA. The largest concentrations of Pakistanis (40 per cent) are found in New York and New Jersey. Some 90 per cent of Pakistanis live in only four states: New York, New Jersey, Texas and California. The Pakistani community is primarily an East Coast community that is growing in the West and the South (Najam 2006).

The age profile of the Pakistani community in Britain and the USA is in marked contrast to the host population, which is an aging population in both countries. Among the White British population of the UK, only 20 per cent are under 16 years of age, and 17 per cent are over 65, making for a median age of 39. Of the total population in the USA, only 25.6 per cent are under 18 and 12.4 per cent are over 65, making for a median age of 35.4. Pakistanis are characterised by large numbers of young people and a dearth of elderly people in both countries. In the UK, over 35 per cent of Pakistanis are aged less than 16 and only 4 per cent above 65, with a median age of 22. In the USA, 32.8 per cent of Pakistanis are aged less than 18, and only 3.0 per cent above 65, giving a median age of 28.7. The fact that there are large numbers of children of school age has numerous social policy implications, particularly in Britain (unlike the USA, where they are dispersed), as they are relatively concentrated in large numbers in a number of cities: parts of London, Birmingham, Leicester, Manchester and Bradford (Dobbs *et al.* 2006: 23–31, 40; Reeves and Bennett 2004: 6).

Human capital and non-material assets such as education and skills have a major impact on employment prospects. In the UK, around 18 per cent of Pakistanis of working age have a degree, which is marginally lower than the education levels found in the White British population (19 per cent). However, a third of Pakistanis have no qualifications, while only a quarter of White British have no qualifications (Dobbs *et al.* 2006: 130, 153). In the USA, 54.3 per cent of Pakistanis are graduates, which is double the rate for the total population. Only 18 per cent of Pakistanis have less than high school education, which is fractionally better than the average for the total population. Pakistanis' educational experience in Britain is highly divergent, with significant numbers experiencing high as well as low outcomes. In the UK, the Pakistani population originally had low qualifications and low skill levels, but the numbers of graduates has increased as a greater number of the younger generation attend university and qualified professionals arrive. In the case of the USA, the original cohort who migrated were highly educated professionals and they were later joined by relatives who were not so well qualified. The evidence shows the main division that is emerging within Pakistanis in the UK and the USA is between those from middle-class backgrounds, who are achieving high levels of education leading into prosperous professions and becoming integrated into multi-cultural societies, and those from the working class. Those from proletarian backgrounds, with poor educational attainment, are subject to uncertain futures and social exclusion and marginalisation, which is more of a problem in Britain (Heath 2001: 128; Reeves and Bennett 2004: 12; Najam 2006).

There is considerable diversity of occupation between Pakistanis in the two countries and amongst Pakistanis in the individual countries. Only 13.8 per cent of Pakistanis are in managerial and professional occupations in the UK, in contrast to White British, of whom 30.3 per cent are professionals. It should be noted that 23.3 per cent of Pakistanis work in routine or manual jobs and 26.3 per cent have never worked or are long-term unemployed (Dobbs *et al.* 2006: 41). In the USA more Pakistanis are professionals – around 43.5 per cent – than the average for all workers (33.6 per cent). Of the rest, 26.2 per cent work in routine or manual work,[1] as opposed to the average for all workers of 38.7 per cent (Reeves and Bennett 2004: 14). Pakistanis in the British labour market are also clustered in certain sectors of the economy and are overrepresented in distribution, restaurants and hotels (28.2 per cent), transport and communication (19 per cent), which covers taxis and chauffeurs, and manufacturing (18.7 per cent) (Annual Local Area Labour Force Survey 2001–2). In the USA there is also clustering, with 26 per cent of Pakistanis finding employment in the retail trade, 17.4 per cent in educational and health services and 11.6 per cent in finance, insurance and the real estate market (US Census, American Community Survey, 2005).

Pakistanis are one of the poorest communities in Britain and two-thirds live under the poverty line and in areas with high-level multiple deprivation (Department of Work and Pensions 2004). A total of 26 per cent of families live in overcrowded conditions (Dobbs *et al.* 2006). In contrast, among Pakistanis in the USA only 16.5 per cent of families are below the poverty line and the median family income is around US $50,189, which is just above the average family median income of $50,046 (Reeves and Bennett 2004: 16–17). Unemployment for this group in the UK is high, with Pakistani male adult unemployment at 16 per cent, while White British unemployment is around 6 per cent, and with male youth unemployment of 26 per cent for 18–24 year olds being considerably higher than the 11 per cent for the equivalent White British age group. Furthermore, 26.3 per cent of Pakistanis have never worked or are long-term unemployed (Dobbs *et al.* 2006: 136, 41). In the USA, 76.6 per cent of men and 36.9 per cent of women are participating in the labour force and unemployment rates are around 4.8 per cent (Reeves and Bennett 2004: 13; US Census, American Community Survey: Pakistanis, 2005).

Housing patterns in the UK and the USA are quite different. In the UK in the northern towns, Birmingham, Luton, Slough and parts of London there are Pakistani enclaves living in overcrowded housing, the result of discrimination in the housing market, a propensity for home ownership (67 per cent own their own homes) and a shortage of suitable social housing that can accommodate large families with an average of 4.4 persons per household (Dobbs *et al.* 2006).

The consequence of this is that parts of some British cites have localities that have high rates of concentration of Pakistanis. In Bradford, Manningham ward, Pakistanis make up 60.1 per cent of the population, while in Birmingham, Washwood Heath, the figure is 56.2 per cent. These are not just Pakistanis, but usually members of the same *biraderis* or social brotherhoods, usually Kashmiri clans (City of Bradford Metropolitan District Council 2004; Birmingham City Council 2006). In the USA, while certain states have a high concentration of Pakistanis, housing concentration does not exist on the same scale. There are some enclaves, but these are not exclusively Pakistani. The trajectory of the Pakistani community is similar to that of Indians. Neither have followed the path of earlier immigrants to the USA or their counterparts in the UK and formed enclaves, primarily due to the suburbanisation of an upwardly mobile community. Decision to purchase a home in a particular locality is predicated by employment opportunities, investment considerations, good quality housing, availability of good education, low levels of crime and ethnic conflict and the desire to maintain privacy while keeping reasonably close to fellow Pakistanis (Helweg and Helweg 1990: 163–7). Home ownership is lower in the USA, running at 41.7 per cent, but that may reflect labour market demands for flexible labour and the desire to work in a professional specialisation (Reeves and Bennett 2004: 19).

Local cultural and social organisations

Pakistanis in Britain are considered to be a disadvantaged community and have benefited from anti-discriminatory legislation and multicultural policy. Social policy dealing with discrimination and disadvantage and cultural diversity in Britain was piecemeal and primarily implemented on the local level. The approach consisted of a series of legal changes against racial discrimination and recognising cultural diversity. The consequence is that there is a proliferation of local service-providing organisations in localities with concentrations of Pakistanis. These include sports activities, day-care centres for children and the elderly, educational services, advice centres, women's groups, health advisors, etc. They also range in size, from large centres providing a range of services and facilities to the locality, which could be exclusively Pakistani or primarily Pakistani along with other South Asian groups, to small single-service providers servicing a neighbourhood.

The key difference with comparable organisations in Britain is that all these organisations in the USA are funded by their members. As a community that is not recognised as a deprived minority, they have no access to state funding. Cities in the USA with significant Pakistani populations have one or more Pakistani organisations. Cities such as New York, Chicago and Los Angles have a dozen or so local organisations, including student organisations that provide space for social and cultural interaction. In areas with smaller populations such as Raleigh, NC, Phoenix, AZ and Boston, MA single organisations are found to operate with a long history and diverse portfolio of activities. They attempt to develop a sense of community in particular localities by holding events on Eid, Muharram and Pakistan Day, music galas and *Basant*. They also act as cultural ambassadors, participating in annual Independence Day Parades in New York and Chicago, acting as key facilitators for philanthropic activities such as raising funds for hospitals, tsunami relief and charitable work for earthquake victims in Gujarat and Kashmir (Najam 2006: 69–71).

Religious organisations

The earliest mosque in Britain dates from 1889, in Liverpool. Today there are around 1,581 mosques, of which 323, the largest number, are considered to be Pakistani mosques

(Naqshabandi 2010). In Britain, mosques are constituted on a sectarian and ethnic basis representing the religious and ethnic preferences of the mosque committees and constituencies. The Imams recruited reflect the social and ethnic background of the mosque committees: they are generally not well educated, quite often have poor English capabilities and are poorly paid. They usually are responsible for leading prayers, running Quran classes for children and burial and marriage services. Only after the 7/7 bombing has there been serious consideration of the training of Imams in the UK, to ensure that they are not only linguistically competent but also familiar with the liberal traditions of democratic society.

The Sunni presence is dominant and within it there are three overlapping categories. Brelvis have the largest number of mosques and a number of subcultures represented by influential *pirs* in some major cities. There are a number of revivalist strands such as the Tablighi Jamat, Deobandis and Ahl-I-Hadith. The third element in the Sunni tradition consists of elite organisations, which aspire for national status and recognition. This includes the UK Islamic Mission and the Islamic Foundation, Dawatul-Islam, the Young Muslim Organisation and the Muslim Women's Association, all affiliates of the Jamati Islami network (Nielsen 1987). The Federation of Students' Islamic Societies represents the amalgamation of the various Islamic groups within the universities, and more radical groups such as Hibzi-ut-Tahrir and Al Mujairoun have gained influence on the campuses. In opposition to these sectarian-based organisations there emerged a number of umbrella organisations such as the Union of Muslim Organisation, the Council of Imams and Mosques and the Muslim Parliament, as well as the defunct Council of Mosques (Nielsen 1992). There is also a Shia presence. In addition, the Agha Khan has a number of organisations, and the Ahmadiyya world-wide headquarters is based in South London.

During the Satanic Verses controversy, most of these organisations cooperated and functioned within the UK Action Committee on Islamic Affairs. This was a confederation, which subsumed the umbrella organisations as well as local institutions (Samad 1992). The significance of the UK Action Committee on Islamic Affairs was that it was the forerunner of the Muslim Council of Britain (MCB), which has 350 affiliates from all across the country. The largest presence in it is Pakistani. The MCB for a while acted as a representative of the Muslim community before it fell out of favour with the government. Arab Muslims who felt that Islam in the country was dominated by South-Asian organisations set up the Muslim Association of Britain (MAB) (Pedziwiatr 2007).

The oldest mosque in the USA was established in 1915 in Maine. Today, there around 1,200 mosques in the country (Ghazali 2001). Around 77 per cent of Imams are degree educated, usually in Islamic studies, and are full-time employees. Among presidents of the mosques, 93 per cent are degree educated, and usually the roles of Imam and president are separate. Immigration requirements make it almost essential that imported Imams are qualified. The mosque has a different role in American Muslim life. Many mosques are Islamic centres and have a wide range of activities: schools, seminaries, inter-faith activity, marriage counselling, wedding facilities, burial services, welfare activities for the poor, prison programmes, soup kitchens, food programmes, anti-drug and crime initiatives, pre-school support and voter registration (Cesari 2004: 137).

The biggest division among Muslims is between Black converts, the Nation of Islam and immigrants. Within the latter group, most Islamic centres are non-denominational or Sunni with some Shia presence. The Brelvi presence is not significant. There are no *pirs* but there are some Sufi orders. The Tabligh-i-Jammat, Jamma-i-Islami, Muslim Brotherhood and Salafi and Wahabi groups are prevalent. Very few of the mosques are ethnically based and many have relocated to serve wider Islamic audiences. Hence, many religious institutions serve Pakistani needs, but most are not specifically Pakistani institutions, even though some may be dependent on their support (Cesari 2004: 25, 51, 85; Najam 2006: 79). On the national level, there are a number of active organisations. Some have elements of South Asian influence, but none are specifically Pakistani. The Muslim Brotherhood influences the oldest organisation, Islamic Society of North America (ISNA) founded in 1972; Islamic Council of North America (ICNA) has Jammat-i-Islami influence; and Council of American Islamic Relations uses existing laws to defend Muslims (Cesari 2004: 81–4).

Professional organisations

Here, there is a clear difference between the two countries. In the UK, there is a dearth of professional associations and only a handful appear to be functioning: the Association of Pakistani Physicians and Surgeons and the British Pakistani Psychiatrist Association are the only organisations that exist, and they act as professional support networks for members and to promote health care in Pakistan. In sharp contrast, there are a considerable number of professional organisations in the USA. The oldest and most well known is the Association of Pakistani Physicians of North America (APPNA), which is a conglomerate of affiliates and regional organisations. It has a youth wing, a Young Pakistani Physicians Resource Centre for the spouses and children of members and numerous affiliates involved in charitable activities. APPNA-Sehat runs integrated health programmes in Pakistan, APPNA charitable foundation projects include free clinics in the USA and educational scholarships for Pakistani Americans and the Human Development Foundation of North America. It has a number of affiliated alumni organisations such as King Edward Medical College Alumni Association of North America and DOW Graduate Association of North America. In the 2005 earthquake, the APPNA conglomerate of associations raised US $10 million and physicians volunteered their services (Najam 2006: 74–5).

The Organisation of Pakistani Entrepreneurs of North America (OPEN) is a different model of organisation and provides a platform for Pakistanis in the high-tech sector. Its activities include networking, mentoring and information sharing and events that bring together professional Pakistanis with high-profile Americans. OPEN–New England runs a competition for entrepreneurs with a US $50,000 prize for the most successful business plan. There are also proliferations of other organisations for engineers, professionals and alumni, such as the Association of Pakistani Scientists and Engineers of North America, DASTAK–Network of Pakistani Professionals and Pakistani American Business Executive Associations (Najam 2006: 76).

Political representation

A number of factors combined in Britain that made it favourable for Pakistanis to make an impact on the political processes. The foremost was that they were concentrated in enclaves in particular localities interconnected by kinship networks. These networks were overlaid by a range of local community organisations that were established by local authorities under policies of multiculturalism and later community cohesion programmes, combined with networks of mosques and religious organisations and local business servicing the community. These interconnecting networks provided the basis from which a local political leadership emerged. The political parties were quick to recognise these vote banks and, even though Pakistanis are conservative and share views with the Tory Party on a range of social issues, they were however alienated by their position on immigration and hence tended to support the Labour Party.

In 2007 there were around 257 councillors and mayors of Pakistani origin and in 2009 there were four members of parliament – two were cabinet minsters, Shahid Malik and Sadiq Khan – and one peer, Lord Nazir Ahmad. With David Cameron and Nick Clegg forming a coalition government in 2010, Baroness Sayeeda Warsi joined the Cabinet and was made Chairperson of the Conservative Party. Sajjad Karim was a Member of the European Parliament. Other influential Pakistani politicians are Qassim Afzal, a senior member of the Liberal Democrat Party and Salma Yaqoob, a significant figure in the Respect Party (Perlez 2007; Travis 2008).

There are also a number of long-distance nationalist organisations based in the UK. The Jammu Kashmir Liberation Front (JKLF) was a secular pro-independence organisation founded in 1977 in Birmingham by Amanullah Khan and Maqbool Butt, which initiated an insurgency in the summer of 1989. The Kashmiri diaspora funded the organisation, supplying it with personnel and leadership. It orchestrated a lobbying campaign in Britain and the USA in order to influence their respective governments. In the 2005 election in Britain, the JKLF extracted concessions from the Labour Party on Kashmir in return for mobilising the Kashmiri vote in the key inner city constituencies of Luton, Bradford, Birmingham and Manchester. The Muttahida Qaumi Mahaz (MQM) leader is in self-imposed exile in the UK and leads the party from its headquarters in Edgware, Middlesex. Also, Hayrbiyar Marri, the Baluch separatist leader, is based in London.

As Pakistanis in the USA develop roots, they have begun to involve themselves in the political process. However, their relative newness, lack of concentration in particular localities and the fact that many were not born in the USA has meant that their attempts have not been successful. Pakistanis raise funds for both of the main political parties, Democrats and Republicans and are involved in voter registration and political awareness campaigns. Candidates unsuccessfully stood for state senate in Brooklyn, New York and City Council and Community Boards. These local public offices do not require a candidate to be a born US citizen (only the President and the VP are required to be born citizens) (Qutabashahi 2008). There are also a number of organisations that lobby the White House and Congress. The Association of Pakistani Physicians of North America has a political lobbying organisation, the Pakistani–American Public Affairs Committee. The Pakistani American Leadership Centre was instrumental in setting up the Congressional Pakistan Caucus (www.pal-c.org/pkamericans.html) and Islamic organisations such as the American Muslim Alliance, American Muslim Council and Muslim Public Affairs Committee (Najam 2006: 74, Cesari 2004: 81–4). Generally Pakistanis' votes have been divided. In the past, affluent Pakistanis supported the Republicans due to their sharing of conservative values and the belief that Republican administrations were more favourable to Pakistan than Democrat ones. In the 2000 elections many Pakistanis voted for the Republicans and they were subsequently disillusioned with their policies.

There are also a number of long-distance nationalists operating within the beltway lobbying Congress. The Sindhi American Political Action Committee and Sindh Monitor promote the concerns of Sindh. The Baluch Society of North America and American Friends of Baluchistan promote Baluch affairs. The Kashmir American Council supports Kashmiris from both India and Pakistan.

Conclusion

There are a number of important structural and policy differences between the UK and the USA, which have an impact on the Pakistani diaspora in the respective countries. The fact that the census in the UK has a category that recognises Pakistanis as well as Muslims allows for the enumeration of the social profile of the community. In the USA, neither Pakistanis nor Muslims are a recognised category in the census and so do not have a specific ethnic recognition in social policy. This is unlike the Indian diaspora, which was recognised as a distinct ethnic category in the 1980 census and in 1982 was recognised as a socially disadvantaged group, receiving the same preference as Blacks and Hispanics in the competition for government contracts (Helweg and Helweg 1990: 72). There are also distinct differences in housing patterns between the diaspora in the two countries. In the UK they are located in enclaves, which are predominantly Pakistani, or especially Kashmiri. While there are enclaves in the USA, they are not exclusively Pakistani, and a considerable number are dispersed in suburbia. This is a reflection of the human capital difference between the diaspora in the two counties. While the educational profile is improving in the UK, the tail is still long. Together these various factors in the UK feed into the development of social policy, which recognised the Pakistani community as a disadvantaged community, while in the USA they have very little visibility in relation to social policy. This has allowed Pakistanis in Britain to develop a network of local organisation to service the community, which has intersected with business and religious networks. Together, this has allowed them to exert some political significance at the local level and now at the national level. This political clout then feeds back into the community in numerous ways, accelerating change in the community. In contrast, Pakistanis in the USA have not yet been able to transfer their associational capacity, nor their cultural, religious and professional identities into political influence. They are less established than their counterparts in Britain and only with time will make inroads into the political sphere.

Note

1   In the US census the categories that have been condensed into routine or manual work are Service; Farming, fishing and forestry; Construction, extraction and maintenance; and Production, transportation and material moving.

References

Annual Local Area Labour Force Survey (2001/02) 'Industry: By Sex and Ethnic Group, 2001/02', London: Office for National Statistics.

Anwar, M. (1996) *British Pakistanis: Demographic, Social and Economic Position*, Centre for Research in Ethnic Relations, Warwick University.

Ballard, R. (1991) 'The Kashmir Crisis: A View from Mirpur', *Economic and Political Weekly*, March 2–9, pp. 513–17.

Birmingham City Council (2006) *2001 Population Census in Birmingham, Ward Profiles*, www.birmingham. gov.uk/cs/Satellite?c=Page&childpagename=Planning-and-Regeneration%2FPageLayout&cid=12230 96353895&pagename=BCC%2FCommon%2FWrapper%2FWrapper, accessed 29/9/2010.

Cesari, Jocelyne (2004) *When Islam and Democracy Meet: Muslims in Europe and the United States*, Palgrave Macmillan, New York.

City of Bradford Metropolitan District Council, Research and Consultation Service (2004) *Census 2001 Bradford District Ward Profiles, 19, Manningham*.

Cohen, Robin (2008) *Global Diasporas: An Introduction* (2nd edn), UCL, London.

Congressional Pakistan Caucus, www.pal-c.org/node/12, accessed 12/9/2013.

Department of Work and Pensions (2004) *Households Below Average Incomes 2002/3*, Crown Copyright.

Dobbs, J., Green, H. and Zealey, L. (2006) *Focus on Ethnicity and Religion*, National Statistics, Palgrave Macmillan, Basingstoke.

Ghazali, Abdus Sattar (2001) 'The Number of Mosque Attendants Increasing Rapidly in America', *American Muslim Perspective*, http://amp.ghazali.net/html/mosques_in_us.html, accessed 24/8/2010.

Government of Pakistan (2004) *Year Book 2004–5*, Ministry of Labour, Manpower and Overseas Pakistanis (Overseas Pakistanis Division), Islamabad.

Heath, A. (2001) *Ethnic Minorities and the Labour Market: Interim Analytical Report*, Performance and Innovation Unit, Cabinet Office.

Helweg, Arthur W. and Helweg, Usha M. (1990) *An Immigrant Success Story: East Indians in America*, Hurst & Co, London.

Kosmin, B. and Keysar, A. (2009) *American Religious Identification Survey (ARIS 2008)*, Institute for the Study of Secularism in Society and Culture, Trinity College, Hartford.

Layton-Henry, Zig (1992) *The Politics of Immigration*, Blackwell, Oxford.

Mohammad-Arif, Aminah (2000) *Salaam America: South Asian Muslims in New York*, Anthem Press, London.

Najam, Adil (2006) *Portrait of a Giving Community: Philanthropy by Pakistani Diaspora*, Harvard University Press, Massachusetts.

Naqshabandi, Mehmood (2010) *UK Masjid Statistics*, http://mosques.muslimsinbritain.org/index.php, accessed 31/8/2010.

Nielsen, Jorgen (1987) 'Muslims in Britain: Searching for an Identity', *New Community* 13(3).

— (1992) *Muslims in Western Europe*, Edinburgh University Press, Edinburgh.

Nimer, M. (2002) *The North American Muslim Resource Guide*, Routledge, New York.

Pedziwiatr, Konrad (2007) 'Muslims in Europe: Demography and Organizations' in *Islam in the European Union: Transnationalism, Youth and the War on Terror*, eds Yunas Samad and Kasutri Sen, Oxford University Press, Karachi.

Perlez, Jane (2007) 'Pakistani Official Tackles Prejudice in Britain' Friday, August 3, *The New York Times*, www.nytimes.com/2007/08/03/world/asia/03iht-profile.1.6970573.html?_r=2&pagewanted=1, accessed 7/9/2010.

Qutabashahi, Feroz (2008) 'Pakistani–Americans or American–Pakistanis?' *Chowk*, www.chowk.com/articles/14749.

Reeves, T. and Bennett, C. (2004) *We the People: Asians in the United States*, CENSR-17, United States Census 2000, US Census Bureau.

Samad, Yunas (1992) 'Book Burning and Race Relations: Politicisation of Bradford Muslims', *New Community*, 18(4).

Travis, Alan (2008) 'Officials Think UK's Muslim Population Has Risen to 2m', Tuesday 8 April 2008, *The Guardian*, www.guardian.co.uk/world/2008/apr/08/population.islam, accessed 7/9/2010.

US Census, American Community Survey (2005) S0201. *Selected Population Profile in the United States, Population Group: Pakistani Alone or in any Combination.*

24

HINDUISM IN THE DIASPORA

John Zavos

In the introduction to his exploration of Hinduism in a British context (1987), Richard Burghart begins with an anecdote about the Maharaja of Jaipur, Madho Singh. When the Maharaja travelled to London in 1902, he recounts, he carried with him a range of indigenous products and undertook a range of ritual acts so that he could maintain some semblance of ritual purity, even though for a Hindu of his status the journey across the *kalipani*, the black waters, away from the Hindu universe of mother India, was a dangerously polluting act. The anecdote is designed to demonstrate the implicit problems associated with the idea of Hinduism on the move. It also points up the intensification of these problems in the modern world. Madho Singh was required to travel as he had been summoned to attend the coronation of his Imperial ruler, Edward VII. Although not exactly typical, the compulsions of this journey represent the realignment of global power structures in the nineteenth century, which invoked not just Madho Singh but many hundreds of thousands of Indians to travel across the network of the British Empire for various reasons associated with the political economy of colonialism. The anecdote, then, helps to bring into focus a question of some relevance to the theme of this chapter. How does a religion which is subject to such ritual constraints, such fastidious observance of purity and pollution regulation related to travel, reconcile itself to the compromises, adaptations and innovations of rapid, forced and/or mass migration in the modern world?

Delving a little deeper into the Maharaja's predicament provides the resources for an opening response. His rule in Jaipur being somewhat unstable due to an unconventional succession, Madho Singh was able to fashion the journey to the metropolis as what one scholar has called a 'carefully crafted propaganda programme' (Belli 2007: 46). Amongst other things, the Maharaja was accompanied by the *murti* of the state deity, Govind dev, who preceded Madho Singh wherever he went, thus providing divine sanction to his journey. A specially commissioned work provided a commentary on what was termed the Maharaja's '*yatra*', culminating in his triumphant return to Jaipur. These examples indicate that the Maharaja was, after all, able to bend the religious ramifications of the journey to his particular political situation. This reading, then, allows us to see how creative adaptation and innovation inspired even this most orthoprax of Hindu travellers, and helps to explain what Burghart goes on to point out: that Hinduism and Hindus can be found across the globe, a result of migrations that stretch back some two millennia.

At the same time, Madho Singh's political opportunism helps to demonstrate the way in which traditional Hindu 'religion' is embedded deeply in social and political life, bound up with caste status and other markers of social and cosmological order. In this sense, the concerns of the Maharaja are rather specific, so there is a question mark over how far his case can be generalised as indicative of 'Hinduism'. As we shall see, for many migrants in the nineteenth and twentieth centuries such refined ritual concerns were of no relevance at all. This observation points us towards a key issue in the exploration of Hinduism in the diaspora: that the idea of Hinduism itself is problematic, barely able to encompass the rich and sometimes conflicting variety of traditions and social positions that it seeks to represent. Much scholarship on Hinduism has of course made this point. What some work has emphasised, however, is that this problem is associated with the processes of abstraction and universalisation through which the notion of religion itself was produced in the modern world. Religion as a single category of human experience, encountered differently in different regions only because of the development of different 'religious systems', is a discourse of modernity (see Asad 1993: 42; King 1999; Zavos 2010a).[1]

However one views this idea, it is certainly the case that the nineteenth and early twentieth century was a period when Hindu traditions were drawn increasingly into a comparative framework and organised in a manner which enabled them to be represented as one of these 'religious systems'. Crucially in the current context, mobility and travel associated with the globalising impulses of the Empire was a significant factor in enabling these processes. In 1893, for example, Swami Vivekananda travelled to Chicago to attend the so-called World's Parliament of Religions, in order to offer Vedantic Hinduism as a spiritual alternative to the materialism and (as he saw it) defunct Christianity of the West. His triumphant speeches and popularity as a representative of Hinduism were widely reported in the press back in the colonised motherland. Such initiatives, then, serve to demonstrate the impact of mobilities on the actual development of Hinduism, its conceptualisation as a religion in the modern world. In this context, the idea of diaspora Hinduism emerges as deeply significant.

It is this significance which the present chapter seeks to explore. I will examine first the historical processes which have fashioned the extent and parameters of Hinduism in the modern diaspora. I will then go on to explore a number of trends through which the diaspora has shaped the religion, as well as the role that Hinduism plays in shaping diaspora consciousness amongst particular South Asian communities.

Labour, trade and mobility in the Empire

In contrast to both Madho Singh and Vivekananda, the majority of migrants during the colonial period were from lower-caste backgrounds, travelling with none of the social and cultural capital which accompanied these two. Indeed, the largest group moved primarily not in a spirit of elitism, but more typically one of desperation. These were indentured labourers: migrants who signed up to a contract of indenture, through which they would be transported to work for a fixed number of years (a minimum of five) on plantations or sometimes infrastructure projects in other parts of the Empire. The indentured labour system was introduced in the 1830s after the abolition of slavery and ran until 1917. During this period, an estimated 1.5 million Indians entered into such contracts. These workers were primarily from agricultural regions, Tamil Nadu in the South and especially from what is today the Indian states of Uttar Pradesh and Bihar, where in the nineteenth century there was considerable pressure due to the fragmentation of land holdings and the commercialisation of agriculture. The primary destinations for such migrants were Mauritius, Guyana, South Africa and Trinidad, although there were plenty of other pockets of the Empire which became home to Indian indentured workers, as well as French and Dutch colonial territories.[2] Some labourers entered into somewhat freer contracts related to specific projects, such as the building of the railway system in East Africa in the 1890s.

In addition to these labour contracts, Indians moved across the web of the Empire due to employment in the armed and associated services, and also as traders and entrepreneurs, providing specific services and building on pre-colonial patterns of movement and business networks. The British colonies in East Africa were a significant site, for example, for the development of Gujarati trade networks which had been evident for many centuries before the Empire became so central to the mechanisms of global connectivity. Whereas in earlier periods these networks were generally confined to coastal regions of East Africa and Zanzibar, the extension of colonial power into the interior was accompanied by a similar extension of trading networks, supplying both infrastructure projects and developing administrative settlements across the region. The impact of this trading network was such that, as Judith Brown notes, by the end of the nineteenth century the rupee had become the most important trade currency in the region (2006: 37).

These different forms of mobility encouraged diverse developments in the articulation of Hinduism. The system of indenture initially produced stratified, sometimes conflictual notions of religious practice, as localised forms associated with different areas of the subcontinent were reproduced partially in the constrained conditions of the plantation. Although sustained by intermittent links to home villages amongst some migrants (Bates 2000: 25–32), the process of reproduction was greatly affected by the relative collapse and/or renegotiation of caste as a means of organising social relations. Indentured labourers came from a variety of castes (many of them low castes unaffected by the issues of purity and pollution that preoccupied Madho Singh) and, in this new context, relations associated with these identities were transformed by the complete restructuring of economic and social life: village and even family structures, along with traditional occupations associated with *jati*, were radically affected by the demands of the plantation (Younger 2009).

Ironically, a key effect of this radical shift in the locus of social life was the gradual emergence of more defined notions of Hinduism as a religion. Van der Burg and van der Veer (1986), for example, note how in Surinam what may be termed localised 'folk practices' were increasingly marginalised as a Brahmanised form of Hinduism came to dominate, driven by the small number of Brahmans present in this plantation society. Hindu practice began to be structured around the ability of Brahmans to conduct ritual based on knowledge of sacred texts, 'so that ritual knowledge replaced purity as the legitimation of the Brahman's status' (Van der Burg and van der Veer 1986: 517). This perhaps surprising dynamic led, then, to a kind of reaffirmation of the position of Brahmans as significant in Hindu society – based not on their localised role in affirming caste relations, but rather on their ability to mediate Hinduism as a religion to the emerging 'Hindu public' (see also Younger 2009: 76–8, 101). In the relative absence of complex caste dynamics, Hinduism appears more clearly as a religion based around specific rituals and knowledge of specific sacred texts. This example, then, already illustrates the role that diaspora can play in the formation of Hinduism as a religion.

Outside the constrained context of indenture, alternative patterns of development are apparent. A significant point here is that freer forms of movement tended to encourage comparatively sustained connectivity with the homeland. Traders with an established business in East Africa in the early twentieth century, for example, were likely to retain strong links including family links to Gujarat, returning intermittently to their home region. One important consequence was that, unlike indentured labourers, these traders were likely to retain a strong sense of their existing caste status, even if such identities were generally operationalised more on visits home than in the context of East Africa itself in this early period. As the number of migrants grew in the 1920s and '30s, these identities became more prominent in East Africa as well, as communities accrued the 'critical mass necessary to make funerary, educational and recreational communalism viable' (Twaddle 1990: 155; see also Younger 2009: 214–5). Hinduism in these contexts, then, tended to be more clearly influenced by the status claims of different caste groups, particularly as these groups developed a strong middle-class, urban consciousness appropriate to their position as mercantile mediators in the peculiar, racialised conditions of the colonial economy.

Post-colonial Indian mobilities

Initially, this caste-configured community consciousness was replicated in the patterns of post-colonial migration and settlement. The early post-colonial period was marked by a sojourner phase of migration, where primarily male migrants from trading communities in Gujarat and rural communities in Punjab travelled mostly to Britain, whilst retaining a strong link to their local caste and kinship networks in the home region. Through processes of chain migration, however, these sojourner mentalities were gradually replaced by a settler orientation which enabled the emergence of what Ballard called 'desh pardesh' (1994), or home away from home. From the 1960s in Britain, families were gradually reconstituted and communities developed around this focus; henceforward cultural practices were increasingly perceived as an affirmative feature of community identity. Hinduism emerged as central to this cultural affirmation, although initially collective forms of practice and consciousness were, as in East Africa, largely configured by specific caste, linguistic and regional identities.

This movement from specific regions of India to the erstwhile colonial metropolis provides us with an initial template of post-colonial migration and settlement, which has since been over-laid by different patterns, both in the context of the UK and beyond. One important factor has been the increasing significance of twice migration, especially from East Africa. Responding to Africanisation policies in various newly independent states, many East African Asians resettled in Britain and North America in the early 1970s. These migrants, of course, were already skilled urban operators, with a strong sense of cultural distinctiveness honed in the minority context of East Africa. This distinctiveness was to manifest itself particularly through the establishment of temples and the promotion of and support for a range of devotional sects.

This trajectory of development has been bolstered by later patterns of direct migration into English-speaking Western countries, primarily the USA. Here, migration has been led primarily by the demand for highly skilled, professionally qualified migrants. These migrants have led the development of an economically successful community, employed primarily in professional sectors such as engineering and medicine, and strongly committed to high levels of education for their children. The economic (and growing political) power of this community has led to the development of some major religious sites and very active religious organisations in the States.

In more recent years, Indian mobilities have been increasingly configured by the demands of transnational corporations. In particular, the global expansion of the IT sector has increased the demand for a mobile and highly skilled English-speaking labour force. IT industries in India, pioneered in Bangalore but now very much part of the economies of Andhra Pradesh, Maharashtra and Gujarat, have encouraged both the presence of transnational corporations and the emergence of an appropriately skilled labour force in these areas. Often building on company links, these workers have demonstrated a capacity for sustained mobility, variously characterised in recent writing as a sense of 'flexible citizenship' (Ong 1999) or 'new cosmopolitanism' (Rajan and Sharma 2006). These migrants have had a major impact on the IT industry in California, for example, but they are not necessarily committed to permanent US settlement, maintaining instead the status of what Bilimoria has called 'transnational cyber settlers in transit' (2007: 317). The mobility of this group draws partly on previously established networks of migration, as they cut across national boundaries to explore and settle fleetingly in Indian localities across the globe, and grounds itself in a strong commitment and frequent returns home to India. This group, as Rajan and Sharma state, 'blur(s) the edges of home and abroad' (2006: 2–3). Interestingly, there is a strong echo of this pattern of movement in some globalised transnational Hindu organisations, to which we will now turn.

Transnational organisations and the emergence of global constituencies

As noted earlier, indentured Hinduism, such as that explored by van der Burg and van der Veer in Surinam, tended to develop a focus on regular, Brahman-mediated rituals associated with sacred texts. This homogenisation of Hindu practice produced what Vertovec has called a kind of 'official Hinduism' (2000: 41), clearly demarcated and identifiable as a religion. Although these developments generally marginalised more fragmented, parochial practices associated with kin, caste or village gods, they provided fertile ground for other forms of Hinduism to emerge. In particular, the delinking of Hinduism from specific, localised practices opened the way for the propagation of so-called 'neo-Hinduism' by a range of new, systematically structured organisations eager to propagate their own forms of Hinduism across the networks of the Empire.

One of the most prominent of these organisations in plantation societies was the Arya Samaj. Established in 1875 by Dayananda Saraswati, and initially successful primarily in Punjab, this organisation was something of a radical departure in nineteenth-century India because of the way in which it focused strongly on specific (Vedic) texts as infallible, universal and accessible to all, and on specific rituals (especially *havan*, the Vedic fire sacrifice) as appropriate to that focus. In this sense, Arya Dharm seems to mirror the emerging structure of indentured Hinduism. As a self-consciously universalist and expansionist movement, the Samaj was also concerned in particular about the plight of those it perceived as Hindus across the globe. As a result, Arya missionaries visited the Caribbean and other plantation societies from as early as 1910, and within 20 years had established branches which challenged the authority of local Brahmans.

In areas where trading connections were more important than indenture to the growth of the Hindu population, specific Hindu sects were also an influential presence from a relatively early period. For example, the Swaminarayan *sampradaya* has had a significant presence in East Africa since the early twentieth century. This is not surprising, as this is a Gujarati *sampradaya*, established in the early nineteenth century by Sahajanand Swami. Raymond Williams describes how Swaminarayan gained popularity in East Africa through the networks of the Empire, as 'temples and centers . . . developed along the railway in conjunction with the growth in trade and commerce among Indian immigrants' (2001: 205). The first Swaminarayan temple in Africa was established in Nairobi in 1945 and, although in India the *sampradaya* was by that stage divided into several competing groups, in Nairobi 'followers of the various branches joined together in building and worshipping in the temple' (Williams 2001: 206).

Since these early developments, certain Swaminarayan organisations have developed a global profile. By far the most prominent has been the BAPS Swaminarayan Sanstha, which is now a vast organisation with major temples in India, the UK and the USA. BAPS Swaminarayan has been particularly successful in attracting devotees amongst twice migrants moving from East Africa to the UK and USA, and also amongst highly skilled migrants to the USA (Williams 2001: 225). The organisation emphasises its global reach through a network of websites and an energetic charitable trust registered in the USA but working across several continents. The 'Annual Review 2009' of the UK Sanstha, for example, highlights charitable activities in Gujarat, Dar-es-Salaam, and even Silicon Valley, where career help forums were held in the wake of the global economic downturn (BAPS n.d: 23). This extensive reach has led Steven Vertovec to describe BAPS as a form of 'cosmopolitan Hinduism' (2000: 164).

The Arya Samaj and the BAPS Swaminarayan Sanstha represent two different types of Hindu organisation prominent in the diaspora: missionary style neo-Hindu organisations and regionally rooted, efficiently managed *sampradayas*. BAPS' careful management strategy has enabled it to expand out of India, mirroring the migration patterns of its key Gujarati constituency. In more recent years it has projected its image beyond this constituency to present itself as representative of modern Hinduism more generally, both in India and (more successfully) in the diaspora. The Samaj's expansion has been less dramatic, after its initial success in plantation societies. This perhaps reflects its rather dry focus on Vedic text. Missionary organisations based on a more emotional theistic devotionalism and spirituality have been more successful. One significant example is the International Society for Krishna Consciousness, or ISKCON. The diasporic intent of this organisation is evident even in its inauguration, which occurred in New York in 1966. Malory Nye (2001) has described how ISKCON has negotiated a prominent position as a provider of devotional infrastructures attractive to Vaishnavite Hindus in the UK.[3] This process has occurred in other parts of the global diaspora, to the extent that ISKCON is a significant Hindu organisation not just in the major Western migration centres, but also in places such as Fiji, where it has been vigorous in its attempts to expand its constituency (Kelly 1995).

Representing diaspora Hindus

Other organisations project the idea of diaspora Hinduism in contemporary social and political environments. These are generally associated with discourses of multiculturalism which have been central to the management of ethnic difference in Western societies over the past 40 years or so, although it is again important to place this in the context of earlier developments. For example, in Trinidad 'official' Hinduism was institutionalised in the early twentieth century through two rival organisations, the Sanatana Dharma Association and the Sanatan Dharma Board of Control, which were unified as the Sanatan Dharm Maha Sabha in 1952. The purpose of these organisations was, as Vertovec notes, 'the unification of Hindu interests' in Trinidad (2000: 55). As in other Caribbean states, this declaration of collective interests provided a basis for the political articulation of Hindu-ness, with the Maha Sabha providing the leadership and ensuring the support base amongst Hindus for the People's Democratic Party.

Although marked by a rather different template of inclusion, and entering the political process in different ways, we can see some similarities between this kind of development and the emergence of representative bodies in the context of Western multiculturalism. For example, in the UK, a body designed to promote the interests of the proliferating number of temples was established in 1978, the National Council of Hindu Temples. In 1994, this organisation was instrumental in the establishment of the Hindu Council UK (HCUK), which pitched itself as a body concerned primarily with the representation of Hindus in national political arenas. This has been followed in 2004 by the establishment of the Hindu Forum of Britain (HFB), a rival organisation to the HCUK and one which has been particularly successful in projecting its image as the 'voice' of UK Hindus to government institutions and other national bodies (see Zavos 2009). Currently, the HFB claims on its website to be 'the largest umbrella body for British Hindus with more then 420 member organisations from around the country. HFB is the first port of call from the central government and the most reported Hindu organisation in the British media' (www.hinduforum.org – accessed 31/8/10).

In America, similar organisations have emerged, driven by protagonists drawn from the sophisticated, largely professional constituency of American Hindus. Most Hindu umbrella organisations are regionally based and pitched in terms of Vedic or Dharmic authority. Since 2003, there has also been a prominent national organisation, the Hindu American Forum (HAF). This organisation describes itself as an 'advocacy group providing a progressive voice for over two million Hindu Americans'. As with umbrella organisations in the UK, the HAF is self-consciously ecumenical, as it seeks to 'serve Hindu Americans across all sampradayas (Hindu religious traditions) regardless of race, color, national origin, citizenship, caste, gender, sexual orientation, age and/or disability' (www.hinduamericanfoundation.org, 'Who We Are' page – accessed 31/8/10). As this statement indicates, such organisations are clearly framed by the language of contemporary multiculturalism. Indeed, Prema Kurien argues that it is this idea of multiculturalism – with its 'pressure to organize into groups on the basis of cultural similarity', its marking of ethnicity as an important source of cultural capital and its demand for authenticity sanctioned by traditional sources of authority – which has invoked the development of such organisations (2007: 4).

In this context, representative organisations develop outside the formal political process (unlike, for example, in Trinidad), so are not constrained by the need for internal democracy and exposure to the normal mechanics of electoral legitimation (although tropes of democratic infrastructure are very much a part of their image). Consequently their representative character is more overtly performative and symbolic, sanctioned by, for example, their ability to demonstrate proximity to political power (as in, for example, HFB-organised Diwali celebrations in the British Houses of Parliament, and the official recognition of this festival by the US Congress, lobbied for by the HAF). High-profile monitoring of commercial and media representations of Hindu symbols and practices is another means of legitimating representative authority (Zavos 2008). The work of organisations such as the HFB and the HAF in this area is supplemented by monitoring organisations less clearly framed by specific national contexts. Hindu Human Rights (HHR), for example, although based in the UK, provides commentary on what it sees as the global abuse of Hindus, with articles on issues such as the persecution of Hindu minorities in Bangladesh and Pakistan and the destruction of Hindu temples in Malaysia, and an archive illustrating the desecration of Hindu imagery from around the world. The organisation has also produced a Charter of Hindu Human Rights which echoes the form of the UN's Universal Declaration of Human Rights (www.hinduhumanrights.org – accessed 31/8/10). HHR, then, is an assertive defender of Hindu 'rights', leading us to consider the role of politicised Hindu nationalism in the projection of this transnational Hinduism.

Hindu (trans)nationalism

Hindu nationalism has been a feature of the public manifestation of Hinduism in India since the late nineteenth century. It is characterised by an intense valorisation of Hindu culture sometimes known as *Hindutva*, accompanied by varying degrees of antagonism towards what are perceived as non-indigenous world views, especially those read as Islamic, Christian or communist. The ideology is propagated in particular by a network of organisations known as the Sangh Parivar, led by the 'parent' Rashtriya Swayamsevak Sangh (RSS). In the diaspora, this network has been a vigorous operator during the post-colonial years, with the first overseas unit of the RSS being established in Kenya in 1947 (Jaffrelot and Therwath, 2007). The relatively low-profile work of the RSS itself has been augmented by more publicly visible Sangh organisations. In particular, the Vishwa Hindu Parishad (VHP) has been an active force in the diaspora, as it seeks to fulfil its objective to work for the 'total welfare of humanity on the basis of the unique cultural ethos of Bharatvarsha' (http://vhp.org, 'Objective' page – accessed 31/8/10). The VHP has established a presence in something like 80 countries around the world (Katju, 2003: 155). Whereas, in the UK, it has a presence which has been intermittently prominent at national level (Zavos, 2010b), in the USA it has been particularly active, providing support and resources for a range of smaller organisations (Kurien, 2007). In Mauritius, Eisenlohr (2006) has demonstrated that the VHP also provides support to a range of organisations such as the Hindu Council and the Hindu Trust, enabling the Sangh to have some influence over individuals and institutions associated with government. A Mauritian government minister, for example, attended the VHP's World Hindu Conference held in Allahabad as long ago as 1979 (Eisenlohr, 2006: 37).

The case of Mauritius demonstrates that the boundaries between *Hindutva* and 'mainstream' representations of Hinduism in diaspora environments can be difficult to locate. There is frequently a blurring and overlap, as some organisations draw on Sangh resources (including people) and speak the language of *Hindutva*, whilst maintaining a position outside the Sangh Parivar. A kind of affinity can emerge between Hindu nationalism and public Hinduism, which springs partly from the conditions of diaspora. In particular, in pluralist environments where religion is recognised as a significant marker of cultural or ethnic identity, key Hindu nationalist tropes such as strong communal unity, the global significance of Hindu ideas and an assertive difference in relation to other communities are easily adopted as a means of negotiating what Kurien calls 'a place at the multicultural table'. In addition, we should note the significance of multilocal connections which link the politics of community in diasporic spaces with politics in India. For example, transnational connections which link Gujarat with its diaspora mean that the dominant politics in that state, which in recent years have been avowedly Hindu nationalist, have a resonance in diaspora communities across the globe.

Views from elsewhere

There are forms of Hinduness emerging in the diaspora which challenge and to some extent subvert the existing dominant formations, both in terms of community identity and notions of Hinduism. Low-caste migrants have organised around specific devotional traditions. The Kabir Panth Association, for example, is particularly active in Trinidad, Canada, Surinam and Guyana. In the UK the Council of Valmiki Sabhas oversees the work of several Valmiki Mandirs. These institutions are significant for their tendency to challenge the established boundaries of religious identity between Hindu and Sikh formations, thus implicitly subverting the religious paradigms underpinning the dominant multiculturalist representation of Hinduism in this country (see Leslie 2003).

Another form of Hindu identity gaining greater prominence in recent years is that of Tamil Hinduism. Of course, Tamil Hindus have always been a feature of the diaspora – the system of indenture operated out of Madras as well as Calcutta, taking Tamil Hindus to plantations in South Africa, Fiji and other destinations. In recent years, however, the presence of Tamil Hinduism in diaspora has expanded greatly due to the civil war in Sri Lanka. Sri Lankan Tamil Hindu refugees have subsequently settled across Europe and the UK, North America and Australia. For example, in Germany and Switzerland Sri Lankan Tamils form the majority Hindu community and so are shaping the public representation of Hinduism in those countries. Temples are generally small-scale and unobtrusive, although the first purpose-built temple was built in Germany in 2002, in the city of Hamm. The Sri Kamadchi Ampal temple is distinguished by two classic southern Indian *gopurams*, reflecting a general trend towards 'visibilisation' amongst Tamil Hindus which echoes a similar move amongst Hindus in Britain in the 1990s.

The Tamil presence in Europe is also significant for its emphasis on procession (*pradakshina*), whereby *murtis* are carried or pulled through streets surrounding temples during festival occasions. Devotional practices associated with procession are sometimes dramatic: Luchesi, for example, describes practices of prostration, 'body-rolling', piercing and even hook-swinging amongst Tamils in Germany (2008: 184–5). Such practices challenge what are becoming established understandings of Hinduism in areas like Europe and North America, where a more sanitised Hinduism drawn from northern/western Indian practices and ideas has been more dominant. It is not just the difference of Tamil Hinduism which provides this alternative perspective. In addition, it is driven by the particularity of the refugee experience. Patterns of (sometimes traumatised) movement and dispersal affect both the cultural capital of Tamil Hindus and their ability to follow paths of chain migration which may bring associated social capital. McDowell, for example, explores Tamil pilgrimage in Switzerland to the shrine of the Black Madonna at the Benedictine Monastery and Church to Our Lady of the Hermits at Einsiedeln. The Black Madonna has been perceived as an incarnation of Mariyammam, a mother goddess who is worshipped at small shrines throughout South India and Sri Lanka. McDowell describes myths circulating amongst Tamils in Switzerland about the shrine's power, many of them related distinctly to the predicament of the refugee (1996: 234–6). This example demonstrates not just an openness to cross-tradition practices in a manner reminiscent of Valmiki temples in Britain, but also an openness to foregrounding what has been described as the kismetic dimension of South Asian religion (Ballard 1996), whereby divine intercession is sought in relation to specific individual predicaments.

Such an approach is also evident amongst Tamil refugees in London. For example, Ann David (2009) examines practices in the East Ham Sakthi Peetham, a small temple in a converted house dedicated to Goddess Adhiparasakthi. This Tamil devotional tradition has been vigorously pursued by Sri Lankan women, and a similar set of kismetic narratives to those noted at the Black Madonna shrine are present here. David comments that narratives of 'miracles' associated with the goddess

> bring power and legitimation, empowering the women and transforming them into religious specialists. Miracles allow the building of faith and indicate that even though this is a small, local site of practice, the devotees will have access to the supernatural realm.
>
> *(2009: 347)*

David also notes the presence of related South Indian practices in the locality. In 2008, for example, the first fire-walking ceremony to be held in the UK took place in an East London park. Significantly, the main agents in this ceremony were a group of Mauritian Tamils, fire-walking being a ritual practice pursued by South Indians in Mauritius since the days of indenture. This indicates the increasingly complex networks which connect Hindu practices across the globe, developing a multidimensional sense of Hindu consciousness which transgresses the idea not just of settled, nationally configured religious communities, but also of what constitutes Hinduism as a religion.

A Hindu diaspora?

In this essay we have seen examples of Hindu organisations with a global profile, invoking an image of global Hinduism: a transnational consciousness which binds Hindus, around the world to one articulated form of identity. Certain features of Hindu-ness may be associated with this identity: the trope of tolerance, for example, the significance of service (*seva*), or the claim of extreme antiquity. Such themes figure highly in the 'Understanding Hinduism' permanent exhibition at the BAPS *mandir* in Neasden, London, where the intention is to bring 'Hinduism to the doorstep of the West who can now appreciate what lofty ideals Hinduism stands for; what it has given in science, medicine and arts, and what is being contributed now to carve a better world for all' (www.mandir.org, 'Exhibition' page – accessed 31/8/10). Some scholars have also pointed to the *Ramayana* as particularly significant to Hindus in diaspora, because of its emphasis on themes of exile, suffering and return (Parekh 1993: 17–20). This is particularly so since this epic was produced as a television series in India and subsequently released on video/dvd, hence becoming universally accessible.

Such examples of a globalised Hindu identity, however, need to be mediated by recognition that the formations of diaspora Hindu-ness are continually being reformulated and reimagined. One interesting feature of recent Hindu practices in diaspora, for example, has been the growth of procession and other public rituals. These were noted in relation to Tamil Hinduism in the previous section, but they have also become increasingly associated with other traditions. Inspired by the Jagannatha Rath Yatra in Puri, for example, ISKCON holds processions in an increasing number of cities around the world, temporarily transforming city spaces into Hindu realms. As P.P. Kumar comments on the procession in Durban, South Africa,

> the ordinary streets in the city centre are turned into a sacred route along which the festival of chariots proceeds. . . . In other words, the sacred steps into the secular path, halting ordinary life while the festival procession moves forward uninterrupted.
>
> *(2008: 208–9)*

Diaspora Hinduism in this way fashions new arenas of sacredness in multiple ways, potentially challenging traditional ideas about the sacred quality of the Indian landscape. This landscape is also decentred in the complex spaces of the internet, where, for example, virtual puja sites allow either active engagement with puja practices, or 'proxy puja' at specific temples in India, verified through images posted on the net. The land itself, it seems, is reimagined through the act of virtual attendance.

Another kind of challenge is presented by the numerous organisations and devotional groups that interrogate the boundaries of the religious. Global networks such as the Sathya Sai Organisation and the Mata Amritanandamayi Math, as well as more multilocal bodies such as the Sakthi Peetham of Melmaruvathur, claim not to be constrained by specific religious identities, as they encourage participation by Hindus and non-Hindus alike. As Sathya Sai Baba says, 'do not give importance to differences of religion, sect, status, or color. Have the feeling of one-ness permeate all your acts' (www.sathyasai.org, 'Sai Organization sites' page –accessed 31/8/10). This approach is frequently linked to a kind of orientalist division between religion and spirituality (see King 1999), which identifies the latter as the focus of contemporary needs, framed by the secularism of modern lives. Sivananda's Divine Life Society, for example, aims to 'remove the unwarranted distinction between the spiritual and the secular, and endeavors to present an integrated view of life as a whole' (McKean 1996: 183). At the same time, many organisations also operate strategically *with* a discourse of religion in particular contexts, when such a status may be considered beneficial (see Kim 2009; Nye 2001).

This kind of strategic movement across modern social relations and cultural forms is indicative of the plasticity of Hindu ideas in contemporary diasporic contexts. There is a sense of movement, of process, which complicates and problematises the idea of the Hindu, and to some extent subverts universalist visions of a global Hinduism. To this extent, the idea of diaspora Hinduism is ironically most appropriate, as it signifies a multiple, processual form, continually open to difference, and challenging established categories which seek to encompass it, in a manner which resonates with late-modern understandings of the diaspora dynamic.

Notes

1   Indeed, it is this idea of 'religion' as a normative set of comparable 'systems' which underpins the presentation of Madho Singh's journey as indicative of the problems of Hinduism on the move.
2   For estimated destination-by-destination figures, see Clarke *et al.* 1990: 9.
3   Nye describes this process as the 'Hinduisation' of ISCKON, due to the initial reluctance of some Hindus to recognise it as Hindu.

References

Asad, T. (1993) *Genealogies of Religion: Discipline and Reasons of Power in Christianity and Islam*, Baltimore, MD: John Hopkins University Press.

Ballard, R. (1994) 'Introduction: The Emergence of Desh Pardesh', in R. Ballard (ed.) *Desh Pardesh: The South Asian Experience in Britain*, London: Hurst.

— (1996) 'Panth, Kismet, Dharm te Qaum: Four Dimensions of Punjabi Religion' in P. Singh (ed.) *Punjabi Identity in a Global Context*, New Delhi: Oxford University Press.

BAPS (n.d.) 'Annual Review 2009', London: BAPS Swaminarayan Sanstha UK.

Bates, C. (2000) *Coerced and Migrant Labourers in India: The Colonial Experience*, Edinburgh: Centre for South Asian Studies (Edinburgh Papers in South Asian Studies).

Belli, M. (2007) 'A Triumphant Homecoming: The Frieze Programme on Maharaja Sawai Madho Singh II's Cenotaph', *Marg: A Magazine of the Arts* 59 (1): 45–53.

Bilimoria, P. (2007) 'Transglobalism of Self-exiled Hindus: The Case of Australia', *Religion Compass* 1 (2): 305–28.

Brown, J. (2006) *Global South Asians: Introducing the Modern Diaspora*, Cambridge: Cambridge University Press.

Burghart, R. (1987) 'Introduction: The Diffusion of Hinduism to Great Britain', in R. Burghart (ed.) *Hinduism in Great Britain*, London: Tavistock.

Clarke, C., Peach, C. and Vertovec, S. (1990) 'Introduction: Themes in the Study of the South Asian Diaspora', in C. Clarke, C. Peach and S. Vertovec (eds) *South Asians Overseas: Migration and Ethnicity*, Cambridge: Cambridge University Press.

David, A. (2009) 'Gendering the Divine: New Forms of Feminine Hindu Worship', *International Journal of Hindu Studies* 13 (3): 337–55.

Eisenlohr, P. (2006) *Little India: Diaspora, Time and Ethnolinguistic Belonging in Hindu Mauritius*, Berkeley, CA: University of California Press.

Jaffrelot, C. and Therwath, I. (2007) 'The Sangh Parivar and the Hindu Diaspora in the West: What Kind of "Long-distance Nationalism"?', *International Political Sociology* 1: 278–95.

Katju, M. (2003) *Vishva Hindu Parishad and Indian Politics*, Hyderabad: Orient Longman.

Kelly, J. (1995) 'Bhakti and Postcolonial Politics: Hindu Missions to Fiji', in P. van der Veer (ed.) *Nation and Migration: the Politics of Space in the South Asian Diaspora*, Philadelphia: University of Pennsylvania Press.

Kim, H. (2009) 'Public Engagement and Personal Desires: BAPS Swaminarayan Temples and their Contribution to the Discourses on Religion', *International Journal of Hindu Studies* 13 (3): 357–90.

King, R. (1999) *Orientalism and Religion: Postcolonial Theory and 'the Mystic East'*, London: Routledge.

Kumar, P.P. (2008) 'Rathayatra of the Hare Krishnas in Durban: Inventing Strategies to Transmit Religious Ideas in Modern Society', in K. Jacobsen (ed.), *South Asian Religions on Display*, London: Routledge.

Kurien, P. (2007) *A Place at the Multicultural Table: The Development of an American Hinduism*, New Brunswick, NJ: Rutgers University Press.

Leslie, J. (2003) *Authority and Meaning in Indian Religions: Hinduism and the Case of Valmiki*, Aldershot: Ashgate.

Luchesi, B. (2008) 'Parading Hindu Gods in Public: New Festival Traditions of Tamil Hindus in Germany', in K. Jacobsen (ed.), *South Asian Religions on Display*, London: Routledge.

McDowell, C. (1996) *A Tamil Asylum Diaspora: Sri Lankan Migration, Settlement and Politics in Switzerland*, Oxford: Berghahn.

McKean, L. (1996) *Divine Enterprises: Gurus and the Hindu Nationalist Movement*, Chicago: University of Chicago Press.

Nye, M. (2001) *Multiculturalism and Minority Religions in Britain*, Richmond: Curzon.

Ong, A. (1999) *Flexible Citizenship: The Cultural Logics of Transnationality*, Durham, NC: Duke University Press.

Parekh, B. (1993) *Some Reflections on the Indian Diaspora*, London: British Organisation of People of Indian Origin.

Rajan, G. and Sharma, S. (2006) 'New Cosmopolitanisms: South Asians in the United States at the Turn of the Twenty-first Century', in G. Rajan and S. Sharma (eds) *New Cosmopolitanisms: South Asians in the US*, Stanford, CA: Stanford University Press.

Twaddle, M. (1990) 'East African Asians through a Hundred Years', in C. Clarke, C. Peach and S. Vertovec (eds) *South Asians Overseas: Migration and Ethnicity*, Cambridge: Cambridge University Press.

Van der Burg, C. and van der Veer, P. (1986) 'Pandits, Power and Profit; Religious Organization and the Construction of Identity among the Surinamese Hindus', *Ethnic and Racial Studies* 9 (4): 514–29.

Vertovec, S. (2000) *The Hindu Diaspora: Comparative Patterns*, London: Routledge.

Williams, R.B. (2001) *An Introduction to Swaminarayan Hinduism*, Cambridge: Cambridge University Press.

Younger, P. (2009) *New Homelands: Hindu Communities in Mauritius, Guyana, Trinidad, South Africa, Fiji and East Africa*, New York: Oxford University Press.

Zavos, J. (2008) 'Stamp it out! Disciplining the Image of Hinduism in a Multicultural Milieu', *Contemporary South Asia* 16 (3): 323–37.

— (2009) 'Negotiating Multiculturalism: The Organisation of Hindu Identity in Contemporary Britain', *Journal of Ethnic and Migration Studies* 35 (6): 881–900.

— (2010a) 'Representing Religion in Colonial India', in E. Bloch, M. Keppens and R. Hegde (eds) *Rethinking Religion in India: The Colonial Construction of Hinduism*, London: Routledge.

— (2010b) 'Situating Hindu Nationalism in the UK: Vishwa Hindu Parishad and the Development of British Hindu Identity', *Journal of Commonwealth and Comparative Politics* 48 (1): 2–22.

25

RITUAL, RELIGION AND AESTHETICS IN THE PAKISTANI AND SOUTH ASIAN DIASPORA[1]

Pnina Werbner

The translocation of culture

As transnational migrants settle in a new country, they transplant and naturalise cultural categories and practices, not simply because this is their 'tradition' or 'culture', but because as active agents they have a stake in particular *aspects* of their culture. The scholarly challenge, then, is one of conceptualising ritual and religious practice, observance and organisation as they respond in the diaspora to the dislocations and relocations of culture initiated by transnational migration. As a medium of social interaction, culture is not inert: it confers agency within a field of sociality and power relations. In this respect culture can be conceptualised first and foremost as a *field of transaction and relatedness*. Second, understood as performance, culture – in being *embodied* – is an experiential force. Finally, as a *discursive imaginary* of selfhood, identity, subjectivity and moral virtue, culture constitutes a field of political power. In these three senses, the cultures of immigrants are 'real', a force generating social conflict, defensive mobilisation and creativity. And because this is so, such cultures cannot be either reified, frozen in time or space, or simply dismissed.[2]

South Asian migrants form 'complex' or 'segmentary' diasporas. By this I mean that the boundaries between Indians, Pakistanis, Bangladeshis and Sri Lankans, Muslims, Hindus, Buddhists or Sikhs, are not fixed or clearly demarcated social entities, but are fluid, situational, context-specific and permeable; they interpenetrate and cross-cut one another depending on whether the analytic lens is directed to religious, national, linguistic or regional divisions. This means that the cultures of any one South Asian diaspora, say Pakistani or Indian, are multiple and sometimes conflicted. Moreover, 'culture' may be used to refer to quite different expressions of migrant cultural performance, from personally focused domestic or healing rituals in the home to collective public religious or ethnic celebrations and mass consumption of imported films and music. Culture may allude to popular or high culture and it includes both locally created diasporic cultural products – novels, films, music, visual arts – and the imported products of transnational culture industries. These different aesthetic expressions all combine to define the 'culture' of transnational migrants.

Any analysis of the cultures of transnational migrants must recognise the different scales and levels of public exposure characterising their ritual and religious observances and celebrations. I begin by considering the domestic, personal or family-focused rituals of South

Asian diasporic migrants. I then move on to discuss the dynamics of migrant public processions, religious networks and, finally, the politicisation of Islam after the Rushdie affair and 9/11.

The naturalisation of ritual: making homes, reconstituting persons and moral communities

The rituals that immigrants celebrate in distant and alien places are usually elaborated with cultural images and objects derived from their homeland. This transfer of images from one cultural context to another is an evident feature of the migration processs. Yet the theoretical questions it raises have been little explored in the literature on migration. Moreover, all too rarely has an attempt been made to interpret transferred ritual fully and systematically, analysing how specific symbols are used during particular sequences of rites in the diaspora.

Anthropological analysis has dominantly been about ritual in its 'natural' setting. In the natural setting the beliefs and concerns underlying the ritual, indeed the very substances and paraphernalia of a performance, are all rooted in the context in which the ritual takes place. Nevertheless, this focus on symbolic performance as enacted by people 'at home', in their country of origin, has also produced seminal insights important for the study of transferred ritual. In particular, studies of cultural revitalisation have shown how a former cultural order has to be renewed or reconstructed in response to the impact of disruptive change (see Fernandez 1982). Similarly, we need to explore how immigrants reconstitute the taken-for-granted features of rites and endow symbols with a direct and immediate bearing on their everyday world. We need, in other words, to examine the ways in which a ritual becomes 'naturalised' in a new setting.

Certain reductive approaches have to be avoided. Perhaps the least fruitful approach is the one which regards transferred rituals solely as a vehicle for boundary marking, meaning that the cultural images which constitute the rituals are considered to be anachronistic and therefore inert, as if the rituals have been 'emptied' in being transferred. This approach, in its obsession with boundaries, denies the continued force that transferred ritual has. Similarly, the 'replication' approach is also misleading: it assumes that cultural dislocation is unproblematic, without any need for cultural innovation. Both approaches obscure the power of the transferred rituals to reconcile past and present in and through metaphors and images.

To highlight this reconciling of past and present requires analysis of how the tropes and symbols of ritual as celebrated in the context of migration give renewed validity to fundamental ideas about the person, gender relations, human fertility, kinship and filiation, culture and nature, moral obligation and ethical dispositions. And it is through performance that rituals regain their sense of validity and naturalness.

If the migration process frequently starts with the arrival of lone migrants, male or female, the translocation and naturalisation of culture usually begins when they are joined by their families. Perhaps the most emotionally compelling events for migrants away from home involve nurture and sociability within the home, whether seasonal holidays like Eid or Diwali, or rites of passage and rituals of sacralisation and votive offerings, which bring together emergent circles of trust: kin, friends and neighbours.

The special ambience of family seasonal holidays and rites of passage is embodied in the tastes and smells of absent homes created by immigrants in their new homes. Immigrants often sacralise these homes, forging another kind of transnational bridge to their country of origin. When British Pakistani migrants move into a new home, they call a *khatam qur'an* ritual, a communal

Koran reading followed by a ritual offering and commensal meal (Werbner 2002/1990, Chapter 5). *Khatam qur'ans* are held on other occasions too – to thank God for recovery from illness or accidents, when starting a new job or to commemorate the dead. Hosts and guests are often women friends, kin and neighbours. They sit on a clean sheet spread on the floor, heads covered, and read all the 30 *siparas* (chapters) of the Koran in one sitting, each woman reading one or two chapters. Participation in such ritual events is regarded as a meritorious service on behalf of the convenor 'for the sake of Allah', requiring no reciprocation. *Khatam qu'rans*, like other such domestic rituals, create circles of trust for incoming immigrants, allowing them to incorporate newcomers and strangers. They are often neighbourhood events, especially so in immigrant residential enclaves, but they are also held among higher-class elite migrants living in suburbs and can include men as well as women. Part of the food blessed would be given away in Pakistan to the poor as an offering to Allah. This creates a dilemma in the diaspora where there are said to be 'no poor': can shared food in communion without expiation constitute an offering (see Werbner ibid.)?

The same dilemma is not present among Hindus in Southern California studied by Mazumdar and Mazumdar (2009), who sacralise their homes with religious artefacts and landscape their gardens with significant trees and plants through which home owners renew their connections to 'home'. Before moving into a new home, an altar is created for the dieties on an auspicious day, and a *puja* offering of music and food is made, attended by invited relatives and friends. In the ritual, overflowing boiling milk symbolises the abundance and prosperity of the new home; a priest sprinkles the rooms with holy water, while the sacred camphor flame is lit and passed to congregants. Its smoke is believed to drive out evil. The owners decorate the entrance to their house with coconut, rice and sacred objects, and anoint the doorway with sandalwood and tumeric in elaborate designs representing flowers or the goddess Lakshmi. Southern Californian Hindu homes are thus transformed, the authors argue, into 'sacred microcosm[s]' (Mazumdar and Mazumdar 2009: 259; see also Raj 2003: 95–8). Home altars, replete with pictures and statues of gods and goddesses, some of them heirlooms, or imported substances like Ganges water, decorate the altars, while multiple statues of gods and goddesses are distributed throughout the house. Sacred plants, bushes and flowers are planted in the garden and used for ritual events, when relatives and friends are invited for devotional singing and music-making on special occasions. These gatherings, with their food, fragrances, visual aesthetics and sound offer participants a multi-sensorial spiritual experience, the authors say, connecting and recreating homes away from home.

The Bene Israel, Indian Jews who have migrated to Israel, hold their own unique version of this immigrant ritual of offering, thanksgiving and purification. The *malida* is a ritual invoking the Prophet Elijah, believed to be still alive, which is followed by an offering containing a sweet rice mixture, five kinds of fruit, scented twigs and flowers, placed on a large platter. A wine libation is spilt on the ground and the prayers are followed by a festive meal. Gabriele Shenar, who studied the ritual, makes the point that Indian Bene Israel immigrants create 'emotional continuity' with India in their 'understanding of emotions as foods … elaborated in terms of nourishment, cooking, ingestion, digesting, and life'. Food rituals are thus a concrete means of experiencing and re-experiencing homage to the prophet or a gift to a deity (Shenar 2004).

Large-scale family rituals, like weddings and funerals, are indexical occasions, which register the full range of a family's network of acquaintances, friends and kin. Often these events consist of a series of rites which effect crucial transitions. Hence, the Pakistani all-female *mehndi* (henna) pre-wedding ritual is the most elaborate within a complex cycle of wedding rites. Through feeding and cosmetic treatment with substances, the symbolic transformations taking effect during the *mehndi* move bride and groom from a state of culturally constrained 'coldness' to framed, safe 'heat', in anticipation of the consummation of the marriage (Werbner 2002/1990). Weddings are occasions for initiating gift exchanges of cloth, gold and money between relatives and friends, part of an elaborate Punjabi gift economy, *len den*, imported into Britain, in which women predominate (see Bhachu 1985; Werbner 2002/1990).

Equivalent female henna rituals known as *kina gecesi, laylat al-henna* or *mehndi*, are held by Hindustani Muslim migrants in the Netherlands (Dessing 2001). As among Pakistanis, weddings involve elaborate exchanges. Importantly also, much like in India (Raheja and Gold 1994), the Pakistani *mehndi* is an occasion for bawdy singing, sexual clowning and transgressive masquerade: a resistive, counter-hegemonic commentary both on the status of women in Muslim Punjabi society and of Pakistani migrants within British society. Such clowning is not simply reflexive; it fulfils an embodied transformational role in the ritual process, occurring at a key liminal moment, before the clown is banished amidst gales of laughter by the women (Werbner ibid.; Werbner 2010a). *Mehndi* rituals allow for creative inventiveness and culturally hybrid objects, songs and dramas, while revitalising through aesthetic performance the substances, foods, music and dance of the homeland. The groom is subjected to hazing, sexually suggestive joking and forced feeding by the female bride receivers, underlining the power and control of Punjabi women over the domestic domain. As Raheja and Gold also argue, such rituals highlight the uninhibited expressive sexuality of South Asian women. Not surprisingly, *mehndis* are disapproved of by Muslim reformists and Islamists.

An important feature of family and domestic rituals is their socialisation of second-generation migrants into the intricate concrete details of their parents' culture through the medium of objects, substances and performances, images, sounds and tastes, as lived experience rather than theoretical dogma or text. Young girls and women figure prominently in Pakistani *mehndi* celebrations. They are the ones who dance, sing and clown, supporting the bride. So too, networks of second-generation girls and younger women are formed around such inter-dometic rituals and celebrations.

But 'culture', once taken as axiomatic in the natural context, can also come to be questioned in the migration context. Young South Asian women may question arranged or 'forced' marriages, accusing their parents of mistaking outmoded Punjabi 'culture' with Islam (Werbner 2007). Quite often in Britain, pubescent girls' movements are restricted and they are chaperoned, with family honour and female modesty repeatedly invoked. Fear of gossip is highly potent in close-knit Pakistani communities, although illicit love affairs do occur (see Shaw 2000: 172–3; Mody, this volume).

Whether due to global trends towards Islamicisation, or the maturation of second-generation migrant women, the spread of the *hijab* (veil) has become increasingly marked in Muslim migrant communities across Western Europe, from Norway, Denmark and Sweden to France, Belgium, the Netherlands, Germany and the UK, along with the proliferation of Islamic study groups (*dars*), as noted by Afshar (1998) and Schmidt (2004). These rotate between women's homes or meet in mosques to interpret Koranic verses or learn classical Arabic, often guided by a woman expert in Islamic studies. Some 'born again' women belong to national and international networks, as in the case of the Al-Huda women's network which has its headquarters in Pakistan. Such networks use email and have their own websites and chat rooms. An increased knowledge of Islam allows young women to resist traditional customs as unislamic and to demand the right to make their own marriage choices (Dwyer 1999; Schmidt 2004; Werbner 2007).

In addition to weddings, funerals or birthday parties, immigrant festivals and holidays are celebrated at home as well in temples, gurdwaras or mosques. Eid, Diwali and a myriad of other communal holidays must all be reconstructed in the migration context. In an overview of such family celebrations, Pleck (2000) shows how past and present cultural tranditions are renegotiated and reinvented in the context of migration. In Trinidad, for example, the descendents of Indian Muslim indentured labourers celebrate Muharram in an elaborate ritual which begins with the building of *imambaras*, large, complex ritual structures that purify the community and are later carried through the streets in procession with carnevelesque drumming and music, before being cast into the sea. Korom investigates the origins of the ritual in India in the light of current attacks on it by Islamic reformers who object to what they see as its illegitimate creolised form (Korom 2003).

One of the paradoxes of immigrant cultural celebrations highlighted by Korom's study is that in some respects immigrant cultures are both the same and different wherever they settle. But they are never beyond place. As Stuart Hall reminds us (1991), they are hybrid formations, created by the encounter with very different receiving contexts. How, then, can they share a single imagination of home, when even the location of immigrant sacred centres differ? Multiplicity is reflected in the diverse ways in which the cultural landscapes of immigrants are reproduced differentially even in a single receiving context, while resembling one another across different places. Religious and cultural movements respect no administrative, territorial or political boundaries. This is what makes diasporas *chaordic* social formations – chaotic orders that reproduce and extend themselves without any centralised command structures, emerging as unique and yet predictable cultural-organisational forms in many different places. Chaorders, I have proposed (Werbner 2002b), are inscribed both materially and imaginatively in space, time and objectifying practices. Chaorder theory implies that, irrespective of receiving contexts, the generative cultural, religious and organisational DNA of diasporas, so to speak, both ignores and transcends context. This is nowhere more evident than in diasporic religious processions and festivals, celebrated in the streets of migrants' new places of settlement.

Sacred Muslim geographies and ritual processions: Sufi migrants

Much immigrant culture is celebrated outside the home, often deliberately so, as migrants take over the streets and parks of their adopted cities and inscribe them with their presence. These public celebrations often follow distinctive patterns wherever migrants settle. Muslim Sufi orders create their own sacred geographies of migration. City-wide processions of Sufi followers commemorate their annual *'urs* festivals and *eid milad un Nabi*, the Prophet's birthday, with processions through the streets of Birmingham, London or Manchester. The processions wend their way for 3 miles through inner-city neighbourhoods to the city or order's mosque where sermons, praise singing, *qawwalis*, prayers and benedictions mingle with civic public speeches by the Lord Mayor, police and local councillors. Several hundred or even thousand strong, the processions include men coming from all over Britain, wherever the order's saint is venerated among UK South Asian Muslims. On both the *'urs* and the Prophet's birthday the marchers process the streets shouting out the name of God; they literally stamp the earth with the name of Allah. In doing so, they sacralise the spaces of the cities and immigrant neighbourhoods they have colonised, linking their domestic homes, mosques and Asian commercial districts as they march along reciting *zikr*, the memorialisation of God. They call people back to the faith, they 'own' the streets of their adopted cities.

In Pakistan and South Asia generally, the movement and settlement of saints which led to the expansion of Sufi cults on the subcontinent, is similarly conceived of as sacralising barren, wild, uninhabited land (Eaton 1993; Gardner 1993; Werbner 2003). In Britain, the land of infidels and unbelievers, indeed of open blasphemers, diasporic migrants inscribe the dangerous and sacrilegious foreign earth they have colonised with God's blessing. God remembers the place where His name has been called out, I was told.

Of course, not all Pakistani immigrants in Britain are followers of Sufi orders. The impact of so-called 'Wahabbi' reformist Islam is said to be growing in the diaspora, especially among young people. The relations between the venerators of Sufi saints and their shrines, and iconoclastic, puritannical Islamists, has been antagonistic and highly politicised for hundreds of years in South Asia, and the battles have carried over into Britain, though in an attenuated form. Pakistani immigrants in Britain have over the years since the early–post-World War II mass migration, replicated and reproduced all the sub-continental religious sectarian streams, denominations, political parties and divisions. The inclusive, mostly peaceful ideology of the hundreds of Sufi orders now present in Britain, some small, some quite large, all focused on shrines and saints in South Asia, is countered by the more exclusive and hardline ideologies of the various reformists and political Islamic groups. Muslim religiosity is thus highly contested and politicised in the diaspora, as it is in South Asia.

From Bollywood to *The Satanic Verses*: religion and aesthetics

A major aspect of immigrant culture relates to the importing and local creativity of diasporic aesthetic products, from music and films to novels or plays. Here debates about cultural hybridity, crossover, reception, interpretation and performance are linked to issues of identity and multiculturalism. A growing literature on Indian popular cinema's reception in the dispersed South Asian diaspora highlights the way in which context and positionality determine the appropriation, interpretation and performance of Bollywood by migrants. An early study by Gillespie (1995) described how Hindus watching the Indian version of the *Mahabharata* in their homes in London adopted devotional attitudes to the deities portrayed on TV. For them, watching was also a performative spiritual act. This is a theme carried over into other studies, such as Dudrah's of South Asian gay clubs where homoerotic dance-and-song video clips of male friendship are performed, against the grain, from films whose overall plot and message is heteronormative (Dudrah 2006, Chapter 5).

Parents and children diverge in their reading of Bollywood movies in Germany (Brosius 2005), South Africa (Hansen 2005), Britain (Kaur 2005), Guyana and New York (Halstead 2005). For the older immigrant generation these films are a source of authentic images set in a safe, 'pure', respectful, sexually modest cultural frame. Against that, young viewers are attracted by Bollywood's colourful and musical aesthetic qualities of stardom, dance and song while often distancing themselves from cinematic plots. Their subjectivities are thus marked, according to one author, by a double subjectivity, a double consciousness (Mishra 2002). Across generations, however, Bollywood is also performed – in Pakistani *mehndis*, Indian and Sikh weddings, club disco-dancing, Indian festivals of song and dance in Israel (Shenar 2013) and even in Hindu temples (Halstead 2005: 278).

By contrast to Bollywood, young South Asian immigrants' films, and TV shows produced by second-generation immigrants *in* the diaspora, usually in English, are far more critical. They challenge the normative gender and generational assumptions upheld by the immigrant generation (for a review see Desai 2004). They contain explicit homoerotic love scenes (e.g. *My Beautiful Laundrette, East is East, Bhaji on the Beach*), inter-racial love (e.g. *Missisipi Masala*), pervasive challenges to religious morality and the authority of the parental immigrant generation (e.g. *East is East, My Son the Fanatic*), women's agency and a subversion of strictly defined gender roles (e.g. *Bhaji on the Beach, Bend it Like Beckham*). They are thus transgressive in the tradition of Punjabi *mehndi* masquerade performances, lampooning hallowed customs and questioning religious authority as they express feminist, gay, liberal, anti-racist or secular attitudes. They deliberately caricature and parody conventional South Asian weddings, the sentimental core of so many Bollywood movies, even as they valorise romantic love. Not surprisingly, many of these culturally hybrid and transgressive films have had a stormy critical reception from older members of the migrant community.

Bakhtin's distinction between organic and intentional hybridities (1981) is relevant here: it allows us to theorise the simultaneous co-existence of cultural change *and* resistance to change in immigrant communities, as well as the way in which immigrant cultures challenge the established cultures that they settle in. A key theorist of hybridity, Homi K. Bhabha, celebrates hybridity as destabilising hegemonic meanings through a 'doubling up of the sign', a 'splitting' which is 'less than one and double' (Bhabha 1994: 119). In other words, the same object or custom translocated and placed in a different context can acquire quite new, transgressive meanings while echoing old ones. Bhabha locates the agency of post-colonial migrants in this act of 'interruptive enunciation', which subverts the possibility of 'pure' narratives of nation (ibid.). However, hybrid aesthetic products can also transgress religious sensibilities within the diaspora itself.

While South Asian immigrants embed themselves in their new homes by appropriating and naturalising homeland rituals and celebrations, what they often find to be most threatening is the deliberate, explicitly provocative aesthetic challenge to a felt social order and religious identity. Such intentional aesthetic hybrid interventions are thus critically different from immigrant routine cultural borrowings and appropriations, which unconsciously create the grounds for future social change. This was evident in the deep offence caused to immigrant Muslim South Asian readers by Salman Rushdie's novel, *The Satanic Verses* (1988). It led to a fierce academic debate about the novel, regarded by postmodern literary critics as a hybrid, postmodern narrative of migration. Anthropologists and sociologists critiqued its non-representativeness, which they argued reflected the alienation of elite diasporic intellectuals, writers and novelists from the wider migrant community (Asad 1990; Friedman 1997; van der Veer 1997; Fowler 2000). Others read the novel differently and argued that it meshed with Muslim traditions celebrating hybrid, liminal moments and spaces of transgressive licence (Fischer and Abedi 1990; Werbner 2002a, Chapters 4 and 5). But the evident offence experienced by working-class immigrants raised the question: what are the *limits* to licensed hybridity (Werbner and Modood 1997)? Most Muslims regarded the *Satanic Verses* as a blasphemous attack on their most sacred religious values, highlighting the fact that hybrid novels or plays can harm vulnerable minorities, even if their offence arises from a misreading of the novel's intentions (Werbner 2002a).

If immigrant identities form hybrid mosaics (Fischer 1986), immigrants also celebrate multiple overlapping identities or identifications – moral, aesthetic, political – as coherent wholes, *situationally*, in discrete social spaces that they create and set apart. In Britain, Islamic piety, South Asian popular culture, cricket as an expression of Pakistani nationalism and Commonwealth citizenship, are selectively foregrounded by British Pakistanis in separated social events and spaces, though there are also contexts in which they *fuse* these different identities (Werbner 2002a, Chapter 2). Spaces of immigrant cultural celebration or devotion require investment in material props, personnel and programmes, if the ambience associated with home is to be embodied and materialised. Nowhere is this more apparent than in the foundation and institutionalisation of religious observance. In the next section I focus specifically on Pakistani religiosity in the diaspora (for Hindus see Zavos, this volume).

Religion and political organisation: processes of community incorporation

While South Asian culture in Britain has been relatively innovative and responsive to diasporic experiences, this has been far less the case for the transnational movement of Islam into Britain. Instead, the wide variety of different religious streams, denominations and movements evident in South Asia has been transposed into Britain almost wholesale, along with the migration of Muslims from the subcontinent. Major religious organisations and movements such as Tablighi-Jama'at, Jama'at-i-Islami (in Britain known as the UK Islamic Mission), Deobandis and Ahl-e-Hadith compete with new Islamic movements such as the Al-Muhajiroun or Hizb-ut-Tahrir, imported from the Middle East, which are attractive to some young South Asian Muslims. All these groups have their institutional embodiments in the UK. In Manchester, for example, a city of some 30,000 Muslims, there are 22 mosques, each representing a stream, sect, nationality and city catchment area. In some neighbourhoods with high concentrations of Pakistanis, there are four or five mosques within walking distance of one another. This reflects also the fact that Islam in Britain remains on the whole nationally and ethnically divided.

Historically, then, as in the case of many immigrant settler groups in the religiously plural West, Islam began for South Asian Muslims arriving in Britain in the post-war era as an acceptable incorporative identity, non-racialised, high cultural and highly valorised. The mosque was the central locus of cultural value, the focus of communal factional politics, a point of mobilisation, a haven for incoming migrants, and a basis for solidarity in times of crisis. It provided a platform for subaltern orators and lay preachers, excluded from British formal political arenas.

Over time, as the settler community grew, there was an efflorescence of religious spaces, with the bewildering variety of different religious streams, denominations and movements in South Asia transposed into Britain. This process of replication was often associated with acrimonious splits so that, by the mid-1970s, most religious groups also had their own mosques. The process could be summed up as follows:

- proliferation (of religious spaces)
- replication (of South Asian Islam's sectarian and ideological diversity)
- diasporic encounter (with Muslims from the Middle East)
- confrontation and dissent (following the Rushdie affair)
- identity-led religiosity
- adoption of Muslim diacritical ritual practices and attire in public
- voluntary 'self-segregation'
- the politicisation and racialisation of Islam in Britain
- confrontation and dissent (following the wars in Afghanistan and Iraq).

Importantly, this was a male-dominated process. Women created Islamic spaces in the home and came to dominate the interdomestic domain, a domain of sociality and of ritual and religious celebration focused on familial, friendship and neighbourhood networks. Women have also been involved in philanthropic work for the home country. Alongside these, newly formed women's Pakistani Islamic movements, such as al Huda, which reject customary traditions and espouse a fundamentalist return to the Koran and veiling, have been imported into the UK since the 1990s.[3]

This points to a further historical process which occurred in Britain – the diasporic encounter with other Muslims coming from the Middle East. This did not lead to convergence, however. Language, culture and nationality have remained a major block to homogenisation of British Islam, despite public invocations of unity and despite the fact that mosques are open for worship to any Muslim, whatever his (and sometimes her) affiliation, kinship or *zat* (Muslim caste). There is, however, evidence of some Saudi-influenced Salafi, born-again conversion among South Asian students at British universities.

Despite wishful talk about the emergence of a 'British Islam' and despite the fact that Pakistanis tend to control central *Jami'a* mosques in almost all the major cities, Islam in Britain at the turn of the twenty-first century remains nationally and ethnically divided. There are Pakistani, Bangladeshi and Arab mosques, as well as Turkish and Shi'a mosques, and the language of sermons and even supplicatory prayers in the Pakistani mosques, whatever their tendency, is Urdu (or English) rather than Arabic. At the same time, children are taught to read the Koran in Arabic, and few can read and write in Urdu unless they study the language in high schools as an examination subject.

While the proliferation of mosques in Britain reflected differences in nationality, language and religious tendency, the main theological divide among Pakistani settlers has been between the majority Barelvis, Sufi followers who endorse the veneration of saints and love of the Prophet, and an array of Islamic reformist groups, some more fundamentalist than others, but none Islamist in the sense of espousing violent revolution. All these groups have continued to be linked through viable and ongoing transnational networks to religious centres or saints' lodges in Pakistan.

Until the 1990s, regional burial societies, known as 'kommittis', ensured that most people who died in Britain were buried in Pakistan. As families have matured, however, the increasing tendency has been to bury in local Muslim cemeteries, allocated by local authorities in Britain, a sure sign that many families are sinking roots in Britain. There has also been an extensive development of federated umbrella organisations uniting various Islamic groups across the whole of the UK.

This was very generally the picture of Islam in Britain before the Rushdie affair, in 1989, and subsequent international conflicts brought Muslims out onto the streets of British cities and onto global television screens. The processes of differentiation and replication outlined here took place relatively peacefully, beyond the public gaze. Since the Rushdie affair, however, and even more so since the September 11 bombing of the Twin Towers in New York city and, in the UK, the bombing of the London Underground on July 7, 2005, a reversal of the usual process of religious incorporation seems to have occurred. Instead of religion being defined as a legitimate source of identity for incoming migrants arriving in an established multi-faith society, Islam has become a flag of political dissent. The growth of specifically anti-Muslim prejudice, Islamophobia, has exacerbated this process. So too has the related perception that mosques are sites of rhetorical vilification of the West and, in a few cases, of incitement to terror. Stripped of its experiential dimensions, beyond personal belief, Islam is now an oppositional badge. One may speak of an identity-led religiosity. This has led to a serious questioning in the British press and media of the loyalty of young, second-generation British Muslims and the extent of their identification with British society (see Werbner 2009, 2010b).

In this context first- and second-generation Pakistanis, men and women alike, are increasingly adopting Islamic diacritical ritual emblems and practices which act as boundary markers, setting them apart from non-Muslim youngsters, including other young South Asians. Whereas the North Indian Islam of the migrant generation, embedded in Sufi traditions, tended to be relatively relaxed, with veiling and purdah abandoned in large measure by the Muslim middle classes when they settled in Britain, in contemporary Britain the wearing by women of burqas, elaborate veils and North African-style headscarves, and of beards by men, are linked also to a total abstinence from drinking alcohol and a refusal to participate in British youth culture which celebrates music, dance, sexuality, drink and drugs (see also Kim and Alexander, this volume).

This has led to a political discourse which accuses Muslims of self-segregation, while Sikhs and Hindu youngsters appear increasingly well-integrated, although evidence exists that they too sometimes support extremist nationalist movements. Despite these accusations, young Pakistanis are, nevertheless, very British. Mosque attendance among the younger generation is a matter of choice and often quite low although as Jacobson's (1998) and Shain's (2000) studies show, most youngsters remain pious and stress their Islamic identity, which they feel to be beleaguered both locally and globally.

The predicament of the Muslim South Asian diaspora in Britain has been that, rather than gradual integration, with Islam accorded respect as a religion of tolerance and peace, the community has been unable to escape the stigma generated by international conflicts with their globally transmitted images of book- or effigy-burning Muslim mobs (Devji, this volume). Conflicts of loyalty and identification create tragic dilemmas for diasporas which are, by definition, transnational communities of co-responsibility. Pakistanis in Britain identify deeply with the plight of Palestinians, Bosnians, Kashmiris, Afghans or Iraqis. Many see the West, and especially the United States, as an oppressor. The result has been that, rather than peaceful integration, Muslim South Asians in Britain have had to lurch from one crisis to another, from the Rushdie affair to the first Gulf War, to September 11, July 7 and the wars in Iraq and Afghanistan.[4] The images of alienation that these conflicts have generated have been exacerbated by the inner-city rioting of young Pakistanis in northern British towns and by the revelation that some young British Muslims had joined the Taliban and other extremist groups. This poses difficulties for Sikhs and Hindus as well, who are often racialised as 'Pakis'. Islamophobia thus has an impact on all South Asians in Britain. The diaspora was, and remains, complex, subject to fission and fusion and not finally segmented once and for all.

Conclusion

It seems, then, that the politicisation of Islam in Britain challenges the view that religion mediates the peaceful integration of immigrants into Western democracies as they strive to achieve equality in the public sphere. But against this relatively pessimistic prognosis is the fact that Pakistanis in Britain have remained, on the whole, peaceful and pragmatic. Islam is a congregational religion which provides a valued identity for immigrants. Much of it is home based, focused around rites of passage or communal Koran readings which mobilise family and friends. Even religious study groups, known as *dars*, which have proliferated, are held in private homes. So, too, some of the smaller Sufi groups have mixed male and female zikr circles. There is little or no purdah practised in homes, beyond formal etiquette. Most second-generation women move around freely, drive and work in salaried employment. They are active in their own philanthropic voluntary associations and have their own religious experts. The younger generation, both male and female, is currently entering the open job market in large numbers. For many, Islam appears to be an adventure of self-discovery, an enjoyable and meaningful alternative to British youth culture.

Notes

1   This paper draws partly on a wider comparative piece, 'Migration and Culture' (Werbner 2012) and partly on an encyclopedia article (Werbner 2005b).
2   For a more extensive discussion of this point see Werbner 2005a.
3   On al Huda in Pakistan, see Ahmad 2009. On veiling in the UK more generally, see Tarlo 2010 and this volume.
4   Other conflicts have included the Danish cartoon affair, for example.

Bibliography

Afshar, Haleh (1998) 'Strategies of Resistance among the Muslim Minority in West Yorkshire: Impact on Women', in Nickie Charles and Helen Hintje (eds) *Gender, Ethnicity and Political Ideologies*. London: Routledge, pp. 107–26.

Ahmad, Sadaf (2009) *Transforming Faith: The Story of Al-Huda and Islamic Revivalism Among Urban Pakistani Women*. Syracuse, NY: Syracuse University Press.

Asad, Talal (1990) 'Multiculturalism and British Identity in the Wake of the Rushdie Affair'. *Politics and Society* 18, 4: 455–76.

Bakhtin, Mikhail (1981) *The Dialogic Imagination*, trans. Caryl Emerson and Michael Holsquist. Austin: University of Texas Press.

Bhabha, Homi K. (1994) *The Location of Culture*. London: Routledge.

Bhachu, Parminder (1985) *Twice Migrants: East African Sikh Settlers in Britain*. London: Tavistock.

Brosius, Christiane (2005) 'The Scattered Homelands of the Migrant: Bollyworld through the Diasporic Lens', in Raminder Kaur and Ajay J. Sinha (eds) *Popular Indian Cinema through a Transnational Lens*. New Delhi: Sage, pp. 207–38.

Desai, Jigna (2004) *Beyond Bollywood: The Cultural Politics of South Asian Diasporic Film*. New York: Routledge.

Dessing, Nathal M. (2001) *Rituals of Birth, Circumcision, Marriage, and Death among Muslims in the Netherlands*. Leuven: Peeters.

Dudrah, Rajinder K. (2006) *Bollywood: Sociology Goes to the Movies*. New Delhi: Sage.

Dwyer, Claire (1999) 'Veiled Meanings: Young British Muslim Women and the Negotiation of Difference'. *Gender, Place and Culture* 6, 1: 5–26.

Eaton, R. (1993) *The Rise of Islam and the Bengal Frontier, 1204–1760*. Berkeley: University of California Press.

Fernandez, James W. (1982) *Bwiti: An Ethnography of the Religious Imagination in Africa*. Princeton, NJ: Princeton University Press.

Fischer, Michael M. J. (1986) 'Ethnicity and the Post-Modern Arts of Memory', in James Clifford and George E. Marcus (eds) *Writing Culture: the Poetics and Politics of Ethnography*. Berkeley: University of California Press, pp. 194–233.

Fischer, Michael M. J. and Mehdi Abedi (1990) *Debating Muslims*. Madison: University of Wisconsin Press.

Fowler, Bridget (2000) 'A Sociological Analysis of *The Satanic Verses* Affair'. *Theory, Culture and Society* 17, 1: 39–61.

Friedman, Jonathan (1997) 'Global Crises, the Struggle for Cultural Identity and Intellectual Porkbarrelling: Cosmopolitans versus Locals, Ethnics and Nationals in an Era of De-Hegemonisation', in Pnina Werbner and Tariq Modood (eds) *Debating Cultural Hybridity: Multi-Cultural Identities and the Politics of Anti-Racism*. London: Zed Books, pp. 70–89.

Gardner, Katy (1993) 'Mullahs, Migrants, Miracles: Travel and Transformation in Sylhet'. *Contributions to Indian Sociology* 27: 213–35.

Gillespie, Marie (1995) *Television, Ethnicity and Cultural Change*. London: Routledge.

Gopal, Sangita and Sujata Moorti (2008) 'Introduction: Travels of Hindi Song and Dance', in Sangita Gopal and Sujata Moorti (eds) *Global Bollywood: Travels of Hindi Song and Dance*. Minneapolis: University of Minnesota Press, pp. 1–60.

Hall, Stuart (1991) 'Old and New Identities, Old and New Ethnicities', in A.D. King (ed.) *Culture, Globalisation and the World System*. London: Sage.

Halstead, Narmala (2005) 'Belonging and Respect Notions vis-à-vis Modern East Indians: Hindi Movies in the Guyanese East Indian Diaspora', in Raminder Kaur and Ajay J. Sinha (eds) *Popular Indian Cinema through a Transnational Lens*. New Delhi: Sage, pp. 261–83.

Hansen, Thomas Blom (2005) 'In Search of the Diasporic Self: Bollywood in South Africa', in Raminder Kaur and Ajay J. Sinha (eds) *Popular Indian Cinema through a Transnational Lens*. New Delhi: Sage, pp. 239–60.

Jacobson, Jessica (1998) *Islam in Transition: Religion and Identity among British Pakistani Youth*. London: Routledge.

Kaur, Raminder (2005) 'Cruising the *Vilayeti* Bandwagon: Diasporic Representations and Reception of Popular Indian Movies', in Raminder Kaur and Ajay J. Sinha (eds) *Popular Indian Cinema through a Transnational Lens*. New Delhi: Sage, pp. 309–29.

Korom, Frank J. (2003) *Hosay Trinidad: Muharram Performances in an Indo-Caribbean Diaspora*. Philadelphia: Pennsylvania Press.

Mazumdar, Shampa and Sanjoy Mazumdar (2009) 'Religion, Immigration, and Home Making in Diaspora: Hindu Space in Southern California'. *Journal of Environmental Psychology* 29: 256–66.

Mishra, Vijay (2002) *Bollywood Cinema: Temples of Desire*. New York: Routledge.

Pleck, Elizabeth H. (2000) *Celebrating the Family: Ethnicity, Consumer Culture, and Family Rituals*. Cambridge, MA: Harvard University Press.

Raheja, Gloria G. and Ann G. Gold (1994) *Listen to the Heron's Words*. Berkeley: University of California Press.

Raj, Dhooleka S. (2003) *Where Are You From? Middle Class Migrants in the Modern World*. Berkeley: University of California Press.

Rushdie, Salman (1988) *The Satanic Verses*. London: Verso.

Schmidt, Garbi (2004) 'Identity Formation among Young Muslims: The Case of Denmark, Sweden, and the United States'. *Journal of Muslim Affairs* 24, 1: 31–45.

Shain, Farzana (2000) *The Schooling and Identity of Asian Girls*. Stoke-on-Trent: Trentham.

Shaw, Alison (2000) *Kinship and Continuity: Pakistani Families in Britain*. London: Routledge.

Shenar, Gabriele (2004) *Aesthetics and Identity among the Bene Israel in Israel*. PhD thesis, Keele University.

—— (2013) 'Bollywood: Transnational Dialogues, Cultural Appropriation and the Aesthetics of Diaspora'. *Ethnos* 76, 3: 226–54.

Tarlo, Emma (2010) *Visibly Muslim: Fashion, Politics, Faith*. Oxford: Berg.

van der Veer, Peter (1997) '"The Enigma of Arrival": Hybridity and Authenticity in the Global Space', in Pnina Werbner and Tariq Modood (eds) *Debating Cultural Hybridity: Multi-Cultural Identities and the Politics of Anti-Racism*. London: Zed Books, pp. 90–105.

Werbner, Pnina (2002/1990) *The Migration Process: Capital, Gifts and Offerings among British Pakistanis*, 2nd edition with new preface. Oxford: Berg.

—— (2002a) *Imagined Diasporas among Manchester Muslims: the Cultural Performance of Transnational Identity Politics*. Oxford: James Currey and Sante Fe: SAR.

—— (2002b) 'The Place which is Diaspora: Citizenship, Religion and Gender in the Making of Chaordic Transnationalism'. *Journal of Ethnic and Migration Studies* 28, 1: 119–34.

—— (2003) *Pilgrims of Love: the Anthropology of a Global Sufi Cult*. London: Hurst and Bloomington: Indiana University Press.

—— (2005a) 'The Translocation of Culture: Migration, Community, and the Force of Multiculturalism in History'. *Sociological Review* 53, 4: 745–68.

—— (2005b) 'Pakistani Migration and Diaspora Religious Politics in a Global Age', in Melvin Ember, Carol R. Ember and Ian Skoggard (eds), *Encyclopedia of Diasporas: Immigrant and Refugee Cultures Around the World*. New York: Kluwer Academic/Plenum Publishers, pp. 475–84.

—— (2007) 'Veiled Interventions in Pure Space: Shame and Embodied Struggles among Muslims in Britain and France', special issue on 'Authority and Islam'. *Theory, Culture and Society* 24, 2: 161–86.

—— (2009) 'Revisiting the UK Muslim Diasporic Public Sphere at a Time of Terror: From Local (Benign) Invisible Spaces to Seditious Conspiratorial Spaces and the "Failure of Multiculturalism" Discourse'. *South Asian Diaspora* 1, 1: 19–45.

—— (2010a) 'The Place(s) of Transgressive Sexuality in South Asia: From Ritual to Popular Culture', *Histories of Intimacies and Situated Ethnography*. Special issue in Honour of Sylvia Vatuk; Karen Isaksen Leonard, Gayatri Reddy and Ann Grodzins Gold (eds). New Delhi: Manohar, pp. 185–208.

—— (2010b) 'Notes from a Small Place: Anthropological Blues in the Face of Global Terror'. *Current Anthropology*, 50, 2: 193–221.

—— (2012) 'Migration and Culture', in Mark Rosenblum and Daniel Tichenor (eds) *The Oxford Handbook of the Politics of International Migration*. Oxford: Oxford University Press, pp. 215–42.

Werbner, Pnina and Tariq Modood (eds) (1997) *Debating Cultural Hybridity: Multi-Cultural Identities and the Politics of Anti-Racism*. London: Zed Books.

329

26

EUROPE'S MUSLIM PASSIONS

Faisal Devji

There exists a literature on Muslim communities in Europe that is so vast as to require bibliographies like Felice Dacetto and Yves Conrad's (1996) now woefully outdated *Musulmans en Europe Occidentale: Bibliographie Commentée* to be adequately surveyed. Despite its great bulk, however, this material dates for the most part to comparatively recent times. Indeed, scholarly, journalistic and policy work on Muslims in Europe only comes to constitute a genre from the 1980s, much after the great waves of migration that established such populations in countries like Britain, France, the Netherlands and Germany after the Second World War, in a context defined by decolonization and the opening of European labour markets. Starting with the study of these migrant communities, the literature on Muslims in Europe has moved on to locate them within a longer history of interactions between Christians, Muslims and Jews on the continent, sometimes stretching as far back as Charlemagne, Arab Spain and the Crusades, but more often beginning with the movement of Muslim diplomats, merchants and adventurers in the eighteenth century. Parallel to this narrative exists another having to do with the Muslim population in those parts of Europe that came under Ottoman rule, and even some work on the long-established communities of Tatars in Russia.

The extensive literature on Muslims in Europe, which in its academic mode emerges from every discipline in the humanities and social sciences, has no doubt opened up new ways of conceiving the continent's history and perhaps even that of the globe. Yet in other respects its focus is so anachronistic as to be dishonest. For, although the individuals and groups described in this literature might well be Muslim, there is no reason to assume that the role they played in Europe, whether in their own eyes or those of their neighbours, had invariably to be defined by Islam. Surely the absence of Muslims as subjects of academic and other interest, at least before the 1980s, demonstrates that whatever the blindness of observers in those times, such a population did not in fact exist politically or culturally at the continental and even national level. By making the false assumption of Muslim continuity, a great deal of the scholarship on such populations is not only unable to see discontinuities in the history of European immigration, but is consequently also capable of systematically underplaying the commonality of migrant experience across religious lines. Is it at all possible to speak of a Muslim population in Europe before the end of the Cold War, given that its religious practices tended to be confined within the discrete bonds of language and locality?

The Cold War was as important an event for Muslim immigrants as it was for the European countries in which they settled. For it was only with the collapse of the Soviet Union that Islam came to assume a role of its own on the continent. Before inquiring into the implications of this emergence, however, I want to point out that the Cold War represented such a disjuncture in Europe's history that very few of the ways in which Muslims had been considered during the imperial past of nations like Britain, France or Holland assumed any importance when they migrated to these countries. So, in the United Kingdom, which became the chief destination of Muslims from South Asia, the categorization of people in religious terms, so familiar from colonial times, was abandoned in favour of racial, regional and national classifications that frequently clubbed Hindus, Sikhs and Muslims, or Indians, Pakistanis and Bangladeshis together under rubrics like 'Asian'. Similarly the narrative of pan-Islamism quite lost its importance in this period, despite its former prominence, and only reappeared as an ally of the West during the Cold War's last battle in Afghanistan. In other words, while it was clear that some migrants to Britain happened to be Muslim, a population dominated by Pakistanis from the Punjab or Kashmir on the one hand and Bangladeshis from Sylhet on the other, their religious identification never assumed sufficient political or cultural importance to pre-empt these migrants' ethnicity or place of origin. Of this the most illustrative example is undoubtedly the slur 'Paki', used in the very recent past to define neither religion nor nationality, but race.

How, then, did a section of South Asian migrants in Britain and increasingly the European continent come to be defined as Muslims? It has become a cliché to note that the terrorist attacks of September 11, 2001 in the United States transformed world politics and, among other things, gave rise to novel security procedures that profiled some Muslims in the West while targeting a number of their coreligionists in military operations elsewhere. Yet I want to argue that such laws and procedures only consolidated existing narratives about Muhammad's followers in Europe and America rather than creating new lines of political reasoning there, thus providing us with one example of how unoriginal the response to global forms of militancy has been on the intellectual front. I do not however mean by this that policymakers and the general public in Western countries simply reached for a common stock of assumptions or prejudices to deal with their Muslim neighbours in the aftermath of 9/11, but want rather to suggest that, despite the rhetoric of novelty in which they are routinely mired, these events were in fact located within a quite different history defined by the end of the Cold War.

My task in this chapter will be to show that Islam and its adherents have neither come to constitute new historical actors after the terrorist attacks in America, nor indeed to serve merely as the victims of stereotyping and discrimination in Europe. Instead I will contend that, apart from its particular implications upon the lives of Muslims resident there, the 'War on Terror' has had little conceptual effect, not least because it has been absorbed by another historical problem, that of rethinking Europe after the collapse of the Soviet Union. Prior to this event, capitalism and communism constituted the globe's only actors, state-based ideologies that had divided its hemispheres into eastern and western halves that had little to do with the orientations by which former empires had defined themselves. I will claim here that Islam has not only emerged as a putative global agent in the wake of the Cold War but, in doing so, has put into question the political status of a newly federated Europe as well. But this means that the more Muslims are invoked in controversies on the continent, the less are such debates about them and the more about Europe itself.

Islam in the global arena

As a political rather than merely demographic entity, Muslims in Europe tend to be viewed not simply as a minority but rather as part of a global constituency. Whatever it owes to earlier worries about pan-Islamism in the days of Europe's empires, this manner of considering the continent's Muslims has to do as much with the creation of the European Union, and therefore the necessity of thinking about politics in a way that is not confined within national boundaries. In this sense debates having to do with Islam, as indeed over other issues seen as being primarily European in character, represent anxieties about the coming to light of new political arenas beyond the nation state (Bunzl 2007). And so Muslims are seen as posing a problem of the same kind as a single currency or laws made in Brussels, though their greater visibility may also render these latter concerns more tolerable as part of 'our' common European civilization under threat from global Islam.

Of course Muslims in Europe are not the passive observers of their transformation into a global threat but have driven this process from the very beginning. So the first manifestation of their emergence as a political constituency of an extra-territorial kind was arguably with the controversy over the British writer Salman Rushdie's book, *The Satanic Verses*, published just as the Cold War ended in 1989. Starting in an unprecedented manner with protests against the author's portrayal of Muhammad among immigrant communities in the north of England, the controversy spread to their places of origin in Pakistan and India, finally becoming the first among several global demonstrations of Muslim solidarity by way of the television and press coverage it received (Devji 2009a). It is interesting to note that subsequent manifestations of such global mobilization, for example the protests over Danish cartoons of the Prophet in 2005, or the Pope's comments about him in 2006, have also originated among immigrant communities in Europe, and all been provoked by insults alleged to have been delivered to Muhammad.

If anything this history of protest tells us how new traditions of Muslim solidarity are formed and makes it clear that their global character is somehow tied up with that of Europe. Indeed, it even seems as if Muslim solidarity can only be manifested in European terms, since no matter how well publicized they might be, similar insults to the Prophet in other parts of the world, not least in Muslim countries, have never achieved global notoriety, however effusive the protests they provoke at the local or national level. Such, for instance, was the case of the Bangladeshi writer Tasleema Nasreen, whose journalism of many years suddenly became controversial in the aftermath of Rushdie's infamy, even though the attempt by Islamic parties in Bangladesh to achieve global celebrity by attacking her did not meet with much success. However, the global nature of these controversies resides not in their geographical dispersal so much as in the fact that they appeal ostensibly to non-political causes like insults to the Prophet that are held to affect Muslims universally and without distinction. Whether or not such insults are viewed as illustrations of a wider political antagonism between the Muslim world and the West, their global character is defined morally, by using the language of 'respect denied', rather than in strictly legal or geopolitical terms.

Unlike protests over the treatment of Muslims in Bosnia, Chechnya or Kashmir, those engaged by insults to the Prophet do not single out a particular place or population that others are meant to identify with, but, in as much as it affects them all universally, move solidarity itself from an international to a global dimension. And though at every level these protests certainly involve political concerns of a more conventional sort, their strictly religious phraseology and global constituency does nothing more than put into question the inherited categories of European politics. And from the Rushdie controversy it became clear that these categories ranged from the nation state itself to those of race, class and region, which had been the political building blocks of post-war Europe. After all, Muslim immigrants in the days before the publication of Rushdie's novel were dealt with by European governments in terms of race or class, nationality or neighbourhood, and not primarily by religion. For even the great debates over Middle Eastern events like the Islamic Revolution in Iran were engaged with along the geopolitical lines of Cold War tradition.

Erupting into a new global arena that came to light with the end of the Cold War, movements of Islamic solidarity transformed the vocabulary of conventional politics. Just as the Soviet collapse resulted in class warfare being downgraded from an international language to a local dialect of politics, so too did the rise of global forms of Muslim protest have as their consequence the dismantling of race as a political category in Europe. So, in Britain, for example, we have seen the collapse of attempts to build a 'Black' political alliance, while more discrete classifications like 'Asian' are also being questioned, with the focus of government as much as media moving to the different religious communities that constitute them. This emphasis on religious groups as a society's basic political actors possesses, of course, a long colonial history, and such definitions are therefore as familiar to Muslim immigrants from places like South Asia as they are to the British state. I shall return to the important role played by this colonial past in the debate over Europe's Muslim populations and want to note here only that this discussion seems caught between racial and religious idioms that cannot be collapsed into a single category. In fact disputes over forms of Muslim visibility like veils or minarets in some parts of Europe might indicate attempts to cling on to some sort of racial script, much as the visibility of poverty, drug-use, teenage pregnancy and crime is used to mark other minority populations without any biological theory of race having to be invoked (Bowen 2010, Scott 2007).

Naturally in arguing that race is being dismantled in Europe I am not suggesting that racism or race consciousness has disappeared from the continent, only that immigrant communities there have been rearranged into a new hierarchy with Muslims occupying its summit of visibility. Moreover, since Islam cannot be racially defined and is seen as a global threat partly because it names a bewildering array of ethnic groups including European converts, even when they are the objects of racial prejudice Muslims end up fragmenting race itself as a political category. And this despite the fact that in Europe followers of the Prophet continue to associate with one another and worship along ethnic and linguistic lines. Only the young and educated, those who are fully integrated into European societies and who communicate in their official languages, are capable of forming ethnically diverse associations of Muslims (EUMC 2006b). And it is precisely from this population that 'militants' and 'moderates' emerge, both groups united by the fact that their ideas of Islam are as likely to come from Western sources, in Western languages and by way of close interaction with the West, than they are to derive from some traditional model of religious education.

But of course the clearest example of the way in which the language of global Islam has triumphed over that of race has to do with the fact that many if not most of Europe's racist parties have redefined their narratives to target Muslims rather than Blacks or Jews as the chief threat to civilized society in the West. Indeed this is so much the case that groups like the English Defence League have welcomed Sikhs, West Indians and others as fellow travellers in the project to defend the world against Islam. By pushing aside the vocabulary of biological determinism, this transformation of racial reasoning ends up evoking not some threatened European purity so much as defending the fairly commonplace 'Western' values of freedom, tolerance and even diversity against Muslim 'totalitarianism'. And, in taking on such values, racist groups are not only coming into the European mainstream by slowly casting off their biological concerns, but also demonstrating that their new passions possess an entirely legitimate provenance. After all it is not coincidental these are the very values that were for so long upheld by capitalist democracies against communism and therefore represent the Cold War's legacy to these new conflicts of religion or civilization that appear to have succeeded it.

Observers at the time noted the specificity of anti-Muslim prejudice in Europe in the wake of the Rushdie controversy, and soon a neologism was coined for it with the word Islamophobia. Whatever the merits of this term, those who deploy it tend to describe Islamophobia as a form of racism, as in the influential report on the phenomenon by the Runnymede Trust in 1997. By tying discrimination against Muslims to the received language of race relations, however, this approach is unable to recognize Islamophobia's role in the breakdown of race as a political category. In fact, racism in Europe seems increasingly to be abandoning its old biological formulae in favour of liberal shibboleths, to the degree that there is often very little rhetorical distance between the two ideological forms. It is as if the victory of liberalism over its Marxist antagonist with the end of the Cold War led to the collapse of all other forms of ideological autonomy as well. But whether racist parties are disingenuous in referring to such liberal verities, or if in doing so they simply reveal the otherwise hidden potential of these principles, the ostensible hegemony exercised by liberalism in its capitalist and democratic aspect needs to be questioned.

Politics without sovereignty

One reason why Islam after the Cold War cannot be said merely to have taken communism's place as the West's new enemy has to do with the fact that this Occident passed into history together with its Marxist rival. For, in retrospect, the supposedly triumphal narrative of Western dominance, as manifested in massively popular books like the American philosopher Francis Fukuyama's *The End of History and the Last Man* (1992), turn out to have been anxious attempts to redefine NATO's role in a new and increasingly unpredictable political landscape marked, among other things, by the 'revival' of xenophobic nationalism and ethnic cleansing in parts of Europe itself. And just as the Occident was being redefined for a global arena in the form of temporary coalitions among a changing list of geographically dispersed countries dedicated to military action against some recalcitrant nation, so too was Islam being defined as an historical actor in equally transitory coalitions of protesting believers. Both cases illustrate that the global arena lacks political institutions of its own and can only be occupied intermittently by actors with pretensions to planetary influence.

This situation was first described in another famous book by an American political scientist, Samuel Huntington's *The Clash of Civilizations and the Remaking of World Order* (1996), which identified in conceptual terms the momentous political consequences wrought by the end of the Cold War. Whatever its other weaknesses, this book, written for a general audience, had the singular merit of pointing out that the global arena coming to light after the Soviet collapse called for a transformation of political agency. Instead of merely celebrating or on the contrary bemoaning the West's triumph and proceeding to analyze the perils of its hegemony, Huntington sought to sketch the theoretical framework for an entirely novel politics. In effect he argued that the global arena could no longer be defined by a statist politics once its hemispheric configuration had come apart with the Cold War's sudden ending. But, having already come into existence, this arena could not give way to the kind of international politics that had preceded it either. And in the absence of conventional institutions to ground it, the global arena came to be defined by struggles that Huntington described as being based upon the values of civilizations instead of the ideologies of states. And on the rhetorical register at least, nothing could characterize the so-called Global War on Terror better than this formulation, fought as its battles are between competing orders of value with no geographical limits.

Now the word civilization, like race, was last deployed as a category of international politics in the days of European imperialism. In a set of lectures collected under the title *Society Must be Defended* (2003), the French historian Michel Foucault argued that race in this period named a 'politics beneath politics', referring in this way to a host of uncharted demographic interactions, in particular countries as much as the world at large, that were held to constitute the unrecognized truth of politics as such. Those who made the racial argument, then, believed that its truth was ignored within the institutions of national and international order, which in their eyes were concerned with superficialities. Not only did the geopolitics of racism, in Foucault's view, delineate the outlines of an emerging global arena that the institutions of Europe's state system were unable to colonize, it also attempted to occupy this new world by giving political life to planetary categories like an Aryan or White brotherhood that had in the past possessed a very limited social existence. While Foucault did not include it in his argument, it is easy to see how civilization, which alongside race was a great staple of European imperialism, has come to play a similar role in our own time by naming another mode of 'politics beneath politics'.

Unlike the more or less constant hierarchies of race, however, civilization represented the liberal aspect of imperialism, because in stereotyped forms such as the 'civilizing mission' it was premised upon the possibility of change and held out the promise of equality for all in some generally undefined future. Indeed, civilization, or rather the time and training needed to inculcate it, provided the only liberal justification for colonialism, as is evident from the works of liberalism's founding fathers, men of such eminence as John Stuart Mill (Mehta 1999). It is also clear that civilization is in this way intimately related to the notions of progress and development, whose promotion is even now used to justify the postponement of political freedom for some. And so, by latching on to this term today, parties on the far right are staking a claim to liberalism in another example of the process of ideological narrowing that I described above. After all, as distinguished from race, civilization has the advantage of shifting political argument from nature to history, so that, even when particular people or their possessions are attacked in ways that have hitherto been called racist, the target is always said to be a set of values that they represent and are asked only to abjure in order to be integrated as Europeans.

Crucial about this demand for integration is that it falls squarely within the tradition of secularism upon which so many states in continental Europe (unlike the United Kingdom with its established church) have been founded, one that in theory seeks to forbid religion any role in public life. For though it may have links with older narratives of integration as a way of erasing visible differences of a secular kind (including language and clothing), today's rhetoric of assimilation prides itself on its tolerance of non-religious differences in conventionally liberal ways and, however disingenuously, returns to the classical theories of secular citizenship for which religion alone is important. Thus, in the furious debate about banning Muslim women's headscarves in France, it is now difficult to tell the difference between high-minded secularists and racist pretenders, both of whom take recourse to the same reasoning. On the other hand, the increasingly common appeal to civilization undermines this secular form of argumentation, since in contemporary debates a suitably sanitized version of Christianity is considered to lie at the heart of Western civilization. Apart from bringing Christianity back to political life in this way, the language of civilization mobilized to face the threat of global Islam is therefore transforming rather than merely defending Europe's secular tradition, in the same way as it has transformed the politics of race there. Just as the debate on integration is no longer linked to some ethnic uniformity of citizenship within the nation state, but rather to a conflict of civilizations for which the latter provides only one site, so too does the argument about secularism now stand apart from a national arena, referring as it does to an encounter of civilizations whose context can only be global.

Musical chairs

Given its imperial lineage, the irony of today's 'clash of civilizations' is that, in the opinion of many of its upholders, Islam is seen as posing Europe the same kind of threat that colonialism had presented to the Muslim world not so long ago. Thus, in the whole series of books detailing this conflict of values, among which the most recent and superior publication is undoubtedly the American journalist Christopher Caldwell's (2009) *Reflections on the Revolution in Europe: Immigration, Islam and the West*, the focus is firmly on the settlement of Muslim populations in Europe, their unwillingness to integrate, attempts at converting Christians to Islam and finally the subversion and even conquest of host societies by a set of alien values. With the necessary transposition of identities, these are exactly the same fears that had once been voiced by colonized peoples in Asia and Africa. Such beliefs were perhaps most famously expressed during the Indian Mutiny of 1857, when the Bengal Army's Hindu and Muslim troops rebelled against their English masters not because they resented the presence of foreigners in India or even their rule over it, but at least rhetorically because they feared the settlement there of Europeans who sought to subvert what today would be called Indian values and replace them with Christian ones (Devji 2009b).

Whether these nineteenth-century Indian fears were more justified than our twenty-first-century European ones, what is interesting about the turn to civilization in discussions of Muslim immigration is the fact that its terms of reference seem to have undergone a strange reversal. Now it is Europe that is portrayed as being under threat from colonial settlement, and Islam's civilizing mission that will end up subverting the continent's indigenous values. Although such warnings about the West's decline have come in many different forms since they were pioneered during the eighteenth century, the mirror image of imperialism that this one in particular offers us deserves scrutiny. Regarded in the image of one of its former colonies, Europe is described as falling under the sway of Muslims neither by design, necessarily, nor even by a clash of arms, but maybe in some version of that famous 'fit of absent-mindedness' that was once said to have procured Britain her empire in India. The problem, in other words, is not Islam so much as Europe's own 'tolerance' and thus inability to defend itself. But what accounts for this desire to turn Europe into a caricature of one of its former colonies?

The answer, as I have suggested, has to do with anxieties about the emergence of Europe as a federated unit. For interesting about the European Union is that it represents a new kind of global polity, one that is extraordinary in that, while being something more than a free-trade zone or alliance of nation states, lacks the kind of sovereignty that has been the hallmark of all political forms in modern times. Europe, in other words, indubitably exists as a polity but at the same times does not, as its much remarked upon inability to act decisively in the global arena demonstrates (Kagan 2004). And in this way it is in many ways like Islam as a global actor, one that also lacks sovereignty and even institutional foundations, thus occupying a curious position between political existence and non-existence. It is because Europe lacks sovereignty that I think it is increasingly defined against its similarly placed Islamic rival in terms of values and civilization. This might also be why the threat of Muslim colonization is seen to affect Europe and not the United States, despite the latter's growing Muslim population and unrivalled status as a target of Islamic militancy. Indeed it is instructive to note that none of the many competing visions of American decline take Islam to be an important factor in their narratives. For, on the domestic front, it is still Mexican and other 'illegal immigrants' who are seen as threatening the American way of life, as Samuel Huntington himself made clear in the last book he wrote, which was devoted to this politically contentious subject. And on the international front it is China and to a lesser degree India that are acknowledged as the chief competitors of the United States, at least in economic terms, with Iran, North Korea and even Al-Qaeda simply posing it a number of dangerous but manageable security threats.

But all this still doesn't explain why it is that colonialism provides the most compelling model of Europe's decline in the face of Muslim assertion. Europe, I would like to claim, has always been united in the form of an empire, whether a religious one, as was the case with the Holy Roman Empire, secular, as with the Napoleonic conquests, or racist as with the Nazis. Indeed it was during its last incarnation as a fascist empire that Europe was conceived as being threatened by immigration and the hybrid values that resulted from it, of which the Jews represented the chief internal example (Mazower 2008). Not the purity of the outsider, then, but rather his amalgamation with European civilization posed the greatest threat to the latter, and it is therefore interesting to note that the guardians of European values today are also concerned with the hybrid mixing of cultures, which is why their favourite terms of opprobrium tend to evoke this non-racial miscegenation. Of these, the three most popular among writers accused of 'Islamophobia' like Bat Yeor (a pseudonym for the polemicist Gisele Littman) are undoubtedly Eurabia (Yeor 2005), a name for the continent under Muslim domination; dhimmitude, a description of those who accept the subordinate status of a 'dhimmi' or non-Muslim in classical Islamic legal theory; and Islamofascism, an ideological category that links Islamic militancy in particular to the history of Europe.

Since it appears to lack sovereignty, Europe receives its political identity from the outside, this time as part of a Muslim empire. The fact that this empire turns out to be a mirror image of Europe's own tells us that colonialism remains an unresolved issue in much of the continent and is able therefore to revisit its politics in such ghostly ways. But the turn to empire also makes it clear that the partisans of a beleaguered West can only think of their victimization in colonial terms. Rather than simply taking the place of their former subjects, however, those Europeans who hold such views appear to be claiming that the true Occidentals in this story are in fact Muslims. After all it is precisely Islam's unwavering confidence and conquering spirit that these men and women both admire and despise, for the lack of such qualities in contemporary Europe is what they constantly bemoan. Muslims may even be said to represent the truest of Europeans in this negative way, constituting as they do a supposedly uniform and universal problem in a continent seen as having lost its own unity, cultural as much as political, in the wake of the Cold War.

Whatever the conflicts that Muslims are part of in Europe's many societies, including street crime, anti-Semitism, patriarchal repression and terrorism, their wealth, influence, numbers and political affiliations cannot by any stretch of the imagination be said to pose an existential threat for the continent or even for its cherished values, constituting as they do less than 5 per cent of the Union's population (EUMC 2006a). Indeed, as I have tried to show above, descriptions of the Islamic threat tend to fall into familiar narratives from other times and places, though they do gesture towards a very real question, that of defining politics for a global arena that possesses none of its own. In any case the list of European values threatened by Muslim immigration is a contradictory one, including as it does historical rivals like Christianity and the Enlightenment, together with a hodgepodge of others such as secularism, humanism, tolerance, democracy and science. The last time such a disparate set of values was deployed in this reified manner to define the essence of Europe, it happened to be in that continent's various colonies and as part of a civilizing mission. And so it is only appropriate that these same values should now return to Europe in all their purity, naming as they do a place lacking sovereignty and without a politics of its own.

It is possible to say that, newly defined by its values, Europe as a civilization transcending all political and even geographical determinations, has returned to the continent from its redoubts in Africa and Asia. Even the word European, after all, which until recently had little currency in the continent itself, has always been used in former colonies to identify the citizens of its several states by a collective name. And then as much as now, the term European did not designate people by race alone, for which other terms were available, and certainly not by geography, since included within its ranks were also Americans, Australians or South Africans, but primarily by the civilization they all were meant to share. And if this is true, then Europe really is a creation of its empire, brought back to the place of its origin by Muslim immigrants.

References

Bowen, J. R. (2010) *Can Islam be French? Pluralism and Pragmatism in a Secularist State*, Princeton, NJ: Princeton University Press.

Bunzl, M. (2007) *Anti-semitism and Islamophobia: Hatreds Old and New in Europe*, Chicago, IL: Prickly Paradigm Press.

Caldwell, C. (2009) *Reflections on the Revolution in Europe: Immigration, Islam, and the West*, New York: Doubleday.

Dacetto, F. and Conrad, Y. (1996) *Musulmans en Europe Occidentale: Bibliographie Commentée*, Paris: L'Harmattan.

Devji, F. (2009a) 'The Mountain Comes to Muhammad: Global Islam in Provincial Europe', in Chris Rumford (ed.) *The Sage Handbook of European Studies*, London: Sage Publications.

— (2009b) 'The Mutiny to Come', *New Literary History*, vol. 40, no. 2.

European Monitoring Centre on Racism and Xenophobia (EUMC) (2006a) *Muslims in the European Union: Discrimination and Islamophobia*, Vienna: EUMC.

— (2006b) *Perceptions of Discrimination and Islamophobia: Voices from Members of Muslim Communities in the European Union*, Vienna: EUMC.

Foucault, M. (2003) *Society Must be Defended: Lectures at the College de France, 1975–1976*, trans. David Macey, New York: Picador.

Fukuyama, F. (1992) *The End of History and the Last Man*, New York: The Free Press.

Huntington, S. (1996) *The Clash of Civilizations and the Remaking of World Order*, New York: Simon and Schuster.

Kagan, R. (2004) *Of Paradise and Power: America and Europe in the New World Order*, New York: Vintage.

Mazower, M. (2008) *Hitler's Empire: How the Nazis Ruled Europe*, New York: Penguin Press.

Mehta, U. S. (1999) *Liberalism and Empire: A Study in Nineteenth Century British Liberal Thought*, Chicago, IL: University of Chicago Press.

Runnymede Trust (1997) *Islamophobia: A Challenge for Us All*, London: Runnymede Trust.

Rushdie, S. (1989) *The Satanic Verses*, New York: Viking.

Scott, J. W. (2007) *The Politics of the Veil*, Princeton, NJ: Princeton University Press.

Yeor, B. (2005) *Eurabia: The Euro-Arab Axis*, Madison, NJ: Farleigh Dickinson University Press.

27

DIASPORIC CITIES IN BRITAIN: BRADFORD, MANCHESTER, LEICESTER, LONDON

William Gould

If peacocks dance in the jungle, who can see them?[1]

Here was a community in Bradford which actually stood up ... the way they look at Bradford, the way they brush Bradford, making it one entity of mad Asians ... which are just myths which are amazingly perpetrated and entertained ... I think Muslims within Bradford are looking internationally at their position in the world ... I think that is the way forward for all of us.

(Aki Nawaz 2009)

The histories of post-war South Asian migration to British cities are intimately wrapped up with the history of British decolonisation itself. Yet, such interconnections have often been overlooked by historians of the Isles themselves, whose histories instead present a movement of Commonwealth peoples to provide the labour for mid-century regeneration – economic sojourners who created specific ethnic enclaves in the hearts of Britain's industrial centres. In mainstream historical narratives, South Asian immigrants are represented as ethnic minorities, whose voices and histories were largely mediated by the state, in the working out of Britain's multicultural experiments (Roger Louis 2005; Sandbrook 2005, 2006). Only recently have some writers begun to disavow the roots of such narratives and the ethnicities that they create.

This chapter will explore how new work and writing has begun to transform our view of the 'British Asian' city, and to connect its histories to longer processes of decolonisation and the end of empire, via literature, art and cultural production. Looking at some of the principal cities of South Asian settlement in the UK from the south, Midlands and north – in this case, London, Leicester, Bradford and Manchester – it becomes difficult to relegate diasporic histories to a framework which just considers the late-twentieth-century projects of race relations and 'multiculturalism'. Instead, as we will argue below, the South Asian presence in these urban centres reveals both an alterative history of the cities themselves, but also simultaneous attachments to different localities and places.

The very idea of 'locality' is significant in this context, and has elicited much interest among scholars working on South Asian and other diasporas in Europe. New work has began to critique the classical 'diaspora studies' projects of the 'memory' of homeland and the 'myth of return'. The work of James Clifford, for example, has suggested that ethnic ties and fixed boundaries in diaspora consciousness might be replaced by notions of hybridity through the lived experience of a locality, where less emphasis is placed on 'home'. Instead of being regarded as simply ethnic minorities displaced from their 'homeland', diasporas might be seen as the product of trans-national capitalism (Clifford 1997). Even more relevant is work that has explored the significance of 'location', border and movement through the idea of 'diaspora space', in which multiple diasporic groups and those considered to be 'indigenous' interact. Here, power is seen to work in a multi-axial way, in which 'minority' status is contingent on location (Brah 2003). As we will see below, this more complex model of the nodalities of power, and their operation in specific localities, is particularly relevant to the South Asian presence in London, Manchester, Bradford and Leicester.

The Commission for Racial Equality's (CRE) electronic 'tour' of 'multi-ethnic Britain' evokes the importance of the urban landscape relative to the countryside in the cartography of South Asian settlement. In the Yorkshire and Humber region, whereas Leeds, Sheffield and Bradford account for about a third of the region's population as a whole, these three cities contain 65 per cent of all South Asians in the region. And this too is related to the projection of the Yorkshire city's image. Instead of local authorities in the region focussing on urban histories and cultures in attempts to push the region as a tourist destination, the attraction of the (largely white) countryside often takes precedence, with (in the case of Bradford) focus on 'Bronte country' (McLoughlin 2006). Urban-rural ethnic divisions are repeated within the city's neigh-bourhoods themselves, with forms of segregation appearing to map onto longer urban traditions of building type and spatial planning (Nasser 2006). Yet also evident is the coincidence of the 'diversity' on the one hand and the international significance of a city on the other. London, Bradford, Manchester and Leicester (and Birmingham) are 'global' cities in a way that goes beyond the connections of international trade and commerce. These cities are also nodes in trans-continental networks of social and cultural capital. All present a particular kind of global and imperial history.

London's international significance, first as imperial capital and then more predominantly as financial capital is well known. But the city can also be seen as a node in a wider set of trans-national or global connections and networks involving South Asians (Westwood and Williams 1997; Eade 2000). The capital stands out above every other city in the UK, if not Europe as a whole, as the site for criss-crossing networks of people, financial resources, information and ideas (Appadurai 1990, 1996). Manchester was the principal centre of imperial capital goods, as the world centre of cotton manufacturing, and, like the other cities discussed here, attracted migrant labour from overseas, whether Irish, Jewish or South Asian (Werbner 1990). Bradford changed from a relatively insignificant market town to a centre of wool production and export, with its population exploding twenty-fold over the nineteenth century, to earn the name of 'Worstedopolis'. Leicester, too, was a magnet for successive waves of migration (particularly Jewish and Irish), attracted by its diverse industries in hosiery, footwear, printing, adhesives and food processing (Herbert 2008: 20). All four cities, then, were already centres of significant migrant populations before the large-scale settlement of South Asians. Equally, some have expe-rienced industrial decline since the 1970s, and the social histories of each urban space reflects such transformations. Unlike Manchester and Leeds, however, Bradford has not experienced the same degree of economic 'regeneration'. The decline in textile-based employment in the city can be measured by the drop in the total workforce of the mills from 73,000 in 1961 to only 20,000 in 1981 (McLoughlin 2006). Relative measures of economic success between the cities have also been important in shifting the identity narratives of South Asians in the UK, as we will see below.

There were significant South Asian populations in the UK (especially London), well before the larger movements of the post-war period (Visram 2002). However, the shaping of the settled British Asian neighbourhoods in these cities began in the 1950s and 1960s and, in the case of

Leicester, accelerated as a result of the forced migration from Uganda after 1972. In this process, the immigration policies of the national government were significant. Migration to 'beat the ban' of the 1962 Immigration Act and the 1968 Commonwealth Immigration Act vouchers was discernible, particularly in the northern and Midlands cities (12,823 South Asians entered the UK in the first two months of 1968). The attractiveness of these cities for South Asians was not just a consequence of chain migration. It was also related to perceptions of the cities themselves. As early as the 1970s, Bradford was developing a cosmopolitan image, later reflected in colloquial names of 'Bradistan', with plentiful mill work in the 1950s and 1960s. London had always been a huge attraction as a global metropolis; Manchester was the commercial centre of the north; and Leicester's industrial success attracted new waves of migrants right until the mid-1970s (Marett 1989: 3). South Asian migration to the UK, then, was not just a response to a post-war labour shortage, but was also driven by multiple forms of network building across cities and continents.

The city and the ethnicity of space

The impact of state-driven ethnic cartographies and measurements of South Asians in the UK has been largely responsible for the production of popular identity boundaries, represented in statistical categories such as 'Asian', 'Pakistani', 'Indian', 'Muslim' or 'Gujarati'. These have, of course, often collapsed differences of religion, language and caste (*biradari*) (kinship network), even though it is well known that, in each of the main localities of settlement, very different groups of South Asians migrated from specific parts of the subcontinent. In these aggregations of ethnic difference, which bear some resemblance to older British colonial ethnographic experiments, differences between each locality have been connected to overarching discourses of achievement and underachievement. These discourses emanate from national and local government and are also appropriated in the popular media and remobilised by community organisations, political lobbying groups and academia. This chapter will look at this process of ethnic aggregation across the four cities and examine its political effects by focussing on a comparison between Bradford and Manchester.

Official and academic attention to ethnicity within the UK has a history that predates post-war Commonwealth migration. 'Scientific' and academic interest centred on cities in the mid-to-late-Victorian era, due to an interest in the 'problem' of urban deprivation and rapid industrialisation. It was in the European city that the Western discourse of 'race' emerged as much as in the colonial empire (Malik 1996). These deeper histories of (and anxieties about) urban sociology have affected changing academic approaches, as they have shifted from an older Weberian urban sociology (for example, the work of Richard Rex in the 1960s), to the more recent Culture Studies approaches. Over the second half of the twentieth century, academic attention has shifted from the examination of 'race', economic stratification and urban location in the 1960s and 1970s (Ballard 1994) to the consideration of cultural hybridity and cultural production (exemplified by the work of Ravinder Dudrah on *Bhangra* in Birmingham – Dudrah 2007) – a shift which has accompanied the moving gaze of policy makers from the politics of race and ethnicity, to religion and culture. At the turn of the millennium attention has shifted back to the idea of the locale and place once again (Kaur and Kalra 1996; Ali *et al.* 2006) and, in these projects, the idea of the 'British Asian' or 'BrAsian' is critiqued anew by looking specifically at cities as repositories of cultural production. Nevertheless, even the cultural turn has to some extent reinstated older discourses of ethnic space and difference. The study of culture has not served significantly to break down the categories of success and failure.

The CRE's ethnic tour of Britain is based on the fact that particular localities of each of our cities have been dominated by specific groups of South Asian migrants from particular regions (although even this detail is generally hidden from view under the category of 'Asian'). In Leicester, Belgrave, Highfields and Rushy Mead, Evington and Latimar are associated with the 'Asian community', which is dominated by Gujaratis either born in India or East Africa. In Manchester, the focal point for the South Asian community is Rusholme and the 'Curry Mile', which runs through Wilmslow Road (with its 80 inaptly named 'Indian' restaurants and takeaways) and connects with the Oxford Road in the centre of the city. Here, the South Asian community is predominantly Pakistani, but has more varied origins than the larger population in Bradford. In the latter, the Mirpuri (Kashmiri) Pakistani population is most numerous, although there are significant populations from other regions of Pakistan and Bangladesh. London has the most diverse South Asian diaspora, but even here the archetypal 'localities' of the South Asian presence are Bangladeshi-dominated Tower Hamlets and Southall ('Little India'), with its large Indian Punjabi population.

Ethnic spaces are not however, represented as static entities. In nearly all cases, the commentaries on these urban locales have taken into account changing socio-economic circumstances, and the issue of 'white flight' or, in the case of Bradford, 'Hindu and Sikh flight'. Moving out of the city, from the inner-city areas around Manningham Lane into the suburbs, has been described as a movement across different South Asian ethnicities, from Bangladeshi, to Pakistani, then to Hindu and Sikh communities in the suburbs of middle-class Bradford (Butto 2005). In contrast to the image of Manningham, Belgrave in Leicester is configured as a locale of regeneration and rising economic prosperity. Leicester's relative 'success' in 'accommodating' communities is also linked to the idea of the cosmopolitan and mixed nature of its Indian communities – particularly the combination of Gujarati, Punjabi and East African migrants (Herbert 2008).

As in Leicester, the apparent 'success' of Manchester's Pakistani communities has been partially explained by some academics with reference to ethnic backgrounds and cultural practices (Werbner 2002: 257). However, partly because of elision with other narratives of the north–south divide, Manchester's Pakistanis have fallen into a general discourse of 'British Muslim' disassociation. The Pakistani population of Greater Manchester was 23,104 in 2001, which, while dominant, accounts for just around 30 per cent of all ethnic minorities in the city. In Bradford, by contrast, with a population of 68,000, Pakistanis represent 77 per cent of all ethnic minorities (CRE). This means that a large proportion of England's urban Pakistani populations outside London and Birmingham live in either Bradford or Manchester. This northern concentration has connected with popular discourses of the 'grim' north and industrial decline – an image recreated in cult films such as *Rita, Sue and Bob Too* (1982), which depicts the tough realities of life on a Bradford council estate, set against the wild (and largely white) Dales countryside (McLoughlin 2006: 3).

The struggle of Bradford to regenerate in the same way as Leeds and Manchester, and its dominance in the official and popular mind about 'British Asians', has meant that some of the differences within the Pakistani community have been glossed over. Narratives of 'Muslim disadvantage', developed within government and often by community organisations themselves (Eade, this volume), do not sit well with the history of the South Asian presence in either Bradford or Manchester, but particularly not the latter, especially if Rusholme and Manningham are the sole basis of analysis. Whilst Manchester was a centre of global manufacturing predominance in the nineteenth and early twentieth centuries, in the immediate post-war period, its strengths were more as a commercial centre. Unlike the mill towns of the north, the attraction of Manchester lay more in the University, and the opportunities in the rag trade, as its previously dominant Jewish businessmen sold up and turned to the supply of credit to the new incomers.

Those coming to Manchester were relatively quickly able to enter market trading and eventually wholesaling. The latter activity, as was evident with Star Hosiery and Joe Bloggs, allowed South Asian traders in the city to form networks connecting to the Midlands (particularly Birmingham) and back to Pakistan. Servicing this South Asian enclave encouraged a wide variety of professionals – travel agents, doctors and lawyers specialising in immigration. Saving and capital accumulation took place as a result of the migration practices of inter-related families, in a collective process of beneficial cycles of investment and internal community trade (Werbner 1990: 327–9).

Wealth, however, did not necessarily create more cultural contact with white communities. Higher incomes could often encourage the assertion of new forms of ethnic consciousness, based on traditional institutions like *zat* (Werbner, 1990). The more complex realities of these 'ethnic enclaves', formed via national and international networks of business, trade and settlement, were also linked to the migrants' origins. Pakistani tailors working in Cyprus were able to bring their skills to Manchester after decolonisation. *Arain* communities originally from Jalandhar, East Punjab, translated their relative success in the subcontinent to the English city. In contrast, a large proportion of Bradford's South Asian migrants arrived in the city in very different circumstances – many got British work permits for displacement after the building of the Mangla Dam in Mirpur,[2] for example, in the 1960s. Here, a degree of relative homogeneity, which emerged against the backdrop of rapid industrial decline, marked Bradford off very sharply from Manchester and Birmingham.

Measures of 'success': a tale of two cities

One of the main ways in which these cities come to our attention as 'British Asian', then, is as a result of the statistical information publicised by the government and the media. Ethnic categorisations are embedded with ideas of the 'success' or 'achievement' of 'communities' on the one hand, and the fortunes of 'multiculturalism' on the other. These measures are often incidental to the immediate concerns of South Asian diasporas themselves, and represent the outsider's concern about an apparent crisis of national belonging. Nevertheless, they have become important points of debate and lobbying for local resources by community organisations, as ethnic 'leaderships' take their places in the political institutions of race relations. Mutually constitutive ideas of 'success' or 'failure' in these cities has been one of the abiding themes of official reports on the South Asian presence in the UK, with Leicester frequently cited as an example of relative 'success' (Cantle 2001) and Bradford as 'failure'(Ouseley 2001). However, these representations obscure more complex and challenging local histories and voices, many of which critique the whole premise of qualitative measures.

The relatively large South Asian minorities in Leicester and Bradford have drawn the attention of local and national governments and the media since the early 1970s. The total Indian population of Leicester in 1991 – 60,279 – represented 22.3 per cent of the city's population and around 8 per cent of the total number of Indians in the UK overall (Vertovec 1994). In 2001, the 'ethnic minority' population of Leicester was roughly 36.1 per cent of the city's total population, and made up roughly 45 per cent of all school children (Singh, G. 2003: 42). After London, Leicester has the largest Hindu population in the UK, totalling 41,248 in the 2011 census. Importantly, the size of the Leicester diaspora has changed over time and space. It has a large 'twice migrant' population, composed for the most part of the expelled 'Asian' Ugandans, ejected under Idi Amin's regime in 1972. The proportion of South Asians in the city increased from roughly 19,000 in 1961, to approximately 42,000 in 1978, with Ugandan Asians and Kenyan Asians making up 21 per cent and 14 per cent of the total 'Commonwealth' immigrant populations, respectively (Marett 1989: 2). The Ugandan community is commonly described as possessing social and cultural capital of economic and business success, as a result of its double displacement and international connections. By comparison, in Bradford, the South Asian population (around 88,000 – over a third of the entire Yorkshire and Humber South Asian population, with nearly 68,000 of Pakistani origin by latest estimates) accounts for around 19 per cent of the total population of the city. Here, the relative homogeneity of the (predominantly Mirpuri) Pakistani community has been associated with material disadvantage, and they are believed to lack the necessary 'social and cultural capital' for upward mobility. This is believed to be a consequence of the unskilled rural backgrounds of the dominant migrant groups (McLoughlin 2006: 113).

However, if we take into account personal and community experiences, the narratives of relative success surrounding Leicester or Bradford do not stand up to close scrutiny. Moments of violence have historically been used by governments as measures of the success or failure of 'multiculturalism' in public policy in cities, and it is for this reason that the 'Leicester model' has been more celebrated in comparison to Bradford, particular since the riots of 2001. There were very specific political factors that contributed to the 2001 violence, not least the growing prominence of the BNP in the north (Bagguley and Hussein 2006). But local authorities have tended to place the blame on the separate development, and disassociation, of different communities, which are seen as as an indication of the failures of multiculturalism (Singh, G. 2003). In contrast, the thriving Asian business enterprises of Leicester and the redeployment of that wealth into cultural events celebrating British Asian life have generated an altogether different image. The image of peace and harmony in Leicester, however, has a shallow history – belied by experiences of racism in the 1970s. The events that followed the settlement of more than 20,000 Indians in the city after their expulsion from Uganda suggest that the 'Leicester model' rests on precarious foundations. Headlines in the *Leicester Mercury* in 1972 belied the mythology of Leicester as a city of accommodation: 'Whitehall told: no more – Leicester is full up' (Singh and Martin 2002). Importantly, fear of racial attacks in the 1970s pushed many Ugandan Asians to avoid council housing in favour of buying up in the inner city (Marett 1989), and this played a large part in creating segmentation in housing in the city along ethnic lines.

The Leicester 'success' story is fragile in other respects. From the late 1970s and early 1980s, Labour's domination of the City Council was based on a diversified recruitment policy. Party-political success depended on access to inner-city development funds, and local authorities developed complex 'patron-client' relationships with community groups (Singh, G. 2003: 44). Yet such co-option was unstable and, since the defeat of Labour in local elections in May 2003, one of the main political vehicles of civic multiculturalism has been undermined. Unemployment in the city is still higher for South Asians than for the white population and, to a great extent, the growth of small-scale South Asian businesses (which largely cater for a specific 'internal' sector of the city) was partly an outcome of manufacturing decline. Indeed, over the same period that Leicester was experiencing racial tension in the early 1970s, Bradford was held up as a shining example of good race relations.

Looking at lived experience, memory and cultural production further complicates narratives of urban 'success' and 'failure'. South Asian sport has been promoted in both cities on the back of memories of racial discrimination. The Red Star youth group and football team in Leicester were established as a reaction to racial incidents, police harassment and riots in the summer of 1981, and to a lack of youth facilities and jobs. The football team regrouped under the name Nirvana FC in 1984 and eventually sponsored 13 teams comprising 33 nationalities and encompassing many new migrant communities bound together by neighbourhood and sport (Westwood 1991). Comparable exclusions in Yorkshire are well known in the world of cricket. Until 2004, no 'British Asian' born in Yorkshire had managed to make it into the Yorkshire team, while before 1992 those not born in Yorkshire were not permitted to play for the team unless, like Sachin Tendulkar, they were admitted as 'overseas players'. In response, hundreds of Asian players have competed in teams in Leeds, Huddersfield and Bradford as part of the Quaid-I-Azam League.

Bradford's literature and art scene also contradicts the national image of racial conflict and economic 'underachievement' to reveal a complex array of voices which challenge the dominant narratives of national belonging. The fiction of Yunus Alam (*Annie Potts is Dead*, 1998 and *Kilo*, 2002) and Tariq Mehmood (*Hand on the Sun*, 1983) emerge from a sense of specific attachment to the city and its particular street politics, engaging with both the themes of diasporic belonging and the experiences of youth in Yorkshire. These books, with their urban themes, represent a strong regional contrast to the UK-based celebrities of South Asian writing – for example, the work of Hanif Kureshi, Rushdie and Monica Ali. This broader industry of South Asian, post-imperial writing represents a commoditised global publishing industry, whereas Alam and Mehmood complicate the exoticisation of ethnic difference with tales of police clashes, drug dealing and inter-generational conflict.

Such city-specific creativity, challenging popular national discourse about British Asian life in the UK, is mirrored in dance and oral history. The eclectic music of Aki Nawaz, in its militant invocation of Ali, connects to a powerful Punjabi sufi tradition, which critiques religious and political establishments over time and space (Kabir 2009). 'Kalasangam', founded in 1993, also seeks to bring the arts of the South Asian diaspora in West Yorkshire to non-South Asian communities. Holding dance performances and exhibitions which originally sought to bring art to the disabled, 'Kalasangam' has more recently worked with youth offenders (www.kalasangam. org). Since the early '80s, the Bradford Heritage Recording Unit has created a collection of oral testimonies of the migrant communities in the city, illustrating the varied and contingent connections of inhabitants to the city. In particular, the dual pictorial volume *Here to Stay*, produced by Irna Qureshi and Tim Smith (1994), traces the life histories of Indian, Pakistani and Bangladeshi families and throws light on the central dynamics of Britain's urban spaces. Such voices deconstruct traditional narratives of urban development/decline, by recounting for example, changes in Bradford's inner city and changes in community relations following the Rushdie affair in the late 1980s.

The city, the local and the global: London and beyond

As previous sections have suggested, it is more fruitful to think about the British South Asian presence in terms of what Rajinder Dudrah has described as 'webbed connections' – contingent identities which never forsake the locality in Britain, but instead rewrite or reinvent it in new ways and which also operate simultaneously in multiple directions across the nation and between continents (Dudrah 2002). This process is not confined to business or the arts, but has been mediated by political institutions. In asserting identities that attempted to move beyond the nationally configured 'minority', secular political movements emerged, which operated along multi-axial indices of power (Brah 2003). The Asian Youth Movements (AYM) represented the most sustained attempts to mobilise against anti-racism, particularly in the late 1970s and early 1980s (Ramamurthy 2011). Although it was in Bradford that the organisation had the biggest impact on local politics, the AYM depended (in both practical and ideological terms) on the maintenance of national and international connections that were intimately tied to streams of South Asian migration. This process was not confined to the post-war 'post-colonial' diasporas either. The Indian Workers' Association (IWA), founded in Coventry in 1937 but which extended across Midlands towns and to Bradford in 1941, was perhaps the earliest manifestation of such secular South Asian political mobilisation and built on the same dual principles of national and international 'webbed connections'. Dominated by Punjabi Sikhs and Muslims, the IWA was formalised in 1942, linking the cities of Birmingham, Bradford, Coventry and London, with additional branches in Manchester, Newcastle and Wolverhampton (Visram 2002: 270–2).

The much-discussed shift from secular 'anti-racism' politics of the 1960s, 1970s and mid-1980s, to religious identity politics, is the best known example of how the local, national and international connections of diasporic communities were transformed over time. Large-scale investment in religious institutions has been a feature in all of the cities since the 1960s. Institutional or voluntary endowment and investment have played an important part in this, as have ceremonial occasions which for many (for example the *Arain* families in Manchester) have served as forms of community empowerment (Werbner 1990: 305–9). Bradford Council's experiment in 'multiculturalism' in the early 1980s provided the context for the formation of the Bradford Council of Mosques (BCM) in 1981. In later years, the BCM championed local community-interest issues (for example the *halal* meat and Honeyford affairs).[3]

Religious observance, then, has been an effective means of challenging outsider views of disunity and weakness. This needs to be borne in mind when considering the decision of members of the BCM to burn a copy of Salman Rushdie's *The Satanic Verses* (1988) on 14 January 1989. While this event, along with the subsequent shifts in post-Cold War US foreign policy, has dramatically shifted public attention to the predicament of the 'British Muslim', this should not obscure the fact that religious mobilisations have long challenged Orientalist trends in British liberal traditions (Mandair 2009). And, as we will see below in the case of the East London Mosque, urban space has been refashioned for religious use through local, national and international negotiation and compromise, particularly with conservative notions of Britain's 'heritage' (Nasser 2006: 380–2).

Other artistic and literary efforts to promote the image of cities to outsiders have helped determine the global significance of each place. London has been subject to especially intense and multi-directional representations (Eade 2000; Eade and Mele 2002). The attempts to 'sell' the city to the wider world in the 2005 Olympics bid as the ultimate multicultural metropolis were part of this, although such projections of London existed even well before Samuel Johnson's famous epigram. The presence of South Asians in the capital was certainly linked to the maritime and imperial histories of London. The pioneering South Asian settlers in London – from the early lascars from Sylhet to the East African twice-migrant Punjabis – concentrated in areas such as Southall, Spitalfields, Poplar, Canning Town, Customs House, Tidal Basin and Plaistow. The presence of lascars in the city dated back to the early eighteenth century (Visram 2002: 15–16; Eade this volume). Significant numbers of these sailors were forced into begging, with little or no knowledge of English and no contacts or relations in the city. Their exclusion from English society epitomised the predicament of South Asian settlers in the UK until 1948 (Visram 2002: 264–5).

It was after decolonisation at the end of the Second World War that the first concentrated settlements of South Asians developed in London. Brick Lane in Spitalfields and the streets around it became one such focus, being close to the garment factories, although many sought employment, too, across the Midlands (Adams 1987: 200–16). Other important concentrations of South Asian settlement were Wembley and Southall, where East African Ramgarhia Sikhs, once a majority in their first point of migration, became a minority within the larger Sikh community on arrival in the UK. One writer has suggested that this led to reassertions of their 'Ramgarhianess', but also to the establishment of strong links to other cities of settlement – Birmingham, Coventry, Leeds and Cardiff. Unlike other South Asian diasporas, not having a 'myth of return' to Punjab where 'the only culture . . . is agriculture', they enhanced their community networks (Bhachu 1985: 40–6).

The second generation of British Asians in Tower Hamlets, London, in the 1970s and 1980s engaged more directly with local politics, forming organisations of left-wing activism and anti-racism campaigns (Eade 1989). In these struggles the politics of the locality were connected to both national and international developments, with flows of ideas and political concerns linking back to Bangladesh. For example, the conflicts between local architectural conservationists in Spitalfields and the Bangladeshi community over the transformation of the Brick Lane Mosque (sited in an old Huguenot chapel) in the 1990s involved the mobilisation of support and sympathy overseas (Eade 2000: 171–2). Such projects were also encouraged by the apparent Islamisation of urban space in the region from the late 1980s to the 1990s. To some extent, the subsequent formation of religious pressure group organisations has been at the cost of syncretic Bengali traditions in the locality – for example *Baul* singing, with its Sufi themes, and the Kobi Nazrul Centre, both of which have been criticised by leaders of the East London Mosque (Eade and Garbin 2002).

In London, as in Leicester, Bradford and Manchester, internal struggles of community definition and representation have been turned outwards to the world. A recent oral history project run by the Swadhininta Trust – *Tales of Three Generations of Bengalis in Britain* – has re-asserted the secular politics of Bangladeshi political activism, and the connections between Islam and cultural production, in opposition to Islamists.

Other representations of community tensions and dichotomies to the wider world have been met with insider opprobrium when they reach beyond the locality itself. Monica Ali's *Brick Lane*, and the alleged 'non-authentic' provenance of the author, created two such protests against the novel in 2002 and 2006. Importantly, these reactions to the book and its screen adaptation focussed on the alleged misrepresentation of the 'place' of Brick Lane, on the one hand, and, on the other, the (false) implied claim of the author to be an 'insider' of the community.

Conclusion

South Asian migrants in Bradford, Leicester, London and Manchester have been represented by state and media as creators and inhabitants of ethnic enclaves, whose relative 'success' in the British Isles has been linked to popular agendas of national belonging. At another level, their fortunes have been tied into the political and ethnic cartographies of the island – the divisions between north and south, or between the affluent white countryside and 'grim' inner cities. But, for the diaspora, the meanings of national belonging are divided and contingent, not least because of the complex dispersals and dislocations thrown up by the end of Empire. For the South Asian settlers in these UK cities, the 'global' has become the gaze of the outsider at one level but, at another, it is about the contingent realities of belonging in more than one place at once: it involves the interconnection between multiple localities, in which status and identity could shift between the streets of London, Kampala and Jalandhar. For South Asians in these UK cities, the global and the local are mutually constitutive, and local space is also always transformed by that which is absent and distant. A sense of this interconnection can be seen in the vernacular descriptions of the South Asian presence, coming from within (and across) communities them-selves. Such cultural products, whether in the form of literature, dance or music, have been celebrated by governments and the media as artefacts of Britain's successful multiculturalism. The political tensions, social conflicts and identity struggles inherent within them, on the other hand, have evoked little official response. However, diasporic histories and voices are striking back (Kalra 2009), taking issue with the crude popular generalisations of the 'Asian' community in the UK.

Notes

1 Punjabi proverb, cited in Werbner, 2002.
2 The Mangla Dam, located on the Jhelum river in Mirpur district, was constructed between 1961 and 1967, leading to the submersion of over 280 settlements: a displaced population of over 120,000.
3 The controversy surrounding *halal* meat followed the introduction of *halal* in state schools with at least ten Muslim students in November 1982. The serving of the food began in September 1983 and sparked protests from animal rights groups. Muslim communities threatened to boycott schools and take legal action and eventually the Council voted to continue the practice. The Honeyford affair surrounded the publication of an article in the *Salisbury Review* in June 1983, by Ray Honeyford, the Head Teacher of Drummond Middle School, Manningham, Bradford. Honeyford argued that white children in schools with a Pakistani majority were at an educational disadvantage and opposed Muslim parents taking children to Pakistan during term time. Views about Honeyford polarised between accusations of racism and support for his 'freedom of speech' (including backing by Margaret Thatcher). Protests from the Muslim community followed, with a demand to have Honeyford removed, eventually resulting in his taking early retirement in December 1985.

Bibliography

Adams, C. (1987) *Across Seven Seas and Thirteen Rivers: Life Stories of Pioneer Sylhetti Settlers in Britain,* London: Eastside Books.
Alam, M.Y., (1998) *Annie Potts is Dead*, Castleford: Route Publishing.
— (2002) *Kilo*, Castleford: Route Publishing.
Ali, N., Kalra, V.S., and Sayyid, S., eds, (2006) *A Postcolonial People: South Asians in Britain,* London: Hurst and Company.
Appadurai, A. (1990) 'Disjuncture and Difference in the Global Cultural Economy', *Public Culture*, 2 (2): 1–23.
— (1996) *Modernity at Large: Cultural Dimensions of Modernity*, London and Minneapolis: University of Minnesota Press.
Bagguley, P. and Hussein, Y. (2006) 'Uprisings', in Ali, Kalra and Sayyid, eds, *A Postcolonial People: South Asians in Britain*, London: Hurst and Company, 340–2.
Ballard, R, ed. (1994) *Desh Pardesh: the South Asian Presence in Britain*, London: Hurst and Company.
Bhachu, P. (1985) *Twice Migrants: East African Sikh Settlers in Britain*, London: Tavistock.
Brah, A. (1997) *Cartographies of Diaspora: Contesting Identities*, London: Routledge.
— (2003) 'Diaspora, Border and Transnational Identities' in Lewis, R. and Mills, S. eds, *Feminist Postcolonial Theory: A Reader,* Edinburgh: Edinburgh University Press.
Butto, S. (2005) Interview with Irna Qureishi, www.leeds.ac.uk/writingbritishasiancities/bradford_voices. htm.
Cantle, T. (2001) 'Community Cohesion: A Report of the Independent Review Team', Home Office.
Clifford, J. (1997) *Routes: Travel and Translation in the Late Twentieth Century,* London: Harvard University Press.
Dudrah, R.K. (2002) 'Birmingham (UK): Constructing City Spaces through Black Popular Cultures and Black Public Sphere', *City*, 6: 3, 335–50.
— (2007) *Bhangra: Birmingham and Beyond,* Birmingham: Birmingham City Council.
Eade, J. (1989) *The Politics of Community: The Bangladeshi Community in East London,* Aldershot: Avebury.
— (2000) *Placing London: From Imperial Capital to Global City,* New York: Berghahn Books.
Eade, J. and Garbin, D. (2002) *Changing Narratives of Violence, Struggle and Resistance: Bangladeshis and the Competition for Resources in the Global City,* Oxford Development Studies, Carfax Publishing, 30: 2, 137–49.
Eade, J. and Mele, C. (2002) *Understanding the City: Contemporary and Future Perspectives*, Oxford: Blackwell.
Herbert, J. (2008) *Negotiating Boundaries in the City: Migration, Ethnicity, and Gender in Britain*, Aldershot: Ashgate.

Kabir, A. (2009) 'The British Asian City and Cultural Production' – working paper, www.leeds.ac.uk/writingbritishasiancities/interactive_papers.htm.

Kalra, V. (2009) 'Writing British Asian Manchester' – working paper, www.leeds.ac.uk/writingbritishasiancities/interactive_papers.htm.

Kaur, Raminder and Kalra, Virinder S. (1996) 'New Paths for South Asian Identity and Musical Creativity', in S. Sharma, J. Hutnyk and A. Sharma, eds, *Dis-Orienting Rhythms: the Politics of the New Asian Dance Music*, London: Zed Books, 217–31.

Malik, K. (1996) *The Meaning of Race: Race, History and Culture in Western Society,* Basingstoke: Macmillan.

Mandair, A.P.S. (2009) *Religion and the Specter of the West: Sikism, India, Postcolonialism and the Politics of Translation,* New York: Columbia University Press.

Marett, V. (1989) *Immigrants Settling in the City: Ugandan Asians in Leicester,* London: Leicester University Press.

McLeod, J. (2004) *Postcolonial London: Rewriting the Metropolis,* London: Routledge.

McLoughlin, S. (2006) 'Writing a BrAsian City: "Race", Culture and Religion in Accounts of Postcolonial Bradford', in Ali, Kalra and Sayyid, eds, *A Postcolonial People: South Asians in Britain,* London: Hurst and Company, 110–40.

Mehmood, T. (1983) *Hand on the Sun,* London: Penguin Books, Ltd.

Nasser, N. (2006) 'Metropolitan Borderlands: The Formation of BrAsian Landscapes' in Ali, Kalra and Sayyid, eds, *A Postcolonial People: South Asians in Britain,* London: Hurst and Company, 374–94.

Nawaz, Aki (2009) 'Bradford Voices', accessed at www.leeds.ac.uk/brasian/assets/Bradford/Bradford%20Voices%20-%20MP3/Aki%20Nawaz.mp3 on 13 May 2013.

Ouseley, H. (2001) *Community Pride Not Prejudice,* Bradford: Bradford 2020 Vision.

Qureshi, I. and Smith, T. (1994) *Here to Stay: Bradford's South Asian Communities,* Bradford: City of Bradford Metropolitan Council Arts, Museums and Libraries.

Ramamurthy, A. (2011) *South Asian Mobilisation in Two Northern Cities: A Comparison of Manchester and Bradford Asian Youth Movements: Race and Ethnicity in a Changing World,* Manchester: Manchester University Press.

Roger Louis, Wm, ed. (2001) *The Oxford History of the British Empire: Volume IV: The Twentieth Century,* Oxford: Oxford University Press.

— (2005) *Yet More Adventures with Britannia: Personalities, Politics and Culture,* London: I.B. Taurus.

Rushdie, S. (1988) *The Satanic Verses,* London: Vintage.

Sandbrook, Dominic, (2005) *Never Had It So Good: A History of Britain from Suez to the Beatles,* London: Little, Brown.

— (2006) *White Heat: A History of Britain in the Swinging Sixties,* London: Little, Brown.

Singh, G. (2003) 'Multiculturalism in Contemporary Britain: Reflections on the "Leicester Model"' *IJMS: International Journal on Multicultural Societies,* 5: 1, 40–54.

Singh, G., Martin, J. (2002) *Asian Leicester,* London: Sutton Publishing Ltd.

Singh, R. (1994) 'Introduction', *Here to Stay: Bradford's South Asian Communities,* Bradford: City of Bradford Metropolitan Council, Arts Museum.

Vertovec, S. (1994) 'Multicultural, Multi-Asian, Multi-Muslim Leicester: Dimensions of Social Complexity, Ethnic Organisation and Local Government Interface', *Innovation: European Journal of Social Sciences,* 7: 3, 259–76.

Visram, R. (2002) *Asians in Britain: 400 Years of History,* London: Pluto Press.

Werbner, P. (1990) *The Migration Process: Capital, Gifts, and Offerings among British Pakistanis,* New York: Berg.

— (2002) *Imagined Diasporas among Manchester Muslims: The Public Performance of Pakistani Transnational Identity Politics,* Oxford: James Currey.

Westwood, S. (1991) 'Red Star Over Leicester: Racism, the Politics of Identity and Black Youth in Britain', in Werbner, Pnina and Anwar, Muhammad, eds, *Black and Ethnic Leaderships,* London, Routledge, 101–16.

Westwood, S. and Williams, J. (1997) *Imagining Cities: Scripts, Signs, Memory,* London: Routledge.

28

DIS/LOCATING DIASPORA

South Asian youth cultures in Britain

Claire Alexander and Helen Kim

I am a British Asian.
My identity and my history are defined only by myself –
Beyond politics, beyond nationality, beyond religion and beyond skin.

(Nitin Sawhney, Beyond Skin*, 1999)*

Introduction

Every Wednesday night the space of Club 49 in the West End of London is temporarily transformed into a South Asian night, catering to the capital's aspirational and affluent British Asian cultural producers and young consumers. The music on rotation includes hip hop chart music as well as the 'hybrid' sounds of bhangra and Bollywood beats, fused with the 'urban' sounds of R&B. Remixes using Asian instrumentation – tabla, sitar, dhol drums – are common and speak to the travelling and fusion of cultural forms in this global city. The crowd is predominantly South Asian, drawn from across the capital and more widely – issues of region, religion, nationality rendered invisible in the melee, and in the creation, consumption and celebration of a shared (generational) identity in this (admittedly transient) diasporic space (Kim 2011a).

The South Asian club scene, and its enactment of everyday forms of social and cultural 'conviviality' (Gilroy 2004), presents a microcosm of the issues and challenges confronting the conceptualisation of South Asian diasporic youth cultures and identities. On the one hand, it points to the formation of an emergent and inclusive 'desi' identity, which, in the contemporary performance of a peculiarly British Asian identity, at once recreates imaginative links to South Asia, homogenises diverse communities and reaches outwards to other desi diasporas, particularly in North America. On the other, it works to contest and disrupt the boundaries of 'community', culture and nation, staking claims for a reimagined Britishness within a complex and contested multicultural terrain. Avtar Brah has thus written of the South Asian diaspora as an 'imagined community' whose identity 'is far from fixed and pre-given. It is constituted within the crucible of the materiality of everyday life; in the everyday stories we tell ourselves individually and collectively' (1996: 183) – or, indeed, in the music we create or listen to, the dances we embody or the spaces we meet and (re)make, where new cultural hybrids emerge as a way of contesting the borders of cultural difference around (or indeed, 'beyond') issues of gender, generation, sexuality, nation, religion, 'skin'.

Youth cultures and identities are often positioned at the centre of this process of continuity and change, with artists, cultural theorists and cultural producers celebrated uncritically as the vanguard of a progressive political project of claims-staking and place-making (Alexander 2002, 2008, 2010), levering open 'diaspora spaces' (Brah 1996) or 'third spaces' (Bhabha 1990) that unsettle and contest the boundaries and narratives of the post-Imperial nations. However, as Paul Gilroy has warned, a flattened-out embracing of the imaginative and narrative force of diaspora as 'libertarian' and 'polyphonic' aesthetics runs the risk of being 'insufficiently alive to the lingering power of specifically "racial" forms of power and subordination' (1993: 123) and to the ambiguous positionalities which persist and resurface. Understanding diasporic youth cultures thus necessitates a recognition not only of the way in which diaspora communities unsettle and dislocate identities but the way in which they take shape in specific and often *local* historical, geographical, social, cultural and political spaces – that is, diaspora identities are simultaneously dislocated and located, transplanted and 'home grown', routed and rooted. They are, to mangle Paul Gilroy's evocative phrase (1993), *both* where you're from *and* where you're at.

Locating diasporic youth cultures thus necessitates a reckoning with the particularities of national contexts and histories, as well as of their subversions and transgressions. It also requires a recognition of the historical, social and political positionings within particular places, times and relationships of power (Hall 1990). Youth cultures – particularly those associated with racial or ethnic minority communities – are often positioned in mainstream discourses as problem and as threat, and South Asian youth cultures are no exception (Alexander 2008). Diaspora can thus work as both a reinscription of, and challenge to, this marginal positioning. Taking as its starting point the construction of Asian youth as 'problem' in the post-war years (Brah 1996; Alexander 2006), this chapter traces both the transformation of the Asian 'folk devil' in the British national imaginary and the emergence of diasporic cultural identities which resist and subvert this positioning. Focusing particularly on some of the multiple, polyphonic and dissonant worlds of British South Asian diasporic cultural production – bhangra, the Asian Underground and the contemporary 'desi' scene – the chapter examines the tension between the borders of the nation-space and travelling diasporic cultures, between the 'orders' and 'disorders' of youth identities and cultural production, between the 'play' of history, culture and power. British South Asian youth cultures provide a powerful insight into the global trajectories of cultural exchange – not just with South Asia itself but across its diasporic communities and spaces in Britain, Canada and America – as well as the local and sub-local histories which shape them. The chapter argues that these youth cultures both draw upon and reinvent the notion of South Asian diaspora, while being alive to some of the ambivalences and silences that these cultural forms produce and maintain (Kalra, Kaur and Hutnyk 2005).

A double dislocation? The 'problem' of British South Asian youth

As Dick Hebdige has argued (in Giroux 1996: 3), 'In our society, youth is only present when its presence is a problem . . . when young people make their presence felt by going "out of bounds"'. In relation to ethnic minority youth, in particular, the visible markers of racial and cultural difference have in and of themselves often been read as being 'out of bounds', and serve to double both the sense of dislocation and threat posed by young people to broader society (Hall *et al.* 1979; Alexander 1996, 2000). Traditionally, black youth cultural expressions have been positioned as either a negative and defensive reaction to social exclusion or as a form of romanticised hyper-political resistance to it (Hebdige 1979), while simultaneously rehearsing negative and stereotypical representations of black cultures and identities (Alexander 2002). While contemporary approaches to black popular culture have tended to de-essentialise black cultural forms and recognise both the global diasporic, highly localised and politically ambiguous contours of black cultural production (Hall 1992; Gilroy 1993, 2010), the same cannot be said of South Asian youth cultural forms until much more recently. Rather, from a position of invisibility, where South Asian youth were considered to be subsumed within the cultural absolutes of authentic 'community', South Asian youth cultural forms have emerged into the mainstream imagination from the mid-1990s onwards as emblematic of civic and civilisational crisis and threat (Alexander 2002, 2008). These threats are both linked to new diasporic religious networks and nationalisms (Bhatt 2001, 2006) and to more national–local versions of the 'clash of civilisations', such as 'the Muslim underclass' (Modood *et al*.1997), 'the Asian gang' (Alexander 2000) or the 'homegrown' terrorist (Kundnani 2007; McGhee 2008).

The focus on youth is perhaps unsurprising when we consider the statistics. According to the Office of National Statistics, in December 2005 the population of the UK stood at just under 60 million people, of which 7.9 per cent (around 4.6 million people) were from 'non-white' ethnic minority backgrounds (Office for National Statistics 2009). Of these, the largest groups were of South Asian descent, with Indians making up 22.7 per cent, Pakistanis 16.1 per cent and Bangladeshis 6.1 per cent of the Black and Minority Ethnic population.[1] A distinctive feature of South Asian diaspora communities in Britain and elsewhere are their markedly younger age profile by comparison with other ethnic majority and minority groups – in 2001, 23 per cent of Indian, 35 per cent of Pakistani and 38 per cent of Bangladeshi communities were aged under 16 years, compared to less than 20 per cent of White Britons. Over half of these communities, and the vast majority of young people, are British born.

Since the start of mass migration from India, Pakistan and Bangladesh to Britain in the post-war years, the dominant (and persistent) representation of Asian young people in Britain has been as 'caught between cultures', the victims of repressive and unchanging parental and community norms and the permissive freedoms of 'modern' British society (Alexander 2006). This portrait of passivity was partially offset by the increasingly active and angry role of South Asian youth in the anti-racist struggles of the 1980s – for example, in the network of Asian Youth Movements which sprang up across the UK (Tower Hamlets, Southall, Leicester, Birmingham, Bradford) in the 1970s and 1980s (Sivanandan 1981; Brah 1996). Of course, such representations were highly gendered, with young women viewed as the passive victims of cultural dysfunction around arranged marriages, domestic violence and self harm, while young men became associated with street violence, criminality and social and political alienation – a mixture which formed the basis of the moral panic over 'Asian gangs' in the 1990s (Alexander 2000). The 1990s saw the reclamation of 'ethnicity' as a positive primary identity with research stressing issues of cultural and intergenerational 'continuity and change' (Anwar 1998) or the Asian 'mode of being' (Modood 1992: 55). Nevertheless, the recognition of different agendas in the wake of the *Satanic Verses* affair of 1989 also highlighted emergent divisions within the South Asian community, along national and then religious lines (Sivanandan 2000). These divisions were underpinned, crucially, by a divergence in the socio-economic positions of (successful) Indians and East African Asians, on the one hand, and (unsuccessful) Pakistanis and Bangladeshis on the other – a division characterised by Tariq Modood as between 'the achievers' and 'the believers' (1992: 43). Muslim youth were positioned as at once more 'conservative' in their outlook than their Hindu and Sikh counterparts (Modood *et al*. 1997; Anwar 1998) and as vulnerable to social marginalisation, crime and alienation, a welter of attributed social and cultural dysfunction which lays the foundation for the newest 'folk devil' – the Islamist/Fundamentalist (Alexander 2006).

There is, however, an alternative story of South Asian youth identities and cultures: one which contests the cultural absolutism of the old ethnicities paradigm and insists instead on the shifting, partial and contingent construction of identity – of 'becoming' rather than 'being', or what Nitin

Sawhney (one of the British South Asian diaspora's most famous sons) might characterise as 'beyond' categorisation. From the 1990s onwards, there has been a flowering of British South Asian cultural expression in literature, comedy, cinema, photography and fashion, and particularly in music. This work has been concerned with the hybrid and diasporic forms of cultural 'cut and mix' which challenge the historic invisibility of South Asian youth cultural expressions and explode the boundaries of narrowly defined ethnic communities, which are at once highly rooted in local and national issues and experiences and look to South Asia and to its other diasporas (both 'old', for example in the Caribbean, and 'new', as in North America) for inspiration and audience (Sharma, Hutnyk and Sharma 1996a; Murthy 2007). These forms highlight the syncretic and globalised nature of South Asian youth identities and the complex and ambiguous ways in which culture 'travels'. Nevertheless, as the groundbreaking collection, *DisOrienting Rhythms* (Sharma, Hutnyk and Sharma 1996a), powerfully warns, what was briefly celebrated in the 1990s as 'the new Asian cool' should not blind us to the ongoing relationships of dominance, discrimination and violence which continue to control the South Asian youth identities and experiences which generate and constrain these cultural expressions.

From Bhangra to Br-Asian: a brief history of British South Asian youth cultures

Out of Handsworth: the rise of British bhangra

One of the earliest 'home-grown' forms of British South Asian youth cultural expression to achieve mainstream notice was bhangra music, which grew out of the working-class and predominantly Sikh communities of Birmingham – most famously, Soho Road, in the multi-racial borough of Handsworth – and London from the 1980s onwards (Dudrah 2007). A traditional form of folk singing and dance rooted in the agrarian communities of the Punjab, bhangra music travelled across to the UK with the first wave of Punjabi immigrants coming to settle in the 1950s and 1960s, while the 1970s saw Punjabi artists travel from India to perform in packed halls in London, Birmingham and Manchester. Rajinder Dudrah (2007) has noted that the traditional themes of bhangra music evocatively capture themes associated with migration and diaspora, and are simultaneously reminiscent of the past as well as signalling hope in the new present and the possible future. The music both looks back to India, rehearsing tropes of loss and feelings of nostalgia for the homeland, as well as forward to joy, revelry and celebration, capturing the excitement of the present, marking celebrations of everyday life and belonging in Britain, such as at weddings and other community gatherings (Banerji and Baumann 1990; Dudrah 2002a, 2002b; Gopinath 1995).

The 1980s saw, however, the emergence of a new 'home-grown' British South Asian bhangra scene, with the rise of British-based bhangra artists such as Heera, Malkit Singh and Apna Sangeet in Birmingham, as well as Alaap based in London (Bauman 1990; Banerji and Bauman 1990; Dudrah 2002b, 2002a). Signalling perhaps the growth of a confident and culturally innovative 'second generation', which mirrored broader shifts in the position and politics of South Asian youth during this period (Brah 1996; Alexander 2006), bhangra club nights became popular, along with live 'daytimer' gigs (Back 1996). As South Asian youth moved centre stage in discussions around Britishness and belonging from the late 1980s and into the 1990s, British bhangra was 'discovered' by mainstream British press, who largely rehearsed recycled notions of repressed Asian youth 'confused' and 'lost', who sought out bhangra music as an escape from their parents and problems (Dudrah 2007; Kalra 2000). From this perspective, bhangra represented a break from, rather than continuity with, the cultures of their parents and their homelands –

a mysterious and over-exoticised expression of youth disaffection and disjuncture which was impenetrable to ethnic 'outsiders' (Baumann 1996; Back 1996).

However, despite what the stereotypes suggested, British bhangra music was articulating a much more complex cultural map of British Asian identities, which drew on, translated and transformed its traditional contours on the streets and in the houses of Handsworth and Southall, and which in turn reflected the emergence of a new British South Asian sensibility and identity. Towards the early 1990s, a new generation of bhangra remix artists came onto the scene who were interested in fusing the dhol beats and sampling vocals with other forms of diasporic youth cultures such as hip hop, reggae and R&B styles of music. Artists such as Steven Kapur, better known as Apache Indian, exemplified a new generation of British Asian music culture that articulated complex fusions of multiple sounds, lyrics and styles that traversed and blended India, the Caribbean, Europe and North America (Dudrah 2007; Back 1996). Back (1996) calls this the creation of an 'intermezzo culture' in which identities forged are no longer intent on purity but about 'becoming more than one' (p. 227) and reflect a more complex and globalised sense of ethnic and national identity.

At the same time, British bhangra was itself taken up and transformed in new diasporic contexts, forming part of a trans- or outer-national youth culture,[2] located both within the larger South Asian diaspora and returning to India itself, with 'nodes' forming in New York, Toronto, Bombay and Delhi (Gopinath 1995). Sunaina Maira (2002) writes that the bhangra remix culture in New York City provided a space for young South Asians to enact and perform localised and specific Indian American identities. However, although bhangra music has travelled across the South Asian diaspora as a potent form of diasporic music and identity – perhaps a form of what Paul Gilroy (2006) has termed the 'connective tissue' of diasporic identity (p. 383) – it is important to remember that its significance and meanings, and the identity practices that develop around this form of cultural production, are not all the same across different diasporic and local contexts. Bhangra music developed distinctive meanings and characteristics as it was taken up by its respective youth cultures, nationally and locally located, and with particular forms of inclusion and exclusion, reflecting the divergent forms of migration and social location. Thus, in stark contrast to the working-class multicultural neighbourhoods and streets of Birmingham, Maira (2002) characterises the bhangra remix culture in New York City as an affluent, predominantly Indian–American youth culture located in the elite spaces of Manhattan night clubs, and sustained in the American university system through cultural organisations, within a broader framework of privileged and commodified American multiculture (Dawson 2002). Within the context of a USA-based racialised hierarchy, as Gayatri Gopinath (1995) has argued, bhangra remix culture provided an alternative and culturally distinct site of identity for Asian–Americans who were eclipsed by the strict black/white binaries of mainstream American popular culture. This cultural formation thus differs sharply from the UK's history of bhangra as emerging from first-generation, working-class South Asian communities, and the cultural innovations of their British born children, and as part of a broader, if sometimes contentious, dialogue with both black Caribbean and white youth cultural forms (Sharma, Hutnyk and Sharma 1996a).

Nevertheless, even within the British context it is important not to over-romanticise the role of bhangra – and to recognise its exclusionary formations, particularly in regard to issues of region, religion and gender. Although Banerji and Baumann (1990) and Les Back (1996) positioned bhangra music as the definitive articulation of British Asian youth identity formation at this period, there were other forms of music practice and cultural engagement that spoke of alternate ways of being diasporic and South Asian in Britain (see Banerjea and Banerjea 1996). The claim that bhangra, once a traditional Punjabi, Northern Indian folk form of music, could stand for all members of the British Asian diaspora is highly problematic, particularly when one considers how bhangra might or might not have held such significance for young people in their actual lives. Different migration histories and experiences amongst South Asian communities in the UK have shaped distinct diasporic identities and cultural histories. British bhangra articulated a very particular South Asian identity rooted in the local and the highly specific regional backgrounds of a Punjabi-based North Indian/Pakistani culture in Birmingham and London, but may not have had similar resonances elsewhere in the UK or amongst other South Asian communities. At the same time, the insistence on the ethnic 'authenticity' of bhangra tended to marginalise other forms of cultural engagement and hybrid formations (Sharma, Hutnyk and Sharma 1996b).

Going overground: the rise of the 'Asian Underground'

In *DisOrienting Rhythms* (1996a) Sharma, Hutnyk and Sharma strongly criticise the marginalisation and ghettoisation of forms of South Asian cultural production, as exemplified particularly through the focus on bhangra music. Sanjay Sharma (1996) also notes that white scholars continually reinforced the 'otherness' of bhangra music in placing it 'squarely within an authenticity problematic that sustains a neo-orientalist understanding' of this cultural formation (p. 36). Meanwhile, other forms of cultural production – both within and outside the 'Asian community' – were significant in shaping and voicing other locations of Asian identities (Banerjea and Banerjea 1996). In particular, from the early 1990s onwards, interest grew in the emerging forms of cultural production and fusion captured in the idea of 'The Asian Underground'.

'Asian Underground' was a term that was originally given to Talvin Singh's famous club night *Anokha* held at London's *Blue Note Club* from 1996 to 1998, but later came to stand for a broad category of new Asian dance music which included artists as disparate as Talvin Singh, Nitin Sawhney, States of Bengal and Black Star Liner, as well as politically outspoken groups such as Fun-da-Mental and Asian Dub Foundation.[3] The mainstream British music press hailed these bands as the voice of a new generation, producing music by and for British Asians, who saw themselves as part of what Asian Dub Foundation called the 'digital underclass' (Asian Dub Foundation 1998). The movement (loosely defined) was celebrated as providing genre-breaking musical fusions that redefined the idea of British Asian cultural identity and placed them at the cutting edge of cultural innovation and political commentary. For instance, Asian Dub Foundation, who came out of the Bangladeshi Muslim community in East London, were identified as producing music with a 'radical edge', representing a 'rich cultural stew' that reflected their multicultural London heritage and a vocal and critical anti-racist politics (Evans 2003). *Rolling Stone* magazine called Asian Dub Foundation 'musical colonization in reverse' – and their lyrics and music full of 'noisy uprising' – whose music was impossible 'not to get swept up in the rush' (Kun, *Rolling Stone*, 10 December 1998).

Many of the Asian Underground reached a level of mainstream success that had not been achieved previously, bringing British South Asian cultural production into the spotlight and into the British cultural mainstream in an unprecedented way. Talvin Singh won the Mercury Prize for Best New Artist in 1999 for his album *OK*, with fellow Asian Underground artist Nitin Sawhney also nominated the same year. At the same time, Asian dance music was also spreading from the UK to cities such as New York and Toronto, which boasted their own scenes of related club nights and renowned DJs (Murthy 2007).

Much lauded for its 'hybrid' sounds and as a vehicle for the expression of 'radical' identities, many of the bands of the Asian Underground articulated a celebratory globalised 'outer-national consciousness' of diasporic connections that went avowedly and deliberately beyond the cultural restrictions of narrowly ascribed ethnic identity, challenging backward-looking notions of tradition within this new electronic music scene. Other bands, such as Asian Dub Foundation or Bradford-based Fun-da-mental, argued more explicitly, and often angrily, for a 'subaltern nationalism' (Dawson 2002) that challenged the racist, and later Islamophobic, British conceptions of a nation that excluded those who were not 'white' (and Christian).

Reflecting the celebratory approach to a commodified multicultural sphere that was typical during this period, the Asian Underground was attributed a postmodern edginess assumed to be more culturally and politically progressive than other, more ethnically marked, cultural forms such as bhangra. Thus, Sanjay Sharma (1996) has commented that 'Asian cultural productions marked as hybrid are celebrated and valorised as being enlightened and politically emancipatory' (p. 21). The legitimacy that, for many fans, music critics and academics, the Asian Underground could claim, was grounded in its harmonious fusion of Asian sounds with Western discourses of marketable protest and commodified youthful rebellion. The Asian Underground can thus be seen as marking the shift from 'old' to 'new' ethnicities (Hall 1992) and cultural practices that was to reflect the emergence of a culturally, politically and economically confident British Asian identity, briefly lauded as 'Cool Britannia' (Alexander 2008). This shift was marked too by the emerging generation of British South Asian academics and cultural commentators who coined the term 'Br-Asian' or 'Transl-Asian' (Kalra and Kaur 1996) to articulate the syncretic cultural formations that were starting to emerge and which challenged the marginalised and essentialised neo-orientalist framework put forward by white academics of Asian popular culture. Reflecting the circulation and exchange of concepts between the academy and cultural practitioners at this time, the use of the term 'Br-Asian' also became more widespread, so that bands and critics started to adopt this term to refer to these complex, 'hybrid' migrating styles of Asian and Western music.

In contrast, bhangra was considered to be more closely associated with homespun, working-class 'authentic' tradition and community 'roots'. This view of bhangra music reduces its potential to being merely 'Asian music for Asians' (see Banerji and Bauman 1990; Bennett 1999). Yet, as has been argued above, these false dichotomies between bhangra and Asian Underground cultural production obscure the similar routes, histories and connections of both cultural forms. Like the Asian Underground, bhangra is a globalised expression of South Asian popular culture, which has become diasporic, remixed and reimagined, much like the diasporic lives of its audiences in the UK and elsewhere, undergoing multiple transformations in the process. The Asian Underground scene, though generated from a specifically second-generation, metropolitan British Asian experience, was also speaking to similar transformations and diasporic flows of people, tradition and experiences, and drawing upon these multiple heritages rooted in the subcontinent. Asian Dub Foundation, for example, used Bengali folk music and language in their material and, in doing so, made visible and aural the different histories, experiences and voices within the British Asian diaspora.

The success of the Asian Underground, moreover, was not without its own ambiguities. As Koushik Banerjea has argued (2000), this success was focused almost exclusively on the cosmopolitan consumption of hybrid music, fashion and food. It has been heavily criticised both for its middle-class and consumerist commercialisation of 'ethnic chic' and its elision of long-standing racial and ethnic inequalities and increasing hostility towards Muslim groups during this period. The commodification of such goods involved refashioning cultural forms into objects of 'exotica'; thus John Hutnyk (2000) discusses how the Asian Underground was packaged and sold under the problematic category of 'world music' – as being outside and marginal to the commercial and cultural mainstream – the timeless artefacts of 'the other' that inscribe rather than contest ideas of ethnic difference. Moreover, as with bhangra, the Asian Underground carried its own exclusions and internal hierarchies, particularly around class, gender and sexuality. Gopinath (1995, 2005) thus explores how concepts of diaspora support heteronormative and male-oriented visions of identity. She has criticised bands such as Fun-da-mental who, despite their anti-racist, oppositional politics also espoused militant and nationalist rhetoric that often reinforced gendered inequalities.

It is important, of course, to recognise that these transitions were not simply 'bottom up' forms of youth cultural transgression, but concretised within, and shaped by, institutional settings and the growing power of the 'brown' economy in Britain. For example, the rise in support for local radio and media to service British Asian communities coincided with, and helped to increase, the diversity of British Asian cultural production and similarly reflected tensions and transitions within the Asian youth popular cultural scene. The late 1970s saw the first specifically Asian programming, with the establishment of BBC Radio Leicester (www.bbc. co.uk/asiannetwork). In the 1980s and 1990s, the British Radio Authority opened up access to ethnic and minority radio stations, offering licences and funding the creation of local radio that would better serve local minority communities (Georgiou 2005). Sunrise Radio (Sina Radio), established in Southall in the late 1980s, was the first to start Asian broadcasting in London, offering 24-hour programming of news, music and talk (Sreberny 2001). While these earlier years of Asian radio were primarily focused on serving the Asian 'communities' as a whole – perhaps reinforcing ideas of internal homogeneity and external difference very much 'in tune' with the rise of multicultural Britain – by the early 2000s, the BBC Asian Network achieved national broadcast and widened its remit by covering the growth of Asian youth music cultures with younger audiences in mind, whose needs and interests were understood to be different from those of the (older) Asian 'communities'. For instance, the BBC Asian Network introduced late-night radio shows that showcased Asian 'Underground' urban music hosted by Asian Underground music DJs such as Bobby (Friction) and Nihal. These popular shows drew in younger, urban Asian music fans. Soon, rival independent stations operating in London such as Club Asia[4] were formed to broadcast contemporary British Asian music for audiences between the ages of 15 and 34. Currently, besides the BBC Asian Network broadcasting, digital radio technology and internet radio have allowed for an even greater diversity of local and regional Asian programming that caters to young and old, offering regional programming from Punjabi talk radio and poetry to Sufi devotionals and South Indian shows, as well as popular Asian music.

Desi beats: the contemporary 'scenes' of South Asian youth culture

Although the Asian Underground was crucial in opening up spaces for Asian artists and producers, and reflected the changing identities of Britain's South Asian diaspora communities, in recent years it has been superceded by other forms of South Asian diasporic popular music, thriving in underground 'scenes'[5] across Britain's towns and cities. These 'scenes' have become more diversified as well as increasingly fragmented, perhaps reflecting the complexity of Britain's South Asian communities themselves. The music of the contemporary Asian urban scene can be identified as 'hybrid' sounds of bhangra and Bollywood beats, and instrumentals fused with 'urban' beats of hip hop and R&B. The use of Asian instrumentation, including the tabla, sitar and dhol, are common. Members of this scene are arguably trying to stake a claim to space beyond what has been achieved before either by bhangra or by the Asian Underground.

The contemporary 'scene' is not limited to any one genre of music, but consists of a series of networks and smaller sub-scenes, often going by many names that reveal the constellation of connections and musical styles that encompass the overall 'scene'. This can be referred to broadly as a 'desi urban music scene', but it is also termed the 'desi beats' scene, 'desi hip hop', sometimes 'post bhangra' or, quite simply, 'Asian music'. The 'Asian' in 'Asian music scene' can sometimes refer to the mostly diasporic Asian audience who support the music. In some cases, it refers not to the sounds produced but rather to the ethnicity of the artist. An artist such as Jay Sean who is considered to make R&B music, who sings in English and whose music does not contain Asian elements, might still be considered to be someone within the Asian urban 'scene'.

This contemporary South Asian 'scene' foregrounds the transnational links that inform how South Asian popular culture makes a space for itself locally, nationally and globally. Thus, while the desi urban music scene is quite firmly locally 'placed' within London, especially West London, it also inhabits a much wider space, which includes other cities, nations and the virtual spaces of the Internet, providing different and challenging conceptions of space criss-crossed by the networks that comprise youth cultural identities (Kahn-Harris 2007; Bennett and Peterson 2004; Kim 2011a).

The term 'desi' (which originates from the word 'desh' to mean 'of the homeland') is used to connote someone of the South Asian diaspora, particularly young people whose parents' moved to the USA, Canada and Britain in the post-1960s wave of migration. This was, in the first instance, adopted by many South Asian American youths to highlight their diasporic or 'hyphen-ated' identities within a context of American multiculturalism (Maira 1998, 2000; Murthy 2007; Shankar 2008). The subsequent appropriation of the term 'desi' to describe contemporary British Asian cultural formations, including music, film, etc., gestures toward a more trans-Atlantic South Asian youth culture emerging within an 'outer-national' frame of connections. Further, the 'desi' scene explicitly draws from the global, migrating syncretic sounds of hip hop and R&B, and often makes explicit connections between a 'desi' set of experiences and specifically African–American histories in the USA against racial discrimination and economic hardships. 'Desi' thus signals a cross-over cultural formation in 'diaspora spaces' (Brah 1996), rooted in the shared experience of racial marginalisation within specific local and national contexts.

While the 'desi' scene in the UK offers counter-hegemonic readings of culture, it also reaffirms certain dominant ideologies of race, religion, gender and class, reflecting the Janus-faced and ambiguous dimensions of diasporic cultural forms. For example, cultural production is often harnessed to the enactment of highly policed forms of cultural authenticity – of what it means to be truly 'Asian' and 'desi' (Kim 2011a, 2012). At the same time, the 'desi' scene can be a site in which claims to 'authentic' Asian identity are actively contested through local, national and transnational definitions and meanings, harnessing ideas of what it means to be a West/East/South Londoner (or from Handsworth, Birmingham, or Leeds or Bradford) as well as wider ideas about Britishness, and also through the evocation of diverse British South Asian community struggles.

At the same time, markers of authenticity within the desi scene are also informed and translated by globalised forms of popular culture and popular music. Its close identification with hip hop and other syncretic musical forms historically rooted in black African or African–American diasporic experiences have been influential in shaping transnational 'desi' diasporic identities and scenes. This has meant that the politics within hip hop, foregrounding notions of working-class 'street' masculine identities as models for racial authenticity, have become embedded within the complex articulations of 'desiness' within the scene. 'Desiness' has come to be dependent upon the performance and validation of a tough, working-class, hyper-masculinity, celebrated within some forms of hip hop culture. Its embrace of hip hop values can also include the materialism and commodification of music often celebrated in mainstream versions of that form.

The 'scene' thus offers more complex readings of youth culture. Too often youth cultures – particularly racialised youth cultures – are analysed within an oversimplified discourse of 'resistance' of oppositional identities against a 'mainstream'. It is undoubtedly true that many 'desi' urban artists are independent, financing themselves the production and distribution of their own music. It is also a fact that the scene relies upon small networks of independent media, independent record shops and social networking sites to promote its music.[6] Live performances are often at local club venues. Yet this does not automatically suggest a commitment to a particular set of politics. Jay Sean's signing to a US hip hop label owned by Universal Records is often seen as an example of the global mainstreaming of British Asian cultural production, shifting its politics and position away from the margins (Kim 2011a). The rise of an Asian middle class in Britain – at least amongst certain sections of the community – has had a profound impact on Asian popular culture, and greater affluence for many within the Asian urban scene has led to a decline in oppositional stances in identities and music. Rather, many in the 'scene' now identify with a mainstream politics and outlook, stressing 'sameness' and assimilation rather than difference (Hall 1990). Rejecting radical politics and positionality has thus become a way of claiming an alternative voice and narrative, setting itself against the discursive construction of young British Asians, in the media and academic literature, as 'problematic' (Alexander 2000, 2002). It is perhaps possible to argue that the assertion of sameness and integration carries a contestatory (anti)politics of its own – a twenty-first-century proclamation of 'here to stay, here to dance'.[7]

However, as argued earlier, the aftermath of 9/11 and 7/7 has precipitated a heightened awareness of difference, and an increased profiling and scrutiny of British Asian Muslims and, consequently, all Asian communities have come under greater scrutiny and misapprehension. This new environment has shaped cultural production within the Asian scene in various ways, fragmenting the scene along religious lines, creating divisions between Muslim, Hindu and Sikh producers and consumers. While some artists have developed and articulated critical, alternative positions against the increased profiling, Islamophobia and the state's draconian measures against terrorism, others within the scene have chosen to develop an image that rejects a politicised Asian identity. Thus, the 'desi' scene challenges the automatic assumption that there needs to be the enactment of a minoritarian politics within 'underground' music cultures. The radical, politicised minority position that was carved out from the Asian Underground has given way to a messier, more ambivalent space that is perhaps less 'militant' (Sharma 1996; Dawson 2002) and less connected to a stable collective 'Asian' identity and politics.

Conclusions: South Asian youth cultures in an age of diaspora

The creation and transformation of South Asian youth cultures in Britain encapsulate both the pleasures and perils of diasporic cultural identities and practices. 'Janus-faced', they look back to the countries and cultures of origin as a source of inspiration for claims-staking and place-making in the diasporic present, perhaps conjuring myths of authentic pasts as part of a polysemous and profligate (multi-)cultural future. Youth cultures thus stand at the uncertain intersection of space – of homeland, nation and global diaspora – and time – of imagined pasts, contested presents and optimistic futures.

At the same time, diasporic youth cultures imagine different ways of being British, perform discordant multicultural citizenships and generate hybrid forms of belonging. However, it is important not to over-emphasise or romanticise the transformative potential of youth cultural forms – in particular the unequal relations of power or patronage within which they are enmeshed or licensed – nor the complex internal exclusions (around gender, class or religion) to which they may give rise. British South Asian youth cultures are not necessarily progressive, nor even (self-)consciously political. Nevertheless, they testify to the complex and shifting terrain of South Asian diasporic identities as a reckoning with history, as mode of 'becoming' and as a way of changing the terms of debate. As Nitin Sawhney has commented in his 1995 album, *Migration*, 'from the anguish, turmoil and pain of our parents' history comes the responsibility to build our own dreams. This is the soundtrack to our journey'.

Notes

1 According to the 2001 Census, 2.8 per cent of Britain's population were Muslim, 1 per cent Hindu and 0.6 per cent Sikhs, with South Asian Muslims making up around 67 per cent of the UK Muslim population (43.2 per cent Pakistani, 16.5 per cent Bangladeshi, 8.3 per cent Indian) (Office for National Statistics 2006).
2 See Paul Gilroy (1993, 2006) for his perspective on outer-national networks and projects with regard to the concept of diaspora.
3 It is worth noting that many, including Talvin Singh, objected to the use of the label 'Asian Underground'.
4 London's Club Asia radio station went into administration in August 2009 (*Media Week* 2009) and was bought by a rival station, Sunrise Radio in September 2009, who renamed it 'Buzz Asia Radio' (*Asians In Media* 2009). It currently operates as Buzz Asia Radio.
5 A music 'scene' can be understood to be inclusive of all 'music making, production, circulation, discussion and texts' (Kahn-Harris 2007, p. 15; Kim 2011a, 2011b, 2011c). The concept of 'scenes' has become the way in which scene members, music journalists and scholars have conceptualised contemporary musical communities.
6 Public relations firms formed within the mid-90s, such as Media Moguls and PR-UK, have generally had a large share of ethnic marketing and the public relations market, particularly for larger campaigns and corporate clients. Within the Asian urban music scene, Asian music industry insiders such as Pedro Carvalho (who was one of the founding members of Media Moguls) and his company, FNIK PR, have become prominent within the growing Asian music industry and have represented artists on the well known Rishi Rich Productions label, as well as Nitin Sawhney and So Solid Crew (see AIM www.asiansinmedia.org for more information on FNIK PR). However, for many of the independent Asian artists within the urban scene, marketing and PR usually tend to be handled by smaller, local PR firms that also provide multiple services such as handling artists' bookings and management.
7 Cf. the 1970s' anti-racist slogan 'Here to stay, here to fight' (Sivanandan 1981).

References

Alexander, C. E. (1996) *The Art of Being Black: The Creation of Black British Youth Identities*, Oxford: Oxford University Press.

— (2000) *The Asian Gang: Ethnicity, Identity, Masculinity*, Oxford: Berg.

— (2002) 'Beyond Black: Re-thinking the Colour/Culture Divide', *Ethnic and Racial Studies*, 25 (4): 552–71.

— (2006) 'Imagining the Politics of BrAsian Youth', in N. Ali, V. Kalra and S. Sayyid (eds) *A Postcolonial People: South Asians in Britain*, London: Christopher Hurst.

— (2008) 'The Problem of South Asian Popular Culture: A View from the UK', *South Asian Popular Culture*, 6 (1): 1–12.

— (2010) 'Diaspora and Hybridity', in P. Hill Collins and J. Solomos (eds) *Handbook of Race and Ethnic Studies*, London: Sage.

Anwar, M. (1998) *Between Cultures: Continuity and Change in the Lives of Young Asians*, London: Routledge.

Asians in Media (2009) 'Sunrise Radio Buys Bankrupt Club Asia, Industry Insiders Say', *Asians in Media*, 17 September. Online. Available at: www.asiansinmedia.org/2009/09/17/sunrise-radio-buys-bankrupt club-asia-industry-insiders-say (accessed 1 May 2013).

Back, L. (1996) *New Ethnicities and Urban Culture: Racisms and Multiculture in Young Lives*, London: UCL Press.

Banerjea, K. (2000) '"Sound of Whose Underground?" The Fine Tuning of Diaspora in an Age of Mechanical Reproduction', *Theory, Culture and Society*, 17 (3): 64–79.

Banerjea, K. and Banerjea, P. (1996) 'Psyche and Soul: A View from the "South"', in S. Sharma, J. Hutnyk and A. Sharma (eds) *Dis-orienting Rhythms: The Politics of the New Asian Dance Music*, London: Zed Books.

Banerji, S. and Baumann G. (1990) 'Bhangra 1984–8: Fusion and Professionalization in a Genre of South Asian Dance Music' in Oliver, P. (ed.) *Black Music in Britain: Essays on the Afro-Asian Contribution to Popular Music*, Milton Keynes: Open University Press.

Baumann, G. (1990) 'The Re-Invention of Bhangra. Social Change and Aesthetic Shifts in Punjabi Music in Britain', *World of Music*, 32 (2): 91–8.

— (1996) *Contesting Culture: Discourses of Identity in Multi-ethnic London*, Cambridge: Cambridge University Press.

Bennett, A. (1999) 'Subcultures or Neo-tribes? Rethinking the Relationship between Youth, Style and Musical Taste', *Sociology*, 33 (3): 599–617.

Bennett, A. and Peterson, A. R. (2004) *Music Scenes: Local, Translocal and Virtual*, Nashville: Vanderbilt University Press.

Bhabha, H. (1990) 'The Third Space', in J. Rutherford (ed.) *Identity: Community, Culture, Difference*, London: Lawrence & Wishart.

Bhatt, C. (2001) *Hindu Nationalism: Origins, Ideologies and Modern Myths*, Oxford: Berg.

— (2006) 'The Fetish of the Margin: Religious Absolutism, Anti-racism and Postcolonial Silence', *New Formation*, 59: 98–115.

Brah, A. (1996) *Cartographies of Diaspora: Contesting Identities*, London: Routledge.

Dawson, A. (2002) '"This is the Digital Underclass": Asian Dub Foundation and Hip-Hop Cosmopolitanism', *Social Semiotics*, 12 (1): 27–44.

Dudrah, R. (2002a) 'Drum'n'dhol: British Bhangra Music and Diasporic South Asian Identity Formation', *European Journal of Cultural Studies*, 5 (3): 363–83.

— (2002b) 'Birmingham (UK): Constructing City Spaces through Black Popular Cultures and the Black Public Sphere', *City*, 6 (3): 335–50.

— (2007) *Bhangra: Birmingham and Beyond*, Birmingham: Birmingham City Council Library and Archive Service.

Evans, S. (October 2003) 'Asian Dub Foundation: Keep Banging on the Walls Music Review', Music OMH, 27. Online. Available at: www.musicomh.com/albums/asian-dub-foundation-2.htm (accessed 25 August 2009).

Georgiou, M. (2005) 'Diasporic Media across Europe: Multicultural Societies and Universalism–Particularism Continuum', *Journal of Ethnic and Migration Studies*, 31 (3): 481–498.

Gilroy, P. (1993) *Small Acts: Thoughts on the Politics of Black Cultures*, London: Serpent's Tail.

— (2004) *After Empire, Melancholia or Convivial Culture?* London: Routledge.

— (2006) 'British Cultural Studies and the Pitfalls of Identity' in Durham, G. and Kellner, D. (eds) (2006) *Media and Cultural Studies KeyWorks*, Oxford: Blackwell Publishing.

— (2010) *Darker Than Blue: On The Moral Economies of Black Atlantic Culture*, Cambridge: Harvard University Press.

Giroux, H. (1996) *Fugitive Cultures*, London and New York: Routledge.

Gopinath, G. (1995) '"Bombay, UK, Yuba City": Bhangra Music and the Engendering of Diaspora', *Diaspora*, 4 (3): 303–321.

— (2005) *Impossible Desires: Queer Diasporas and South Asian Public Cultures*, Durham: Duke University Press.

Hall, S. (1990) 'Cultural Identity and Diaspora', in J. Rutherford (ed.) *Identity: Community, Culture, Difference*, London: Lawrence & Wishart.

— (1992) 'New Ethnicities' in J. Donald and A. Rattansi (eds) *Race, Culture and Difference*, London: Sage.

Hall, S., Critcher, C., Jefferson, T., Clarke, J., Roberts, B. (1979) *Policing the Crisis*, London: Macmillan.

Hebdige, D. (1979) *Subculture: The Meaning of Style*, London: Methuen.

Hutnyk, J. (2000) *Critique of Exotica: Music, Politics and the Culture Industry*, London: Pluto Press.

Kahn-Harris, K. (2007) *Extreme Metal: Music and Culture on the Edge*, Oxford: Berg.

Kalra, V. S. (2000) 'Vilayeti Rhythms: Beyond Bhangra's Emblematic Status to a Translation of Lyrical Texts', *Theory Culture and Society*, 17 (3): 80–102.

Kalra, V. S. and Kaur, R. (1996) 'New Paths for South Asian Identity and Musical Creativity' in S. Sharma, J. Hutnyk and A. Sharma (eds) *Dis-Orienting Rhythms: The Politics of the New Asian Dance Music*, London: Zed Books.

Kalra, V. S., Kaur, R. and Hutnyk, J. (2005) *Diaspora and Hybridity*, London: Sage.

Kim, H. (2011a) *'Desis Doing it Like This' Diaspora and Spaces of the Asian Music Scene in London*, PhD thesis, London School of Economics and Political Science.

— (2011b) 'It's Desi-licious: Space and London's "Desi" Urban Music Scene' in Alexander, C. and James, M. (eds) *New Perspectives, New Voices*, London: The Runnymede Trust.

— (2011c) '"Keeping it Real" Bombay Bronx, Cultural Producers and the Asian Scene', in Toynbee J. and Dueck, B. (eds) *Migrating Music*, London: Routledge.

— (2012) 'A "Desi" Diaspora? The Production of "Desiness" and London's Asian Urban Music Scene', *Identities* 19 (5): 555–75.

Kun, J. (10 December 1998) 'Rafi's Revenge', *Rolling Stone*. Online. Available at: www.rollingstone.com/reviews/album/118730/review/5946549/rafisrevenge.

Kundnani, A. (2007) *The End of Tolerance*, London: Pluto Press.

Maira S. (1998) 'Desis Reprazent: Bhangra Remix and Hip Hop in New York City', *Postcolonial Studies* 1 (3): 357–70.

— (2000) 'Henna and Hip Hop: The Politics of Cultural Production and the Work of Cultural Studies', *Journal of Asian American Studies*, 3 (3): 329–69.

— (2002) *Desis in the House: Indian American Youth Culture in New York City*, Philadelphia: Temple University Press.

McGhee, D. (2008) *The End of Multiculturalism?*, Maidenhead: Open University Press.

Media Week (2009) 'Club Asia Radio Station Goes into Administration', *Media Week*, 21 August. Online. Available at: www.mediaweek.co.uk/news/928618 (accessed 1 May 2013).

Modood, T. (1992) *Not Easy Being British: Colour, Culture and Citizenship*, Stoke-on-Trent: Trentham.

Modood, T., Berthoud, R., Lakey, J., Nazroo, J., Smith, P. (1997) *Ethnic Minorities in Britain: Diversity and Disadvantage*, London: Policy Studies Institute.

Murthy, D. (2007) 'A South Asian American Diasporic Aesthetic Community? Ethnicity and New York City's "Asian Electronic Music" Scene', *Ethnicities*, 7 (2): 225–47.

Office for National Statistics (2006) *Focus on Ethnicity and Religion*, Basingstoke.

— (2009) *Population and Social Trends*, London.

Sawhney, Nitin (1999) Beyond Skin (CD), London: Pias UK.

Shankar, S. (2008) *Desi Land: Teen Culture, Class, and Success in Silicon Valley*, Durham: Duke University Press.

Sharma, S. (1996) 'Noisy Asians or "Asian Noise"?', in S. Sharma, J. Hutnyk and A. Sharma (eds) *Dis-orienting Rhythms: The Politics of the New Asian Dance Music*, London: Zed Books.

Sharma, S., Hutnyk, J. and Sharma, A. (eds) (1996a) *Dis-orienting Rhythms: The Politics of the New Asian Dance Music*, London: Zed Books.

— (1996b) 'Introduction' in *Dis-orienting Rhythms: The Politics of the New Asian Dance Music*, London: Zed Books.

Sivanandan, A. (1981) *From Resistance to Rebellion: Asian and Afro-Caribbean Struggles in Britain*, London: Institute of Race Relations.

— (2000) 'A Radical Black Political Culture' in K. Owusu (ed.) *Black British Culture and Society*, London: Routledge.

Sreberny, A. (2001) 'The Role of the Media in the Cultural Practices of Diasporic Communities', in Bennett, T. (ed.) (2001) *Differing Diversities: Transversal Study on the Theme of Cultural Policy and Cultural Diversity*, Strasbourg: Council of Europe Publishing.

29

DRESS AND THE SOUTH ASIAN DIASPORA

Emma Tarlo

The distinction between frames and their contents is less stable than may at first appear; they challenge each other, transforming themselves into new entities with new meanings. Women wearing their shalwar kameez in British city streets change the meaning both of shalwar kameez and British city street.

(Helen Scalway 2010)

It would be impossible to ignore the presence of South Asian textiles and dress in Britain – visible not only in overt and easily recognisable forms such as the sari and shalwar kamiz, displayed most spectacularly at weddings or in Bollywood movies, but also in plainer forms of everyday dress and in more subtle ways through shawls, prints, patterns, colour, ornament and clothing combinations which have entered mainstream fashion and are no longer associated only with South Asians. Garments like the 'pashmina shawl' have, for example, become a ubiquitous feature of the wardrobes of women from a variety of backgrounds. Conversely, men and women of South Asian origin often wear globally popular garments, many of which do not have overt South Asian connotations, although they may have been fabricated in South Asia or make reference to South Asian patterns and designs. These two examples serve as reminders that the relationship between ethnicity and clothing is multifaceted in a cosmopolitan post-colonial context where both people and goods circulate with ease, though at different rhythms and speeds, recalling diverse histories and memories and heralding new experiences. How, then, can we understand the relationship between South Asian peoples in diaspora and the textiles and fashions we call South Asian? What insights might be gained from considering the entangled histories of the diasporas of South Asian people and their clothes?

Historic legacies

Indo-British textile relations have long been caught up in complex historic cycles of admiration, competition, adoption, rejection and reinvention. Long before South Asians arrived in Britain in significant numbers, Indian textiles entered the repertoire of British fashions, admired for their superior technological brilliance, complexity of pattern and vibrancy of colour. In the sixteenth century, most British clothes were made from wool or silk and were often plain or containing patterns incorporated into the weaving process and thereby restricted by the geometric structure of the warp and weft. India however offered cotton textiles decorated using block printing and wax-resist techniques. These enabled a diverse range of complex patterns, colours and motifs which excited British tastes (Crill 2010). Printed cottons known as chintzes became so popular in British clothing and furniture that by the late seventeenth century they were considered a threat to local textile production and laws were introduced banning their import in 1701 and 1722. Once forbidden, such cloth continued to enter Britain through the black market, no doubt only adding to its exoticism and desirability.

By the early twentieth century, however, suspicions were reversed and nationalists in India sought to protect local Indian textile production through placing bans on the import of foreign machine-made cloth and machine-spun yarn from Britain and Europe, which was undercutting local production. Gandhi's elevation of khadi (hand-spun, hand-woven cloth) to the status of a national uniform in the 1920s and '30s was part of this rejection of imported foreign cloth and clothes in favour of a newly defined idea of authentic Indian dress (Tarlo 1996: ch. 3). That such an invention emerged out of Gandhi's experiences in Britain and South Africa is a reminder of the difficulty and indeed futility of drawing rigid distinctions between British and Indian textiles and tastes that had emerged through histories of mutual interaction.

The precise meanings accorded to Indian fashions have varied not only in time and place but also in relation to the identities of wearers with their particular and sometimes contradictory aspirations and projections. Whilst Indian nationalists were busy redefining Indian dress in terms of simplicity, social solidarity and rural tradition in the 1920s and '30s, the British upper-class intelligentsia and literati of the same period were sporting sumptuous fabrics and loose cuts of Indian inspiration as an expression of individualism, eccentricity and liberated modernity. Similarly, in the 1960s and '70s, at the same time that many South Asian migrants to Britain were experiencing racist abuse and mockery partly on account of their distinctive clothes and food which marked them out as different, many young people in Britain, Europe and the United States, most noticeably those identified with the hippy movement, adopted Indian clothes as a means of expressing self-chosen nonconformity, sensuality and exoticism (Ashmore 2010). Such juxtapositions hint both at the huge diversity of fashions and textiles available on the subcontinent as well as the diversity of interpretations of them which take on different meanings for different actors in different spaces.

The story of South Asian diaspora fashion and dress can best be understood in terms of a series of interlocking themes, some of which correspond to particular moments of diasporic experience. Whilst life in diasporic circumstances may vary considerably according to particular migration paths, social and cultural backgrounds, and moments and locations of settlement, certain elements of experience may also be shared in common amongst people of South Asian origin scattered in different parts of the world. The following account relies heavily on British and American experiences from the 1950s onwards with more limited reference to other times and contexts.

Early adaptations

In his autobiography, Gandhi famously recalled his embarrassment at arriving in England in late September dressed in white trousers, having misinterpreted local sartorial codes for the early autumn. This sense of unwanted conspicuousness and wearing clothes ill suited to the local climate was something later faced by many South Asian migrants who came to Britain in the 1950s and '60s in search of prosperity and to fill gaps in the labour market and, in the 1970s, in response to political circumstances in East Africa. Unlike Gandhi, many first generation migrants, particularly those coming directly from India, Pakistan and Bangladesh were from less educated rural backgrounds and would not have had much knowledge of the intricacies of British sartorial codes. However, like Gandhi, they soon became aware of the disadvantages of conspicuousness and, whilst South Asian clothing traditions were not abandoned, they were rapidly modified in the interests of minimising racist attention and maximising chances in the labour market. Most Sikh men in Britain in the early 1960s did, for example, remove their beards and turbans, with half of them doing so within just a few months of their arrival in England. Many had found themselves simply unable to get jobs or accommodation on account of negative responses to their distinctive appearance (Helwig 1979; Beetham 1970).

Managing what the sociologist, Erving Goffman (1963) identifies as the stigma of 'shameful differentness' became an important practical step towards acceptability and partial integration at a time when identifiable forms of South Asian dress such as the sari, shalwar kamiz, kurta pyjama and turban were associated with foreignness, fancy dress, exoticism and even nightwear. This downplaying of markers of ethnic, regional, religious and caste identity was an adaptive strategy which many of the older generation experienced as a painful but necessary compromise but which was sometimes welcomed by their offspring. Accounts of the experiences of immigrant women and children highlight the extent to which their dress codes were constrained both by the external environment of the work place or school and by patriarchal authority structures within the family. For example, factory labourers of Gujarati origin working in the garment-manufacturing industry in the British Midlands in the 1970s and early '80s found that they were not permitted to wear saris to work. This was justified by employers on the grounds of health and safety. Many of the older-generation women resented this and felt deeply uncomfortable wearing 'English clothes'. They tended to favour trousers with long smock tops, creating outfits which to some extent respected cultural ideas of modesty and were not far removed from the shalwar kameez in terms of the covering they offered (Westwood 1984). At home, they would return to their saris, just as many Indian men in colonial India had maintained a strict division between a public Westernised self in the work place and street and a private Indianised self in the home (Tarlo 1996: ch. 2). However, many of the younger South Asian women working in the same British factories apparently welcomed the opportunity to wear 'Western dress' to work, perceiving it as a form of emancipation from restrictive cultural constraints. For them, the sari represented restriction and many expressed resentment at the attempts of fathers, husbands and mothers-in-law to impose sari wearing on them (ibid). Just as women's bodies had been made sites for the preservation of tradition and the elaboration of cultural authenticity in the context of nationalist responses to colonialism in India, so they were expected to perform the role of keepers of tradition in new diasporic contexts, even as they were experiencing startling changes in their everyday lives.

Intergenerational tensions and concerns frequently emerge in ethnographic, sociological and autobiographical writings about first-generation South Asian immigrants and their children. Concerns about preserving female modesty and chastity, considered by many to be central to the maintenance of family honour, combined with fear of the possible negative effects of 'Westernisation', led many parents to expect their daughters to wear long sleeves and trousers under their school uniform skirts. This was a cause of embarrassment for many, and some recall desperately wanting to look like white British peers at a time when there were few alternative role models. Strategies for doing so often involved minor acts of subversion such as rolling down socks, pushing up sleeves or removing the unwanted trousers. Humorous accounts of such yearnings to 'fit in' whether by the writer, Meera Sayal, in her novel, *Anita and Me*, or performer, Shazia Mirza, in her stand up comedy are often highly poignant (Sayal 1996; Tarlo 2010a: ch. 2). One survey made of dress changes amongst British Asian families suggests a loosening of parental attitudes over time, with 38 per cent of parents objecting to their children wearing so-called

'Western clothes' in 1975, but only 27 per cent doing so in 1983 (Anwar 1998: 138–147). Religious rituals, family occasions and especially weddings were and still are the domain where South Asian clothing and textiles were worn most abundantly and, whilst some children seem to have enjoyed the sensual experience of dressing in silky fabrics, bright colours and sequined outfits (Puwar 2002), others experienced the pressure to wear 'traditional' cultural dress as a burdensome obligation which seemed to impose an unnecessary and alienating level of ethnic identification (Tarlo 2010a: ch. 2).

Hybridity

The idea that South Asian children of the diaspora found themselves caught between two cultures has in recent years given way to the notion that, rather than experiencing cultural conflict, they have developed bi-cultural competence which enables them to draw on different cultural repertoires simultaneously, switch codes and blend cultural symbols in new hybrid ways. The focus on hybridity takes inspiration from Stuart Hall's conceptualisation of identity in terms of positioning rather than origins (Hall 1990) as well as on anthropology's well-established critique of the notion of bounded cultures. A number of studies demonstrate that, for South Asian diasporic youth, it is not so much a question of choosing between between Asian or Western clothes as of developing new and unexpected combinations. Bakirathi Mani, for example, interprets the juxtaposing of Western and Indian clothing styles by students of South Asian origin in the United States as a deliberate attempt to disrupt biologically inscribed racial categories and to challenge the often assumed connection between skin colour and ethnic identity (Mani 2003). Similarly Clare Dwyer has shown how British Muslim schoolgirls of Pakistani origin in the early 1990s negotiated religious, ethnic and national categories of clothing with relative ease, experimenting with different combinations in different spaces and questioning common assumptions about what constitutes 'Muslim', 'English' and 'Pakistani' cultural dress (Dwyer 1999). More recently, Tarlo has documented the emergence of what has become known as 'Islamic fashion' amongst young Muslims in Britain and elsewhere in Europe, showing how designers and wearers of new Western Islamic fashions often draw simultaneously on several different clothing repertoires including South Asian, Middle Eastern and North African fashions as well as mainstream global fashions and those of other diasporic communities (Tarlo 2010a). Many of those developing and wearing Muslim fashions in Britain are from British Asian backgrounds, but the outfits they develop are often based more on what are perceived as Islamic and Western styles than South Asian ones. By creating fashionable new forms of modern Western Muslim dress, they challenge bounded ideas of what constitutes 'Asian', 'Western' and 'Islamic' dress, whilst at the same time expanding the repertoire and possibilities of contemporary British fashion.

The mixing and matching of fabrics and styles from Asian and non-Asian fashion regimes has therefore become an important means by which many second- and third-generation British and American South Asians escape being defined and perceived as 'traditional' and assert their modernity and individualism as well as their knowledge, sartorial competence, familiarity and aesthetic appreciation of different clothing traditions and fashion regimes. More generally, such outfits can be read as an expression of the biographical experience of being raised in bi- and multicultural contexts and forging new hyphenated identities in the process.

Simultaneous to the South Asian diasporic adoption, adaptation and incorporation of global fashions alongside South Asian ones has been the mainstream fashion industry's appropriation and adaptation of elements of South Asian clothing traditions. Some scholars perceive this as a superficial form of cultural appropriation and an example of capitalism's voracious and undiscriminating appetite for diversification (Puwar 2002). Here, ethnicity is commodified and culturally essentialist ideas of exoticism reinforced through the market and sold to new consumers, including non-resident Indians who are often attracted to idealised images of tradition (Subbaraman 1999). But, as suggested earlier, South Asian textiles have a long and complex history of entanglement with British and European fashions, and these latest incursions might equally be read as just another episode in this complex history of mutual appropriation, reinterpretation and recontextualisation. Recent fashions on the global high street such as the wearing of tunics and dresses over trousers or the popularity of bindis and pashminas as fashion accessories could also be interpreted as examples of cultural hybridity and as a demonstration of the successful reach of South Asian fashions and aesthetics (Bhachu 2004) rather than simply in terms of capitalist greed and cultural exploitation (Puwar 2002). What is clear, however, is that ethnic stereotypes persist in interpretations of the relationship between people and what they wear. It remains the case that, if a woman of South Asian skin colour wears a sari to a social event where she is in an ethnic minority, she is likely to be stereotyped as 'foreign' and 'traditional', labels she may wish to avoid. The same garment worn by a white woman might be interpreted as an eccentric, imaginative, attractive or inappropriate choice but it would not be considered a defining feature of her identity. Interviews with non-Asian British women reveal how many are reluctant to wear a sari or shalwar kamiz on the ground that it would feel like stepping into someone else's clothes (Jackson *et al.* 2007). This reveals the extent to which ethnic associations continue to cling to particular styles even in the context of multicultural urban environments.

Sartorial biographies

One fertile line of enquiry has been the focus on sartorial biographies and narratives as a means of gaining access to how individuals position themselves in terms of discourses of class, race, racism, politics, nationalism, ethnicity, religion and fashion. Such an approach allows space for exploration of how individual clothing choices are transformed over time and how different elements of life experience take on material and visual form in different social contexts. Viewed from this perspective, wardrobes and their contents can be interpreted as a form of personal archive in which different social relationships and contexts are embodied and imagined (Woodward 2007). Throughout South Asia, gifts of clothing and jewellery have long been integral to the consolidation and celebration of social relationships such as betrothal and marriage and, in the case of families spread around the globe, such gifts continue to play an important role in maintaining social relationships and embodying memories of people and places. The wardrobes of people from diasporic backgrounds lend rich insights into issues of impression management in a multicultural context. For example, in Sophie Woodward's study of British women's clothing practices we learn of Mumtaz who has three wardrobes containing what she calls 'Western clothing' and one wardrobe containing 'Indian clothing'. Mumtaz maintains these categories as distinct in the way she classifies her clothing, yet her dress practices are eclectic as she plays up and plays down her Indianness in different contexts through the manner in which she creates new combinations by selecting from both categories in inventive ways. Woodward shows how different elements of Mumtaz's biography – her past, her ethnicity, her global travels, her social world, her creativity – are objectified in the wardrobe. Here, items of South Asian provenance, pattern or design have become a cultural resource on which she draws, rather than a frame which fixes her identity and look. At the same time, her background has given her particular competence and knowledge of colour combinations and stylistic possibilities which have a distinctive Indian inflection.

Exploration of how people of South Asian descent select and negotiate clothing choices in diasporic contexts reveals a complex and often ambivalent relationship to cultural heritage involving elements of memory, nostalgia, loss and desire. How people feel about their clothing heritage is strongly linked to how others respond to them in particular contexts. Experiences of racism and stereotyping may lead some to reject certain clothing choices or restrict them to particular milieu where they are surrounded by people of similar backgrounds. Describing her adaptation to life in the United States, Sivagami Subbaraman writes:

> As I struggled to evolve a style of clothing that would allow me to mingle unnoticed in daily American life, and yet continue to preserve something of my own self-image from the past, what became clear was that the process of Americanisation not only involved forging a new style and space, but also losing my place in a special locale and historical context in India.
>
> *(1999: 578)*

Learning to identify and inscribe herself with the generic national category of 'Indian' in the United States simultaneously meant de-emphasising markers of caste, region and religion which had been important to her in the Indian context. Her argument is that, for second-generation South Asians in the United States, their acceptance as Americans relies on their relocation as 'Indian' and their capacity to demonstrate this visually and through their consumption choices. Other sartorial biographies suggest different trajectories. For example, an ethnography of the sartorial biographies of professional, university-educated Muslim women of different backgrounds in London, shows how many downplay markers of ethnic origin in favour of markers of religious affiliation such as hijab and jilbab through which they express feelings of belonging to a transnational Muslim community or global 'umma' (Tarlo 2010a). Taken together, these different biographical experiences of dress reveal the extent to which individuals and groups use clothing as a means of forging complex identities, negotiating different social and imaginary landscapes and positioning themselves in the world around them and in relation to different actors.

Rights

Although today a wide variety of clothing styles of South Asian resonance are visible in the streets, shops, schools and public spaces of multicultural British cities, this was not always the case. As suggested earlier, turbans and saris acted as barriers to employment and sometimes made finding accommodation difficult as they seemed to embody all that was different about people coming from the subcontinent. The idea that visible markers of difference symbolise mixed loyalties and indicate a refusal to integrate on the part of immigrant communities continues to plague political debates about migration and multiculturalism and has led to the banning of certain forms of Islamic dress in public spaces in Europe over the last decade. Whilst discourses of suspicion and condemnation relating to the headscarf worn by some Muslim women were already prevalent in France in the 1990s, it was the terrorist attacks of 9/11 that acted as a trigger and catalyst for a more systematic resurgence of suspicion concerning the popularity of various forms of Islamic dress, leading to the introduction of legislation prohibiting their wearing in public contexts in a number of European countries. For example, in 2004 the French government introduced legislation to ban the wearing of religious symbols in state schools and, in 2010, passed a law banning the concealment of the face in public space. The suggestion that Islamic dress symbolises the oppression of women, the spread of a threatening political Islamist movement and the refusal of Muslims to become modern European citizens haunts public debates about visibly Muslim appearances. British Muslims, many of whom have over the past decade or more adopted markers of religious affiliation such as hijab, jilbab and, to a lesser extent, niqab, occupy an interesting position in these debates. Whilst opinions divide considerably over what 'Muslim dress' should consist of or look like, there is a strong consensus amongst British Muslims concerning the importance of maintaining the right to dress in accordance with one's faith. Whilst the full length jilbab and face-concealing niqab have been subject to controversy and restrictions, especially in schools, the headscarf has to a large extent become well integrated into the dress practices of young British Muslims and is an object of considerable aesthetic attention, contributing to the development of urban Muslim youth styles and to multicultural fashions more generally (Tarlo 2010a). Outraged by restrictions on the wearing of Islamic dress in Europe, many young British Muslims, a large proportion of whom are from South Asian backgrounds, have joined campaigns for the protection of hijab and participated in protest marches and online forums opposing restrictive legislation and expressing solidarity with their European sisters (ibid).

The opposition and defence of Islamic dress practices in Britain today echoes debates and struggles waged several decades earlier concerning the rights of Sikh men to wear turbans and grow beards. And it is largely due to the persistent legal battles pursued by some tenacious community members that a space was created in Britain for the expression of religious and ethnic difference through dress. The first major public dress controversy involving British South Asians began in 1959 with the case of one Mr Sagar, who was rejected for the job of bus conductor by the Department of Transport in Manchester on the grounds that his turban did not conform to conditions of service. A local councillor's proposal of a compromise, consisting of a navy blue turban worn with a Department of Transport badge, was also rejected as inappropriate. The dispute, which was much publicised, lasted several years. It became an occasion for wider discussions on the meaning of 'integration' with some MPs, both Labour and Conservative, arguing that Sikhs could only become integrated into British society if they abandoned their turbans (Poulter 1998; Beetham 1970). The dispute led Mr Sagar to make the dramatic announcement that he would rather die for the turban than live with such dis-crimination. By the time he won his case in 1967, he was too old for employment. In the same year, a 23-year-old Sikh man, Mr Sandhu in Wolverhampton, was turned away from his work in the transport department on account of the beard he had grown for spiritual reasons during a period of sick leave. In the two-year dispute that followed, Sikh networks were activated both in Britain and India, with the Indian Government getting directly involved and with threats of suicide from some Sikh activists. The opposition of local authorities in Britain to visible markers of Sikh identity had the effect of encouraging several mass baptisms of Sikhs in the UK, encouraging increasing numbers of men to chose to readopt the turban and beard in solidarity with other Sikhs.

There are many parallels between the Sikh and Muslim cases, both in the discourses of suspicion opposing their dress practices and in the development of local and international activist networks in response to the threat of suppression. In both cases, attempts to ban the wearing of certain forms of dress encouraged a more enthusiastic adoption of them, giving the dress forms themselves heightened importance as symbols of community. Recognition of some of these parallels was expressed at a pro-hijab conference held in London in 2004, when a Sikh dignitary shared a platform with Muslim women activists campaigning for the protection of hijab in Europe. What is striking in both cases is that the forms of turban and hijab that have become most valorised as symbols of community stem not from some pristine era prior to British intervention in India but from contexts of cultural interaction. Images of Sikhs in turbans in

India in the early nineteenth century give an idea of the wide variety of different turban styles worn by Sikh men on the subcontinent at the time. Yet such diversification ceased with the development of a standardised turban style for Sikhs serving in the British army and it is this style that has now become emblematic of Sikh identity (Cohn 1989) even if the reasons people give for wearing it vary considerably (Singh 2010). Similarly, the closely wrapped and pinned hijab which tightly conceals a woman's hair, neck and front and which many British Asians today consider a defining feature of Muslim identity, takes inspiration from Islamic revival movements in North Africa and the Middle East (El Guindi 1999) and is quite unlike the forms of loose head covering popular historically in India where the use of the cloth was far more relaxed and fluid. In both cases, there is a discrepancy between the culturally eclectic history of the garments and the way in which their forms have become standardised.

Where Sikh and Muslim struggles for the right to wear particular items of clothing differed in the past was in their treatment by the law. For example, when Sikhs struggled for the right to abstain from wearing motorbike helmets in the early 1970s, their rights became enshrined in the Motor Cycle Crash Helmets (Religious Exemption) Act in 1976, and were later incorporated in the Road Traffic Act in 1988 (Poulter 1998). Whilst clothing disputes involving Sikh and Muslim dress were both covered by the Race Relations Act of 1976, which made indirect discrimination to members of any minority group unlawful, the level of cover provided to Sikhs was greater than that to Muslims, as the former were classified as an ethnic or racial rather than religious group. Under the the Equality Act 2010, however, categories of race and religion gain equal recognition and protection. How far religious rights are respected in practice and what counts as indirect discrimination remain contentious issues, as the many clothing disputes involving forms of visibly Muslim dress in schools and public places in Britain and Europe demonstrate. What is clear is that a number of European countries, especially those with highly developed secular constitutions, are becoming increasingly intolerant of visible expressions of faith and legislating against the wearing of them, using arguments about health and safety, security (in the case of face coverings) and the preservation of secularism (Moors and Tarlo in press).

Transnational fashion

Simultaneous to the homogenisation of certain clothing styles and forms in the context of diaspora has been the diversification of South Asian fashions in diaspora spaces and through transnational networks. Most major cities which have established populations of South Asian descent have developed commercial spaces in which South Asian food, clothing, jewellery, music and other commodities are readily available and where a sense of South Asianness is inscribed in the urban landscape through shop fronts, street names, sounds and dress practices. Analysis of the commercial makeup of such spaces reveals complex networks of trade between South Asia, the place of settlement and South Asian diasporic communities elsewhere. The shopping centres of Green Street, Southall and Wembley in London or Soho Road in Birmingham and Belgrave Road in Leicester, all of which have developed in areas with large concentrations of people of South Asian origin, contain shops selling saris, shawls, jewellery, shoes, ready-made shalwar kamizes, lengha and choli combinations, and so forth, imported directly from South Asia, as well as boutiques selling clothes designed by a new generation of fashion designers and entrepreneurs located both in Asia and in the diaspora. Some of these boutiques are highly luxurious, stocking upmarket fashions and offering promotional sales at festival times such as Diwali or Ramadan. Such boutiques stand in sharp contrast to the unglamorous sales out of back bedrooms and suitcases through which both imported and home-made South Asian fashions circulated amongst South Asian immigrants in the 1960s and 70s (Bhachu 2004; Dwyer 2010).

In her book, *Dangerous Designs*, Parminder Bhachu pays homage to this first generation of South Asian migrants, including the 'twice migrants' who came to Britain from East Africa, arguing that it was their assiduousness at keeping alive a culture of stitching and sewing which provided the foundations and conditions out of which the women-led South Asian diaspora fashion industry has emerged.

The thriving transnational industry for South Asian fashion is part of a wider resurgence of South Asian self-expression found also in the success of both Bollywood and British Asian films, Asian cable TV channels, popular forms of South Asian and Asian-inspired music and South Asian lifestyle, film and fashion magazines, all of which forms part of a transnational media scape (Appadurai 1996). Diasporic fashion designers draw widely from these and other mainstream fashion and media sources in their creation of fusion styles of shalwar kamiz, some of which are designed directly according to customer specifications. Bhachu's ethnography reveals the speed with which global networks are mobilised. It is possible, for example for a client based in Trinidad or New York to call up a London designer giving details of the colour, design, material and style of outfits they require for some special event. Within hours, the designer will have made sketches and faxed these off to her production unit in India. If necessary, outfits can be returned via international courier service within a matter of a few days. For such designers, India remains not only a source of spectacular fabrics but also of cheap labour and high levels of skill. Whilst some studies suggest that local craftspeople in India and Bangladesh have been able to improve their lifestyles and incomes through participation in the fashion industry, other studies suggest that high levels of exploitation and poor working conditions and pay are a ubiquitous element of the industry (Phizacklea 1990). That many South Asian immigrants and their descendents participate as pieceworkers in such fashion economies is also a reminder that diaspora experiences are to some extent fragmented by class differences.

Contrary to what some theorists of globalisation might have predicted, the ease and speed with which people, patterns, designs and fashions travel has not led to the formation of homogenous transnational South Asian fashions. Comparative studies of fashion practices and preferences amongst South Asians in London, Delhi and Mumbai reveal how choices remain localised. Interestingly, many fashionable young people in India consider their relatives in England old-fashioned or at least behind the times in their choice of garments (Jackson *et al.* 2007). Some also suggested that relatives abroad were 'more Indian' in their choices, suggesting a strong element of nostalgia and a desire to maintain an attachment to their real or imagined homelands on the part of diaspora peoples. Similarly, many hijab-wearing Muslims in Britain recount how their relatives in Bangladesh and Pakistan consider them old-fashioned and traditional, and often encourage them to remove their headscarves and dress in what they perceive to be more fashionable clothes (Tarlo 2010a). Conversely, it is not uncommon for those living in Britain to be disconcerted by the fashions favoured by relatives in South Asia.

In conclusion, dress provides an interesting lens into the lives and experiences of people of South Asian origin living in the diaspora. It should, however, be acknowledged that the category of 'South Asian' merges and to some extent obscures differences of class, location and religion which may be highly significant to people. For example, some young Sikh men are particularly keen that their style of beard should not be mistaken as Islamic (Singh 2010), and some Muslim women reject the shalwar kamiz on the grounds that is also worn by Hindus and Sikhs (Tarlo 2010a: ch. 5). All of this suggests fragmentation which is not easily captured by the category 'South Asian'. Similarly the relationships of cultural exchange and shared symbolism which may emerge between people of different ethnic origins in diaspora spaces are also excluded or obscured by the category. One study of shopping practices and identity in London (Miller *et al.* 1998) has suggested the emergence of a new generalised category to which people from different migrant backgrounds relate, the key defining feature of membership being identification with the notion of 'not-English'. How far new dress practices are emerging which reflect such an idea is a matter for further investigation. What remains beyond doubt, however, is that South Asian dress, fashions and textiles, however defined, have a distinctive place not only in the places where South Asians have settled but also in the global fashion economy.

Bibliography

Anwar, M. (1998), *Between Cultures: Continuity and Change in the Lives of Young Asians*, London: Routledge.

Appadurai, A. (1996), *Modernity at Large: Cultural Dimensions of Globalization*, Minneapolis: University of Minnesota Press.

Ashmore, S. (2010), 'Hippies, Bohemians and Chintz' in C. Breward, P. Crang and R. Crill (eds), *British Asian Style: Fashion and Textiles Past and Present*, London: V&A.

Beetham, D. (1970), *Transport and Turbans: A Comparative Study in Local Politics*, Oxford: Oxford University Press.

Bhachu, P. (2004), *Dangerous Designs: Asian Women Fashion the Diaspora Economies*, London: Routledge.

Breward, C., P. Crang and R. Crill (eds) (2010), *British Asian Style: Fashion and Textiles Past and Present*, London: V&A.

Cohn, Bernard S. (1989) *Colonialism and Its Forms of Knowledge: the British in India*, Princeton, NJ: Princeton University Press.

Crill, R. (2010), 'Trading Materials: Textiles and British Markets' in C. Breward, P. Crang and R. Crill (eds), *British Asian Style: Fashion and Textiles Past and Present*, London: V&A.

Dwyer, C. (1999), 'Veiled Meanings: Young British Muslim Women and the Negotiation of Differences', *Gender, Place and Culture*, vol. 6, no. 1, 5–26.

— (2010), 'From Suitcase to Showroom: British Asian Retail Spaces' in C. Breward, P. Crang and R. Crill (eds), *British Asian Style: Fashion and Textiles Past and Present*, London: V&A.

El Guindi, F. (1999), *Veil: Modesty, Privacy and Resistance*, Oxford: Berg.

Goffman, E. (1963), *Stigma, Notes on the Management of a Spoiled Identity*, Harmondsworth: Penguin.

Hall, S. (1990), 'Cultural Identity and Diaspora' in J. Rutherford (ed.), *Identity: Community Culture Difference*, London: Paul and Co. Publishing Consortium.

Helwig, A.W. (1979), *Sikhs in England: The Development of a Migrant Community*, Delhi: Oxford University Press.

Herrera, L. and A. Moors (2003), 'Banning Face-veiling: The Boundaries of Liberal Education', ISIM Newsletter 13, 16–17.

Jackson, P., N. Tomas and C. Dwyer (2007), 'Consuming Transnational Fashion in London and Mumbai', *Science Direct*, vol. 38, no. 5, 908–24.

Jones, C. and A.M. Leshkowich (2003), 'Introduction: The Globalization of Asian Dress: Re-Orienting Fashion or Re-Orienting Asia?' in S. Niessen, A.M. Leshkowich and C. Jones (eds), *Re-orienting Fashion: The Globalization of Asian Dress*, Oxford: Berg.

Mani, B. (2003), 'Undressing the Diaspora' in N. Puwar and P. Raghuram (eds), *South Asian Women in the Diaspora*, Oxford: Berg.

Miller, D., P. Jackson, N. Thrift, B. Holbrook and M. Rowlands (1998), 'Englishness and Other Identities', in *Shopping, Place and Identity*, London: Routledge.

Moors, A. and E. Tarlo (2007), Introduction, Special Issue, *Muslim Fashions, Fashion Theory*, vol. 11, no. 2/3: 133–41.

— (in press), 'Introduction' in *Islamic Fashion and Anti-Fashion: New Perspectives from Europe and America*, Oxford: Berg.

Phizacklea, A. (1990), *Unpacking the Fashion Industry: Gender, Racism and Class in Production*, London: Routledge.

Poulter, S. (1998), *Ethnicity, Law and Human Rights*, Oxford: Clarendon.

Puwar, N. (2002), 'Multi-Cultural Fashion … Stirrings of Another Sense of Aesthetics and Memory', *Feminist Review*, 71.

Puwar, N. and P. Raghuram (eds) (2003), *South Asian Women in the Diaspora*. Oxford, Berg.

Sayal, Meera (1996), *Anita and Me*, Flamingo.

Scalway, H. (2010), 'South Asian Patterns in Urban Spaces' in C. Breward, P. Crang and R. Crill (eds), *British Asian Style: Fashion and Textiles Past and Present*, London: V&A.

Singh, J. (2010), 'Head First: Young British Sikhs, Hair, and the Turban', *Journal of Contemporary Religion*, vol. 25, no. 2, 203–20.

Subbaraman, S. (1999), 'Cataloguing Ethnicity: Clothing as Cultural Citizenship', *Interventions*, vol. 1, no. 4, 572–589.

Tarlo, E. (1996), *Clothing Matters: Dress and Identity in India*, London: Hurst.

— (2010a), *Visibly Muslim: Fashion, Politics, Faith*, Oxford: Berg.

— (2010b), 'The South Asian Twist in British Muslim Fashion', in C. Breward, P. Crang and R. Crill (eds), *British Asian Style: Fashion and Textiles Past and Present*, London: V&A.

Westwood, S. (1984), *All Day Every Day: Factory and Family in the Making of Women's Lives*, London: Pluto.

Woodward, S. (2007), *Why Women Wear What They Wear*, Oxford: Berg.

30

MARRIAGES OF CONVENIENCE AND CAPITULATION

South Asian marriage, family and intimacy in the diaspora

Perveez Mody

This chapter uses the debate about the legal redress against 'forced marriages' in the UK to explore the fuzzy spaces between consent and coercion in South Asian or '*desi*'[1] arranged marriages.[2] It suggests that, whilst the social construction of consent has received some attention in recent years (notably, Anitha and Gill 2009), 'force' and capitulation are just as important to understanding South Asian kinship and marital arrangements. The word 'capitulation' comes from the Latin *capitulare* – 'to treat upon terms' – and indicates a surrender that has been suitably negotiated and whose terms are to be upheld by conventions of honour. This chapter seeks to understand the significance of capitulation in the realm of South Asian marriage and kinship.

This chapter explores 'force' and capitulation in relation to the emergence of a new form of marital arrangement amongst South Asians – 'Marriages of Convenience' (known most commonly on the internet by their acronymn 'MoC').[3] These are self-arranged marriages for those whose intimate bonds are, for one reason or another, socially inconvenient. Rather than allowing such inconveniences to destroy the familial and kinship bonds through coming-out or problematic 'love-marriages', numerous websites have proliferated that enable South Asians to arrange suitable marriages of convenience for themselves.[4] Superficially, the posts on these sites appear to parody 'arrangement' with knowing youth seeking out those whose kinship identity would suffice to assuage parents and make a reasonable social match (so, for example, one post is entitled 'Jatt Sikh Guy Wanted for MoC', another 'Brahmin Girl for MoC'). For their success, however, they share a fundamental principle with arranged marriages that these are not ideal 'dream' matches, where all criteria of desirability are imagined to be fulfilled, but rather arrangements that work only if both sides are willing to see marriage (even 'convenient' ones) as a series of mutual compromises. In this sense, MoC marriages are simply a new form of self-arrangement. However, what they reveal is an increasing desire (in the words of an informant) not to 'spoil innocent lives' through agreeing to a parentally arranged marriage, but rather arranging to make compossible an authentic private intimacy with a mutually beneficial public facade of obligation and the display of the primacy of kinship over the subjective self. As Das has shown in her exploration of the moral projects that love-marriage couples pursue in their everyday lives, the intimate aspirations of South Asians seeking MoCs are not fully governed by any 'pre-given grid' of rules (Das 2010: 398). This chapter explores the moral projects revealed by MoC-seeking *desis* through local and transnational arrangements of convenience in marriage.

'Forced marriage': 'honour . . . at the expense of *human* sentiments'[5]

First, however, this chapter must engage with the debates surrounding 'forced marriage', particularly in Britain. In recent years, the high profile of certain crimes (Briggs and Briggs 1997; Sanghera 2007, 2009[6]) has led the British state to intervene on the issue of 'forced marriages' and to develop legislation to tackle it in the form of the Forced Marriage (Civil Protection) Act 2007. This act was designed to signal the state's intolerance of families coercing their children to marry against their wishes and to prevent such marriages from taking place. It makes provision for 'protecting individuals against being forced to enter into marriage without their free and full consent and for protecting individuals who have been forced to enter into marriage without such consent'.[7] Furthermore, at the time of writing there are moves afoot to criminalise forced marriage altogether and to introduce a new bill in 2013 to this effect.

But these interventions have attracted a great deal of criticism. One critique of the new civil law is that its definition of 'force' hinges around notions of consent, force and coercion that are hard to define and distinguish (Ballard 2006a; Anitha and Gill 2009). The Home Office report into 'Forced Marriages' in 2000 (co-authored by Lord Ahmed and Baroness Uddin) emphasises the problematic definitional boundaries between arranged marriages and forced marriages. Arranged marriages are described as 'traditional' and legitimate forms of marriage in numerous parts of the world and within certain minority communities in Britain. Such marriages are arranged by the parents, but nonetheless require the consent of both partners to the marriage. 'Forced marriage' is sharply distinguished from arranged marriage as something of a mutation from the (approved or tolerated) arranged set-up, in which one or both parties to the marriage do not consent or have been coerced or forced into giving consent (Uddin and Ahmed 2000).

However, the interpretive burden placed upon judges to decide what counts as legitimate parental pressure and what counts as psychological coercion is very great indeed. Take this extract from a judgment cited by Anitha and Gill – though note that it concerns a case in 1994, prior to the passing of the 'forced marriage' law in 2007. In *Mahmud v Mahmud*, the judge ruled that 'if under pressure – and perhaps very considerable pressure – a party does indeed change his or her mind and consents to a marriage, with however ill a grace and however resentfully, then the marriage is in my opinion valid'[8] (2009: 172). However, the judge also went on to conclude that consent 'had been vitiated by *pressure amounting to force*' and a decree of nullity was granted. Interestingly, the comment on the case goes on to say:

> But the judge also stressed that parents are entitled to apply pressure upon a person refusing to marry, with a view to producing a change of mind. '(I)f under pressure – and perhaps very considerable pressure – a party does indeed change his or her mind and consents to a marriage with however ill a grace and however resentfully, then the marriage is in my opinion valid' [italics mine].[9]

The judge thus annulled the marriage in one breath, but recognised the possibility that pressure is perfectly legitimate in kinship relations and that it need not amount to coercion if the person capitulates to that pressure, even if it is with 'ill grace'. Thus, capitulation to intense pressure can, in legal terms, both count as consent, as well as consent that has been vitiated by force.

The categorisation of 'forced marriage'

Uddin and Ahmed's Parliamentary Working Group's report *A Choice by Right* (2000) set the stage for the 'cultural' phenomenon of 'forced marriage' as being defined by coercion. Notably, it firmly defended religion (it states gallantly that it found that 'no major world faith condones forced marriage'). In this way, it placed 'blame' for such practices on 'culture' and, by implication, on the sending regions from which concerned migrants originate. Here, 'religion' is reified and reduced to bodies of textual sources, and culture is abstracted from it, so that it is taken to bear the burden of responsibility for such renegade actions when they occur. Such 'culturalisation' characterises the men of these communities as violent and 'backward'; it also presents culture as anaesthetised from other forms of domination (class, race and so on), thus justifying measures designed to control such groups (Razack 2004: 131; Wilson 2007).

The discussion of 'forced marriage' has become highly gendered. In popular perception, it is something that South Asian (and 'other') men do to their daughters, and for this reason it is especially condemned.[10] It is not viewed within the same frame as, say, domestic violence that might be taking place at the same time in other homes on the same street in urban Britain.

The public discussion in Britain of 'forced marriage' as an 'Asian problem' has led a number of feminist academics and political theorists to express concern about the 'cultural deficit' argument that 'South Asian culture is backward and lacking', that such characterisations imply (Razack 2004: 129; Dustin and Phillips 2008). These responses are partly reactions against earlier policies that failed to recognise gendered violence within the South Asian community under the pretext of 'cultural sensitivity'.[11] In an article on her role representing Southall Black Sisters on this Parliamentary Working Group, Siddiqui (2003: 81) noted that, 'The Home Office does not promote mediation for women experiencing domestic violence in the wider community, so why do so for Asian and other minority women?' and, in an unprecedented move, she resigned from the Home Office Working Group on 'forced marriages'. As Amrit Wilson (2007) has argued – the 'ethnicisation' of coercion is enormously problematic and forces women to become complicit in wider racist practices. Furthermore, it belies a more fundamental desire of the British state better to police South Asian communities, by representing Asian women as helpless victims with the 'White Knight of the British State' coming to their rescue (Wilson 2007: 30). As Razack argues in the context of 'forced marriage' legislation in Norway, fighting violence against women with racism is likely to strengthen men in communities perceived to be under siege (2004: 132).

The conflicts in question are also increasingly coded by the media, activists and policy makers in such a way as to imply that pre-modern cultural values inhere within certain cultural groups or ethno-religious communities (Werner 2009; Wilson 2007; Werbner 2005). Framing 'forced marriages' as a cultural practice rather than an individual crime (such as domestic violence) means that the events in a few families come to *adhere* to the rest of the community, making 'forced marriage' a particularly tricky subject for South Asians keen on arrangement. It also creates an ambivalence in the way concerned non-government organisations respond to the problem. So, for instance, Shaheen Taj of the Henna Foundation, based in Cardiff, makes it clear that she regards the many forms of violence that she encounters in her local South Asian community (which include the full spectrum of familial violence, sexual abuse by fathers-in-law of daughters-in-law, coercion in marriage and abuse of the elderly), as instances of 'bad behaviour' that need civil and criminal redress rather than cultural stereotyping or manipulation.[12] Such careful discursive strategies, borne from years of work within British South Asian communities, demonstrate the extent of the unease being generated by the public discourse on 'forced marriage', which presents British South Asians with a particularly hegemonic conception of their social and marital world. South Asians struggle with the term as it does not map easily onto their own ideas of how marriages are arranged and their own conceptions of the proper obligations of the younger generation towards their elders, as well as the care, sacrifice and love that go into creating and sustaining relations within a family.

Force, coercion and loving coercion

The social anthropologist Roger Ballard has worked extensively within the British South Asian community and has also been an expert witness in over 300 cases concerning South Asians in British courts (1994, 2006a, 2006b). He has argued that the distinguishing feature of South Asian kinship is that it conceives of the social order holistically rather than the more individualistically constructed 'Euro-American' moral world around them. He writes: 'persons ... gain their social being not so much from their uniquely constituted personal qualities ... but rather from their participation [in] a network of reciprocities, such that their personhood ... arises from their fulfilment of their rights and obligations within that network' (2006a: 5). In this vein, young people sacrifice their 'short-term interests' for the greater good of the group as a whole, on the further understanding that there will be sufficient 'long-term pay-backs' for their compliance and co-operation. Note here the implication that 'Euro-Americans' can just do as they please, that their love and 'choice' aren't socially constructed and economically mediated, an essentialism that has been successfully rejected by the academic literature (Illouz 1997; Zelizer 2005). Whilst there is certainly some element of truth in Ballard's construction, there is a danger in subscribing to this idealised Dumontian wholism uncritically, not least because it elides the fact that British South Asians are both British *and* South Asian.

The many instances of 'loving coercion' that litter the anthropological record and that remain undetected to the legal gaze alert us to the inherent confusion between kinship coercion and the practice that is short-handed as 'arrangement'. The paradox is encapsulated by the frequently heard and telling slippage amongst informants who seek redress from a forced marriage and who describe their situation as one in which they have been 'forced into an arranged marriage'. As two important recent studies of Britain show, South Asians who themselves are complicit in forceful arrangements, nonetheless condemn 'forced marriages' as they find it difficult to 'see themselves in the picture' (Khanum 2008: 10; Samad and Eade 2002: vi[13]). Whilst government and legal luminaries are keen to emphasise that the new law is about 'force' not 'arrangement', in practice the forcefulness of obligation, the internally coercive nature of kinship and the sexual and romantic attachments of lovers are often difficult to disentangle. Forceful arrangement may be the outcome of the sudden discovery of romantic love, or other signs of a loss of parental control (for instance, sexuality and independence amongst young women, as well as children getting involved in drugs and petty crime, see Samad and Eade 2002: 53–67; Khanum 2008: 6–10); equally, young people may find themselves morally and psychologically bound to follow a course of arrangement they say they want no part in.

The elasticity, or reflexivity, of coercion may well express itself in the form of freer secondary marriages that may often follow more socially constrained (even forced) primary marriages – indeed, as I will show in the case of some *desis* arranging MoCs, they may simply wish to have an appropriate primary marriage and then effect an immediate (or near immediate) divorce. With their duties fulfilled, they feel freer to seek personal fulfilment elsewhere. Forcefulness clearly need not be violent; South Asian parents are widely viewed to be *the* legitimate authority to arrange marriages, so that 'force' is in fact stereotypically portrayed as a sort of profound fatalism that forecloses dissent – refusing to consider that obligation can be questioned. As Nazia Khanum notes in her detailed case study of 'forced marriage' in Luton, preventing a love-marriage or forcing someone not to marry is as great a violation as forcing the person into an arrangement not of their making (2008). Furthermore, loving coercion is the bedrock of many forms of parenting, South Asian and otherwise. Whilst this may have been projected onto British South Asians in recent years, the psychoanalytic literature is full of reflections on such relations between mothers, fathers and children in European societies. As Judith Butler has argued, as children the people whom we love most and on whom we depend the most also dominate us the most (1997).

Manipulating gender and sexuality in South Asian marriages

The misleading gendered stereotype of South Asian kinship being characterised by young girls coerced by their heavy-booted and tradition-minded fathers has been successfully challenged by recent ethnographic work on diverse forms of marital arrangements for South Asians in the UK (see Charsley 2005; Prinjha 1999). In fact, in more than 15 per cent of all reported 'forced marriage' cases in the UK, it is the sons who are being forced, and the Crown Prosecution Service suspects this figure is a gross underestimation of the problem.[14] There is sufficient evidence now that the coercion comes equally and perhaps more forcefully from mothers, who, by virtue of their intimacy with their children, are often more expert in getting their way through the full spectrum of coercion, from loving coercion to violence (see also Samad and Eade 2002: 74). Whilst there is undoubtedly a gender imbalance in terms of the repercussions of unsuitable romantic liasons for sons and daughters, there is also the concern that young men may be less forthright in accepting that they have been coerced into unwanted marriages and, consequently, less willing to seek help. Furthermore, recent literature on 'forced marriage' (Gangoli *et al.* 2006; Gill and Anitha 2011; Sharma and Gill 2006) is for good reason heavily focused upon transnational marriages, or arranged marriage within so-called 'BME communities' ('Black and Minority Ethnic') nevertheless leaving a discernible gap in the literature about the large number of South Asians whose loving relations with non-south Asian partners often end when the South Asian partner comes under intense pressure to find a more appropriate or 'suitable' spouse. The extent of this problem can be seen by the fact that South Asian and non-South Asian boyfriends and girlfriends are increasingly contacting British agencies to complain about 'forced marriages', often without the support of the person being so forced. Again, this calls into question issues of agency in assessing what counts as 'coercion' as well as homogenising discourses that imply that 'forced marriages' affect only the South Asian community. The excessive emphasis on young South Asian women in need of rescue by the state has also meant that there are no mixed-sex refuges in the UK that can provide refuge to a couple escaping violence or threats of violence, even though many of those supporting such couples have increasingly noted this need.[15]

The issue of 'forced marriage' amongst British South Asian men is only beginning to be discussed in public.[16] A support group working with South Asian and Middle Eastern gay men in Britain ('*Himat*' – 'courage' or 'resolve' in Hindi/Urdu) notes that, of the 150 people on their list, 'about 80%' have been coerced into marriages. Even more striking is the advice they give young people, telling them not to 'come out' to their families as it will inevitably mean that they will lose their kinship ties. Ali, a member of the *Himat* network says this:

> When they do find out, they're basically going to go against it. My relationship with them is not going to be the same, the respect they have for me is going to be different and I'm going to miss that relationship. You see people being killed for being gay and stuff. I think I'd be vulnerable if people knew about me.[17]

These complex motivations that generate forms of coercion that are as internal as they are external, inflicted less by others and more upon the self, are poignant and revealing examples of the challenges of legal regulation of these arrangements. It is partly to address this intractable problem that Marriages of Convenience have emerged in recent years.[18] My own research suggests that young British South Asian gays and lesbians (or those with inconvenient love-choices) are increasingly seeking to arrange marriages amongst themselves to keep their parents at bay. In these cases, arranged marriages are being used to create options for these young people, rather than to close them down. Internet websites describe 'MoCs' ('Marriages of Convenience') between two British South Asian subjects or, indeed, between *desis* transnationally, as 'normal looking' marriages based on the premise that it is in the interests of both the gay man and the lesbian woman to keep their sexuality secret from their kin.[19] Here, a normative façade of public heterosexuality is crafted to facilitate a continued private sexual subjectivity. As we can see, arranged marriage thus allows a patterned combination of both constraint and sexual freedoms and, unlike the wider ('white') gay and lesbian population, these freedoms are attendant on precisely *not* coming out publicly or, in many instances, even (or indeed, especially) to one's closest kin.

MoC marriages: surrendering on terms

'MoC(k) Marriages' (as one website helpfully puts it) are marriages that young *desis* secretly set up with suitable gay or lesbian partners of the opposite sex. These can sometimes be transnational, but this is relatively rare, given the suspicion of South Asians living in the wealthy West for partners from South Asia for whom the marriage would represent both convenience and social and economic mobility. While the term 'Marriage of Convenience' in academic and popular discourse is used largely to describe marriage entered into for immigration purposes (Wray 2006), in the cases I am about to describe, whilst immigration issues may well play a part, it is a marriage of convenience for other reasons too. The two people embarking on these 'arrangements' bring to their parents suitable marriage proposals, so as to fulfil simultaneously parental ambitions for proper arrangement as well as to develop the potential for their own intimate aspirations after marriage. As one blogger says:

> I am a 33 yr st [straight] acting hindu gay guy from Europe, educated professional and independent. Looking for a good respectful long-term relation in the name of MOC to come out of pressure [sic]. To me it would be a marriage with concern, respect and freedom. If you are going through the same pressure, may be we could be of mutual help.

Many South Asians – whether in blogs or in everyday speech – use the untranslated English words 'pressure' or being 'pressurised' to describe their domestic circumstances *vis-à-vis* marriage arrangements. It is likened to a pressure-cooker, whistling away in most South Asian homes, a perpetual metaphor for the discomfort they feel through the build up of heat and steam. Informants describe the persistent questions from parents, kin, neighbours and even work colleagues, who expect that, when young South Asians have completed their education and have good jobs, they will 'naturally' progress to a marital arrangement, thus allowing economic capital to be transformed into kinship capital. In other words, education and jobs are often valorised by South Asians because they aid in the upward mobility of obtaining a spouse. Arranged marriages are markedly public events, celebrated with loud drumming, music, dancing and large numbers of guests brought together for a feast. The palpable sense of friends and family itching to 'dance at the wedding' is a common source of pressure for those seeking MoCs and helps to fuel the precipitation of capitulation and the urgency of the search.

Pressure in the shape of being asked constantly 'when you are going to get married' *is* nevertheless, qualitatively different from physical coercion, though, evidently, it may also turn coercive. Pressure mounts but, with proper interventions, it can be turned off, managed or released. One website, GayLesbianMOC.com, devoted to match-making MoCs for gays and lesbians reassures those enrolling on their site (and paying the US $18 sign-up fee) with this advice on their home page:

> Some of us are lucky enough that they can become themselves, by coming out to family members, friends, and/or their community, without facing too much problem/ pressure. However, some homosexuals (like us), have to hide our sexual orientation, due to various factors (eg. religion, family, community, etc).
>
> As we get older, people close to us will keep on asking; 'Dear . . . when are you going to get married?' We know deep in our heart, that we have little/no sexual attraction at all towards an opposite sex. And we also know; that getting married with a heterosexual can cause more harm than good to both parties, but due to the continuous pressure from the surrounding (esp. people whom we love), and to save face, we finally succumb to these pressures, and decide to get married. . . . Nowadays, no more. With the help of internet technology, we can now be connected to millions of other homosexuals worldwide, who are in the same situation like us.
>
> [T]he moment you found your partner thru GayLesbianMOC.com and get married, you will no more hear people asking about when you are going to get married. No one will ever question your sexuality again. No more pressure, as if like a heavy burden has been lifted off your shoulders.

There is a growing consensus, then, that 'pressure from people you love', as the website above puts it, is impossibly hard to deflect. MoC marriages, when successful, publicly concede to normative ideals of arranged marriages by taking on an acceptable marital 'mask' whilst simultaneously ensuring a private 'face' that is expressive of an inner subjectivity. As Das has argued in the context of urban Punjabi kinship in joint family households in India, 'maintaining honour is often at the expense of *human* sentiments' (1994: 213, emphasis hers) and, at its extreme, runs the risk of 'irredeemable alienation from the true self' (ibid: 222). MoCs are instances of negotiation between kinship morality and the sustenance of a true self, but what they show us is that cultivating one's true self need not be at the expense of honour, and vice versa.

Thus, one informant, whom I will call Jahan, wrote to explain why he was seeking out an MoC:

> [W]ell, [I] am 27 years old, as u know for many religions and cultures homosexuality is not accepted, . . . in Islamic religion Homosexuality as an act is a sin, but people do not differentiate between a homosexual and the act it self . . . [w]hen my family asked me to search for a girl or that they even offered to search for me . . . i did not know what

to say, and start saying excuses, like i still did not find the one, or am still building my career and my life may be later and so on, but i realized that i have to do it one day, but how shall that happen?!!! i am not attracted to girls, and if i got married to any one i would ruin her life and hurt her, so i started thinking, and searching on the internet about someone who would marry me infront my family in most of cases i was looking for some one western as to be more open minded, and while searching i discovered that there is something called cover marriage, and gay lesbian marriage and lot of staff [sic: 'stuff'] more and i start posting and emailing and getting replies back.

Jahan found that many of the girls with whom he corresponded (whom he marked as genuine because they were so suspicious of him!) were intensely afraid 'cause of fake people or straight guys who pretend to be gay just either to blackmail or get their citizenship'. This was a frequent complaint, and it was plainly a cause of such frustration that many potential MoC partners sought out verifiable 'proofs' of each other's sexuality. Furthermore, unless one lived in the same region and could meet face to face, it was hard to tell over emails and chat who was simply seeking out vulnerable others and those who were 'genuine'. Whilst informants claimed that this was 'understandable' because there were so many 'creeps' and 'fake responses' out there in the virtual world, it seemed to undermine the trust that was a prerequisite of any successful MoC coming to fruition. Clearly, these young people were also concerned about immigration legalities, adjustment and the possibility of 'downward mobility' through such alliances. But it is striking that people whose entire purpose in a MoC is to conceal a private intimacy or sexuality are forced to seek 'proofs' of their sexuality from others who are often in the same veritable boat, but who seek evidence of authentic sexual *dis*interest.

In a short film entitled 'MOC' by Faisal Jahan, a Muslim lesbian protagonist (living in the USA) says of her own MoC marriage to a young South Asian gay doctor: 'In our society, marriages were usually marriages of consensus and convenience anyway and not necessarily for love.'[20] The film describes a female protagonist who falls in love with a girlfriend called Najma. It movingly depicts how her parents start receiving proposals for her marriage, each one bringing her 'close to madness' and generating regular panic attacks. Her girlfriend then saw a webpost from a young gay Muslim South Asian doctor seeking a female 'friend' for a MoC and she responded and agreed to meet him. They felt instantly that they were kindred spirits and he arranged for a proposal to be sent to her parents who were elated to receive one from a Muslim doctor and instantly accepted. In the film, she and her 'hubby' have a house together, with him having his own space upstairs and she and her girlfriend sharing the areas downstairs. The film opens with her tenderly hugging her partner at the door as she leaves and the 'husband' shouting down the stairs (in a perfect simulacrum of ordinary marital domesticity!): 'Has Najma left?! My parents are on their way!'

Most people seeking partners through MoC websites frequently mention in their posts that they expect 'no physical contact' with their marriage partners and, in some cases, even outline plans for divorce a few years down the line. For instance, one lesbian blogger from New Delhi writes candidly about her own 'sham'-marital aspirations:

An ideal situation would be to get married in arya samaj (with a hindu gay man) or registered marriage (with hindu or christian – I do not have anything against Muslim men, however I cannot marry one) and eventually divorce through mutual consent.

It is also noteworthy that many people embarking on MoCs expect to divorce a few years down the line. Louis Dumont, in his magnum opus *Homo Hierarchicus,* famously argued that, in caste

Hindu society, primary marriages are the marriages par excellence, where status and honour are exchanged, whilst secondary marriages are far less prestigious and, consequently, less elaborate events (Dumont 1988: 114). Parry's work in Chhattisgarh in India corroborates this – primary marriages where the stakes are high are ideologically 'forced' (for both men and women), whilst secondary unions involve a much greater level of individual freedom, sexual freedom and, consequently, freedom in the choice of spouse (Parry 2001). So, for instance, Parry found that out of 116 inter-caste marriages he encountered, nearly 90 per cent of these were secondary unions. Again here, the normative model of Hindu kinship serves as a wider resource where young gay or lesbian South Asians gamble on the possibilities of greater sexual and intimate freedom once the self-arranged MoC has been dissolved through a divorce. Here a marriage of convenience is the precursor of a divorce of convenience.

Many MoC seekers clearly have liberal attitudes to the religion or caste of their sexual partners and this is brought into focus through apologetic revelations about parental expectations: 'Looking for a MoC with a hindu lesbian (I am sorry to bring this up but preferably a rajput)'. Here, the calculation of what one type of marriage implies for a future intimacy and subjectivity has interesting implications on the type of marriage arranged, as well as the sort of wider family being imagined, shaped and brought into being. As Kath Weston's ground-breaking ethnography on gay and lesbian kinship in California shows, many of her informants repudiated their blood family's rejection of their sexuality by asserting kinship with their self-chosen families – their friends (1992). The *desi* case of MoC marriages draws attention to a newer form of kinship and family that is simultaneously attentive to the expectations of blood kin and of the intimate self. These too are 'families [they] choose', but they choose them to present conventional tradition alongside a hidden interior kinship of intimacy, trust, care and friendship. This adds a new twist to the love-cum-arranged form of marriage documented with increasing frequency across South Asia and in the diaspora (Mody 2008; Uberoi 2006, Ballard 2006a: 6) with what I would call 'arranged-Marriages-of-Convenience' or even 'self-forced' marriages. Here, kinship, gender and sexuality do not exclude one another but rather are made possible through a clever manipulation of apparently 'traditional' forms.

However, my research also revealed that there were many frustrations that came along the path of true MoC. Take one of my gay informants, a Pakistani called Humayun, whose entire social world appeared to be 'pressuring' him to marry. Humayun advertised on an MoC site looking for a lesbian, but received a flood of what he described as fake replies from women offering him heterosexual services. He did, however, receive some 'genuine responses'. One was from a heterosexual Muslim girl who was in love with a Hindu and unable to marry her boyfriend with parental consent. She categorically told Humayun that she wished to have an MoC and then get a speedy divorce, all the while maintaining her relationship with her Hindu boyfriend. Humayun expressed indignation at this suggestion. Despite wanting to go for a completely unconventional MoC marriage, Humayun still held firmly to notions of heterosexual exclusivity for his future wife. Like many people posting on sites for MoCs he wanted a life-partner and a 'normal' facade of a marriage. As in other posts for MoCs, Humayun said that he didn't want his MoC to involve any physical relationship for the moment. Cyrus, another MoC seeker, presents his view of an MoC with the following:

> I'm a 21 year old guy and I'm currently a Law student from London and I'm looking to offer a MOC with the right girl. I'm not particularly religious even though I was raised in a moderately muslim home. I'm looking for a moc/friendship kinda deal that can benefit us both. I'm aware that some people are in need of a MOC because of family pressures so if I can find the right girl where we click well together, then I'm

offering a working marriage (non-physical of course) where we can be friends with the economic benefit of sharing a place like buddies and also maintaining a longterm friendship which will hopefully look like a brilliant marriage just for appearances in front of friends and family.

Humayun (like Cyrus) wants a 'traditional looking wife' but without the sexual intimacy. Unlike Cyrus, by stating that he doesn't want physical closeness 'for the moment', he raises suspicions that he may be bisexual or even heterosexual.[21] This ambivalence turned out to be disconcerting to his respondents because they were seeking reassurances that any MoC they embark upon is firmly devoid of sexual intimacy (the expression of sexual *dis*interest mentioned earlier, being vital to building trust). Humayun's experiences of seeking a MoC have not been successful thus far, but perhaps he will find someone who is similarly open, honest and tentative about exploring and navigating through their own future marital MoC-based intimacy with him.

'When it comes to marriage, there is nothing much new under the sun'[22]

In exploring 'capitulation', and in highlighting the phenomenon of arranged MoCs, I have sought to draw attention to the myth of group homogeneity, underlining the particular vulnerabilities and marginalisations inherent in the intersections of race and class with gender (e.g. Parmar 1989; Amos and Parmar 2005; Phillips 1995). Anthropologists have long deconstructed the 'given-ness' of both kinship, gender and the family for decades and have viewed 'the family' as an ideological construct best associated with the modern state (Collier, Rosaldo and Yanagisako 1997: 71) and with labour, economy and consumption (White 1997; Kondo 1990). This literature has influenced my interpretation of the terms 'marriage' and 'family' in the context of 'South Asian kinship', which I have sought to denaturalise in order to explore their contours. There is no easy suture that can stitch together into a seamless fabric the genders, sexualities, age groups, ethno-religious communities and the vast and expansive social, political and ideological terrain and 'ethnoscapes' (Appadurai 1996) captured by the term the 'South Asian diaspora'. As Phillips and Dustin have argued, it is by questioning the internal homogeneity of cultural communities that we can draw attention to the complex ways in which socially ascendant and powerful members of minority communities come to act as gatekeepers, presenting their own priorities and perspectives in public domains and often leading to 'conservative codifications to group norms' (2004: 532). By presenting an account of MoCs, I have sought to show a vulnerable constituency of transnational *desis* who are *not* obviously resisting these 'conservative cultural codifications' but who have found a tentative way between resistance and unqualified acceptance through what I have characterised as *capitulation* on their own terms.

South Asian communities in the diaspora have forged their identities in the face of considerable socio-economic hardship and a history of struggle against discriminatory immigration laws. Indeed, the most recent effect of the UK government's push against 'forced marriage' has resulted in a raising of the minimum age for a marriage-related visa of both sponsor and spouse from 18 to 21, thus creating an anomaly between the legal age of marriage in England and Wales (in Scotland it is even lower at 16) and the age of legal permissible transnational-marriage migration. As Wray has shown, the British state has been historically cynical of South Asian forms of arrangement that appear overly pragmatic and out of keeping with dominant UK values of love as the basis of marriage.[23] In fact, this puts the machinations of those seeking MoCs into sharp relief, because communities in the diaspora have been documented as responding to different regimes of cynicism about their marital forms by increasingly incorporating 'rituals of integration' into their marriage rites so that they appear to be 'smiling at the [British] state' through specially posed wedding photos designed to signal happiness, consent and intimacy in a visualised marital language that 'white' neighbours, friends, colleagues and immigration officials might recognise as devoid of even the slightest whiff of coercion or 'force' (Gell 1994). MoCs by contrast, appear to be 'smiling at the family' – they 'smile and wave', presenting a coherent image of conjugal unity, assuaging their parents' own social pressures and anxieties about their children's marriages, whilst concealing deep and *happy* secrets.

By tacking back and forth between two polarities of kinship coercion and kinship manipulation (neither of which have received the scholarly attention they warrant), kinship is seen as a vessel in which South Asians arranging MoCs refine and pronounce their 'emplacement' in families and kin groups, and their sense of a more expansive, 'global' citizenship encountered in *desi* communities on the World Wide Web. Whilst withholding consent to marriages that their parents are seeking to arrange, they capitulate and give consent to a self-arranged marriage where they have taken the initiative to find (but not fall in love with!) a suitable spouse, likely to fulfil their parents' dreams. Since all consent implies the surrender of one choice in favour of another, I have shown that capitulation emerges as a solution to otherwise intractable problems and sits rather closer to consent than we have hitherto conceded. Capitulation (here, bending under the pressure to marry even though one does not want to do so) is generally *not* born of coercion or force, but rather is a solution to that whistling pressure-cooker of kinship which defines new grounds upon which to base future cares and intimacies.

Notes

1 The word 'desi' (meaning of the 'desh' or land) is used to denote a common secular and non-nationalistic identity for South Asians in the diaspora – a term that emphasises their shared cultural heritage rather than the more narrow identities of nation state or religion. It is used in various South Asian languages to refer to other South Asians and colloquially stands in for the English term 'South Asian' or 'subcontinental'.

2 This paper draws on ethnographic work on the phenomenon of 'forced marriages' in the UK since 2006. This has consisted of following debates on the legislation prohibiting 'forced marriages', attending road shows, women's meetings, community events and legal surgeries to see how the new law has been presented, received and implemented on the ground, as well as interviewing 'forced marriage' survivors and following their lives over some years. I am using inverted commas for the words 'forced marriage' because I am seeking to explore what counts as 'force' and what is better explained as 'capitulation'. I do not wish to suggest that 'forced marriage' is either a fiction or somehow non-existent, but rather seek to draw attention to the ambivalent ways in which force can be construed, experienced and explained.

3 MoCs are also described on websites and by my informants as 'cover marriage', 'gay lesbian marriages', 'mutually beneficial arrangements' (or 'MBAs') and 'Lavender Marriages'. The phrase 'Lavender Marriage' apparently came into usage in the 1920s when morality clauses in actors' Hollywood contracts caused some actors to enter into marriages of convenience to protect their careers (Wikipedia, accessed 14/1/13).

4 Most of these websites are free, but some are subscription based (to discourage 'potential creeps from spoiling your search'). To be clear, these sites are not exclusively South Asian, but through clever plays on 'searchable' words in South Asian languages or words that have commonly recognisable cultural connotations, South Asians manage to aggregate on particular sites, some of which have hundreds of posts. So, for example, a word like *saathi*, which means date, friend, mate, partner in Hindi, is a likely word that South Asians might use to seek out a date or a mate online. It is also the name of a 1968 Bollywood film whose plot is based on a love triangle and which features the hit song '*mere jeevan saathi*' ('my life companion') by Lata Mangeshkar, the 'queen' of Hindi playback music – in these subtle ways these websites have emerged without becoming so visible as to be found by potential spoilers.

5 Das 1994: 213.

6 Jasvinder Sanghera is a survivor of a 'forced marriage' and *Shame* (2007) is her account of it. She also set up Karma Nirvana, a support group for survivors of 'forced marriages' and *Daughters of Shame* (2009) is an account of their stories. Sanghera is perhaps one of the most publicly visible and articulate of survivors, speaking on the television, Radio 4 and, most recently, at the Labour Party conference (2012) in the UK.

7 The law is entitled the Forced Marriage (Civil Protection) Act 2007. For a full version of the Act, see www.legislation.gov.uk/ukpga/2007/20/contents (last accessed 3/10/12).

8 *Mahmud v Mahmud* [1994] SLT 599.

9 See http://webdb.lse.ac.uk/gender/Casefinaldetail.asp?id=122&pageno=1 (accessed 7/10/12).

10 Though note that the judgment in *Mahmud v Mahmud* cited earlier draws special attention to the 'emotional pressure' faced by older men too.

11 In an attempt to both draw attention to and shake off this legacy, Mike O'Brien, Home Office minister and Labour MP, memorably said in Parliament: 'Multi-cultural sensitivity is not an excuse for moral blindness' (House of Commons Adjournment Debate on Human Rights (Women) 10 February 1999).

12 Apna Haq event, 'Is there more to Domestic Violence and Forced Marriage?' 24/5/08, Derby.

13 For example, Samad and Eade say: 'The general consensus is that force is unacceptable but community understanding of coercion does not include emotional and psychological pressure' (2002: vi).

14 Interview with Nazir Afzal OBE, Chief Crown Prosecutor and Director of Crown Prosecution Service (CPS), national lead for the CPS on 'forced marriage' and 'honour' crimes (UK); 22/7/08.

15 This was brought home to me by a volunteer who has been working with men affected by 'forced marriage' in the north of England, fieldwork interview 3/12/10.

16 See 11/1/10 'Gay Muslims Made Homeless by Family Violence' on http://news.bbc.co.uk/1/hi/8446458.stm (accessed 8/2/10).

17 Ibid.

18 For news reports on the phenomenon of MoCs see Lovejit Dhaliwal's piece in *The Guardian* 'Across the last gay frontier' 29/9/02 on www.guardian.co.uk/world/2002/sep/29/race.uk and Sandy Bains, 'Desi Marriages of Convenience' 15/6/09 on www.desiblitz.com/content/desi-marriages-of-convenience (both accessed 7/10/12).

19 Not all such marriages involve partners living in the same jurisdiction. Many gay men and lesbians in South Asia seek migration to a 'gay-friendly' country. It is paradoxical that British South Asian gays and lesbians (unlike their counterparts in the Indian subcontinent and in other diasporic settings like Africa) have the legal facility for civil partnership to a same sex-partner in the UK but instead choose a form of heterosexual marital arrangement that better suits cultural expectations and their own ideas about their sexual agency and personhood.

20 The film entitled 'MOC' is by Faisal Jahal.

21 One other possibility is that he may be referring to a future scenario of having children with his 'convenient' spouse.

22 Ballard 2006a: 3.

23 Interestingly, Wray argues that marriages of convenience are valid under UK law; but whether or not they allow claims for immigration is dependent on the immigration laws (2006: 304).

Bibliography

Ahmad, Ali Nobil 2011. *Masculinity, Sexuality and Illegal Migration: Human Smuggling From Pakistan to Europe.* Oxford: Ashgate.

Amos, V. and Parmar, P. 2005. 'Challenging Imperial Feminism' *Feminist Review*, 80, pp. 44–63.

Anitha, Sundari and Gill, Aisha 2009. 'Coercion, Consent and the Forced Marriage Debate in the UK' *Feminist Legal Studies*, 17, pp. 165–84.

Appadurai, Arjun 1996. *Modernity at Large: Cultural Dimensions of Globalisation.* Minneapolis: University of Minnesota Press.

Ballard, Roger 1994. *Desh Pardesh: The South Asian Presence in Britain.* London: Hurst.

—— 2006a. 'Forced Marriages: Just Who is Conspiring against Whom?' Conference Paper presented at the University of Roehampton, www.casas.org.uk/papers/pdfpapers/forced.pdf (last accessed 10/1/10).

— 2006b. 'Ethnic Diversity and the Delivery of Justice: The Challenge of Plurality' in Shah, Prakash (ed.) *Migrations, Diasporas and Legal Systems in Europe*. London: Cavendish, pp. 29–56.

Briggs, Jack and Briggs, Zena 1997. *Runaways: A True Story of Love and Danger*. London: Orion Publishing.

Butler, Judith 1997. *The Psychic Life of Power: Theories in Subjection*. Stanford: Stanford University Press.

Charsley, K. 2005. 'Unhappy Husbands: Masculinity and Migration in Transnational Pakistani Marriages' *Journal of the Royal Anthropological Institute (n.s.)*, 11, pp. 85–105.

Collier, Jane, Rosaldo, Michelle and Yanagisako, S. 1997. 'Is there a Family' in Lancaster, R. and di Leonardo, M. (eds) *The Gender Sexuality Reader*. London: Routledge, pp. 71–81.

Das, Veena 1994. 'Masks and Faces: An Essay on Punjabi Kinship' in Uberoi, P. (ed.) *Family, Kinship and Marriage in India*. New Delhi: Oxford India Paperbacks.

— 2010. 'Engaging the Life of the Other: Love and Everyday Life' in Lambek, M. (ed.) *Ordinary Ethics: Anthropology, Language, and Action*. New York: Fordham University Press, pp. 368–99.

Dumont, Louis 1988. *Homo Hierarchicus*. New Delhi: Oxford University Press.

Dustin, Moira and Phillips, Anne 2008. 'Whose Agenda Is It? Abuses of Women and Abuses of "Culture" in Britain', *Ethnicities*, 8 (3), pp. 405–24.

Gangoli, Geetanjali, Razak, Amina and McCarry, Melanie 2006. 'Forced Marriage and Domestic Violence among South Asian Communities in North East England'. Joint report of School for Policy Studies, University of Bristol and Northern Rock Foundation.

Gell, Simeran 1994. 'Legality and Ethnicity: Marriage among the South Asians of Bedford' *Critique of Anthropology*, 14 (4): pp. 355–92.

Gill, A. and Anitha, S. 2011. 'Introduction: Framing Forced Marriage as a Form of Violence against Women' in *Forced Marriage*. London: Zed Books.

Illouz, Eva 1997. *Consuming the Romantic Utopia: Love and the Cultural Contradictions of Capitalism*. Berkeley: California University Press.

Khanum, Nazia 2008. *Forced Marriage, Family Cohesion and Community Engagement: National Learning through a Case Study of Luton*. Watford: Equality in Diversity.

Kondo, Dorinne 1990. *Power, Gender, and Discourses of Identity in a Japanese Workplace*. London: University of Chicago Press.

Mody, Perveez 2008. *The Intimate State: Love-Marriage and the Law in Delhi*. Delhi: Routledge.

Parmar, P. 1989. 'Other Kinds of Dreams' *Feminist Review*, No. 31 (Spring), pp. 55–65.

Parry, Jonathan 2001. 'Ankalu's Errant Wife: Sex, Marriage and Industry in Contemporary Chhatisgarh', *Modern Asian Studies*, 35 (4), pp. 783–820.

Phillips, A. 1995. 'Democracy and Difference: Some Problems for Feminist Theory' in Kymlicka, W. (ed.) *The Rights of Minority Cultures*. Oxford: Oxford University Press.

Phillips, A. and Dustin, M. 2004. 'UK Initiatives on Forced Marriage: Regulation, Dialogue and Exit' *Political Studies*, 52, pp. 531–51.

Prinjha, Suman 1999. 'With a View to Marriage: Young Hindu Gujaratis in London'. Unpublished PhD dissertation, London School of Economics and Political Science.

Razack, Sherene 2004. 'Imperilled Muslim Women, Dangerous Muslim Men and Civilised Europeans: Legal and Social Responses to Forced Marriage' *Feminist Legal Studies*, 12, pp. 129–74.

Samad, Yunas and Eade, John 2002. *Community Perceptions of Forced Marriage*. Community Liason Unit, Foreign and Commonwealth Office.

Sanghera, Jasvinder 2007. *Shame*. London: Hodder & Stoughton.

— 2009. *Daughters of Shame*. London: Hodder & Stoughton.

Sharma, Kaveri and Gill, Aisha 2006. 'Protection for All? The Failures of the Domestic Violence Rule for (Im)migrant Women' in Thiara, R. and Gill, A. (eds) *Violence against Women in South Asian Communities*. London: Jessica Kingsley Publishers.

Siddiqui, Hannana 2003. '"It Was Written in Her Kismet": Forced Marriage' in Gupta, Rahila *From Homebreakers to Jailbreakers: Southall Black Sisters*. London: Zed Books, pp. 67–91.

Uberoi, Patricia 2006. *Freedom and Destiny: Gender, Family and Popular Culture in India*. Delhi: Oxford University Press.

Uddin, Paola and Nasir, Ahmed 2000. *A Choice by Right: The Report of the Working Group on Forced Marriage*. London: Home Office Communications Directorate.

Werbner, Pnina 2005. 'The Translocation of Culture: Migration, Community, and the Force of Multiculturalism in History' *Sociological Review*, 53 (4), pp. 745–68.

Werner, Cynthia 2009. 'Bride Abduction in Post-Soviet Central Asia: Marking a Shift towards Patriarchy through Local Discourses of Shame and Tradition' *Journal of the Royal Anthropological Institute* (n.s.) 15, pp. 314–31.

Weston, Kath 1992. *Families We Choose: Lesbians, Gays, Kinship*. New York: Columbia University Press.

White, Jenny 1997. *Money Makes Us Relatives: Women's Labor in Urban Turkey*. Austin: University of Texas Press.

Wilson, Amrit 2007. 'The Forced Marriage Debate and the British State' *Race and Class*, 49 (July), pp. 25–38.

Wray, Helena 2006. 'An Ideal Husband? Marriages of Convenience, Moral Gate-keeping and Immigration to the UK' *European Journal of Migration and Law*, 8: pp. 303–20.

Zelizer, Viviana 2005. *The Purchase of Intimacy*. New Jersey: Princeton University Press.

31

LITERATURE OF THE SOUTH ASIAN DIASPORA

Ananya Jahanara Kabir

> It is the sounds we hear as children that shape us.
>
> It is the snap-crush of spices under the heel of my grandmother's hand. It is the slip-splash of her fingertips, sliding fish into turmeric water. It is the thwack of her palms, clapping chapattis into life on her flat stone, a perfect circle, every time. It is the swish of her sari, the click of her knitting needles, the tap-tap of the soles of her feet hitting the soles of her sandals. There lies my grandmother's Morse code.
>
> . . . Listen carefully. These are the sounds of my house.
>
> *(Sadia Shepard,* The Girl from Foreign, *2008)*

Sadia Shepard's *The Girl from Foreign* (2008), which narrates (according to its subtitle) a 'search for shipwrecked ancestors, forgotten histories, and a sense of home', offers a useful starting point for an exploration of South Asian diasporic literature. Written by an American author of South Asian heritage – Shepard's mother is Pakistani – the memoir opens by conflating the sounds of childhood, the sounds that signify a South Asian habitus, and 'the sounds of my house'. This soundscape, displaced onto American space, confirms our understanding of a diasporic literary endeavour as necessarily enacting the search, hopefully successful, for a home away from the homeland. The comforting figure of the grandmother, the author's link to an anterior family history located in that homeland, confirms this expectation that a diasporic text has come to generate in the minds of critics and scholars as well as lay readers: it must engage creatively, philosophically, historically and emotionally with 'a sense of home'.

If the modern condition is characterised by alienation, the literary text born out of and speaking back to a diasporic history is increasingly seen as emblematic, even revelatory of that condition. Diasporic literary texts by writers of South Asian heritage, from V. S. Naipaul to Salman Rushdie, from Hanif Kureshi to Jhumpa Lahiri, writing from locations as diverse as Trinidad, New York, London and Boston, have offered, through the robustness of critical reception and popularity, some of the most meaningful and illuminating commentaries on modernity's intimate relationship to diaspora. Within literary critical explorations of 'diaspora', a term of Greek etymology whose original application has been to the perpetual dispersion of the Jews under different, hostile, political regimes, we now observe a gradual privileging of authors belonging to various South Asian diasporas (Kabir 2010). This paradigm shift has been encouraged by the emergence of post-colonial studies as a discipline (Ashcroft *et al.* 1995) and the Indian (diasporic) post-colonial theorist Homi Bhabha's highly influential formulations of 'hybridity' and 'third space', which, primarily through readings of Rushdie's novels (Bhabha's fellow diasporic subject), proposed the diasporic subject as exemplary of modernity's migrant state (Bhabha 1994: 7–8, 239–43, 320–4, inter alia).

Yet, returning to Shepard's memoir, it is no accident that the sounds of South Asian domesticity that define the grandmother, 'Nana', are also her 'Morse code', tapping out a secret that demands decipherment. Nana is no 'ordinary' grandmother, and this is no 'ordinary' narrative of a subject born in diaspora now seeking her roots. Shepard's memoir reveals Nana, the mother of her Muslim Pakistani mother, as having been born into an Indian Jewish family. Rahat Siddiqui was also Rachel Jacob, part of the Bene Israeli group whose ancestors purportedly sailed from the Holy Land to fetch up on India's Konkan coast in pre-colonial times. These 'shipwrecked ancestors' contributed to the multi-ethnic mosaic of India's Western seaboard which fed into the metropolis of imperial Bombay. If that space of commerce and modernity allowed individuals such as Shepard's Jewish grandmother and Muslim grandfather to meet, fall in love, and marry, it was Partition which took the couple to Karachi in the new Pakistan and forced them to adhere to more rigid conceptions of identity predicated on nation and religion. The granddaughter's cultural inheritance now emerges as the convergence of multiple diasporas – of Jews to India in pre-modern times, of Indians to Pakistan under the sign of Partition and of Pakistanis to North America as part of a white-collar transnationalism spearheaded by the pursuit of higher education.

Through it all, however, she still evokes the 'chapatti' (South Asian unleavened bread), 'turmeric' (a South Asian spice) and the sari (South Asian feminine garb) as primary markers of identity. The 'Morse code' of the Indian kitchen – and, here, 'India' is used advisedly, as an originating space before the creation of post-colonial national boundaries – forms a stable emotional core for South Asian diasporic authors. This core contrasts with the myriad affiliations and journeys, undertaken in historical time, which form them as displaced subjects. In this essay I focus on the dialogue between the myth making of a stable core, which repeatedly returns to the dark interiority of the kitchen as the heart of the domestic and memorial realm – and the outward-facing routes which the South Asian diasporic author also inherits and is created by. It is not my intention to offer an exhaustive list of authors writing from and for the South Asian diaspora; such a task would rapidly deteriorate into a laundry-list of names and locations. Rather, I use this central tension that I have identified between 'the sounds of my house' – the tactile, shaping world of South Asian childhoods – and the transoceanic, transnational webs in which the diasporic subject is suspended. I thereby tease out the South Asian literary diaspora's version of that perennial preoccupation of all diasporas: the relationship between roots and routes. In the process, I will pinpoint some significant authors and seminal texts of the South Asian diaspora, as well as locate them within discrete historical movements of people to and from the Indian subcontinent.

Who is (not) in the South Asian diaspora?

As noted above, Bhabha's theorisation of the migrant condition has motivated the analysis of literature produced by South Asian diasporic authors as exemplary creations arising from the 'in-between', 'interstitial' or 'third space', marked by the condition of 'hybridity' both on textual and authorial levels (Bhabha 1994). Novels by authors who came into prominence around the same historical moment as Bhabha's theories, particularly Salman Rushdie (1988), Hanif Kureishi (1990), and Meera Syal (1996), located in Britain, and some American authors, such as Bharati Mukherjee (1989) and, slightly later, Chitra Banerjee Divakaruni (1997), have proven particularly amenable to this model of interpretation. Critics have analysed their novels as responding to multiple cultural affiliations through their narratives of movement and the stories of displacement from South Asian homelands and adaptation to new environments in the 'West', be it Britain or the United States of America. Such analyses focus on their engagement with comedic romance plots that end in 'happily ever after' scenarios, as seen in Mukherjee's novels (e.g. Mukherjee 1989), or which deflect attention from darker narrative resolutions through linguistic wizardry, such as in Rushdie's novels (e.g. Rushdie 1981, 1988), and humour, such as in Kureishi's *The Buddha of Suburbia* (Kureishi 1990). This privileging of a group of authors, writing in English from metropolitan locations in the 'West', can produce the impression that literature of the South Asian diaspora is confined to a handful of authors who grew up in India or in a Britain which still shared affective ties with a recently decolonised India – and, most importantly, whose primary output is literature in English.

This impression is, however, founded on a restricted view of what constitutes the South Asian diaspora. More useful as an analytical model for understanding what motivates the imaginative production of South Asian diasporic authors is the Indo-Fijian literary theorist Vijay Mishra's differentiation between two 'interlinked but historically separated diasporas' (Mishra 1996: 421–2). The first was constituted through the movement of indentured labour, after the end of slavery, from British India to the sugar plantations of Trinidad, Guyana, Surinam, Mauritius, Fiji and South Africa; it was augmented by movements of labour to East Africa, Sri Lanka and Malaya to work on the railways, tea and rubber plantations respectively (see also Lal and Sen, this volume). These 'older diasporas of classic capitalism' (Mishra 1996: 421) were coterminous with the peak of the British Empire's power: the first shipload of indentured labourers arrived in Mauritius in the 1830s and the system ended in 1917, by which time approximately a million people had been displaced from India, mainly the North, across the transoceanic trade routes. Mishra's second category comprises 'the mid- to late twentieth-century diasporas of advanced capital to the metropolitan centres of the Empire, the New World and the former settler colonies' (Mishra 1996: 421) – tracing, in other words, an Anglophone web. If the pre-eminent author of the first diaspora is the Trinidadian novelist V. S. Naipaul, the second diaspora's concerns have been best articulated by Rushdie and Kureishi. Mishra's overview does not simply offer an anterior supplement to the Bhabha-derived analytical model of diasporic literature as a product of 'hybridity' (Bhabha 1994: 245–82). Rather, he seeks to complicate analysis reliant solely on literary production by representatives of the second diaspora – Rushdie's 'love-song to our mongrel selves' (Mishra 1996: 441, quoting Rushdie 1991: 394) – by insisting on a dialectical relationship between these two different historical stages which constitute the South Asian diasporic population worldwide.

This relationship has been enabled by the complicated vectors of multiple displacement which have brought South Asians of the first and second diasporas in proximity to each other, usually in the cities of the Anglophone 'first world' (including Australia). Thus Mishra devotes considerable attention to Canada as a space of encounter for South Asian authors drawn from different streams of migration (Mishra 2007: 133–84). Strong geopolitical ties between Canada and the Caribbean have ensured the prominent presence of Indo-Trinidadian and Indo-Guyanese writers in Toronto, including the poets Cyril Dabydeen (1986, 1989) and Peter Jaillal (2010), and the novelist Ramabai Espinet (2003). Toronto is also home to the Bombay-born Rohinton Mistry, exemplary of Mishra's second diaspora but, in his fiction about the Parsi community (e.g. Mistry 1987, 2002), a voice for an earlier journey of a community to (rather than away from) India – similar to Shepard's narrative of her Bene Israeli ancestors. Yet other literary presences in Canada complicate further Mishra's two-diaspora model. Where does M. G. Vassanji belong, writer of East African Gujarati heritage, whose novels (1989, 1993, 2003) reflect his experience and historical consciousness of arriving in Canada in the wake of the expulsion of

Indians from the newly independent East African nations of Uganda, Tanzania and Kenya, to which his ancestors had been brought both by colonial labour movements and pre-colonial trade between Gujarat and Africa? Likewise, writings by the Sri-Lankan born, Canadian novelists Shyam Selvadurai (1995, 2000) and Michael Ondaatje (e.g. 1993, 2000) remind us that 'South Asia' is not restricted to the subcontinental landmass; while Sikh Canadian author Shauna Singh Baldwin's novel *What the Body Remembers* (1999) speaks to the labour trajectories radiating from the Punjab, which included early settlements by Sikh men in Vancouver as railway workers for Empire. These authors also share an interest in excavating the colonial period as a common history of the post-colonial diasporic subject (Selvadurai 2000; Singh Baldwin 2004; see also Ghosh 2009, 2012).

As the example of the Punjab reminds us, 'diaspora' should not imply only the long-distance, transoceanic and transcontinental displacement of South Asian peoples. Many readers will be aware that the province of Punjab was divided in 1947, as part of the Partition of India (Chatterji, this volume). The literature of the South Asian diaspora includes the prolific literary responses to the migration triggered by the Partition of India and the further creation of Bangladesh in 1971. Indeed, the work of many writers already considered as 'diasporic' under Mishra's second category, such as Rushdie, Ghosh and a new generation of writers, such as Kamila Shamsie (2000, 2002), Siddhartha Deb (2002) and Tahmima Anam (2007), also enter the category of 'Partition literature': literature that narrates and reflects upon this event and its consequences. But there are other authors writing about these consequences, who were displaced not away from South Asia, but from one South Asian region to another, because of those historical circumstances. Thus, the lens of diaspora can be used to analyse novelists such as Qurratulain Hyder, who moved between Pakistan and India in search of a home, Jyotirmoyee Devi, who left East Bengal as it became East Pakistan to become a refugee in the Indian state of 'West' Bengal, and Attia Hossain, who left the subcontinent to move to London rather than choose one or the other post-Partition country. In Hyder's *River of Fire* (originally written in Urdu; 2003), Devi's *River Churning* (originally written in Bengali; 1995), and Hossain's *Sunlight on a Broken Column* (1961), we encounter the historical and philosophical dimensions of a diasporic existence triggered by the displacements of Partition. The short stories of Saadat Hasan Manto (2004) who, like Shepard's grandmother, moved from Bombay to Pakistan, likewise comment not only on the ethical ruptures of Partition, but, simultaneously, on his separation from a city which has functioned as a creative hub for the production of popular modernity.

Partition created the modern South Asian subject as perpetually fugitive and fragmented (Das 1991: 65); these terms also circulate within the wider discourse on diasporic subjectivity (Tölölyan 2007). Thinking of Partition literature as part of South Asian diasporic literature helps explicate the interest in Partition displayed by another category of diasporic South Asian writer: one whose life is based in several locations, including those in South Asia, and who is, hence, transnational. Exemplary here is Amitav Ghosh, all of whose novels narrate stories of transnational scope. The life and writing of the transnational author straddle the binaries of 'homeland' and 'diaspora' and, indeed, may extend to imaginative investment in diasporas not 'properly' his or her own. Such an investment is demonstrated throughout Ghosh's novels, which have narrated the movement of individuals across the medieval Arabian Sea (Ghosh 1992), the trek of refugees from Burma to British Bengal during the Second World War (Ghosh 2000), the displacements caused by the Bengal Partition (Ghosh 1988) and, most recently, in the novels published to date comprising his *Ibis Trilogy* (Ghosh 2009, 2012) the movement of South Asians across the Indian Ocean through indentured labour and imperial trade. Ghosh's abiding concern is the fugitive and fragmented South Asian subject, whose estrangement from the homeland, under diverse historical catalysts, encodes the lesser-known narratives of South Asian modernity.

This perspective is shared by non-Anglophone writers belonging to the older diaspora, such as Nathacha Appanah (2010) and Abhimanyu Unnuth (1977), both from Mauritius and writing about the history of indentured labour, but in French and Hindi respectively. These diverse writings under the rubric of 'diasporic literature' enlarge and vivify the commonly understood remit of that phrase within literary critical, historical and social scientific approaches to the South Asian diaspora. Histories of displacement, longing and loss can be marshalled into thinking comparatively about writing from different locations, and in different languages, but with certain features in common.

Challenging the nation: South Asian diasporic literature and 'India'

We now turn to these commonalities. All creative writing catalysed through diaspora arises out of the tension between memory and nostalgia. This preoccupation with belonging is figured through a characteristic dialogue, from a distance, with the concept of 'homeland': often, as my introduction suggested, via an interrogation of 'home' and a reconstruction of history. The diasporic novel rewrites the master narrative of official histories of how diasporas came to be, by focusing on the micro-histories of families and individuals, located at home, dislocated in the world. In addition, lyric poetry, such as that of Sujata Bhatt (1988, 2000), or short stories, like Aamer Hussein's lingering evocations of Karachi (2002) and Jhumpa Lahiri's crystallised glimpses of Bengali American life (1999, 2008), proffer snatches of sensory recall, fragments of things remembered, of routes taken and belongings sought. It must be noted, however, that very few comprehensive historiographies of South Asian diasporic populations exist to date. Although the movement of indentured labour to Mauritius, and the migrations and displacements caused by Partition, have respectively attracted solid historiographic attention, these insights have not been reconceptualised to illuminate the 'diasporic' as a master-signifier for understanding the formation of South Asian culture and history through the ruptures of modernity. There is, thus, an even greater burden on the literary text to fill the resultant gaps. Whether it is prose, poetry or short story, these literary responses are characterised by an assessment of diaspora as traumatic. The refraction of trauma through the prism of the literary must engage with the original traumatic loss, even if – as is frequently the case – this engagement is figured through strategies of evasion.

Very few literary works about diaspora narrate or evoke directly the cause of trauma; instead, they displace the marks of trauma onto the level of form. Symptomatically reading these traces across the different categories of diasporic literature, we can observe a repeated preoccupation with the homeland interpreted as nation. South Asian diasporic literature insistently routes the characteristics of a literature of trauma through this filter. Whether the text evokes the old diaspora, the new diaspora, the transnational condition or Partition migration – that which is left behind, and which has scarred the subject formed in and through displacement, emerges as the nation: a phantom, yet palpable, force that is political as much as, and indeed because, it is emotional. 'Damn you, India, Saladin Chamcha cursed silently' in Rushdie's *Satanic Verses*, 'sinking back into his seat. To hell with you, I escaped your clutches long ago, you won't get your hooks into me again, you cannot drag me back' (Rushdie 1988: 35). Despite this resistance, the novel ends with Saladin back in India; in fact, it ends with him turning away from his childhood view of the Arabian Sea with all its outward-facing possibilities. Rushdie's earlier novel *Midnight's Children* (Rushdie 1981) wielded a magic realist style to depict another Bombay-born protagonist, Saleem Sinai, as physically cracking as he narrates the story of his grandfather's departure from Kashmir to the cities of North India at the height of the anti-colonial movement and his parents' migration from Delhi to Bombay because of Partition riots. In both novels, the idea of India is intimately bound up with the idea of migration. Not merely the fact of migration, but the difficulty of disentangling the self from either of these histories, proves to be the deepest trauma of all. The 'in-between space' that Bhabha (1994) extrapolated from these very novels by Rushdie might then be reinterpreted as simultaneously traumatic and liberating.

Vassanji, an author whose personal history is 'multiply diasporic', has offered precisely such a reinterpretation, claiming his writing as both emerging from 'an in-between space', and as trying to 'nullify in-between-ness by constructing an imaginative continuity between me and my history'.[1] His novel *The Book of Secrets* (Vassanji 1993) reconstructs the genealogy of the arche-typal diasporic condition of 'in-between-ness' as arising from the complicated trajectory of the subject, born at the endpoint of Empire to Indian parents in British East Africa. The inability of 'homeland' to crystallise distinctively as 'nation' arises from the multiple post-colonial nations to which the subject, now citizen of yet another post-colonial nation, Canada, may attempt an imaginative return: in this case, to Tanzania, where he was born, and to India, his ancestral land. These complications splinter the desire for a unilinear genealogy connecting 'homeland' to 'diasporic subject' into a variegated set of emotional attachments. The in-between space, which threatens to stall the emergence of a coherent subject, is thus also the force that can challenge the emotional demands made by a coherent nation. The process that is stalled, then, is the reaffirma-tion and reification of those contours through the unitary longing of the diasporic subject for home. This subversive challenge to the 'nation' can take the form, equally, of a close-up focus on region, which jostles with and even threatens to overtake the nation for interpretation as 'homeland'. Thus, in a later novel, *The Assassin's Song* (2007), Vassanji transports the reader to the region of his ancestors, Gujarat, and its medieval histories of syncretism, as they inhere in the practices of the Ismailis, a Shia sect into which Vassanji himself was born. The narrative's privileging of a historical period anterior to the modern nation-state and its endorsement of religious heterodoxies encode its deeper struggle with a different orthodoxy: the expectation that the South Asian diasporic subject's relationship to 'homeland' must articulate itself as affiliation to the, indeed, *a*, post-colonial nation.

The diasporic text's challenge to the nation through imaginative returns to the region set into motion other dialectical relationships between region, nation and South Asian diasporic subjectivity. When a partitioned region such as Bengal is narrated by a range of diasporic authors, such as Ghosh, Lahiri, Anam and Monica Ali, 'Bengal' is recalled through multiple sites – Indian West Bengal (Lahiri 1999; 2008), Bangladesh (Anam 2007, 2011; and Ali 2003) and even the in-between borderlands of the Sunderbans (Ghosh 2004). Each author articulates differently 'Bengal' the region vis-à-vis the nation – whether it be the Indian nation into which Bengal is folded through the federal system, or the Bangladeshi nation into which Bengal is subsumed through a hegemonic congruence of ethnicity and national belonging. The locations of the authors also diverge – Anam and Ali live in Britain, Ghosh and Lahiri in the United States – as do their attachments, political, juridical and emotional, to the countries in which they live.[2] 'Bengal' in their writings is produced through an intricate algorithm of colonial and post-colonial histories of mobility. Compositely, this Bengal challenges the reified nation. Other diasporic texts mount a similar challenge to the idea of Pakistan. Kamila Shamsie's novels have repeatedly prised open the sealed contours of the nation to reveal its formation in the shadow of family histories that seep across national borders and, most recently with *Burnt Shadows* (2009), even across continents. As with Anam's novels, which evoke the histories of migration within South Asia without meta-commentary on the author's own transnational location, Shamsie's narratives, while often dealing with the migrant subject, do not offer explicitly autobiographical echoes of her transnational trajectory. Nevertheless, the echoes and dissonances between the diasporic histories of authors and those of the characters they create further complicate the idea of nation. Alternative spaces of longing and memory are produced, which range from the region within the nation, to the city within the region – as with Hussein's Karachi; indeed, the emotional focus can even shift to a single urban neighbourhood as with Anam's Dhanmondi.

These alternative forms of myth making challenge also the hegemony of 'India' within South Asia. The 'India' that the older diasporas wrote back to was, although post-colonial, still tied through memory to British India; likewise, when Kureishi evoked 'mystic India' in his *Buddha of Suburbia* (Kureishi 1990) he was bringing in a South Asian Muslim's claim to this construct regardless of the Pakistani citizenship of his family members in post-1947 South Asia. But it is the dynamics of the market that have increasingly cleared space for diverse forms of South Asian-ness commodified through the favoured literary form of the novel (Kabir 2013). In the past decade, Pakistani novelists in English, a number of them diasporic, have emerged in concert with the attention garnered by Pakistan on the global stage, albeit for reasons more negative than positive (Shah 2009). Likewise, Sri Lankan diasporic authors, including Selvadurai (1995, 2000), Ondaatje (1993, 2000), Romesh Gunesekera (1994) and A. Sivanandan (1997), have long engaged with the problems of nationhood as produced by the insular history of Sri Lanka and the bitter post-colonial conflict between Tamil and Sinhalese ethno-political positions. This conflict, as indeed the colonial history of Sri Lanka, is regionally tied to that of India, but the weight of storytelling demands it to be read in its own right as a product (and critique) of the Sri Lankan nation. The enabling distance of diaspora has precipitated clarity of stance on other post-colonial conflicts, including that over the disputed region of Kashmir; hence the preeminent poet of Kashmiri origin, the late Agha Shahid Ali, could call himself a 'Kashmiri–American' living in multiple exile and write his poems to the 'country without a post office' – an immanent Kashmir stripped of the markers of nationhood but taking shape through the exiled poet's emotion. While Ali wrote his poems to a ravaged Kashmir in English from his American location, his peers, Kashmiri Pandits who left their homes in the early 1990s under controversial circumstances and are internally displaced in various Indian cities, cultivated in Hindi a 'literature of displacement' through which they rearticulated strategic alignment with the Indian national establishment (Kabir 2009: 166–8).

Marginal spaces of regress and recuperation: diasporic sites of memory

The diasporic text's imaginative dialogue with the homeland as nation, whether to reject, endorse, or quarrel with it, reveals how the modern South Asian subject was formed through the overlapping stories of those who left and those who remained. This mutual dependence is the secret that diasporic writing plays with and wields as its trump card, because it can threaten the perceived stability of the bourgeois South Asian subject secure in a sense of undisturbed entitlement to 'home/land'. The interplay of caste, gender and religion in the formation of the South Asian subject is crucial here, because it is the particular convergence of these identity markers that triggers migration and determines how it is experienced as well as how it is remembered. During Partition, religious identity dictated the direction of movement between the new borders, but how one moved was impacted profoundly by whether one was a woman or a man, whether one possessed the resources to secure an air passage or whether one had no option but to make the trek on foot, whether one had property to leave behind and therefore mourn, or whether one's concern was more basic: personal safety. The authors who write about Partition have been those whose class privileges lessened their vulnerability as well as granted them the fluency to write, in any language, that is a mark of access to resources. This double guilt of the survivor is marked by Bapsi Sidhwa's novel *Ice-Candy-Man* (Sidhwa 1988) in her upper-class Parsi protagonist Lenny's desire to tear out the tongue that betrays her Hindu ayah to

Muslim mobs and bears witness to her subsequent migration from Pakistan to India. The same contradiction, between female authors cushioned by class privilege and the stories they narrate of women who experienced violence because their class positions made them particularly vulnerable, characterises South Asian feminists' concerted recovery of women's oral histories of Partition. Nevertheless, it is the literary text, with its capacities of characterisation, plot and description, that can best acknowledge these ironies of privileged authors giving voice to the subaltern subject, whose precarious position was exacerbated by the conditions of diaspora.

Indeed, those who formulated the revisionist historiography around the subaltern and theorised the (im)possibility of the subaltern's ability to speak (Spivak 1988), themselves benefited from a post-colonial transnational mobility that either arises from the privileges arrogated by those of higher caste/class (Chaturvedi 2012; Dube 2010) or has been seized through rising through the ranks of a deeply segmented society, where class colludes with the contours of caste. Within the old labour diasporas, in contrast, those who risked the passage across the traumatic, caste-erasing *kala pani* (black waters) often had little caste to lose, themselves being the classic subalterns; those who crossed the *kala pani* despite being privileged by higher-caste status were subalternised nonetheless (Niranjana 2006: 55–84). The new *communitas* of *jahaji-bhai/ jahaji-behen* ('ship brothers'/ 'ship sisters'), formed through the ship's crossing, transmits transgenerationally both the promise of new beginnings and the burden of infinite loss; gravitation towards one or the other emotional pole shapes the mood of the literary text looking back to the moment of departure that is also its origin. Driven equally by the fear of dying 'unaccommodated' (Naipaul 1961: 13–14) and the urge to evade the cavernous, demanding recesses of his wife's family home, Hanuman House, Naipaul's Mr Biswas relentlessly seeks his own house, burdened with bitterness towards an inherited history of 'small places, places of limited scope, of brutal past, hesitant present and uncertain future' (Bissoondath 1988: 123), while India emerges through the allegory of Hanuman House as a welter of oppressive custom. The same ambivalence towards a history of colonialism and diaspora generates, in Shani Mootoo's novel *Cereus Blooms at Night* (1996), a dystopic family riven by incest and the utopic possibilities of escape. Mootoo counters the heternormative Indo–Caribbean family, with its violently suppressed memories of Indian-ness, by twinning queer desire with the lush natural resources of the Caribbean. Likewise, in Appanah's *Last Brother* (Appanah 2010), Mauritius's lushness counters the protagonist's brutalisation by the father and the colonial system, although nature's capriciousness also imprisons him within the island and its traumatic histories.

But does escape from the diaspora as incarceration imply untroubled return? Mona, the protagonist of Espinet's *Swinging Bridge* (Espinet 2003) observes her diplomat relative break down while narrating his unsuccessful reunion with Indian members of his family back in the village his ancestors left (89–91). This difficult episode is not followed through; its intrusion into the narrative is a mark of trauma. However, the Indian author who, out of place, discovers descendants and cultures of the old diaspora seems compelled to follow through lost trails of how that diaspora happened, as does Rahul Bhattacharya's semi-autobiographical novel, *The Sly Company of People who Care* (Bhattacharya 2011) that narrates a post-colonial Indian's fascination with the old diaspora in Guyana. In the magisterial hand of Ghosh, a similar discovery takes epic form as we follow the sea routes backward into the hinterland that sent out the labourers from Bihar, downstream on the Ganges, to the port of Calcutta and the bowels of the ship (Ghosh 2009). Both novels distort received narratives of Indian-ness to register the imprint of hitherto excluded subaltern histories that have unfolded unpredictably in distant locations overseas. This fascination with the morphed South Asian subject is figured through the diasporic woman as exemplary subaltern, the ultimate site of diasporic transformation. In

Jaillal's anthology, *Sacrifice* (Jaillal 2010), poems memorialising indenture are juxtaposed with photographs of coolie women, strong arms akimbo, adorned with jewellery 'made by the hands of artisans who had melted down the silver shillings given to indentured workers on payday into these filigreed works of art' (Espinet 2003: 302). Heads bare, eyes defiant, these women look at the camera with a frankness unseen in studio photographs of the colonial era taken in British India. The literary text of the old diaspora excavates how the modern subject is fashioned through both the exclusionary tactics of an intricate moral code based on shame and the female diasporic subject's resistance to that code.

Espinet pays homage to this female agency by adducing her protagonist's ancestry to a young woman who boarded a ship bound for Trinidad to escape the Hindu widow's life of perpetual restriction. 'The rand, casting her vivid shadows upon the face of indenture' (Espinet 2003: 297) is the point at which micro- and macro-histories converge and diverge – even in the differential semantic evolution of the word *rand* (widow in the Indo–Caribbean Bhojpuri; prostitute in Indian Hindi). To bring her 'vivid shadows' to play on a narrative of diasporic South Asian-ness is to celebrate the marginalised sites of memory where women worked, cooked and played – most importantly, the dark recesses of the kitchen, the same space where Shepard heard the Morse code of her Jewish–Muslim–Indian–Pakistani grandmother, in the extract with which we began this essay. While foodways and their preparation in the kitchen are a privileged site of memory across diasporic literature, their recuperation in South Asian diasporic contexts – Rushdie's exemplary 'chutnification of history' (Rushdie 1981) – is additionally shot through with the frisson of recovering regional nuances otherwise subsumed within the nation. *The Swinging Bridge* (Espinet 2003) stages an elaborate validation of this world of subaltern labour through an exhibition of kitchen implements, transcriptions of indentured women's songs and their jewellery. The text revels in recording 'objects brought from India once or made here out of skills that had survived the crossing', from 'chuntas, calchuls, a whole clay chullah, peerhas, pooknis, belnas, tawas, lotas, tarias, hammocks' (Espinet 2003: 283) and 'lotahs, tariahs, and other brassware' to the 'nakphuls, chakapajee, and chandhar necklaces, beras, churias, armbands, and ankle bracelets, ornately worked pieces that had to be priceless, now that they had disappeared from modern life' (Espinet 2003: 301). The cadences of these inventories enshrine words and objects hidden from modernity's linguistic standardisations in post-colonial South Asia. That the exhibition coincides with the Hindu festival of Diwali further suggests the diasporic text's investment in relocating sacrality from the realm of religion to that of labour.

The sacred for the South Asian diasporic text does not preclude the religious. But from the sacred fire of the Parsis (Zoroastrians), brought over to medieval India through that community's flight from Muslim Persia, which forms the affective core of Mistry's *Family Matters* (Mistry 2002), to the syncretic Caribbean devis of Lelawattee Manoo-Rahming's poetry (2011: 19–22), the sacred's differentiated articulation constitutes a spectrum of affective engagements with the imperatives of memorialisation. A broad distinction persists between the transnational and new diasporic author's tendency to keep the sacred close to, but bracketed off from, the everyday world and the text from the old diaspora which uses the sacred to leaven the work of the body. For Banerjee Divakaruni (an example of the former category) the 'mistress of spices' (1997) is a romantic, self-exoticised vision; but for the Indo–Caribbean writer Rosanne Kanhai (an example of the latter), 'the song of the masala stone' (Kanhai 1999) which both traps and frees the woman through rhythmic corporal movement, performs a hard-won recuperation as resistance. For the writer of the older diaspora, a stubborn poetics of labour raises even the humble 'poi bhajee' (Jaillal 2010) to a transcendent level: the journey of the poi seeds, sewn into pouches for transoceanic transportation, and lovingly cultivated in vegetable patches bordering the cane fields, figure in several of Jaillal's poems as the surplus that survives the plantation to irradiate the everyday; they are the trace of 'home' retained through further diasporic journeys to adorn windowsills in Canadian cities. Cultivating the poi bhajee, rolling out rotis/chapattis and singing folk songs during masala grinding are celebrated as work which is transformed into play through the subaltern's pride in physical labour – 'I man Coolie man/baan fu wuk' (Jaillal 2010: 2), he declares with pride. The sacred as privileged site of memory is smuggled in through the small narratives of the everyday.

'*Mon pays n'aura pas de statue / de l'homme de l'orage aux pieds nus*' ('my country will have no statue / of the man of storm with bare feet'). Thus declares the Mauritian poet who formulated the concept of 'coolitude', Khal Torabully (Torabully and Carter 2002: 39). Coolitude, the project and the poetry, reclaims from '*les archives des miettes*' ('the archives of dust'; Torabully and Carter 2002: 29–30) a counter-memorial to the grand monuments commemorating battles won, independence gained and leaders of anti-colonial movements. In commemorating instead the people of storm and bare feet, the poet resurrects the subaltern formed through diaspora as the quintessence of modernity. This diasporic subject, transported packed in ships, co-opted into modernity at the moment of being registered at the colonial port, is worlds removed from the transnational subject of late capitalism, boarding an aeroplane, armed with degrees and a mobile phone, connected to 'back home' through increasingly efficient cyberspace. At another remove stands the subject formed through cartographic rearrangements in South Asia itself and their attendant violence. Yet these categories and temporalities of diasporic South Asians are constituted alike through longing, the affect which medieval poets and their counterpart lyricists in Bollywood together name as 'viraha' (Sangari 2011). Equally, this longing shapes the geopolitical entity we know as 'South Asia': 'My attention wanders to my country / I wish I could go there!', laments an otherwise laconic character in an Urdu Partition narrative (Fatima 1994: 282). It is that shimmering ambiguity around 'country', which, in its most ubiquitous South Asian translation, 'des', could equally well stand for 'region' and 'nation', and its teasing, elusive, yet ultimately productive relation to the subject excluded from it, the 'pardesi', the foreigner, the alien, the exile, which the South Asian diasporic text, in all its avatars, strives to capture and to which it pays homage.

This essay has aimed to introduce readers to the richness of diasporic literature produced by authors of South Asian heritage, whose personal histories participate in widely different trajectories of movement and resettlement. It has also offered different literary critical models for the analysis and appreciation of this body of imaginative expression, which, on perusal, goes far beyond its best-known example: the novel written in English by an Indian-born author living in the Anglophone West. Indeed, I have argued that the concept of 'diaspora' may fruitfully be considered as a master-signifier for our literary analysis of South Asian modernity at large, as it offers a framework for analysing comparatively literary responses to events usually studied separately, such as the Partition of India in 1947 and the phenomenon of indentured labour; equally, 'diaspora' allows us a framework for studying together literature produced by South Asian heritage authors writing in diverse languages, including French and Bhojpuri. In this capacity, literature of the South Asian diaspora also offers new perspectives on the categories of 'nation' and 'region' which have been central to the study of South Asia. Finally, through an emphasis on the emotional worlds and memory work of the South Asian diaspora reflected in these literary texts, the essay has recovered hidden histories of the everyday, which survive the ruptures and traumas of modernity and which generate narratives of South Asian-ness in unpredictable and evolving dialogue with their counterparts emerging from the homeland left behind.

Notes

1 M. G. Vassanji, 'Writing from an In-Between Space', The Ravenscroft Memorial Lecture, University of Leeds, 13 November 2012. See also Vassanji 2003.
2 I am grateful to Antara Chatterjee for this point.

Bibliography

Ali, A. S., 1998. *The Country without A Post Office: Poems*. New York: Norton.
—, 2003. *Rooms are Never Finished*. New York: Norton.
Ali, M., 2003. *Brick Lane*. London: Doubleday.
Anam, T., 2007. *A Golden Age*. London: John Murray.
—, 2011. *The Good Muslim*. Edinburgh: Canongate.
Appanah, N., 2010. *The Last Brother*. Translated from French by Geoffrey Strachan. London: Quercus.
Ashcroft, B., Griffiths, G. and Tiffin, H., eds, 1995. *The Post-Colonial Studies Reader*. London: Routledge.
Banerjee Divakaruni, C., 1997. *The Mistress of Spices*. New York: Anchor.
Bhabha, H., 1994. *The Location of Culture*. London: Routledge.
Bhatt, S., 1988. *Brunizem*. Manchester: Carcanet.
—, 2000. *Augatora*. Manchester: Carcanet.
Bhattacharya, R., 2011. *The Sly Company of People who Care*. New Delhi: Penguin India.
Bissoondath, N., 1988. *A Casual Brutality*. New York: Minerva.
Chaturvedi, V., ed., 2012. *Mapping Subaltern Studies and the Postcolonial*. London: Verso Books.
Dabydeen, C., 1986. *Islands Lovelier than a Vision*. Leeds: Peepal Tree.
—, 1989. *Coastland: Selected Poems*. Oakville: Mosaic Press.
Das, V., 1991. 'Composition of the Personal Voice: Violence and Migration'. In *Studies in History* ns 7: pp. 65–77.
Deb, S., 2002. *The Point of Return*. London: Picador.
Devi, J., 1995. *The River Churning: A Partition Novel*. Translated from Bengali by E. Chatterjee. Delhi: Kali for Women.
Dube, S., 2010. 'Critical Crossovers: Postcolonial Perspectives, Subaltern Studies and Cultural Identities'. In M. Whetherell and C. Talpade Mohanty, eds. *The Sage Handbook of Identities*. Thousand Oaks: Sage Publications, pp. 126–45.
Espinet, R., 2003. *The Swinging Bridge*. Scarborough: HarperFestival.
Fatima, A., 1994. *The One Who Did Not Ask*. Translated from Urdu by R. Ahmed. London: Heinemann.
Ghosh, A., 1988. *The Shadow Lines*. Delhi: Ravi Dayal.
—, 1992. *In an Antique Land*. Delhi: Ravi Dayal.
—, 2000. *The Glass Palace*. Delhi: Ravi Dayal.
—, 2004. *The Hungry Tide*. London: HarperCollins.
—, 2009. *Sea of Poppies*. London: John Murray.
—, 2012. *River of Smoke*. London: John Murray.
Gunesekera, R., 1992. *Monkfish Moon*. London: Granta.
—, 1994. *Reef*. London: Granta.
Hossain, A., 1961. *Sunlight on a Broken Column*. London: Chatto.
Hussein, A., 2002. *Turquoise*. London: Saqi Books.
—, 2009. *Another Gulmohar Tree*. London: Saqi Books.
Hyder, Q., 2003. *River of Fire*. Delhi: Kali for Women.
Jaillal, P., 2010. *Sacrifice: Poems on the Indian Arrival in Guyana*. Missisauga: In Our Words.
Kabir, A. J., 2009. *Territory of Desire: Representing the Valley of Kashmir*. Minneapolis: University of Minnesota Press.
—, 2010. 'Diasporas, Literatures and Literary Studies'. In K. Knott and S. McLoughlin, eds, *Diasporas: Concepts, Identities, Intersections*. London: Zed Books, pp. 145–50.
—, 2013. 'Literary and Cultural Production in British–Asian Diasporas'. In S. McLoughlin *et al.*, eds, *Writing the City in British-Asian Diasporas*. London: Routledge.
Kanhai, R., 1999. 'The Masala Stone Sings'. In R. Kanhai, *The Politics of Identity for Indo-Caribbean Women*. Mona: University of the West Indies, pp. 209–38.
Kureishi, H., 1990. *Buddha of Suburbia*. London: Faber and Faber.
Lahiri, J., 1999. *The Interpreter of Maladies*. Boston: Houghton Mifflin Harcourt.

—, 2008. *Unaccustomed Earth: Stories*. New York: Knopf.

Manoo-Rahming, L., 2011. *Immortelle and Bhandaaraa Poems*. Hong Kong: Proverse.

Manto, S. M., 2004. *Mottled Dawn: Fifty Sketches and Stories of Partition*. Translated from Urdu by Khalid Hassan. New Delhi: Penguin India.

Mishra, V., 1996. 'The Diasporic Imaginary: Theorizing the Indian Diaspora'. In *Textual Practice*, 10 (3): pp. 421–47.

—, 2007. *The Literature of the Indian Diaspora: Theorizing the Diasporic Imaginary*. New York: Taylor & Francis.

Mistry, R., 1987. *Tales from Firozsha Baag*. Toronto: Penguin.

—, 2002. *Family Matters*. London: Faber and Faber.

Mootoo, S., 1996. *Cereus Blooms at Night*. London: Granta.

Mukherjee, B., 1989. *Jasmine*. New York: Grove Press.

Naipaul, V. S., 1961. *A House for Mr Biswas*. New York: Knopf.

Niranjana, T., 2006. *Mobilizing India: Women, Music and Migration between India and Trinidad*. Durham, NC: Duke University Press.

Ondaatje, M., 1993. *Running in the Family*. London: Vintage.

—, 2000. *Anil's Ghost*. London: Bloomsbury.

Rushdie, S., 1981. *Midnight's Children*. New York: Knopf.

—, 1988. *The Satanic Verses*. London: Viking Penguin.

—, 1991. *Imaginary Homelands: Essays and Criticism 1981–1991*. London: Granta.

Sangari, K., 2011. 'Viraha: A Trajectory in the Nehruvian Era'. In K. Panjabi, ed., *Poetics and Politics of Sufism and Bhakti in South Asia: Love, Loss and Liberation*. Delhi: Orient Blackswan, pp. 256–87.

Selvadurai, S., 1995. *Funny Boy: A Novel in Six Stories*. London: Vintage.

—, 2000. *Cinnamon Gardens*. New York: Harvest.

Shah, S., 2009. 'As their Country Descends into Chaos, Pakistani Writers are Winning Acclaim'. *The Guardian* [online] 17 February. Available at: www.guardian.co.uk/books/2009/feb17/fiction-pakistan-hanif [Accessed 3 January 2013].

Shamsie, K., 2000. *Salt and Saffron*. London: Bloomsbury.

—, 2002. *Kartography*. London: Bloomsbury.

—, 2009. *Burnt Shadows*. London: Bloomsbury.

Shepard, S., 2008. *The Girl from Foreign: A Search for Shipwrecked Ancestors, Forgotten Histories, and a Sense of Home*. New Delhi: Penguin India.

Sidhwa, B., 1988. *Ice-Candy-Man*. London: Heinemann.

Singh Baldwin, S., 1999. *What the Body Remembers*. Delhi: Rupa and Co.

—, 2004. *Tiger Claw*. New York: Knopf.

Sivanandan, A., 1997. *When Memory Dies*. London: Arcadia Books.

Spivak, G. C., 1988. 'Can the Subaltern Speak?' In C. Nelson and G. Grossberg, eds, *Marxism and the Interpretation of Culture*. London: Macmillan, pp. 24–8.

Syal, M., 1996. *Anita and Me*. London: Harper Collins.

Tölölyan, K., 2007. 'The Contemporary Discourse of Diaspora Studies'. In *Comparative Studies of South Asia, Africa and the Middle East* 27 (3): pp. 647–55.

Torabully, K. and Carter, M., eds, 2002. *Coolitude: An Anthology of the Indian Labour Diaspora*. London: Anthem Press.

Unnuth, A., 1977. *Lal Pasina*. New Delhi: Rajmahal Prakashan.

Vassanji, M. G., 1989. *The Gunny Sack*. London: Heinemann.

—, 1993. *The Book of Secrets*. Toronto: McClelland and Stewart.

—, 2003. *The In-Between Life of Vikram Lall*. Toronto: Doubleday, Anchor.

—, 2007. *The Assassin's Song*. Toronto: Doubleday.

32

INDIAN FOOD IN THE USA

Adapting to culinary eclecticism

Jayanta Sengupta

Any discussion of Indian food in the United States has to take note of the fact that any strict definition of 'Indianness' in this context is vulnerable to essentialisation. The relationship between food and nationality is quite frequently seen as isomorphic, and such a view may well get reified in a society like the United States where ethnic cultural practices – including food and cooking, dress, music, etc. – are often the principal means for diasporic communities to retain a sense of 'indigenous' identity.

Strictly speaking, the emergence of Indian food items and cooking styles among North American foodways long predated the formation of an Indian diaspora. Colleen Taylor Sen has shown that, in the decades leading into the American Revolution, wealthy American colonists imported, via England, Indian food ingredients including 'tea, pepper, ginger, cardamom, saffron, turmeric, cumin and curry powder'. Following the loss of the East India Company's India monopoly in 1813, Indian spices became more easily accessible to the middle classes, especially in New England, as indicated by the emergence of chicken curry, curried veal and lobster curry as standard items dished out by taverns and eating houses in Boston in the first decades of the nineteenth century. Significantly, recipes for a chicken curry 'after the East Indian manner', for a similarly spiced catfish curry and for curry powder were contained in a pioneering American cookbook – Mary Randolph's *The Virginia Housewife, or Methodical Cook* – as early as 1824. Similar Indian dishes like Mulligatawny soup and chicken *pulao* – and, later, the Anglo-Indian classic 'country captain chicken' – continued to feature in such cookbooks through the nineteenth century, indicating a rising interest in Indian food, though principally as an object of curiosity (Sen 2009: 52–4).

In contrast to the 'exotic' or 'foreign' element that was always involved in the American reproduction of 'Indian' food, the growth of an Indian diaspora in the USA made possible the development of distinctively ethnic Indian food habits. The migration of Indians to the United States began in a small trickle in the nineteenth century, but by and large this migration remained limited up to the second half of the twentieth century (Jensen 1988). Prior to the introduction of restrictive immigration laws in 1917, only a small number of immigrants – mostly unskilled agriculturalists and small entrepreneurs – had begun arriving on the West Coast of the United States in the late 1890s. They were almost all men and from only one region of India, the Punjab province from the northwestern parts of the subcontinent, where the Punjabi language was spoken by Sikhs, Hindus and Muslims (Leonard 2005: 65). Possessing little knowledge of English and often at the receiving end of racial prejudice, these immigrants lived in isolated, self-sufficient communities – most of them in California – in which Sikhs, Hindus and Muslims were forced to live together because of housing difficulties. Religious taboos against beef and pork, as well as against food prepared by people of different religions, limited their food choices and influenced dietary practices. Within the communities, each religious subgroup formed separate eating arrangements with the food prepared by one of its own members. Muslims avoided any meat that had not been prepared by a co-religionist and stuck to poultry and lamb butchered by themselves (Melendy 1977: 238–9). Hindus were mostly vegetarians and usually had their own cooks in the camps. Sikhs subsisted chiefly upon vegetables, fruit and *roti*, and consumed large quantities of milk (one to two quarts a day per person) and butter (at least fifteen pounds per person each month) (Takaki 1995: 56). In general, these Indian immigrants heavily spiced up their food with curry powder, coriander, cumin, cayenne and black pepper (Takaki 1998: 305). Also, by and large, their diet was low on meat, and their cooking method rudimentary. They usually cooked upon a grate placed over a hole in the ground and frequently ate standing, without plate, knife or fork (Melendy 1977: 239).

It has been contended that it was through these Punjabis, in a small pocket of agricultural California during the 1910s and '20s that 'Indian food originally found its way into North American food culture' (Collingham 2006: 218–9). Lizzie Collingham's speculative contention that chicken curry probably first appeared on an American restaurant menu at some Mexican restaurant in California – where curry and *rotis* were served alongside Mexican enchiladas – may have some substance (Takaki 1998: 63–5, 295–312). In a social setting characterised by racial hostility, discriminatory laws barring immigration from 1917 onwards, as well as preventing wives from joining their husbands in the United States, and a post-1924 revocation of citizenship for Indians who became naturalised Americans, quite a few immigrants sought the consolation and stability of a family life by marrying Mexican women (see Leonard, this volume). Thus, there emerged, in California by the 1930s, a sizeable Punjabi–Mexican community that came to be described as 'Mexican Hindus' by Americans. The culinary practices of this community gave birth to probably the first Indian fusion cuisine in the United States – 'Mexican Hindu' dishes, in which traditional Mexican cooking, heavy and spicy and dependent on bread, vegetables and meat, was adapted to a broadly similar Punjabi cuisine. The Mexican wives in these families cooked chicken curry, *roti* (bread), *saag* (greens) and other Punjabi dishes, and dinner guests were frequent, consisting mostly of Indian travellers and bachelors (Leonard 2000: 192–202). Though women bore the larger burden of food preparation, quite frequently Sikh men cooked ceremonial meals for religious occasions, prepared Punjabi meals for family and friends, and made pickles, *lassis* or traditional desserts like *kheer*. The 'Hindus' – in reality a group mostly of Sikhs, along with some Muslims and Hindus – adapted easily enough to a greater use of corn, though there were occasional controversies over the cooking and serving of beef products in Sikh homes and pork in Muslim homes (LaBrack and Leonard 1984: 533; Collingham 2006: 220). In these biracial homes, breakfasts were typically non-Indian, including items such as cornflakes and oatmeal, and Mexican-style beans and pasta were cooked quite regularly. But second- and even third-generation children from these families continued to relate to their 'heritage' through their professed love for ethnic Indian food of the Punjab region, cooked by their Hispanic or Euro–American mothers.[1]

The only other Indians that had a distinctive group identity among immigrants during this period were students who in the first couple of decades in the twentieth century found their way into the United States in search of a practical education in agriculture and engineering. By 1911, there were approximately 100 students from India, mostly men, scattered across the country, but with the majority enrolled in universities of the Pacific coast. Many students shared with working-class immigrants of the period the experience of racial hostility, being turned away regularly from boarding houses, hotels and public restaurants. The 'typical fare for the Indian college student was graham bread, fruit, milk, eggs, and nuts' (Jensen 1988: 170–1).

By 1910, a significant number of Indians in the West Coast were shifting from quasi-industrial work on the railroads and in iron foundries to agricultural work and, by World War I, they even began to lease land for themselves. In northern and central California, a small but enterprising Indian farming community started to grow beans, celery, onions and potatoes, and quickly developed into rice-growers, making good use of the increased wartime demand for food; their success, and business skills were such that they came to be described in local newspapers as 'Hindu rice kings'. By 1920, Indians were cultivating approximately 45,000 acres of rice, 35,000 acres of vegetables, and 3,000 acres of fruit trees (Chandrasekhar 1945: 148). It is quite possible that in these early decades of the century, Indian food in the United States continued to revolve round these very basic staples. The incidence of migration for Indian women was extremely low in this period, accounting for only 1 per cent of all Indian migrants to the United States between 1820 and 1928 (Gabaccia 1996: 92; Takaki 1998: 308). There is little doubt that this severely circumscribed the growth of the ethnic Indian family unit, and limited the cooking of a wider range of traditional Indian food. On the other hand, the shortage of women and the severe housing constraints contributed to a loosening of caste distinctions and taboos with regard to food (Melendy 1977: 239). Interestingly, the first journalistic accounts of Indian food made their way into newspapers in Chicago and New York in the first two decades of the twentieth century. In his two contributions to the *Chicago Daily Tribune* in 1909, the Punjabi journalist Saint Nihal Singh acknowledged that 'the spicy flavored dishes of Hindostan are practically unknown in this country', and called upon Americans to try out a variety of dishes, including spicy vegetables using cauliflower, spinach or mushroom, an array of pickles and condiments, desserts like *halwa*, and – significantly – a *pulao* using hamburger steak meat, a *kachori* with a filling of pork sausage meat and a 'fried chicken à la Hindoo' that involved the frying of chicken pieces already cooked in a spicy gravy (Singh 1909a; Singh 1909b). The fact that Singh's recipes accommodated ingredients like beef and pork provided further indication that religious and caste taboos relating to food counted for little in a foreign setting.

By and large, the data on Indian food in the United States in these early decades of immigration is slight and episodic, because Indians were a dwindling minority during this period. In 1946, the Indian population had a total strength of only about 1,500 (Takaki 1998: 445). It was only from the 1960s, with changes in the politics of immigration and race relations, and also the demand for skilled labour, that this flow began significantly to increase. As the United States loosened its control and gave access to people who had relevant skills and/or a family already settled in the country, a sizeable South Asian – and particularly Indian – population began to make their way into the country. After 1965, changes in immigration law, the abolition of national origins quotas, the emigration of highly qualified young people from India (Washbrook, this volume) and the flight or expulsion of most Indians from the newly-independent East African countries in the 1960s and '70s, contributed significantly to this trend. As a result, the number of Indians in the United States swelled dramatically in the last quarter of the twentieth century, rising to 525,000 by the mid-1980s (Takaki 1998: 445) and reaching over 800,000 by 1990 (Brown 2006: 26). In the present century, this population has really exploded, touching 1.8 million in 2000 (Barnes and Bennett 2002) and moving upwards of 3 million in 2010 (Hoeffel, Rastogi, Kim and Hasan 2012).

How has this substantial, increasingly visible and relatively prosperous diasporic population expressed its 'ethnic' roots through food? The answer to this question is more complex than is immediately apparent. As such, it is common enough for migrants to seek to preserve their ties to a homeland through their preservation of and participation in traditional customs and rituals of consumption. The work of Donna R. Gabaccia has shown how ethnic cuisines have historically contributed to the emergence of food as a powerful marker of identity in the multicultural setting of the United States (Gabaccia 1998). As Arjun Appadurai has also noted, food in the migrant/diasporic subject's cosmos becomes – whatever it might have been at its place of putative origin – tenaciously tethered to economies that are simultaneously and irreducibly national and moral (Appadurai 1988: 1). Indian migrants, of course, are no exception to this, and a number of studies have attested to the strong connection between Indian ethnic food in the United States and the national self-identification of diasporic Indians. The literary critic Ketu Katrak, for instance, has written how – on coming to the United States as a graduate student – her childhood disinterest in food 'was transformed into a new kind of need for that food as an essential connection with home' (Katrak 2005: 270; for similar arguments, see Narayan 1997; Mankekar 2005; Sen 2005). This connection has many facets – from the cooking of Indian meals at home to the increasing number and popularity of Indian restaurants and the growing availability of the specialised ingredients of Indian cooking in not only specialty ethnic grocery stores but supermarkets. This certainly gives an impression of the growing size and influence of the Indian diaspora and, accordingly, a corresponding 'mainstreaming' of Indian cuisine alongside the other major American ethnic cuisines – whether Mexican, Italian or Chinese. While there is an element of truth in this, this chapter contends that the theory of a steady rise in the stature and importance of Indian food in the United States is more complicated than it appears at first glance. The following passages examine these complications about Indian food as the vehicle for the expression of diasporic identity.

Two particular aspects of this larger diasporic population deserve our attention, because both of them have a bearing on food culture. First, unlike the first wave of generally uneducated and working-class Indian immigrants, the more recent arrivals are mostly from the educated middle class. In recent decades, they have secured the highest percentage of employment as managers and professionals among all Asian American groups, this number rising from a little less than 50 per cent to nearly 60 per cent through the 1990s (Takaki 1998: 446; Reeves and Bennett 2004: 14). Based on median income, Indian-born residents in the United States comprise the highest-paid ethnic group in the country (Panagariya 2001), and this relative affluence naturally means the availability of a larger disposable income to spend on food and on eating out at ethnic restaurants. Also, the newfound wealth of many of these immigrants has had an impact on the nature of their cooking. 'Able to afford lavish amounts of fresh vegetables and lots of butter', as Lizzie Collingham has pointed out, 'their cooking has become much more sumptuous' (Collingham 2006: 251). Second, in sharp contrast to the all-male character of the early immigrants, above two-thirds of the Indians currently resident in the United States are married and more than 70 per cent of them live in family households. Notably, both percentage figures are the highest among all Asian American groups (Reeves and Bennett 2004: 7–8). Moreover, these Indian immigrant families are not exclusively nuclear in form, because it is quite common for parents or parents-in-law to arrive for lengthy stays, or for nieces, nephews or the children of cousins to be informally adopted into US households for the duration of their college-going years, as they are in India. The size of South Asian households in the USA has been going up in recent decades owing to the presence of grandparents and non-nuclear kin, as well as the development, especially among wealthier South Asians, of the phenomenon of peripatetic parents who travel between their children's households in the worldwide diaspora for visits (Brown 2006: 77; Visweswaran 2001). This specificity of the social composition and economic background of the new Indian immigrants in the United States also prevented the growth of an all-pervasive 'curry culture', the sort of boom in Indian 'curry houses' or middle-range restaurants that spread across Britain in the last decades of the twentieth century.

The first Indian chef in North America, J. Ranji Smile, left the Savoy Hotel in London in 1899 to take up a job in the Sherry's Restaurant in New York, 'initiating the fashionable set in New York into the mysteries and delights of East Indian cooking' (*Harper's Bazaar* 1899). But the first restaurants under Indian management appeared slightly later, also in the heart of New York City, where the Ceylon Restaurant opened in 1913 and the Taj Mahal Hindu Restaurant in 1918. Both these places quickly became quite popular with Indian students, many of whom were nationalists attracted to the ideals of revolutionary terrorism in colonial India (Bald 2007: 67–70). After World War II Bengali seamen from erstwhile East Pakistan, who had jumped ship and settled in the Harlem area, opened small eating houses in New York's Upper West side (Sen 2009: 58). Right down to the 1960s, the Indian restaurant business in the USA retained this kind of a fringe existence, catering to a limited clientele in mainly downscale establishments and noticed by Americans very rarely, and mainly for their curiosity value.

Unlike the less skilled immigrants to Britain, who often had to fall back on the catering business in order to earn a living, Indian immigrants to the United States in the wake of the US Immigration and Naturalization Act of 1965 were mostly highly educated and skilled professionals who did not turn to catering as an occupation, nor did they live in the highly localised urban clusters of working-class South Asian migrants that sustained the original demand for curry houses in Britain. As Jo Monroe has noted, it was with the newfound American interest in Asian 'fusion food' that curry first came into focus in the United States in the 1980s and '90s, when it developed as a sophisticated, even 'incredibly glamorous' dining experience in chic restaurants in big cities. From these haughty heights, the Indian restaurant experience has gradually trickled down to smaller-scale, though Michelin-starred New York restaurants like Devi, Junoon, Tamarind Tribeca and Tulsi have in recent years added an element of upscale Indian fine dining to this experience. On the whole, however, this business depends primarily on budget curry houses in smaller cities, and has stopped short of spawning a 'tandoori' or 'tikka' revolution of the kind witnessed in contemporary Britain (Monroe 2005: 240–1).

Quite frequently, the US-born children of first-generation Indian immigrants are expected – especially by their immediate family – to develop an awareness of 'Indian values' and 'Indian culture' and, as can be expected, regional foodways become as important a part of such socialisation as traditional music and dance, or religious and ceremonial practice (Visweswaran 2001). By and large, the presence of the extended family has often helped to maintain a connection with Indian ethnic food traditions, has spawned the growth of a sizeable genre of Indian cookery books and an exchange of authentic Indian recipes through internet blogs and has led to an increasing demand for South Asian ethnic food products and grocery stores. Indeed, Indian grocery stores are now available in every state and in every major metropolitan area and are frequently found in smaller towns as well – a significant change from earlier times when Indian immigrants used to bring back from home large supplies of groceries including spices, pickles and other ingredients that were difficult to obtain in the United States.[2] Some areas with especially dense concentrations of Indian grocery stores – including Jackson Heights in New York City, Devon Avenue in Chicago, Oak Tree Road in Edison, New Jersey, Moody Street in Waltham near Boston, Pioneer Boulevard in Artesia in California and the Mahatma Gandhi District in Houston – have carved out a niche for themselves on the culinary map of the United States as representations of 'Little India'. Indian spices, sauces, packaged meals and other ingredients regularly adorn the shelves of large supermarket chains like Giant, Whole Foods, Costco and Wegmans (Bhide 2007). The availability of mail-order delivery of Indian groceries from stores located in cities ranging from New York and Chicago to El Cerrito in California further testifies to the increasing accessibility and catchment area of Indian food in the United States (Bladholm 2000: 254–5). As more North Americans become better accustomed to the cuisines of India, the once-obscure ethnic groceries have joined their shopping destinations, and this is precisely what has led to the demand not only for Indian cookbooks but also for pre-culinary 'orientation guides' like Linda Bladholm's *The Indian Grocery Store Demystified*. It is an indication of the growing demand for Indian food that more than 1,200 Indian food products have been introduced into the United States in the last decade alone (Bhide 2007).

However, it would be incorrect to assume that the food habits of the Indian diaspora in the USA are dominated by 'traditional' Indian cuisine alone. Indeed, for a cuisine that has borrowed unabashedly from outside and is based on turning the 'blatantly exogenous' into the 'prototypically authentic', the very concept of 'traditional' itself can be misleading (Nandy 2004: 11). Though many of the basic staples of Indian cuisine – including potatoes, tomatoes, kidney beans, maize, bell peppers and, most importantly, chilli peppers – are indigenous to the Americas, and other ingredients are widely available, significant changes in dietary practices, including a shift from vegetarianism to non-vegetarianism and a general adaptation of American food, are still quite common among Indian immigrants, especially Hindus. This is in sharp contrast to, for instance, Trinidadian Christian Indians born of parents who converted from Hinduism, who share a repugnance towards eating beef (Niehoff and Niehoff 1960: 93). A 1969 sociological survey on the food habits of a socially diverse group of Asian Indian immigrants in central Pennsylvania revealed that 'non-vegetarian Hindus started eating beef soon after their arrival' in the USA, and that, even among many vegetarians, there was a gradual shift through the eating of eggs to full-scale non-vegetarianism. The Indian Muslims covered by the survey, however, were united in observing their prohibition against pork and pork products (Gupta 1975: 90–1). On the whole, the survey indicated a broad 'Americanisation' of food habits at work, visible especially in a breakfast and lunch fare dominated by cereal, toast, milk, juice, eggs, sandwiches, soups, and tea or coffee, and qualified only by an Indian-style, home-cooked dinner that was cooked with traditional Indian spices and was usually shared by most members of the household.

Perhaps the only full-length and in-depth study of the eating habits of Indian immigrants to the US – based on a survey conducted among Bengalis from West Bengal – also confirms that breakfast and lunch 'both reflect global trends that are making the world the same place', while 'dinner . . . stems these homogenising tides of change. . . . [and] puts us back in our places' (Ray 2004: 48). Centring on rice and fish cooked with traditional spices on most days of the week, their dinner-time meals have not really changed since migration to the USA, with the exception of the addition of more meats, pasta and salads to accommodate second-generation preferences. By and large, it 'has moved to the center of the re-enactment of ethnicity and "culture"' among these Bengalis (Ray 2004: 52). To a slightly greater or lesser degree, this movement towards a practical-minded Americanisation – qualified by the quintessentially ethnic family dinner – has characterised the food habits of most Asian Indian communities in the United States. Though the extent of this 'Americanisation' has varied according to age, regional cultural background and length of time spent in the USA, there is no denying the fact that men have adapted more readily than women to American food habits and that children have done so most easily and happily (Ray 2004: 92–3). A survey similar to the one mentioned above – conducted in 1993 among Caucasian and Asian Indian women in Knoxville, Tennessee – reveals a broad similarity between the two groups in levels of consumption of fast food such as pizza, burger, fried chicken and fried fish, but the biochemical breakdown of their respective diets indicates a greater divergence in the intake of protein, carbohydrates, fat and cholesterol (Sachan and Samuel 1999: 165–8).

This confirms the need to guard against overemphasising the role of ethnic food as a strictly demarcated and exclusivist enclave of 'Indian-ness' for diasporic Indians. The rigid boundaries assumed in such a theory seem to be blurred in reality by a greater acculturation, openness and flexibility in the food habits of these Indians. The presence of a substantial 'American' element – notwithstanding the term's amorphousness – in the average Indian's diet testifies to the fact that the ethnic distinctiveness of Indian cuisine in the United States has come to terms with multiculturalism, or at least culinary eclecticism.

Along with this Indian diaspora in the United States, American consumers have played their own part in the growing popularity and visibility of Indian food. A survey by the National Restaurant Association in 2000 revealed that consumer awareness of Indian cuisine increased by 74 per cent between 1981 and 1996, a period during which nearly half a million Indians – according to the federal Immigration and Naturalization Service (INS) – immigrated to the United States (National Restaurant Association Survey 2000, cited in American Planning Association 2007). Insofar as a diversification within the family kitchen is concerned, this boom in immigration has certainly spawned the growth of several types of regional cuisines – North Indian, South Indian, Tandoori (clay oven), Bengali, vegetarian, etc. The case of the Indian food business in the United States is, however, a more complex one. On the one hand there is a noticeable increase in the number of Indian restaurants, which, along with motels and petrol stations, have been one of the mainstays of the Indian business community in the United States (Brown 2006: 73–4). Immigrants from other South Asian countries like Pakistan, Sri Lanka and Bangladesh have added their own spices to this mix. On the other hand, despite its relative growth in the last three decades, Indian food continues to lag way behind the most popular ethnic-restaurant options, such as the Italian and Chinese. The huge popularity of Indian restaurants in Britain has not been replicated in the United States. With some notable recent exceptions, the Indian restaurants in the United States have been unable, or even unwilling, to serve food that genuinely represents the huge regional diversity of subcontinental cuisine. The misguided expectation of American customers that all Indian food is very spicy has encouraged many Indian cooks to cater to this image by 'heating up' their own recipes, regardless of tradition. The first great wave of Indian restaurants in the United States were mostly from northern India or from Pakistan and, consequently, the first Indian dishes introduced to the American palate were typically mainstays of Mughlai cuisine, for instance *shish kebabs* slow-roasted in a clay oven (*tandoor*) or *biriyanis* made with basmati rice. With the exception of the cities with larger Indian populations – where some restaurants may define their cuisine more specifically in terms of regional traditions – the majority of Indian restaurants in the United States generally only describe themselves as northern or southern in style (Zibart 2001: 196). Such underrepresentation of regional diversity continues to be the major drawback of the Indian restaurant business in the United States, one that is only inadequately compensated for by the increasing availability of a wide array of regional dishes in the form of precooked and packaged ready-to-eat single-serving meals manufactured by processed food companies like House of Spices, Deep Foods, MTR, and – increasingly – the British giant, Patak's.

Indian food in the United States thus continues to hover at the edges of the mainstream ethnic foodways. Significantly, it fails to feature among the ethnic cuisines surveyed in Donna R. Gabaccia's influential historical study of the influence of such cuisines in the making of the American identity (Gabaccia 1998). Though not fully integrated in the American cultural landscape, Indian food has, however, served an important purpose by making it possible for Indian immigrants to preserve their ties to a homeland – real or imagined – through participation in traditional rituals of consumption. As the Indian diaspora keeps growing in size and visibility, so do Indian restaurants and grocery stores, and an ever larger array of packaged sauces, pickles, curry pastes, ready made snacks and similar other food ingredients make their way onto the shelves in specialty grocery stores or 'world foods' sections of major supermarkets. At the same time, however, the status of Indian food as a sheltered niche of ethnic cultural practices is complicated by the changing patterns of acculturation and 'Americanisation' that impact family life, community practices and intergenerational relations within the diaspora itself. The fate of Indian food in the US, like that of many other varieties of ethnic food, will doubtless be shaped by the dynamic adaptations that it makes – or fails to make – with these forces of change.

Notes

1   For a set of interviews with the grown-up children of these 'first-generation' immigrants, all of whom related to their 'Indian-ness' through nostalgic memories of food, see Lavina Dhingra Shankar and Pallassana R. Balgopal, 'South Asian Immigrants before 1950: The Formation of Ethnic, Symbolic, and Group Identity' in *Amerasia Journal*, vol. 27, no. 1 (2001), pp. 55–85, esp. 62–4.
2   The restaurateur Neela Paniz writes, for instance, that she brought several Indian spices and food items for her aunt when travelling to the United States in 1968, but that the subsequent emergence of nearly 9,000 Indian food markets in that country had made such efforts unnecessary. Neela Paniz, 'Foreword', to Linda Bladholm, *The Indian Grocery Store Demystified* (Los Angeles: Renaissance Press, 2000), p. ix.

References

American Planning Association 2007, *Policy Guide on Community and Regional Food Planning*, accessed online at www.planning.org/policy/guides/adopted/food.htm on 5 December 2009.

Appadurai, Arjun 1988, 'How to Make a National Cuisine: Cookbooks in Contemporary India', *Comparative Studies in Society and History*, vol. 30, no. 1, pp. 3–24.

Bald, Vivek 2007, '"Lost in the City": Spaces and Stories of South Asian New York, 1917–1965', *South Asian Popular Culture*, vol. 5, no. 1 (April), pp. 59–76.

Barnes, Jessica S. and Bennett, Claudette E. 2002, *The Asian Population: 2000 (Census 2000 Brief)*, US Department of Commerce, Economics and Statistics Administration, US Census Bureau. Available online at www.census.gov/prod/2002pubs/c2kbr01–16.pdf, accessed on 26 October 2009.

Bhide, Monica 2007, 'Tikka in No Time: Convenient Ingredients Make Indian an Instant Cuisine', *The Washington Post*, 24 January, viewed online at www.washingtonpost.com/wp-dyn/content/article/2007/01/23/AR2007012300296_pf.html, on 20 May 2010.

Bladholm, Linda 2000, *The Indian Grocery Store Demystified*, Renaissance Press, Los Angeles, CA.

Brown, Judith M. 2006, *Global South Asians: Introducing the Modern Diaspora*, Cambridge University Press, Cambridge.

Chandrasekhar, S. 1945, 'The Indian Community in the United States', *Far Eastern Survey*, vol. 14, no. 11, pp. 147–9.

Collingham, Lizzie 2006, *Curry: A Tale of Cooks and Conquerors*, Oxford University Press, New York and Oxford.

Gabaccia, Donna 1996, 'Women of the Mass Migrations: From Minority to Majority, 1820–1930', in Dirk Hoerder and Leslie Page Moch (eds), *European Migrants: Global and Local Perspectives*, Northeastern University Press, Boston, MA.

— 1998, *We Are What We Eat: Ethnic Food and the Making of Americans*, Harvard University Press, Cambridge, MA.

Gupta, Santosh P. 1975, 'Changes in the Food Habits of Asian Indians in the United States: A Case Study', *Sociology and Social Research*, vol. 60, no. 1, pp. 87–99.

Harper's Bazaar 1899, 'Oriental Cookery in New York', 28 October.

Hoeffel, Elizabeth M., Rastogi, Sonya, Kim, Myoung Ouk and Hasan, Shahid 2012, *The Asian Population: 2010 (2010 Census Briefs)*, US Department of Commerce, Economics and Statistics Administration, US Census Bureau. Available online at www.census.gov/prod/cen2010/briefs/c2010br-11.pdf, accessed on 25 January 2013.

Jensen, Joan M. 1988, *Passages from India: Asian Indian Immigrants in North America*, Yale University Press, New Haven, CT.

Katrak, Ketu 2005, 'Food and Belonging: At "Home" and in "Alien-Kitchens"', in Arlene Voski Avakian (ed.), *Through the Kitchen Window: Women Explore the Intimate Meanings of Food and Cooking*, Berg, Oxford and New York, pp. 263–75.

LaBrack, Bruce and Leonard, Karen 1984, 'Conflict and Compatibility in Punjabi–Mexican Immigrant Families in Rural California, 1915–1965', *Journal of Marriage and Family*, vol. 46, no. 3, pp. 527–37.

Leonard, Karen 2000, 'Punjabi Mexican American Experiences of Multiethnicity', in Paul Spickard and W. Jeffrey Burroughs (eds), *Narrative and Multiplicity in Constructing Ethnic Identity*, Temple University Press, Philadelphia, pp. 192–202.

— 2005, 'Asian Indian Americans', in John D. Buenkar and Lorman A. Ratner (eds), *Multiculturalism in the United States: A Comparative Guide to Acculturation and Ethnicity*, Greenwood Press, Westport, CT, pp. 65–78.

Mankekar, Purnima 2005, '"India Shopping": Indian Grocery Stores and Transnational Configurations of Belonging', in James L. Watson and Melissa Caldwell (eds), *Cultural Politics of Food and Eating: A Reader*, Blackwell, Oxford, pp. 197–214.

Melendy, H. Brett 1977, *Asians in America: Filipinos, Koreans, and East Indians*, Twayne Publishers, Boston, MA.

Monroe, Jo 2005, *Star of India: the Spicy Adventures of Curry*, Wiley, Chichester, UK, and Hoboken, NJ.

Nandy, Ashis 2004, 'The Changing Popular Culture of Indian Food: Preliminary Notes', *South Asia Research*, vol. 24, no. 1, pp. 9–19.

Narayan, Uma 1997, 'Eating Cultures: Incorporation, Identity, and Indian Food', in *Dislocating Cultures: Identities, Traditions, and Third World Feminism*, Routledge, London, pp. 159–88.

Niehoff, Arthur H. and Niehoff, Juanita 1960, *East Indians in the West Indies*, Public Museum Publications in Anthropology, Milwaukee, WI.

Panagariya, Arvind 2001, 'The Indian Diaspora in the United States', *Economic Times*, 23 May, accessed online at www.columbia.edu/~ap2231/ET/et26-may01.htm on 27 August 2009.

Ray, Krishnendu 2004, *The Migrant's Table: Meals and Memories in Bengali–American Households*, Temple University Press, Philadelphia, PA.

Reeves, Terrance J. and Bennett, Claudette E. 2004, *We the People: Asians in the United States*, a Census 2000 Special Report of the US Census Bureau, p. 14. Accessed online at www.census.gov/prod/2004pubs/censr-17.pdf on 26 October 2009.

Sachan, Dileep S. and Samuel, Priscilla 1999, 'Comparison of Dietary Profiles of Caucasians and Asian Indian Women in the USA and Asian Indian Women in India', *Journal of Clinical Biochemistry and Nutrition*, vol. 26. no. 2, pp. 161–71.

Sen, Colleen Taylor 2009, *Curry: A Global History*, Reaktion Books, London.

Sen, Sharmila 2005, 'Indian Spices across the Black Waters', in Arlene Voski Avakian and Barbara Haber (eds), *From Betty Crocker to Feminist Food Studies: Critical Perspectives on Women and Food*, University of Massachusetts Press, Amherst and Boston, pp. 185–99.

Shankar, Lavina Dhingra and Balgopal, Pallassana R. 2001, 'South Asian Immigrants before 1950: The Formation of Ethnic, Symbolic, and Group Identity', *Amerasia Journal*, vol. 27, no. 1, pp. 55–85.

Singh, Saint Nihal 1909a, 'Dishes New to the Occident', *Chicago Daily Tribune*, 3 June.

— 1909b, 'Dainty Dishes of the Hindoo Pleasing to American Palates', *Chicago Daily Tribune*, 3 October.

Takaki, Ronald 1995, *India in the West: South Asians in America*, Chelsea House Publishers, New York and Philadelphia, PA.

— 1998, *Strangers from a Different Shore: A History of Asian Americans*, Little, Brown and Co., Boston, MA, New York, Toronto and London.

Visweswaran, Kamala 2001, 'Families in the US Indian Diaspora', South Asia Women's Forum, 19 March, online portal accessed at www.sawf.org/newedit/edit03192001/womensociety.asp on 27 August 2009.

Zibart, Eve 2001, *The Ethnic Food Lover's Companion: Understanding the Cuisines of the World*, Menasha Ridge Press, Birmingham, AL.

33

BOLLYWOOD'S EMPIRE

Indian cinema and the diaspora

Rachel Dwyer

Today Indian cinema almost needs no introduction in the West, where 'Bollywood' is now widely used as a synonym of Indian cinema. The term, much debated by academics, most recently by Vasudevan 2011, is disliked by members of the industry who feel that it belittles what they prefer to call the 'Hindi mainstream' film industry. Although many histories of the word have been suggested, it seems to have been used mostly in the British South Asian diaspora and then to have spread back to India where it is now the usual term for referring to the Bombay (Mumbai) film industry and its associated media, so Bollywood music, Bollywood news, etc. This chapter uses 'Bollywood' to refer approximately to the mainstream Hindi cinema made in Bombay (Mumbai), mostly since 1991. It examines the role it plays in the South Asian diaspora, the depictions of this diaspora and the impact of the diaspora on the film industry itself.

Indian cinema

Indian cinema has an acknowledged unique form, distinctive styles and genres which arose from a combination of Western technologies and modes such as melodrama, with indigenous visual and performative traditions. With the coming of sound in the 1930s, Indian cinema soon devolved into many cinemas, mostly divided by language, including major cinemas in Bengali, Tamil, Marathi and Telugu. However, cinema also united the incipient nation as it spread the use of the lingua franca, 'Hindustani', a language which can be loosely identified as the colloquial form both of Hindi, which became the national language of India after independence, and also of Urdu, later the national language of Pakistan. After independence and Partition in 1947, other popular national cinemas evolved, notably in Pakistan, based in Lahore ('Lollywood'), and important 'regional' cinemas, notably in south India, continued to develop. Hindi cinema, which aspires to be India's national cinema, finds major audiences across the entire region, even where there have been attempts to restrict it, such as in Pakistan.

India has other cinemas that have different production and distribution circuits from the Hindi cinema, notably a realist cinema encompassing the films of Satyajit Ray, one of world cinema's most acclaimed directors, the 'middle cinema' (also known as new cinema, parallel cinema), typified by the work of Shyam Benegal, and the multiplex and *hatke* cinema of the present (Dwyer 2011). This realist cinema is aimed at an audience familiar with world cinema;

though their films are not usually released beyond the festival circuit, they can be seen via other media.

Indian cinema is also a global phenomenon, though different in scale from that of Hollywood. It is hugely popular outside Western Europe and the USA, where it is often preferred to local and Hollywood cinemas. Some Hindi films have proved to be massive international hits such as *Awaara/The vagabond* (dir. Raj Kapoor, 1951). One of the reasons for the wide appeal of Hindi cinema used to be that it was cheaper than Hollywood, but it is also celebrated as a non-Western form, upholding other traditions and values, in particular its depiction of love within the larger family and changing, often Westernising, society.

Hindi cinema had little recognition in the West (Europe and North America) until the 1990s. Hindi films were screened here only for the diasporic Asian markets, but since the 1990s they have begun to find a niche interest and are now viewed in multiplex theatres, although they have only a limited penetration of mainstream audiences in Europe and America. This move was part of the massive changes that occurred in the India of the 1990s, including the media explosion, the shifts that took place within the films and the film industry and a reorientation of government policy towards its relations with the global Indian diaspora.

International distribution of Indian cinema

Indian films have been exported since the early days of silent cinema. Film was imported and distributed as other commodities, in one of the older diasporas, that of East Africa. Gujarati cloth merchants, Ismaili Khojas, Bohras and Hindu Lohanas, brought film from Bombay which they showed in informal screenings in temporary tent theatres, later building permanent single-screen theatres in the 1920s and 1930s. Hindi films were initially bought second-hand in Bombay, but by the 1940s filmmakers were signing international distribution deals with Bombay-based companies such as the Savanis' Shyamji Kalidas & Co. International Film Distributors. The Hindi films were then re-exported to the rest of the world, including other major African centres, the Middle East, and, by the 1960s, to London. Other families, mostly Gujarati or Sindhi, were active in this distribution network, including the Hinduja family, who distributed Indian cinema in Iran and the Middle East from the 1950s to 1970s, and the Lullas whose Eros International, founded in London in 1977, is now the major distributor of Hindi film internationally. In a similar manner, other family groups organised distribution of Hindi and Tamil films to the remaining parts of the world where the Indian diaspora was settled, such as Malaysia and the Caribbean.

In the UK, it was in the 1950s that Indian films began to be screened for Asian audiences. These were mostly on Sunday mornings and other 'off-peak' times at cinemas that mostly showed mainstream cinema. There were occasional events where the stars came over from India for 'premieres' and, though these attracted large audiences, they were few and far between and mostly ignored by the mainstream press. The 1960s saw the increasing presence of British Asians with major migrations from East Africa. These 'twice migrants' arrived already knowing how to develop infrastructures for maintaining their culture in alien environments and continued to watch Hindi films. In the 1980s, some Hindi films were screened on the BBC's Network East, while Channel 4 showed programmes of song and dance numbers as well as full-length films. Asian radio stations, notably Sunrise Radio, founded in 1989, played the latest film songs, increasing the audience for the VHS cassettes that could be hired from grocers and *paan* shops in every Asian neighbourhood. Similar patterns of film exhibition and viewing are reported in areas of large South Asian migration, such as the USA (Punathambekar 2005).

The explosion of new media changed the whole consumption pattern of Indian cinema from the early 1990s. Newly established cable and satellite television companies beamed South Asian channels to diasporic audiences, which precipitated a massive upsurge in film viewing. This, accompanied by the practice of 'video holdback', whereby release of VHS copies was deliberately postponed, although piracy was rife, led to the return of the cinema audience in the mid-1990s as theatre halls improved, Dolby sound was installed and the films themselves showed higher production values. CDs replaced cassette tapes and the VHS shops closed as quickly as they had opened

Ashish Rajadhyaksha (2003: 29) notes:

> Until 1992, the government of India had maintained their control over film production in India through their own Indian Motion Picture Export Corporation, accountable to the State Reserve Bank of India, and later, the state-run Film Development Corporation. They had also regulated the export of films until 1992, when they opened the domain of film to private investors.

Since 1992, other Bombay-based companies have distributed Hindi films internationally through overseas branches, notably Yash Raj Films (since 1997), in the UK, North America and the Gulf. There are separate circuits of international distribution from other major film centres, for example for Tamil films, reaching the diaspora of 8 million Tamil speakers through its own circuits, such as Ayngaran in the UK.

India's domestic distribution networks were set up before independence (as seen in the names still used today, such as Nizam, Bombay, UP and CP, etc.). The creation of Pakistan, and later Bangladesh, has made surprisingly little difference to the diasporas who migrated before 1947, who were part of the circuit of Hindi cinema. Even in India's new neighbours, where Indian films were banned, pirates found the border porous from all sides where Hindi films were viewed, while Indian television was easily picked up near the border. Once VHS and digital technology appeared, films appeared in Pakistan on the day of release, usually imported from the Gulf. Pakistani films, in Pushto and Punjabi, are low-quality productions and have not found audiences in the diaspora. The occasional high-quality film, such as *Khuda kay liye/For the sake of God* (dir. Shoaib Mansoor, 2007) has found markets among all South Asians, as it engages with key issues such as Islamaphobia and fear of proselytising radical Islam in a family drama. Internationally produced Pakistani films with some Indian actors have been well regarded, including *Khamosh pani/Silent water* (dir. Sabiha Sumar, 2003) about a Partition survivor in Islamicising Pakistan and *Ramchand Pakistani* (dir. Mehreen Jabbar, 2008) about Pakistani Hindus who inadvertently cross the border.

The much smaller Nepali and Sri Lankan cinemas do not seem to have such organised distribution circuits. Nepali cinema has always felt under threat from Hindi cinema, and the few Nepalis in the UK probably continue the national obsession with Hindi cinema. Many of the diasporic Sri Lankans are Tamils so are part of the global circulation of Tamil film, although films are also made in India about Sri Lankan Tamils and Sri Lanka has been making Tamil films since the 1960s, while Malaysia started making Tamil films in the 1980s (Velayutham 2008). Little has been written about popular cinema in Sinhala, although it seems not to have found many overseas audiences. Art films, never popular in Sri Lanka, have been screened at Cannes since the 1950s, famously *Rekava* (dir. Lester James Peries 1956). Contemporary Sinhala cinema has received international recognition, notably *Sulanga enu pinisa/The forsaken land* (dir. Vimukti Jayasundara, 2005), which won the Caméra d'Or at Cannes in 2005, and become more popular in Sri Lanka, but runs into censorship problems when it engages with political issues.

In Bollywood the usual modus operandi is for distribution companies to buy the overseas rights for theatrical releases, DVD, television and other screenings from film producers. The various distribution circuits are grouped as a single 'Overseas Territory' when rights are sold, similar to the five major territories into which India is divided for the purposes of Hindi film distribution. In recent years, the overseas market has become more important than any of the Indian territories, with the UK being the most profitable, followed by the USA. These two territories have come to form independent territories, while the other overseas circuit is usually not subdivided. In other words, the diaspora market, in particular that of the UK and North America, is now the core market for Hindi films.

However, piracy became rampant once DVD entered the market and excellent copies of the latest releases appeared at low prices to be viewed on the new home cinemas. Specialist stalls and shops sold DVDs and music in Asian areas, while major music stores also kept them, and the sales moved swiftly onto the Internet. While multiplex cinemas have grown, there has been a decline in cinema attendance except for big releases, probably due to Internet piracy, in particular of MP3s and downloadable films.

Now so much viewing of Hindi film is on digital media, little can be said about the audiences in terms of statistics, but key work on film-viewing and circulation among diasporic audiences has been conducted across the South Asian diaspora. These include studies of the prestigious and lucrative diasporas in the USA (Punathambekar 2005) and in the UK (Banaji 2006; Dudrah 2006; Dwyer 2006); old diasporas in Guyana (Narain 2007; Ramnarine 2001), in South Africa (Hansen 2005) and in East Africa (Bertz 2008); Israel (Gabriele 2009); and the markets in the Gulf, including the Emirates (Arora 2009). There have been a number of publications on Indian cinema among non-diasporic populations in German-speaking Europe (Mader and Budka 2009), Nigeria (Larkin 2008), Turkey (Gürata 2010), the former USSR (Rajagopalan 2008) and Tibet (Morcom 2011).

Little scholarly research has been published on the circulation of the cinemas other than Hindi overseas (see Velayutham 2008 on Tamil). Radhakrishnan 2009 analyses the interrelation-ship between Malalayam cinema made in Kerala and the Malayali diaspora in the Gulf. He shows how the Gulf-migrant features in art and commercial cinema and how the Gulf has shaped the idea of the region and impacted on film-making in India, while the figure of the diasporic Malayali has been so important in shaping the economics of the region.

Indian cinema in the diaspora post-1991

However, the 1990s saw not only a radical change in the circulation of Indian cinema and the formation of new audiences in the diaspora as media became digital and circulated more freely, they also revealed a surprising element in that the audience for these films was no longer the first generation, viewers often supposed to consist of bored housewives and the elderly, who watched Hindi films to while away the time and whose English was too poor for them to enjoy foreign films and television. Instead, a new, young generation of Hindi filmgoers emerged in the diaspora. This second, and even third, generation of the diaspora has highly complex cultural patterns. Educated in non-Asian schools, working among non-Asians, interacting with other communities, they have grown up with Hollywood and other cinema as well as other forms of television and media.

The private sphere of the diaspora consists of a dynamic mixture of South Asian and local elements, creating a wide spectrum of interaction with different cultural possibilities. While many thought that in the West the young were shifting towards speaking English, relinquishing traditional family values, losing their religion, and so on, something more complex was happening. New diasporic forms of culture, including religion, language use and music, began to emerge, mediated largely by, and reflective of, Hindi cinema.

One of the most important roles of the films, and one which is usually identified as attracting diasporic audiences, is the depiction of love and romance, an element which has made the films popular in the world outside India in areas such Zanzibar (Fair 2009), as well as creating the current wave of fans in the German-speaking world (Mader and Budka 2009). The melodrama of Hindi film, which is about love and often about the family, along with the music and the 'magic' of the movies, is usually mentioned as the main attraction. The younger generation says that the issues of the family are still relevant even though most of them have 'love marriages'. Although couples view the films, the family audience remains the norm, and the focus on the erotic rather than the explicitly sexual or on niche audiences is appreciated in Bollywood family blockbusters.

The audiences enjoy the Hindi films' depictions of Asians, who are still shown in limited roles in non-South Asian media. Shah Rukh Khan, the major star, is particularly popular in the diaspora as a light-hearted and 'modern' male, while the female stars are admired for their beauty and styling, which are much imitated by the audiences.

For many of the second- and third-generation diaspora, the public sphere is mostly non-Asian: schools, workplaces, streets and shops, in which there is only limited Asian public space. This used to be Asian shopping streets and restaurants, buildings converted into places of worship and Asian districts of cities. However, in the last 20 years there are new purpose-built religious centres, such as the Swaminarayan temple in North London, and a whole range of areas for Asian social life, from nightclubs and cinema halls in town centres as well as the Asian suburbs, to suburban shopping malls. The new malls built in areas where the Asian diaspora live around the world have multiplexes screening Bollywood films, 'Indian' restaurants and other Asian public spaces. These malls allow for a diasporic South Asian consumerism, creating a global South Asian lifestyle, whether in Bombay, Nairobi, New Jersey or London. Like the images in the films, the malls are away from decaying cities and the poor.

Hindi films are important in the diaspora for creating a queer public space and alternatives to heteronormativity (not so much in the content of the films, although films such as *Dostana* (dir. Tarun Mansukhani, 2008) have knowingly played to this audience with some artful distancing). The Bollywood style is claimed for queer spaces in clubs, as well as for private and online activities (Dudrah 2006).

The Indian cinema also forms a major part of the programming of the Indian television channels that are available to the diaspora. Televisions, which seem to be on constantly in South Asian houses, play songs from recent Hindi films, and these are also to be found on the ringtones on mobile phones. Computer screens show downloaded movies and clips and trailers from new films or film fandom and gossip sites, including the important Twitter and social networking sites which connect the stars closely to their audiences.

Hindi film has played an important role in bringing together the various members of the diaspora. For example, the British South Asian diaspora is largely Punjabi- or Gujarati-speaking, with a significant number of Sylheti speakers from Bangladesh. There are very few mother-tongue Hindi speakers in this diaspora, although many people of Pakistani origin learn Urdu, the national language of Pakistan, which in its colloquial spoken form is largely identical to Hindi, the national language of India. The second and third generations of people of Indian origin know Hindi almost exclusively through watching Hindi cinema, and young people are often encouraged by their parents to watch movies in order to improve their language skills.

Although the films often have strong nationalist rhetoric about what it is to be Indian, the Indian diaspora are included in this new Indianness and, surprisingly, other South Asians do not feel isolated from this. Nor, even, do they feel threatened by films which suggest the permeability of the borders between often hostile nations, notably India and Pakistan, in major hits such as *Veer Zaara* (dir. Yash Chopra, 2004), which promotes a sense of Punjabiness almost above the nation.

This shift in the role of cinema in the diaspora is very much part of the post-1991 changes in media, liberalisation and the content of cinema. Till then, the Asian media, whether provided by the host nation (usually concentrating on language-learning and 'adjusting') or created by the diaspora (mostly in non-English newspapers), put together digests of news from South Asia with local community stories. However, in recent years, the diasporic Asian media is increasingly in English and about Bollywood, the new releases and the stars. It would not be an exaggeration to say that the Hindi film's audience forms an Asian public, different from the individual, enabling a mass public sphere to coalesce. The films link the diaspora to the South Asian middle classes and elites in the metros, just as these people are becoming more detached from others in their cities, as the poor and illegal squatters are condemned for breaking the law, as the films' consumers 'rip' their own digital media. This new public sphere differs from the other Asian public spheres in the diaspora which are often formed around religious communities (temples, mosques, etc.), or caste (community halls) and is one which is heavily mediated through a wide range of technologies, from the Internet to the mobile phone.

Indeed, in the diaspora, Indian cinema now represents Indian culture, and other forms of South Asian culture are being 'Bollywoodised' from fashion, to weddings and music. Even at religious events, such as the dances during the Navratri festival, Bollywood influences the clothes, the music and the dance style of participants and is regarded by some as a cultural tsunami. Bollywood has also become part of the new national Indian culture, as manifested at the closing of the Games in Australia in 2006: the Indian taster for the 2010 Commonwealth Games held in Delhi was a Bollywood spectacular with major stars.

The diasporic Indian in Indian cinema

While film has circulated among the diaspora, the diaspora has featured in the films themselves over the first century of Indian film-making. The earliest films featured the 'foreign-returned' Indian, notably in *Bilet pherat / The England returned* (dir. NC Laharry, 1921), where Dhirendranath Ganguly satirises the Westernised Bengali. Many films have a hero who spends time on an overseas visit, often for education. *Junglee / The savage* (dir. S. Mukherji, 1961) begins with Shammi Kapoor's return, showing Westernised habits that are still a source of great amusement 40 years later. This foreign-returned figure represents the threat of Westernisation within India, often presented as comedy, but a melodramatic crisis usually makes him 'Indianise'. In some cases the consequences of Westernisation are actually dangerous, especially when they apply to a woman, such as in Mehboob's *Andaz / Style* (1949), where the heroine realises her prison sentence for murder is due to errors arising from her Westernised behaviour, even though it is her husband who has travelled overseas rather than she.

The 1960s sees a new kind of Indian overseas, this time the Indian who travels overseas, in films such as *Sangam / Union* (dir. Raj Kapoor, 1964), while *Love in Tokyo* (dir. Pramod Chakravorty, 1966) and *An evening in Paris* (dir. Shakti Samanta, 1967), evoke exoticism with their English titles and songs. Overseas locations are used in these films as spectacle and often meaningless space, showing the Indian moving on the world stage. This was the time at which only very rich Indians could travel overseas because of currency exchange controls, while even in India there was a lack of consumerist choice and access to the 'world'. These films promote the idea of the spiritual but impoverished East and the material and corrupt West, none more so than *Purab aur Pachhim / East and West* (dir. Manoj Kumar, 1970).

In *Purab aur Pachhim*, the pious Indian arrives for an education at Magdalen College, Oxford, but also to rescue an Overseas Indian family, which has forgotten its culture and needs to be reconnected with Indian culture and values, especially their daughter who has to switch from smoking, drinking and wearing miniskirts to being a sari-clad *bahu* ('daughter-in-law'). On the way the Indian hero sees the glittering temptations of the West, including 'loose' women, but his values are never shaken as he always remembers his father, a martyr in the freedom struggle. This figure is seen in other films such as *Hare Krishna Hare Ram* (dir. Dev Anand, 1971), where Indians who have migrated to Canada end up in Nepal, the girl becoming a hippy.

However the figure of the NRI (Non-Resident Indian), as the Overseas Indian became known in the 1980s and 1990s, changed drastically, as he (usually) came to represent the global transnational Indian. His first big role was in the blockbuster, *Dilwale dulhaniya le jayenge/DDLJ/ The braveheart will take the bride* (dir. Aditya Chopra, 1995), where he was played by Shah Rukh Khan. This film shows the heroine's father as the Indian who wants to keep his Indian culture and values intact while living in London, even if it means forcing them on his daughter. The mother supports the daughter, suggesting the values are not 'Indian' as much as patriarchal, while the hero and his father have a strong sense of honour, wanting the bride's father's consent, but they realise that the hero must struggle to show his true, modern Indianness. After the first half of the film, set in Europe, the second half is filmed in India, although there is no indication that the couple will not return to London. In recent films, there is no indication of any intention to return to India, the future clearly lying in the West. Patricia Uberoi (1999: 305, 308) notes that, after *DDLJ*, Indianness is no longer dependent on being resident in India, but now it is about Indian Family Values:

> the specificities of family life, the institutions of courtship and marriage in particular . . . whether at home or abroad, it is the *Indian family system* that is recognized as the social institution that quintessentially defines being Indian.

Indeed, the figure of the Person of Indian Origin (the new name for the NRI) is soon seen as being more than just equal to the resident Indian as he/she is soon to represent, as Prasad (2003) argues, 'a more stable figure of Indian identity than anything that can be found indigenously', while Punathambekar (2005) notes that this diasporic Indian actually shapes the idea of Indianness in films such as *Kabhi khushi kabhie gham/Sometimes happiness sometimes sorrow* (dir. Karan Johar, 2001).

These depictions are all from Hindi cinema. However, different cinemas of India show their own diasporic populations, e.g. *Parasakthi* (dir. R. Krishnana and S. Panju, 1952), in which the central characters are three Tamil brothers who worked in Burma until the Second World War. Even Hindi cinema has a hierarchy of diasporas with the European and North American being the most frequently depicted, with fewer images of the others, although the luxury and shopping malls of the Gulf States sometimes feature, though tinged with an air of gangsterism (*Welcome*, dir. Anees Bazmee, 2007), while the poor or majority of South Asians in the Gulf are invisible. The African diaspora features rarely, or again as villains (*Vishwatma*, dir. Rajiv Rai, 1992, or *Company*, dir. Ram Gopal Varma, 2002). Velayutham 2008 observes that in Tamil cinema one never sees the descendants of the indentured diaspora even when films are shot in those locations.

Films avoid depictions of the poor or unsuccessful diasporic Indian, unless this is part of the plot in which the migrant is restored to consumerist splendour, just as poverty in India is ignored in the Bollywood film. There is outright hostility in India to films which show poverty and are labelled 'poverty porn', notably *Slumdog Millionaire* (dir. Danny Boyle, 2009). As Arvind Rajagopal (2001: 241) argues

> NRIs know they are 'an apotheosis of the Indian middle class, exemplifying what "Indians" could achieve if they were not hampered by an underdeveloped society and an inefficient government'.
>
> In other words, the middle class and the rich are the transnational Indians, while the poor are not part of this world.

These changes in the relationship of the diaspora to Indians, making them part of the same social group, have mostly been mediated through film, the central part of this transmedia world, where it forms the backbone of a whole range of media. Ashish Rajadhyaksha (2003: 32) notes that this Bollywoodisation is 'a freer form of civilizational belonging explicitly delinked from the political rights of citizenship', and also (2003: 25) that it is an instance 'of cultural nationalism in a global arena'.

Although dual citzenship is not yet available, the Person of Indian Origin, whose PIO card gives more rights to travel and invest in India, is now able to apply for Overseas Indian Citizenship and is welcomed back to India on a specially designated Pravasi Bharatiya Divas (Day for Overseas Indians), when they are invited to invest in the motherland. Well aware of the soft power of the Hindi film, the government invites film stars to the PBD, showing this tie-up between the state, the diaspora and the media.

Indeed, the film industry is now courted by the state, which seeks to acquire its global status, its sheen of success, as part of its searching for a global role for itself. The cinema is no longer national and the state's concerns are also spreading. As Bollywood becomes a corporate culture industry, so the state wishes to see its boundaries change and move sociocultural boundaries.

Hindi cinema dominates 'regional' cinema in India, despite massive loyalty to other cinemas and their stars. It also dominates other forms of Hindi cinema, not least because Bollywood is the major cinema of the South Asian diaspora, whether they hail from India or elsewhere in the region (Dwyer 2011; Dwyer and Pinto 2011). However, some of the films that show most clearly how India is changing today and growing away from its diaspora are from the non-Bollywood cinema, the *hatke* ('different') or multiplex film – that is not screened in the diaspora. This is how another section of the globalised Indian sees him/herself, as its audience comprises the old upper classes, the educated film-viewer, rather than the mass audience for the Bolly-wood product, but this internationally informed section of Indian media and audience is not connected to the diaspora, and indeed this cinema is barely seen outside of India at all, where it is further confined to the multiplexes of the metropolises.

Although there are close connections between the Indian and diasporic Bollywood audiences, there are important differences in that the diaspora is surrounded by other cultures and cinemas – usually in the English language – and the films often engage with the concerns of the Indian audience, rather than of the diaspora, despite the popular belief in India that some films are specifically tailored for diaspora audiences. Indeed, few of the characters in the films would even be recognisable as diasporic, given their facility with Hindi, their Indian English accents and their lifestyles. However, this lack of realism is not an issue for Indian or diasporic audiences, who are happy to have the emblematic Bollywood diasporic Indian played by Shah Rukh Khan, who remains by far their most popular hero.

While the diasporic population forms the bulk of the overseas audience, there is also a significant section formed by other ethnic groups. For example, Shah Rukh Khan is known to have a fanatical following in the German-speaking world, while Rajnikant, the superstar of

Tamil cinema, had a hit in Japan with his film *Muthu* (dir. K.S. Ravikumar, 1995), which was the biggest hit there after *Titanic* (Rajadhyaksha 2003: 28), and Hindi films starring Mithun Chakraborty flourished in the USSR (Rajagopalan 2008).

Indian cinema is never purely Indian, as it has always had foreigners working in it, notably the Germans in Bombay Talkies in the 1930s and 'Fearless' Nadia at Wadia Movietone. It is now attracting overseas film producers such as Warner Brothers and Twentieth Century Fox to India, who may use their clout to influence the films' content and marketing. Conversely, Indian film financiers, such as one of the richest Indians, Anil Ambani, whose Reliance Big Pictures has been hugely successful in India and has taken a share in Stephen Spielberg's DreamWorks, have invested in Hollywood.

While Hollywood and world cinema are screened in India, they play to relatively limited audiences, India remaining unique in its preference for non-Hollywood cinema. The much hoped for 'crossover film', that is an Indian film that does well in India and overseas, remains to be seen. Films rarely work in both markets and, although Bollywood blockbusters find success among the diaspora, regularly appearing in the overseas top box office lists for the week, the returns are small compared to Hollywood hits, as the films are not reaching mainstream audiences. Films about India made outside India are rarely popular in India, whether the work of European art house directors (Jhaveri 2010) or heritage film makers such as Merchant Ivory, or the three (at least partly) diasporic female directors (Desai 2003), Mira Nair, Gurinder Chadha and Deepa Mehta, although their films have seen critical and commercial success in the West, notably *Monsoon wedding* (dir. Mira Nair, 2001) and *Bend it like Beckham* (dir. Gurinder Chadha, 2002). Only Chadha's films seem to have been particularly popular among the diaspora themselves, with these films finding audiences who may be partly identical with the readers of the South Asian novels in English, which continue to dominate awards, though increasingly those from Pakistan.

The Bollywood brand is getting stronger and stronger, moving from a household name in the West in the last ten years, to a significant media presence. Shah Rukh Khan's latest film, *My name is Khan* (dir. Karan Johar, 2010), picked up diasporic concerns from the perception of all Muslims as terrorists in the West, to racism in the treatment of a disaster in a city not unlike New Orleans in the American South, to an interest in Manchester United. The media savvy of RK and KJo was seen in their media presence from SRK's 'Lunch with the *FT*' (19 February 2010), to his appearance on the Jonathan Ross Show (5 February 2010). Bollywood is being taken seriously at last, mostly because of the increasing media presence of South Asians in the West and comcomitantly because of India's growing significance as a global economic power. However, given the rapid shifts of the last ten years it is not possible to say what the future will hold other than that this is only the trailer and *abhi picture baaki hai* ('the feature film will follow').

Bibliography

Arora, Poonam (2009) '*Indian cinema in the Gulf: encounter between Beduins, shaikhas and tawaifs*'. Conference paper presented at www.westminster.ac.uk/schools/media/cream/events. Viewed 26 June 2009.

Banaji, Sakuntala (2006) *Reading 'Bollywood': the young audience and Hindi films*. Basingstoke: Palgrave Macmillan.

Bertz, Ned (2008) *Race, nationalism, and urban space in Indian Ocean world history: schools, cinema and the Indian diaspora of Tanzania, 1920–2000*. Unpublished PhD, University of Iowa.

Desai, Jigna (2003) *Beyond Bollywood: the cultural politics of South Asian diasporic film*. London: Routledge.

Dudrah, Rajinder Kumar (2006) *Bollywood: sociology goes to the movies*. New Delhi: Sage Publications.

Dwyer, Rachel (2006) 'Planet Bollywood: Hindi film in the UK'. In Nasreen Ali, Virinder Kalra and S. Sayyid (eds) *Postcolonial people: South Asians in Britain*. London: C. Hurst & Co: 366–75.

— (2010) 'Hindi films and their audiences'. In *Being here, now: some insights into Indian cinema*. Guest ed. Shanay Jhaveri. Special volume of *Marg*, 61 (3), March: 30–9.

— (2011) '*Zara hatke!*: The new middle classes and the segmentation of Hindi cinema'. In Henrike Donner (ed.) *A way of life: being middle-class in contemporary India*. London: Routledge.

Dwyer, Rachel and Jerry Pinto (eds) (2011) *Beyond the boundaries of Bollywood: the many forms of Hindi cinema*. Delhi: Oxford University Press.

Fair, Laura (2009) 'Making love in the Indian Ocean: Hindi films, Zanzibar audiences and the construction of romance in the 1950s and 1960s'. In Jennifer Cole and Lynn M. Thomas (eds) *Love in Africa*. Chicago, IL: Chicago University Press: 58–82.

Gabriele, Shenar (2009) '*Consuming Bollywood in Israel: performance, creativity and aesthetics beyond India*'. Conference paper presented at www.westminster.ac.uk/schools/media/cream/events. Viewed 26 June 2009.

Gürata, Ahmet (2010) '"The Road to Vagrancy": translation and reception of Indian cinema in Turkey'. *BioScope*, 1 (1): 67–90.

Hansen, Thomas Blom (2005) 'In search of the diasporic self: Bollywood in South Africa'. In Raminder Kaur and Ajay J. Sinha (2005) *Bollyworld: popular Indian cinema through a transnational lens*. New Delhi: Sage Publications: 239–60.

Jhaveri, Shanay (ed.) (2010) *Outsider films on India, 1950–1990*. Mumbai: Shoestring Publishers.

Larkin, Brian (2008) *Signal and noise: media, infrastructure and urban culture in Nigeria*. Durham: Duke University Press.

Mader, Elke and Philipp Budka (2009) 'Shah Rukh Khan @Berlinale. Bollywood fans im Kontext medienanthroplogischer Forschung'. In Clause Tieber (ed.) *Fokus Bollywood: das indische Kino in wissenschaftlichen Diskursen*. Berlin: Lit Verlag: 117–33.

Morcom, Anna (2011) 'Film songs and the cultural synergies of Bollywood in and beyond South Asia'. In Rachel Dwyer and Jerry Pinto (eds) *Beyond the boundaries of Bollywood: the many forms of Hindi cinema*. Delhi: Oxford University Press.

Narain, Atticus (2007) 'Indian movies, narratives of dissent and objectification'. *Journal of Creative Communications* (2): 57–77.

Prasad, M. Madhava (2003) 'This thing called Bollywood'. www.india-seminar.com/2003/525/525%20madhava%20prasad.htm. Viewed 6 April 2010.

Punathambekar, Aswin (2005) 'Bollywood in the Indian–American diaspora; mediating a transitive logic of cultural citizenship'. *International Journal of Cultural Studies*, 8 (2): 151–73.

Radhakrishnan, Ratheesh (2009) 'The Gulf in the imagination: migration, Malayalam cinema and regional identity'. *Contributions to Indian Sociology*, 43 (2): 217–45.

Rajadhyaksha, Ashish (2003) 'The "Bollywoodization" of the Indian cinema: cultural nationalism in a global arena'. *Inter-Asia Cultural Studies*, 4 (1): 25–39.

Rajagopal, Arvind (2001) *Politics after television: Hindu nationalism and the reshaping of the public in India*. Cambridge: Cambridge University Press.

Rajagopalan, Sudha (2008) *Leave disco dancer alone!: Indian cinema and Soviet movie-going after Stalin*. New Delhi: Yoda Press.

Ramnarine, Tina (2001) *Creating their own space: the development of an Indian–Caribbean musical tradition*. Kingston: University of the West Indies Press.

Uberoi, Patricia (1999) 'The diaspora comes home: disciplining desire in *DDLJ*'. *Contributions to Indian Sociology* (n.s.), 32 (2): 305–36.

Vasudevan, Ravi (2011) 'The meanings of "Bollywood"'. In Rachel Dwyer and Jerry Pinto (eds) *Beyond the boundaries of Bollywood: the many forms of Hindi cinema*. Delhi: Oxford University Press.

Velayutham, Selvaraj (2008) 'The diaspora and the global circulation of Tamil cinema'. In Selvaraj Velayutham (ed.) *Tamil cinema: the cultural politics of India's other film industry*. London: Routledge: 172–88.

INDEX

Note: Page numbers in **bold** type refer to **figures**
Page numbers in *italic* type refer to *tables*
Page numbers followed by 'n' refer to notes